FINE

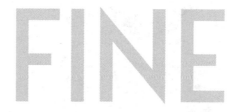

FINE

A COMIC ABOUT GENDER

RHEA EWING

LIVERIGHT PUBLISHING CORPORATION

A Division of W. W. Norton & Company

Independent Publishers Since 1923

Note to Readers: *Fine* is a work of nonfiction. Certain names, dialogue, and potentially identifying visual depictions have been changed. Some factual statements have been changed or conflated for clarity and discretion.

For information about permission to reproduce selections from this book, write to Permissions, Liveright Publishing Corporation, a division of
W. W. Norton & Company, Inc., 500 Fifth Avenue, New York, NY 10110

For information about special discounts for bulk purchases, please contact
W. W. Norton Special Sales at specialsales@wwnorton.com or 800-233-4830

Manufacturing by Versa Press
Production managers: Anna Oler, Joe Lops, Nat Kent

Library of Congress Cataloging-in-Publication Data

Names: Ewing, Rhea, author.
Title: Fine : a comic about gender / Rhea Ewing.
Description: First edition. | New York : Liveright Publishing Corporation, [2022]
Identifiers: LCCN 2021043275 | ISBN 9781631496806 (paperback) |
    ISBN 9781631496813 (epub)
Subjects: LCSH: Ewing, Rhea. | Cartoonists—United States—Biography—
    Comic books, strips, etc. | Gender identity—Comic books, strips, etc. |
    LCGFT: Autobiographical comics. | Graphic novels.
Classification: LCC PN6727.E98 F56 2022 | DDC 741.5/973 [B]—dc23
LC record available at https://lccn.loc.gov/2021043275

Liveright Publishing Corporation, 500 Fifth Avenue, New York, N.Y. 10110
www.wwnorton.com

W. W. Norton & Company Ltd., 15 Carlisle Street, London W1D 3BS

1 2 3 4 5 6 7 8 9 0

This book is dedicated to everyone who wonders if they are enough.

You are enough.

CONTENTS

CONTENT WARNINGS

Gender dysphoria, transphobia, racism, ableism, and body-image issues are discussed throughout the book.

Drug use, sex work, and suicidal ideation are mentioned briefly in some stories. There is one depiction of a suicide attempt on page 185 that may be especially challenging to some readers.

WHERE TO ACCESS SUPPORT

Trans Lifeline

Nonprofit organization offering direct emotional and financial support to trans people in crisis—for the trans community, by the trans community.

https://translifeline.org

US 1-877-565-8860

CAN 1-877-330-6366

The Trevor Project

Mental health crisis assistance for LGBT and questioning folks under 25.

https://www.thetrevorproject.org

Call 1-866-488-7386

Text START to 678-678

National Suicide Prevention Lifeline

https://suicidepreventionlifeline.org

1-800-273-8255

Crisis Text Line

Text HOME to 741-741

INTRODUCTION

Madison, Wisconsin
Mid-August 2012, afternoon

I was sitting in my car just before one of my interviews. My head was buzzing. I'd talked to about a dozen people so far, mostly friends and family. This felt different. I had driven out to OutReach, the nearby LGBT center nestled quietly inside of a shopping center. A few women from one of the transgender support groups had agreed to participate in what was supposed to be a short comic capturing the essence of what gender is, how it works, and my place in it.

I had thought about attending several of the transgender support groups myself, but always backed out at the last second. After all, such spaces should be for transgender people only. Since I didn't know I was trans, I felt like I would be an intruder. But I longed for it. I longed to sit in a room and speak honestly with people about this mixed-up thing called gender, to exist without a sense that I was failing at my part in life. This is what pushed me to start this project in the first place, to find a pathway into that space.

There was still a solid ten minutes before the building opened, so my mind spent that time fixating on all the ways I might screw this up. It was a highlight reel of every naive and ignorant thing I've ever said regarding gender, race, and ability. I tend to perform better once I'm actually in motion, when the soundtrack of my self-criticism can be drowned out by action and conversation. For now, I was stuck: in my car and in my own head.

Why was I doing this again?

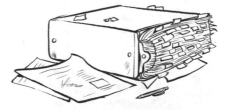

Over the decade I worked on *Fine*, I spoke with fifty-six people and gathered hundreds of pages of transcribed interviews. The transcripts barely fit into a massive three-ring binder, bursting with Post-it Notes marking ideas that stood out to me. It was impossible to fit every person and idea into the book in any coherent or meaningful way. Brevity does not come naturally to me, and editing the content down into something digestible was a herculean task that took years. There were many comic pages I drew that had to be scrapped along the way.

Initially, this was supposed to be a little college project, something I'd turn into a twenty-four-page zine and then move on with my life. But once I started, questions kept coming up that I couldn't let go. The project grew. I'm trained as a visual artist, and my work is all about finding stories and connections between people and ideas. I have no academic training in gender studies, research design, or journalism. This is not formal study or a comprehensive look at gender identity. Take this book for what it is: My own attempt to understand and connect with other people. No more, no less.

These interviews were conducted both online and in person, primarily in the midwestern United States, highlighted in the map below. I was living in Wisconsin, and this is what was feasible for me at the time. Interviewees themselves hailed from all over the United States. While I think the stories in this book are widely applicable, I encourage readers to consider how this project might have been subtly different had I conducted my interviews primarily in the South or on one of the coasts.

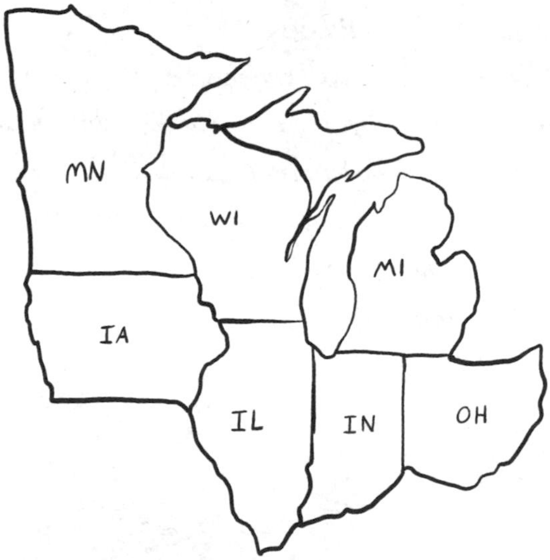
MN
WI
MI
IA
IL
IN
OH

I interviewed people of all gender identities and histories. I chose to include cisgender people (loosely defined here as people who *do* identify as the gender they were assigned at birth) in addition to transgender people (loosely defined here as people who *do not* identify as the gender they were assigned at birth), because gender is something we all grapple with. I do not identify who is transgender and who is cisgender, unless it happens to come up in the story the person is sharing.

Some of my participants wanted their names and appearances included in the book as is. Some of my participants opted to be interviewed under a pseudonym, or simply wanted to be marked as "Anonymous." Others asked for their appearance to be changed. Some people wanted complete anonymity. Places and names in many stories have been changed. While this is a work of nonfiction, resemblance to real people may not be accurate or intentional.

My own story was hardest for me to tell. The earliest drafts didn't include anything about me at all. Eventually I realized I should mention who was behind the editing and framing of all this information, since no one is truly objective. Then I came out as trans, and things got even more personal. The bulk of my own story had to be coaxed out of me by early test readers and my editor. I am immensely grateful for their kindness and patience, and for the reassurance that, yes, I counted.

The language we use to discuss gender and the social landscape of identity has evolved and continues to evolve quickly, with wide regional differences. I'm not a huge fan of prescriptive approaches to language. Even if I were, it is not my place to decide what language is "correct" for the transgender community. To that end, some words will mean different things to different people.

Time is a peculiar factor when discussing gender, for reasons beyond evolving language. Many would now describe their lives and experiences with different words, and many identify differently now than they did at the time we first spoke. For this reason I have included the year each interview occurred, to help orient the reader in time. I encourage readers to contemplate how their own sense of self and their answers to questions like the ones posed in this book may have evolved over time.

Sometimes my interviewees don't agree with each other. With that in mind, you will likely read things in this book that you don't quite agree with. I have approached contradictory statements with the view that life is complicated and it's important to build conversations and visions of gender that make room for varied human experiences. I believe that gender theories should fit people, and not the other way around.

Mid-August 2012, evening

When I stepped out of the OutReach center, I felt lighter. Everyone I spoke to had been so kind and so patient with me. They shared so much of themselves.

There's a unique feeling of ignorance that comes with learning new things—the unnerving realization of how little you actually know. But with this also comes a curiosity for what else is to come. Suddenly, gender felt more mysterious to me than ever. Maybe my little comic project was going to need a few more pages than I thought.

I didn't get closer to a simple, easy explanation of gender that night. But I did get something that I needed more.

Back in the car, I unrolled a little flyer that had been handed to me. It was a calendar of events at the LGBT center, including transgender support group meetings. A woman had handed it to me with encouragement to attend. It felt like I had been given a gift.

FINE

Rhea, 2005

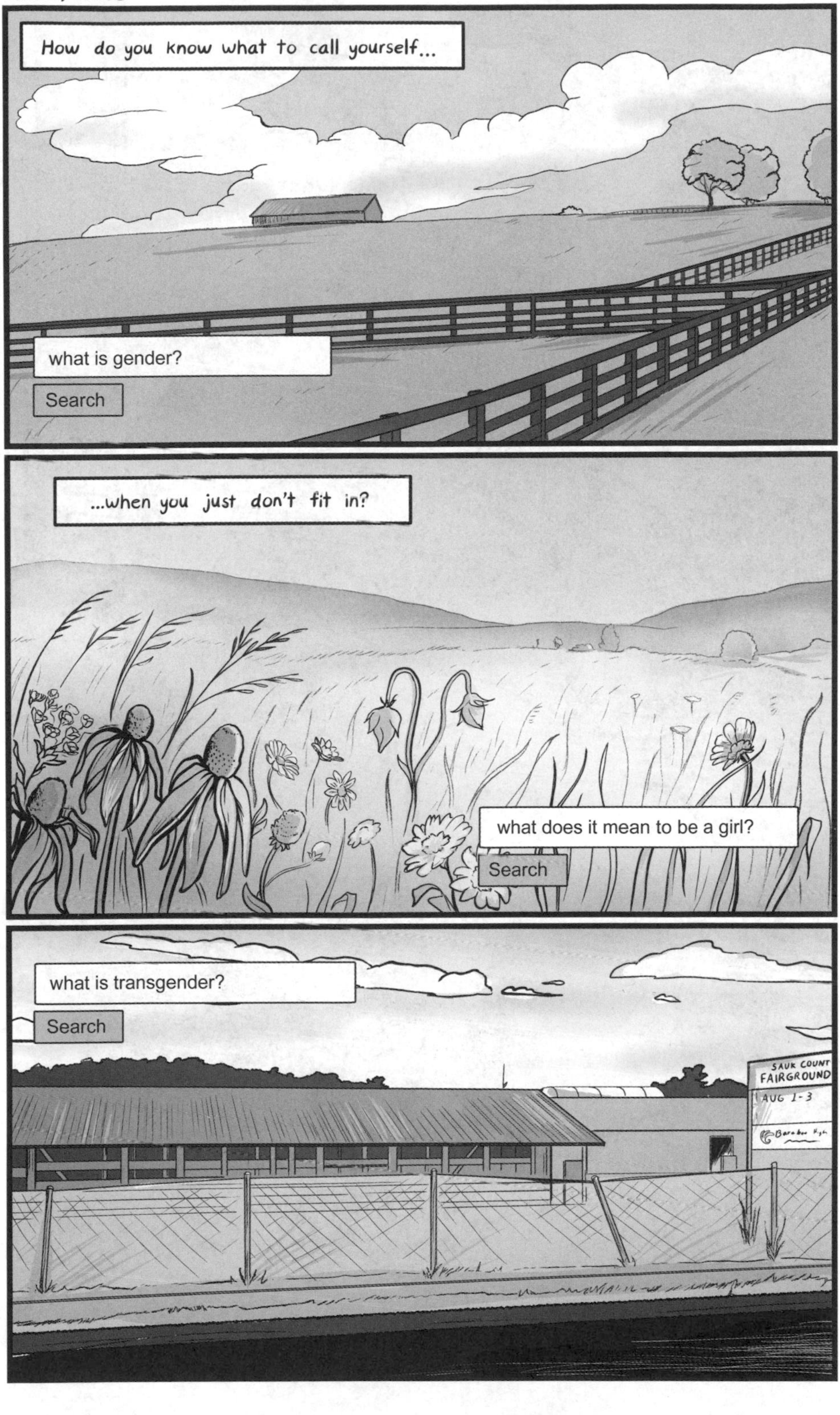
How do you know what to call yourself...
what is gender?
Search
...when you just don't fit in?
what does it mean to be a girl?
Search
what is transgender?
Search
SAUK COUNT
FAIRGROUND
AUG 1-3

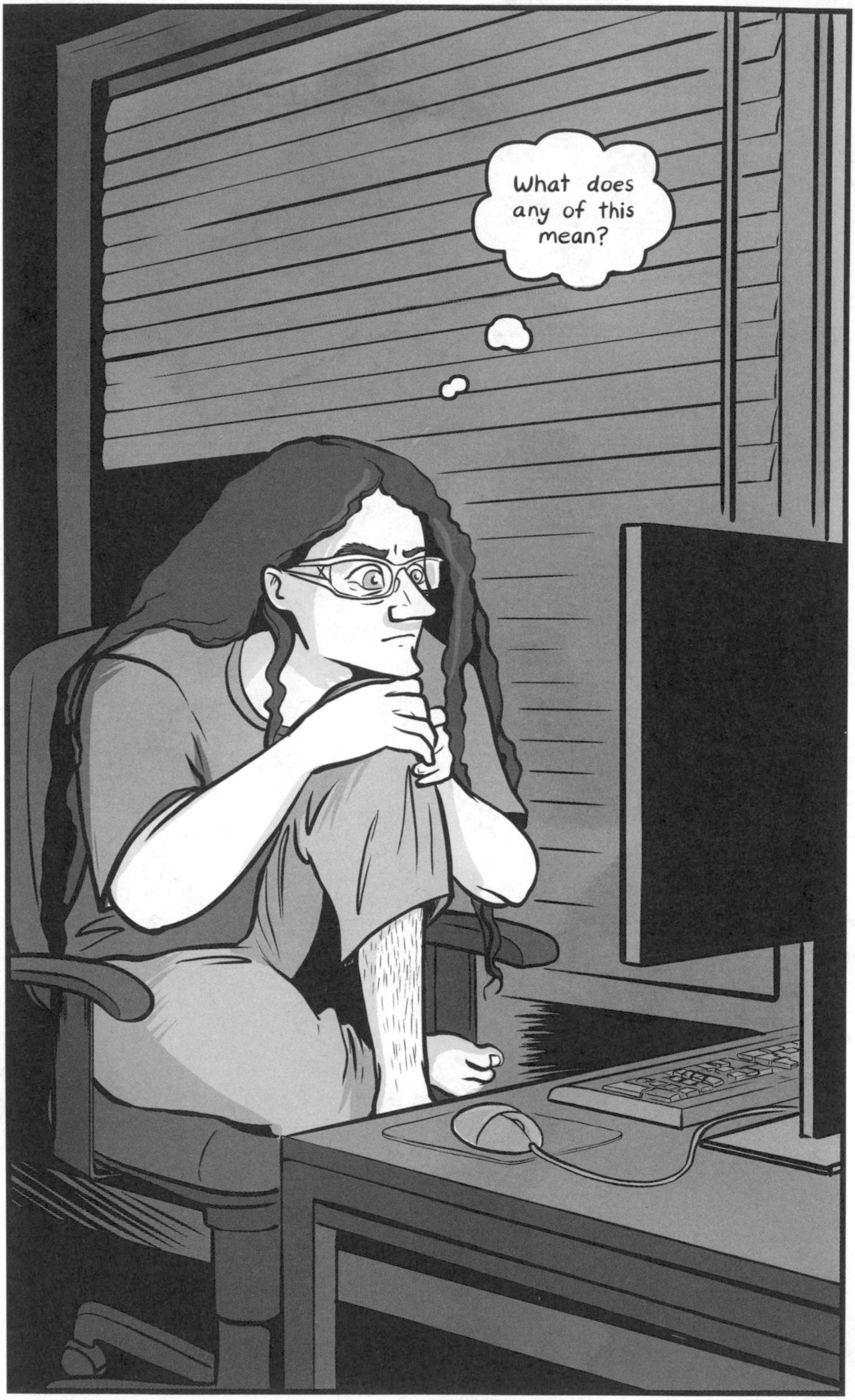
What does any of this mean?

Rhea, 2010

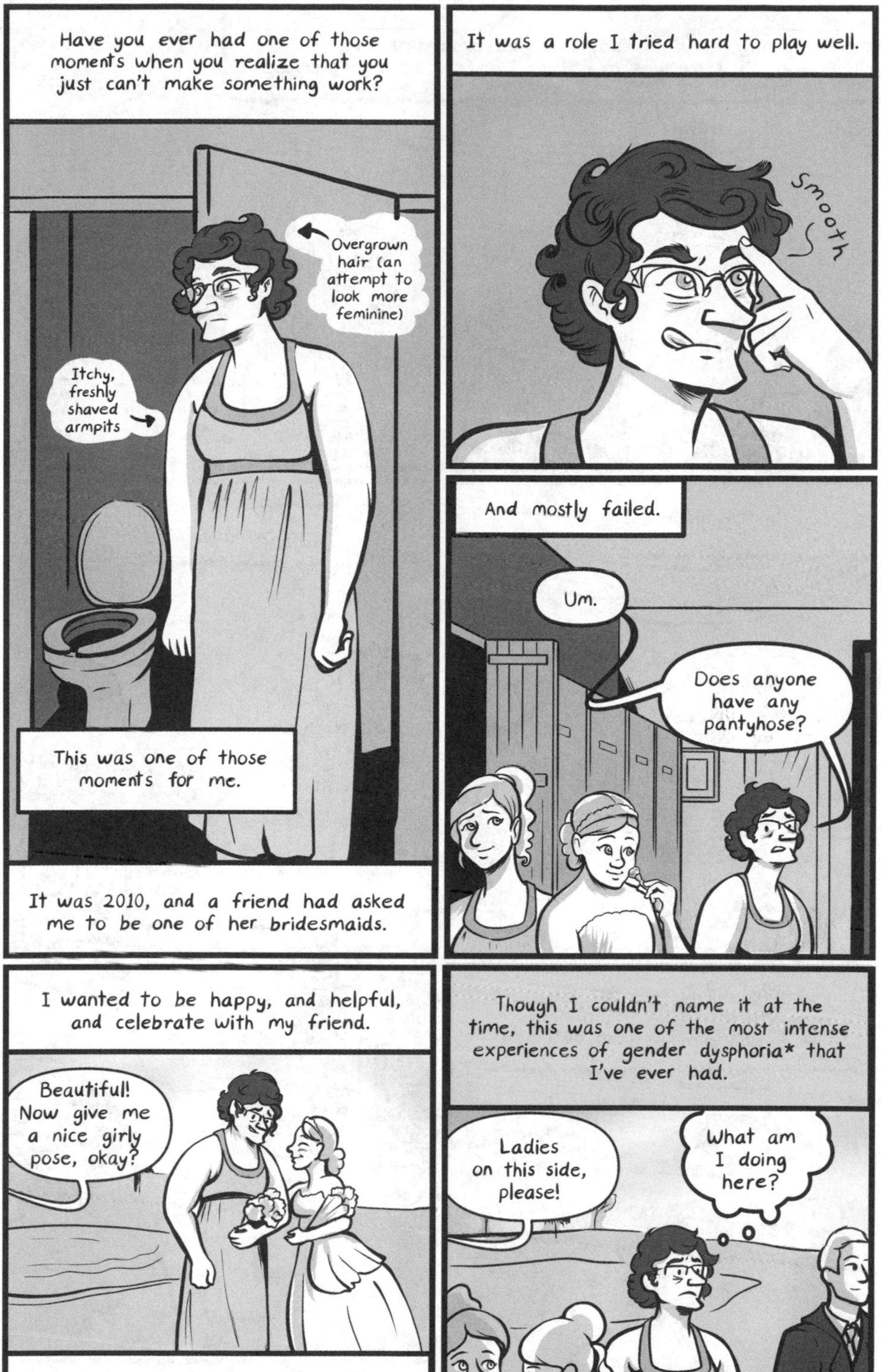
Have you ever had one of those moments when you realize that you just can't make something work?
Overgrown hair (an attempt to look more feminine)
Itchy, freshly shaved armpits
This was one of those moments for me.
It was 2010, and a friend had asked me to be one of her bridesmaids.
It was a role I tried hard to play well.
Smooth
And mostly failed.
Um.
Does anyone have any pantyhose?
I wanted to be happy, and helpful, and celebrate with my friend.
Beautiful! Now give me a nice girly pose, okay?
But instead I wound up barely staving off a panic attack the whole day.
Though I couldn't name it at the time, this was one of the most intense experiences of gender dysphoria* that I've ever had.
Ladies on this side, please!
What am I doing here?

*The despair and alienation many transgender people can feel when there is a disparity between our internal sense of identity and how we look or are being treated.

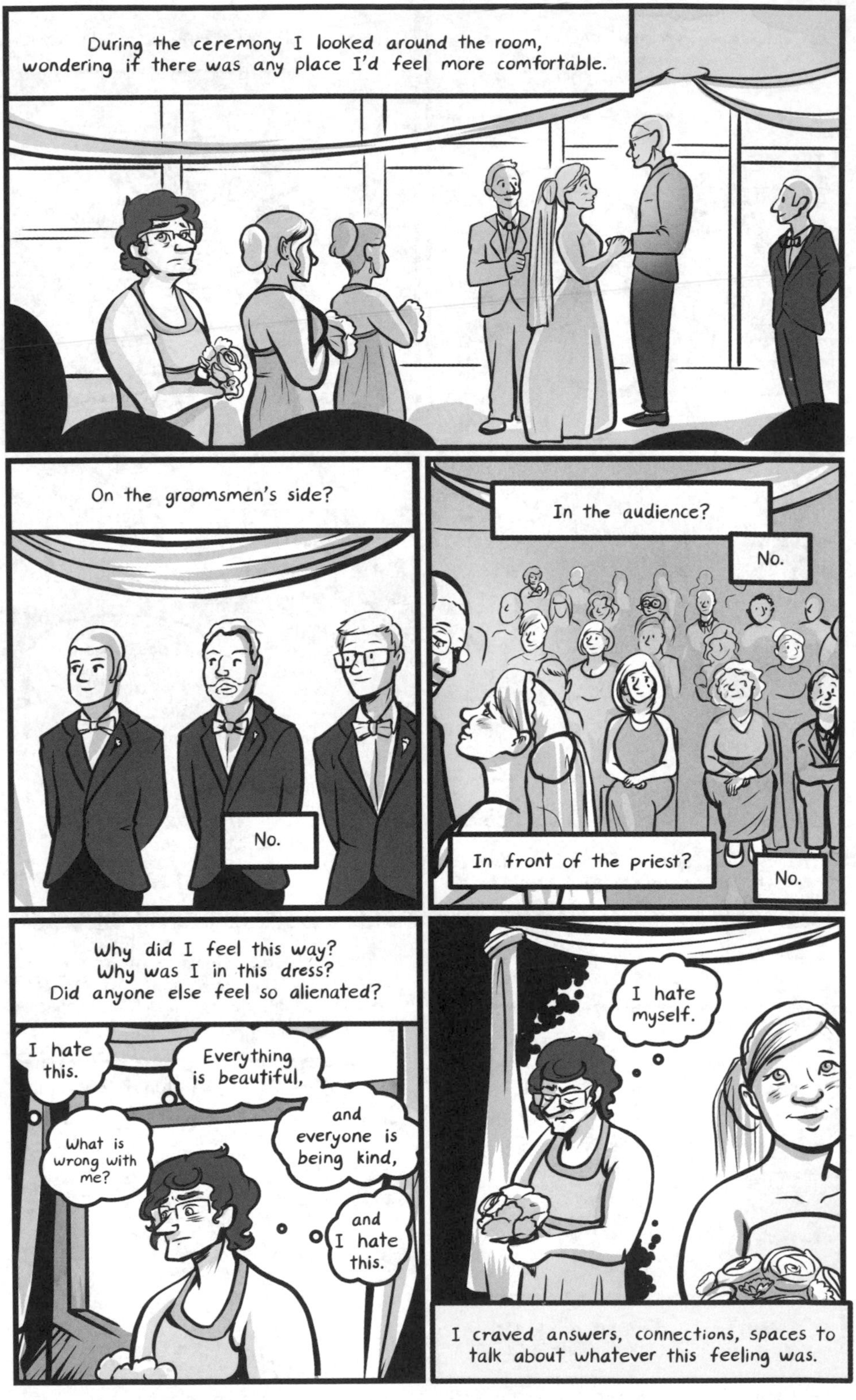

During the ceremony I looked around the room, wondering if there was any place I'd feel more comfortable.
On the groomsmen's side?
No.
In the audience?
No.
In front of the priest?
No.
Why did I feel this way? Why was I in this dress? Did anyone else feel so alienated?
I hate this.
Everything is beautiful,
What is wrong with me?
and everyone is being kind,
and I hate this.
I hate myself.
I craved answers, connections, spaces to talk about whatever this feeling was.

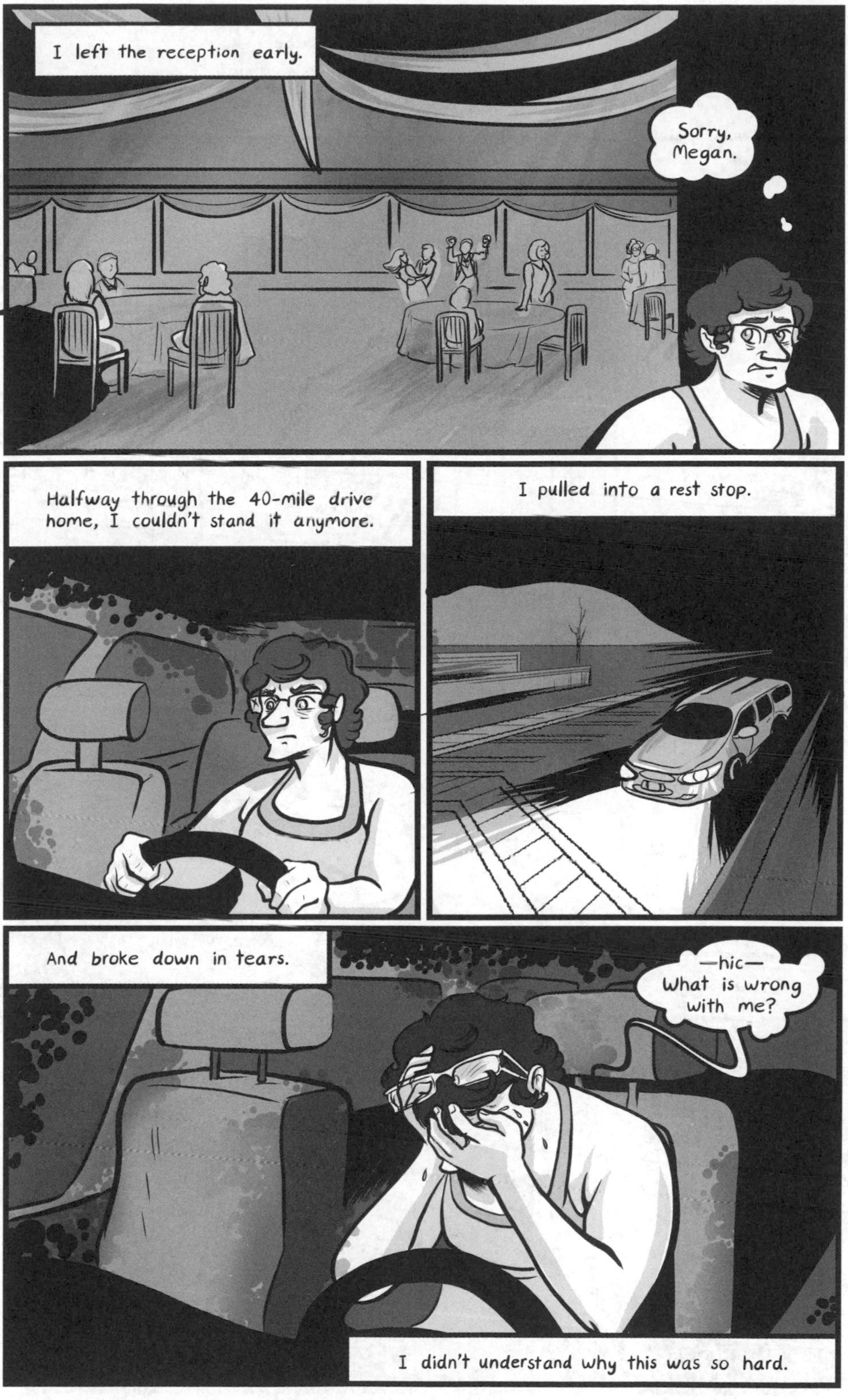
I left the reception early.
Sorry, Megan.
Halfway through the 40-mile drive home, I couldn't stand it anymore.
I pulled into a rest stop.
And broke down in tears.
—hic— What is wrong with me?
I didn't understand why this was so hard.

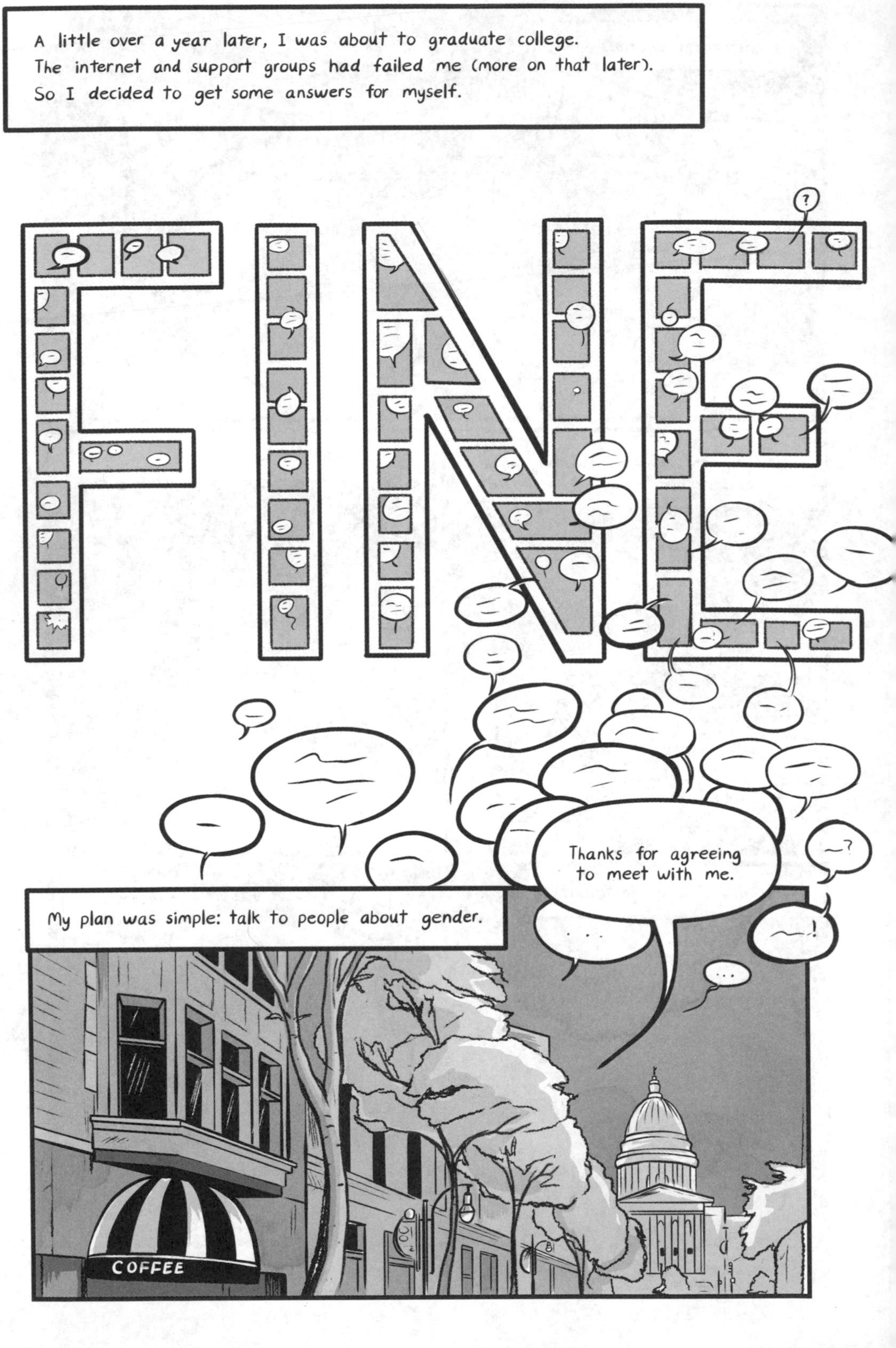
A little over a year later, I was about to graduate college.
The internet and support groups had failed me (more on that later).
So I decided to get some answers for myself.
FINE
My plan was simple: talk to people about gender.
Thanks for agreeing to meet with me.
COFFEE

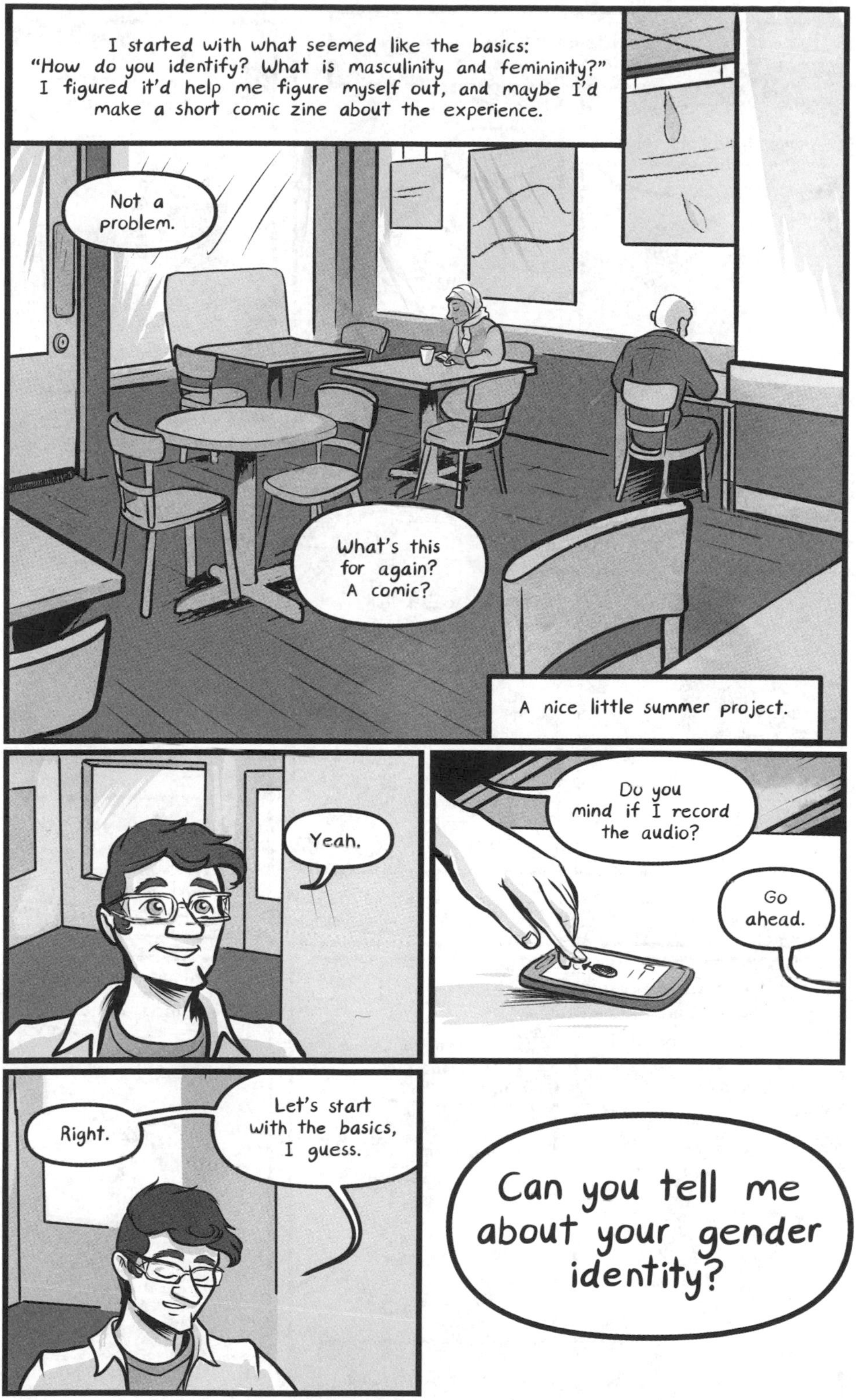
I started with what seemed like the basics: "How do you identify? What is masculinity and femininity?" I figured it'd help me figure myself out, and maybe I'd make a short comic zine about the experience.
Not a problem.
What's this for again? A comic?
A nice little summer project.
Yeah.
Do you mind if I record the audio?
Go ahead.
Right.
Let's start with the basics, I guess.
Can you tell me about your gender identity?

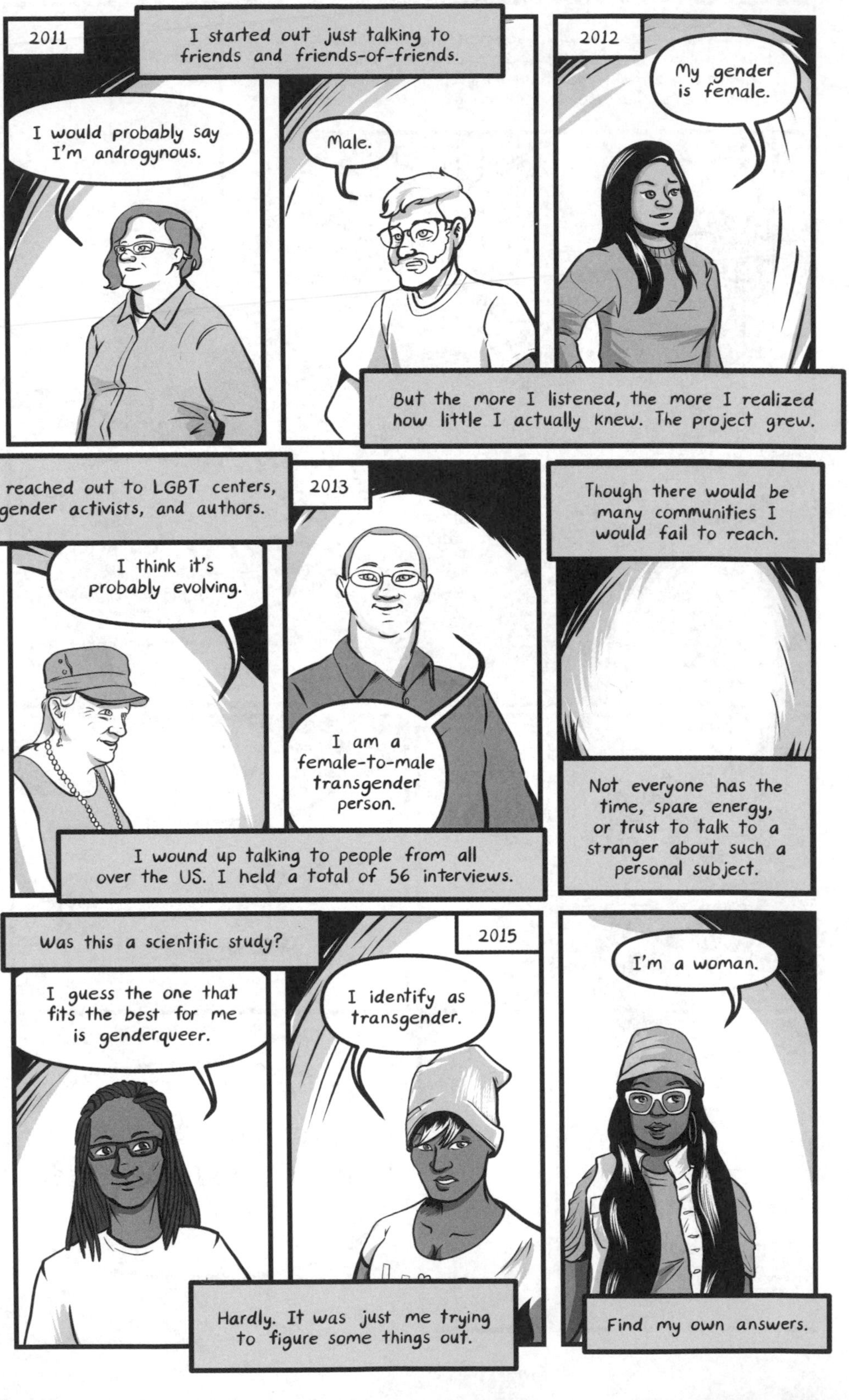
2011
I started out just talking to friends and friends-of-friends.
I would probably say I'm androgynous.
Male.
2012
My gender is female.
But the more I listened, the more I realized how little I actually knew. The project grew.
I reached out to LGBT centers, gender activists, and authors.
2013
I think it's probably evolving.
I am a female-to-male transgender person.
I wound up talking to people from all over the US. I held a total of 56 interviews.
Though there would be many communities I would fail to reach.
Not everyone has the time, spare energy, or trust to talk to a stranger about such a personal subject.
Was this a scientific study?
2015
I guess the one that fits the best for me is genderqueer.
I identify as transgender.
Hardly. It was just me trying to figure some things out.
I'm a woman.
Find my own answers.

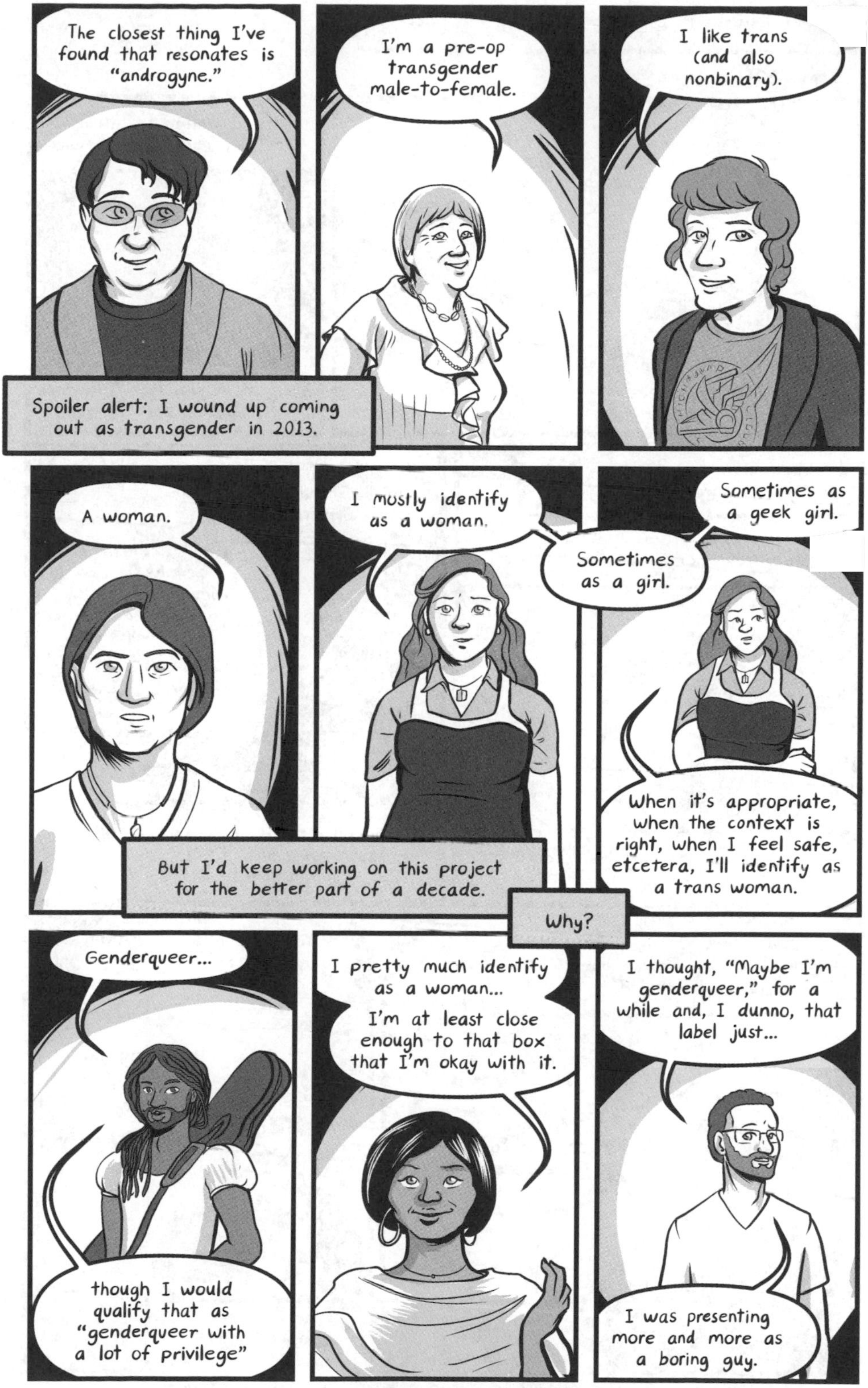
The closest thing I've found that resonates is "androgyne."
Spoiler alert: I wound up coming out as transgender in 2013.
I'm a pre-op transgender male-to-female.
I like trans (and also nonbinary).
A woman.
I mostly identify as a woman.
Sometimes as a girl.
Sometimes as a geek girl.
When it's appropriate, when the context is right, when I feel safe, etcetera, I'll identify as a trans woman.
But I'd keep working on this project for the better part of a decade.
Why?
Genderqueer...
though I would qualify that as "genderqueer with a lot of privilege"
I pretty much identify as a woman...
I'm at least close enough to that box that I'm okay with it.
I thought, "Maybe I'm genderqueer," for a while and, I dunno, that label just...
I was presenting more and more as a boring guy.

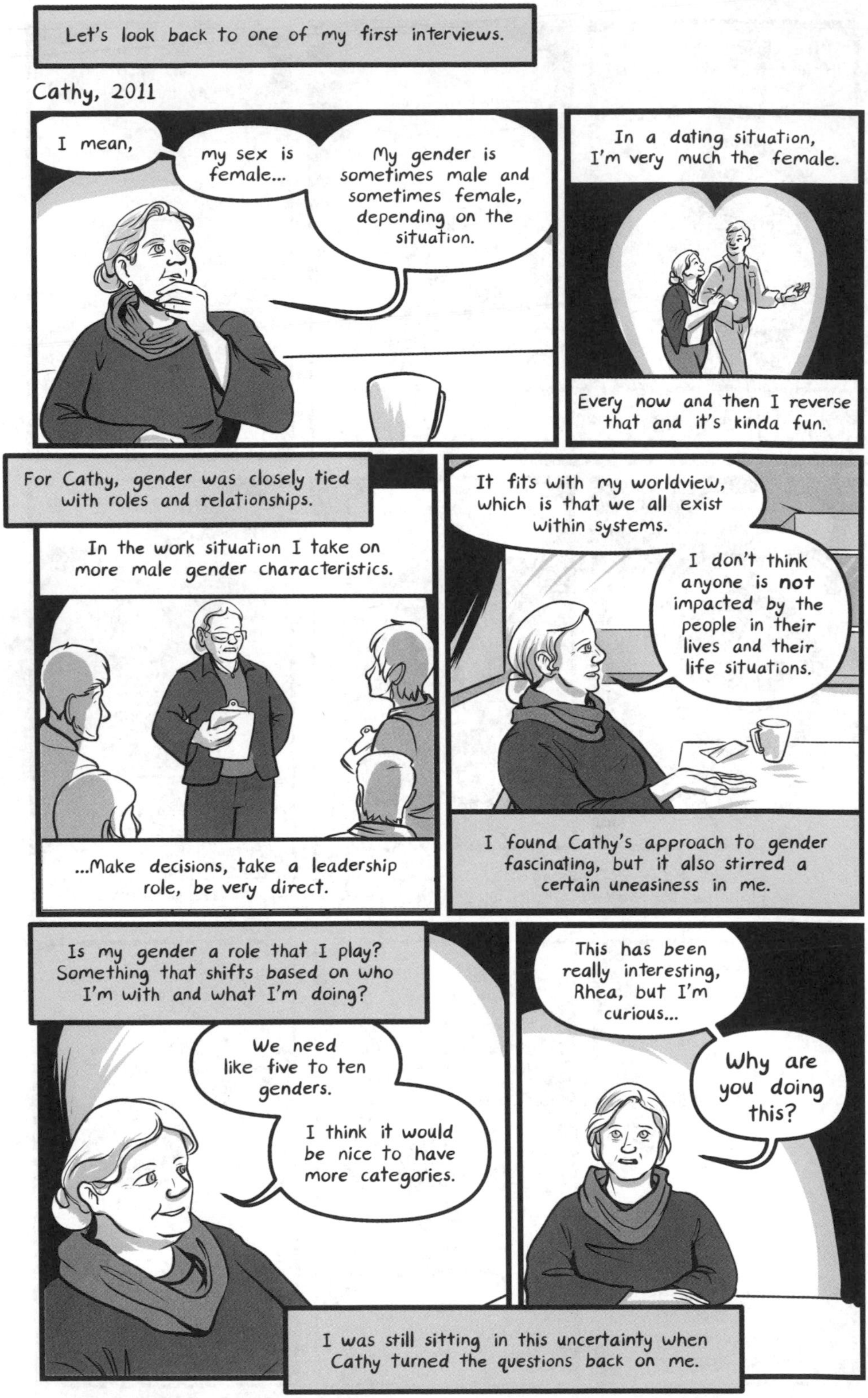
Let's look back to one of my first interviews.
Cathy, 2011
I mean,
my sex is female...
My gender is sometimes male and sometimes female, depending on the situation.
In a dating situation, I'm very much the female.
Every now and then I reverse that and it's kinda fun.
For Cathy, gender was closely tied with roles and relationships.
In the work situation I take on more male gender characteristics.
...Make decisions, take a leadership role, be very direct.
It fits with my worldview, which is that we all exist within systems.
I don't think anyone is **not** impacted by the people in their lives and their life situations.
I found Cathy's approach to gender fascinating, but it also stirred a certain uneasiness in me.
Is my gender a role that I play? Something that shifts based on who I'm with and what I'm doing?
We need like five to ten genders.
I think it would be nice to have more categories.
This has been really interesting, Rhea, but I'm curious...
Why are you doing this?
I was still sitting in this uncertainty when Cathy turned the questions back on me.

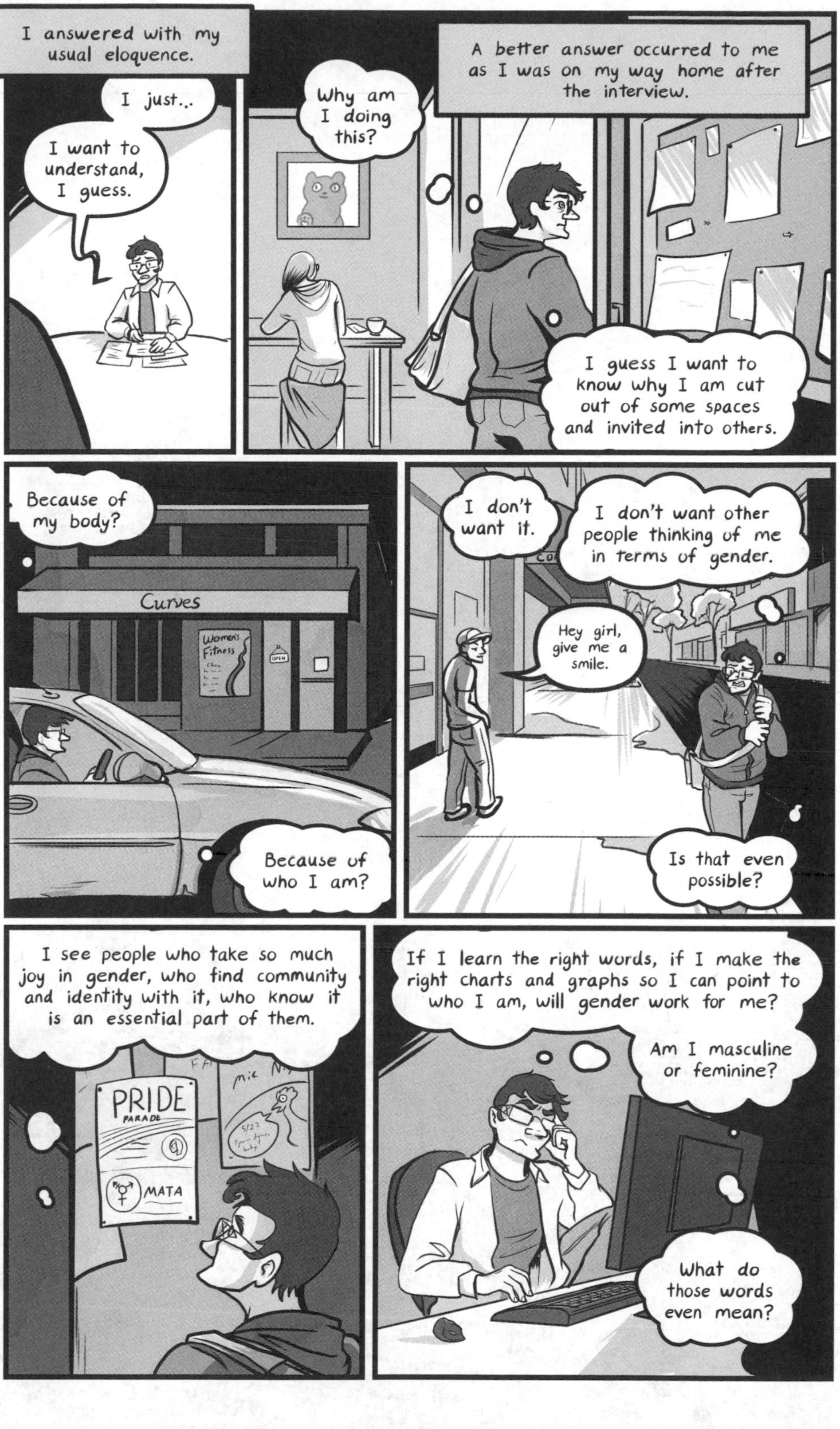
I answered with my usual eloquence.
I just...
I want to understand, I guess.
Why am I doing this?
A better answer occurred to me as I was on my way home after the interview.
I guess I want to know why I am cut out of some spaces and invited into others.
Because of my body?
Curves
Women's Fitness
OPEN
Because of who I am?
I don't want it.
I don't want other people thinking of me in terms of gender.
Hey girl, give me a smile.
Is that even possible?
I see people who take so much joy in gender, who find community and identity with it, who know it is an essential part of them.
PRIDE
PARADE
MATA
5/22
If I learn the right words, if I make the right charts and graphs so I can point to who I am, will gender work for me?
Am I masculine or feminine?
What do those words even mean?

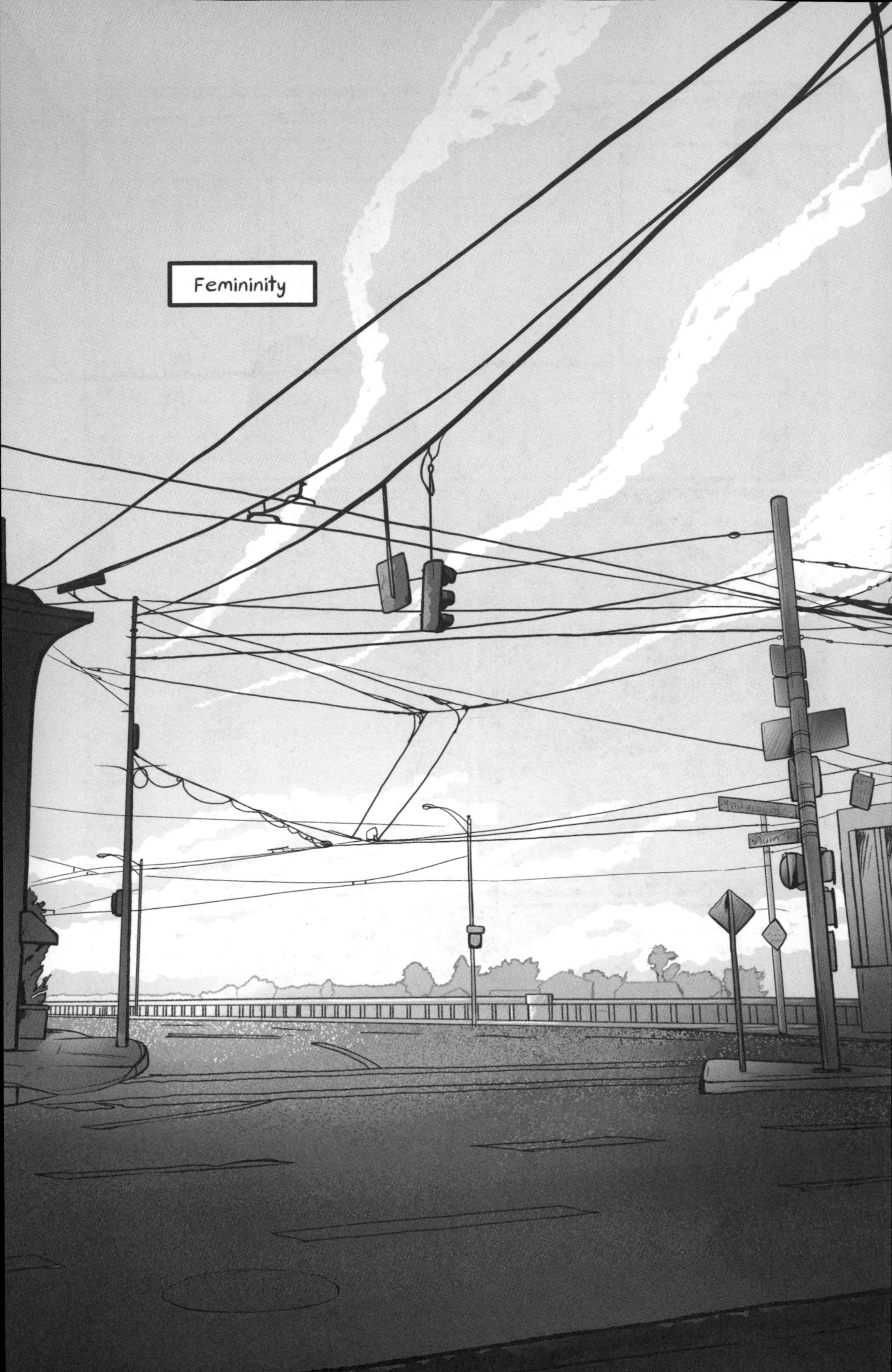
Femininity

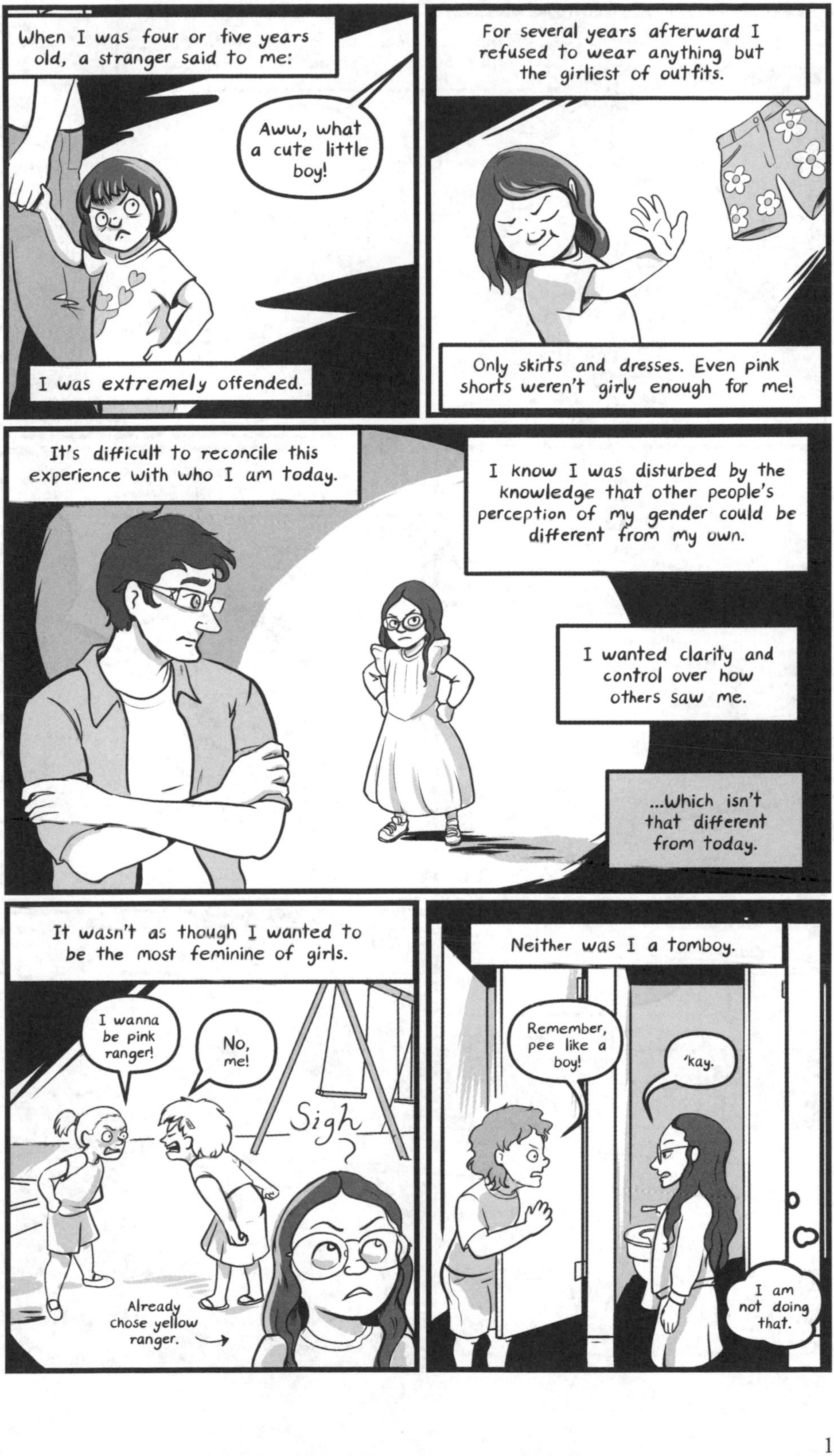
When I was four or five years old, a stranger said to me:
Aww, what a cute little boy!
I was extremely offended.
For several years afterward I refused to wear anything but the girliest of outfits.
Only skirts and dresses. Even pink shorts weren't girly enough for me!
It's difficult to reconcile this experience with who I am today.
I know I was disturbed by the knowledge that other people's perception of my gender could be different from my own.
I wanted clarity and control over how others saw me.
...Which isn't that different from today.
It wasn't as though I wanted to be the most feminine of girls.
I wanna be pink ranger!
No, me!
Sigh
Already chose yellow ranger.
Neither was I a tomboy.
Remember, pee like a boy!
'kay.
I am not doing that.

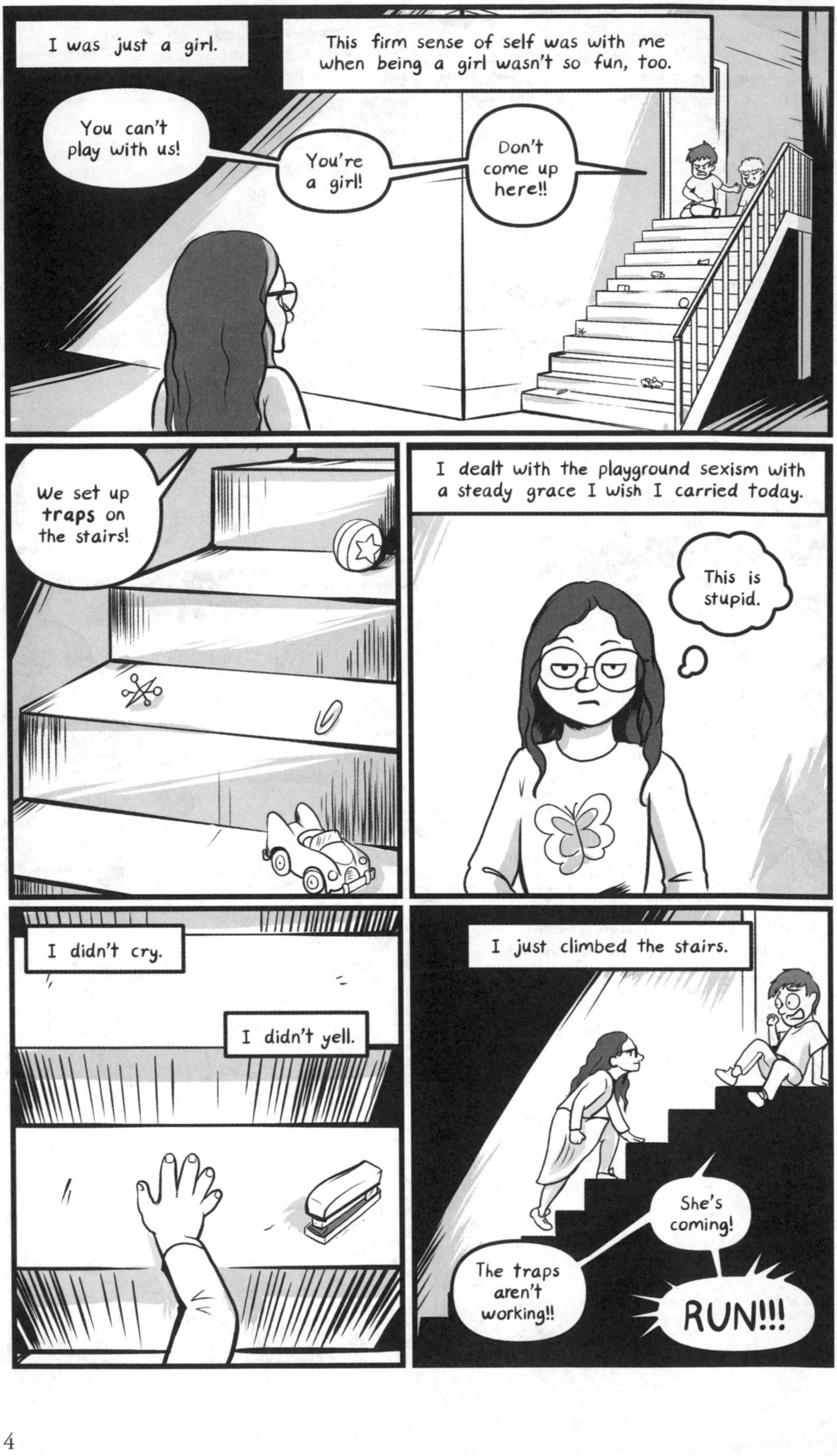
I was just a girl.
This firm sense of self was with me when being a girl wasn't so fun, too.
You can't play with us!
You're a girl!
Don't come up here!!
We set up traps on the stairs!
I dealt with the playground sexism with a steady grace I wish I carried today.
This is stupid.
I didn't cry.
I didn't yell.
I just climbed the stairs.
She's coming!
The traps aren't working!!
RUN!!!

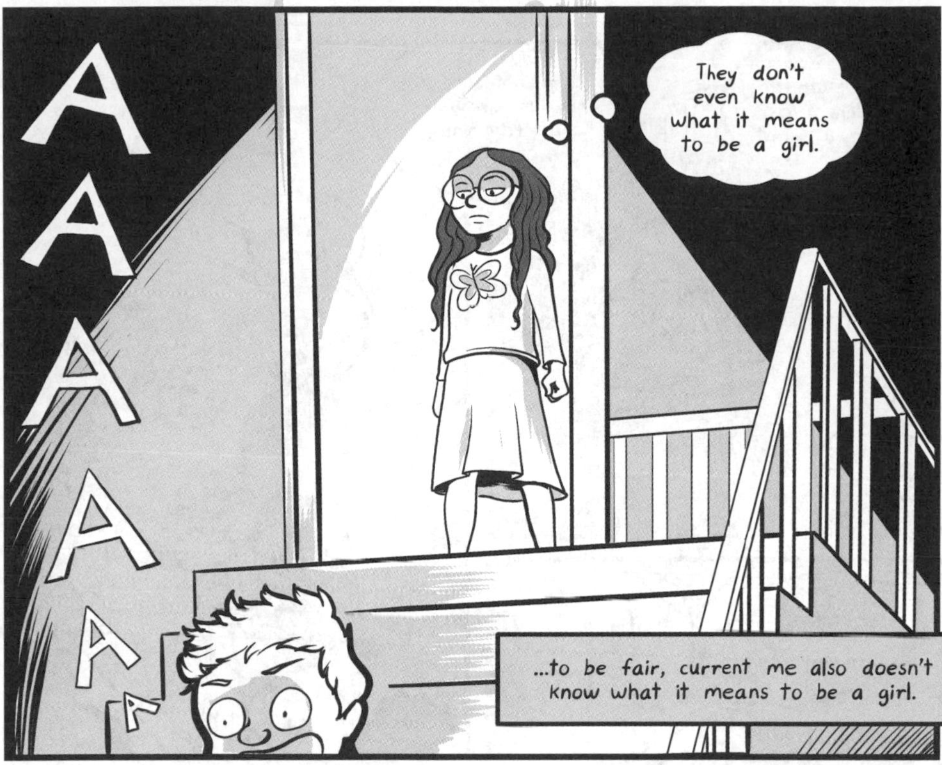
AAAAAAA
They don't even know what it means to be a girl.
...to be fair, current me also doesn't know what it means to be a girl.

Ginger, 2012

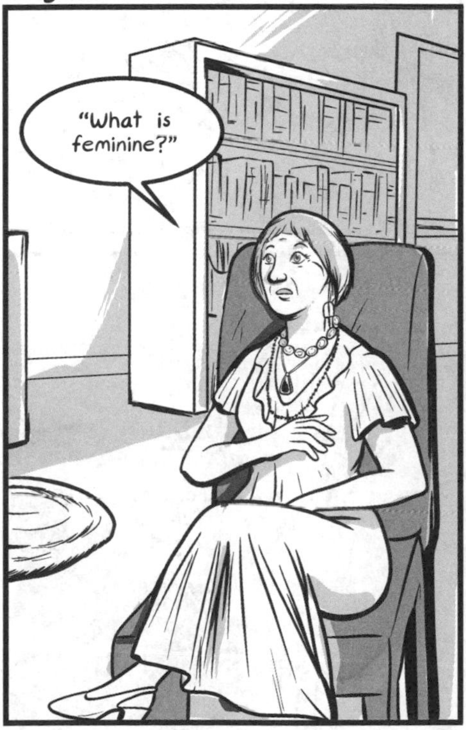
"What is feminine?"

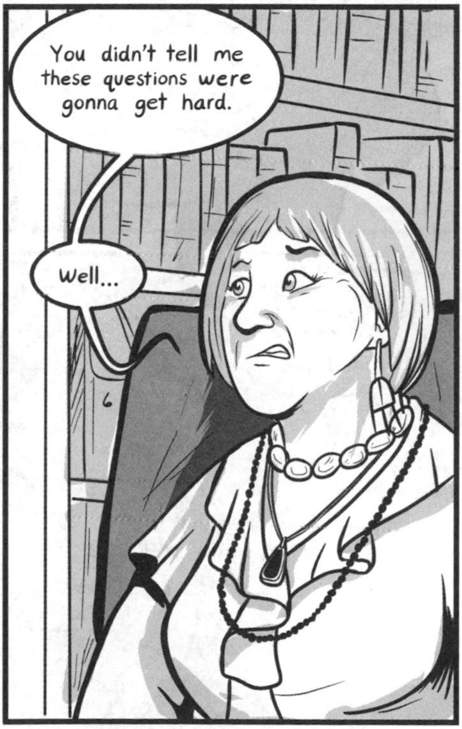
You didn't tell me these questions were gonna get hard.
Well...

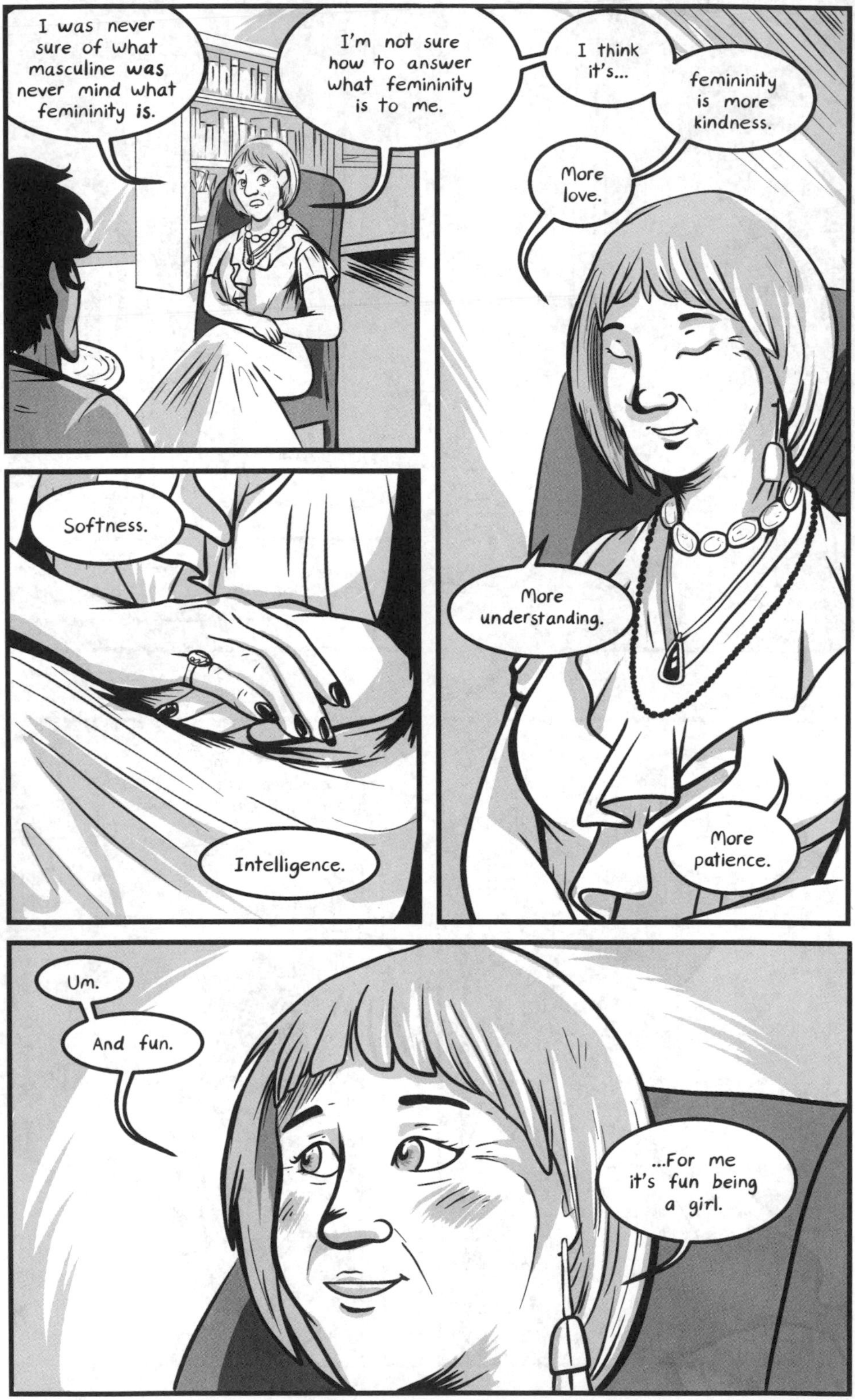
I was never sure of what masculine **was** never mind what femininity **is**.
I'm not sure how to answer what femininity is to me.
I think it's...
femininity is more kindness.
More love.
Softness.
Intelligence.
More understanding.
More patience.
Um.
And fun.
...For me it's fun being a girl.

LaShawn, 2013

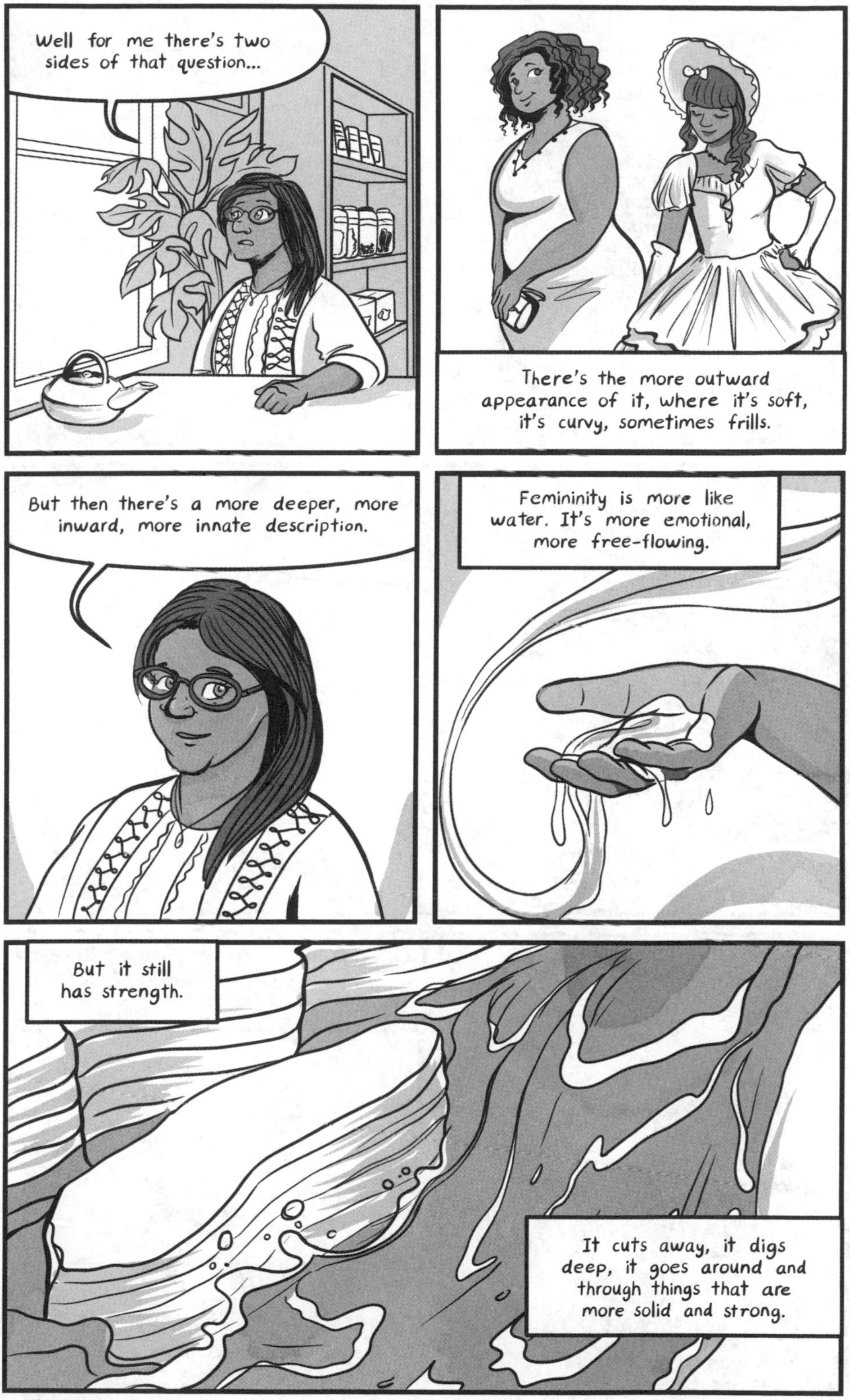
Well for me there's two sides of that question...
There's the more outward appearance of it, where it's soft, it's curvy, sometimes frills.
But then there's a more deeper, more inward, more innate description.
Femininity is more like water. It's more emotional, more free-flowing.
But it still has strength.
It cuts away, it digs deep, it goes around and through things that are more solid and strong.

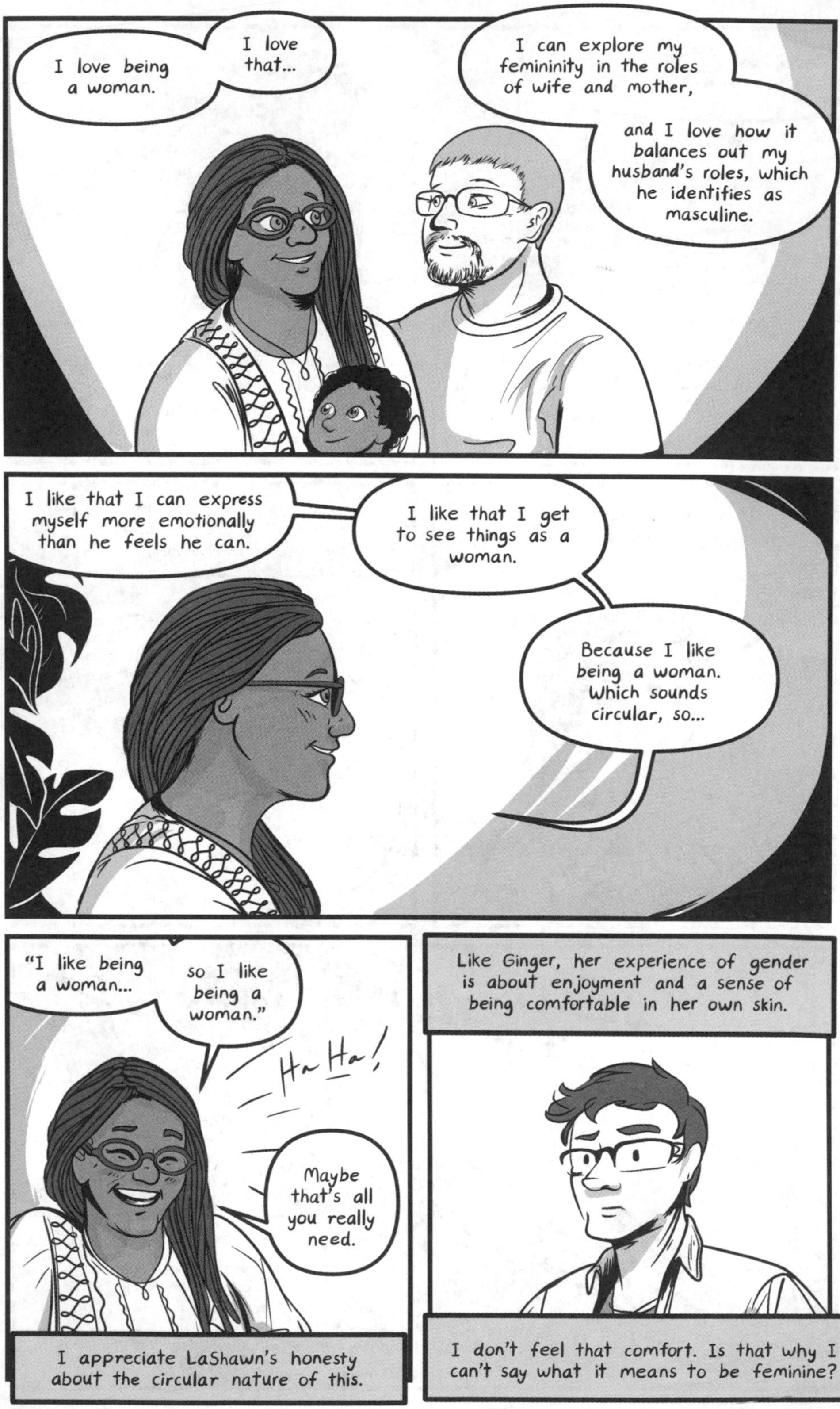

I love being a woman.
I love that...
I can explore my femininity in the roles of wife and mother,
and I love how it balances out my husband's roles, which he identifies as masculine.
I like that I can express myself more emotionally than he feels he can.
I like that I get to see things as a woman.
Because I like being a woman. Which sounds circular, so...
"I like being a woman...
so I like being a woman."
Ha Ha!
Maybe that's all you really need.
I appreciate LaShawn's honesty about the circular nature of this.
Like Ginger, her experience of gender is about enjoyment and a sense of being comfortable in her own skin.
I don't feel that comfort. Is that why I can't say what it means to be feminine?

Marie, 2013

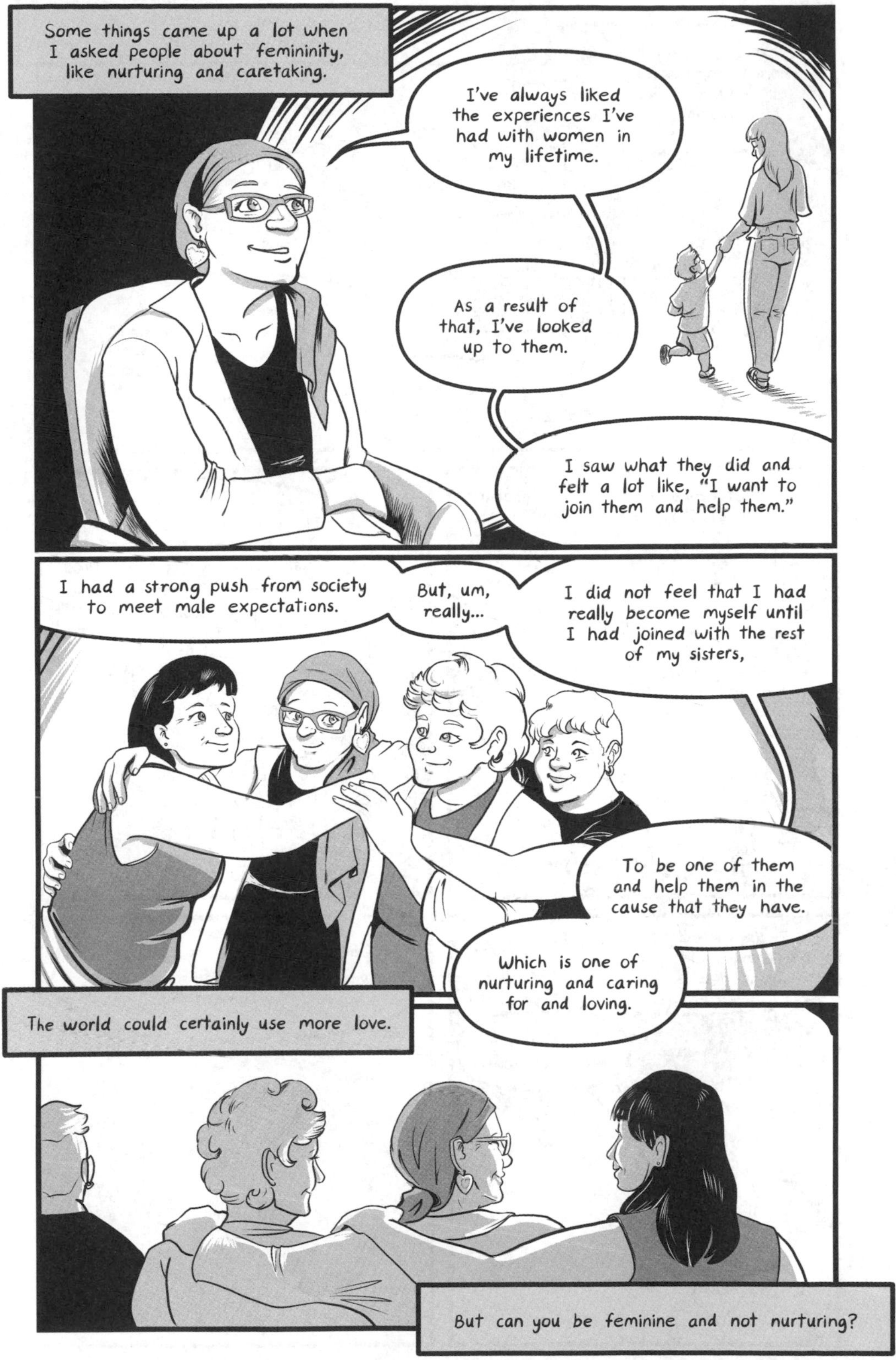
Some things came up a lot when I asked people about femininity, like nurturing and caretaking.
I've always liked the experiences I've had with women in my lifetime.
As a result of that, I've looked up to them.
I saw what they did and felt a lot like, "I want to join them and help them."
I had a strong push from society to meet male expectations.
But, um, really...
I did not feel that I had really become myself until I had joined with the rest of my sisters,
To be one of them and help them in the cause that they have.
Which is one of nurturing and caring for and loving.
The world could certainly use more love.
But can you be feminine and not nurturing?

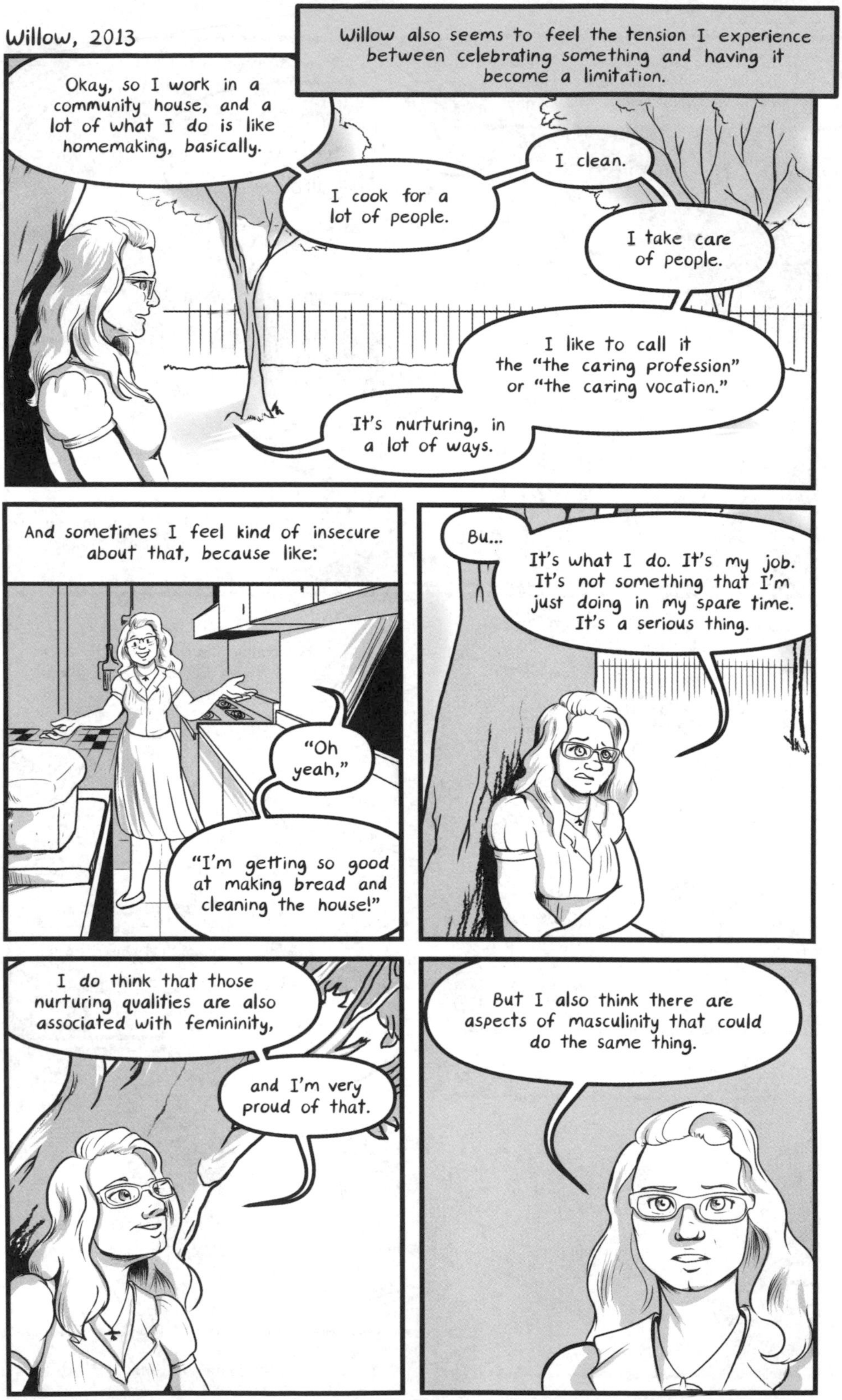

Willow, 2013
Willow also seems to feel the tension I experience between celebrating something and having it become a limitation.
Okay, so I work in a community house, and a lot of what I do is like homemaking, basically.
I cook for a lot of people.
I clean.
I take care of people.
I like to call it the "the caring profession" or "the caring vocation."
It's nurturing, in a lot of ways.
And sometimes I feel kind of insecure about that, because like:
"Oh yeah,"
"I'm getting so good at making bread and cleaning the house!"
Bu...
It's what I do. It's my job. It's not something that I'm just doing in my spare time. It's a serious thing.
I do think that those nurturing qualities are also associated with femininity,
and I'm very proud of that.
But I also think there are aspects of masculinity that could do the same thing.

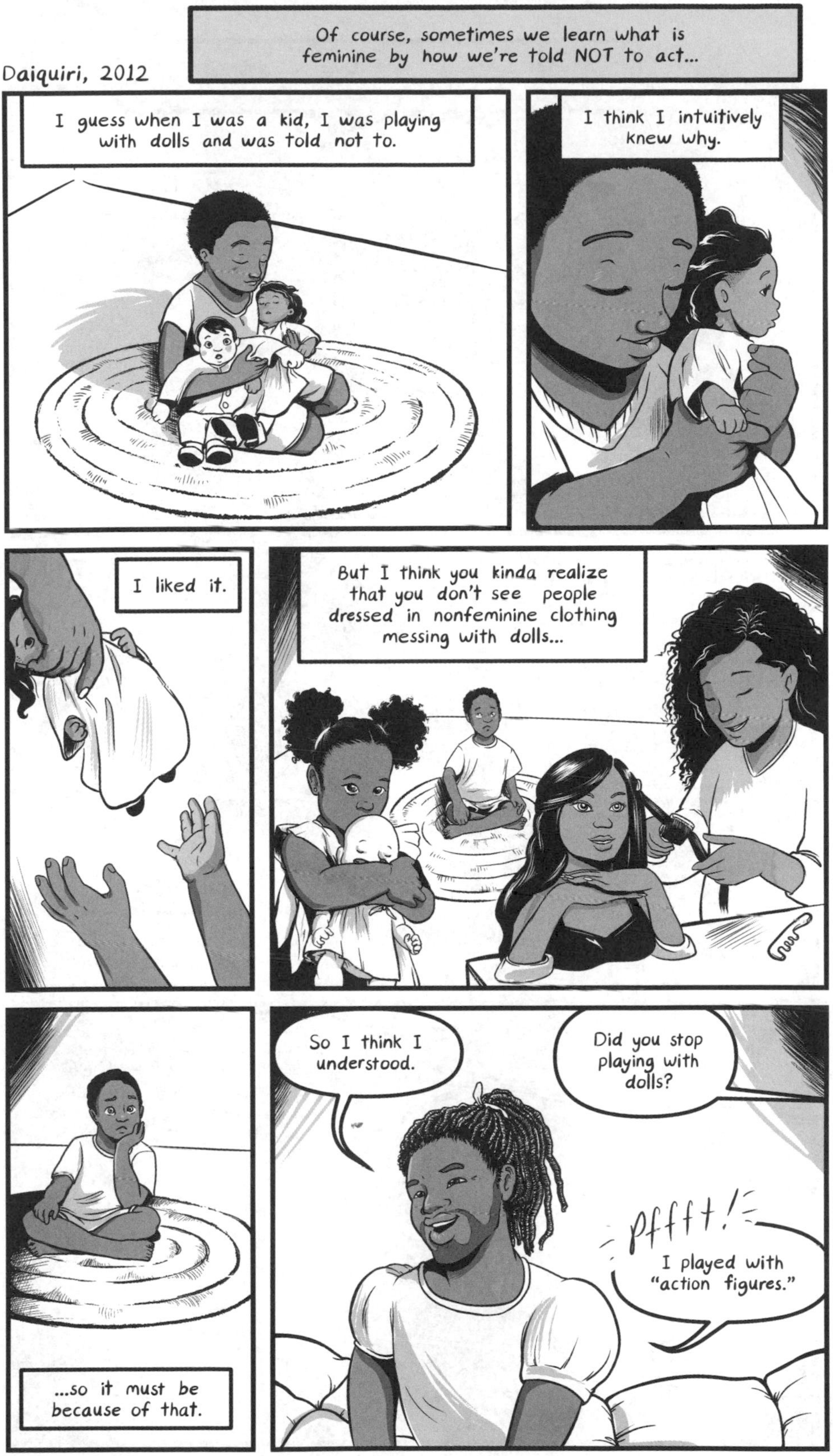
Daiquiri, 2012
Of course, sometimes we learn what is feminine by how we're told NOT to act...
I guess when I was a kid, I was playing with dolls and was told not to.
I think I intuitively knew why.
I liked it.
But I think you kinda realize that you don't see people dressed in nonfeminine clothing messing with dolls...
...so it must be because of that.
So I think I understood.
Did you stop playing with dolls?
pffft!
I played with "action figures."

Monei, 2015

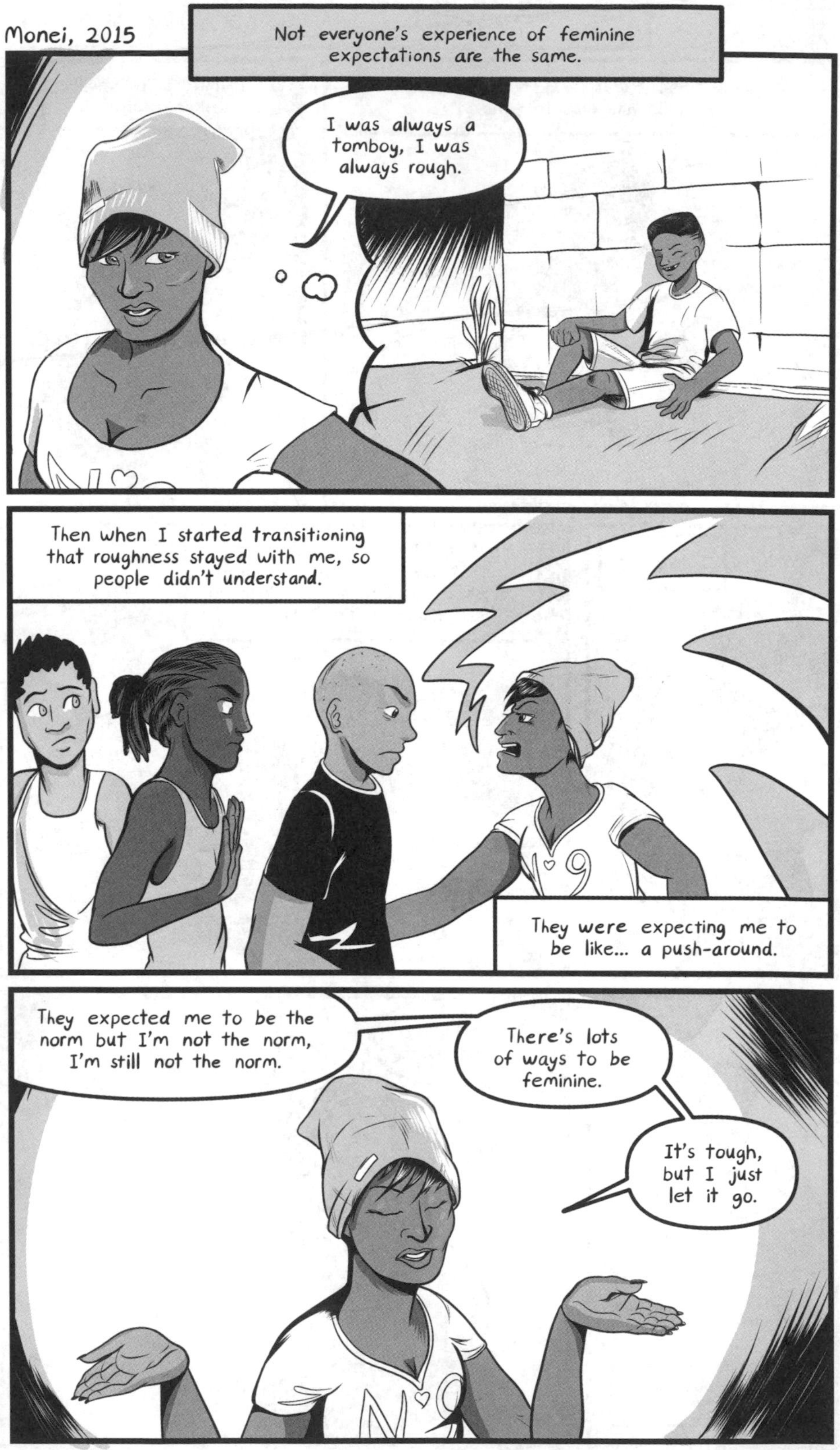
Not everyone's experience of feminine expectations are the same.
I was always a tomboy, I was always rough.
Then when I started transitioning that roughness stayed with me, so people didn't understand.
They were expecting me to be like... a push-around.
They expected me to be the norm but I'm not the norm, I'm still not the norm.
There's lots of ways to be feminine.
It's tough, but I just let it go.

Kai, 2012

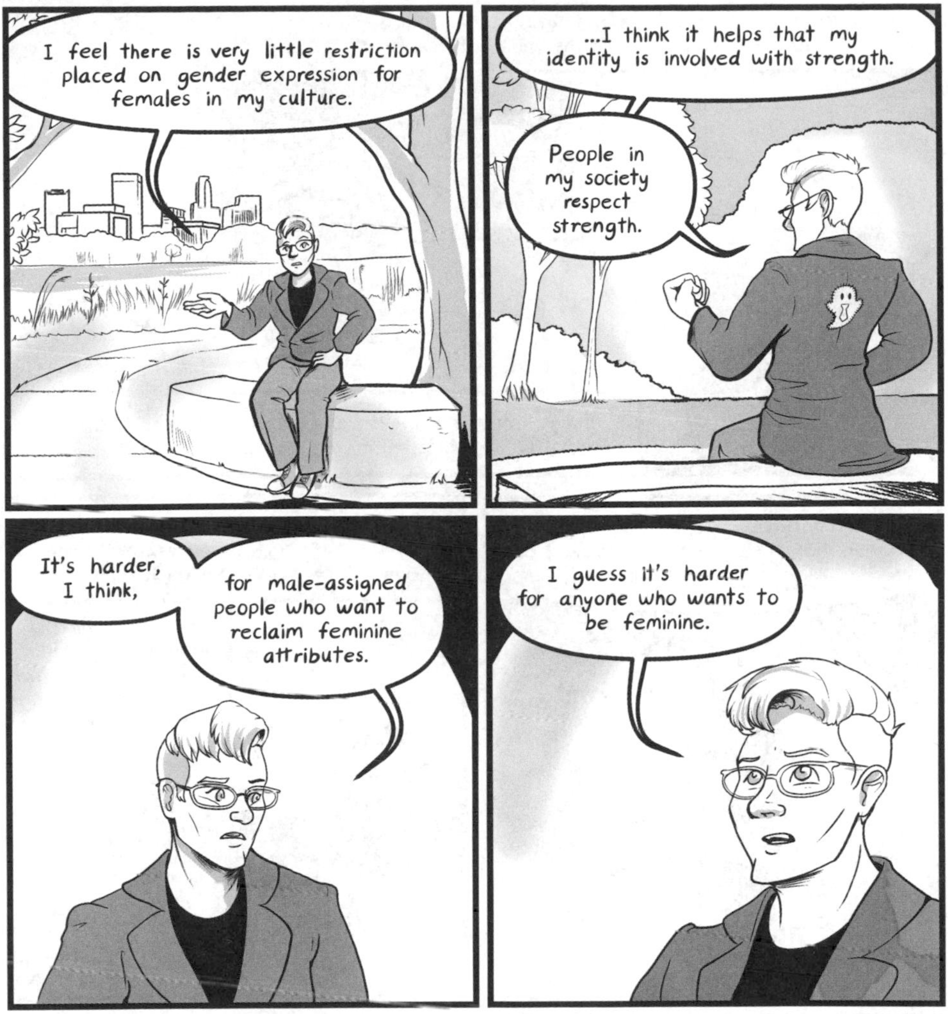
I feel there is very little restriction placed on gender expression for females in my culture.
...I think it helps that my identity is involved with strength.
People in my society respect strength.
It's harder, I think,
for male-assigned people who want to reclaim feminine attributes.
I guess it's harder for anyone who wants to be feminine.

Kim, 2011

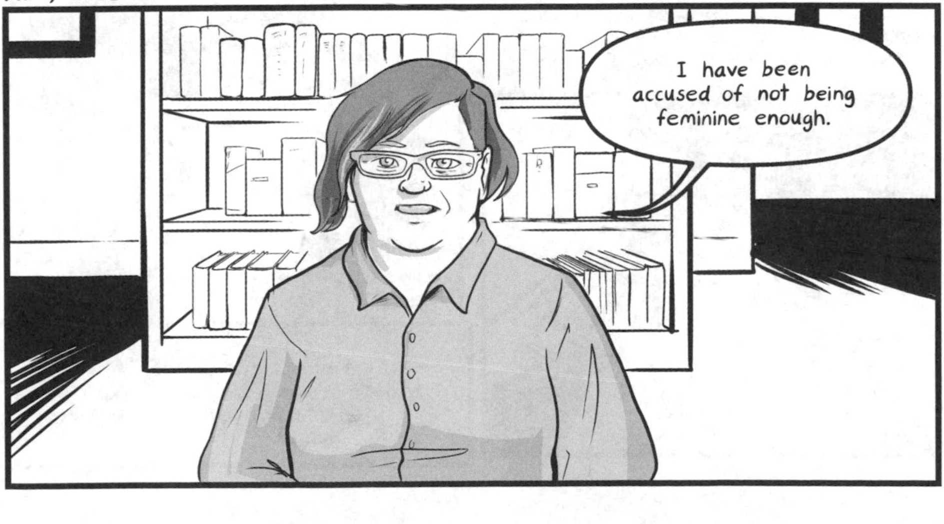
I have been accused of not being feminine enough.

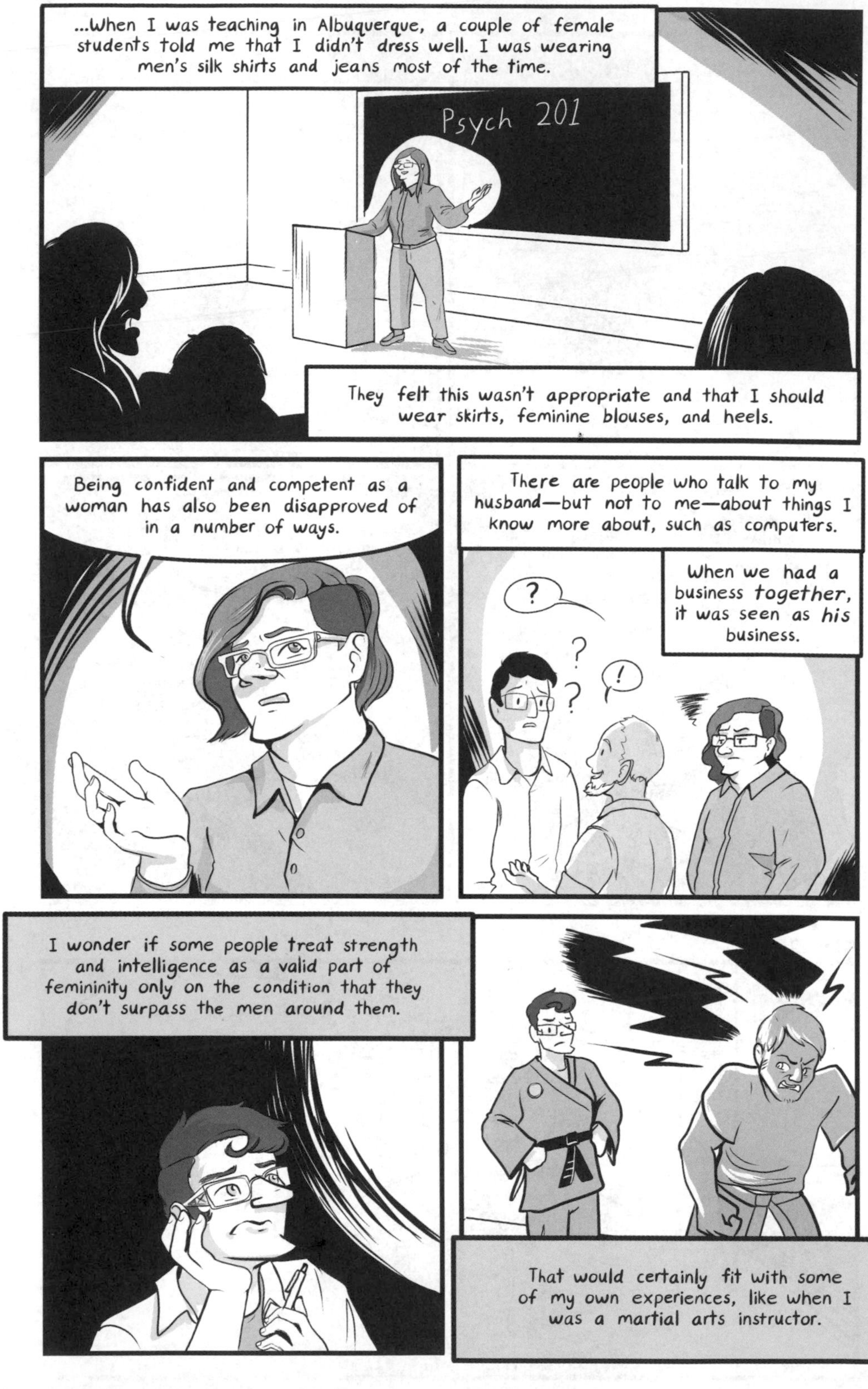

...When I was teaching in Albuquerque, a couple of female students told me that I didn't dress well. I was wearing men's silk shirts and jeans most of the time.
Psych 201
They felt this wasn't appropriate and that I should wear skirts, feminine blouses, and heels.
Being confident and competent as a woman has also been disapproved of in a number of ways.
There are people who talk to my husband—but not to me—about things I know more about, such as computers.
When we had a business *together*, it was seen as *his* business.
?
?
?
!
I wonder if some people treat strength and intelligence as a valid part of femininity only on the condition that they don't surpass the men around them.
That would certainly fit with some of my own experiences, like when I was a martial arts instructor.

Anne, 2012

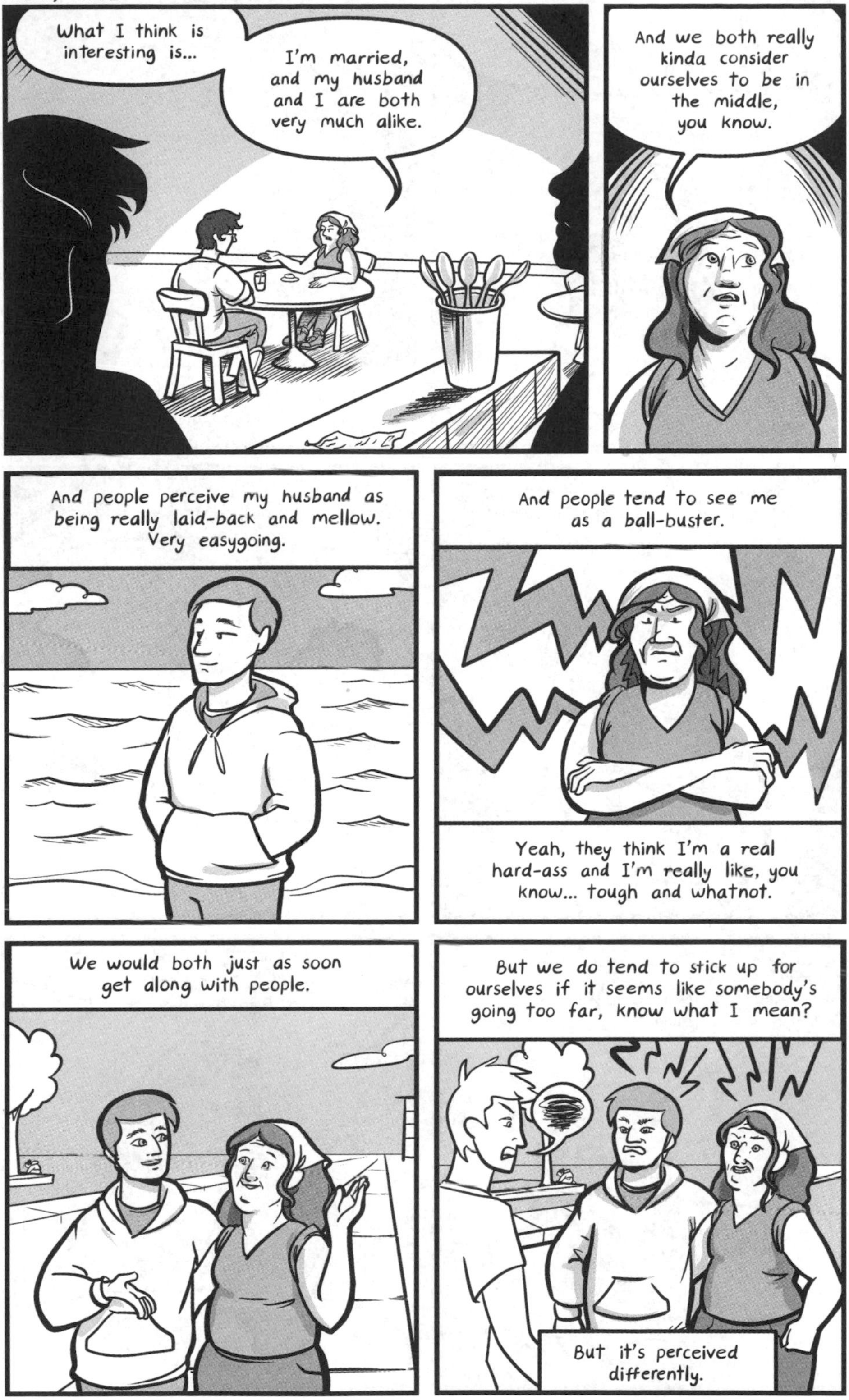
What I think is interesting is...
I'm married, and my husband and I are both very much alike.
And we both really kinda consider ourselves to be in the middle, you know.
And people perceive my husband as being really laid-back and mellow. Very easygoing.
And people tend to see me as a ball-buster.
Yeah, they think I'm a real hard-ass and I'm really like, you know... tough and whatnot.
We would both just as soon get along with people.
But we do tend to stick up for ourselves if it seems like somebody's going too far, know what I mean?
But it's perceived differently.

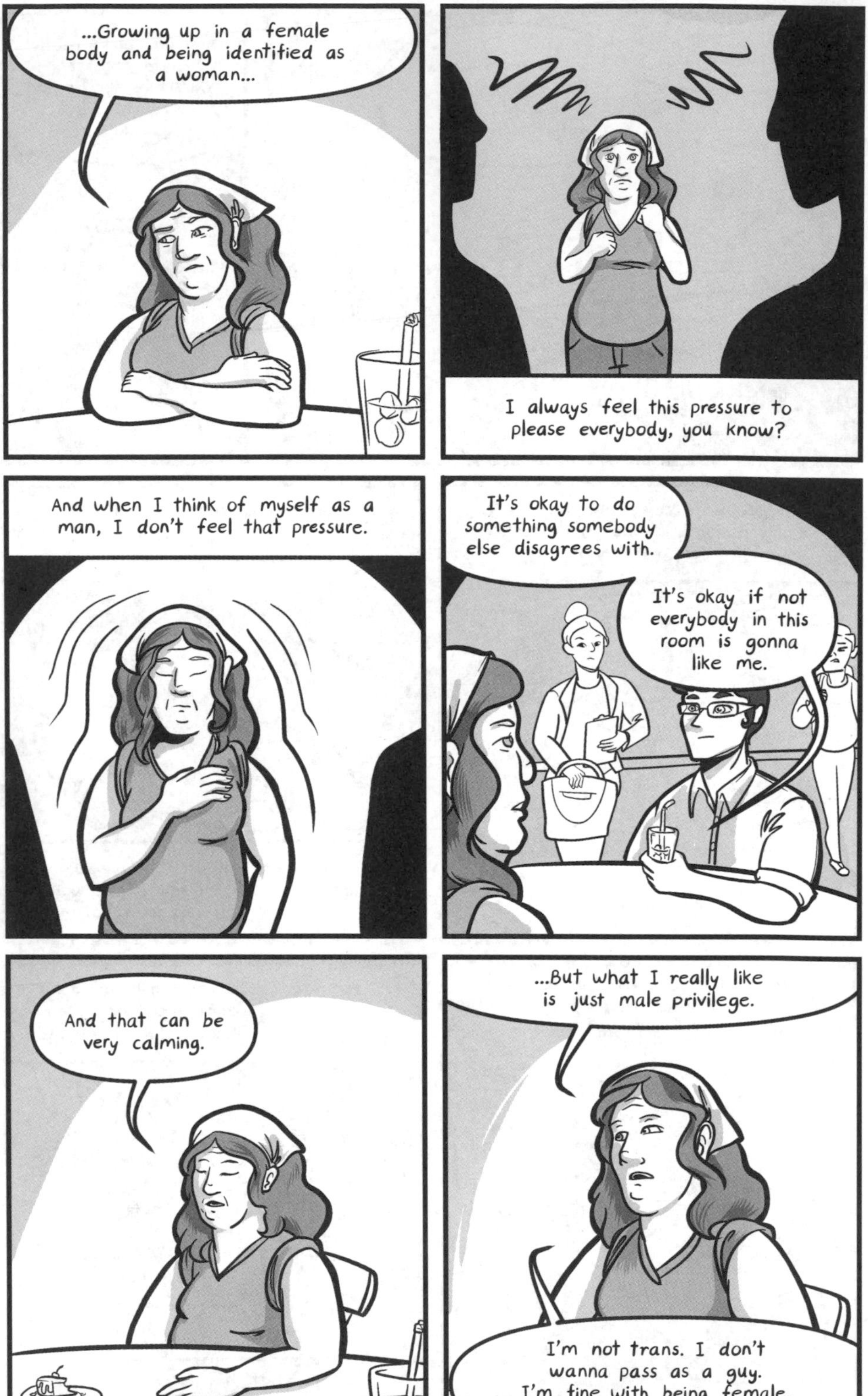

...Growing up in a female body and being identified as a woman...
I always feel this pressure to please everybody, you know?
And when I think of myself as a man, I don't feel that pressure.
It's okay to do something somebody else disagrees with.
It's okay if not everybody in this room is gonna like me.
And that can be very calming.
...But what I really like is just male privilege.
I'm not trans. I don't wanna pass as a guy. I'm fine with being female.

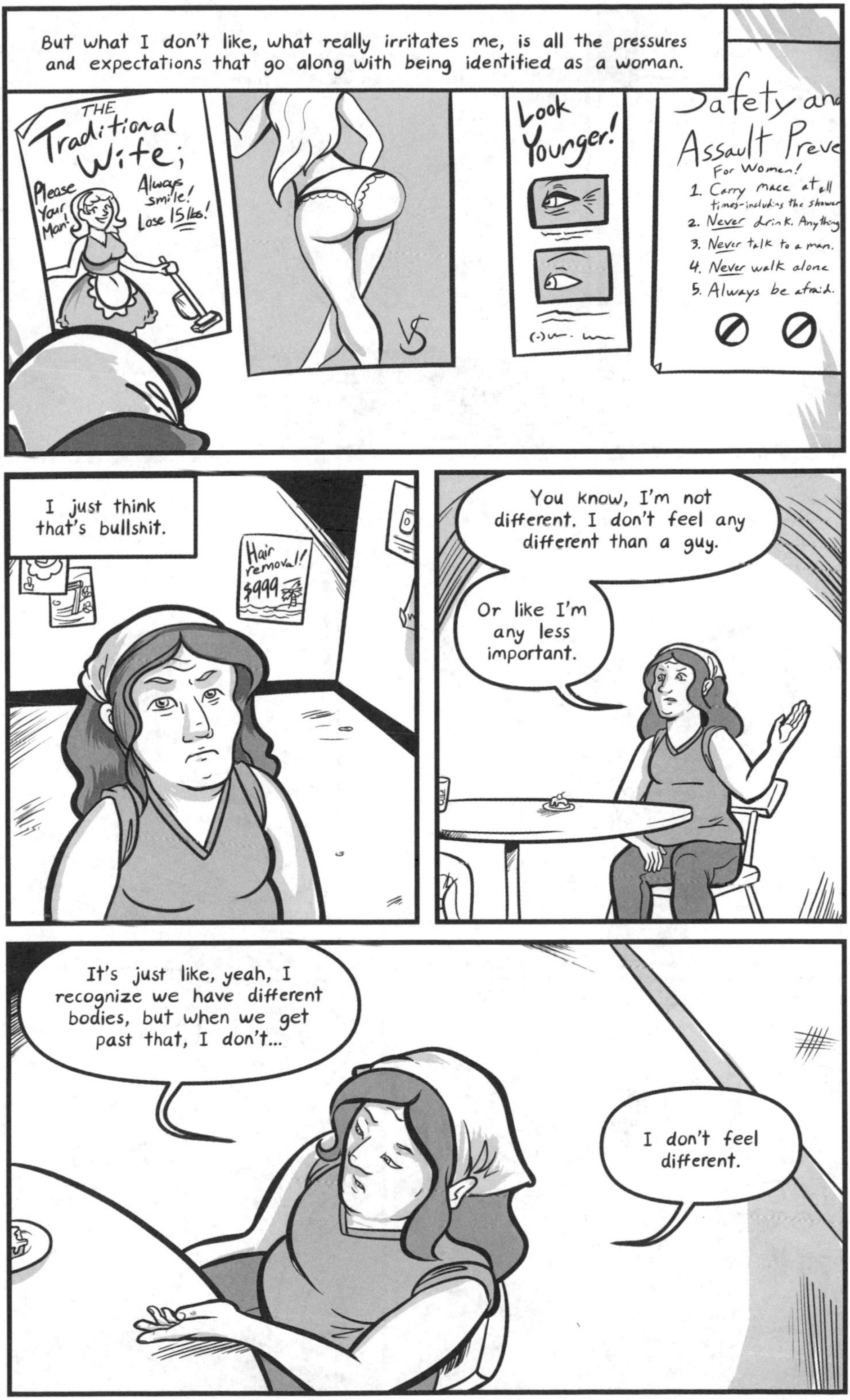

But what I don't like, what really irritates me, is all the pressures and expectations that go along with being identified as a woman.
THE Traditional Wife;
Please Your Man!
Always smile!
Lose 15 lbs!
Look Younger!
Safety and Assault Preve
For Women!
1. Carry mace at all times-including the shower
2. Never drink. Anything
3. Never talk to a man.
4. Never walk alone
5. Always be afraid.
I just think that's bullshit.
Hair removal! $999
You know, I'm not different. I don't feel any different than a guy.
Or like I'm any less important.
It's just like, yeah, I recognize we have different bodies, but when we get past that, I don't...
I don't feel different.

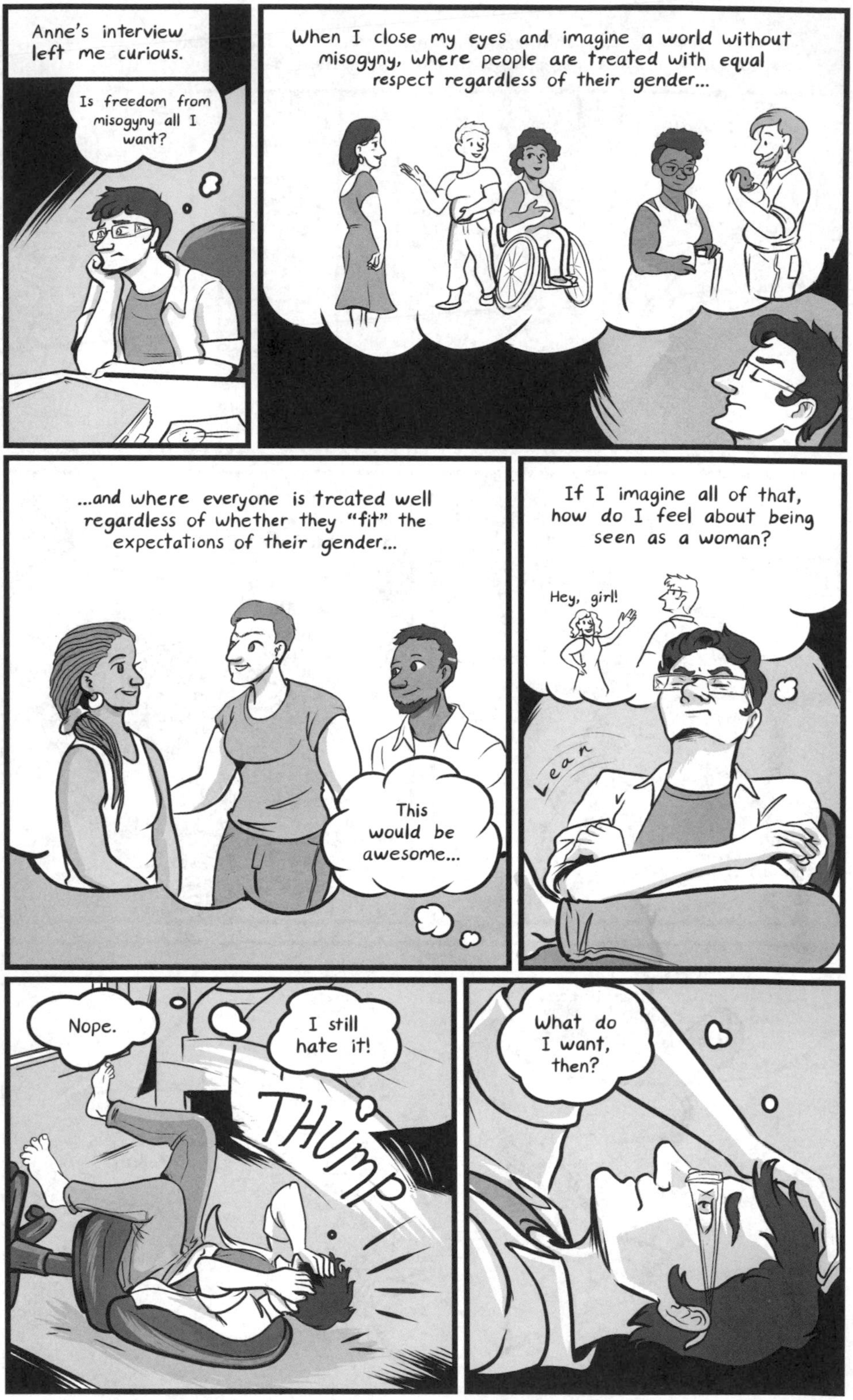

Anne's interview left me curious.
Is freedom from misogyny all I want?
When I close my eyes and imagine a world without misogyny, where people are treated with equal respect regardless of their gender...
...and where everyone is treated well regardless of whether they "fit" the expectations of their gender...
This would be awesome...
If I imagine all of that, how do I feel about being seen as a woman?
Hey, girl!
Lean
Nope.
I still hate it!
THUMP!
What do I want, then?

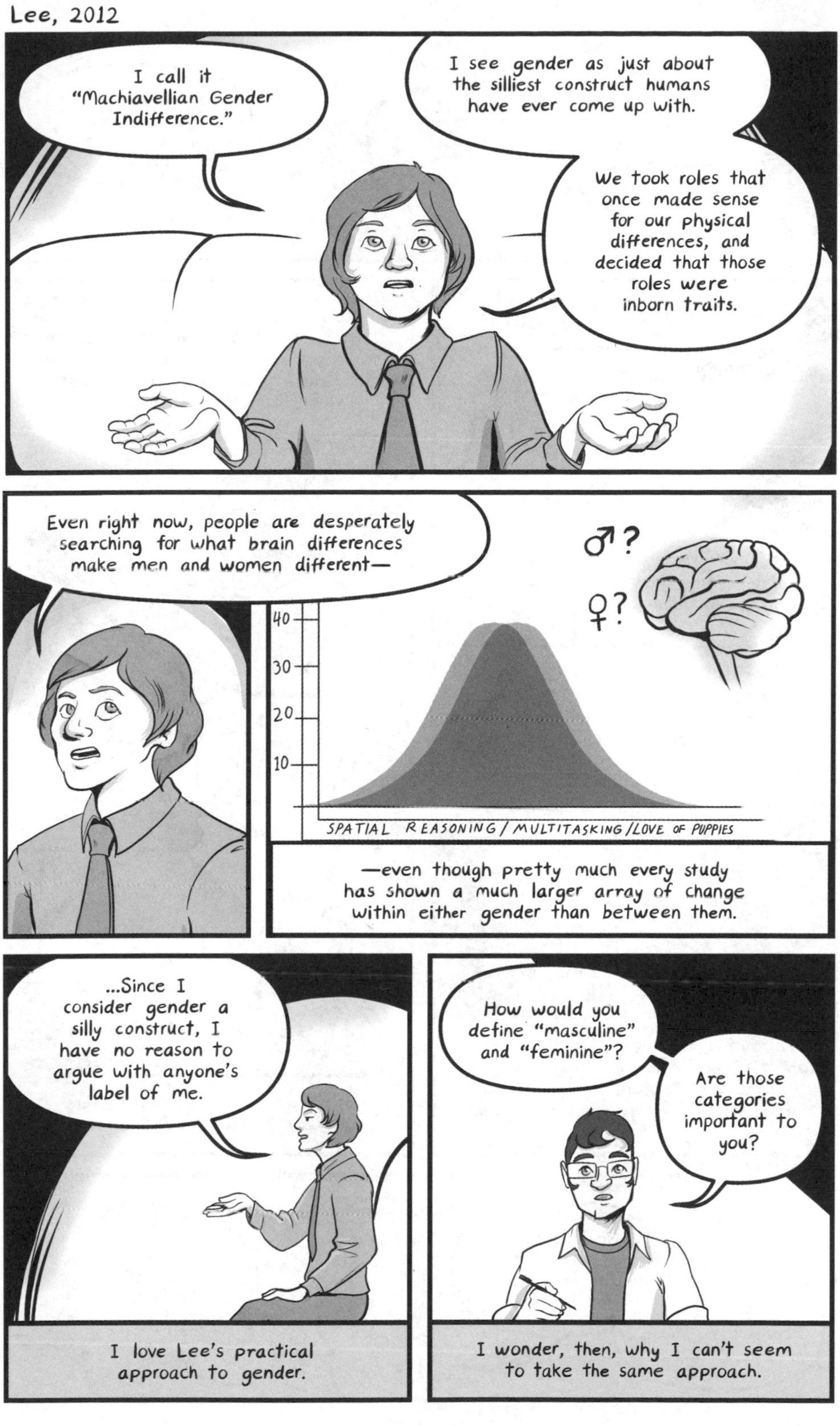
Lee, 2012
I call it "Machiavellian Gender Indifference."
I see gender as just about the silliest construct humans have ever come up with.
We took roles that once made sense for our physical differences, and decided that those roles were inborn traits.
Even right now, people are desperately searching for what brain differences make men and women different—
♂?
♀?
40
30
20
10
SPATIAL REASONING / MULTITASKING / LOVE OF PUPPIES
—even though pretty much every study has shown a much larger array of change within either gender than between them.
...Since I consider gender a silly construct, I have no reason to argue with anyone's label of me.
I love Lee's practical approach to gender.
How would you define "masculine" and "feminine"?
Are those categories important to you?
I wonder, then, why I can't seem to take the same approach.

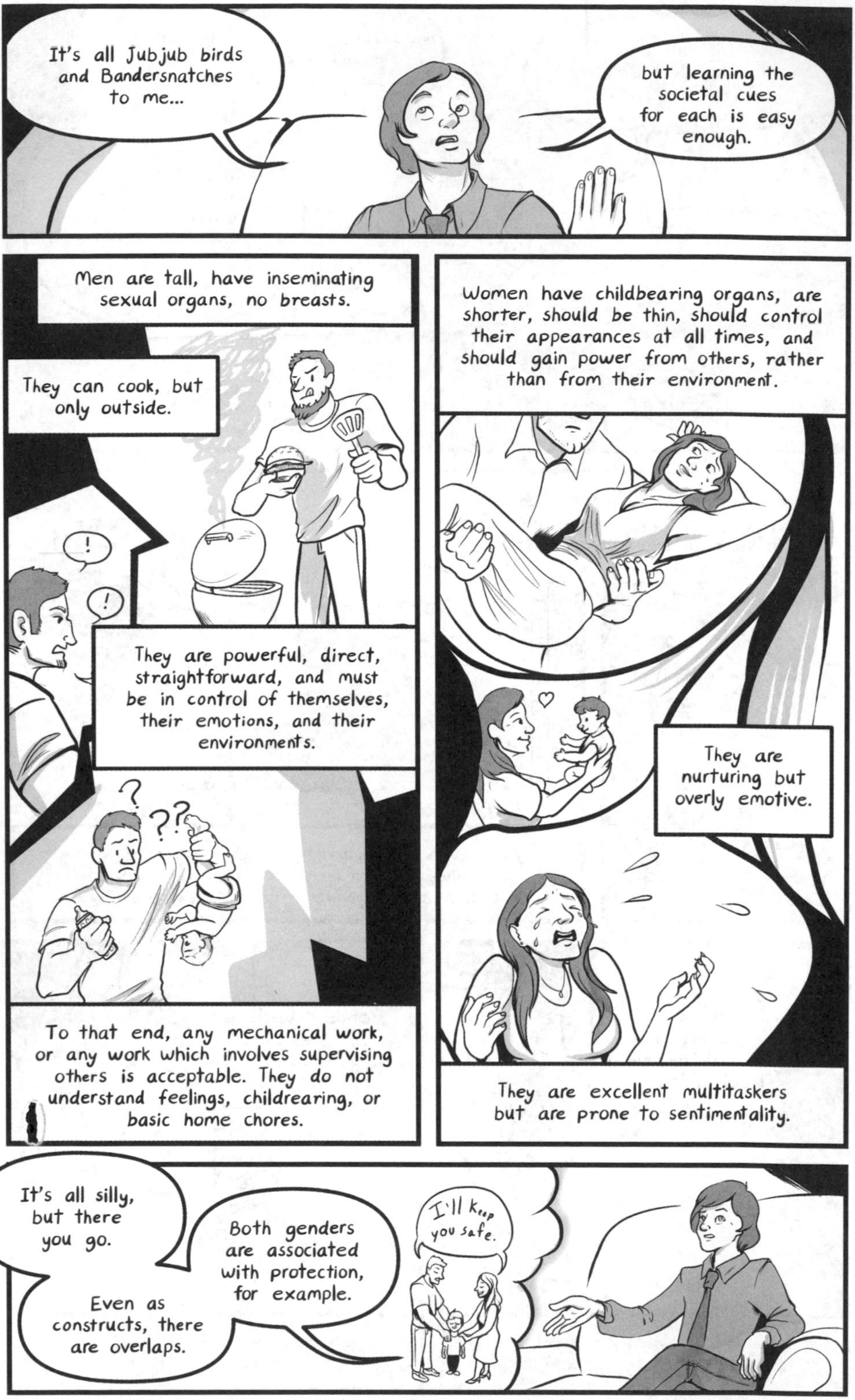
It's all Jubjub birds and Bandersnatches to me...
but learning the societal cues for each is easy enough.
Men are tall, have inseminating sexual organs, no breasts.
They can cook, but only outside.
!
!
They are powerful, direct, straightforward, and must be in control of themselves, their emotions, and their environments.
?
??
To that end, any mechanical work, or any work which involves supervising others is acceptable. They do not understand feelings, childrearing, or basic home chores.
Women have childbearing organs, are shorter, should be thin, should control their appearances at all times, and should gain power from others, rather than from their environment.
They are nurturing but overly emotive.
They are excellent multitaskers but are prone to sentimentality.
It's all silly, but there you go.
Even as constructs, there are overlaps.
Both genders are associated with protection, for example.
I'll keep you safe.

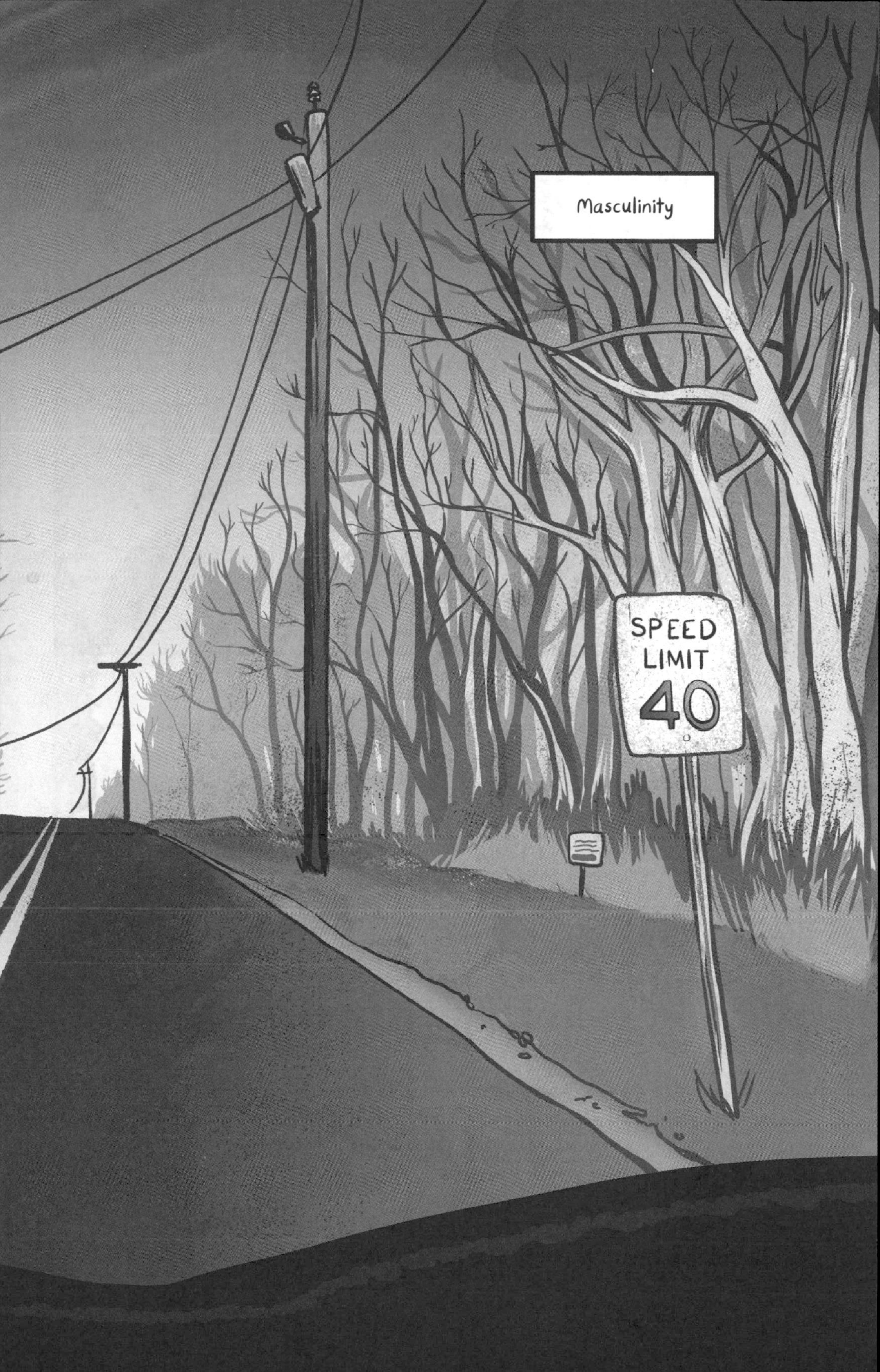
Masculinity
SPEED LIMIT 40

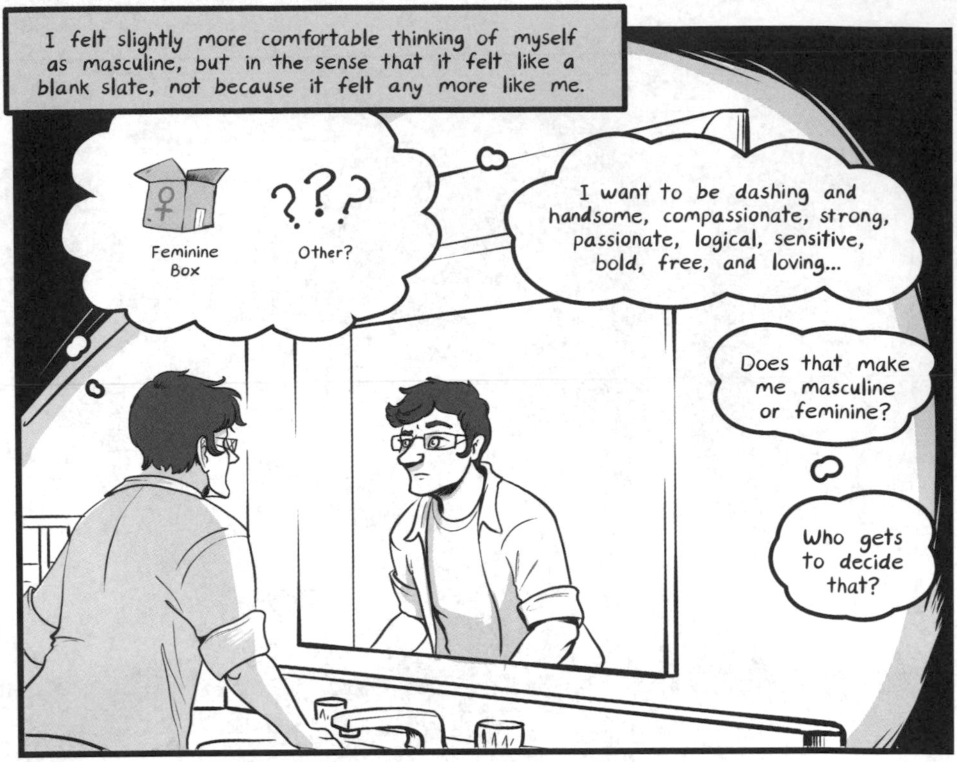
I felt slightly more comfortable thinking of myself as masculine, but in the sense that it felt like a blank slate, not because it felt any more like me.
Feminine Box
???
Other?
I want to be dashing and handsome, compassionate, strong, passionate, logical, sensitive, bold, free, and loving...
Does that make me masculine or feminine?
Who gets to decide that?

Eli, 2013

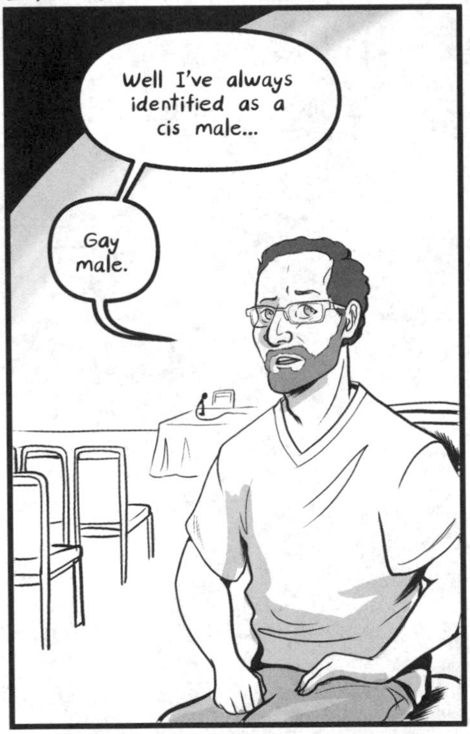
Well I've always identified as a cis male...
Gay male.

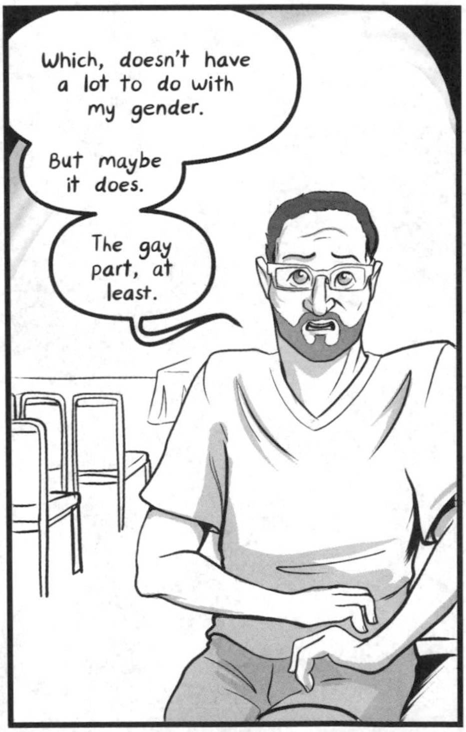
Which, doesn't have a lot to do with my gender.
But maybe it does.
The gay part, at least.

"Cis" here means "cisgender," generally someone who identifies as the gender assigned to them at birth.

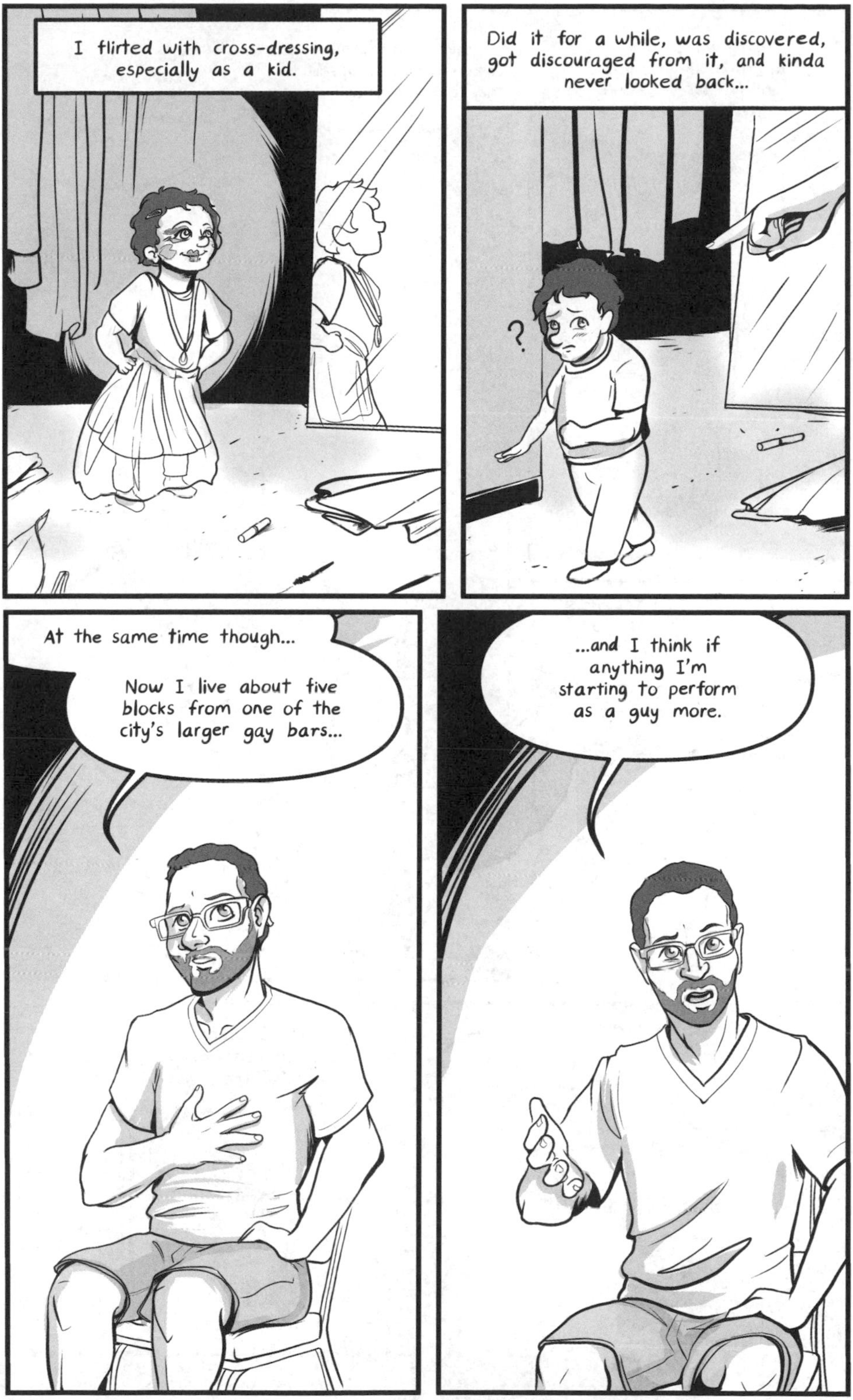
I flirted with cross-dressing, especially as a kid.
Did it for a while, was discovered, got discouraged from it, and kinda never looked back...
?
At the same time though...
Now I live about five blocks from one of the city's larger gay bars...
...and I think if anything I'm starting to perform as a guy more.

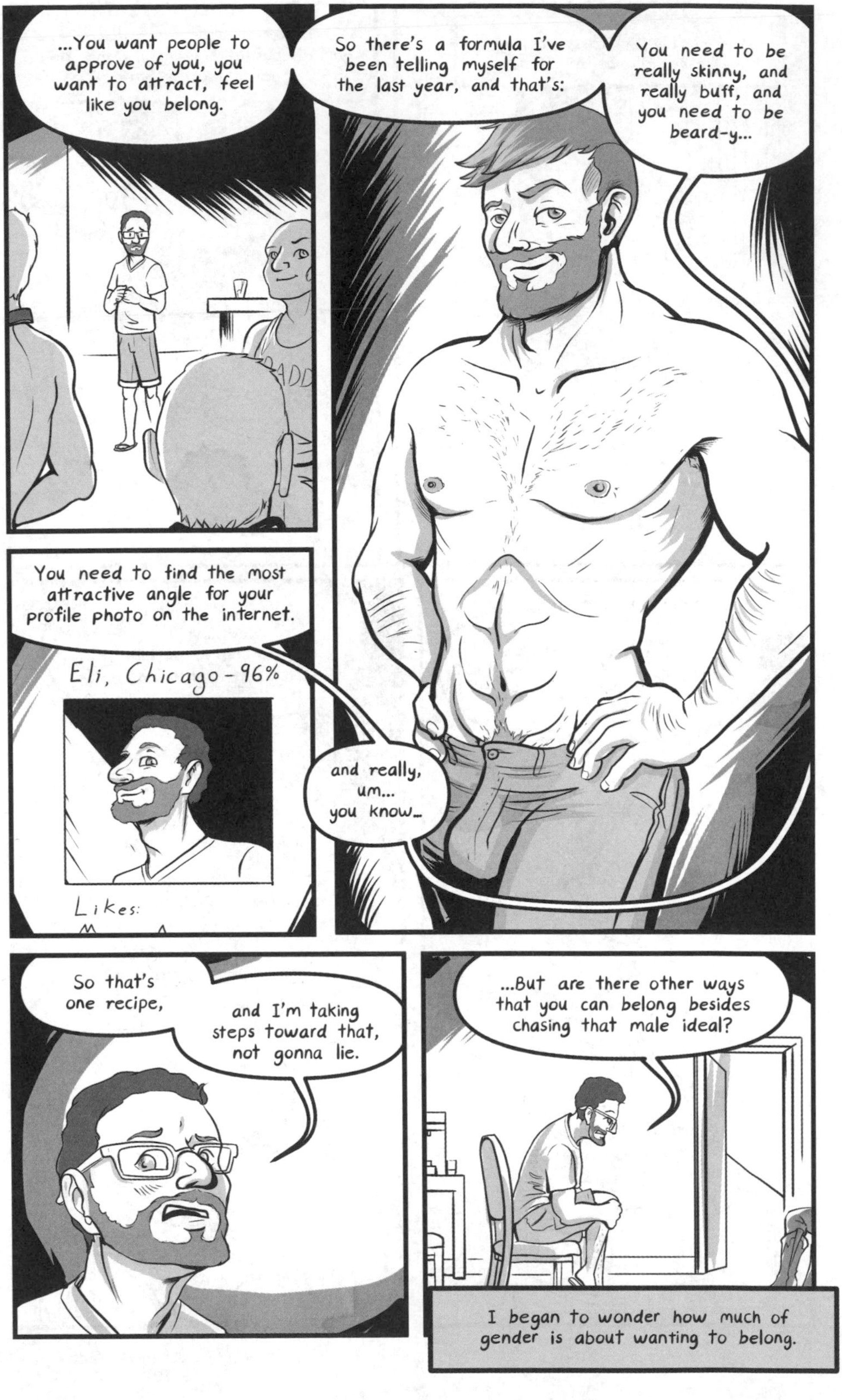
...You want people to approve of you, you want to attract, feel like you belong.
So there's a formula I've been telling myself for the last year, and that's:
You need to be really skinny, and really buff, and you need to be beard-y...
You need to find the most attractive angle for your profile photo on the internet.
Eli, Chicago-96%
Likes:
and really, um... you know...
So that's one recipe,
and I'm taking steps toward that, not gonna lie.
...But are there other ways that you can belong besides chasing that male ideal?
I began to wonder how much of gender is about wanting to belong.

J, 2013

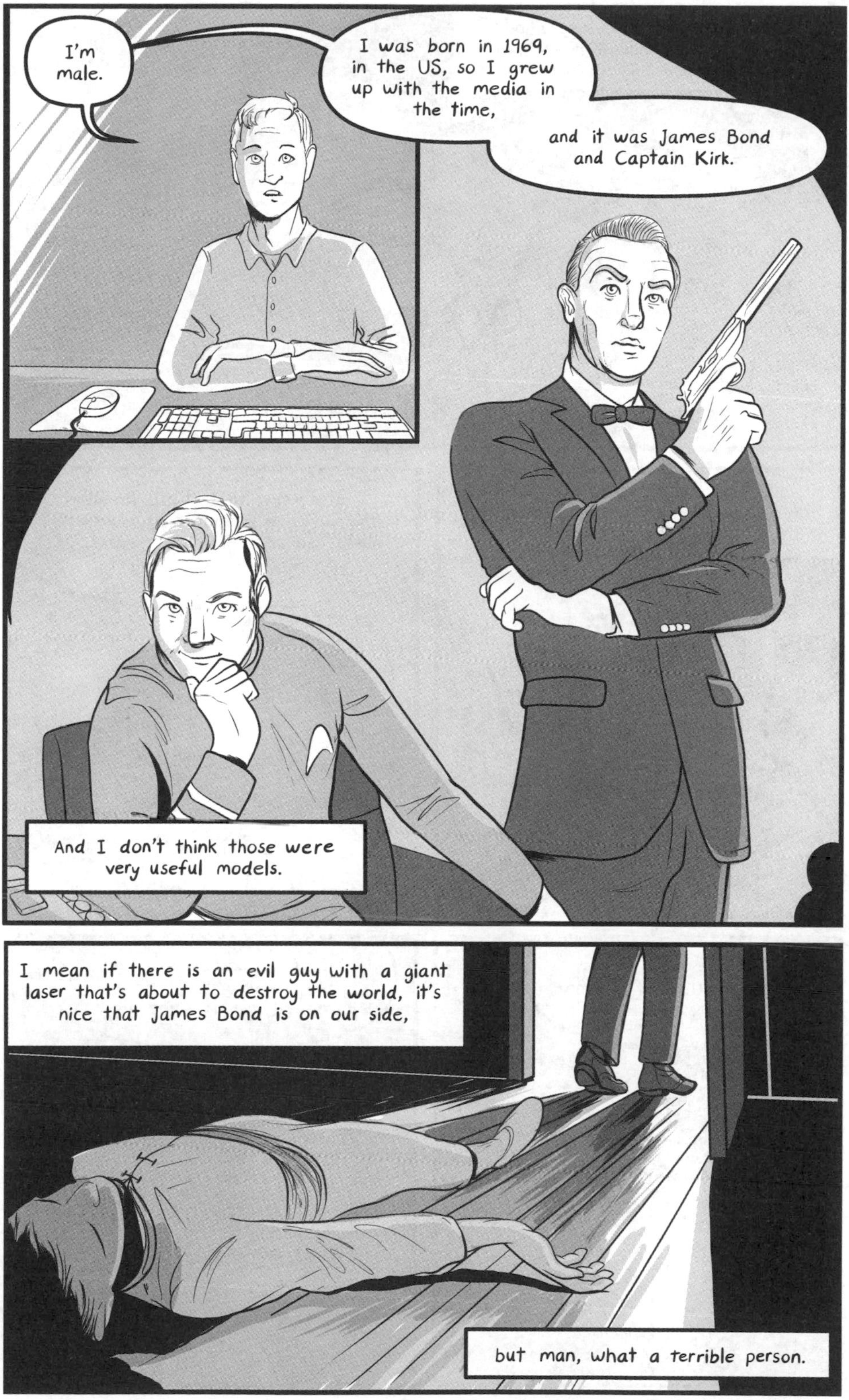
I'm male.
I was born in 1969, in the US, so I grew up with the media in the time,
and it was James Bond and Captain Kirk.
And I don't think those were very useful models.
I mean if there is an evil guy with a giant laser that's about to destroy the world, it's nice that James Bond is on our side,
but man, what a terrible person.

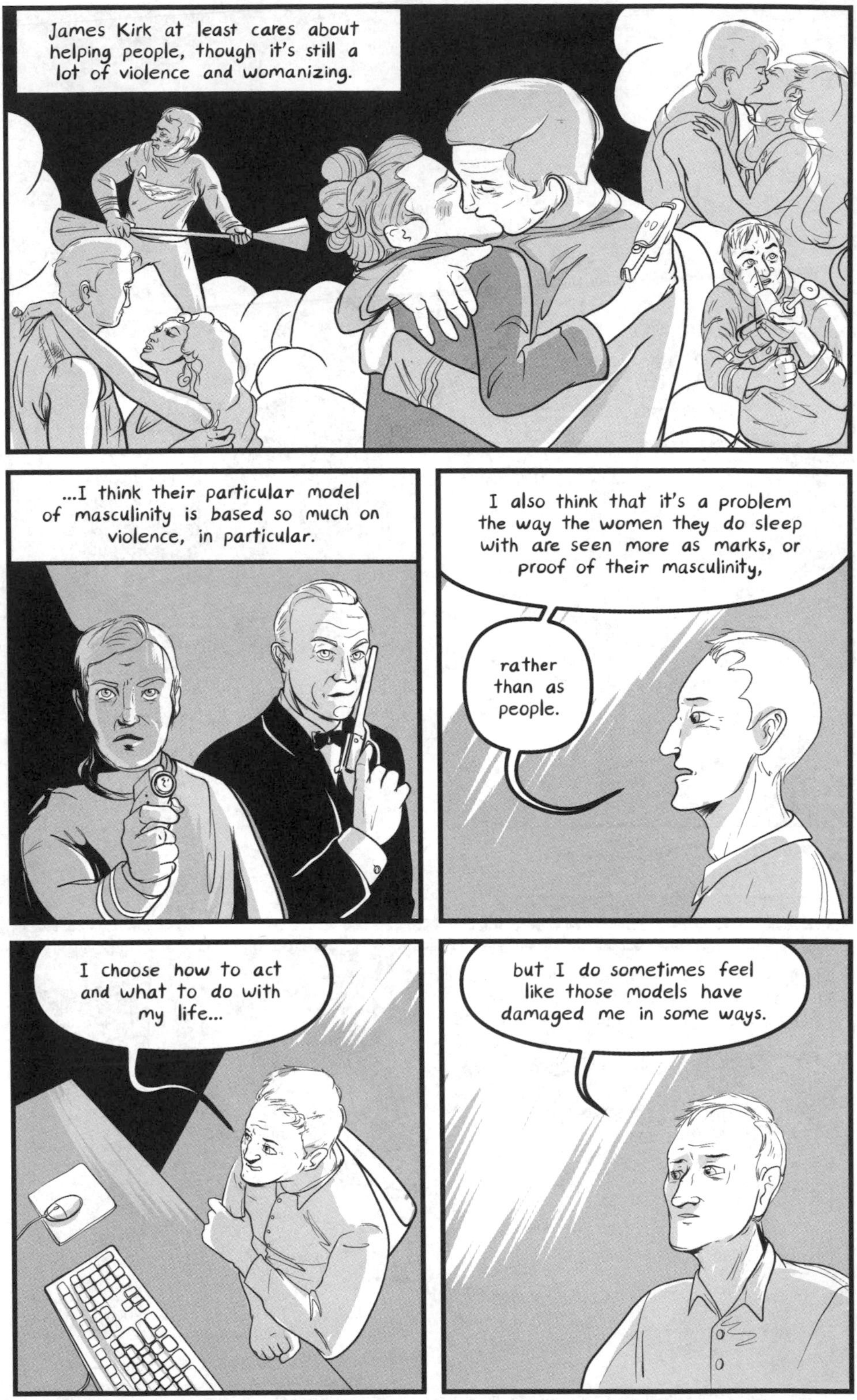
James Kirk at least cares about helping people, though it's still a lot of violence and womanizing.
...I think their particular model of masculinity is based so much on violence, in particular.
I also think that it's a problem the way the women they do sleep with are seen more as marks, or proof of their masculinity,
rather than as people.
I choose how to act and what to do with my life...
but I do sometimes feel like those models have damaged me in some ways.

"A Person," 2012

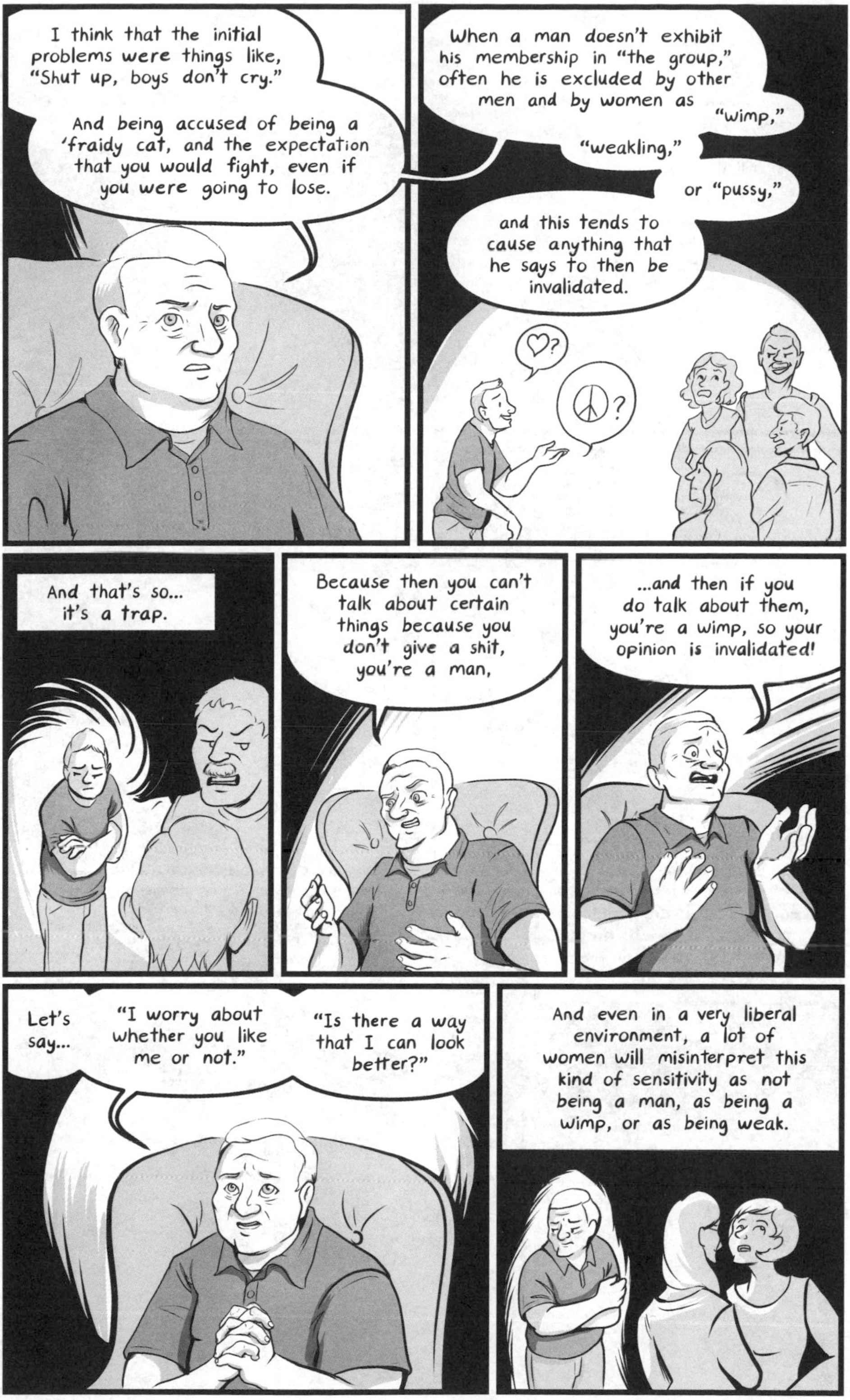
I think that the initial problems were things like, "Shut up, boys don't cry."
And being accused of being a 'fraidy cat, and the expectation that you would fight, even if you were going to lose.
When a man doesn't exhibit his membership in "the group," often he is excluded by other men and by women as
"wimp,"
"weakling,"
or "pussy,"
and this tends to cause anything that he says to then be invalidated.
?
?
And that's so... it's a trap.
Because then you can't talk about certain things because you don't give a shit, you're a man,
...and then if you do talk about them, you're a wimp, so your opinion is invalidated!
Let's say...
"I worry about whether you like me or not."
"Is there a way that I can look better?"
And even in a very liberal environment, a lot of women will misinterpret this kind of sensitivity as not being a man, as being a wimp, or as being weak.

Corrine, 2012

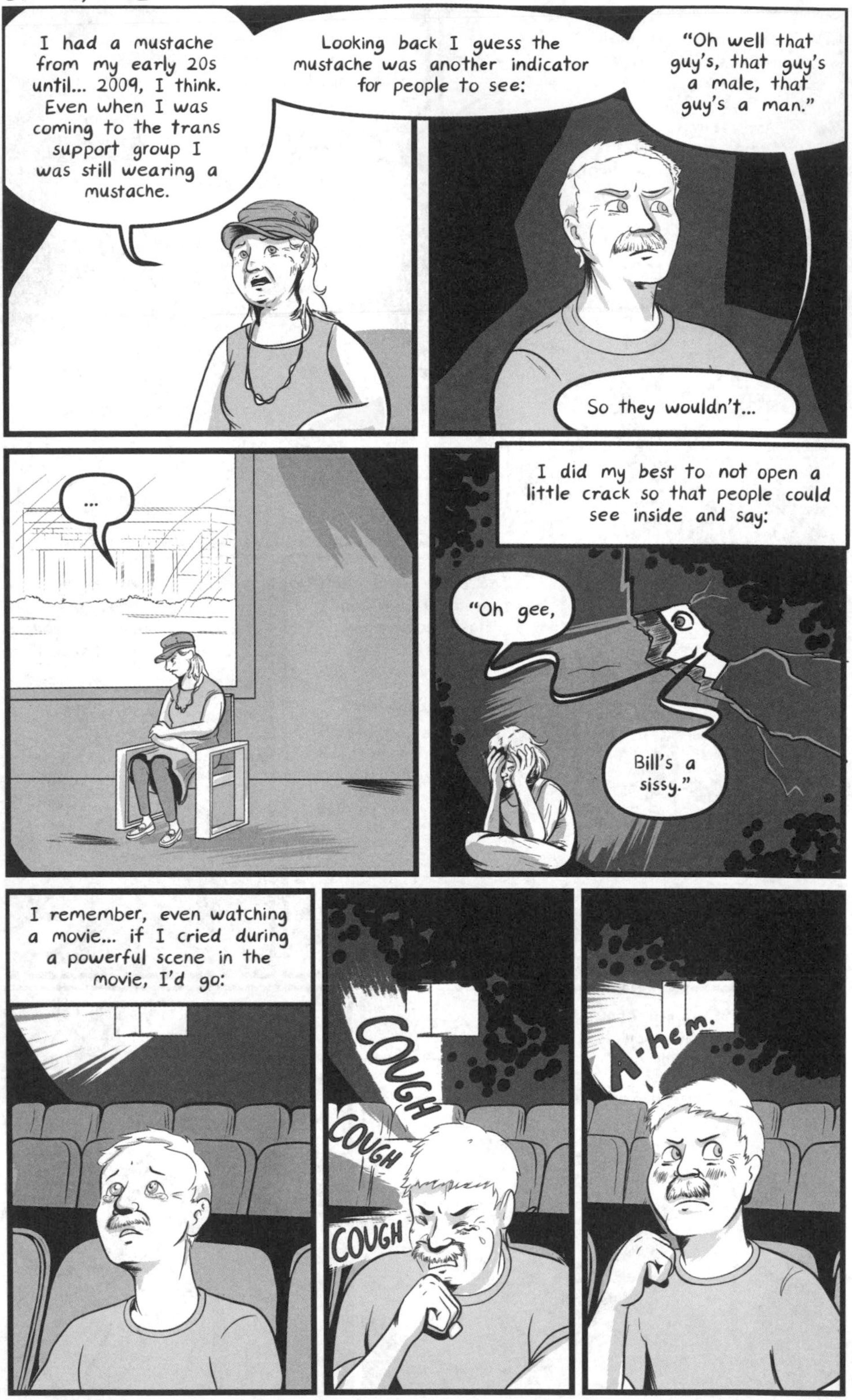
I had a mustache from my early 20s until... 2009, I think. Even when I was coming to the trans support group I was still wearing a mustache.
Looking back I guess the mustache was another indicator for people to see:
"Oh well that guy's, that guy's a male, that guy's a man."
So they wouldn't...
...
I did my best to not open a little crack so that people could see inside and say:
"Oh gee,
Bill's a sissy."
I remember, even watching a movie... if I cried during a powerful scene in the movie, I'd go:
COUGH
COUGH
COUGH
A-hem.

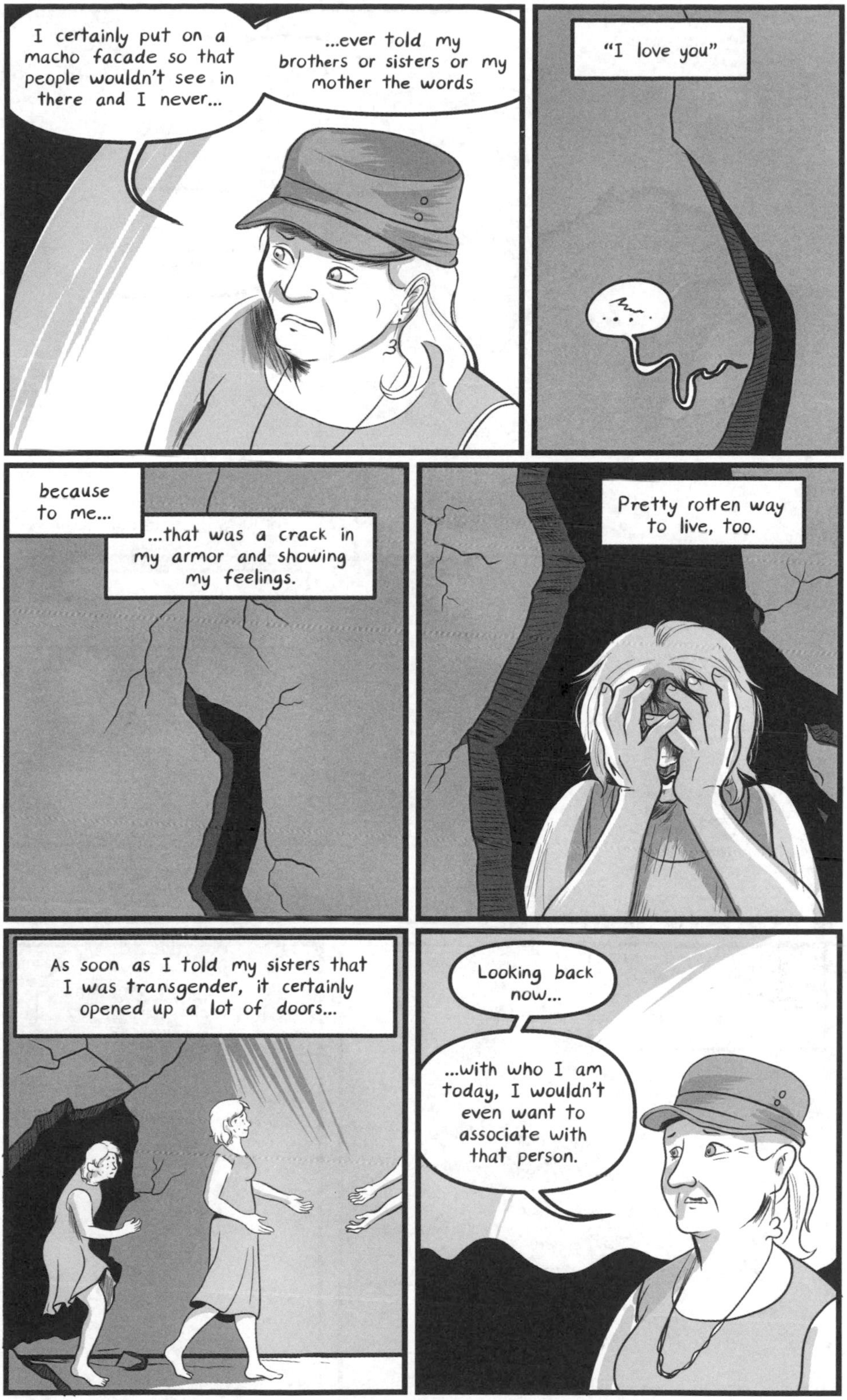

I certainly put on a macho facade so that people wouldn't see in there and I never...
...ever told my brothers or sisters or my mother the words
"I love you"
because to me...
...that was a crack in my armor and showing my feelings.
Pretty rotten way to live, too.
As soon as I told my sisters that I was transgender, it certainly opened up a lot of doors...
Looking back now...
...with who I am today, I wouldn't even want to associate with that person.

Lauren, 2012

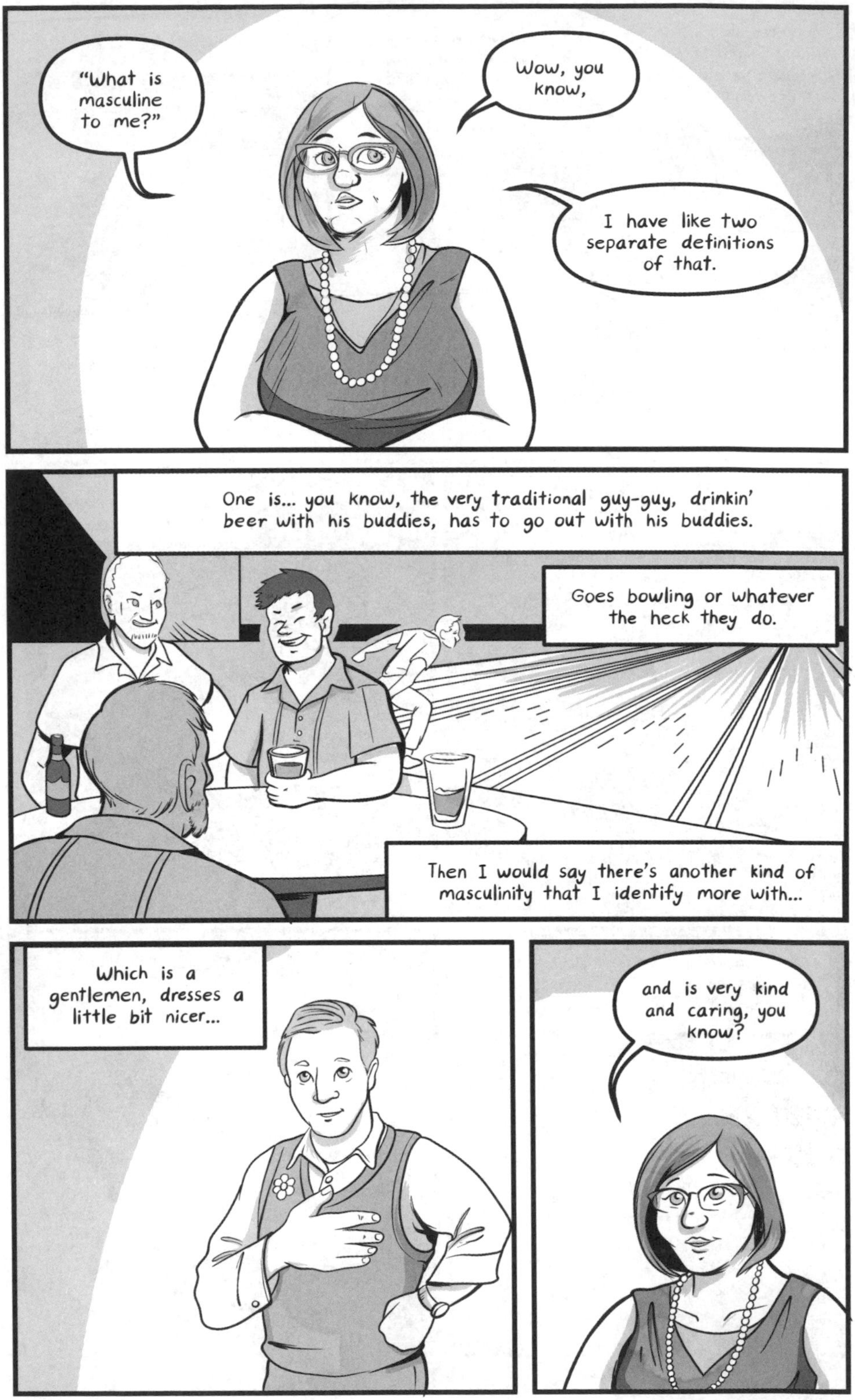
"What is masculine to me?"
Wow, you know,
I have like two separate definitions of that.
One is... you know, the very traditional guy-guy, drinkin' beer with his buddies, has to go out with his buddies.
Goes bowling or whatever the heck they do.
Then I would say there's another kind of masculinity that I identify more with...
Which is a gentlemen, dresses a little bit nicer...
and is very kind and caring, you know?

Ignacio, 2013

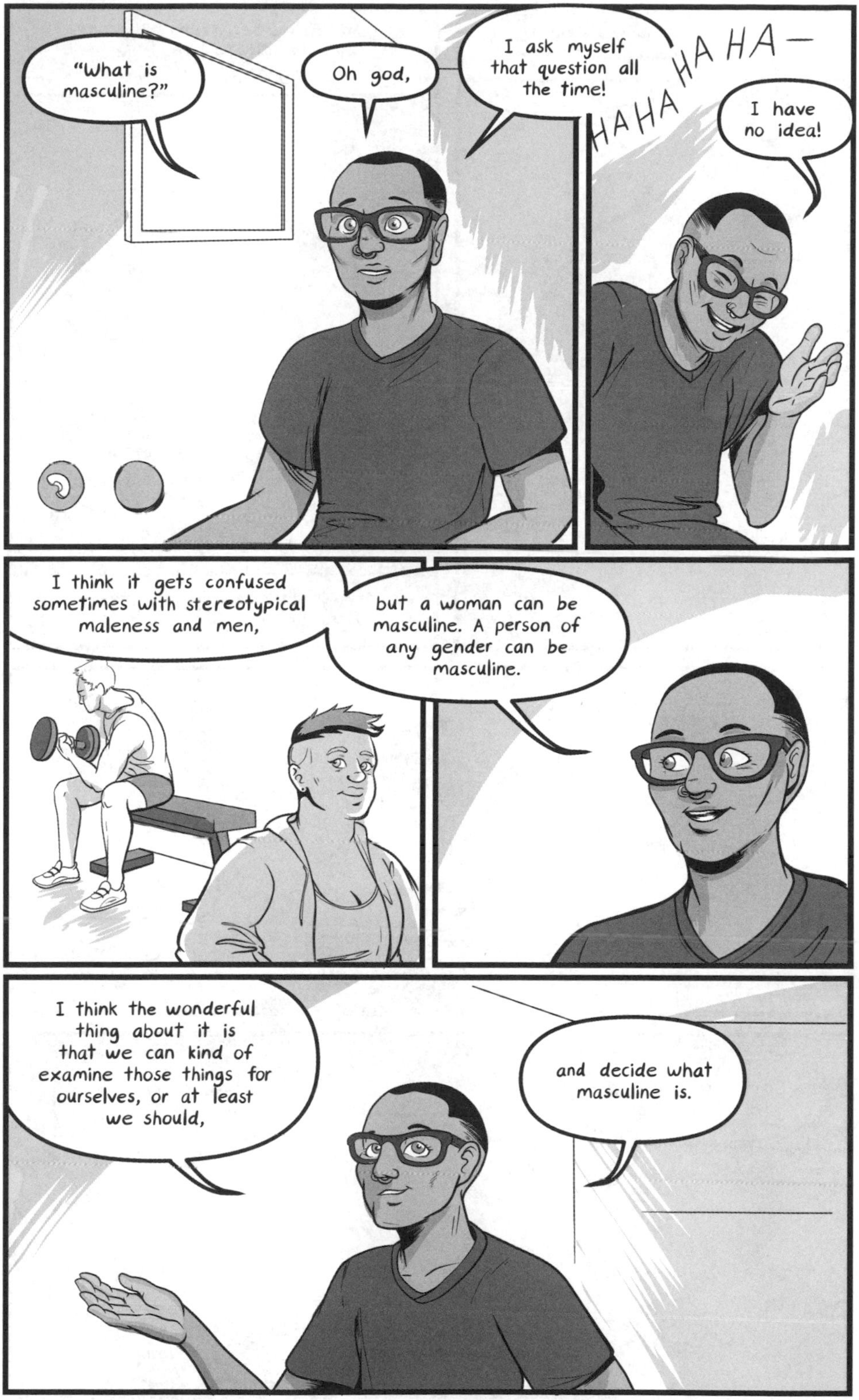
"What is masculine?"
Oh god,
I ask myself that question all the time!
HAHAHAHA HA—
I have no idea!
I think it gets confused sometimes with stereotypical maleness and men,
but a woman can be masculine. A person of any gender can be masculine.
I think the wonderful thing about it is that we can kind of examine those things for ourselves, or at least we should,
and decide what masculine is.

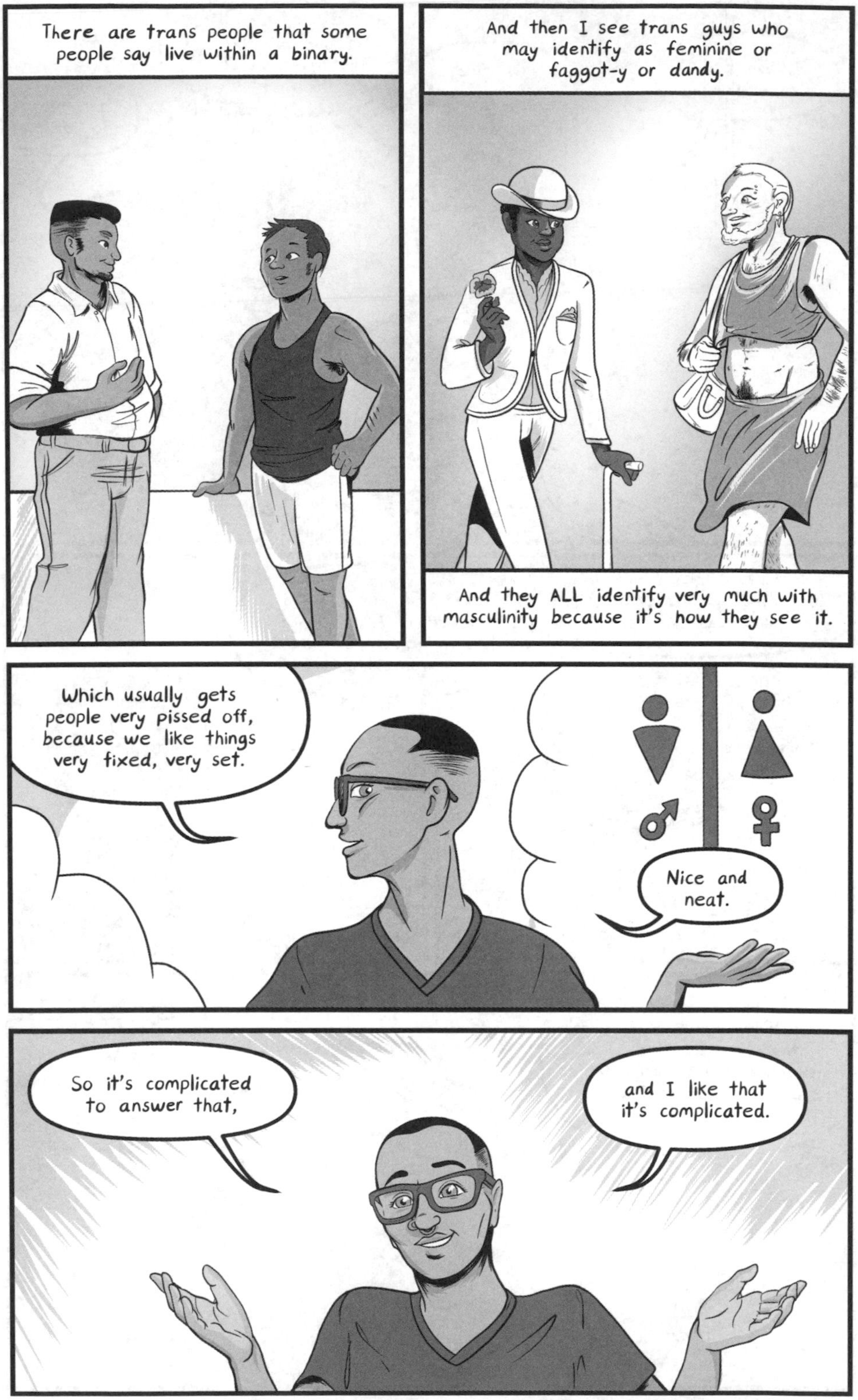
There are trans people that some people say live within a binary.
And then I see trans guys who may identify as feminine or faggot-y or dandy.
And they ALL identify very much with masculinity because it's how they see it.
Which usually gets people very pissed off, because we like things very fixed, very set.
Nice and neat.
So it's complicated to answer that,
and I like that it's complicated.

Mo, 2013

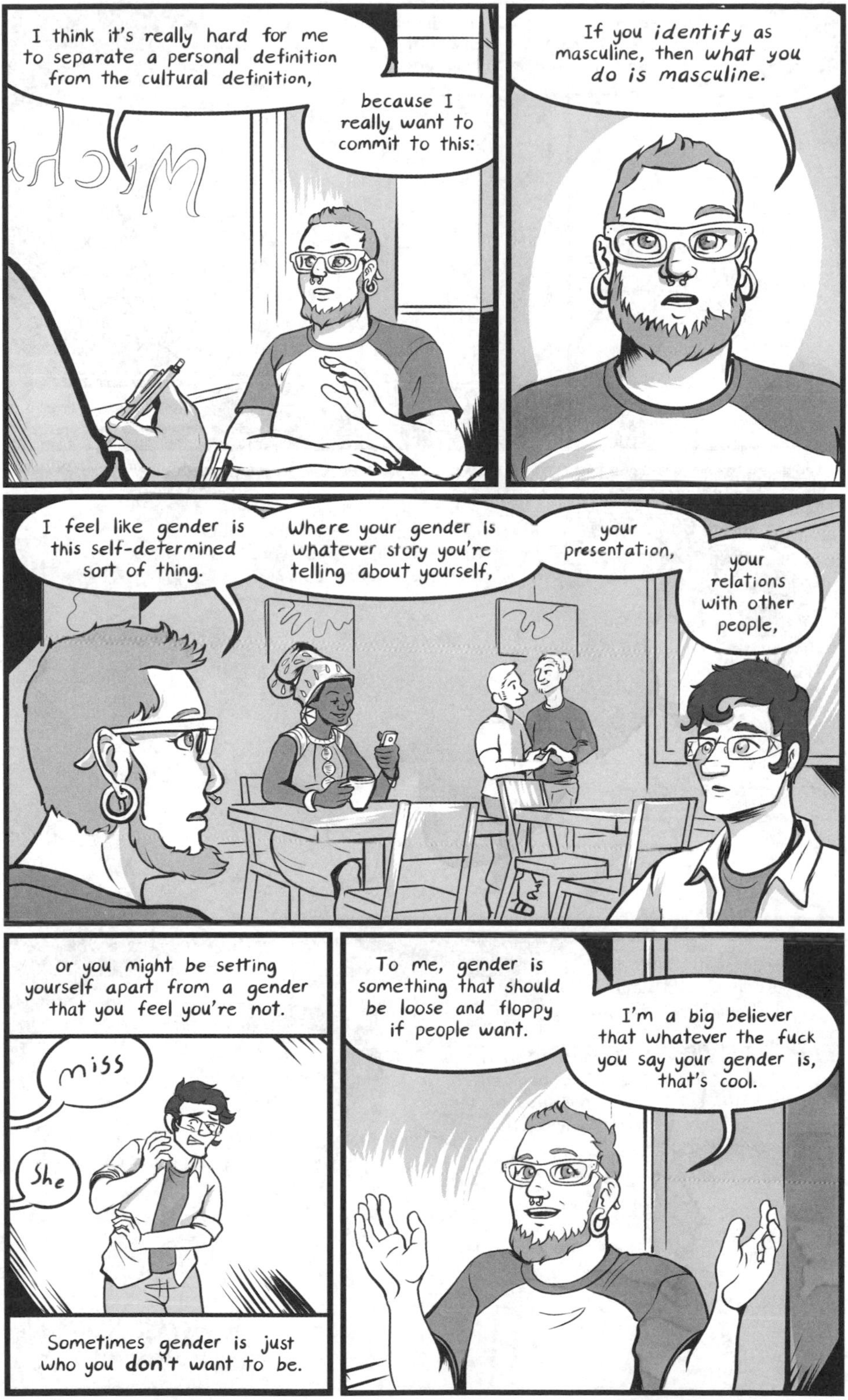
I think it's really hard for me to separate a personal definition from the cultural definition,
because I really want to commit to this:
Michu
If you *identify* as masculine, then *what you do is masculine.*
I feel like gender is this self-determined sort of thing.
Where your gender is whatever story you're telling about yourself,
your presentation,
your relations with other people,
or you might be setting yourself apart from a gender that you feel you're not.
miss
She
Sometimes gender is just who you **don't** want to be.
To me, gender is something that should be loose and floppy if people want.
I'm a big believer that whatever the fuck you say your gender is, that's cool.

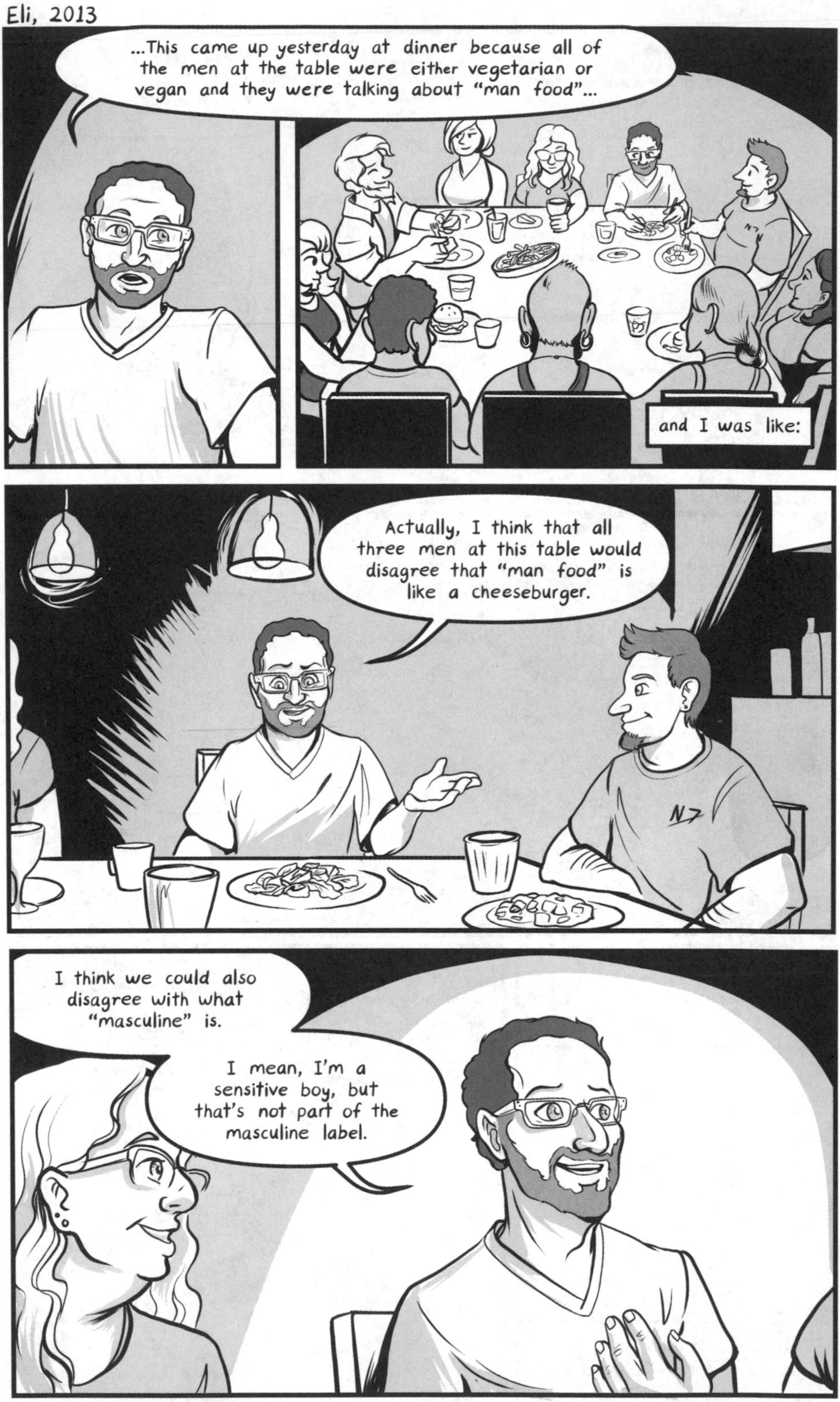
Eli, 2013
...This came up yesterday at dinner because all of the men at the table were either vegetarian or vegan and they were talking about "man food"...
and I was like:
Actually, I think that all three men at this table would disagree that "man food" is like a cheeseburger.
N7
I think we could also disagree with what "masculine" is.
I mean, I'm a sensitive boy, but that's not part of the masculine label.

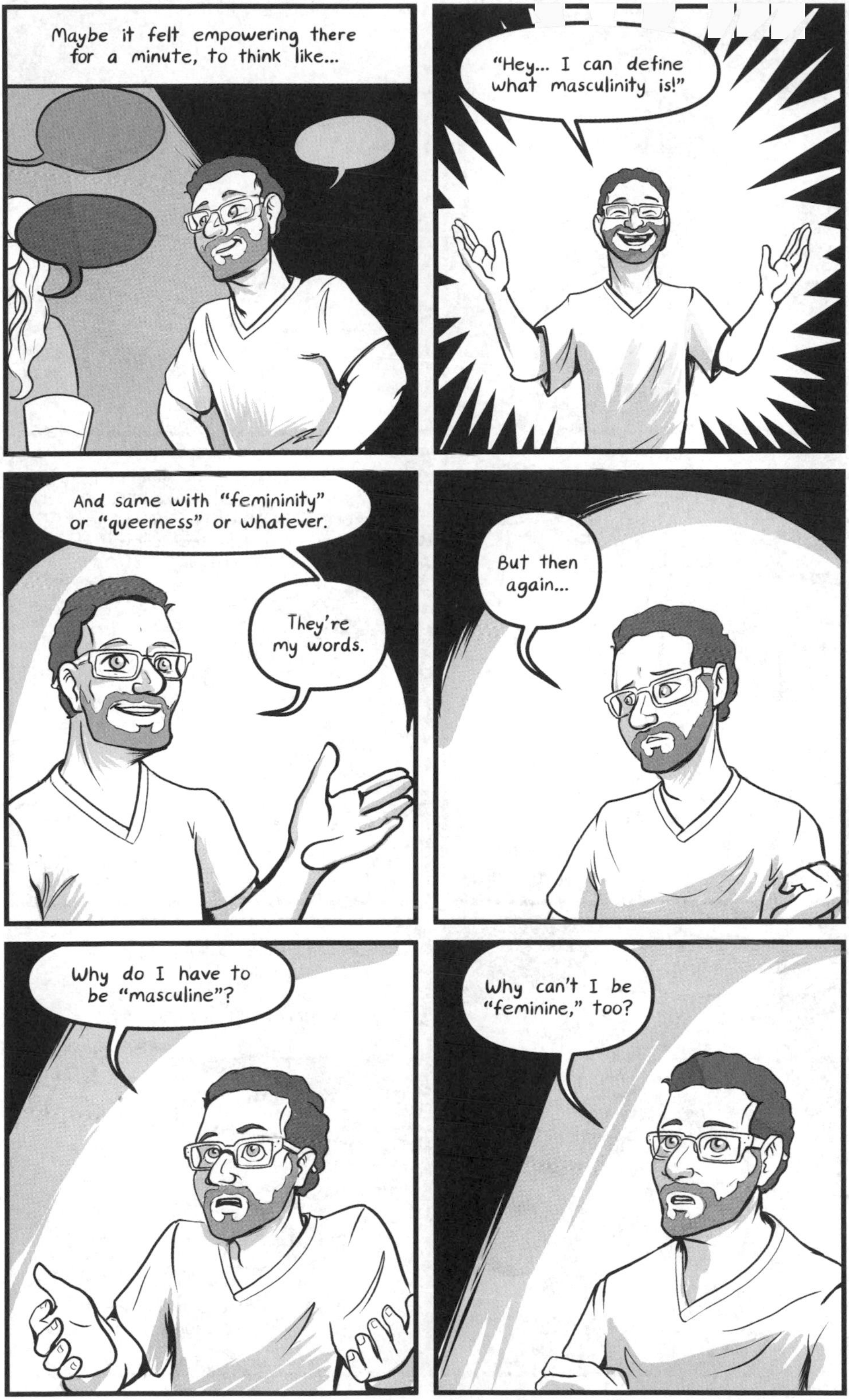
Maybe it felt empowering there for a minute, to think like...
"Hey... I can define what masculinity is!"
And same with "femininity" or "queerness" or whatever.
They're my words.
But then again...
Why do I have to be "masculine"?
Why can't I be "feminine," too?

Rhea, 2012

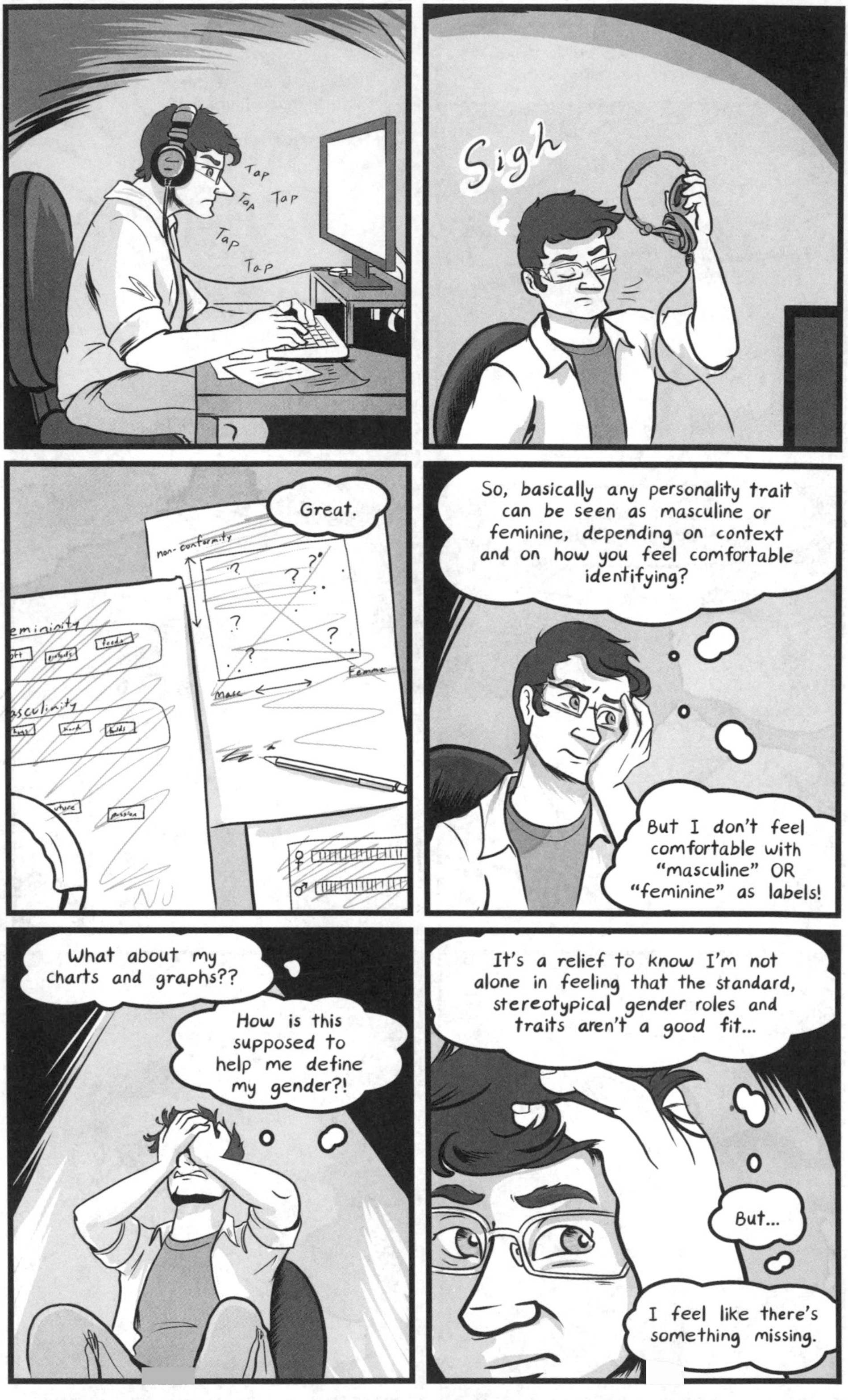
Tap
Tap
Tap
Tap
Tap
Sigh
Great.
So, basically any personality trait can be seen as masculine or feminine, depending on context and on how you feel comfortable identifying?
But I don't feel comfortable with "masculine" OR "feminine" as labels!
What about my charts and graphs??
How is this supposed to help me define my gender?!
It's a relief to know I'm not alone in feeling that the standard, stereotypical gender roles and traits aren't a good fit...
But...
I feel like there's something missing.

Kai, 2012

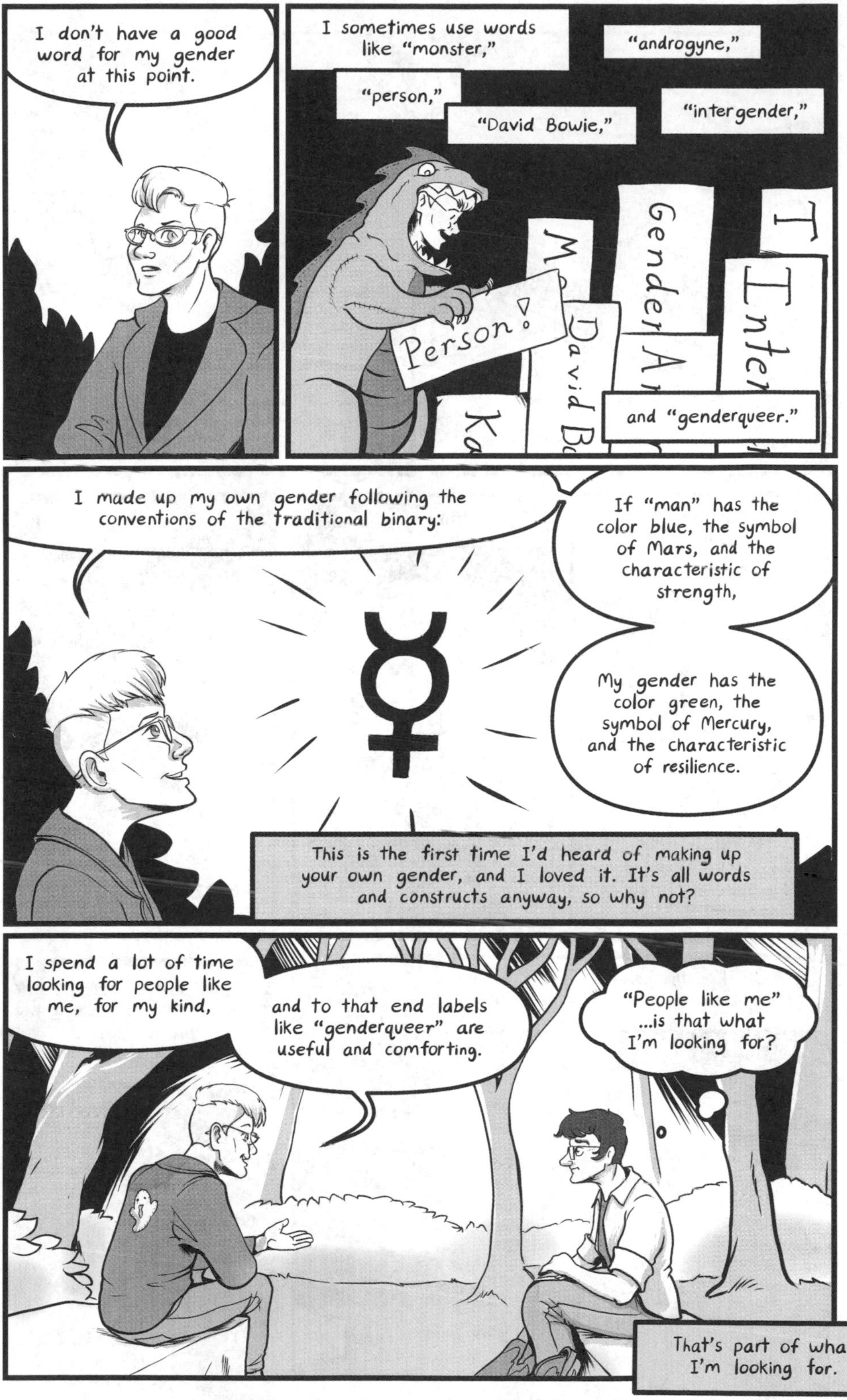
I don't have a good word for my gender at this point.
I sometimes use words like "monster,"
"androgyne,"
"person,"
"David Bowie,"
"intergender,"
Person!
and "genderqueer."
I made up my own gender following the conventions of the traditional binary:
If "man" has the color blue, the symbol of Mars, and the characteristic of strength,
My gender has the color green, the symbol of Mercury, and the characteristic of resilience.
This is the first time I'd heard of making up your own gender, and I loved it. It's all words and constructs anyway, so why not?
I spend a lot of time looking for people like me, for my kind,
and to that end labels like "genderqueer" are useful and comforting.
"People like me" ...is that what I'm looking for?
That's part of what I'm looking for.

Daiquiri, 2012

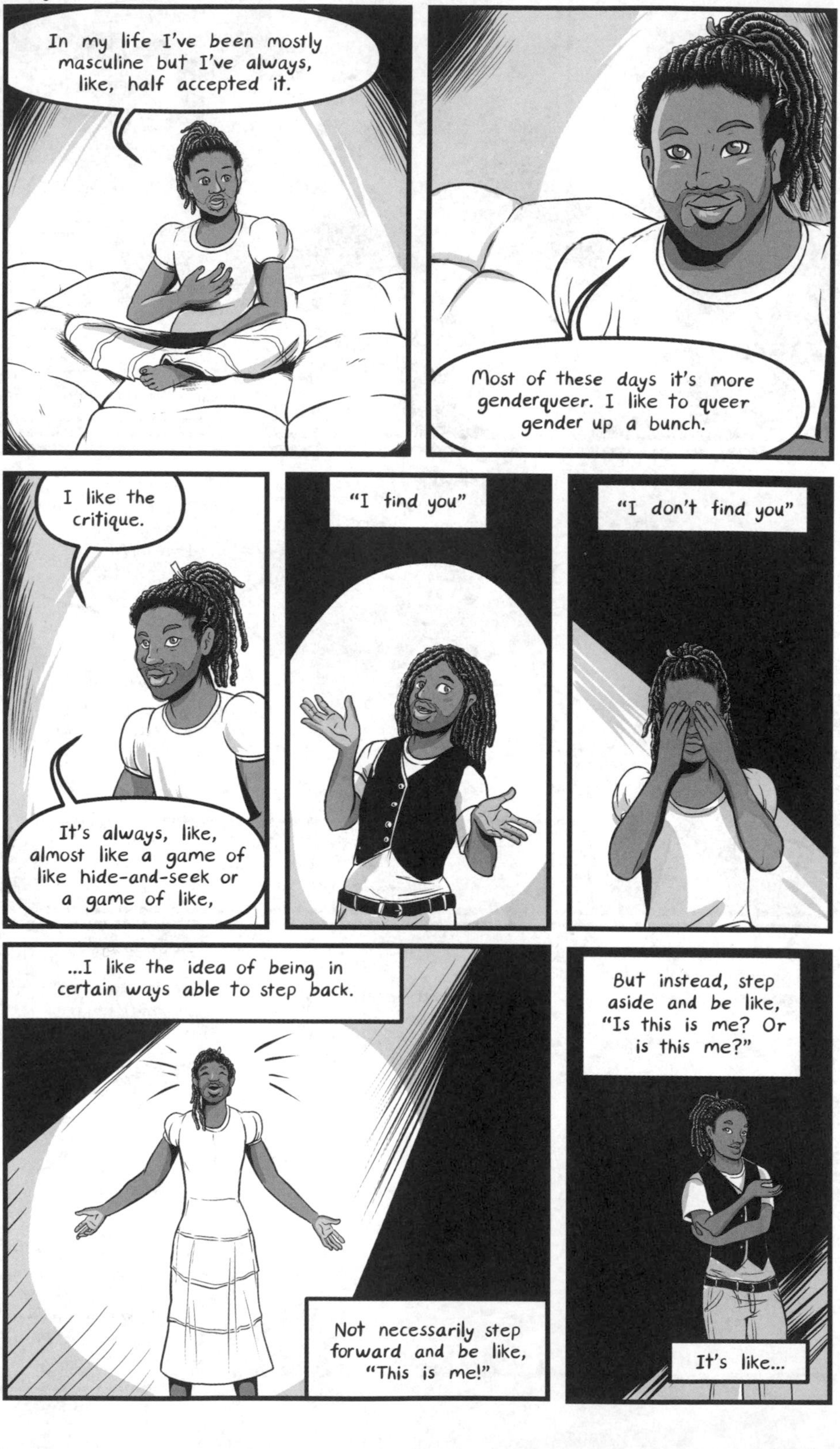
In my life I've been mostly masculine but I've always, like, half accepted it.
Most of these days it's more genderqueer. I like to queer gender up a bunch.
I like the critique.
It's always, like, almost like a game of like hide-and-seek or a game of like,
"I find you"
"I don't find you"
...I like the idea of being in certain ways able to step back.
Not necessarily step forward and be like, "This is me!"
But instead, step aside and be like, "Is this is me? Or is this me?"
It's like...

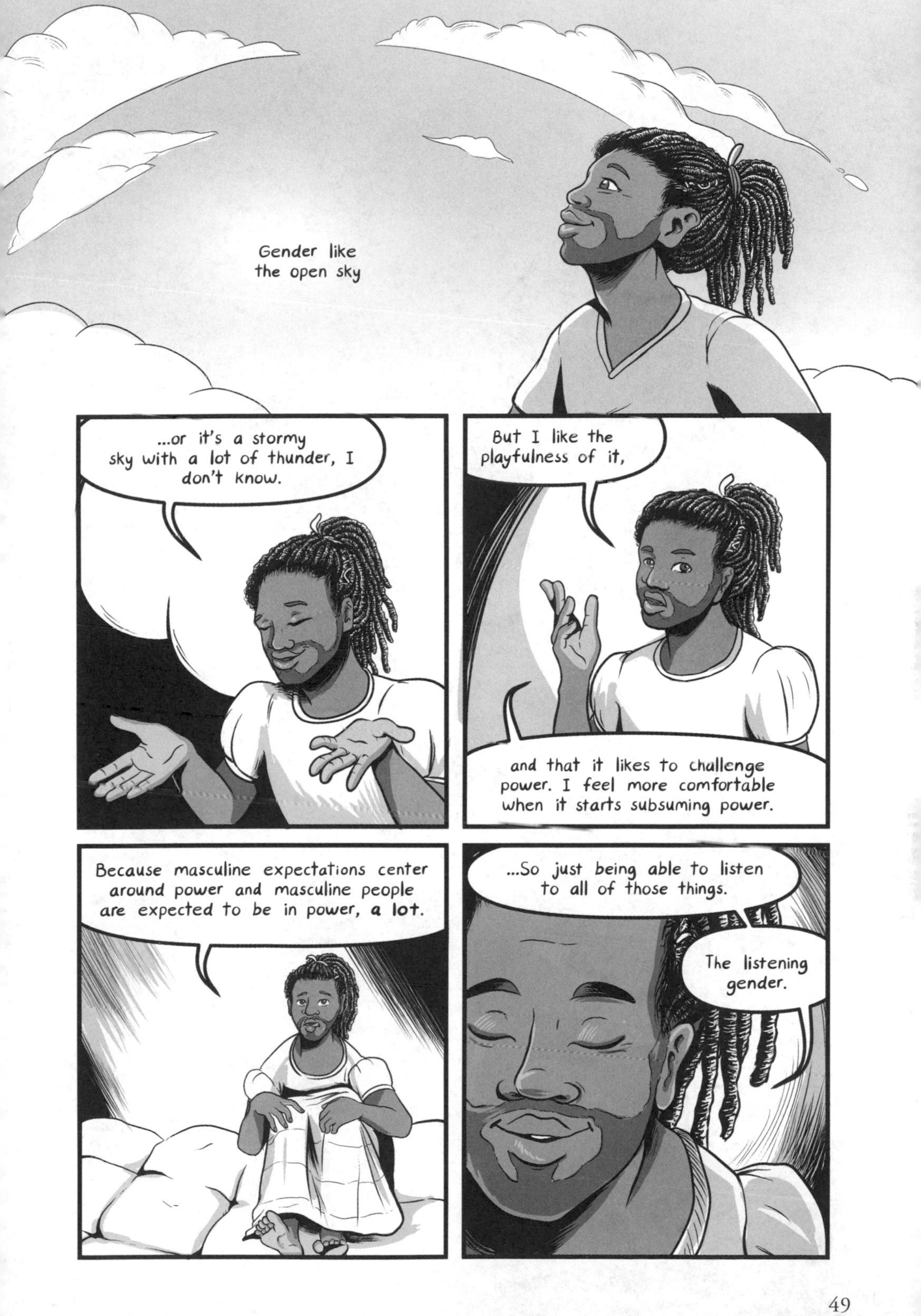
Gender like the open sky
...or it's a stormy sky with a lot of thunder, I don't know.
But I like the playfulness of it,
and that it likes to challenge power. I feel more comfortable when it starts subsuming power.
Because masculine expectations center around power and masculine people are expected to be in power, a lot.
...So just being able to listen to all of those things.
The listening gender.

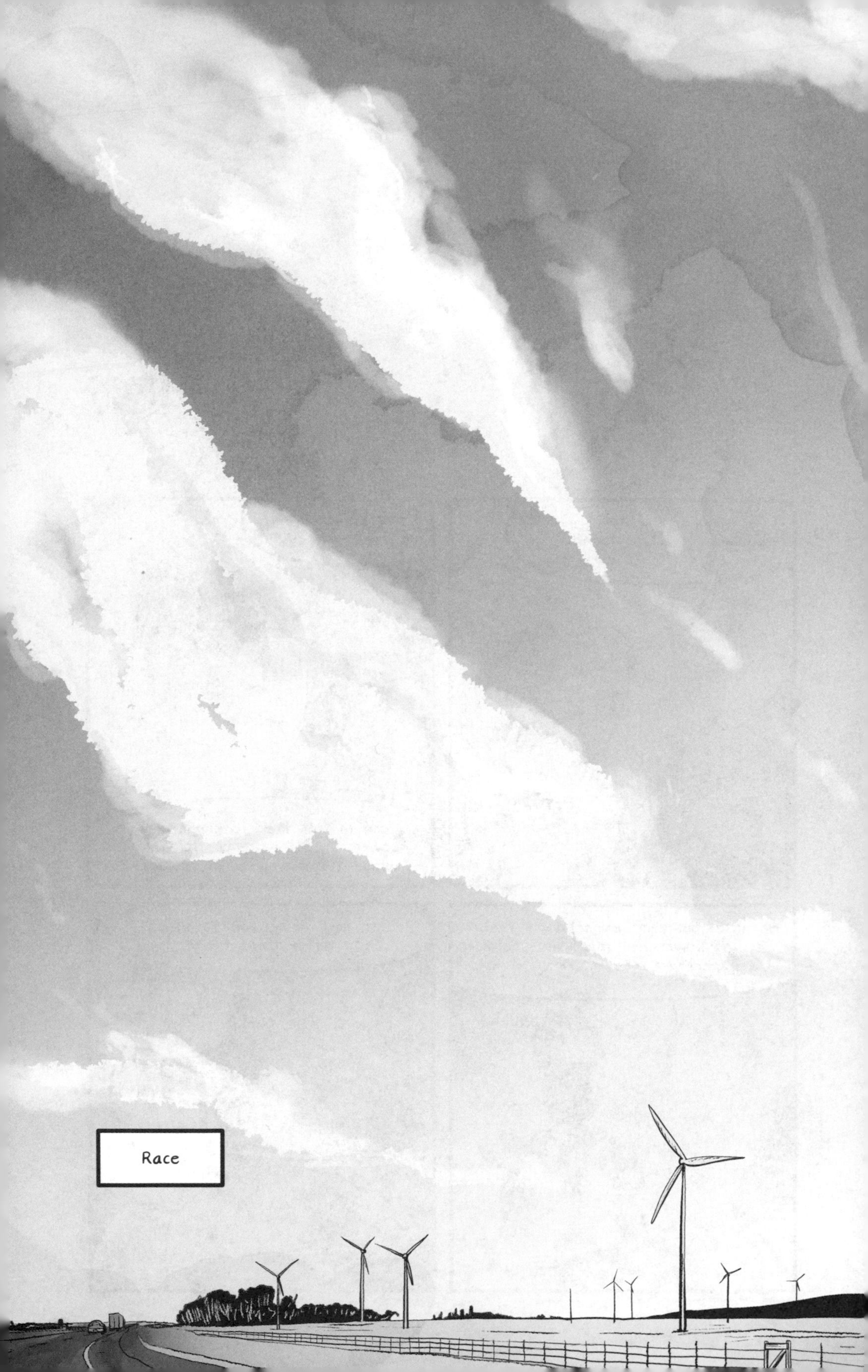
Race

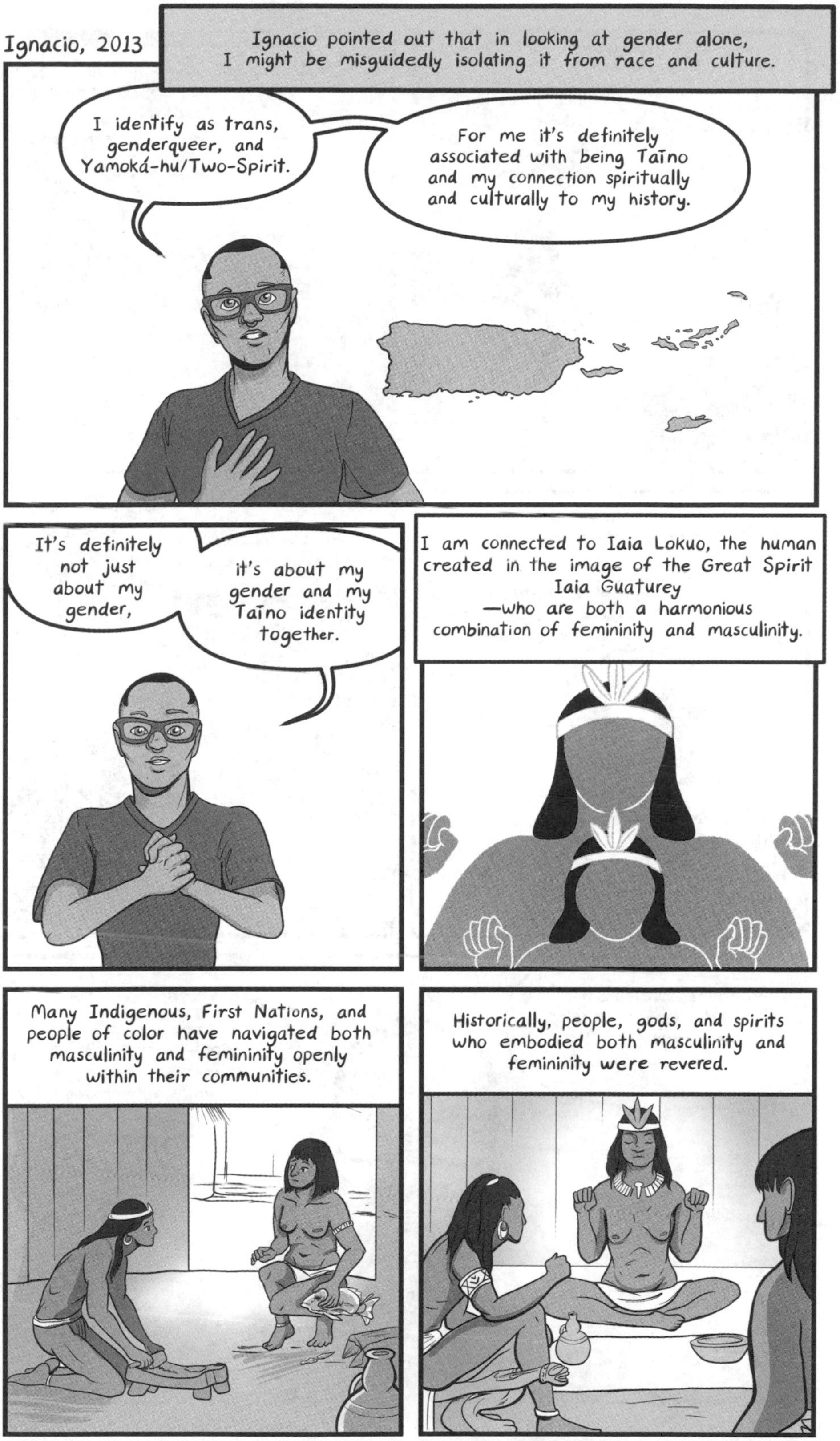
Ignacio, 2013
Ignacio pointed out that in looking at gender alone, I might be misguidedly isolating it from race and culture.
I identify as trans, genderqueer, and Yamoká-hu/Two-Spirit.
For me it's definitely associated with being Taīno and my connection spiritually and culturally to my history.
It's definitely not just about my gender,
it's about my gender and my Taīno identity together.
I am connected to Iaia Lokuo, the human created in the image of the Great Spirit Iaia Guaturey —who are both a harmonious combination of femininity and masculinity.
Many Indigenous, First Nations, and people of color have navigated both masculinity and femininity openly within their communities.
Historically, people, gods, and spirits who embodied both masculinity and femininity were revered.

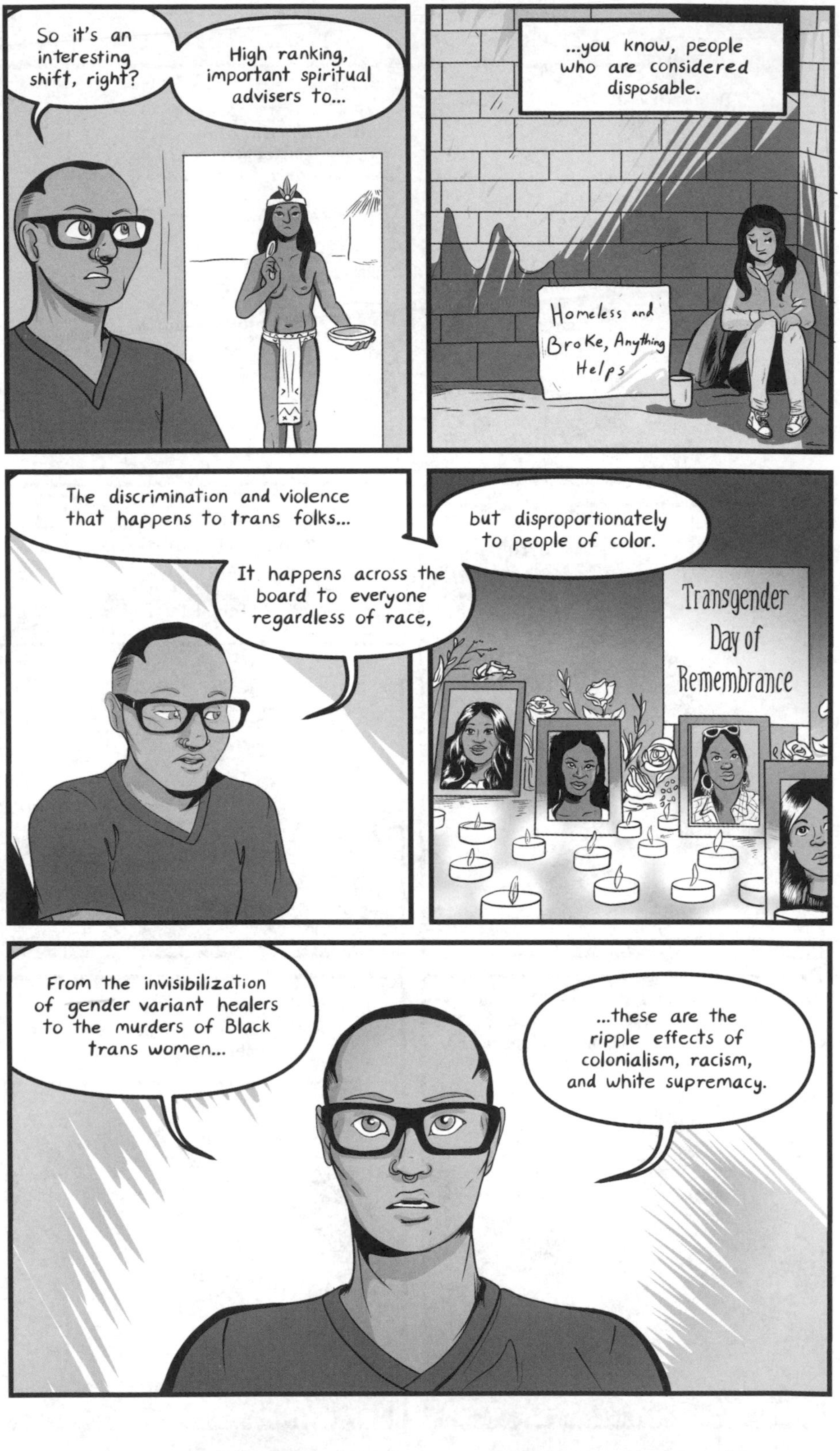
So it's an interesting shift, right?
High ranking, important spiritual advisers to...
...you know, people who are considered disposable.
Homeless and Broke, Anything Helps
The discrimination and violence that happens to trans folks...
It happens across the board to everyone regardless of race,
but disproportionately to people of color.
Transgender Day of Remembrance
From the invisibilization of gender variant healers to the murders of Black trans women...
...these are the ripple effects of colonialism, racism, and white supremacy.

Rhea

I think it says a lot about my white privilege that I didn't even think to include any questions about race, language, or culture when I first started this project.

No wonder I can't come up with a good model for all of this stuff.

In hindsight my questions seem so narrow, trying to take gender out of context.

2013

When a few early interviewees mentioned race, I realized I needed to make sure that I talked to as wide a range of people as possible.

Age		Race		Area
<18	3	White	20	WI
18-20	4	Black	7	MI
20-30	4	Asian	2	IA
-40	5	Indig.	1	MN
0-50	7	Latinx	2	CA
60	5	Other	1	IL
0+	3	Unknown	4	IN
				FL
				MA
				MO
				TX

Even if someone didn't bring up race directly in their interview answers, those experiences inform their opinions.

2014

The project took longer as I searched for a broader range of interviewees and tried to unpack some of my own assumptions.

There's so much in the world I don't know how to cover.

Daiquiri, 2013

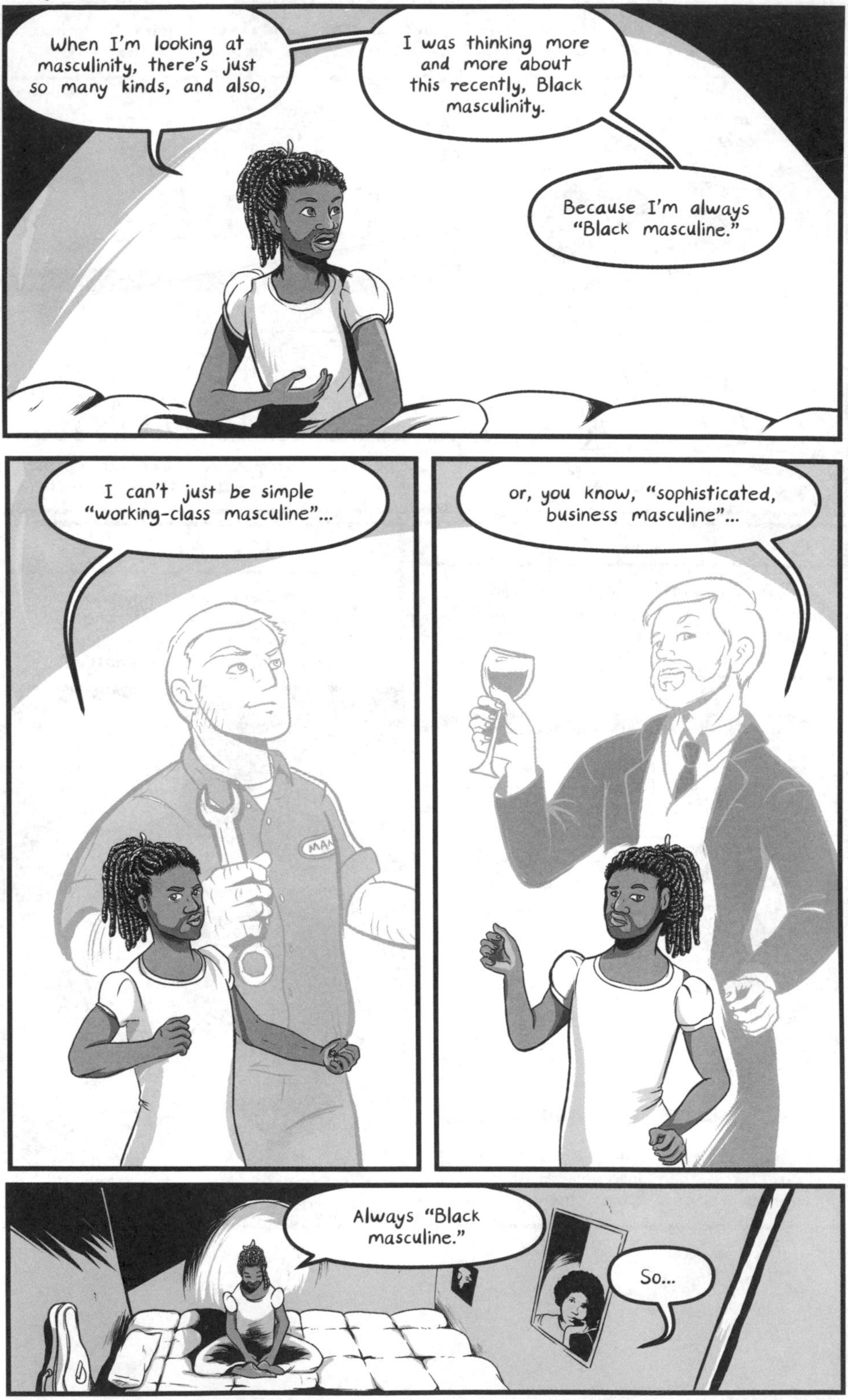

When I'm looking at masculinity, there's just so many kinds, and also,
I was thinking more and more about this recently, Black masculinity.
Because I'm always "Black masculine."
I can't just be simple "working-class masculine"...
MAN
or, you know, "sophisticated, business masculine"...
Always "Black masculine."
So...

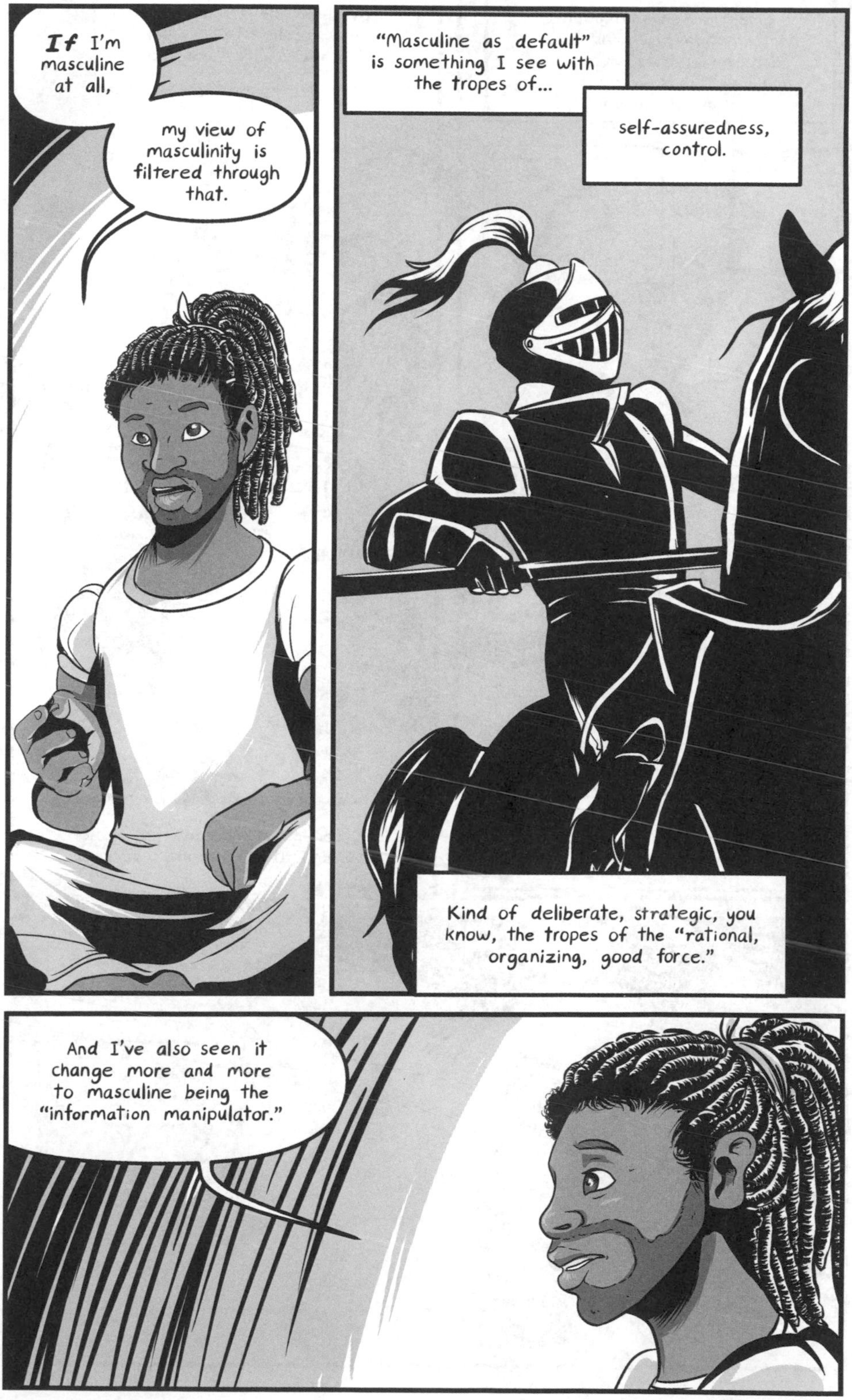
If I'm masculine at all,
my view of masculinity is filtered through that.
"Masculine as default" is something I see with the tropes of...
self-assuredness, control.
Kind of deliberate, strategic, you know, the tropes of the "rational, organizing, good force."
And I've also seen it change more and more to masculine being the "information manipulator."

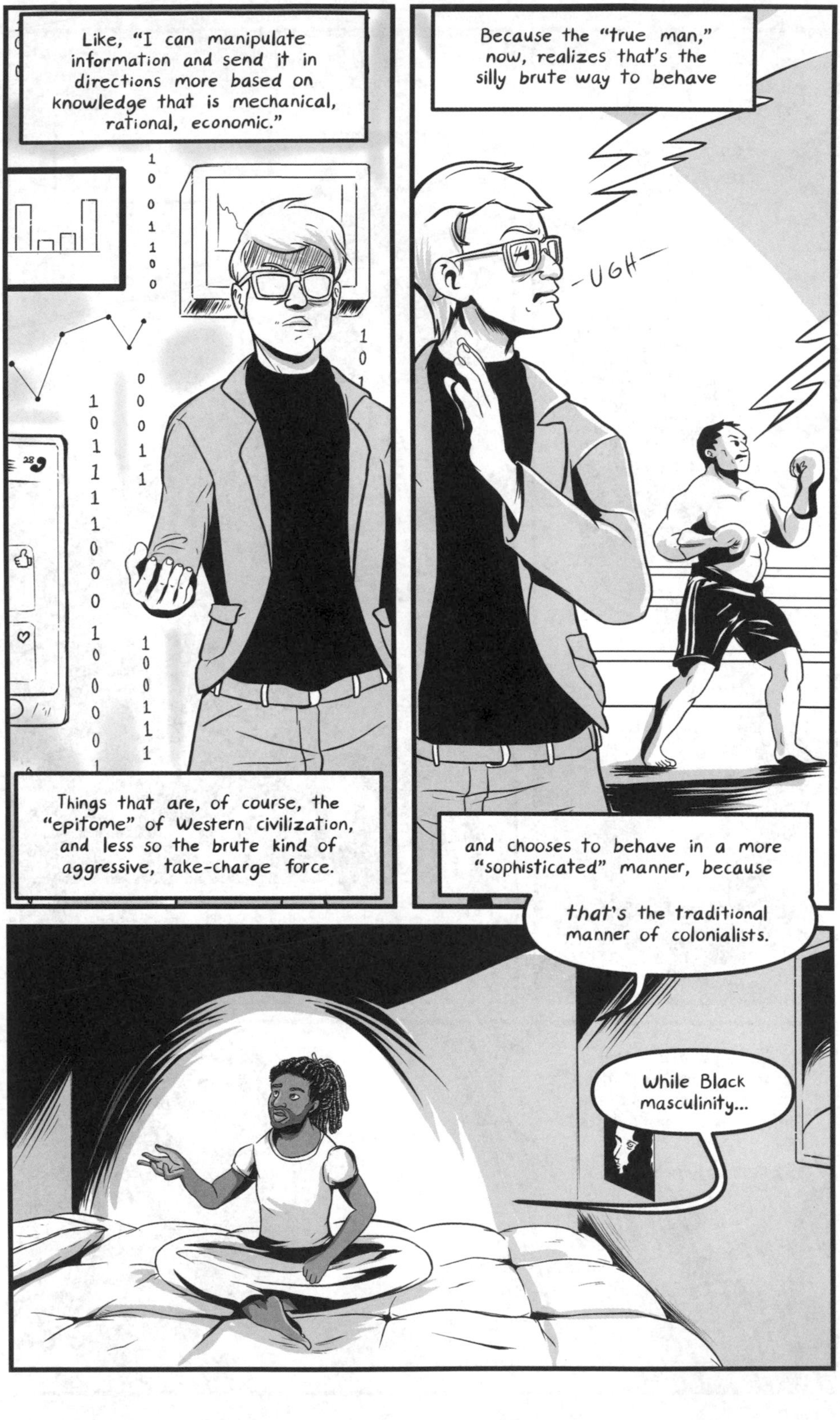

Like, "I can manipulate information and send it in directions more based on knowledge that is mechanical, rational, economic."
Things that are, of course, the "epitome" of Western civilization, and less so the brute kind of aggressive, take-charge force.
Because the "true man," now, realizes that's the silly brute way to behave
UGH
and chooses to behave in a more "sophisticated" manner, because
that's the traditional manner of colonialists.
While Black masculinity...

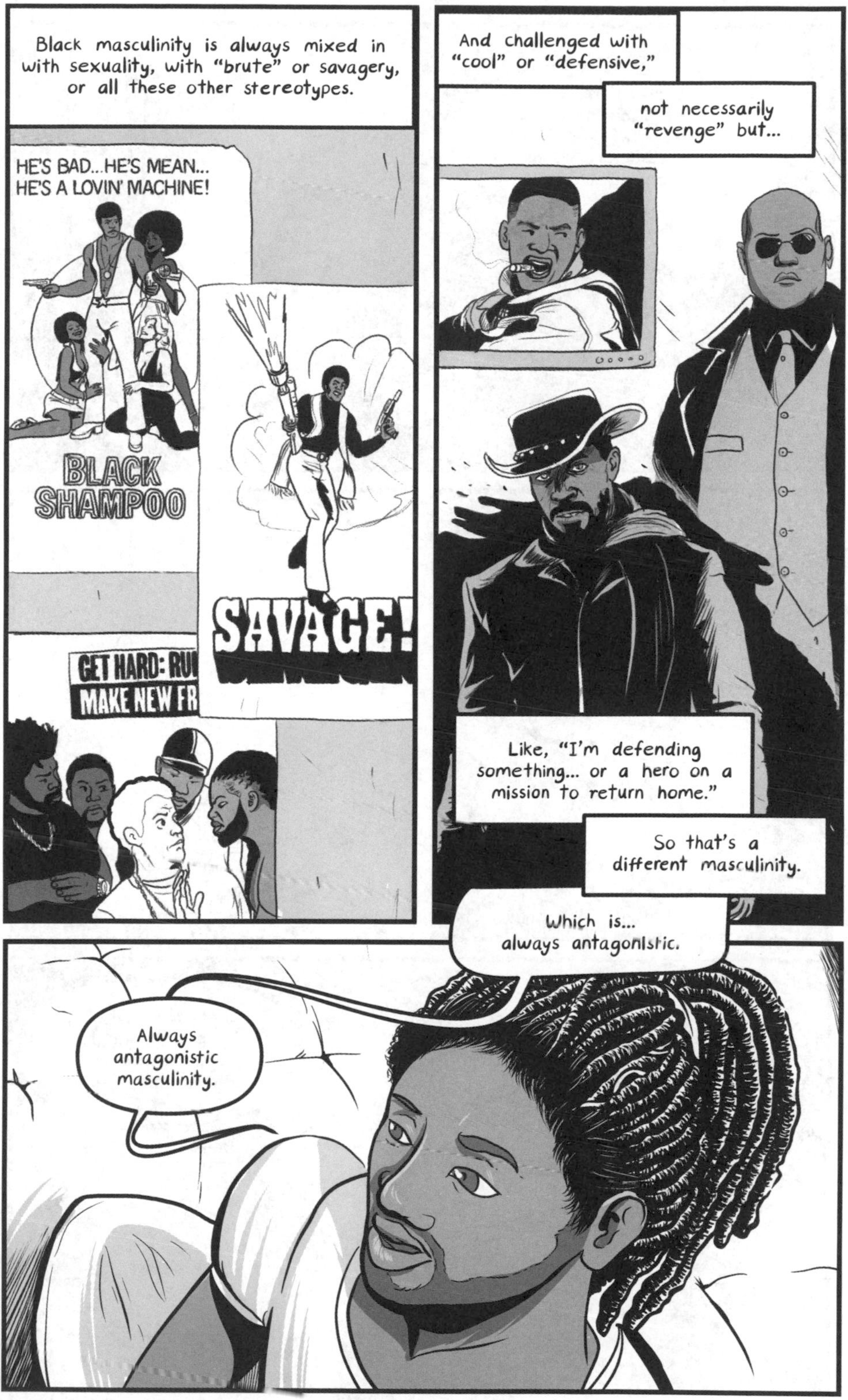
Black masculinity is always mixed in with sexuality, with "brute" or savagery, or all these other stereotypes.
HE'S BAD...HE'S MEAN...
HE'S A LOVIN' MACHINE!
BLACK SHAMPOO
SAVAGE!
GET HARD: RU
MAKE NEW FR
And challenged with "cool" or "defensive,"
not necessarily "revenge" but...
Like, "I'm defending something... or a hero on a mission to return home."
So that's a different masculinity.
Which is... always antagonistic.
Always antagonistic masculinity.

Jonah, 2013

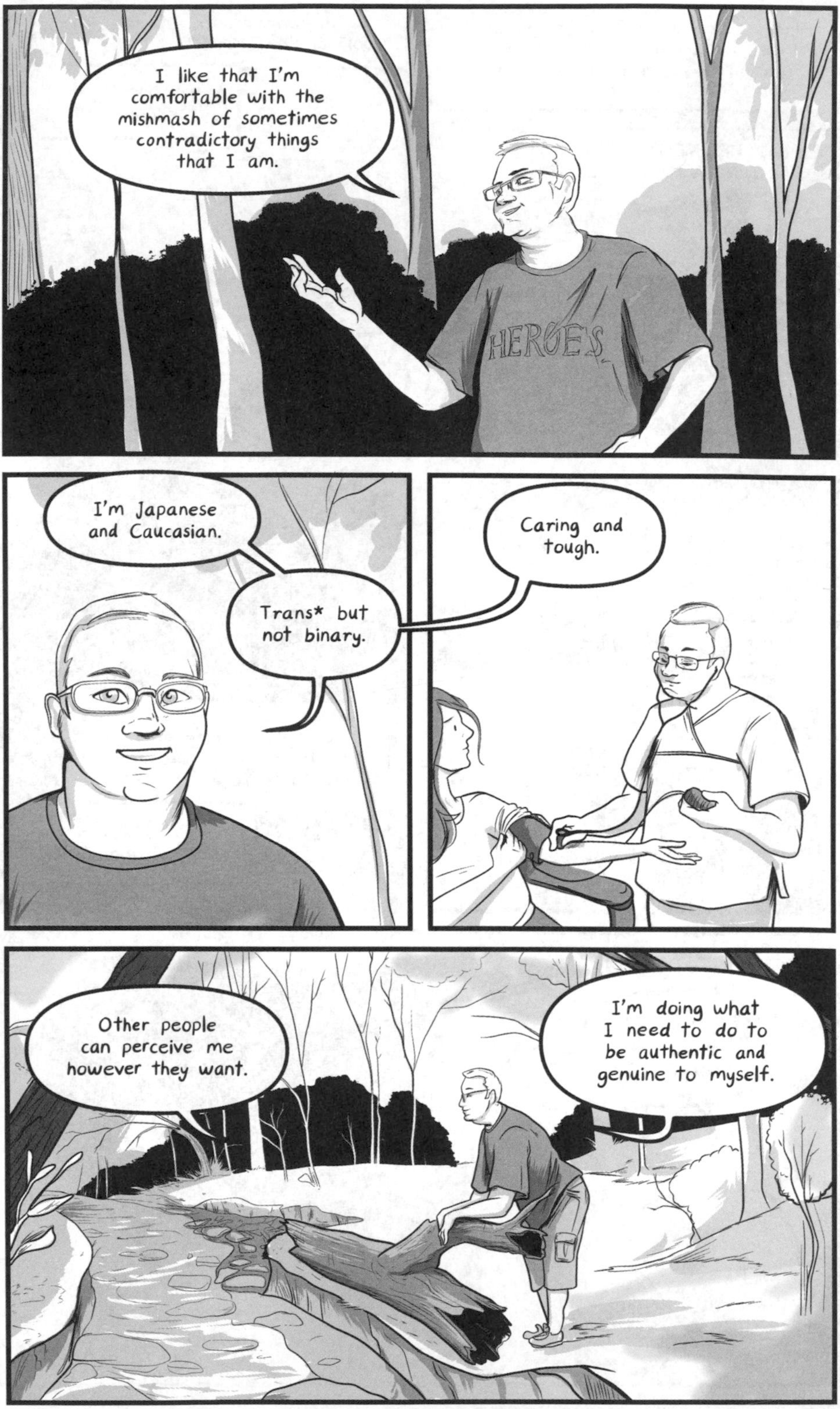
I like that I'm comfortable with the mishmash of sometimes contradictory things that I am.
HEROES
I'm Japanese and Caucasian.
Trans* but not binary.
Caring and tough.
Other people can perceive me however they want.
I'm doing what I need to do to be authentic and genuine to myself.

"Trans*" is sometimes used with an asterisk like this to more clearly indicate a broad range of gender-diverse experiences, identities, and expressions.

LaShawn, 2013

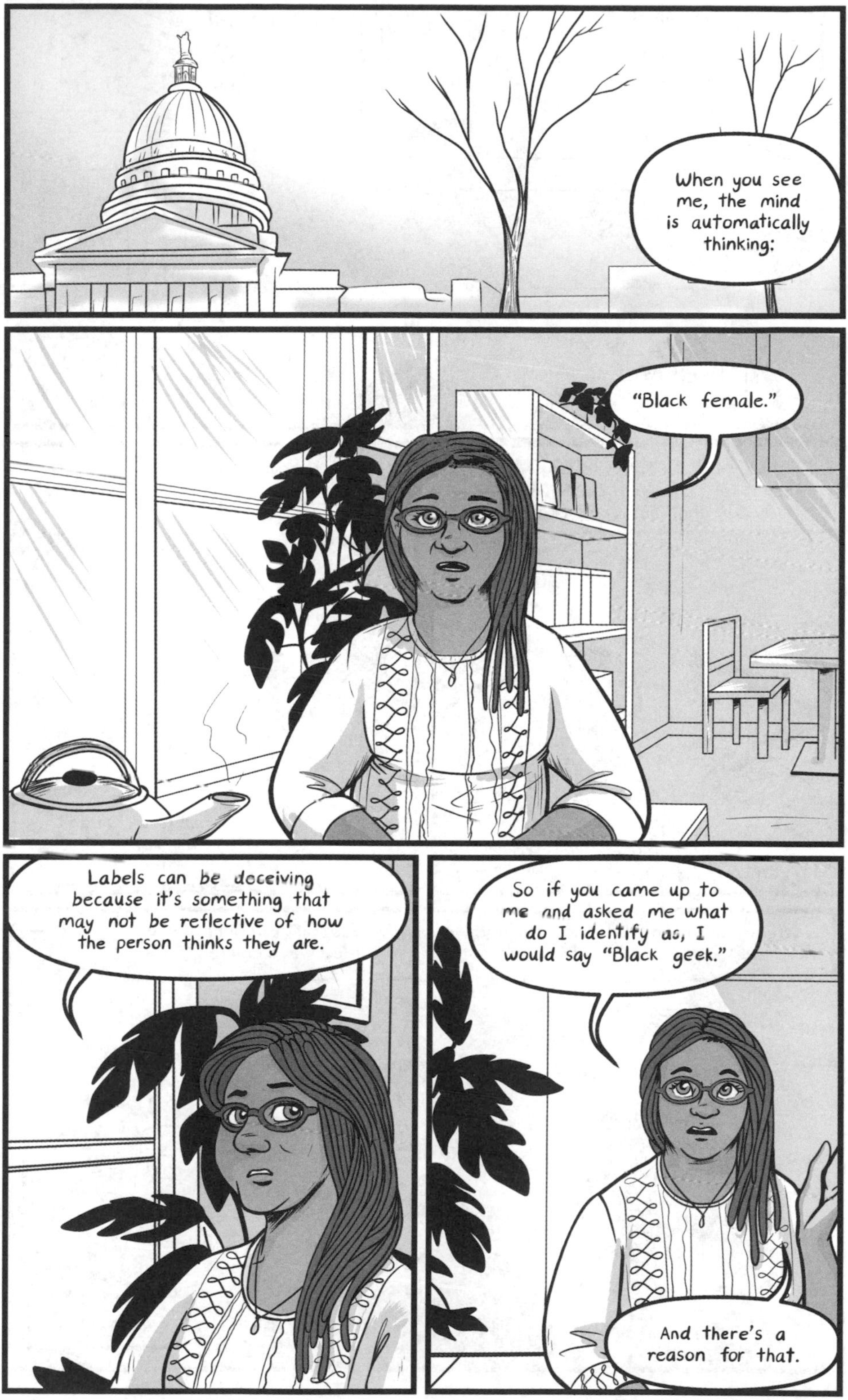
When you see me, the mind is automatically thinking:
"Black female."
Labels can be deceiving because it's something that may not be reflective of how the person thinks they are.
So if you came up to me and asked me what do I identify as, I would say "Black geek."
And there's a reason for that.

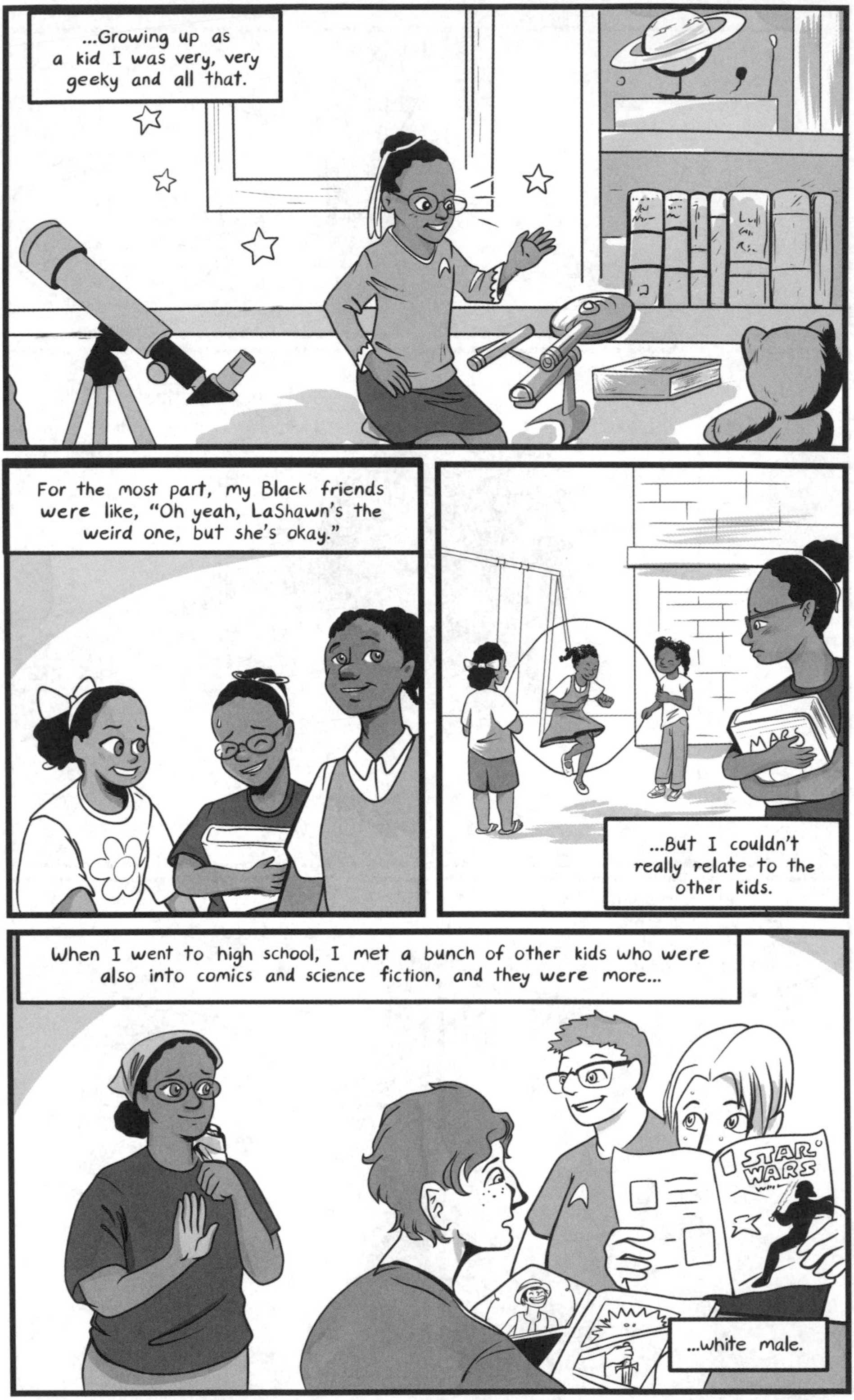
...Growing up as a kid I was very, very geeky and all that.
For the most part, my Black friends were like, "Oh yeah, LaShawn's the weird one, but she's okay."
MARS
...But I couldn't really relate to the other kids.
When I went to high school, I met a bunch of other kids who were also into comics and science fiction, and they were more...
STAR WARS
...white male.

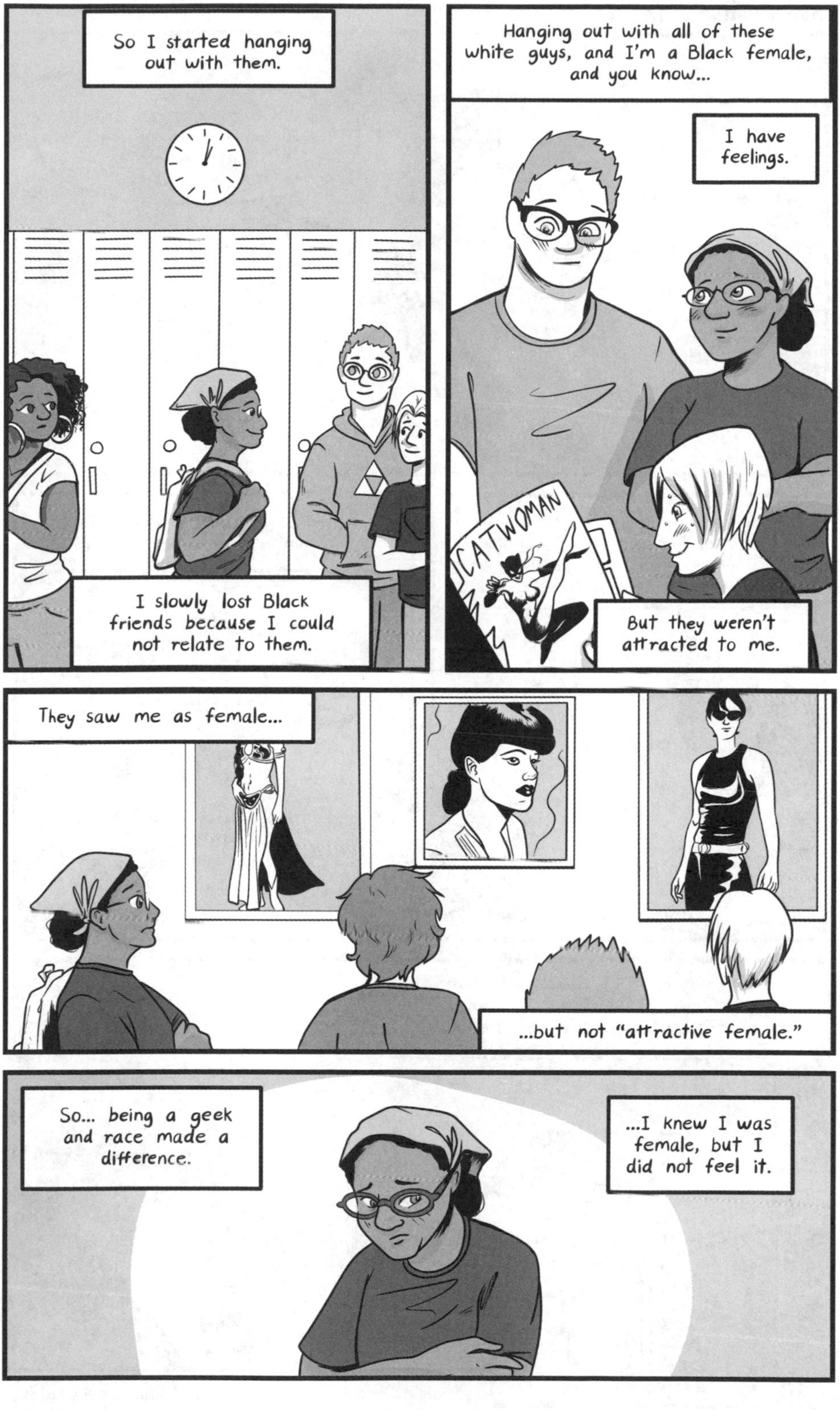
So I started hanging out with them.
I slowly lost Black friends because I could not relate to them.
Hanging out with all of these white guys, and I'm a Black female, and you know...
I have feelings.
CATWOMAN
But they weren't attracted to me.
They saw me as female...
...but not "attractive female."
So... being a geek and race made a difference.
...I knew I was female, but I did not feel it.

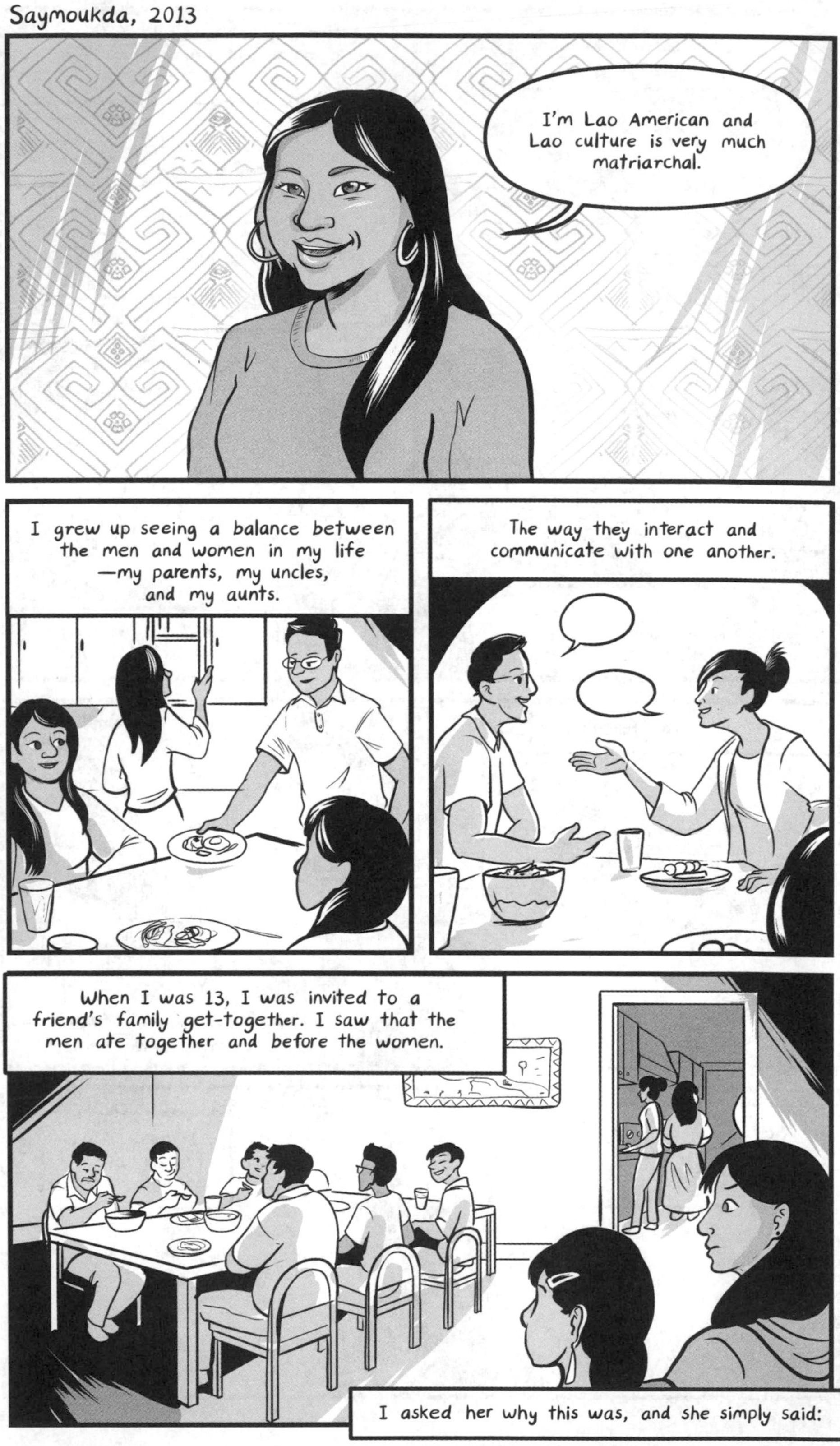
Saymoukda, 2013
I'm Lao American and Lao culture is very much matriarchal.
I grew up seeing a balance between the men and women in my life —my parents, my uncles, and my aunts.
The way they interact and communicate with one another.
When I was 13, I was invited to a friend's family get-together. I saw that the men ate together and before the women.
I asked her why this was, and she simply said:

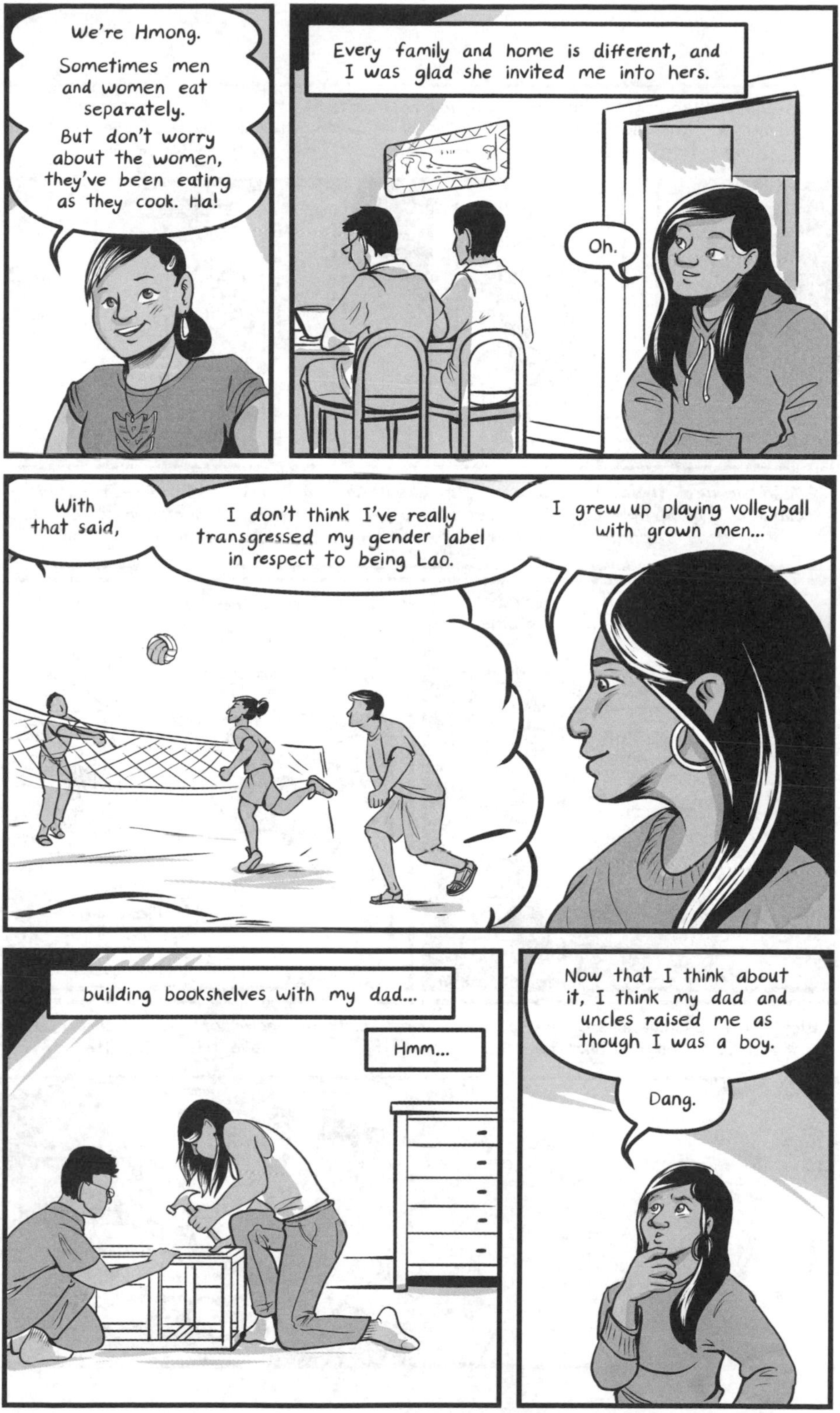
We're Hmong.
Sometimes men and women eat separately.
But don't worry about the women, they've been eating as they cook. Ha!
Every family and home is different, and I was glad she invited me into hers.
Oh.
With that said,
I don't think I've really transgressed my gender label in respect to being Lao.
I grew up playing volleyball with grown men...
building bookshelves with my dad...
Hmm...
Now that I think about it, I think my dad and uncles raised me as though I was a boy.
Dang.

Rhea, 2013

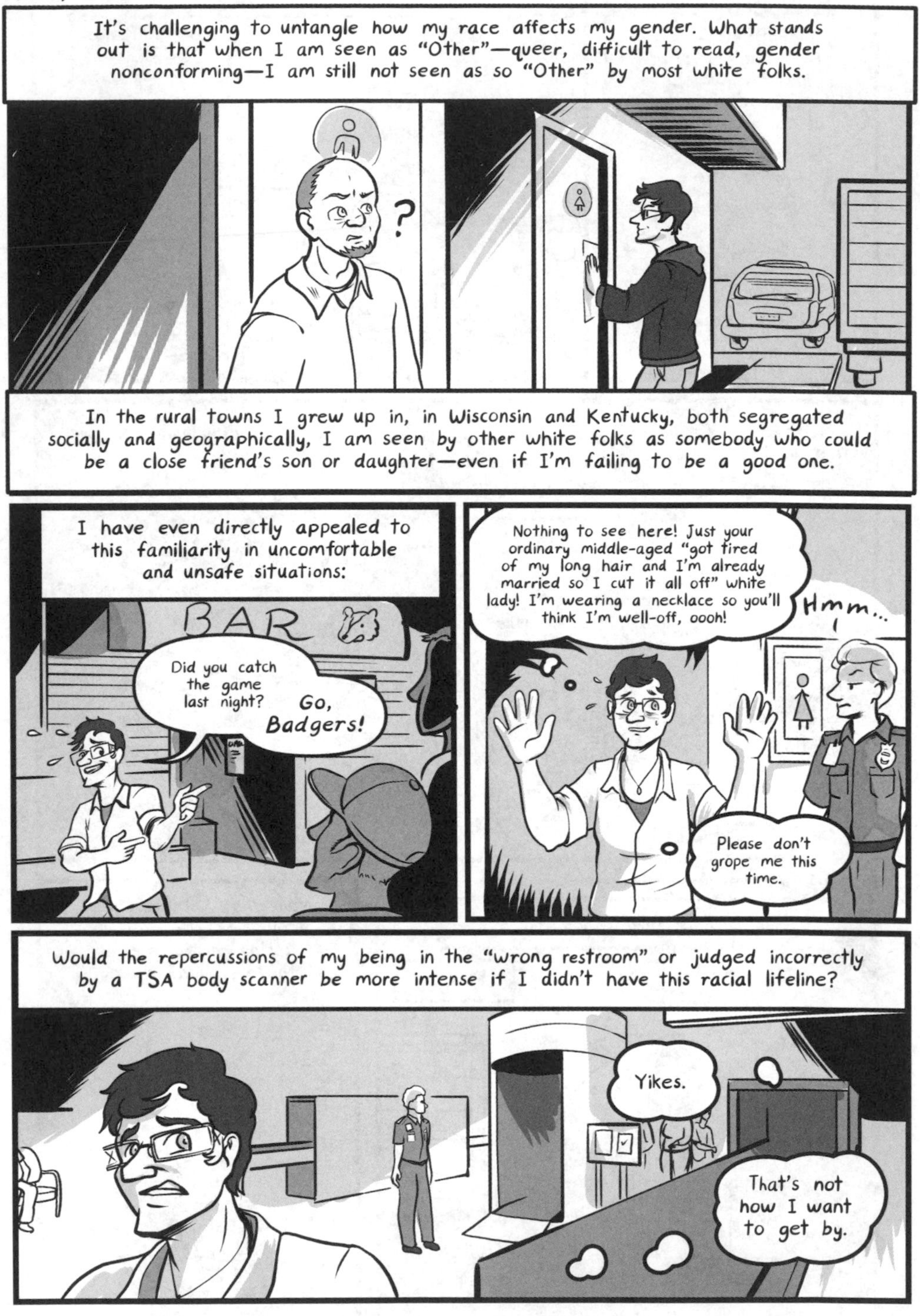
It's challenging to untangle how my race affects my gender. What stands out is that when I am seen as "Other"—queer, difficult to read, gender nonconforming—I am still not seen as so "Other" by most white folks.
?
In the rural towns I grew up in, in Wisconsin and Kentucky, both segregated socially and geographically, I am seen by other white folks as somebody who could be a close friend's son or daughter—even if I'm failing to be a good one.
I have even directly appealed to this familiarity in uncomfortable and unsafe situations:
BAR
Did you catch the game last night?
Go, Badgers!
Nothing to see here! Just your ordinary middle-aged "got tired of my long hair and I'm already married so I cut it all off" white lady! I'm wearing a necklace so you'll think I'm well-off, oooh!
Hmm...
Please don't grope me this time.
Would the repercussions of my being in the "wrong restroom" or judged incorrectly by a TSA body scanner be more intense if I didn't have this racial lifeline?
Yikes.
That's not how I want to get by.

Rhea, 2019

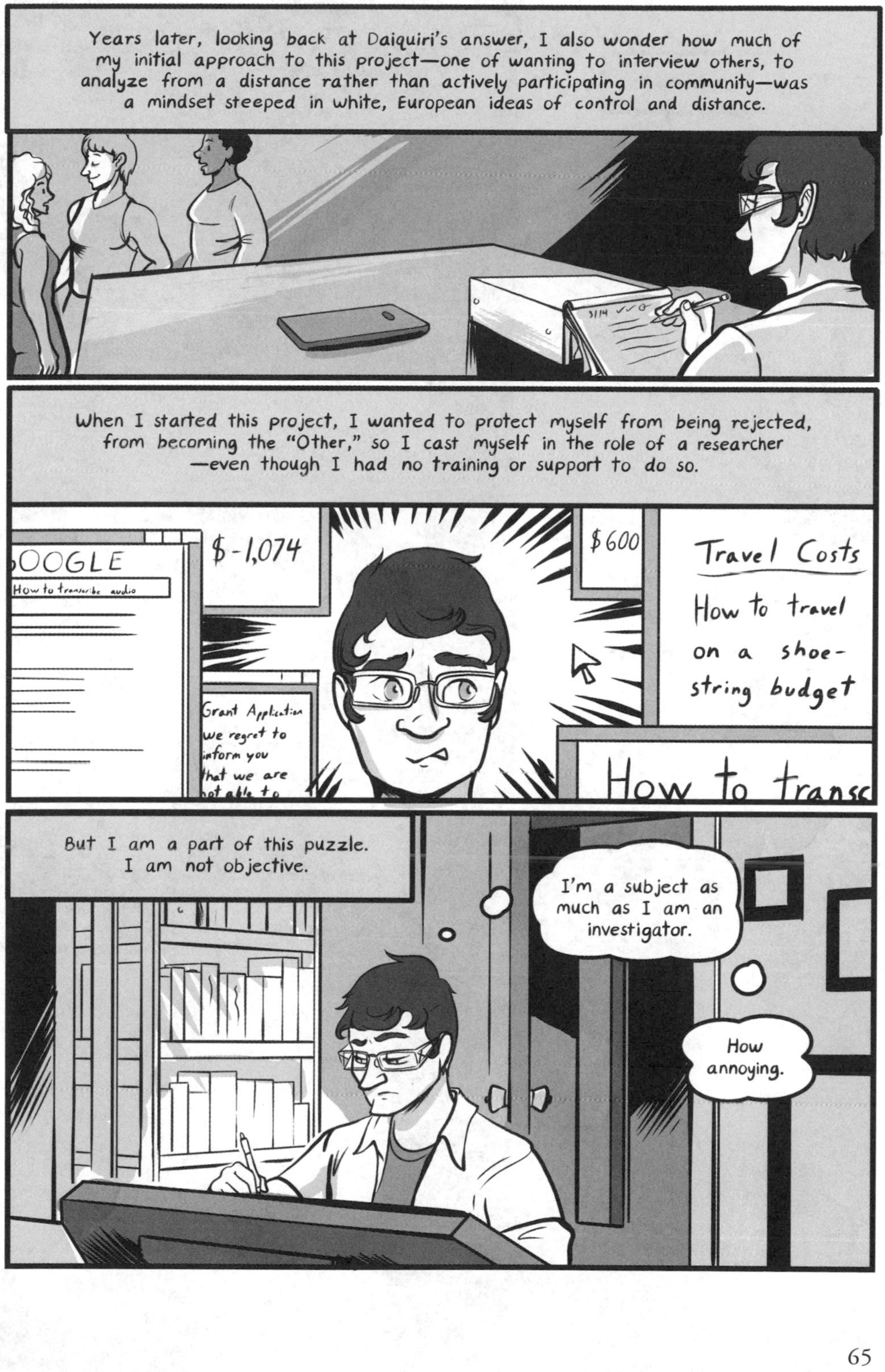
Years later, looking back at Daiquiri's answer, I also wonder how much of my initial approach to this project—one of wanting to interview others, to analyze from a distance rather than actively participating in community—was a mindset steeped in white, European ideas of control and distance.
When I started this project, I wanted to protect myself from being rejected, from becoming the "Other," so I cast myself in the role of a researcher —even though I had no training or support to do so.
How to transcribe audio
$-1,074
$600
Travel Costs
How to travel on a shoe-string budget
Grant Application
But I am a part of this puzzle. I am not objective.
I'm a subject as much as I am an investigator.
How annoying.

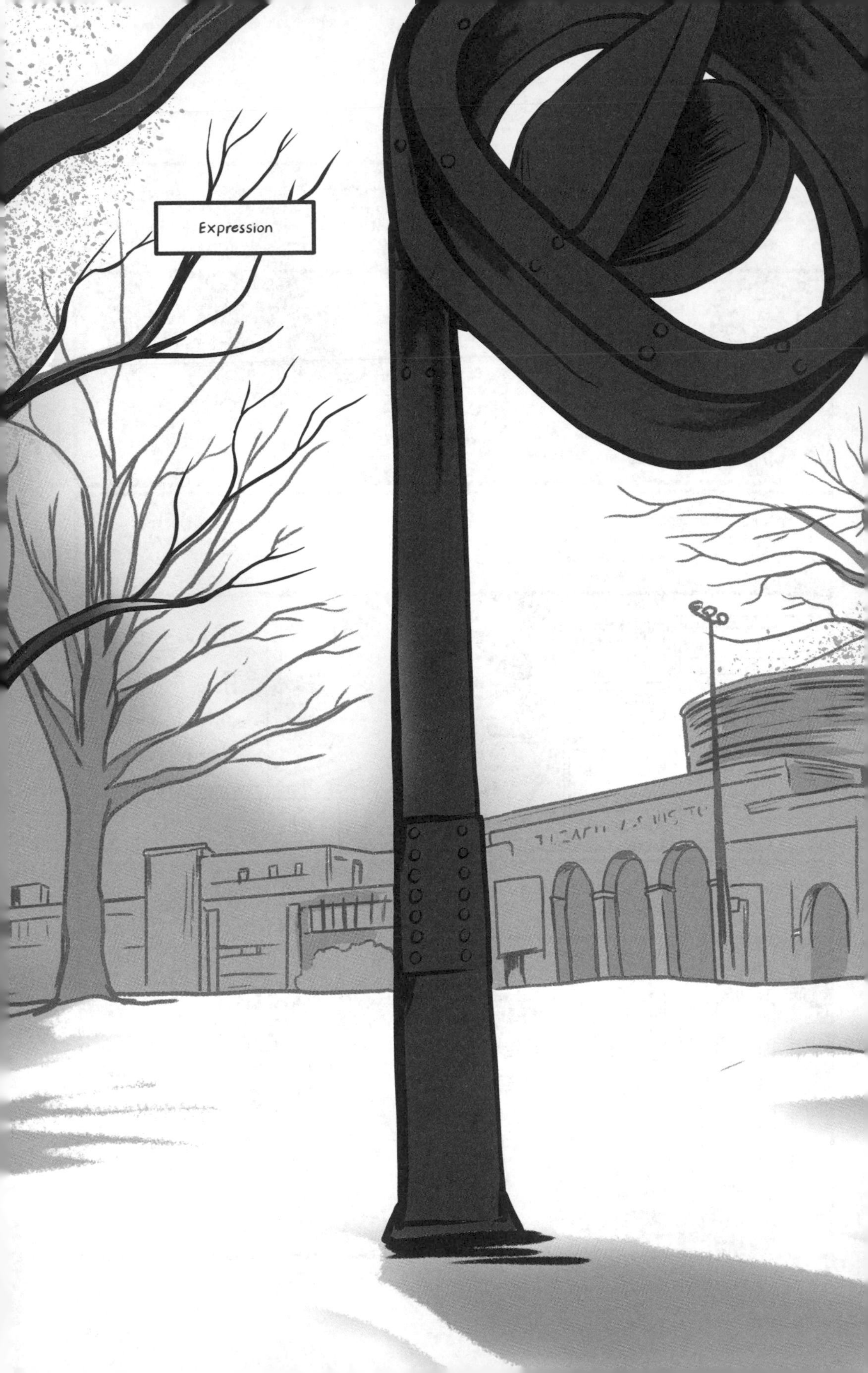
Expression

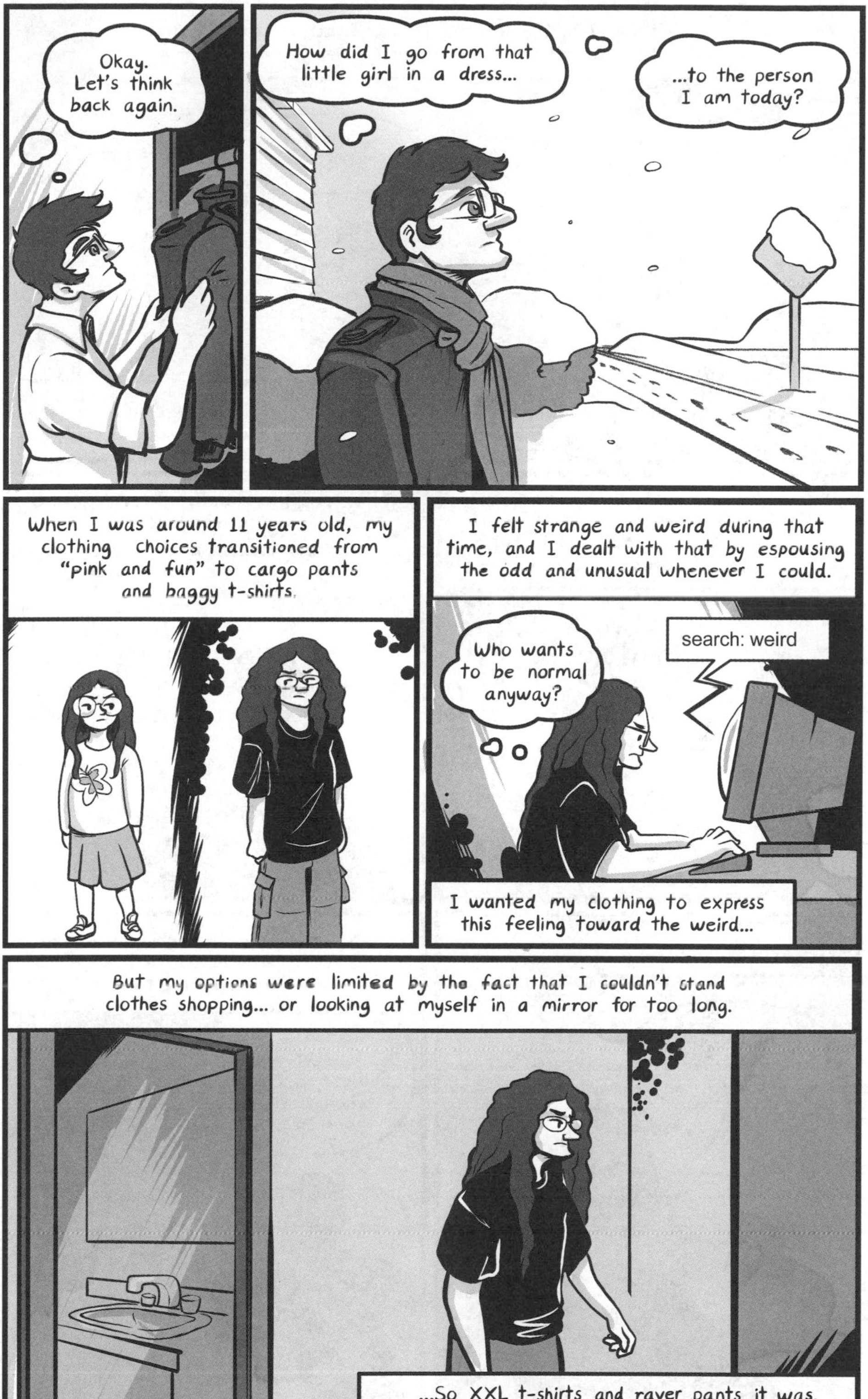
Okay. Let's think back again.
How did I go from that little girl in a dress...
...to the person I am today?
When I was around 11 years old, my clothing choices transitioned from "pink and fun" to cargo pants and baggy t-shirts.
I felt strange and weird during that time, and I dealt with that by espousing the odd and unusual whenever I could.
Who wants to be normal anyway?
search: weird
I wanted my clothing to express this feeling toward the weird...
But my options were limited by the fact that I couldn't stand clothes shopping... or looking at myself in a mirror for too long.
...So XXL t-shirts and raver pants it was.

Teenage me didn't know how I wanted to come across, exactly. But I did successfully convey a rejection of femininity and young womanhood.

Maybe you can perm her hair?

She has her daddy's eyebrows...

Do you think Rhea might be... like *that*?

Adults noticed.

Never shown an interest in boys...*

My parents didn't worry, but other people did.

In college I worked up the courage to cut my hair short, going from waist-length locks to a fluffy pixie cut. I loved it.

Other people's reactions were mixed. From Midwest polite...

Well. That's... certainly a different look.

...to supportive...

You look like a butch Betty Boop!

...to what were probably intended to be cutting remarks that somehow felt complimentary to me.

...Rhea?!? I thought you were a boy when I first walked in!

Well, good!

Wait, why does that feel good?

*This assumption was and is blatantly untrue. I'm bisexual, but assumptions about my gender presentation often make it difficult for some people to believe I could have any interest in men.

68

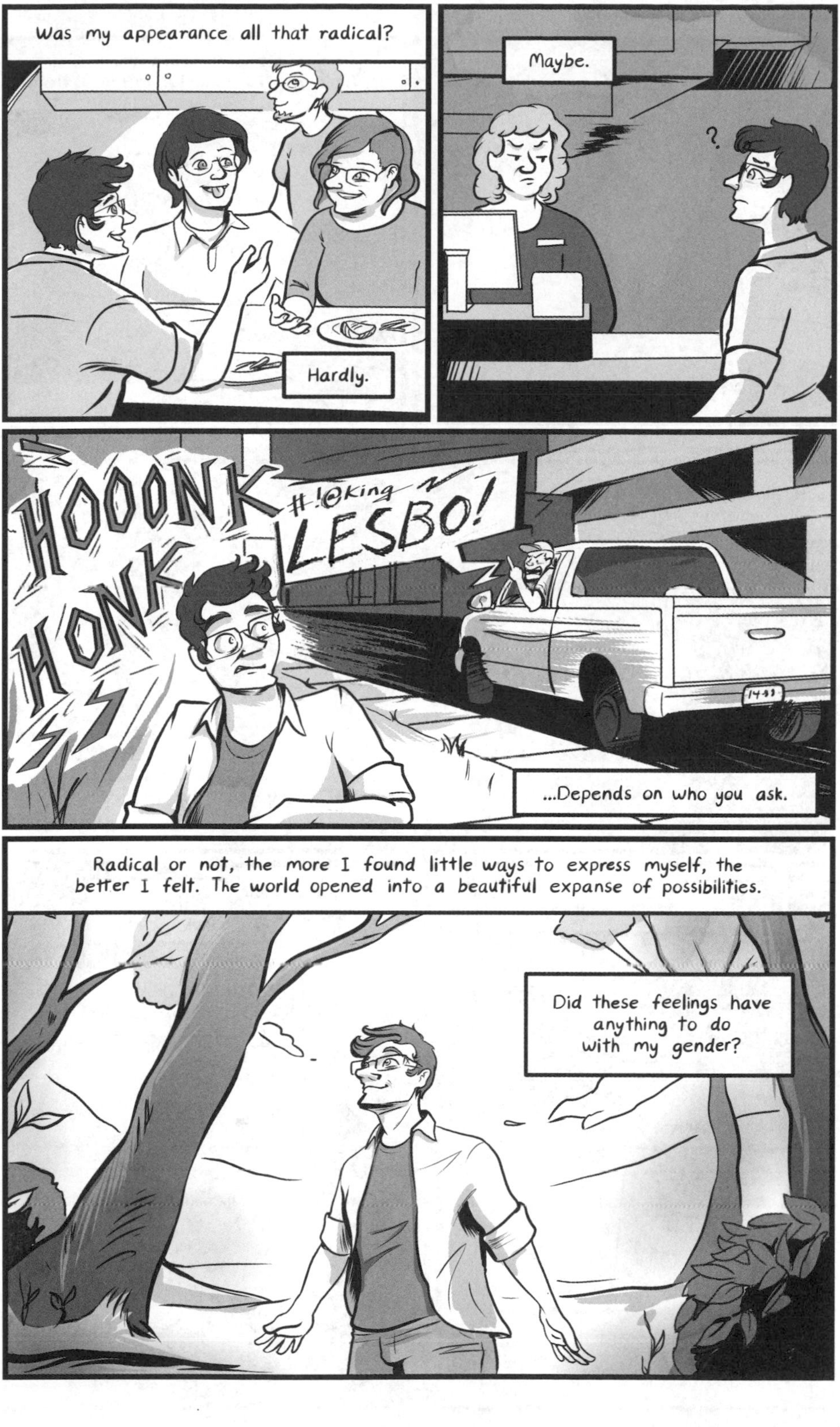
Was my appearance all that radical?
Hardly.
Maybe.
?
HOOONK
HONK
#!@king LESBO!
...Depends on who you ask.
Radical or not, the more I found little ways to express myself, the better I felt. The world opened into a beautiful expanse of possibilities.
Did these feelings have anything to do with my gender?

Haley, 2012

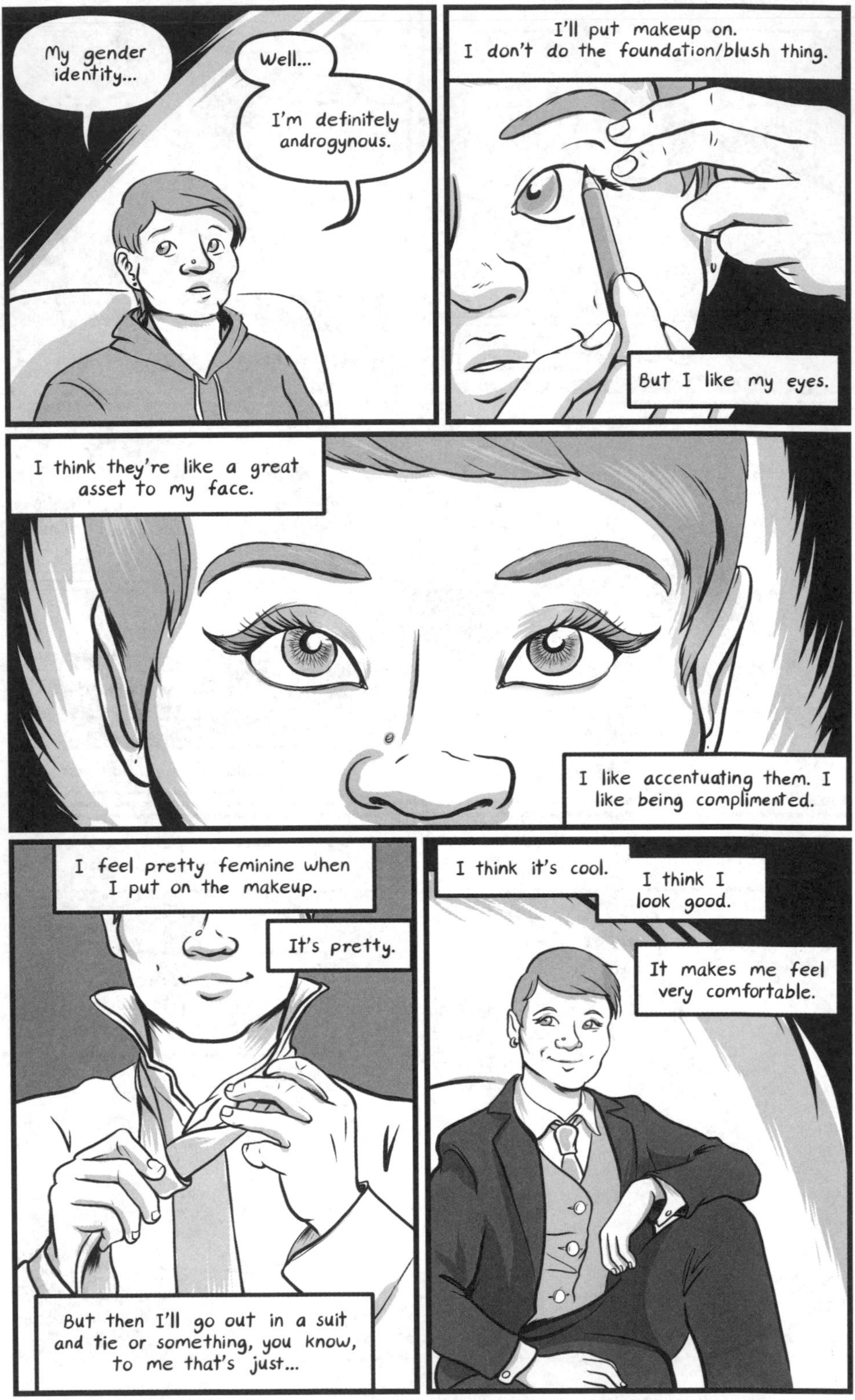
My gender identity...
Well...
I'm definitely androgynous.
I'll put makeup on. I don't do the foundation/blush thing.
But I like my eyes.
I think they're like a great asset to my face.
I like accentuating them. I like being complimented.
I feel pretty feminine when I put on the makeup.
It's pretty.
But then I'll go out in a suit and tie or something, you know, to me that's just...
I think it's cool.
I think I look good.
It makes me feel very comfortable.

Kelly, 2011

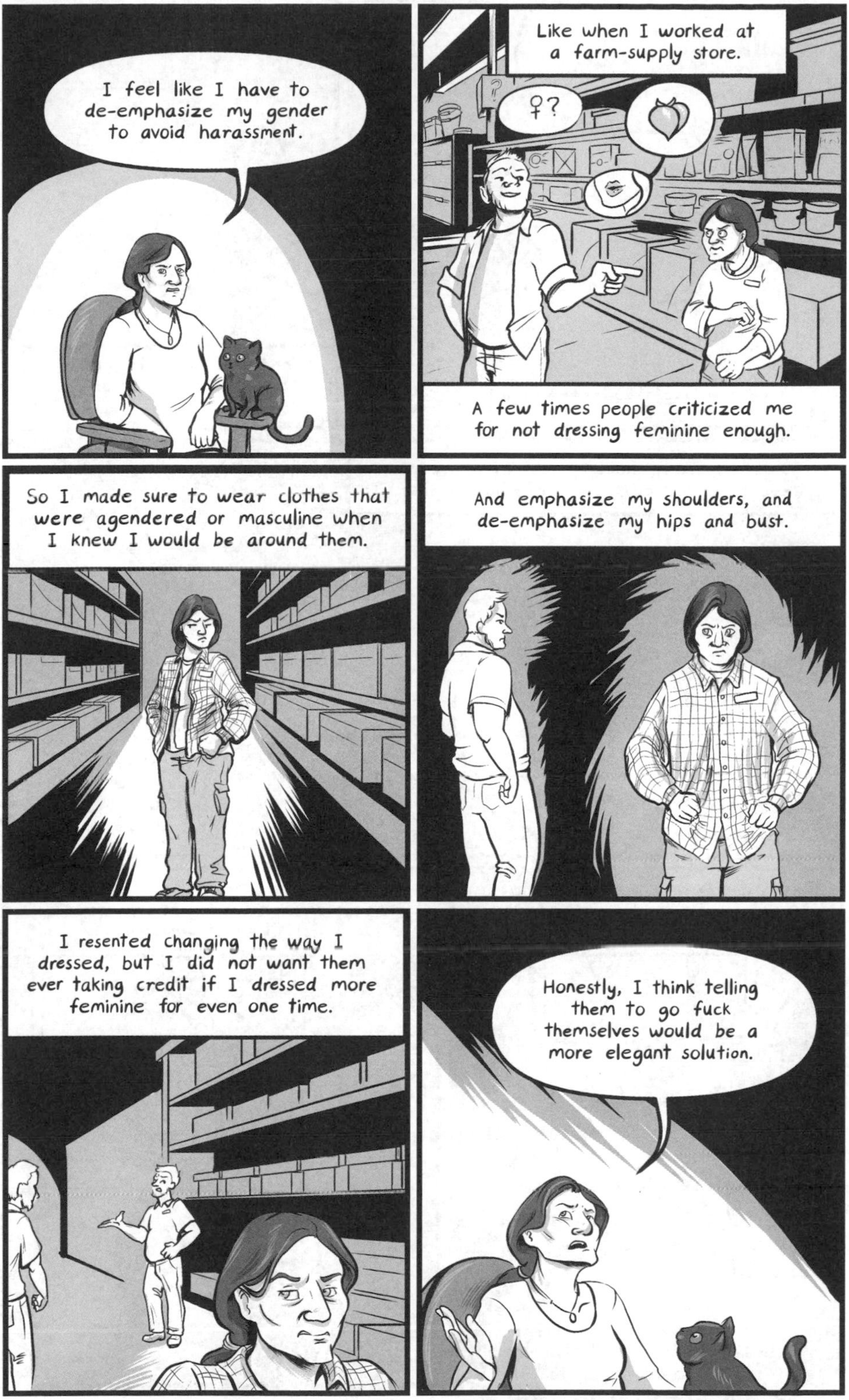
I feel like I have to de-emphasize my gender to avoid harassment.
Like when I worked at a farm-supply store.
♀?
A few times people criticized me for not dressing feminine enough.
So I made sure to wear clothes that were agendered or masculine when I knew I would be around them.
And emphasize my shoulders, and de-emphasize my hips and bust.
I resented changing the way I dressed, but I did not want them ever taking credit if I dressed more feminine for even one time.
Honestly, I think telling them to go fuck themselves would be a more elegant solution.

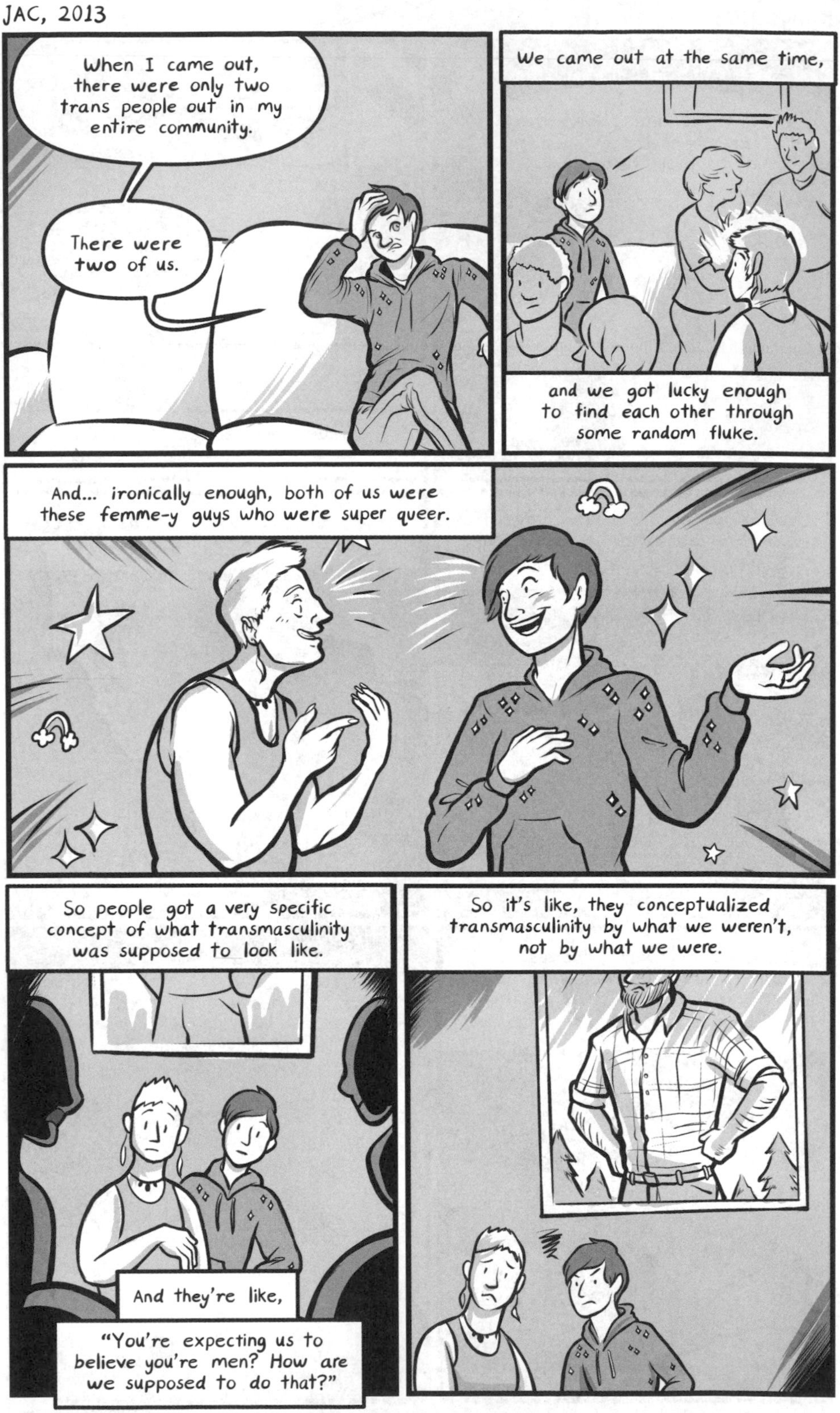
JAC, 2013
When I came out, there were only two trans people out in my entire community.
There were two of us.
We came out at the same time,
and we got lucky enough to find each other through some random fluke.
And... ironically enough, both of us were these femme-y guys who were super queer.
So people got a very specific concept of what transmasculinity was supposed to look like.
And they're like,
"You're expecting us to believe you're men? How are we supposed to do that?"
So it's like, they conceptualized transmasculinity by what we weren't, not by what we were.

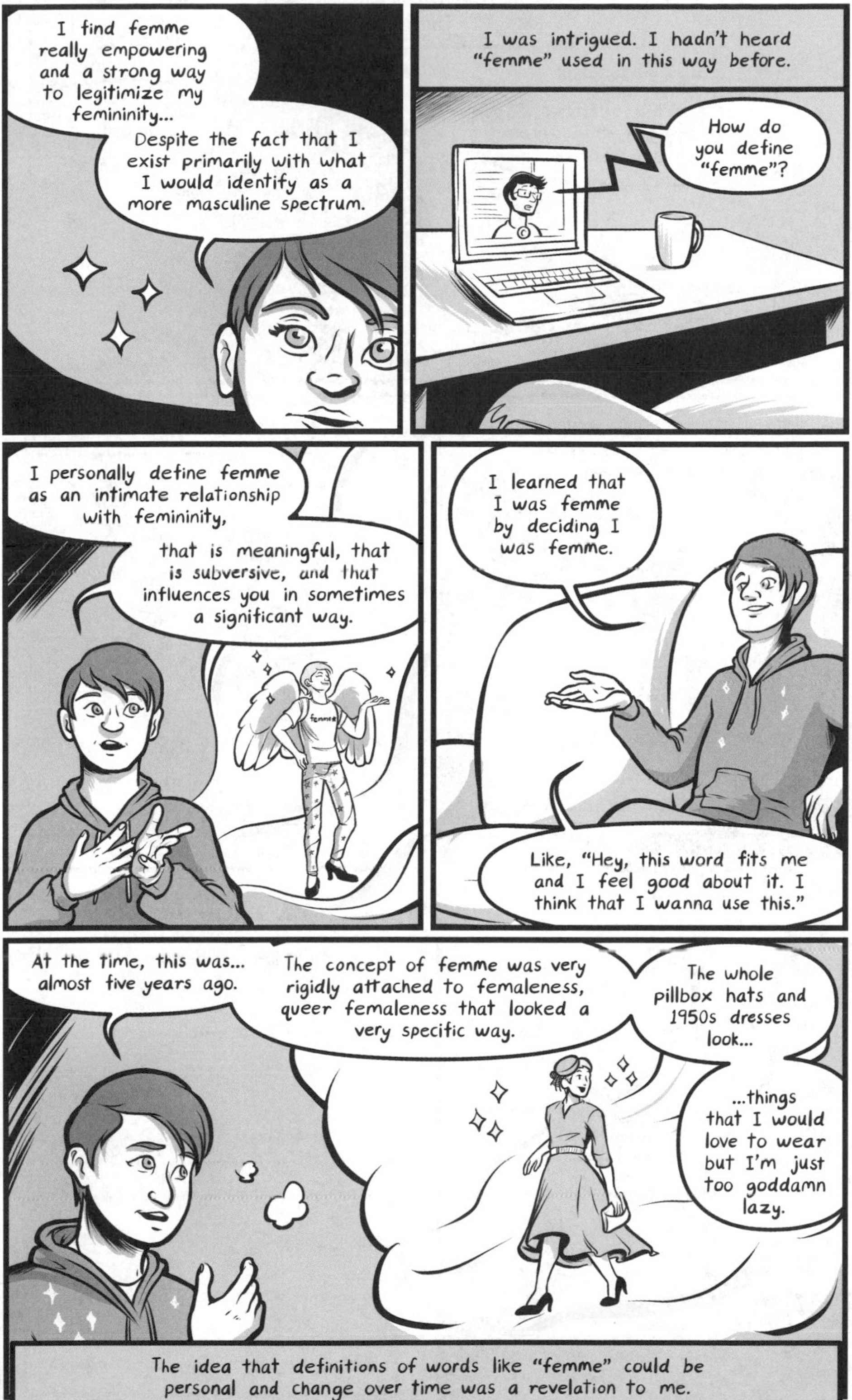
I find femme really empowering and a strong way to legitimize my femininity...
Despite the fact that I exist primarily with what I would identify as a more masculine spectrum.
I was intrigued. I hadn't heard "femme" used in this way before.
How do you define "femme"?
I personally define femme as an intimate relationship with femininity,
that is meaningful, that is subversive, and that influences you in sometimes a significant way.
femme
I learned that I was femme by deciding I was femme.
Like, "Hey, this word fits me and I feel good about it. I think that I wanna use this."
At the time, this was... almost five years ago.
The concept of femme was very rigidly attached to femaleness, queer femaleness that looked a very specific way.
The whole pillbox hats and 1950s dresses look...
...things that I would love to wear but I'm just too goddamn lazy.
The idea that definitions of words like "femme" could be personal and change over time was a revelation to me.

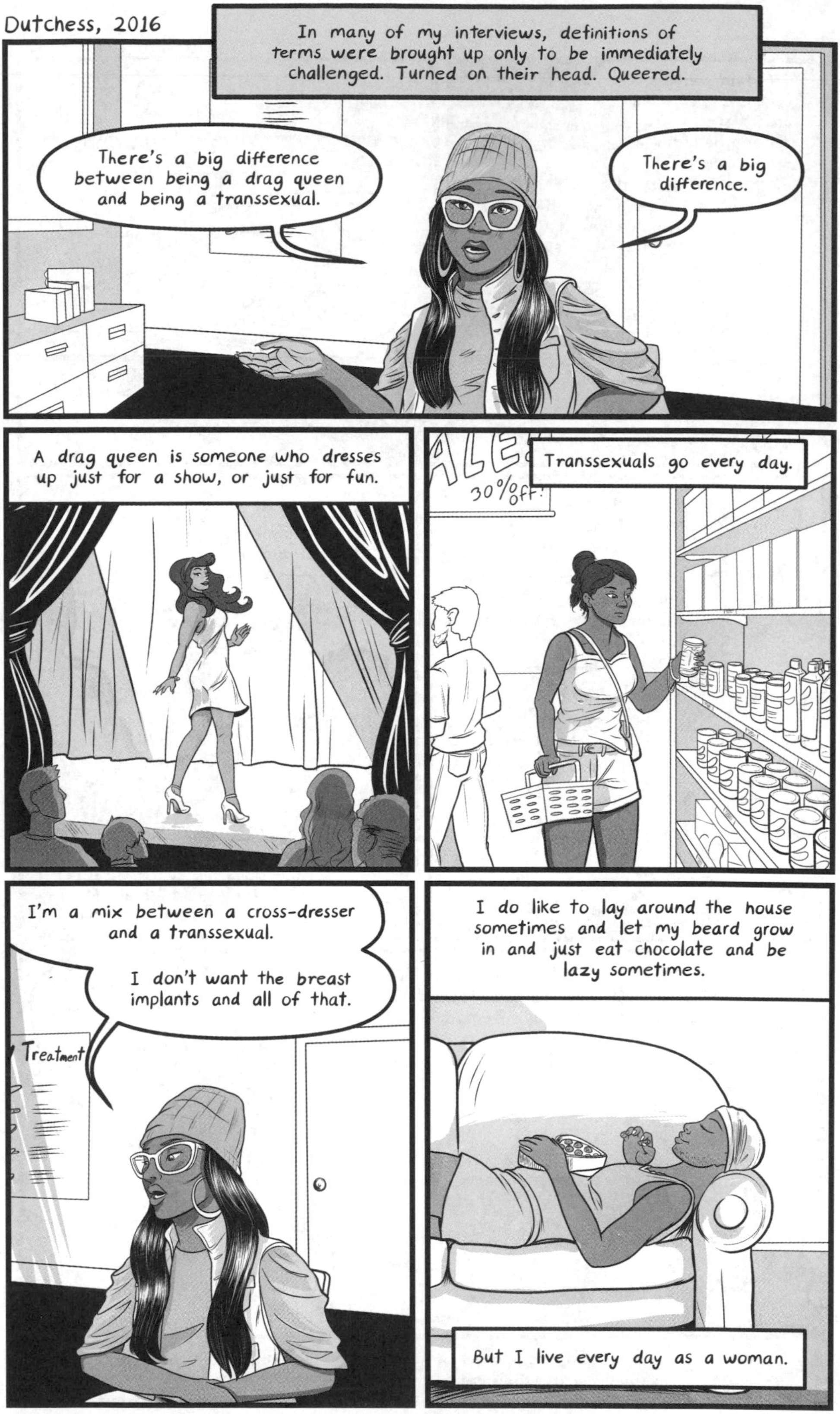
Dutchess, 2016
In many of my interviews, definitions of terms were brought up only to be immediately challenged. Turned on their head. Queered.
There's a big difference between being a drag queen and being a transsexual.
There's a big difference.
A drag queen is someone who dresses up just for a show, or just for fun.
Transsexuals go every day.
30% off!
I'm a mix between a cross-dresser and a transsexual.
I don't want the breast implants and all of that.
Treatment
I do like to lay around the house sometimes and let my beard grow in and just eat chocolate and be lazy sometimes.
But I live every day as a woman.

Wayne, 2012

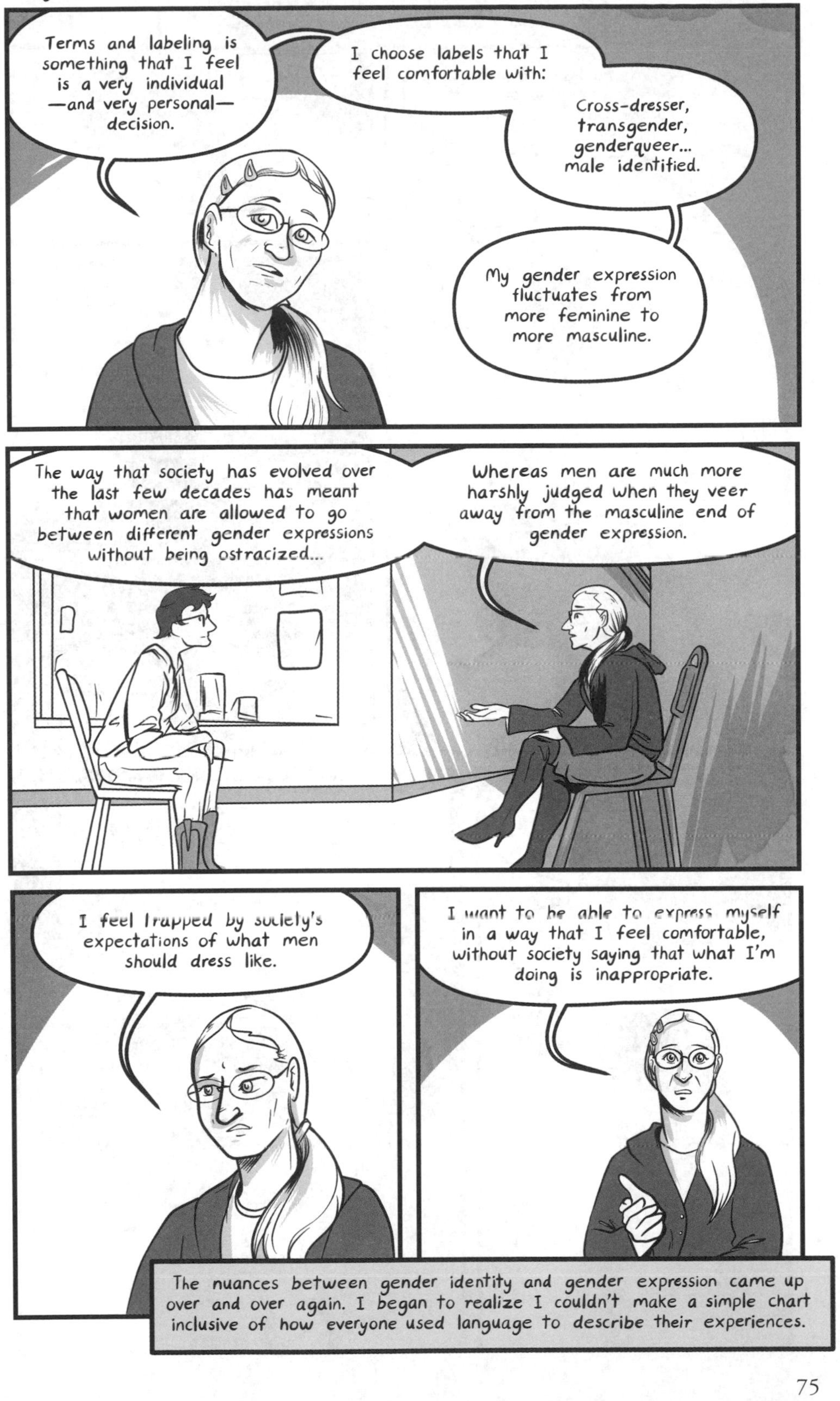
Terms and labeling is something that I feel is a very individual —and very personal— decision.
I choose labels that I feel comfortable with:
Cross-dresser, transgender, genderqueer... male identified.
My gender expression fluctuates from more feminine to more masculine.
The way that society has evolved over the last few decades has meant that women are allowed to go between different gender expressions without being ostracized...
Whereas men are much more harshly judged when they veer away from the masculine end of gender expression.
I feel trapped by society's expectations of what men should dress like.
I want to be able to express myself in a way that I feel comfortable, without society saying that what I'm doing is inappropriate.
The nuances between gender identity and gender expression came up over and over again. I began to realize I couldn't make a simple chart inclusive of how everyone used language to describe their experiences.

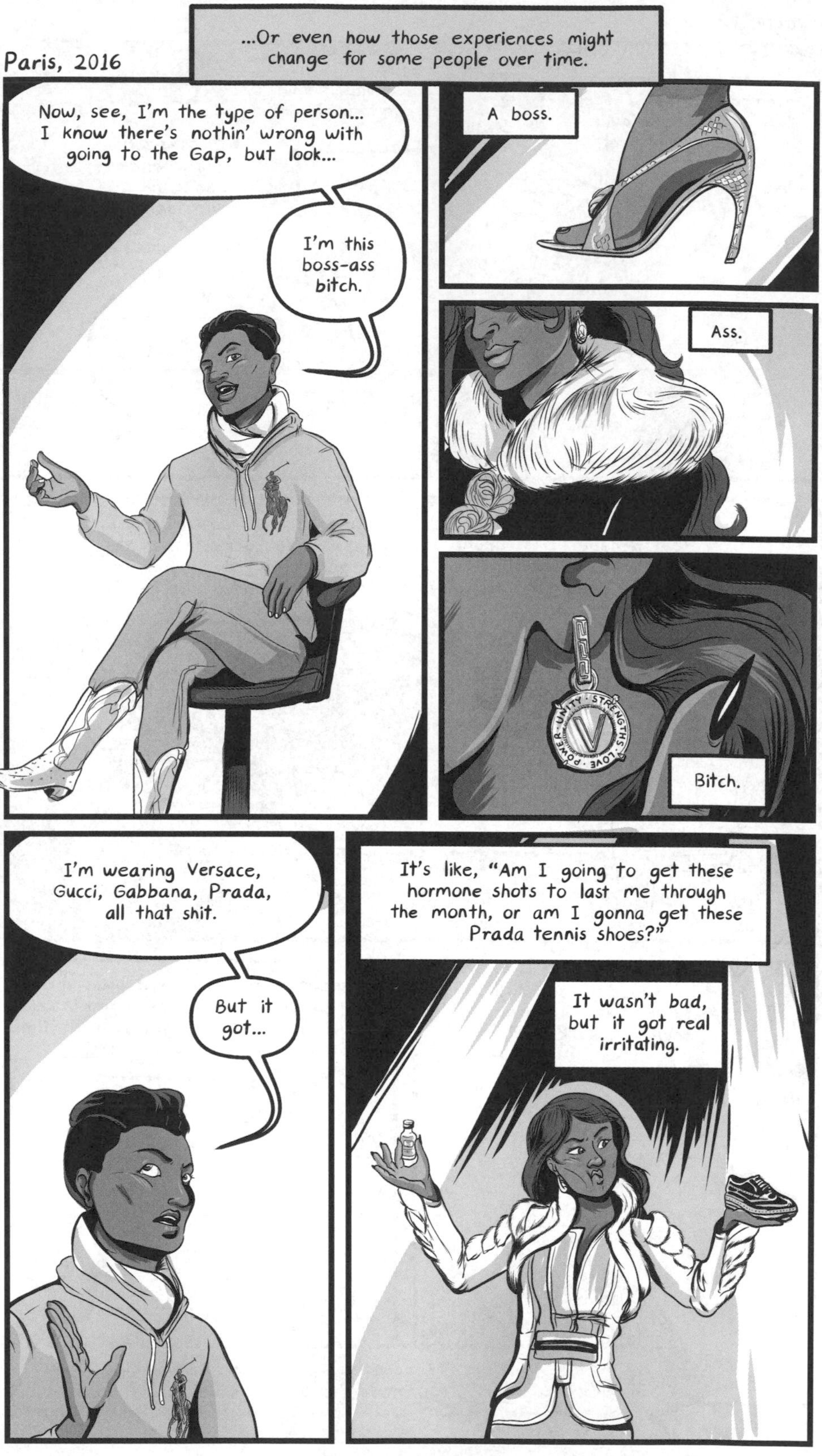
...Or even how those experiences might change for some people over time.
Paris, 2016
Now, see, I'm the type of person... I know there's nothin' wrong with going to the Gap, but look...
I'm this boss-ass bitch.
A boss.
Ass.
UNITY · STRENGTHS · LOVE · POWER
Bitch.
I'm wearing Versace, Gucci, Gabbana, Prada, all that shit.
But it got...
It's like, "Am I going to get these hormone shots to last me through the month, or am I gonna get these Prada tennis shoes?"
It wasn't bad, but it got real irritating.

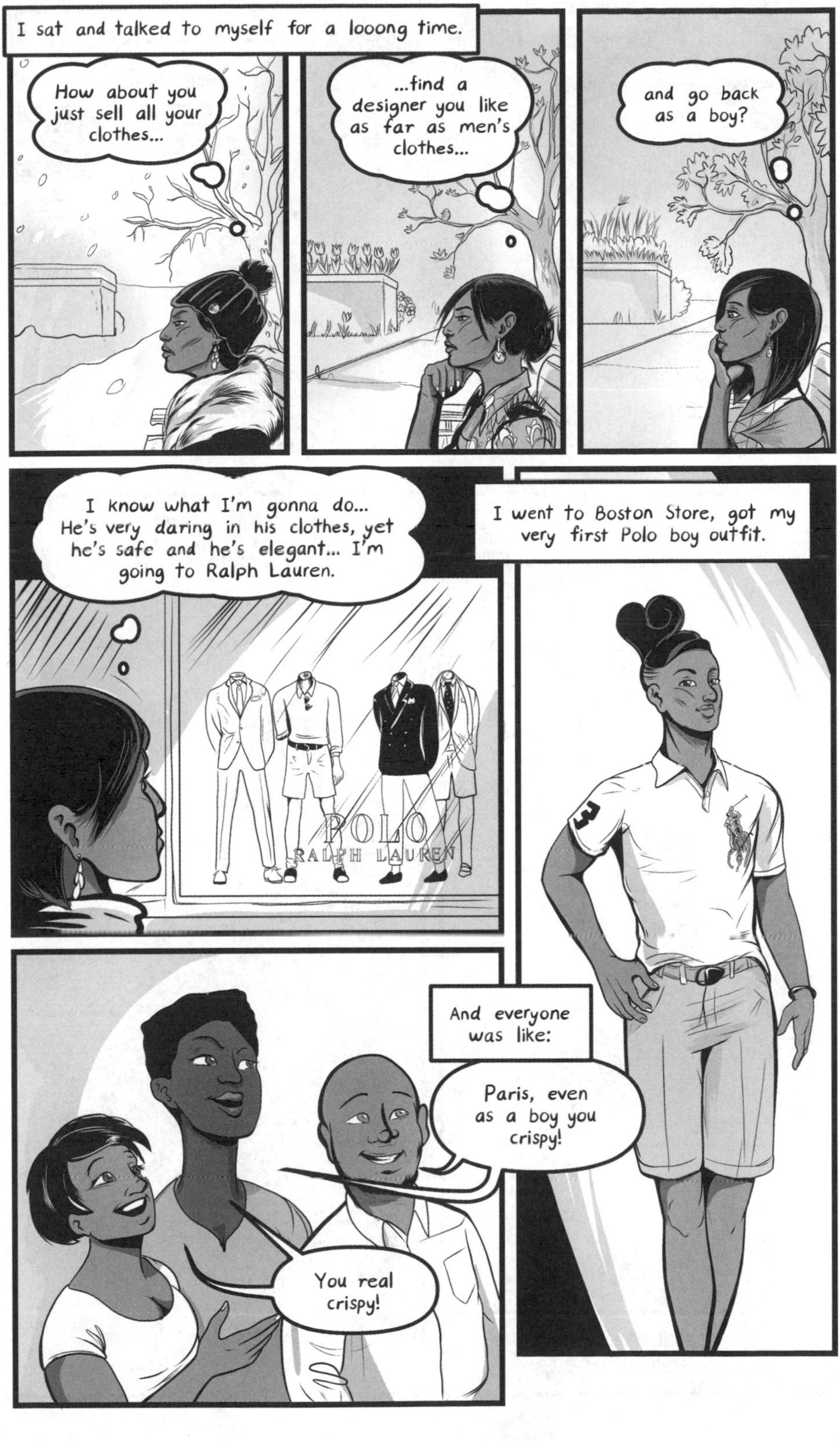
I sat and talked to myself for a looong time.
How about you just sell all your clothes...
...find a designer you like as far as men's clothes...
and go back as a boy?
I know what I'm gonna do... He's very daring in his clothes, yet he's safe and he's elegant... I'm going to Ralph Lauren.
POLO
RALPH LAUREN
I went to Boston Store, got my very first Polo boy outfit.
And everyone was like:
Paris, even as a boy you crispy!
You real crispy!

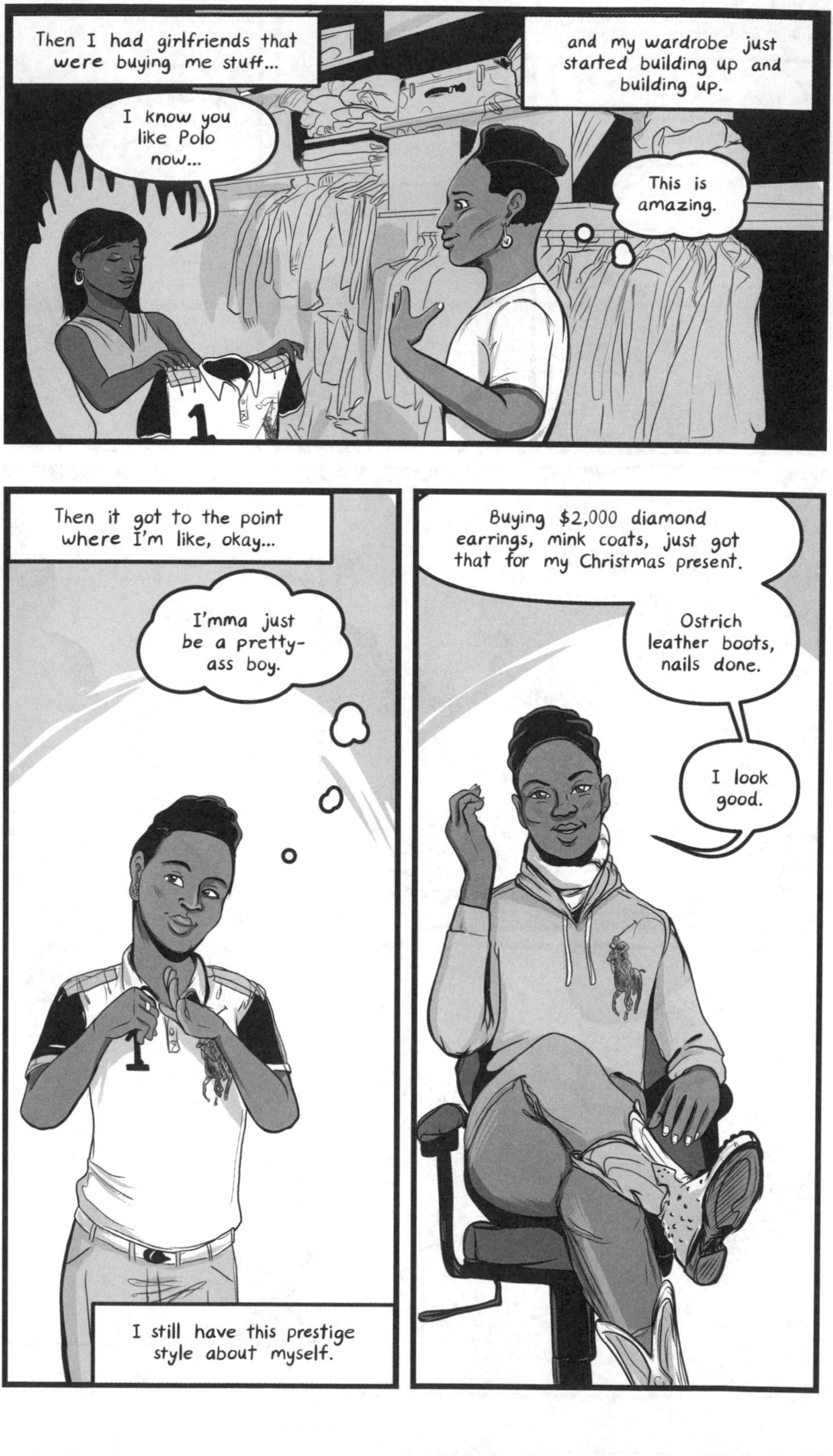

Then I had girlfriends that were buying me stuff...
I know you like Polo now...
and my wardrobe just started building up and building up.
This is amazing.
Then it got to the point where I'm like, okay...
I'mma just be a pretty-ass boy.
I still have this prestige style about myself.
Buying $2,000 diamond earrings, mink coats, just got that for my Christmas present.
Ostrich leather boots, nails done.
I look good.

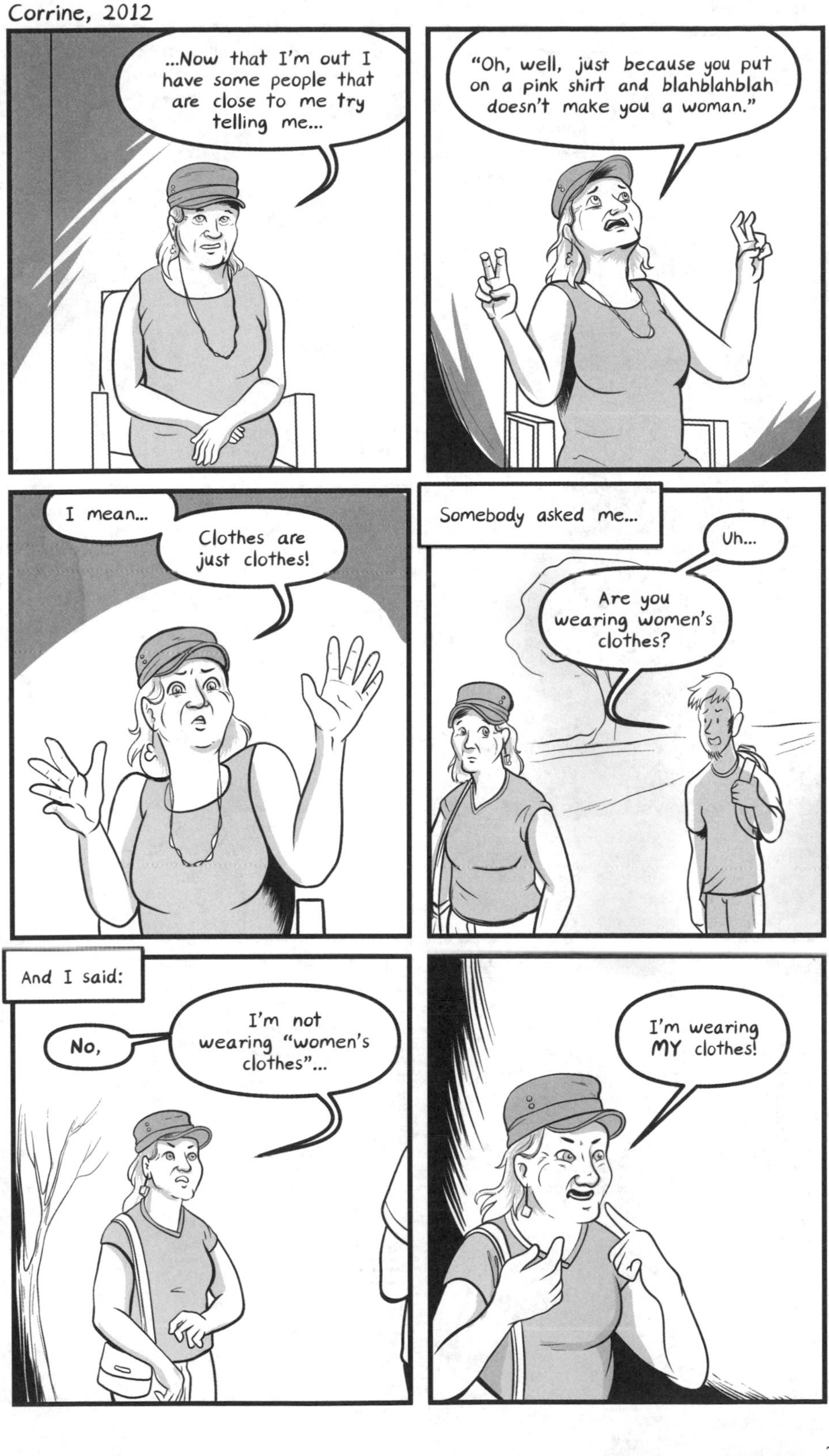
Corrine, 2012
...Now that I'm out I have some people that are close to me try telling me...
"Oh, well, just because you put on a pink shirt and blahblahblah doesn't make you a woman."
I mean...
Clothes are just clothes!
Somebody asked me...
Uh...
Are you wearing women's clothes?
And I said:
No,
I'm not wearing "women's clothes"...
I'm wearing MY clothes!

Rhea, 2014

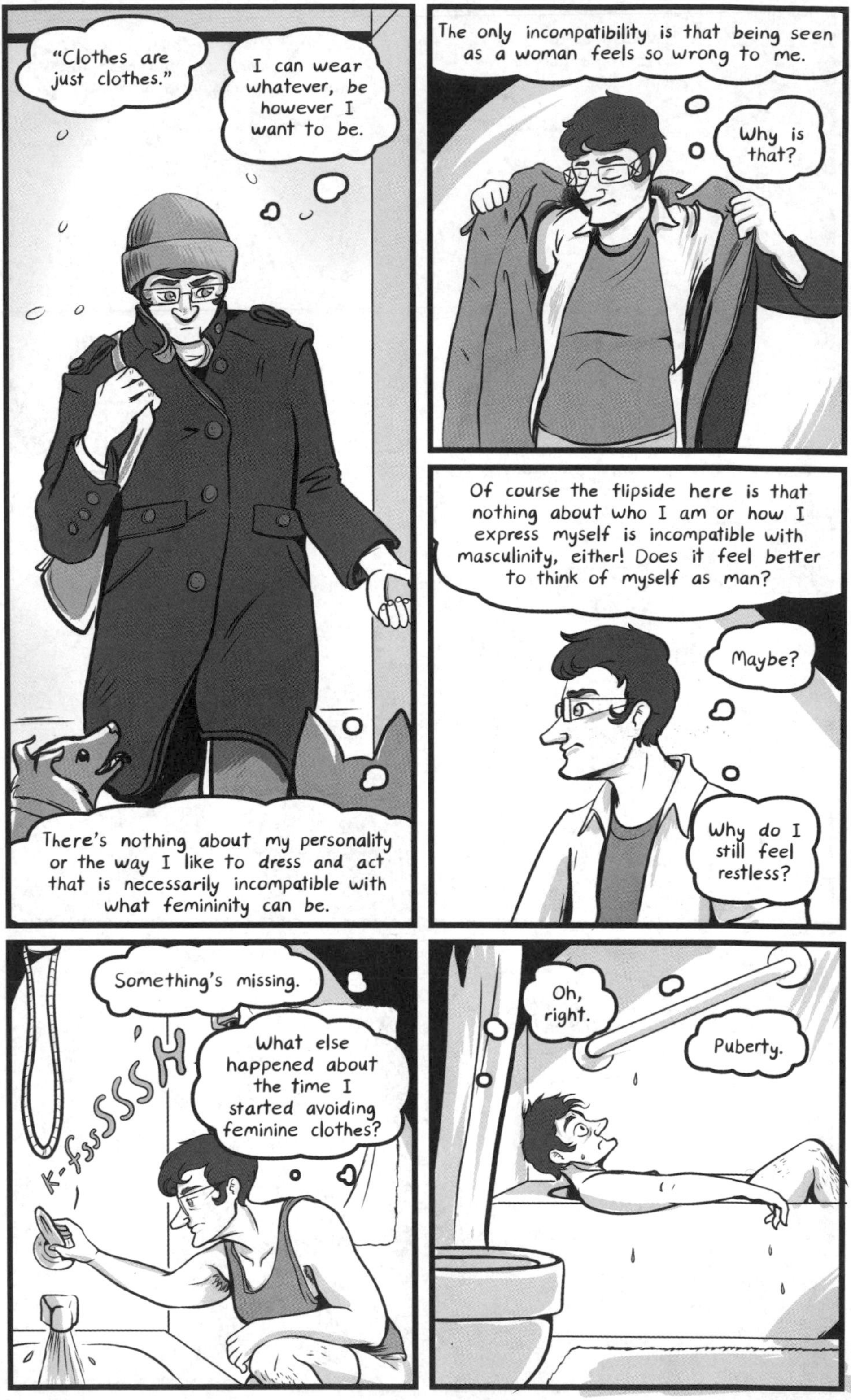
"Clothes are just clothes."
I can wear whatever, be however I want to be.
There's nothing about my personality or the way I like to dress and act that is necessarily incompatible with what femininity can be.
The only incompatibility is that being seen as a woman feels so wrong to me.
Why is that?
Of course the flipside here is that nothing about who I am or how I express myself is incompatible with masculinity, either! Does it feel better to think of myself as man?
Maybe?
Why do I still feel restless?
Something's missing.
What else happened about the time I started avoiding feminine clothes?
K-fssSSSSH
Oh, right.
Puberty.

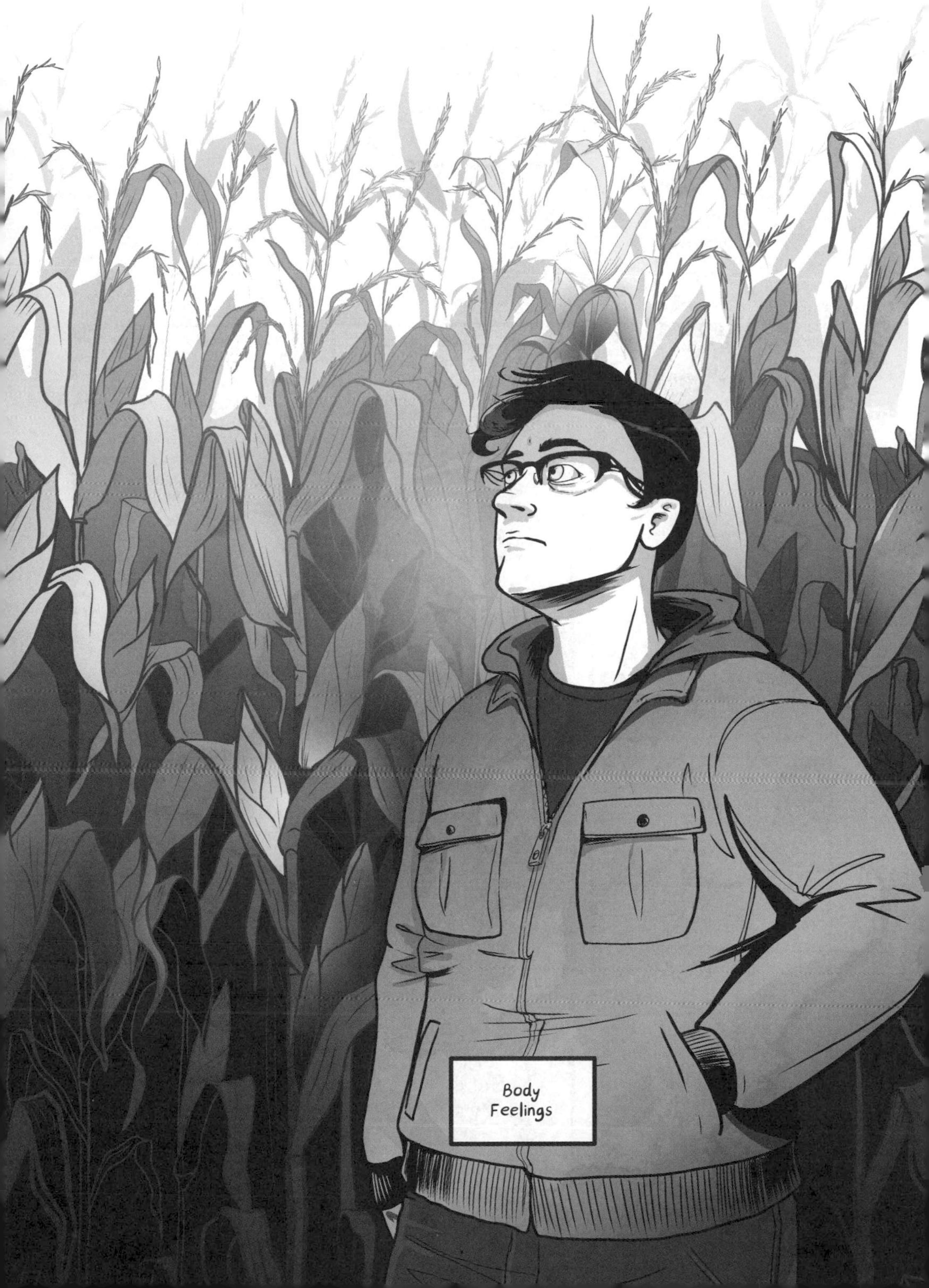
Body
Feelings

What is the difference between gender and sex?

Erik, 2011

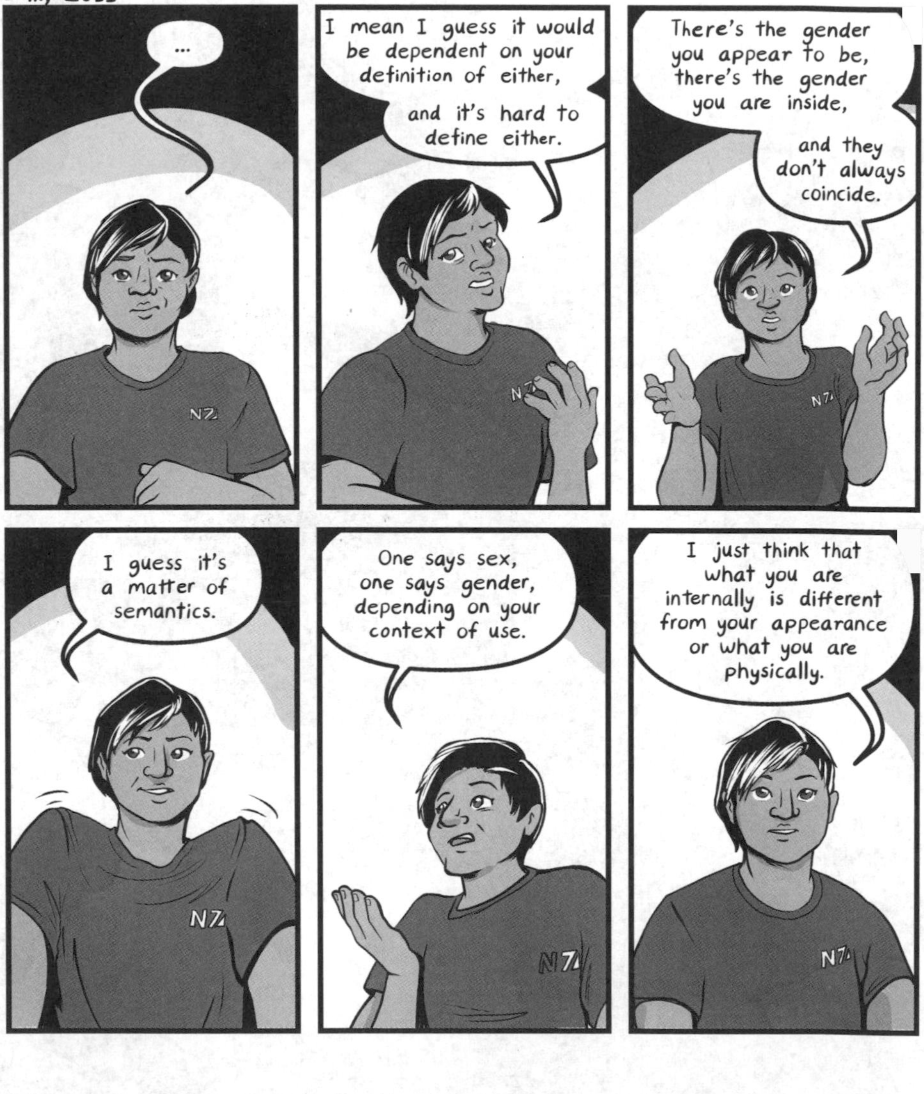

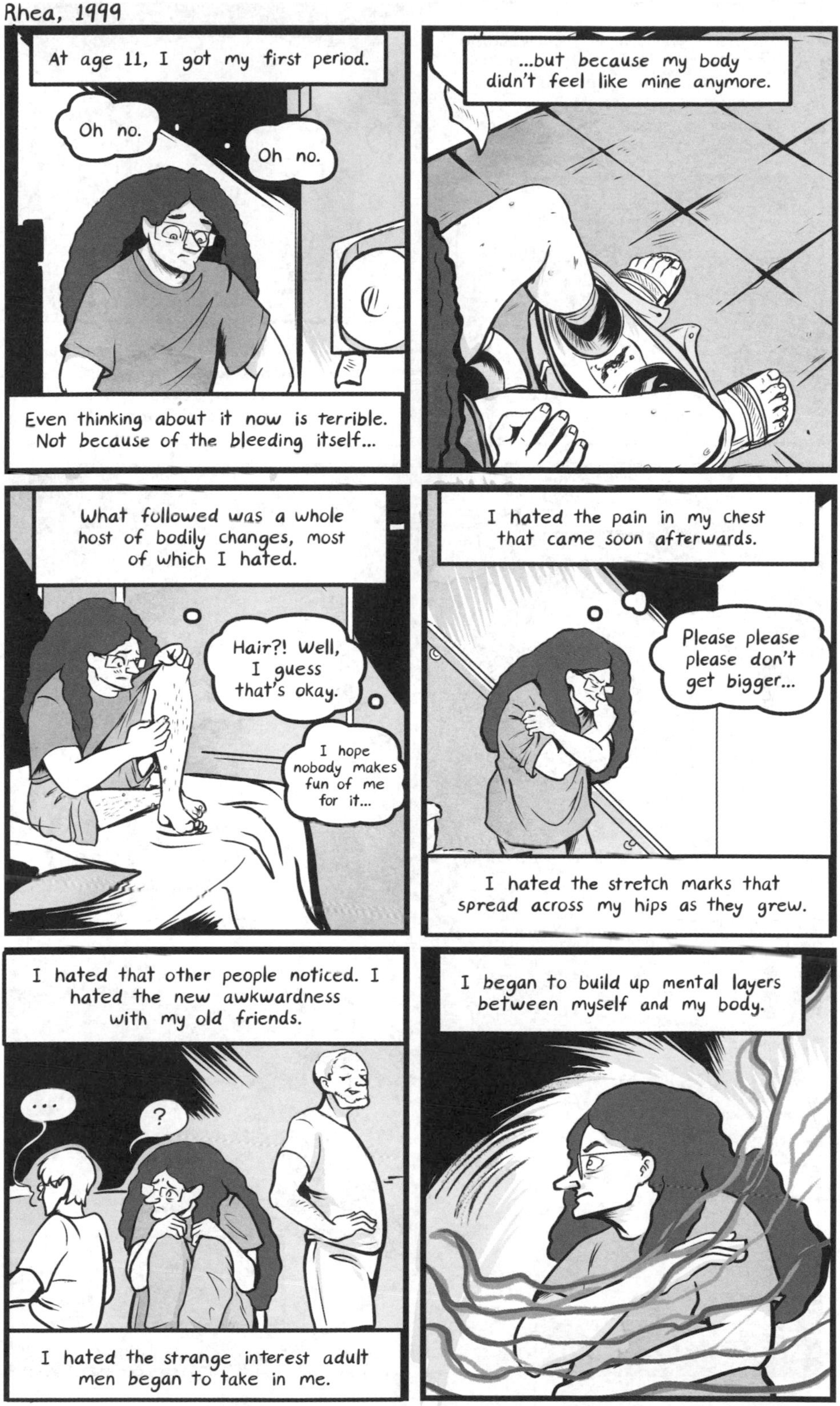
Rhea, 1999
At age 11, I got my first period.
Oh no.
Oh no.
Even thinking about it now is terrible. Not because of the bleeding itself...
...but because my body didn't feel like mine anymore.
What followed was a whole host of bodily changes, most of which I hated.
Hair?! Well, I guess that's okay.
I hope nobody makes fun of me for it...
I hated the pain in my chest that came soon afterwards.
Please please please don't get bigger...
I hated the stretch marks that spread across my hips as they grew.
I hated that other people noticed. I hated the new awkwardness with my old friends.
...
?
I hated the strange interest adult men began to take in me.
I began to build up mental layers between myself and my body.

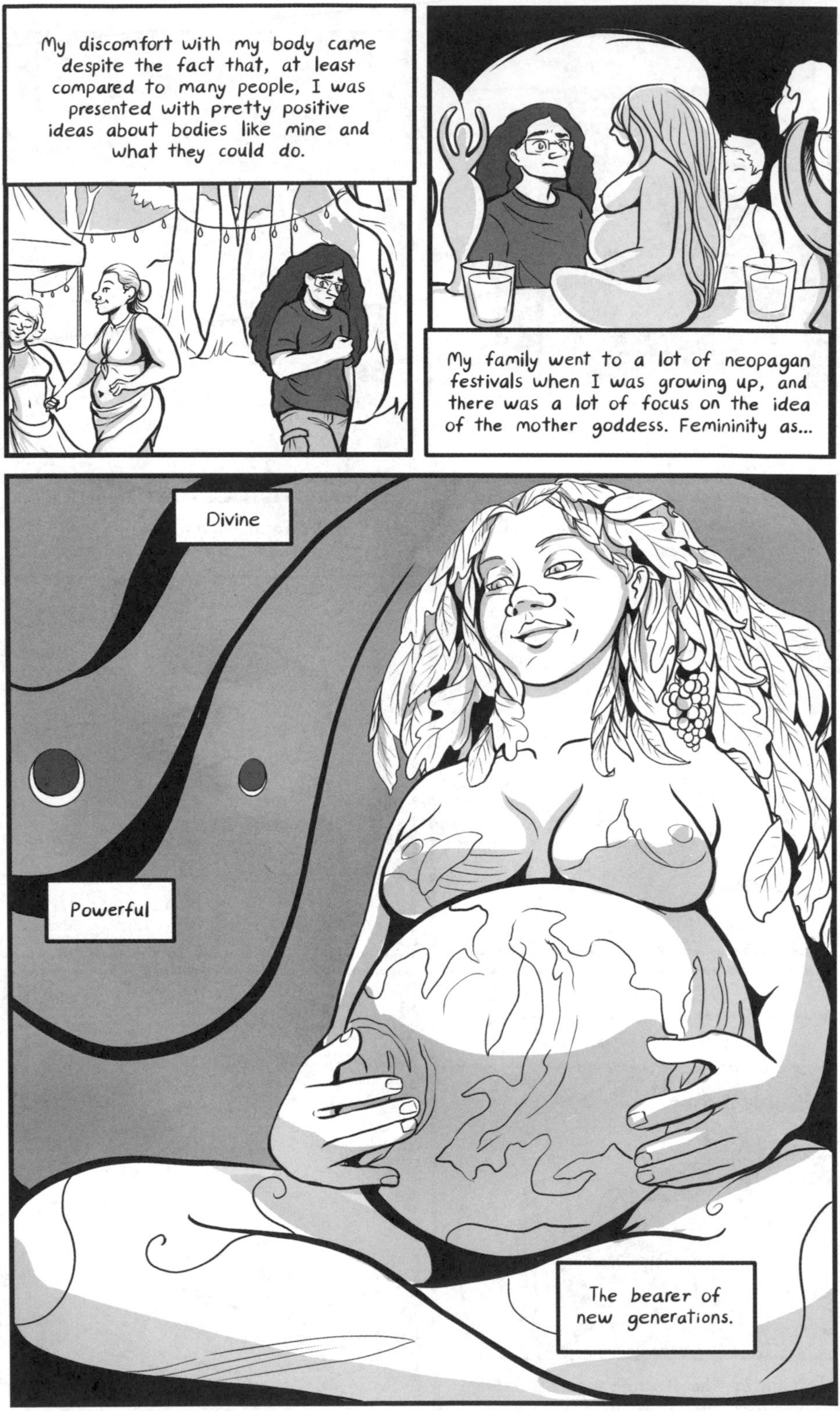
My discomfort with my body came despite the fact that, at least compared to many people, I was presented with pretty positive ideas about bodies like mine and what they could do.
My family went to a lot of neopagan festivals when I was growing up, and there was a lot of focus on the idea of the mother goddess. Femininity as...
Divine
Powerful
The bearer of new generations.

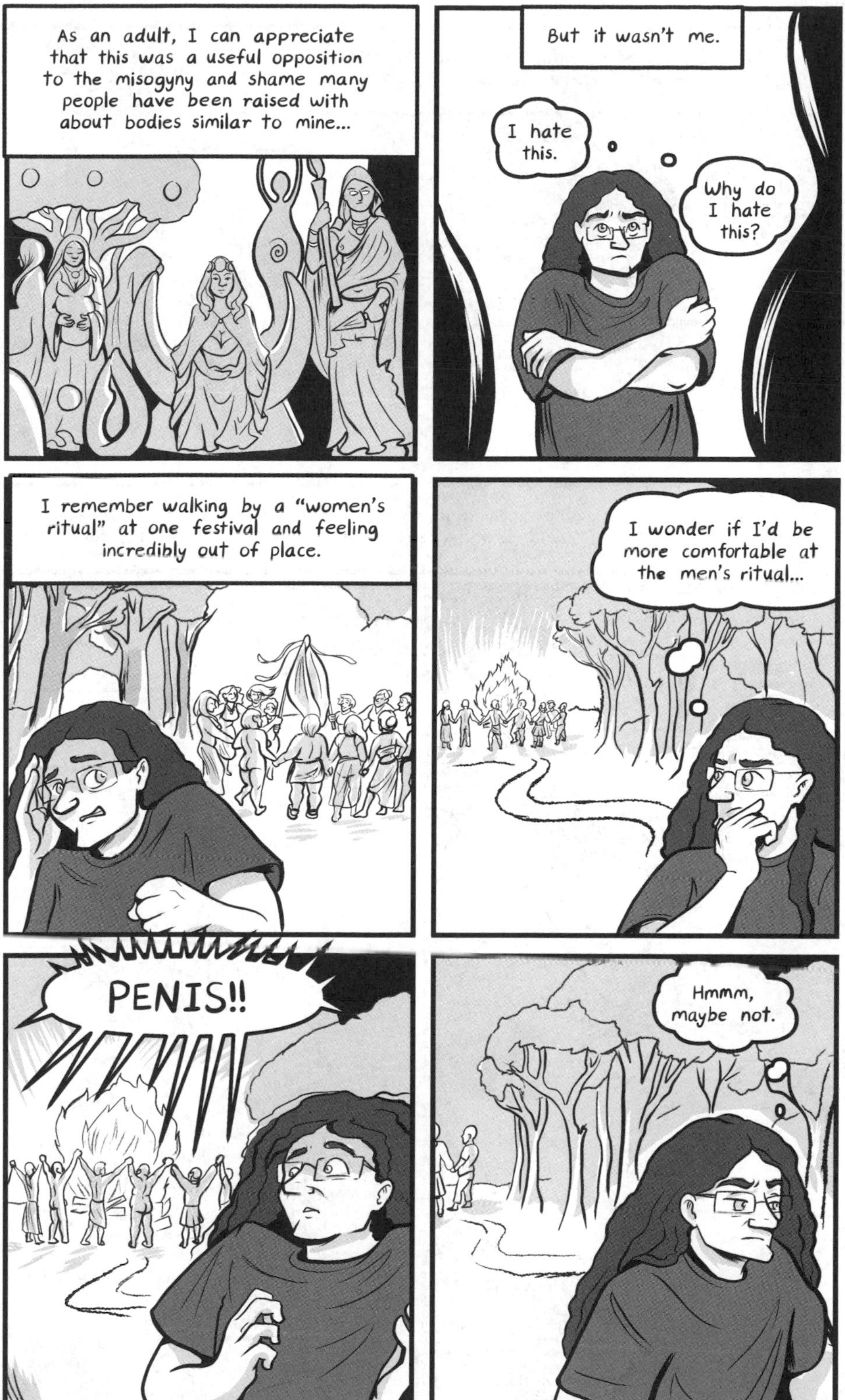
As an adult, I can appreciate that this was a useful opposition to the misogyny and shame many people have been raised with about bodies similar to mine...
But it wasn't me.
I hate this.
Why do I hate this?
I remember walking by a "women's ritual" at one festival and feeling incredibly out of place.
I wonder if I'd be more comfortable at the men's ritual...
PENIS!!
Hmmm, maybe not.

Rhea, 2011

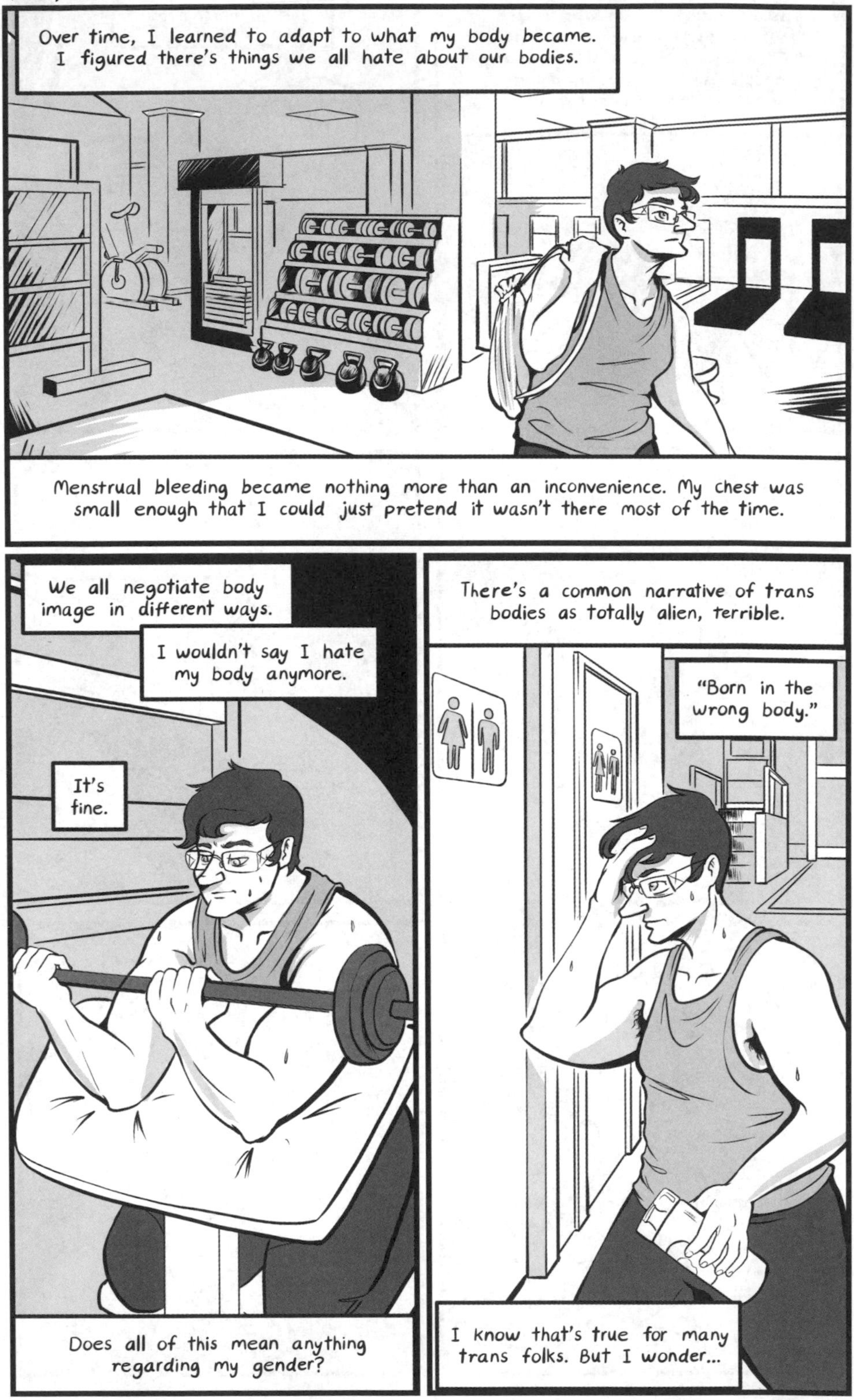
Over time, I learned to adapt to what my body became. I figured there's things we all hate about our bodies.
Menstrual bleeding became nothing more than an inconvenience. My chest was small enough that I could just pretend it wasn't there most of the time.
We all negotiate body image in different ways.
I wouldn't say I hate my body anymore.
It's fine.
Does all of this mean anything regarding my gender?
There's a common narrative of trans bodies as totally alien, terrible.
"Born in the wrong body."
I know that's true for many trans folks. But I wonder...

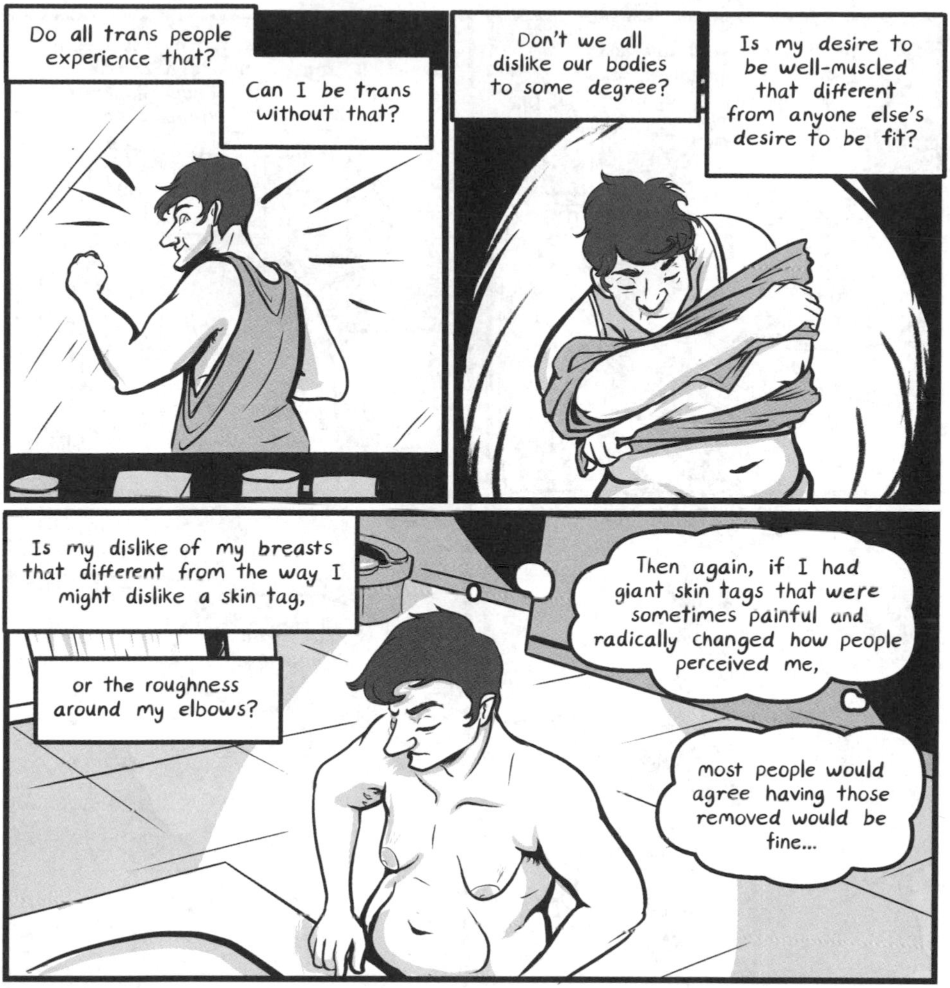
Do all trans people experience that?
Can I be trans without that?
Don't we all dislike our bodies to some degree?
Is my desire to be well-muscled that different from anyone else's desire to be fit?
Is my dislike of my breasts that different from the way I might dislike a skin tag,
or the roughness around my elbows?
Then again, if I had giant skin tags that were sometimes painful and radically changed how people perceived me,
most people would agree having those removed would be fine...

Ginger, 2012

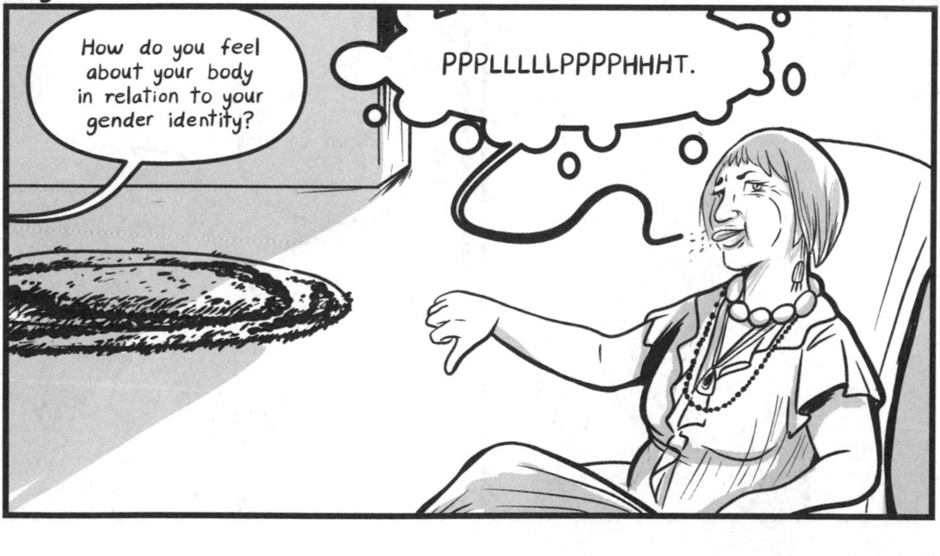
How do you feel about your body in relation to your gender identity?
PPPLLLLLPPPPHHHT.

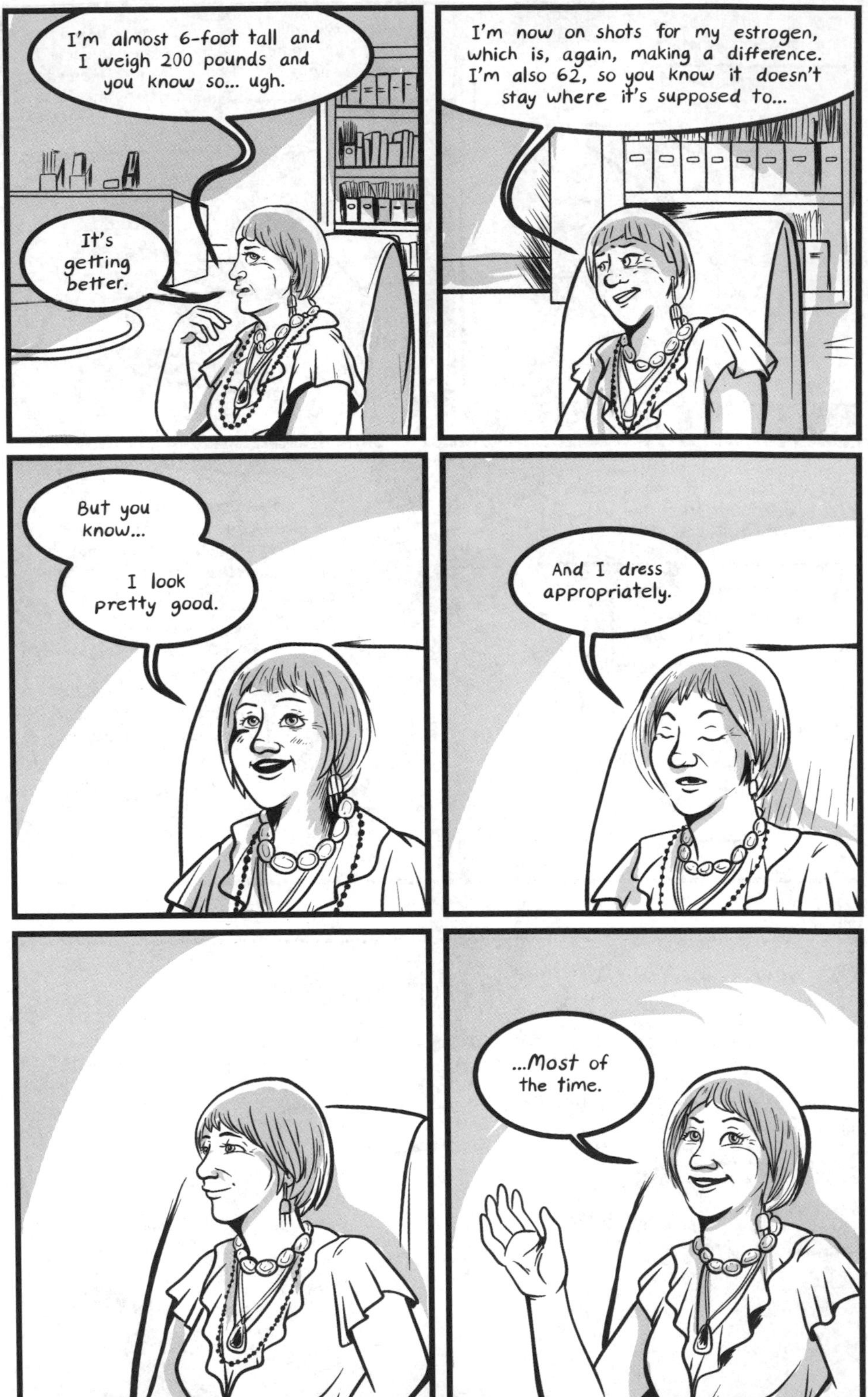
I'm almost 6-foot tall and I weigh 200 pounds and you know so... ugh.
It's getting better.
I'm now on shots for my estrogen, which is, again, making a difference. I'm also 62, so you know it doesn't stay where it's supposed to...
But you know...
I look pretty good.
And I dress appropriately.
...Most of the time.

Kelly, 2011

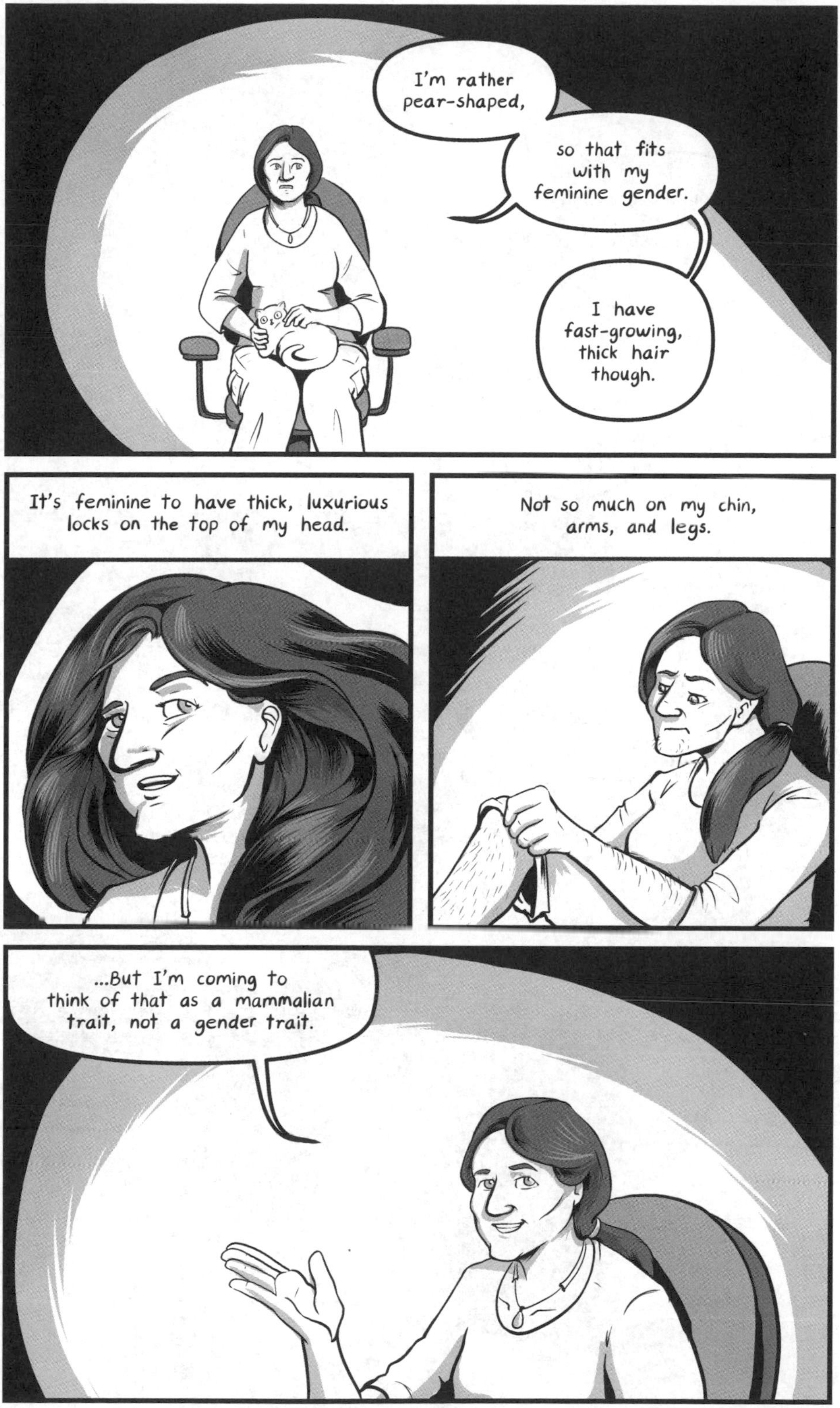
I'm rather pear-shaped,
so that fits with my feminine gender.
I have fast-growing, thick hair though.
It's feminine to have thick, luxurious locks on the top of my head.
Not so much on my chin, arms, and legs.
...But I'm coming to think of that as a mammalian trait, not a gender trait.

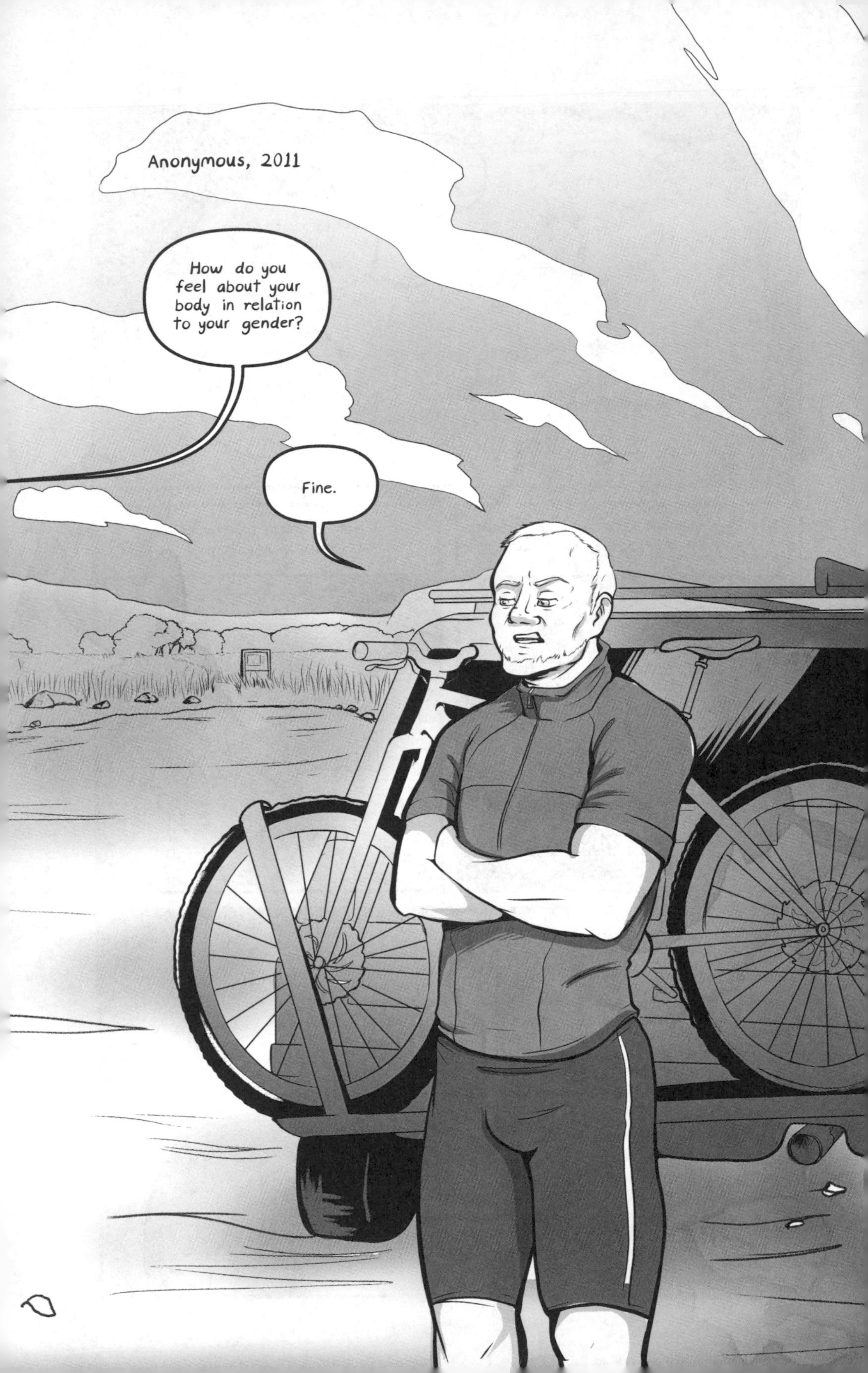
Anonymous, 2011
How do you feel about your body in relation to your gender?
Fine.

Anonymous, 2011

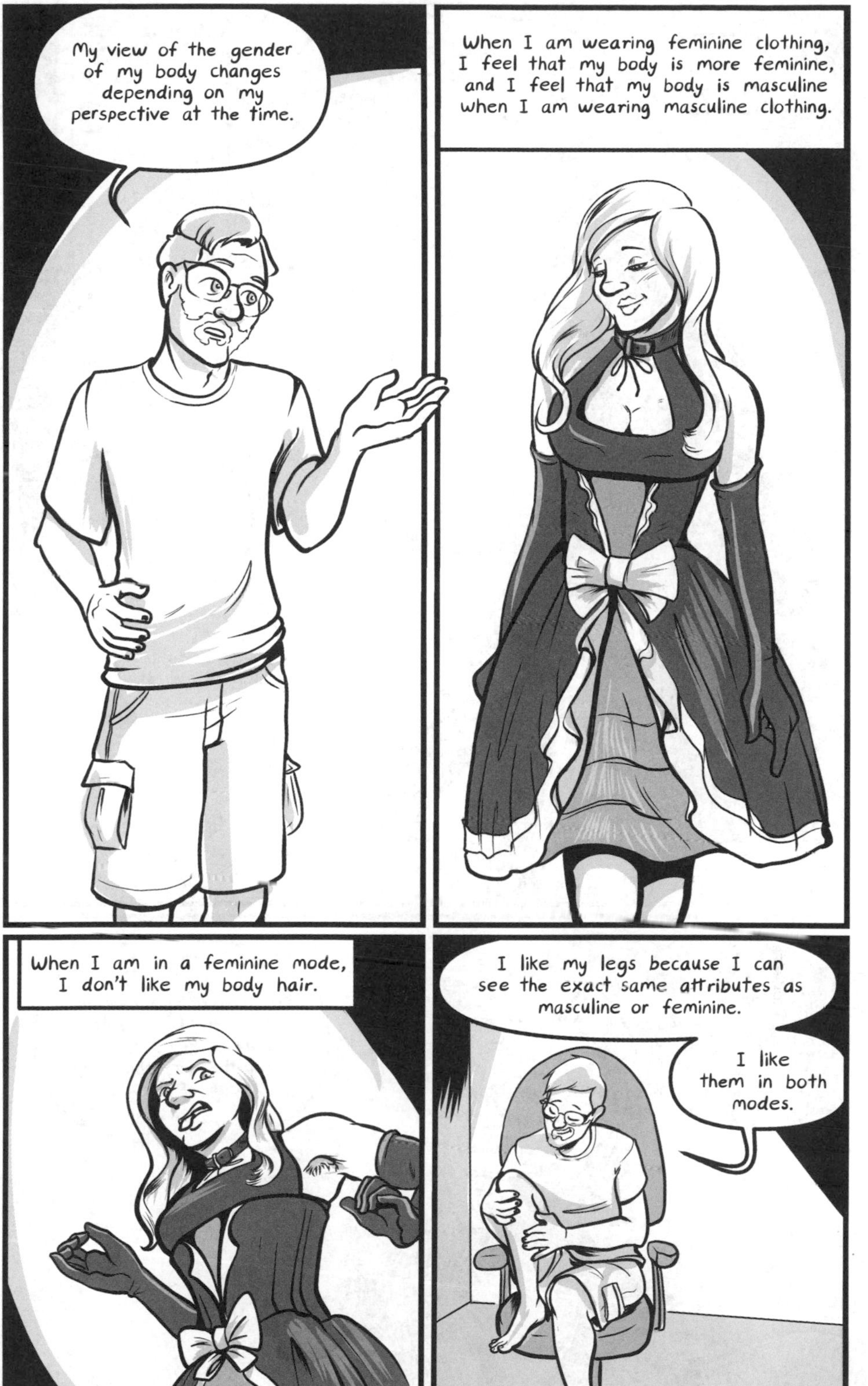
My view of the gender of my body changes depending on my perspective at the time.
When I am wearing feminine clothing, I feel that my body is more feminine, and I feel that my body is masculine when I am wearing masculine clothing.
When I am in a feminine mode, I don't like my body hair.
I like my legs because I can see the exact same attributes as masculine or feminine.
I like them in both modes.

Wayne, 2012

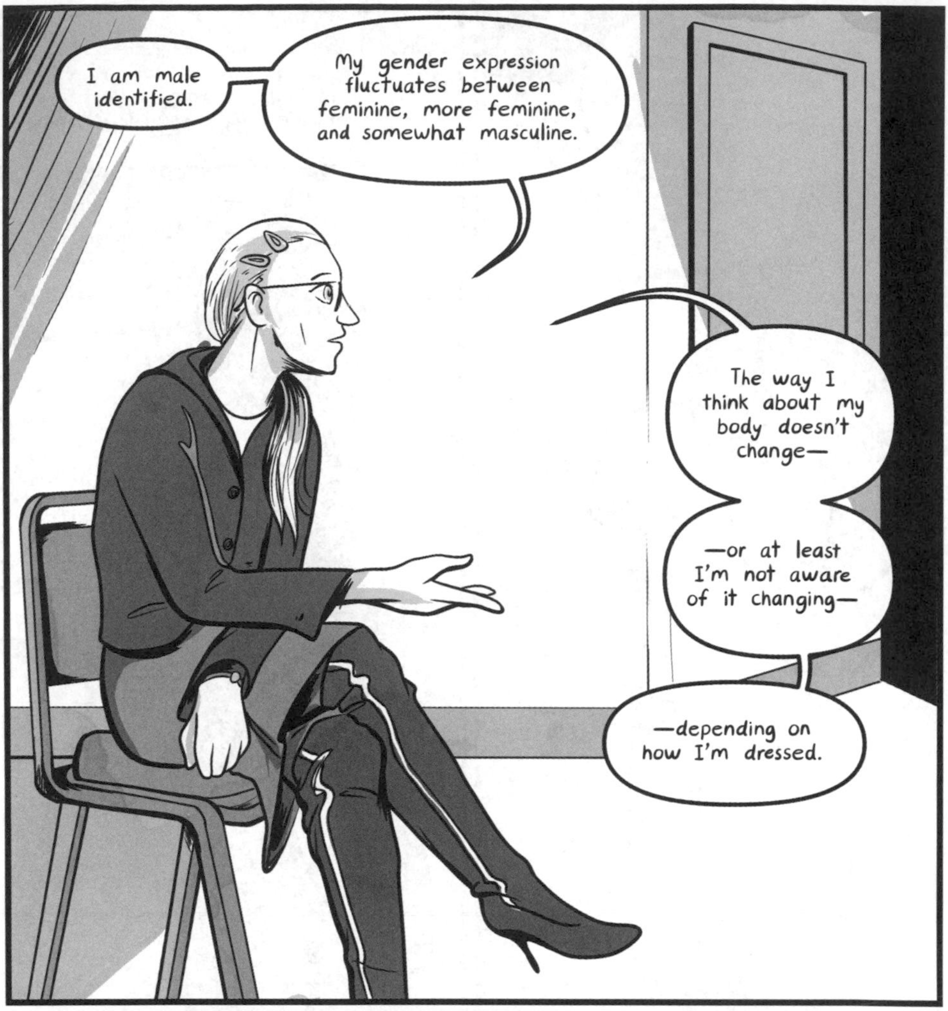
I am male identified.
My gender expression fluctuates between feminine, more feminine, and somewhat masculine.
The way I think about my body doesn't change—
—or at least I'm not aware of it changing—
—depending on how I'm dressed.

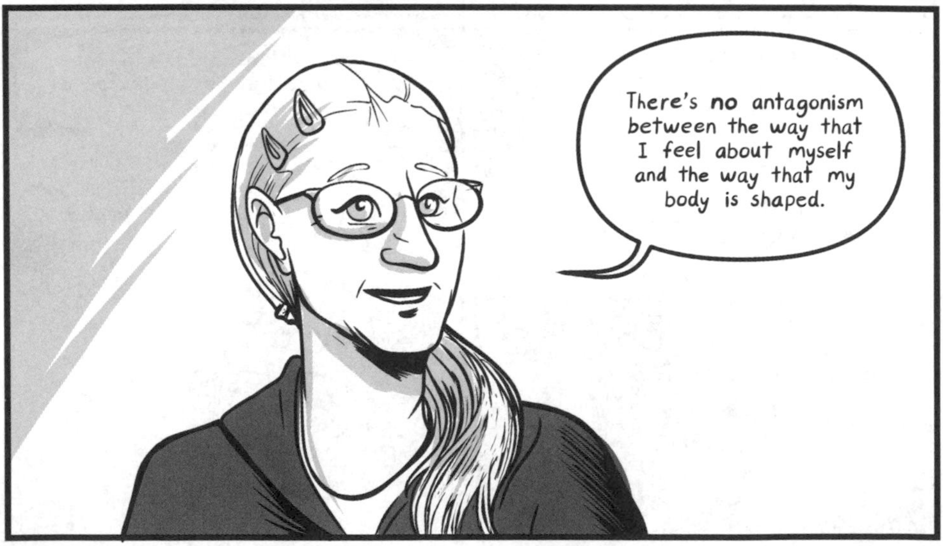
There's **no** antagonism between the way that I feel about myself and the way that my body is shaped.

JAC, 2013

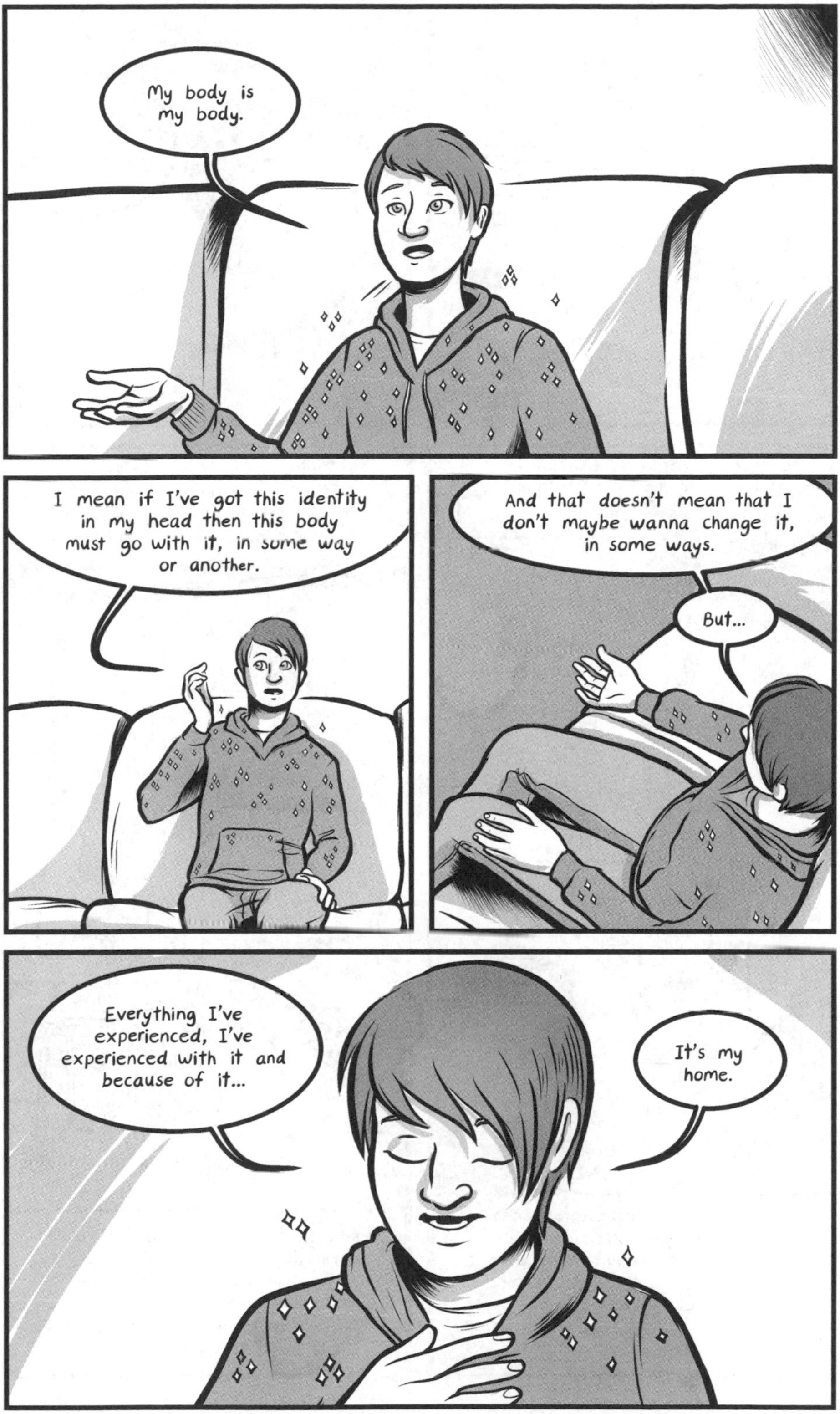
My body is my body.
I mean if I've got this identity in my head then this body must go with it, in some way or another.
And that doesn't mean that I don't maybe wanna change it, in some ways.
But...
Everything I've experienced, I've experienced with it and because of it...
It's my home.

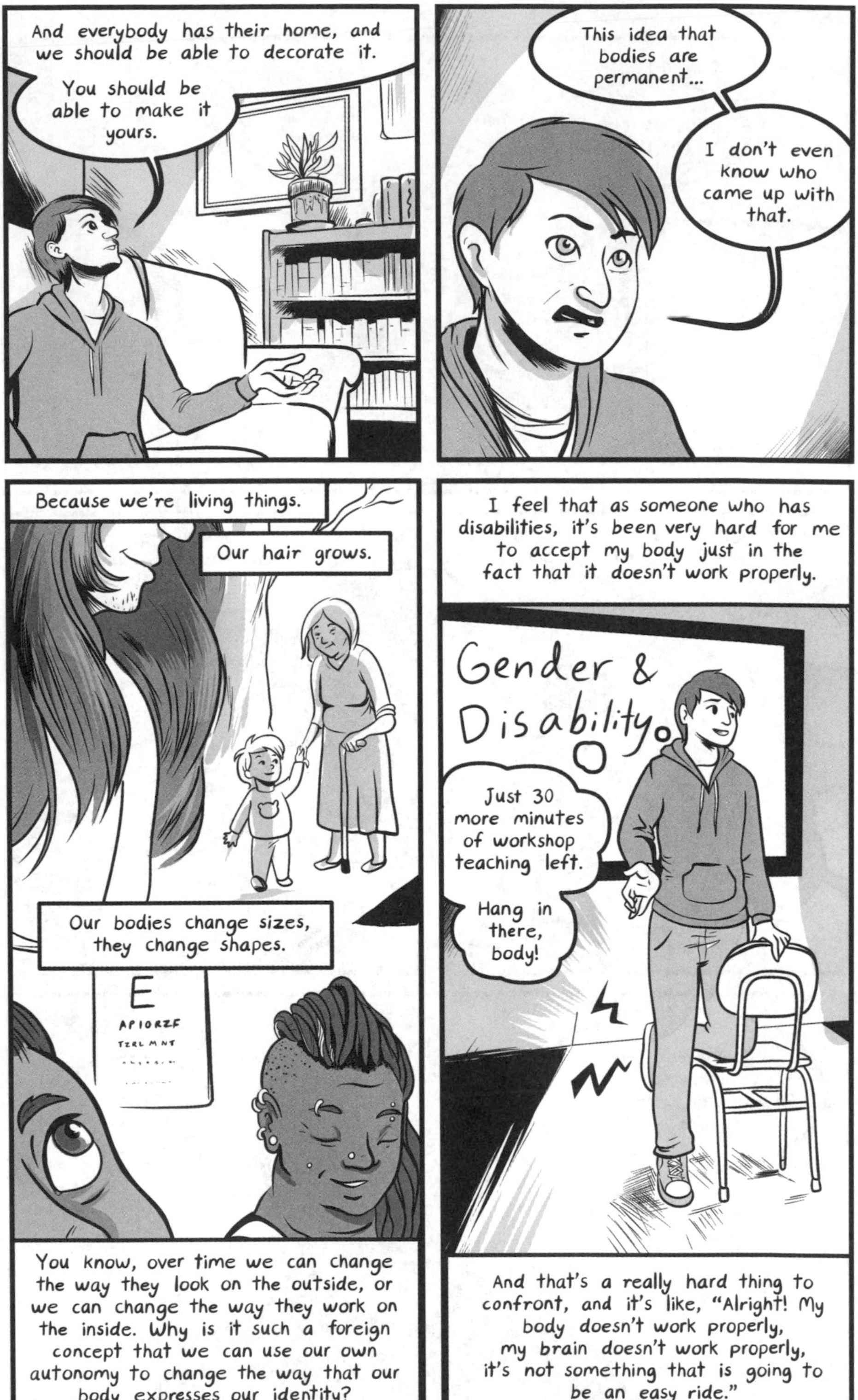
And everybody has their home, and we should be able to decorate it.
You should be able to make it yours.
This idea that bodies are permanent...
I don't even know who came up with that.
Because we're living things.
Our hair grows.
Our bodies change sizes, they change shapes.
You know, over time we can change the way they look on the outside, or we can change the way they work on the inside. Why is it such a foreign concept that we can use our own autonomy to change the way that our body expresses our identity?
I feel that as someone who has disabilities, it's been very hard for me to accept my body just in the fact that it doesn't work properly.
Gender & Disability
Just 30 more minutes of workshop teaching left.
Hang in there, body!
And that's a really hard thing to confront, and it's like, "Alright! My body doesn't work properly, my brain doesn't work properly, it's not something that is going to be an easy ride."

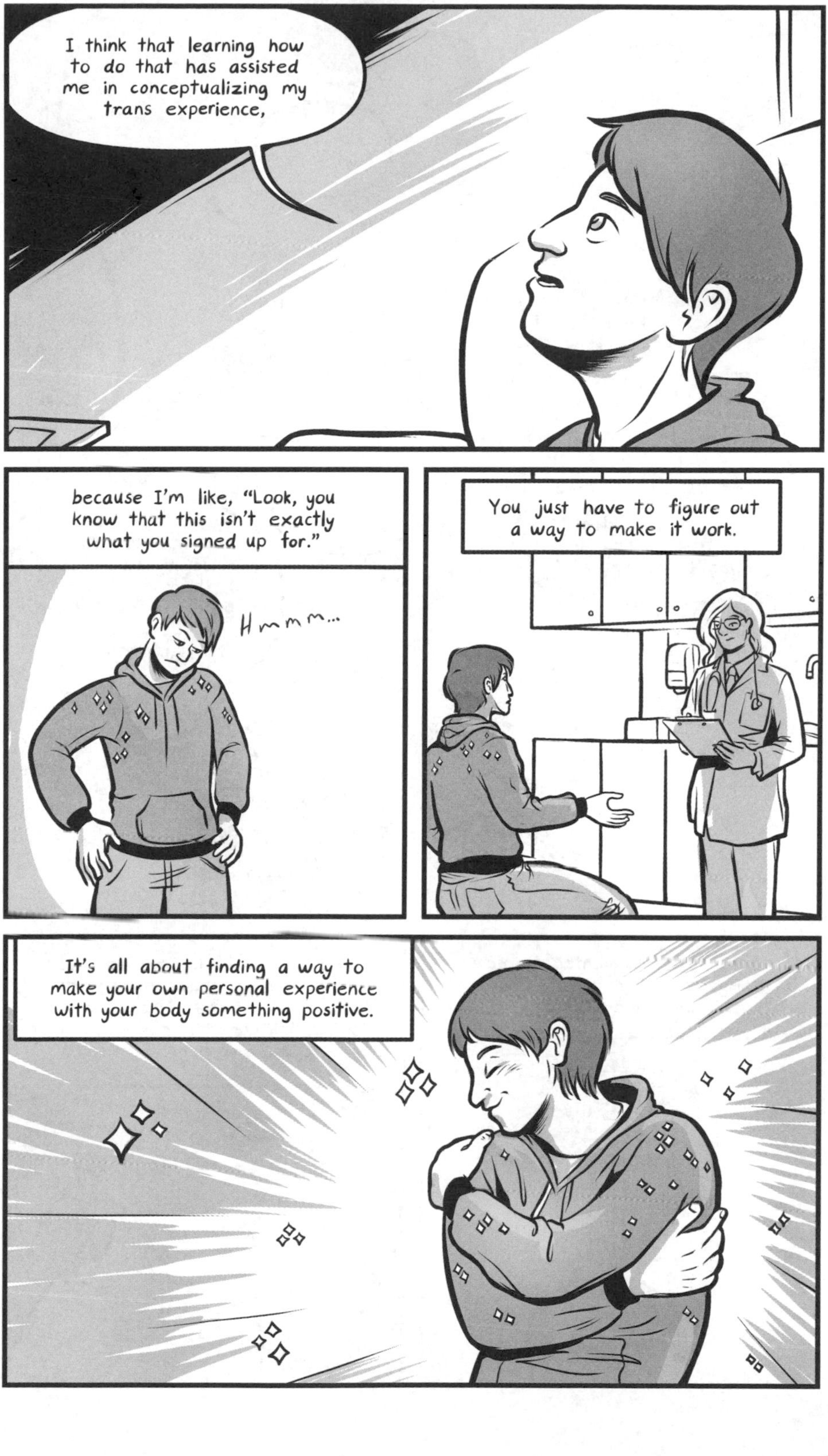
I think that learning how to do that has assisted me in conceptualizing my trans experience,
because I'm like, "Look, you know that this isn't exactly what you signed up for."
Hmmm...
You just have to figure out a way to make it work.
It's all about finding a way to make your own personal experience with your body something positive.

Anne, 2012

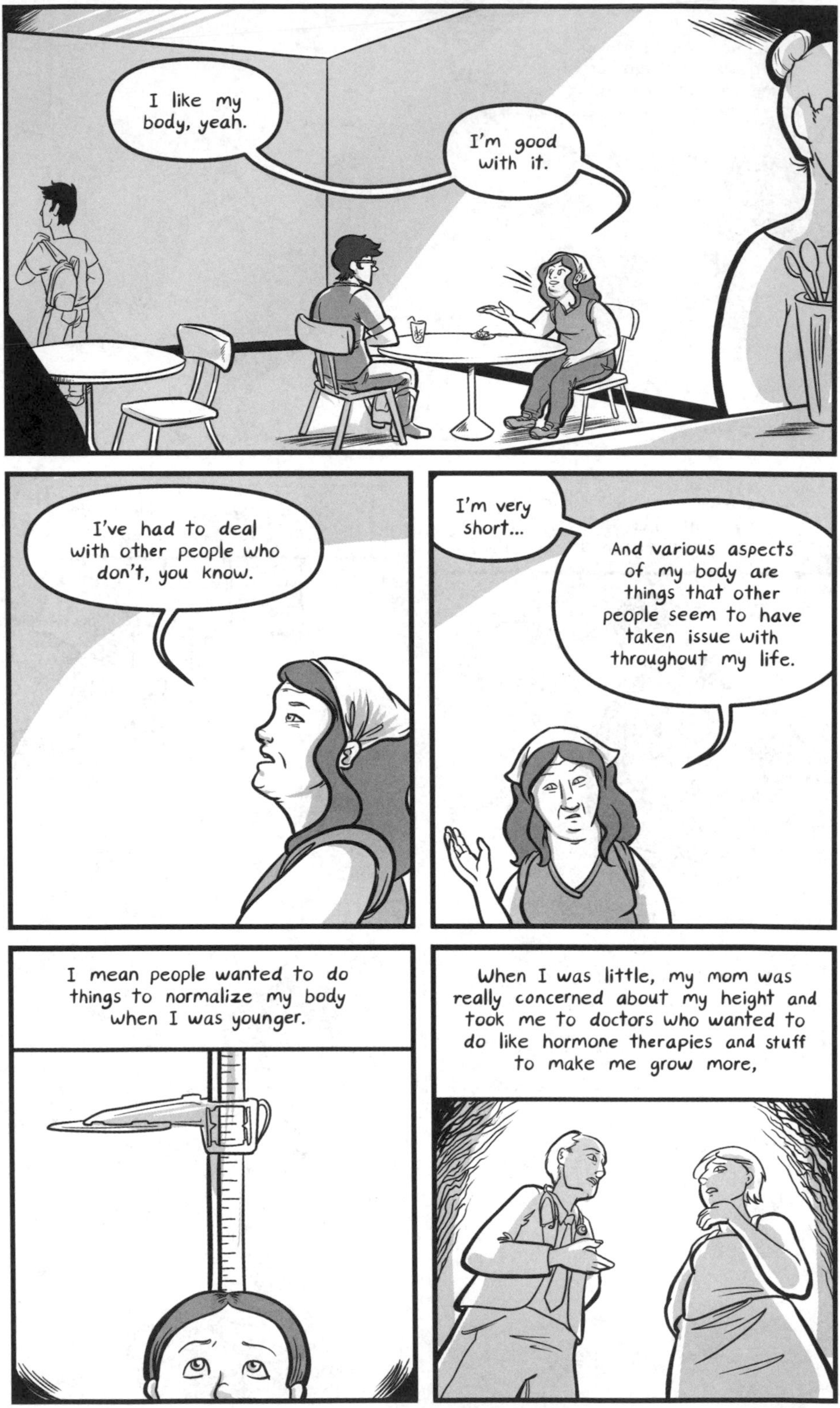
I like my body, yeah.
I'm good with it.
I've had to deal with other people who don't, you know.
I'm very short...
And various aspects of my body are things that other people seem to have taken issue with throughout my life.
I mean people wanted to do things to normalize my body when I was younger.
When I was little, my mom was really concerned about my height and took me to doctors who wanted to do like hormone therapies and stuff to make me grow more,

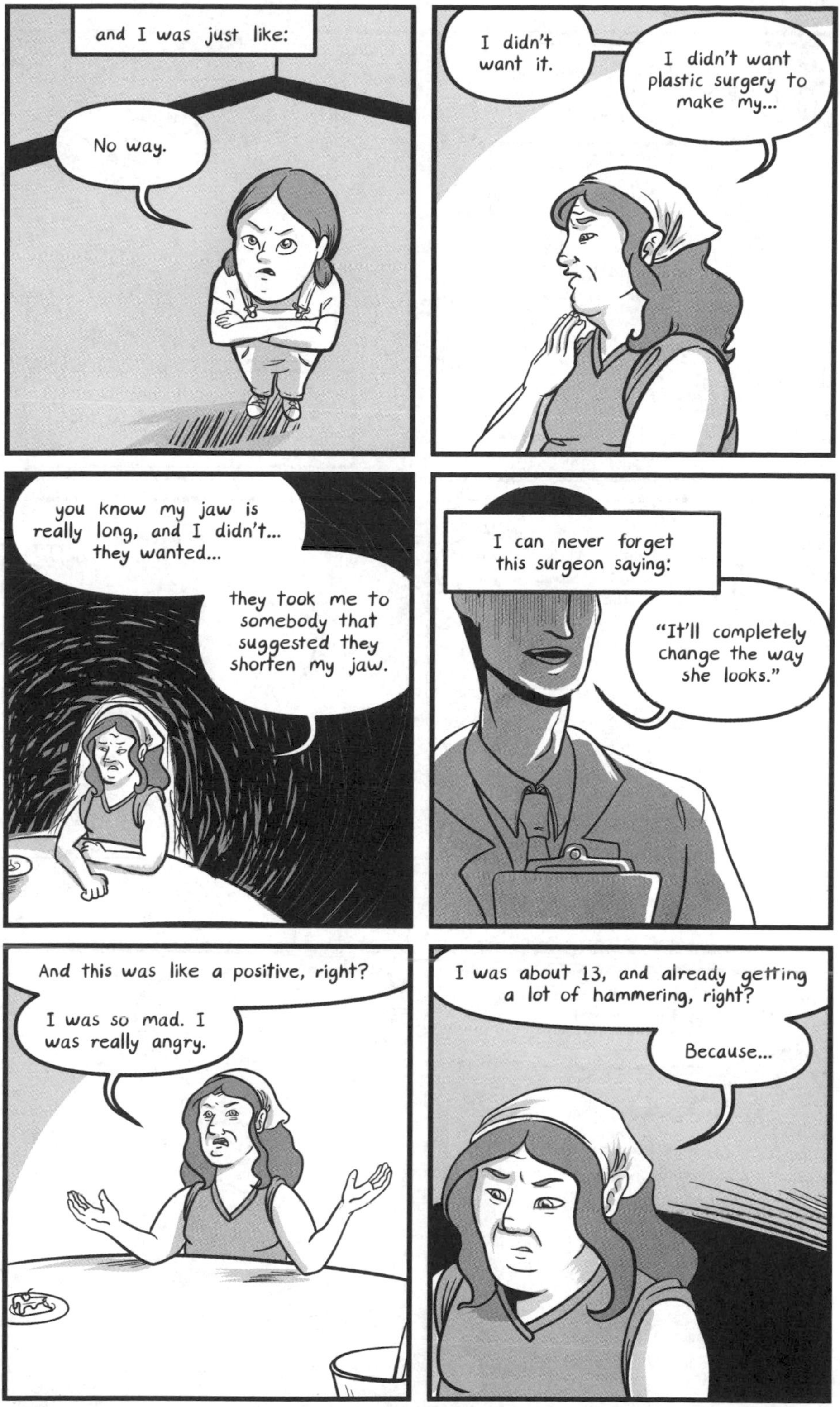
and I was just like:
No way.
I didn't want it.
I didn't want plastic surgery to make my...
you know my jaw is really long, and I didn't... they wanted...
they took me to somebody that suggested they shorten my jaw.
I can never forget this surgeon saying:
"It'll completely change the way she looks."
And this was like a positive, right?
I was so mad. I was really angry.
I was about 13, and already getting a lot of hammering, right?
Because...

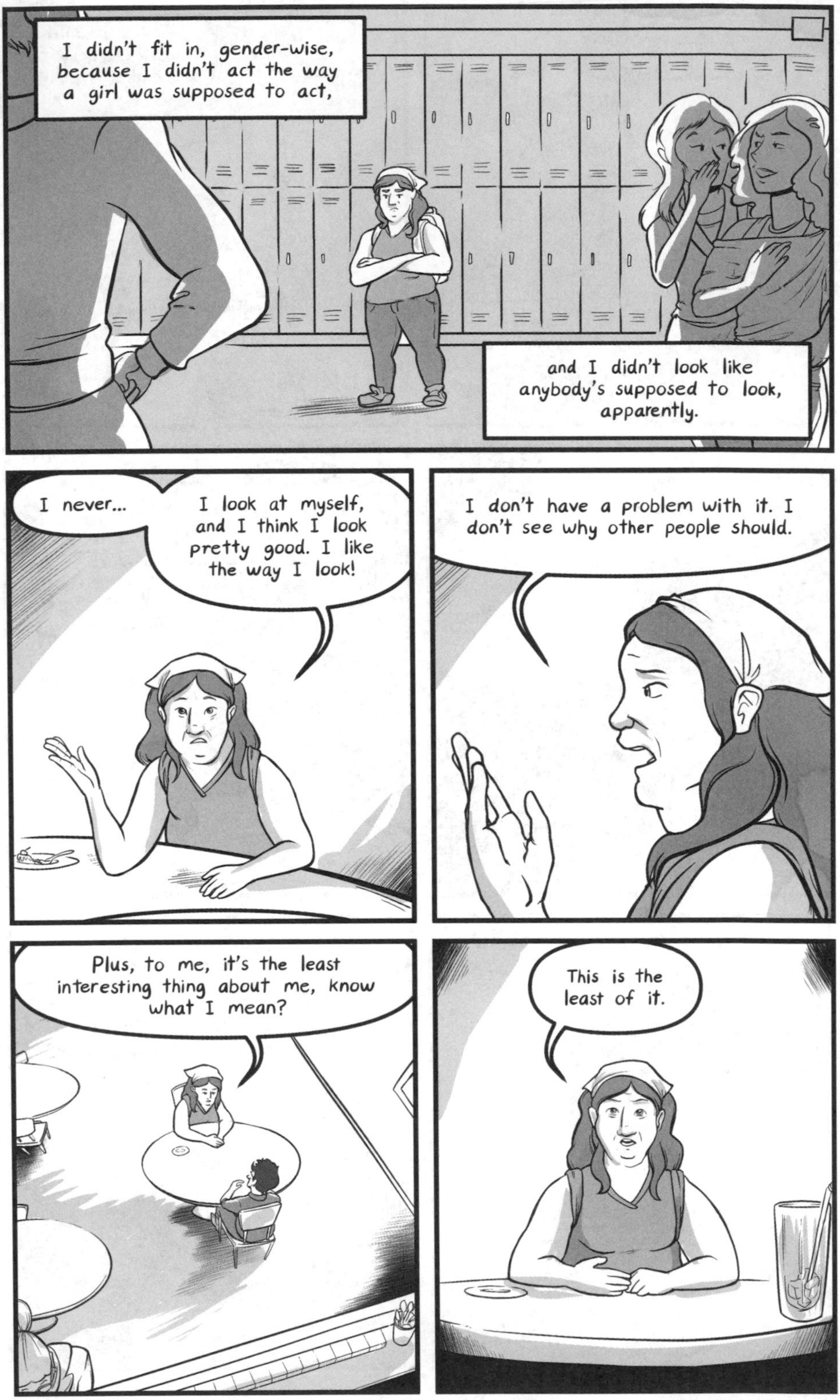
I didn't fit in, gender-wise, because I didn't act the way a girl was supposed to act,
and I didn't look like anybody's supposed to look, apparently.
I never...
I look at myself, and I think I look pretty good. I like the way I look!
I don't have a problem with it. I don't see why other people should.
Plus, to me, it's the least interesting thing about me, know what I mean?
This is the least of it.

Daiquiri, 2012

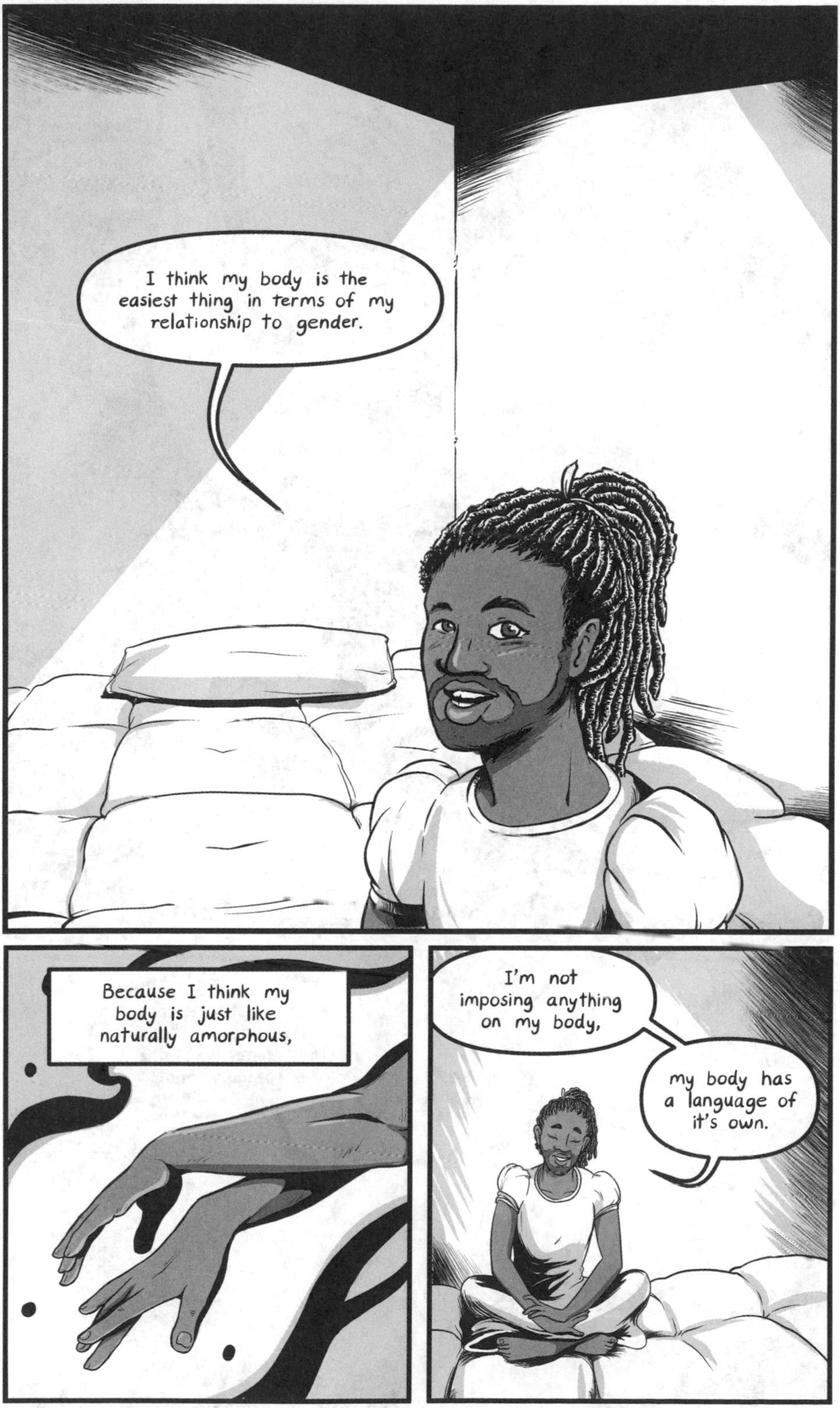
I think my body is the easiest thing in terms of my relationship to gender.
Because I think my body is just like naturally amorphous,
I'm not imposing anything on my body,
my body has a language of it's own.

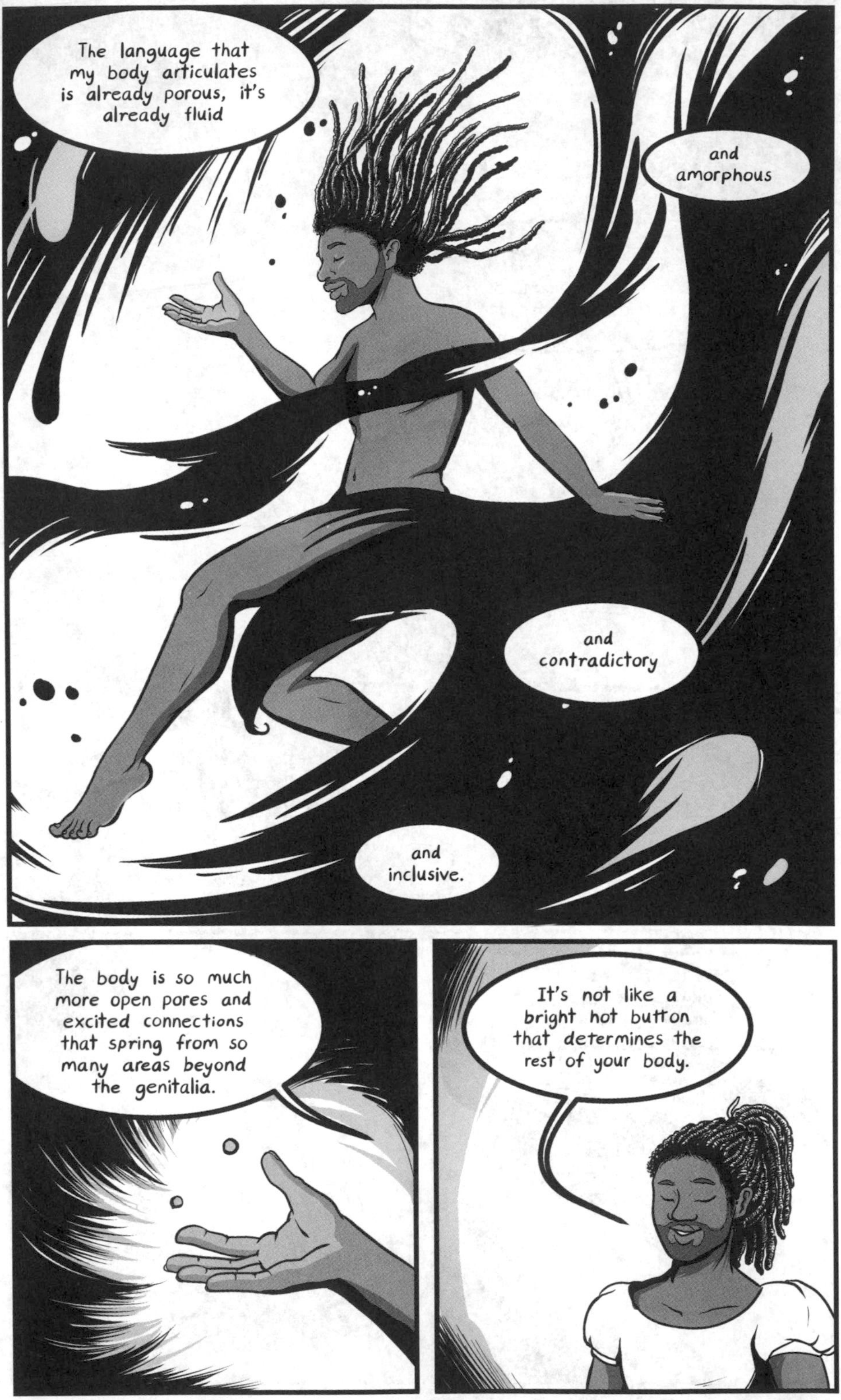
The language that my body articulates is already porous, it's already fluid
and amorphous
and contradictory
and inclusive.
The body is so much more open pores and excited connections that spring from so many areas beyond the genitalia.
It's not like a bright hot button that determines the rest of your body.

Enne, 2013

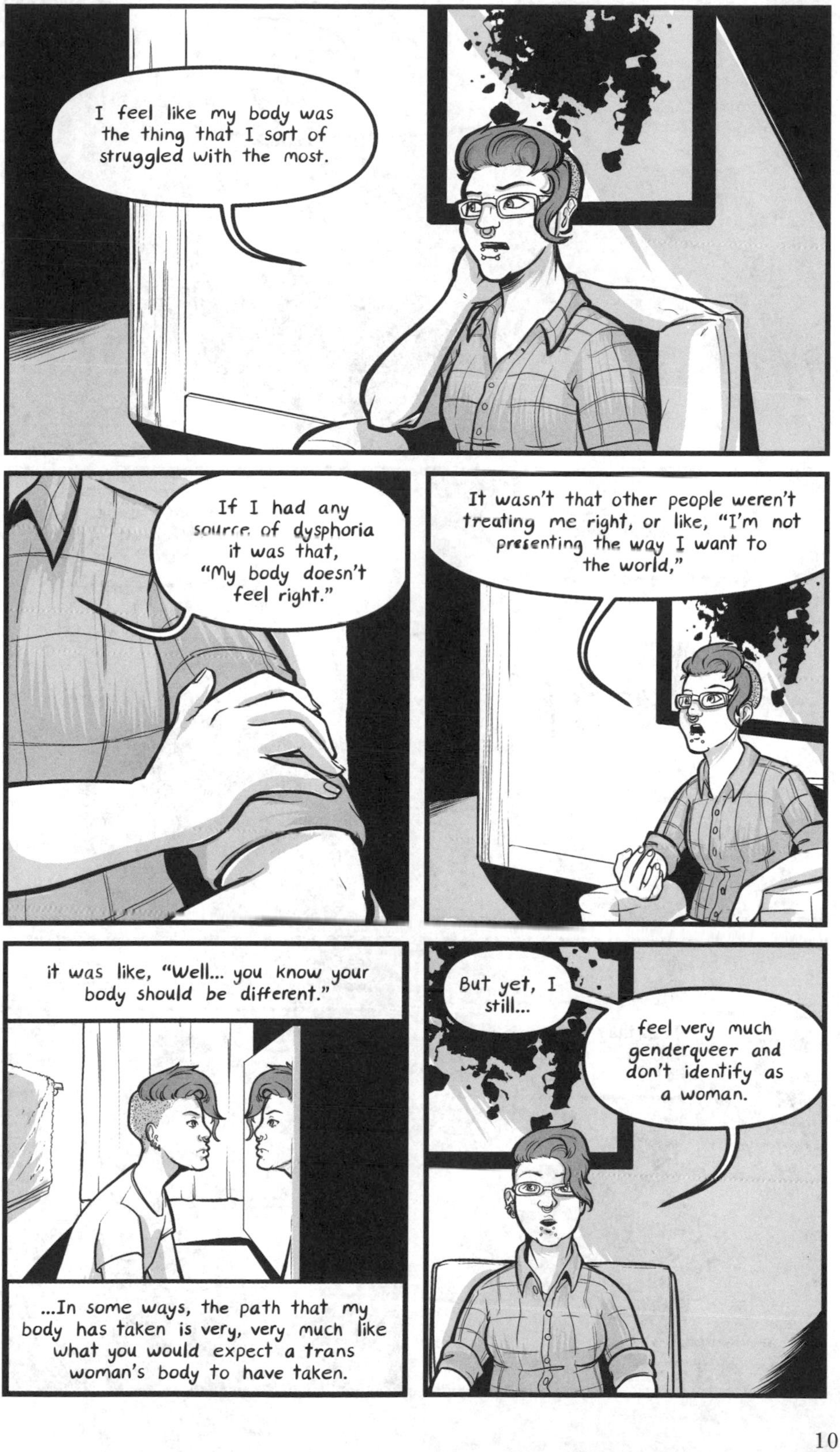
I feel like my body was the thing that I sort of struggled with the most.
If I had any source of dysphoria it was that, "My body doesn't feel right."
It wasn't that other people weren't treating me right, or like, "I'm not presenting the way I want to the world,"
it was like, "Well... you know your body should be different."
...In some ways, the path that my body has taken is very, very much like what you would expect a trans woman's body to have taken.
But yet, I still...
feel very much genderqueer and don't identify as a woman.

Ignacio, 2013

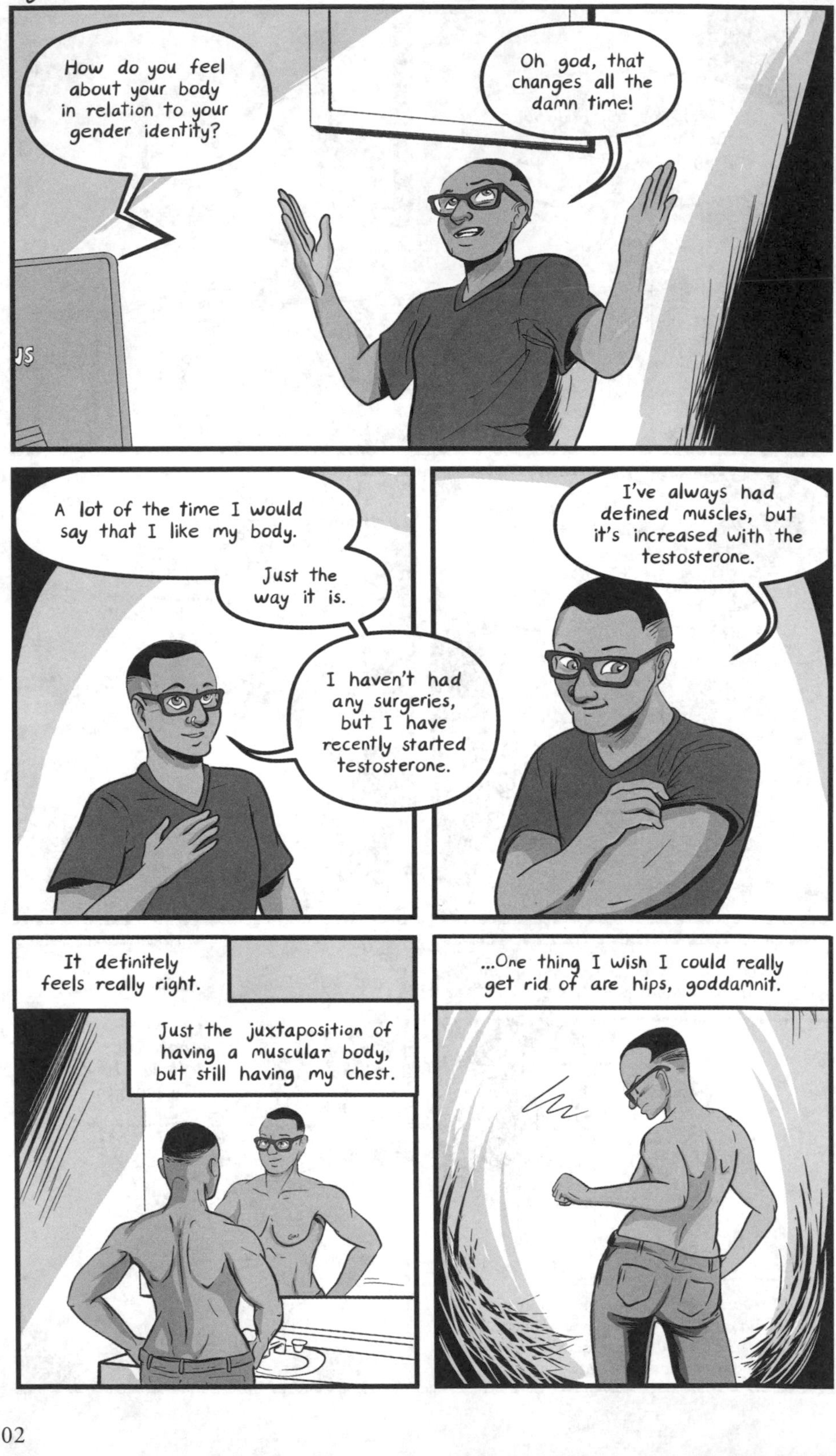
How do you feel about your body in relation to your gender identity?
Oh god, that changes all the damn time!
A lot of the time I would say that I like my body.
Just the way it is.
I haven't had any surgeries, but I have recently started testosterone.
I've always had defined muscles, but it's increased with the testosterone.
It definitely feels really right.
Just the juxtaposition of having a muscular body, but still having my chest.
...One thing I wish I could really get rid of are hips, goddamnit.

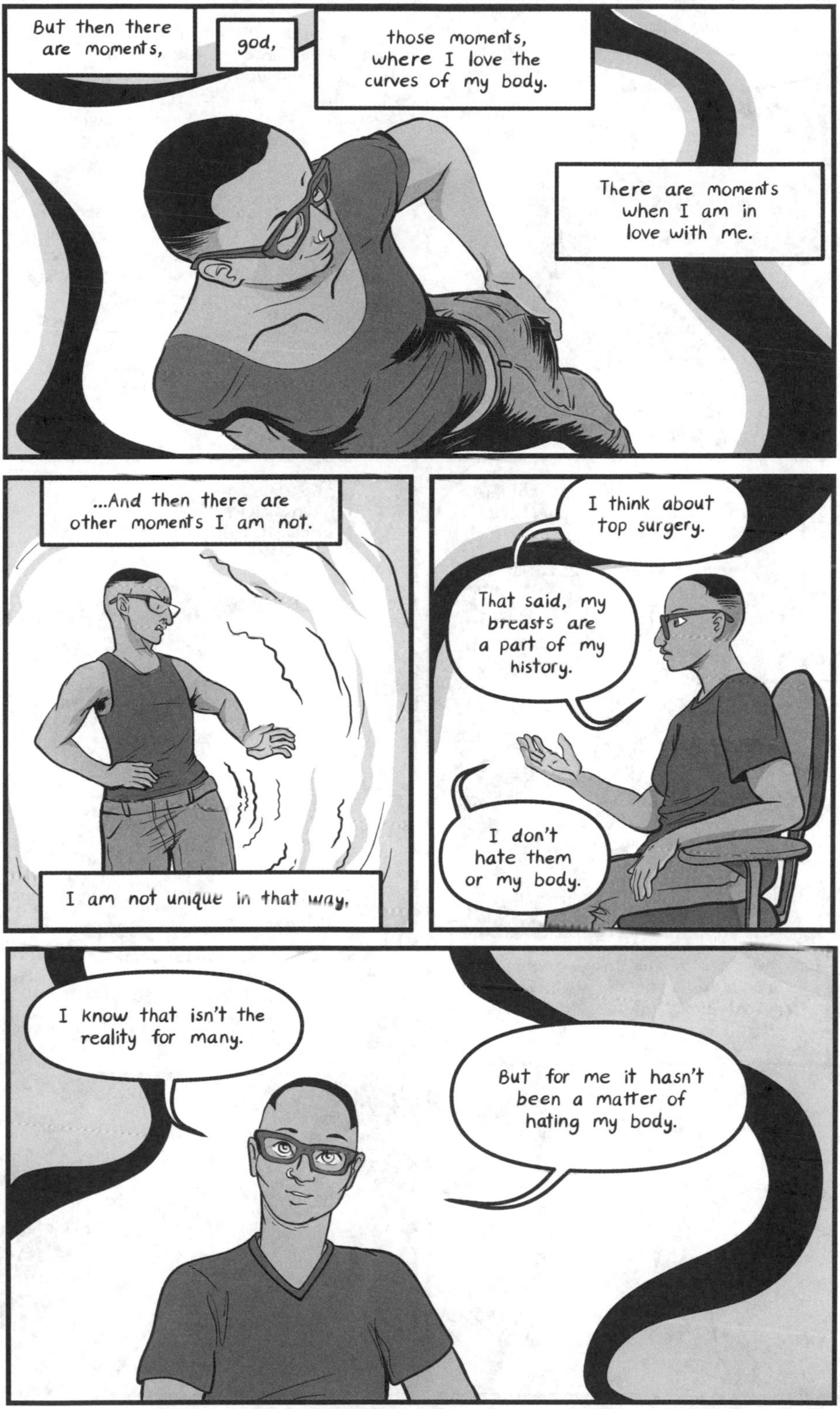
But then there are moments,
god,
those moments, where I love the curves of my body.
There are moments when I am in love with me.
...And then there are other moments I am not.
I am not unique in that way.
I think about top surgery.
That said, my breasts are a part of my history.
I don't hate them or my body.
I know that isn't the reality for many.
But for me it hasn't been a matter of hating my body.

Klara, 2013

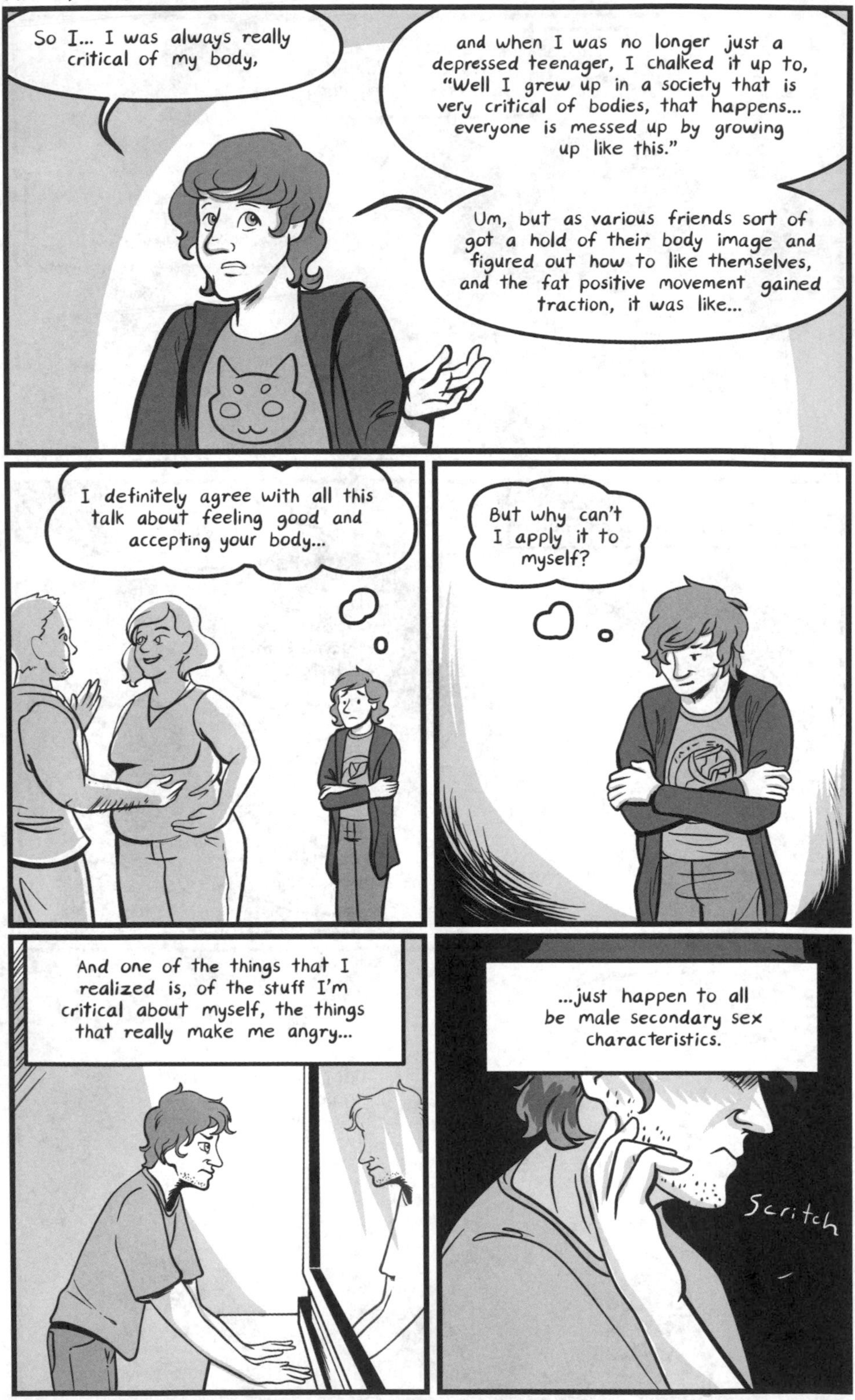

So I... I was always really critical of my body,
and when I was no longer just a depressed teenager, I chalked it up to, "Well I grew up in a society that is very critical of bodies, that happens... everyone is messed up by growing up like this."
Um, but as various friends sort of got a hold of their body image and figured out how to like themselves, and the fat positive movement gained traction, it was like...
I definitely agree with all this talk about feeling good and accepting your body...
But why can't I apply it to myself?
And one of the things that I realized is, of the stuff I'm critical about myself, the things that really make me angry...
...just happen to all be male secondary sex characteristics.
Scritch

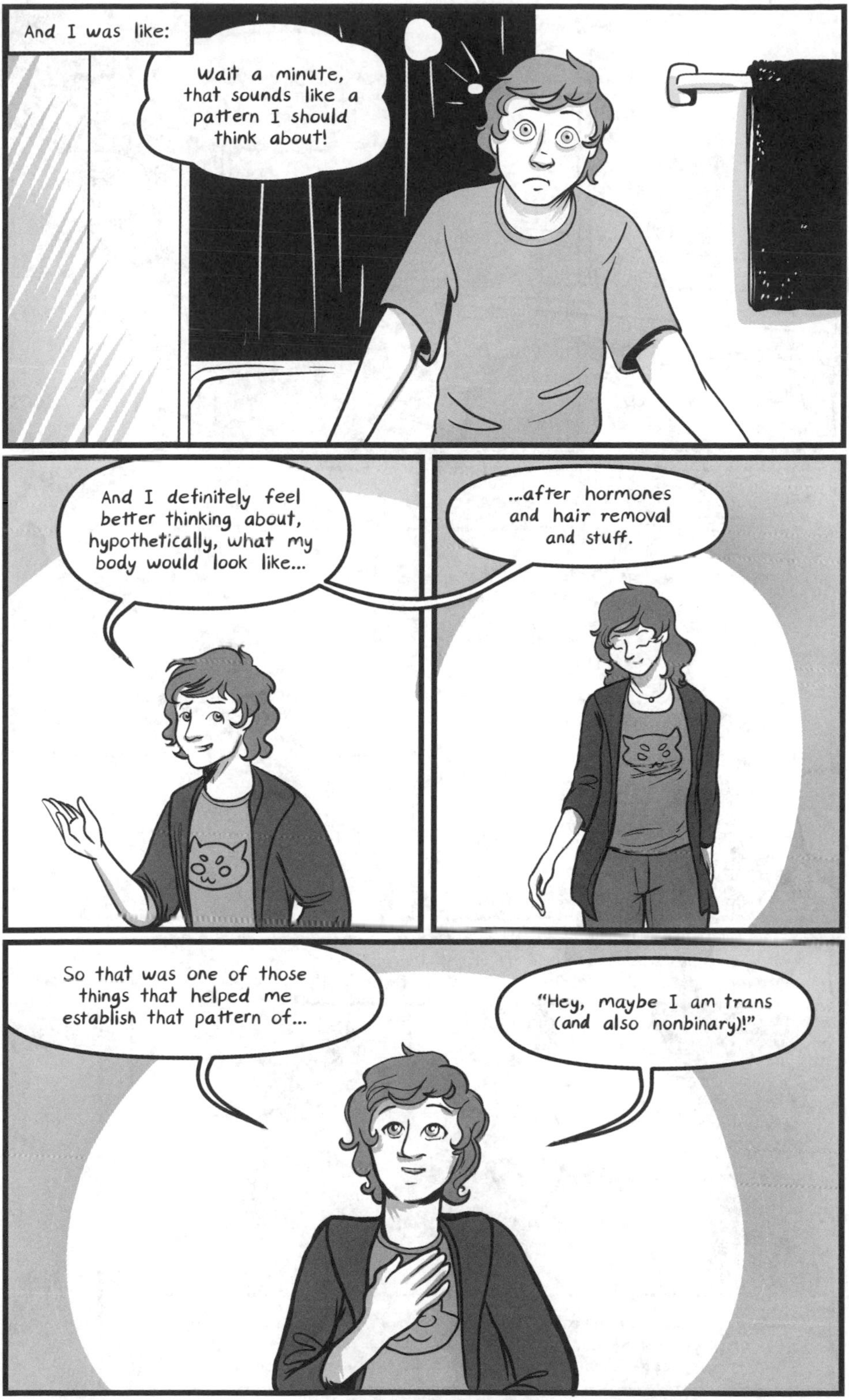
And I was like:
Wait a minute, that sounds like a pattern I should think about!
And I definitely feel better thinking about, hypothetically, what my body would look like...
...after hormones and hair removal and stuff.
So that was one of those things that helped me establish that pattern of...
"Hey, maybe I am trans (and also nonbinary)!"

Gerbil, 2012

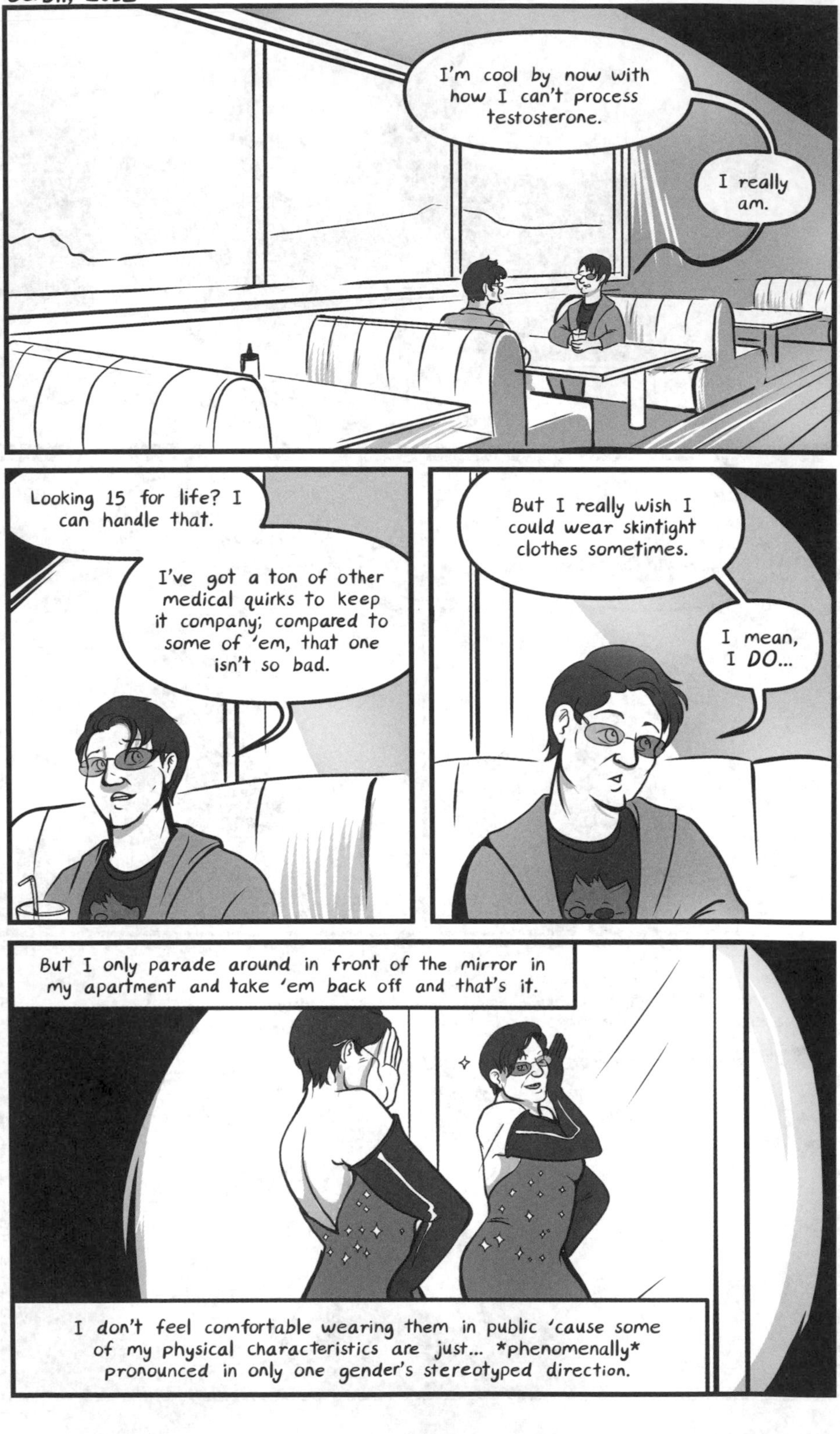
I'm cool by now with how I can't process testosterone.
I really am.
Looking 15 for life? I can handle that.
I've got a ton of other medical quirks to keep it company; compared to some of 'em, that one isn't so bad.
But I really wish I could wear skintight clothes sometimes.
I mean, I *DO*...
But I only parade around in front of the mirror in my apartment and take 'em back off and that's it.
I don't feel comfortable wearing them in public 'cause some of my physical characteristics are just... *phenomenally* pronounced in only one gender's stereotyped direction.

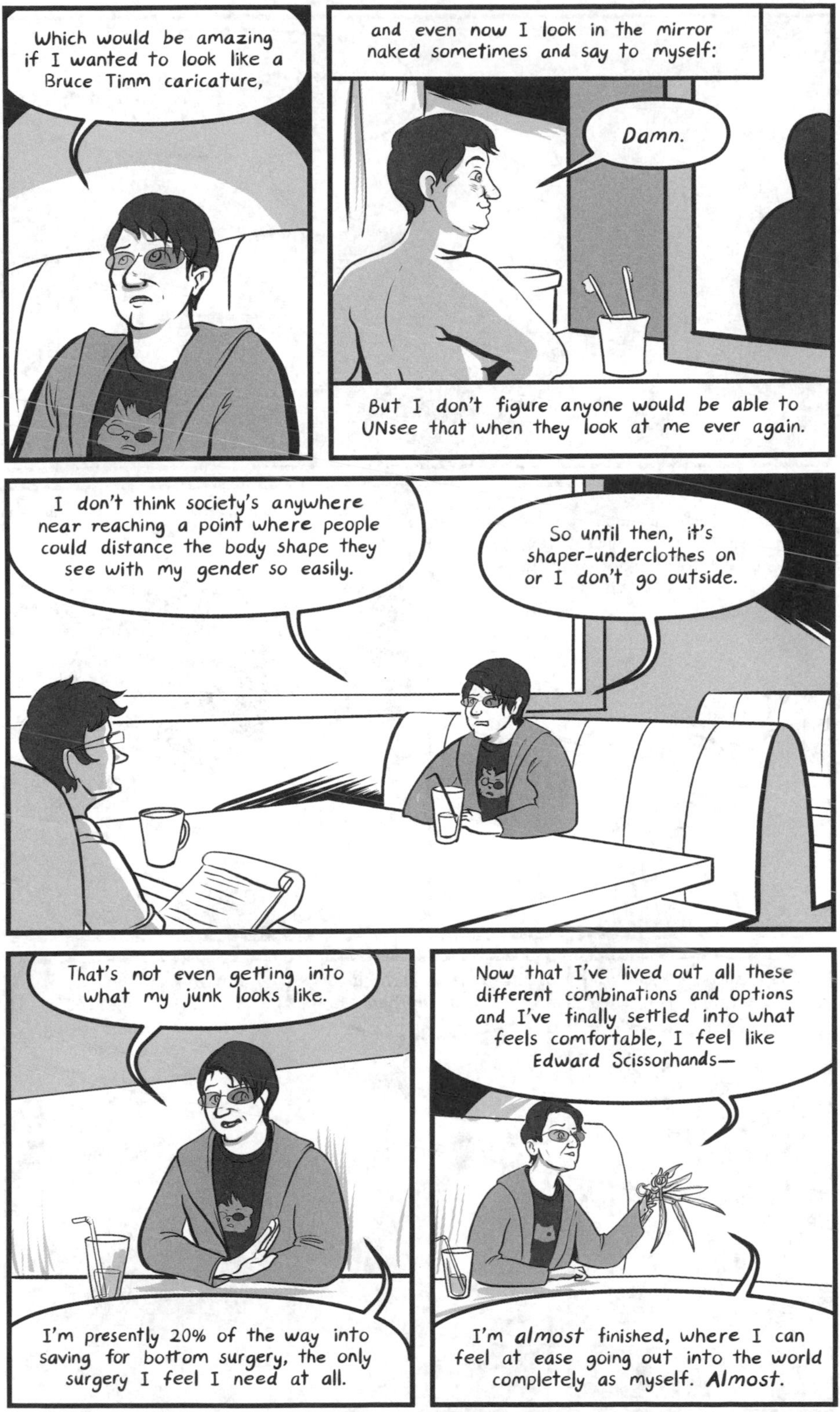
Which would be amazing if I wanted to look like a Bruce Timm caricature,
and even now I look in the mirror naked sometimes and say to myself:
Damn.
But I don't figure anyone would be able to UNsee that when they look at me ever again.
I don't think society's anywhere near reaching a point where people could distance the body shape they see with my gender so easily.
So until then, it's shaper-underclothes on or I don't go outside.
That's not even getting into what my junk looks like.
I'm presently 20% of the way into saving for bottom surgery, the only surgery I feel I need at all.
Now that I've lived out all these different combinations and options and I've finally settled into what feels comfortable, I feel like Edward Scissorhands—
I'm *almost* finished, where I can feel at ease going out into the world completely as myself. *Almost*.

Corrine, 2012

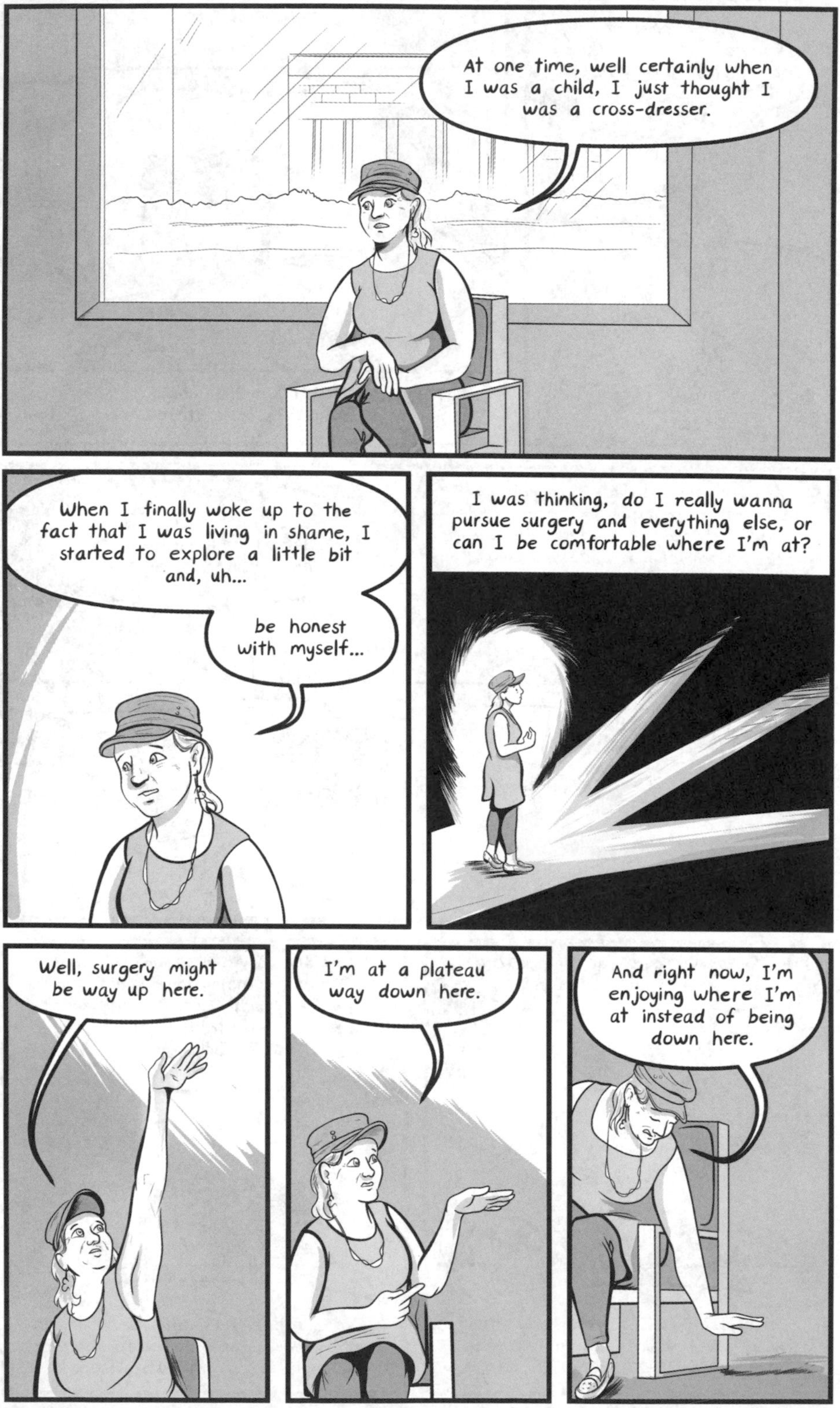

At one time, well certainly when I was a child, I just thought I was a cross-dresser.
When I finally woke up to the fact that I was living in shame, I started to explore a little bit and, uh...
be honest with myself...
I was thinking, do I really wanna pursue surgery and everything else, or can I be comfortable where I'm at?
Well, surgery might be way up here.
I'm at a plateau way down here.
And right now, I'm enjoying where I'm at instead of being down here.

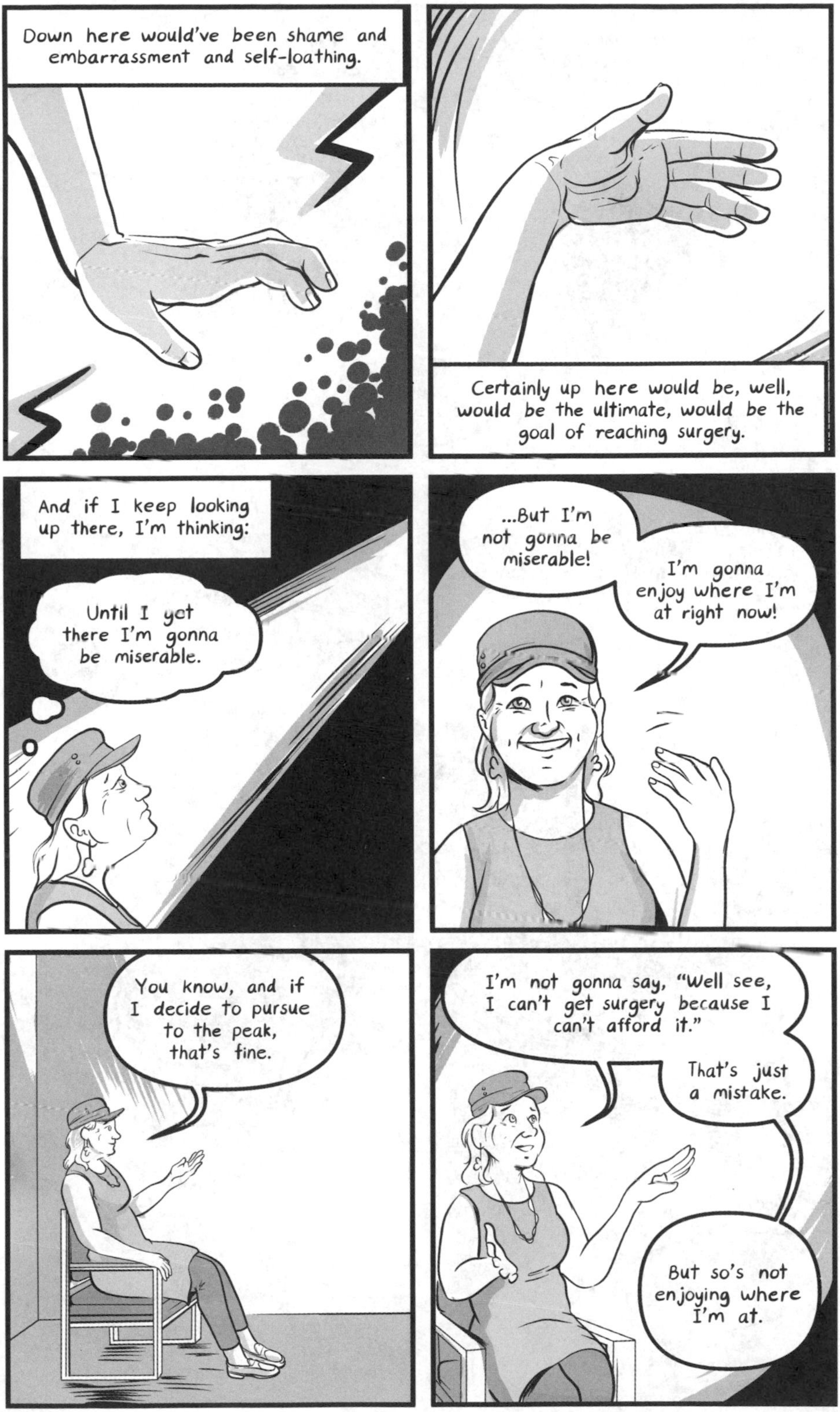
Down here would've been shame and embarrassment and self-loathing.
Certainly up here would be, well, would be the ultimate, would be the goal of reaching surgery.
And if I keep looking up there, I'm thinking:
Until I get there I'm gonna be miserable.
...But I'm not gonna be miserable!
I'm gonna enjoy where I'm at right now!
You know, and if I decide to pursue to the peak, that's fine.
I'm not gonna say, "Well see, I can't get surgery because I can't afford it."
That's just a mistake.
But so's not enjoying where I'm at.

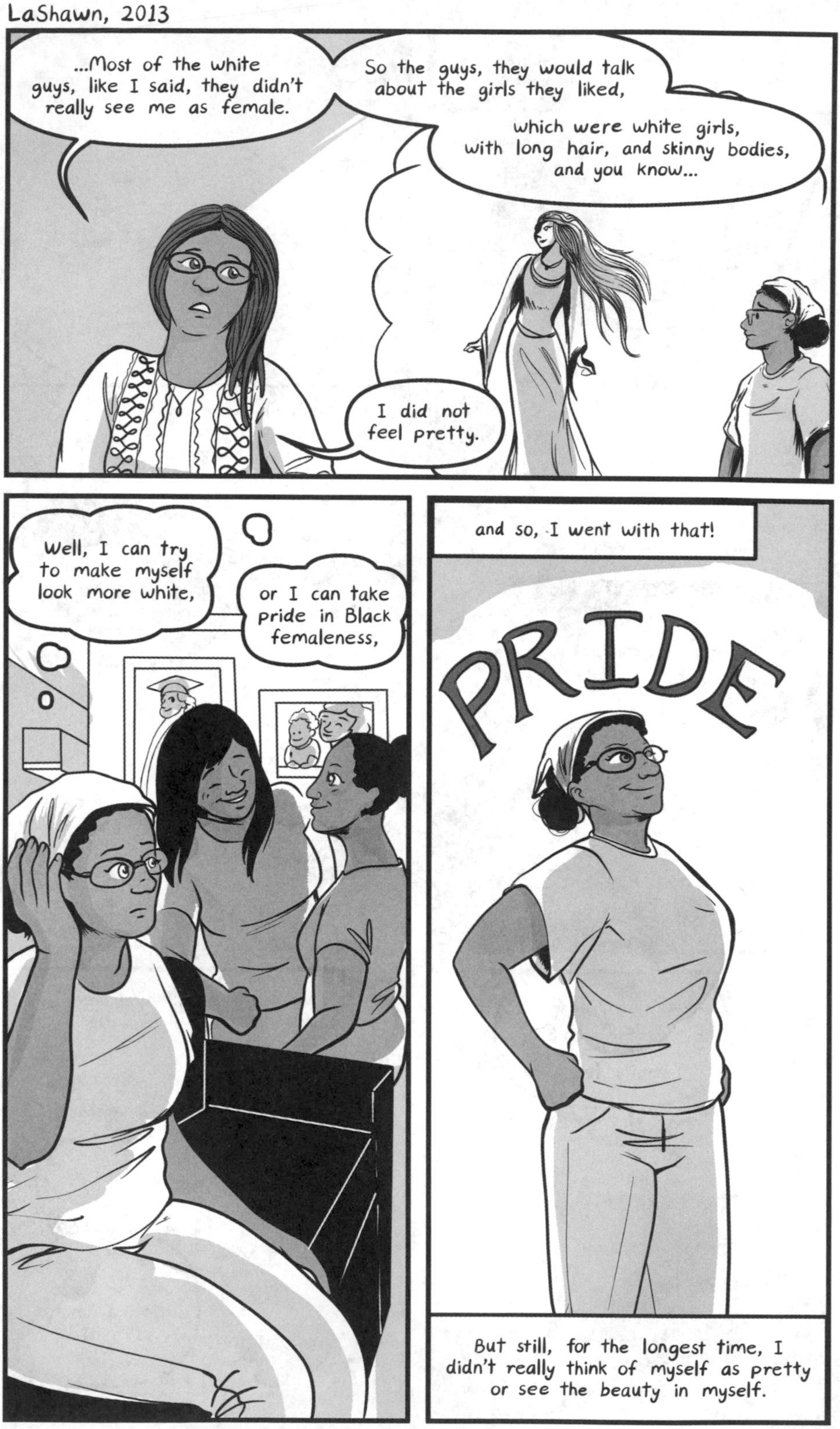
LaShawn, 2013
...Most of the white guys, like I said, they didn't really see me as female.
So the guys, they would talk about the girls they liked,
which were white girls, with long hair, and skinny bodies, and you know...
I did not feel pretty.
Well, I can try to make myself look more white,
or I can take pride in Black femaleness,
and so, I went with that!
PRIDE
But still, for the longest time, I didn't really think of myself as pretty or see the beauty in myself.

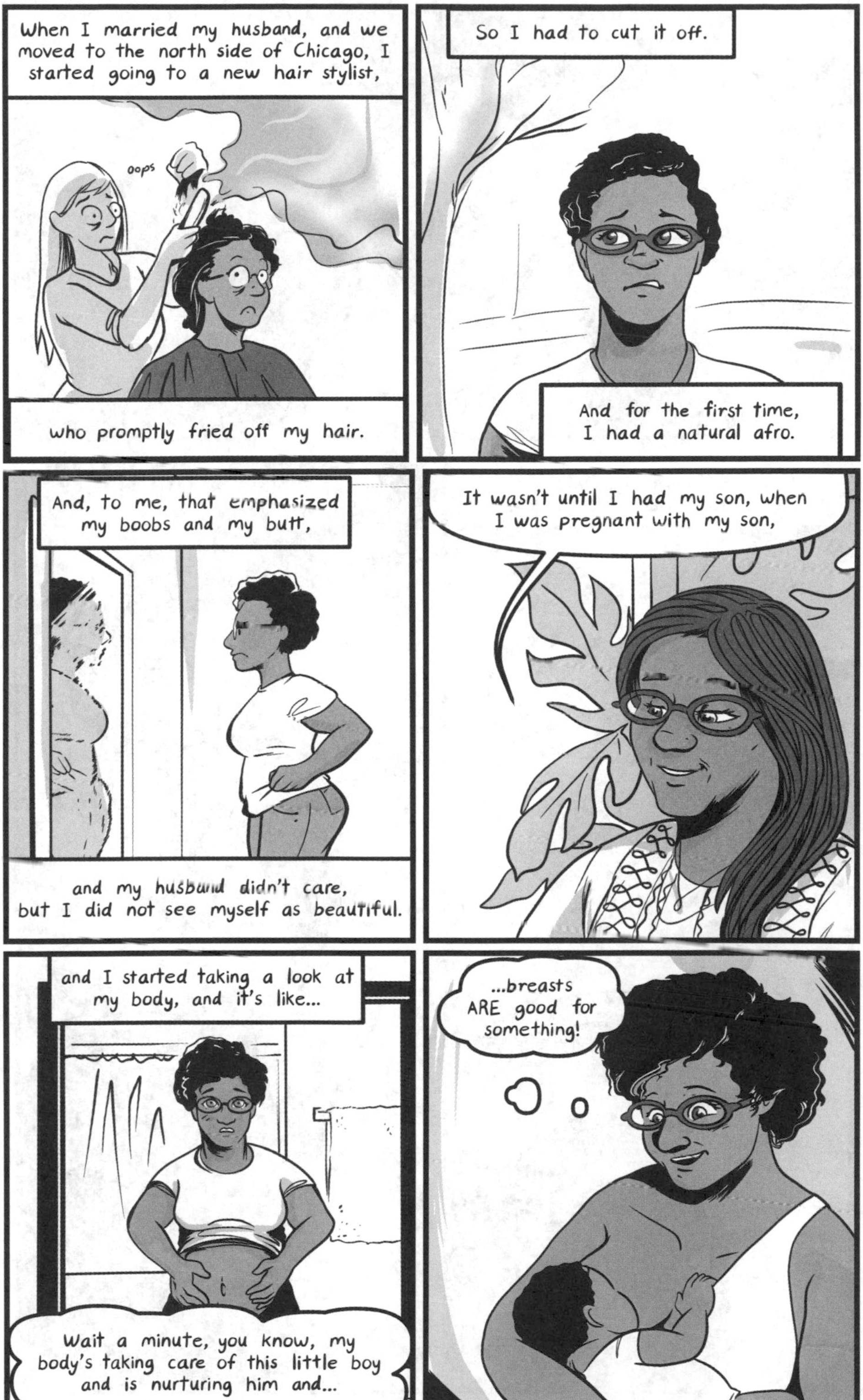
When I married my husband, and we moved to the north side of Chicago, I started going to a new hair stylist,
oops
who promptly fried off my hair.
So I had to cut it off.
And for the first time, I had a natural afro.
And, to me, that emphasized my boobs and my butt,
and my husband didn't care, but I did not see myself as beautiful.
It wasn't until I had my son, when I was pregnant with my son,
and I started taking a look at my body, and it's like...
Wait a minute, you know, my body's taking care of this little boy and is nurturing him and...
...breasts ARE good for something!

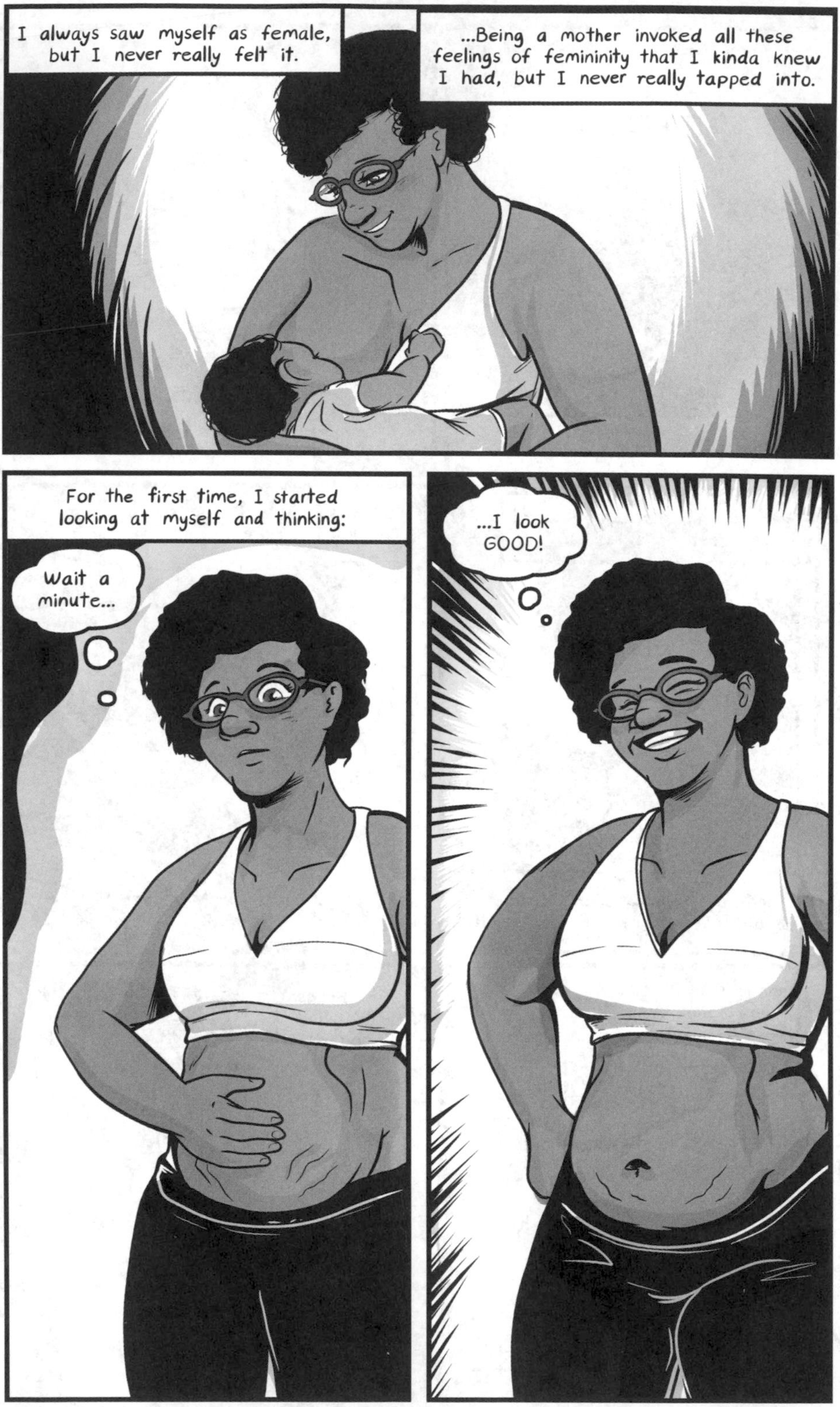
I always saw myself as female, but I never really felt it.
...Being a mother invoked all these feelings of femininity that I kinda knew I had, but I never really tapped into.
For the first time, I started looking at myself and thinking:
Wait a minute...
...I look GOOD!

What is the difference between gender and sex?

Kim, 2011

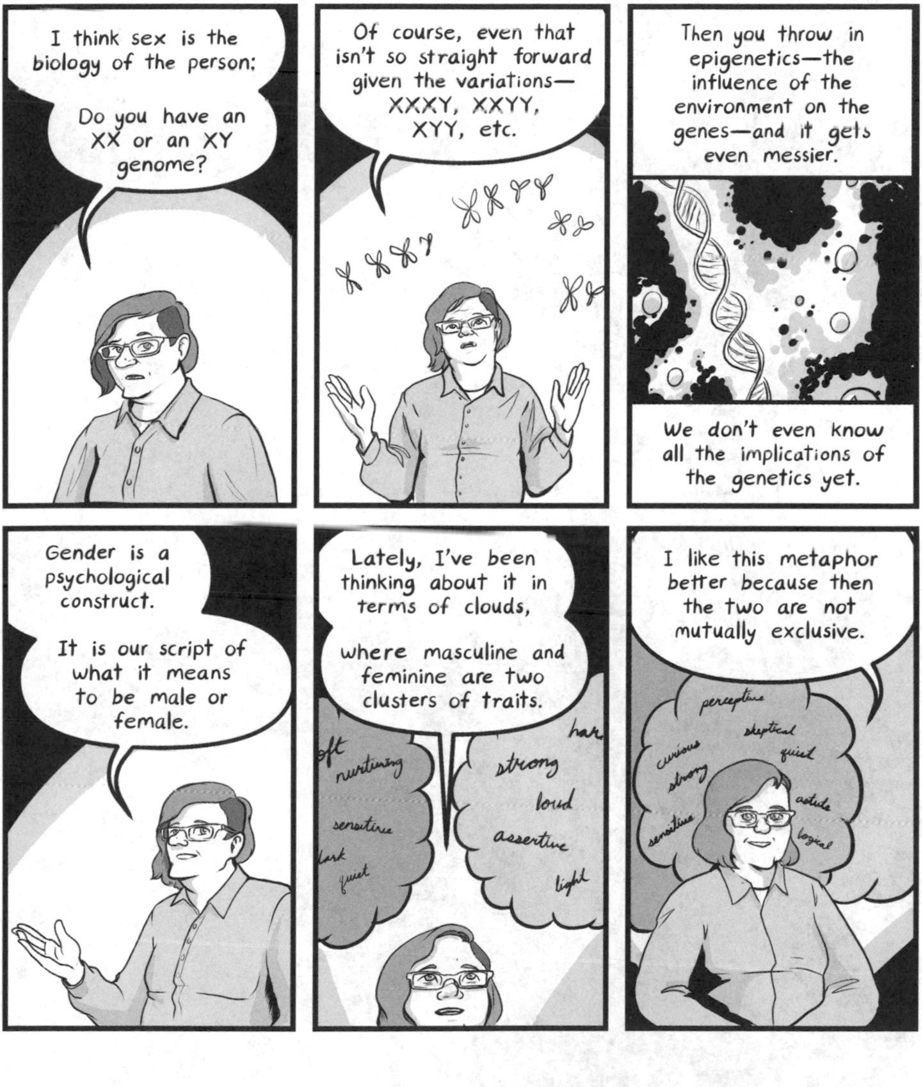

I think sex is the biology of the person;
Do you have an XX or an XY genome?
Of course, even that isn't so straight forward given the variations—XXXY, XXYY, XYY, etc.
Then you throw in epigenetics—the influence of the environment on the genes—and it gets even messier.
We don't even know all the implications of the genetics yet.
Gender is a psychological construct.
It is our script of what it means to be male or female.
Lately, I've been thinking about it in terms of clouds,
where masculine and feminine are two clusters of traits.
nurturing
sensitive
quiet
strong
loud
assertive
light
I like this metaphor better because then the two are not mutually exclusive.
perceptive
skeptical
curious
strong
quiet
astute
sensitive
logical

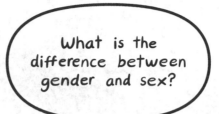

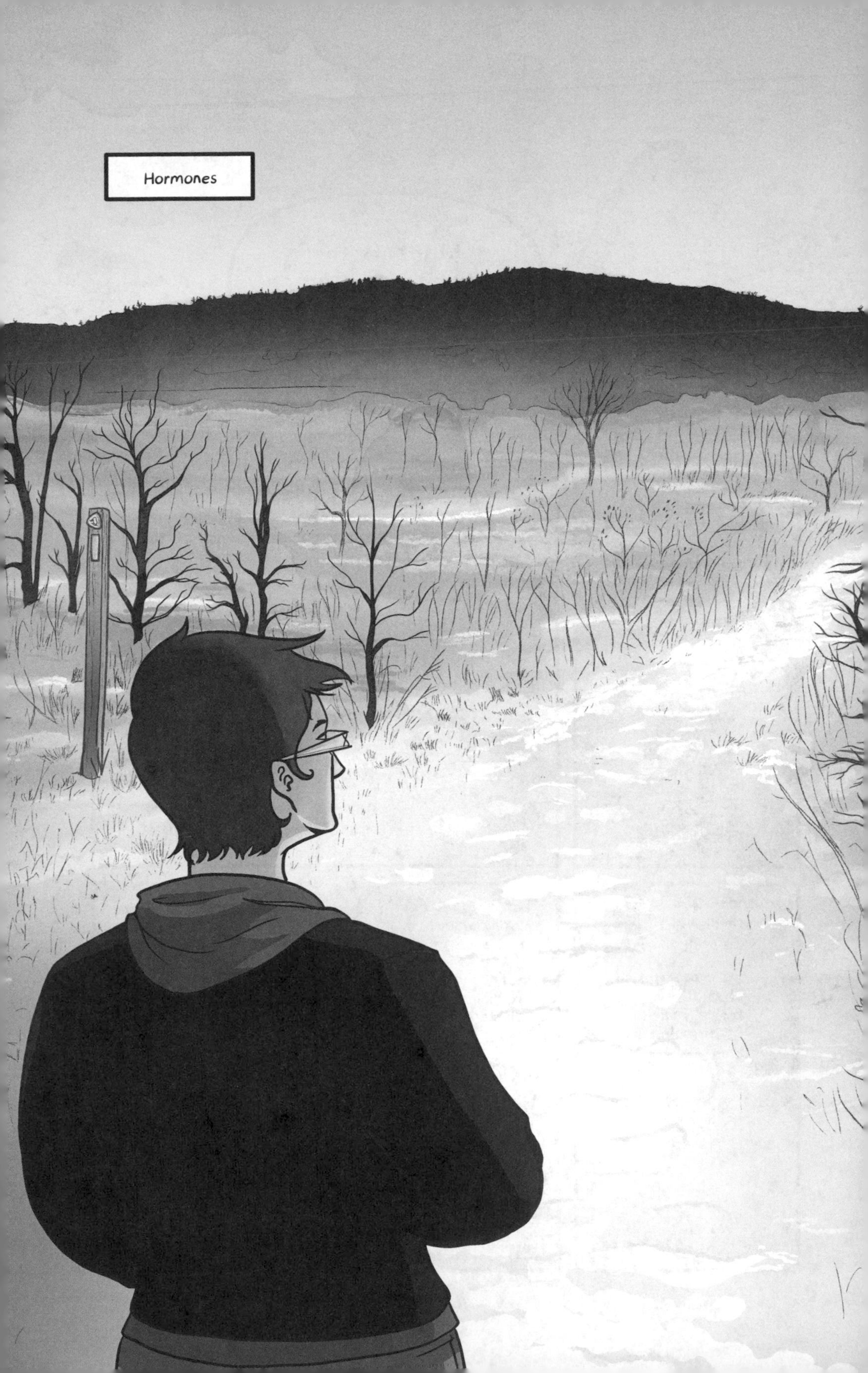
Hormones

Rhea, 2011

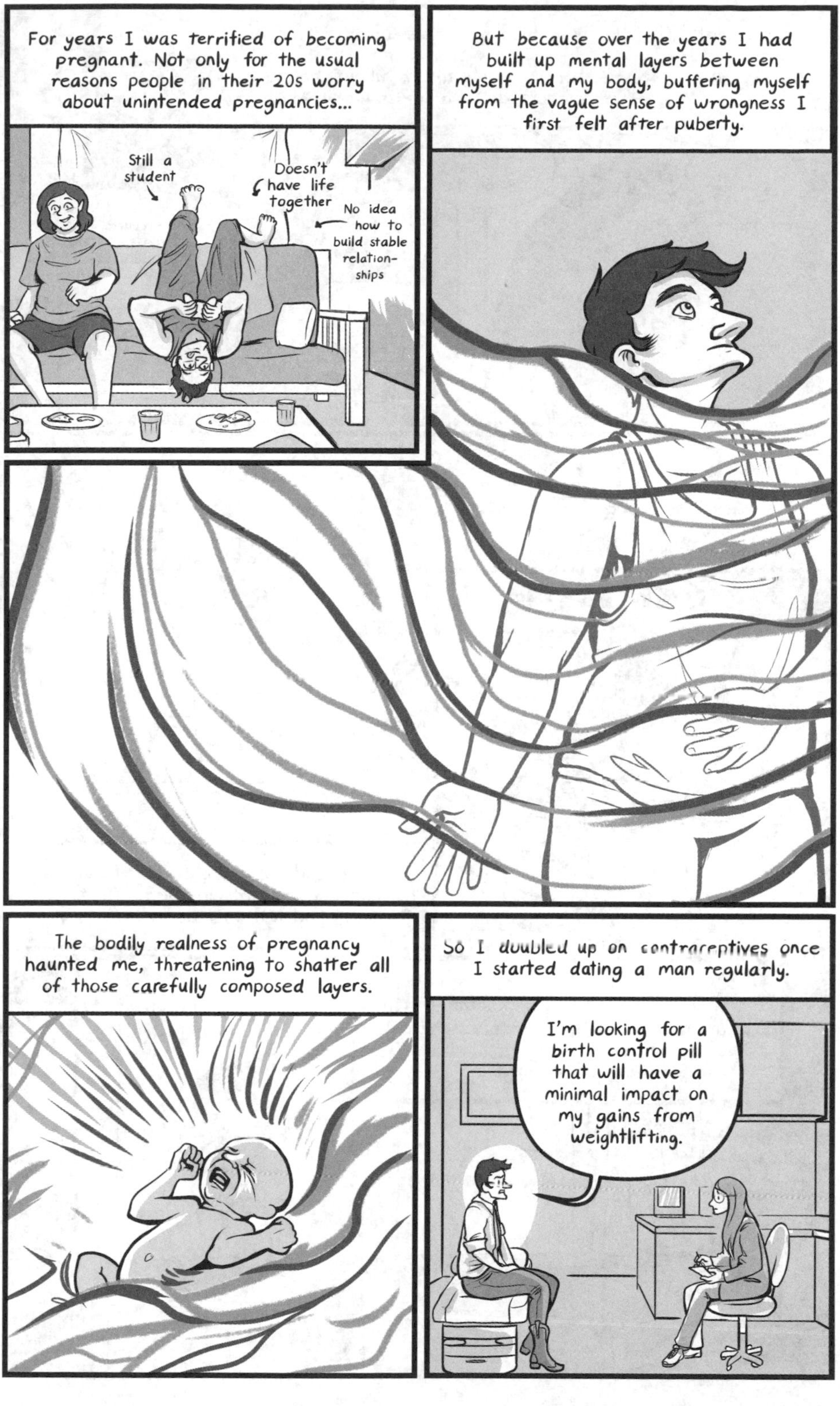
For years I was terrified of becoming pregnant. Not only for the usual reasons people in their 20s worry about unintended pregnancies...
Still a student
Doesn't have life together
No idea how to build stable relation-ships
But because over the years I had built up mental layers between myself and my body, buffering myself from the vague sense of wrongness I first felt after puberty.
The bodily realness of pregnancy haunted me, threatening to shatter all of those carefully composed layers.
So I doubled up on contraceptives once I started dating a man regularly.
I'm looking for a birth control pill that will have a minimal impact on my gains from weightlifting.

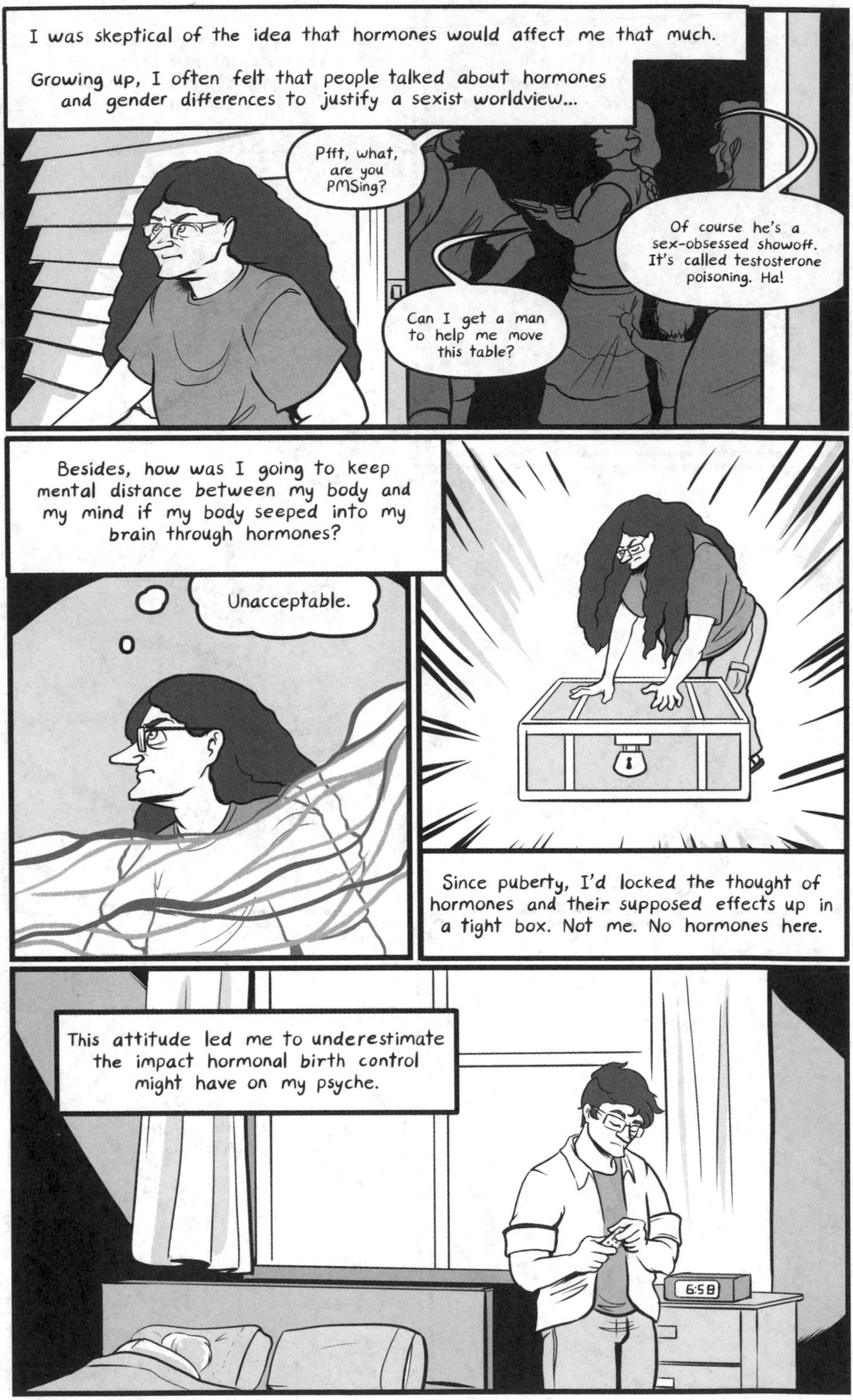
I was skeptical of the idea that hormones would affect me that much.
Growing up, I often felt that people talked about hormones and gender differences to justify a sexist worldview...
Pfft, what, are you PMSing?
Of course he's a sex-obsessed showoff. It's called testosterone poisoning. Ha!
Can I get a man to help me move this table?
Besides, how was I going to keep mental distance between my body and my mind if my body seeped into my brain through hormones?
Unacceptable.
Since puberty, I'd locked the thought of hormones and their supposed effects up in a tight box. Not me. No hormones here.
This attitude led me to underestimate the impact hormonal birth control might have on my psyche.
6:58

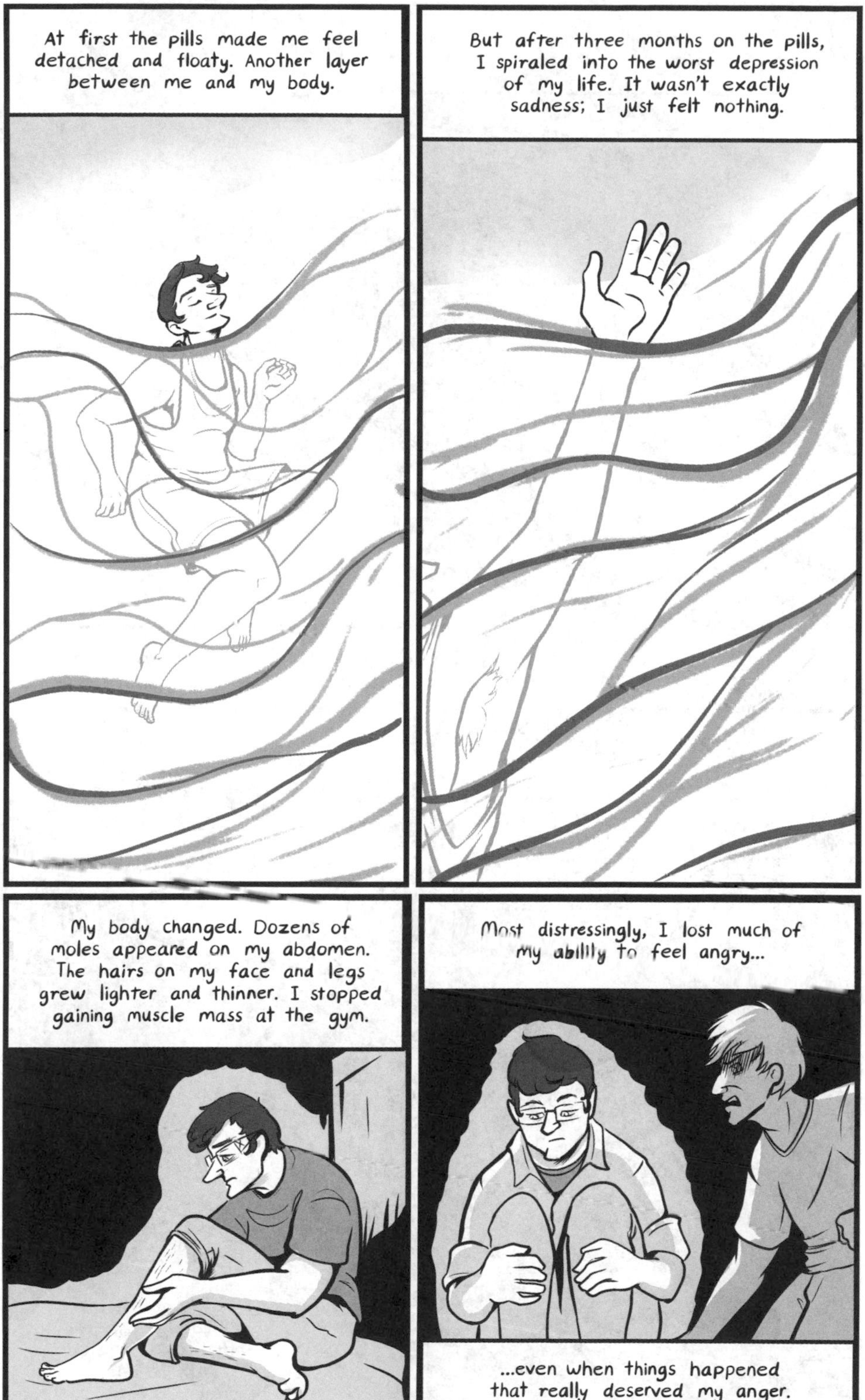
At first the pills made me feel detached and floaty. Another layer between me and my body.
But after three months on the pills, I spiraled into the worst depression of my life. It wasn't exactly sadness; I just felt nothing.
My body changed. Dozens of moles appeared on my abdomen. The hairs on my face and legs grew lighter and thinner. I stopped gaining muscle mass at the gym.
Most distressingly, I lost much of my ability to feel angry...
...even when things happened that really deserved my anger.
Fun fact: This can be a sign of depression!

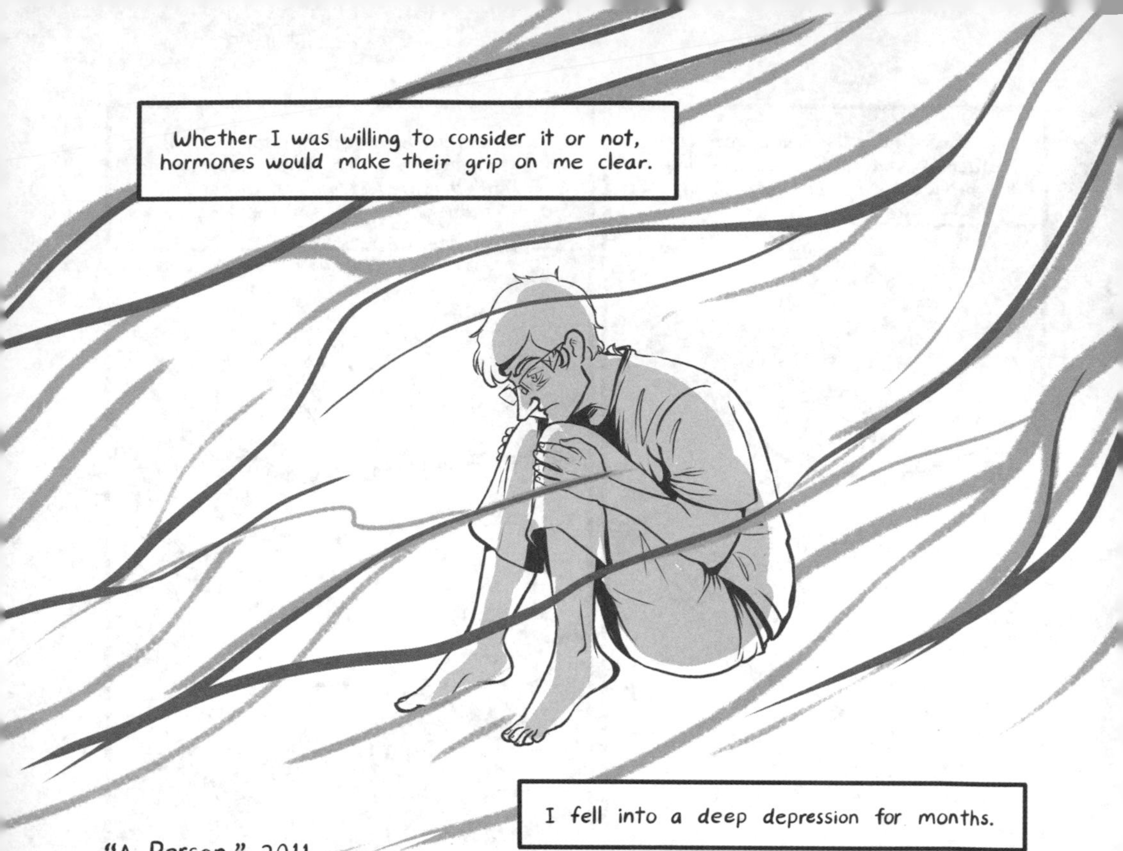
Whether I was willing to consider it or not, hormones would make their grip on me clear.
I fell into a deep depression for months.

"A Person," 2011

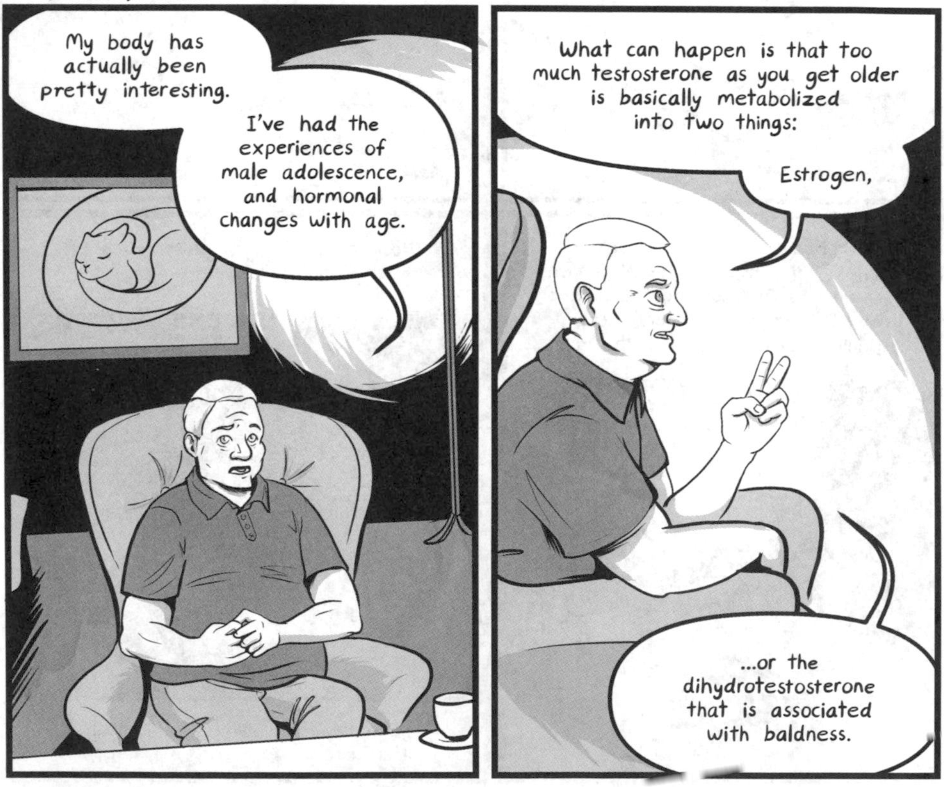
My body has actually been pretty interesting.
I've had the experiences of male adolescence, and hormonal changes with age.
What can happen is that too much testosterone as you get older is basically metabolized into two things:
Estrogen,
...or the dihydrotestosterone that is associated with baldness.

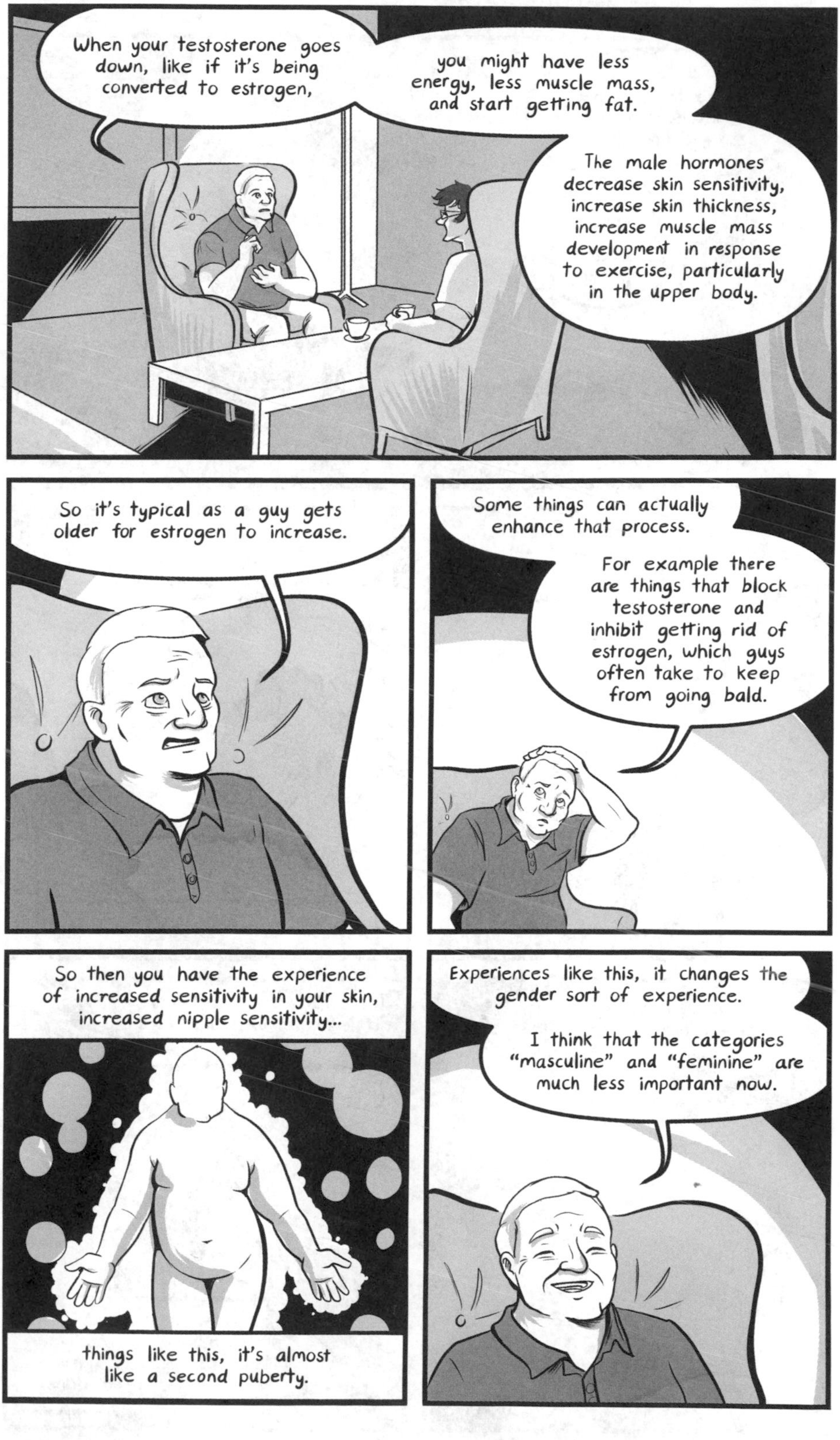
When your testosterone goes down, like if it's being converted to estrogen,
you might have less energy, less muscle mass, and start getting fat.
The male hormones decrease skin sensitivity, increase skin thickness, increase muscle mass development in response to exercise, particularly in the upper body.
So it's typical as a guy gets older for estrogen to increase.
Some things can actually enhance that process.
For example there are things that block testosterone and inhibit getting rid of estrogen, which guys often take to keep from going bald.
So then you have the experience of increased sensitivity in your skin, increased nipple sensitivity...
things like this, it's almost like a second puberty.
Experiences like this, it changes the gender sort of experience.
I think that the categories "masculine" and "feminine" are much less important now.

Ginger, 2012

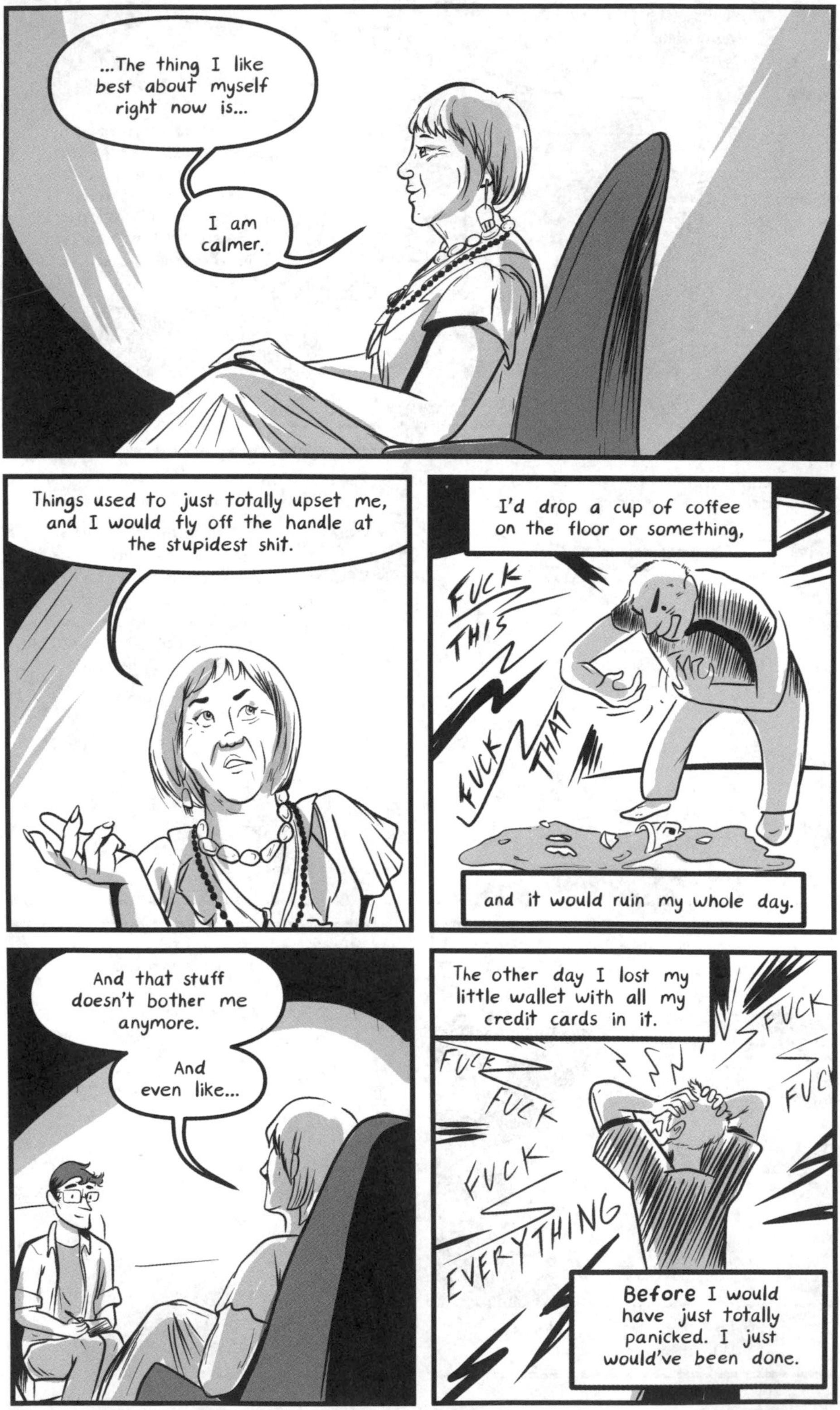
...The thing I like best about myself right now is...
I am calmer.
Things used to just totally upset me, and I would fly off the handle at the stupidest shit.
I'd drop a cup of coffee on the floor or something,
FUCK THIS
FUCK THAT
and it would ruin my whole day.
And that stuff doesn't bother me anymore.
And even like...
The other day I lost my little wallet with all my credit cards in it.
FUCK
FUCK
FUCK
EVERYTHING
Before I would have just totally panicked. I just would've been done.

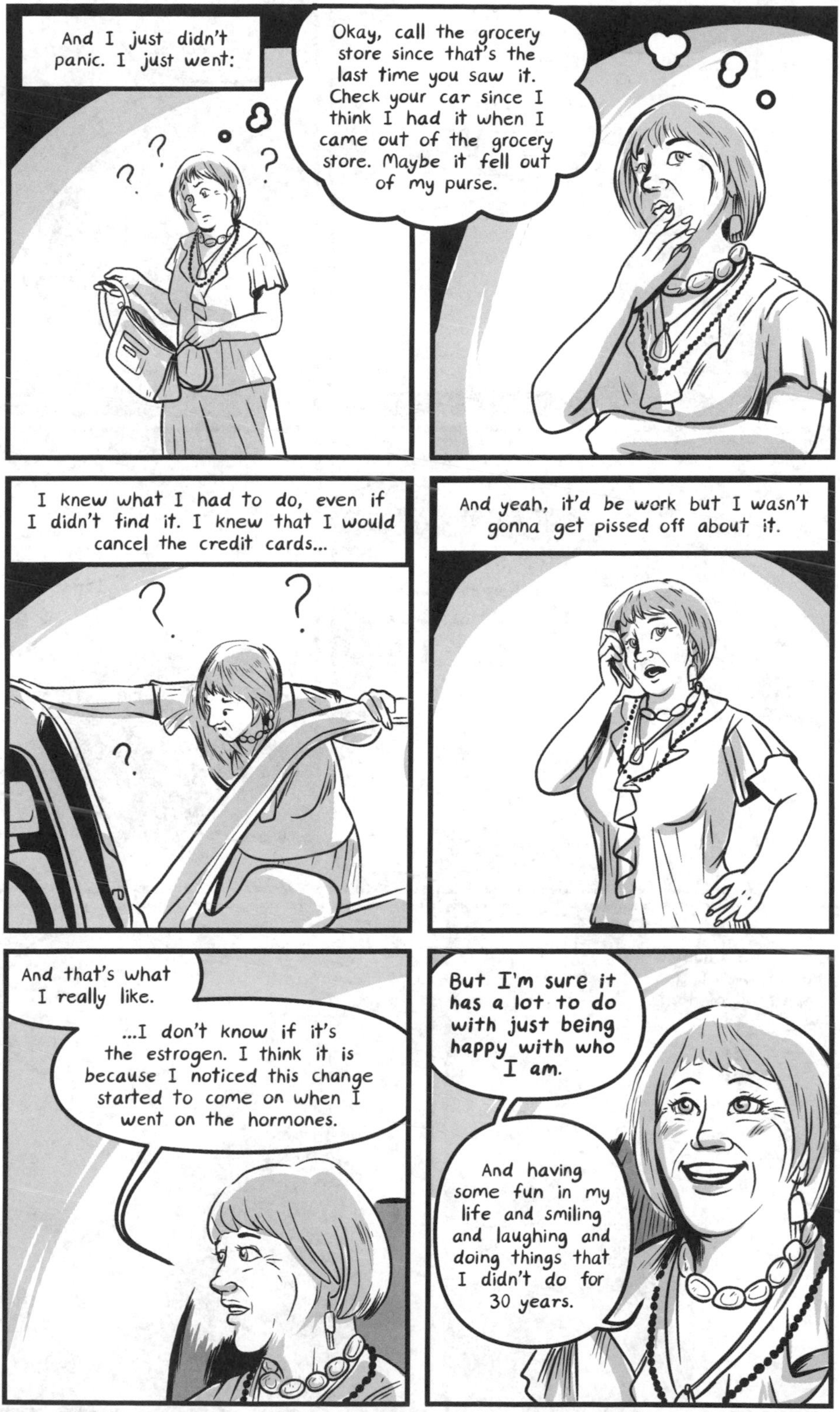

And I just didn't panic. I just went:
Okay, call the grocery store since that's the last time you saw it. Check your car since I think I had it when I came out of the grocery store. Maybe it fell out of my purse.
I knew what I had to do, even if I didn't find it. I knew that I would cancel the credit cards...
And yeah, it'd be work but I wasn't gonna get pissed off about it.
And that's what I really like.
...I don't know if it's the estrogen. I think it is because I noticed this change started to come on when I went on the hormones.
But I'm sure it has a lot to do with just being happy with who I am.
And having some fun in my life and smiling and laughing and doing things that I didn't do for 30 years.

Dutchess, 2015

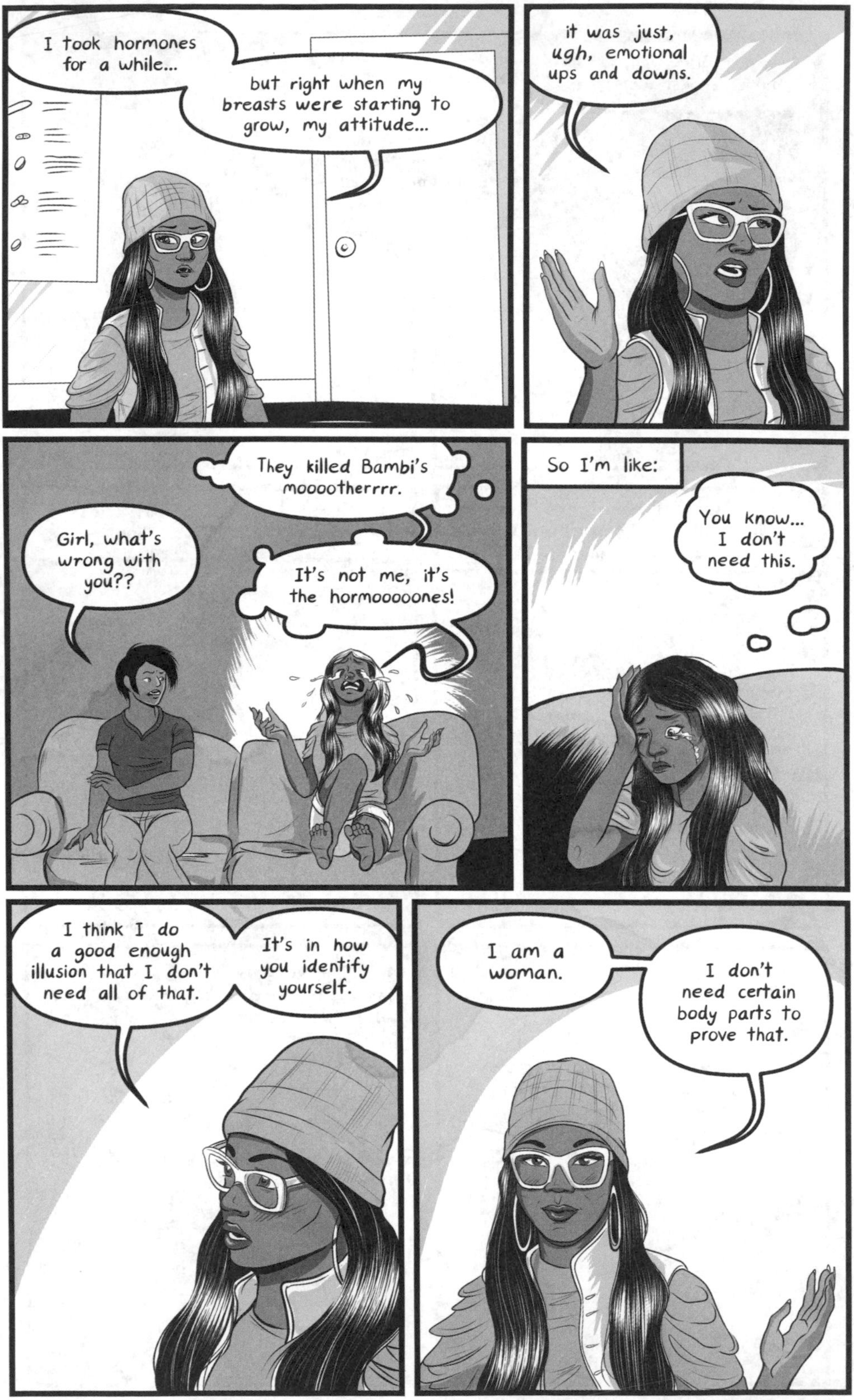
I took hormones for a while...
but right when my breasts were starting to grow, my attitude...
it was just, ugh, emotional ups and downs.
They killed Bambi's moooootherrrr.
Girl, what's wrong with you??
It's not me, it's the hormooooones!
So I'm like:
You know... I don't need this.
I think I do a good enough illusion that I don't need all of that.
It's in how you identify yourself.
I am a woman.
I don't need certain body parts to prove that.

Lauren, 2012

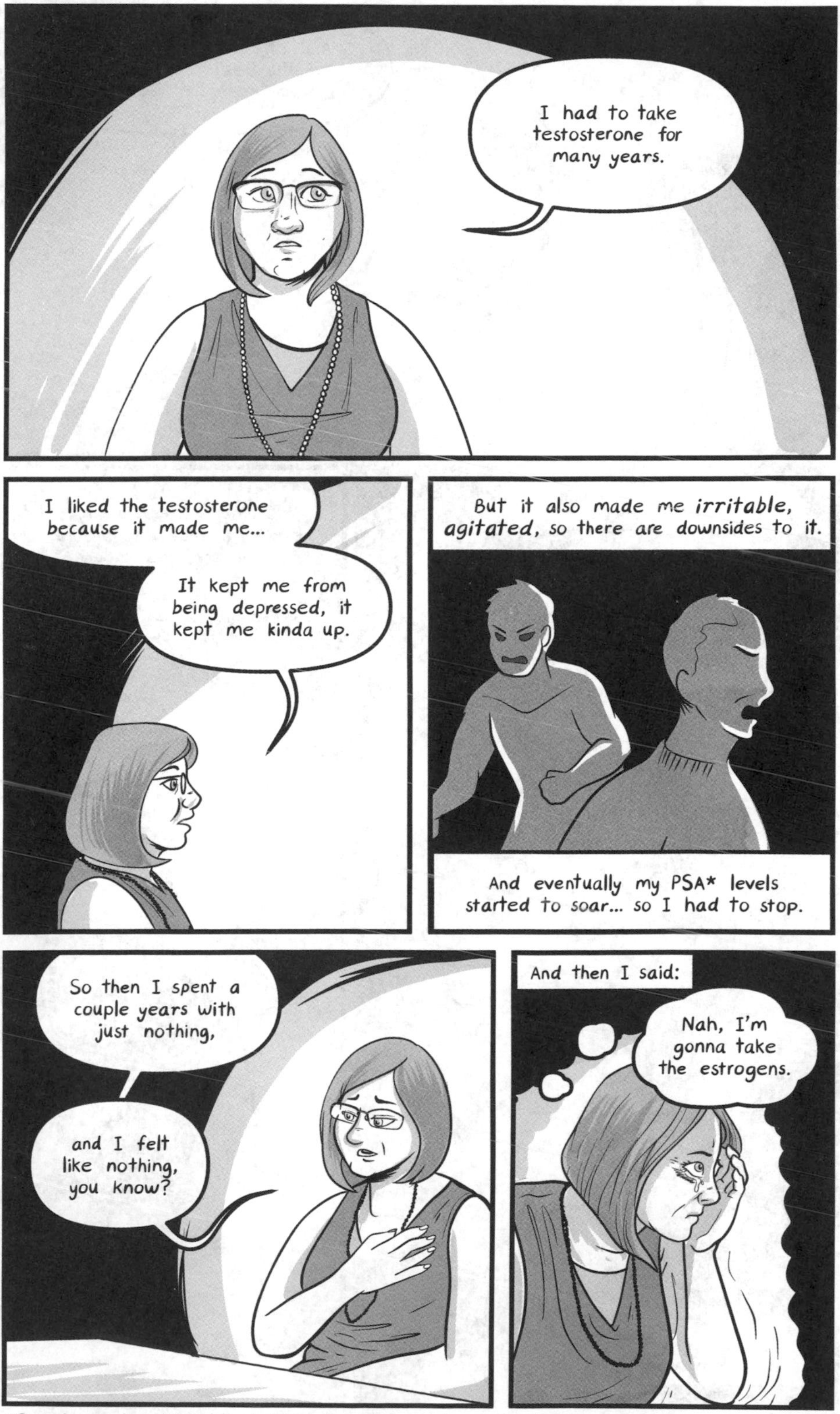
I had to take testosterone for many years.
I liked the testosterone because it made me...
It kept me from being depressed, it kept me kinda up.
But it also made me *irritable, agitated,* so there are downsides to it.
And eventually my PSA* levels started to soar... so I had to stop.
So then I spent a couple years with just nothing,
and I felt like nothing, you know?
And then I said:
Nah, I'm gonna take the estrogens.

*Prostate-specific antigen. Elevated PSA increases prostate cancer risk.

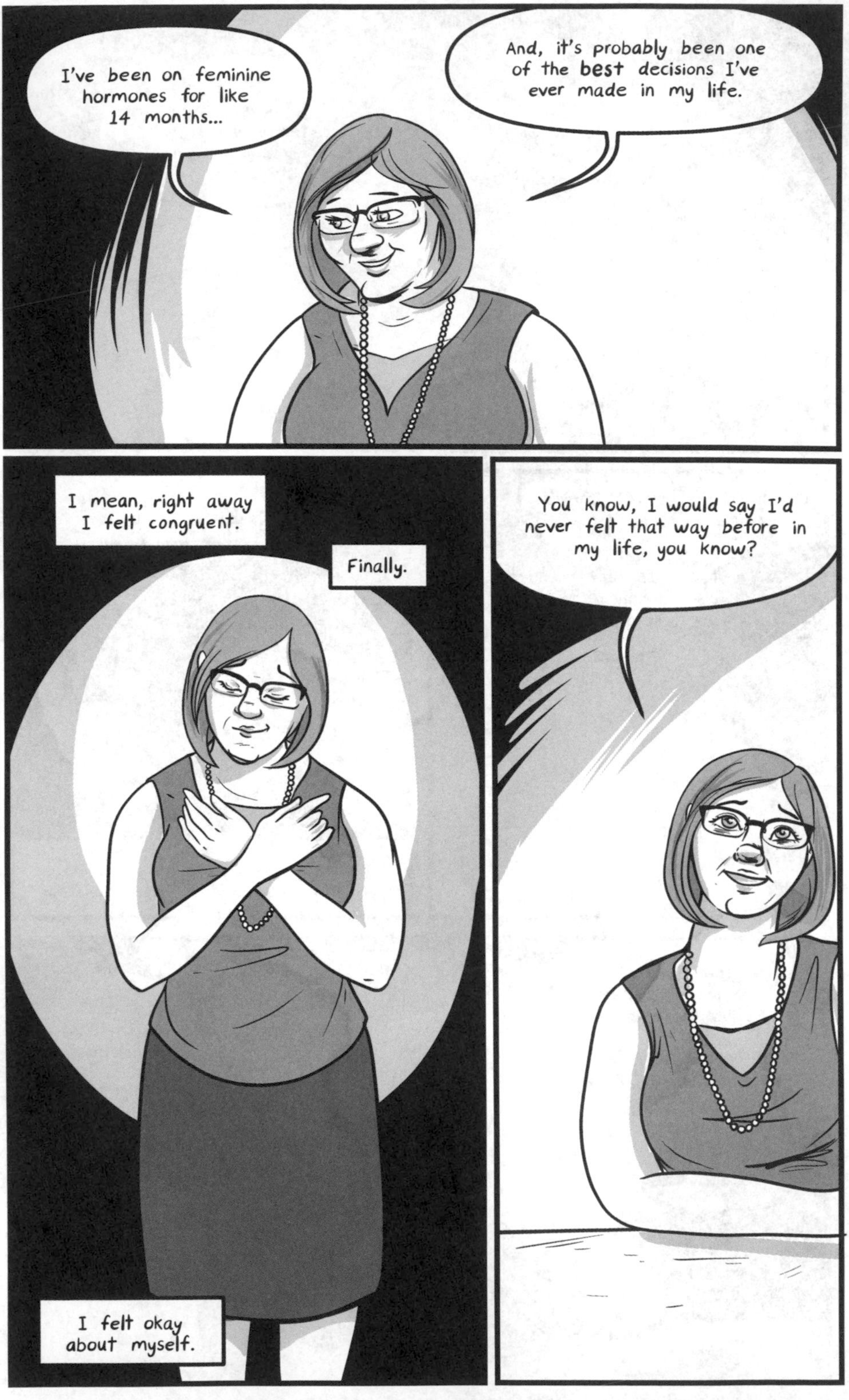
I've been on feminine hormones for like 14 months...
And, it's probably been one of the **best** decisions I've ever made in my life.
I mean, right away I felt congruent.
Finally.
I felt okay about myself.
You know, I would say I'd never felt that way before in my life, you know?

Lauren, 2018

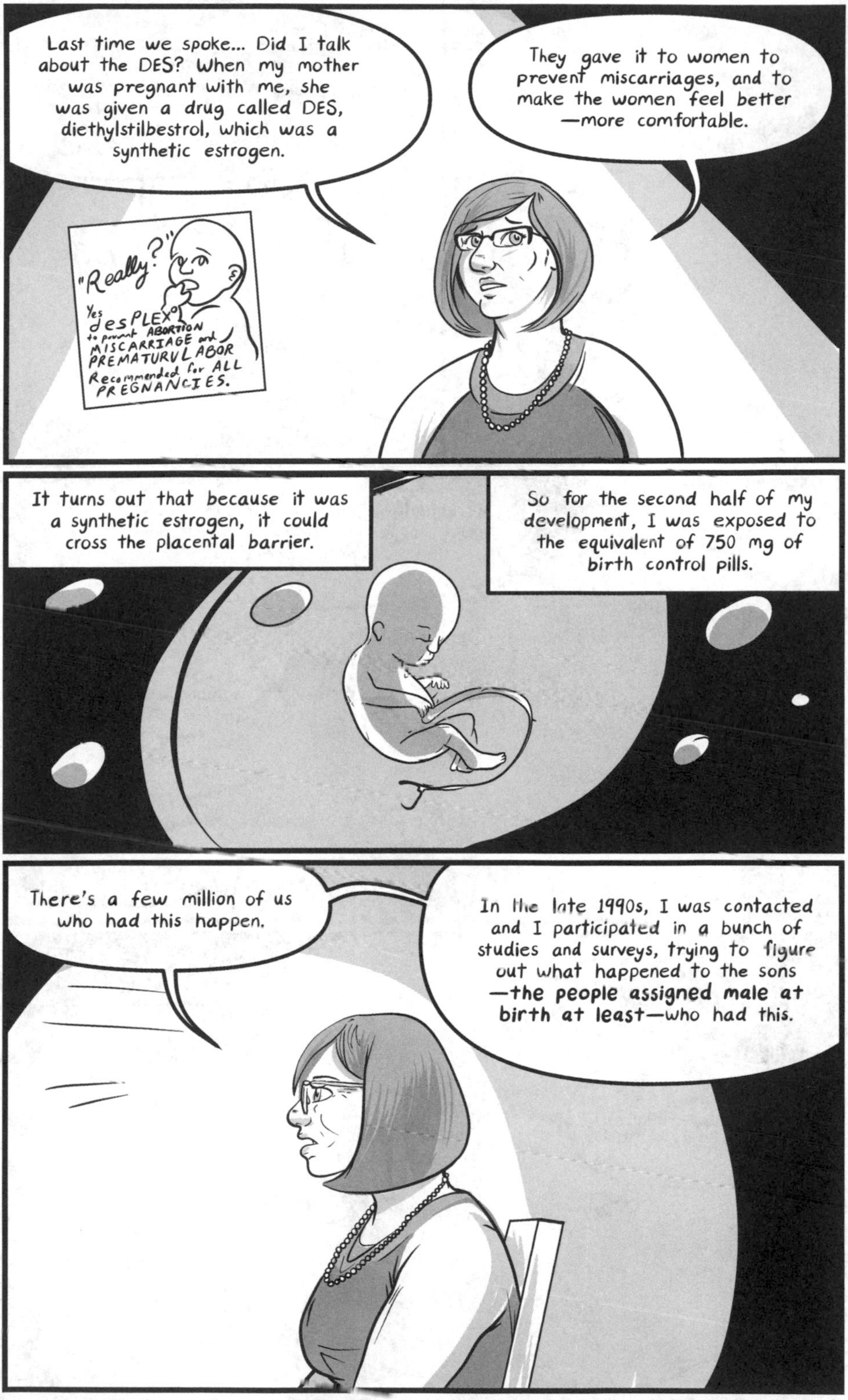

Last time we spoke... Did I talk about the DES? When my mother was pregnant with me, she was given a drug called DES, diethylstilbestrol, which was a synthetic estrogen.
They gave it to women to prevent miscarriages, and to make the women feel better —more comfortable.
"Really?" Yes desPLEX to prevent ABORTION MISCARRIAGE and PREMATURUL ABOR Recommended for ALL PREGNANCIES.
It turns out that because it was a synthetic estrogen, it could cross the placental barrier.
So for the second half of my development, I was exposed to the equivalent of 750 mg of birth control pills.
There's a few million of us who had this happen.
In the late 1990s, I was contacted and I participated in a bunch of studies and surveys, trying to figure out what happened to the sons —**the people assigned male at birth at least**—who had this.

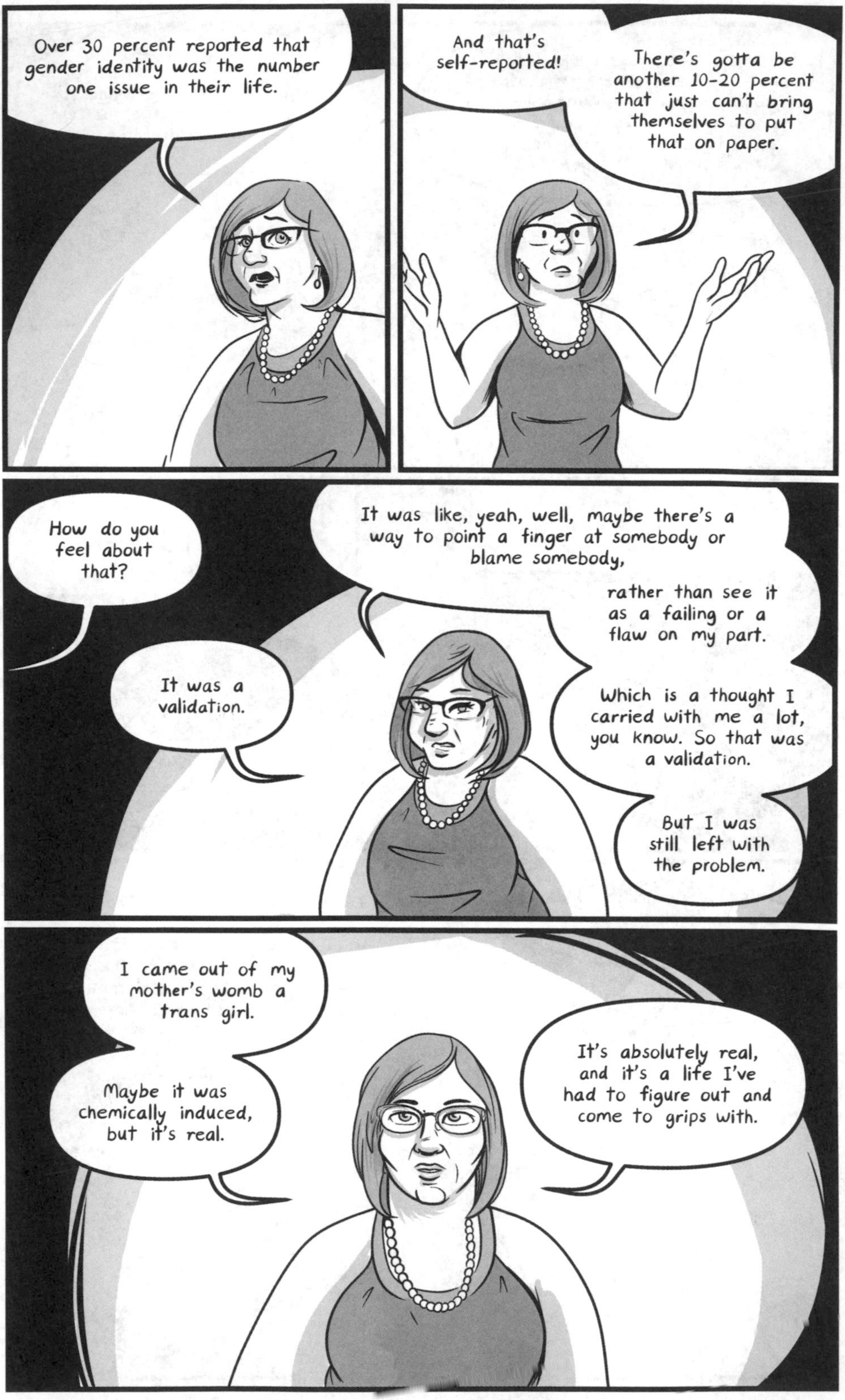

Over 30 percent reported that gender identity was the number one issue in their life.
And that's self-reported!
There's gotta be another 10-20 percent that just can't bring themselves to put that on paper.
How do you feel about that?
It was a validation.
It was like, yeah, well, maybe there's a way to point a finger at somebody or blame somebody,
rather than see it as a failing or a flaw on my part.
Which is a thought I carried with me a lot, you know. So that was a validation.
But I was still left with the problem.
I came out of my mother's womb a trans girl.
Maybe it was chemically induced, but it's real.
It's absolutely real, and it's a life I've had to figure out and come to grips with.

Anonymous, 2013

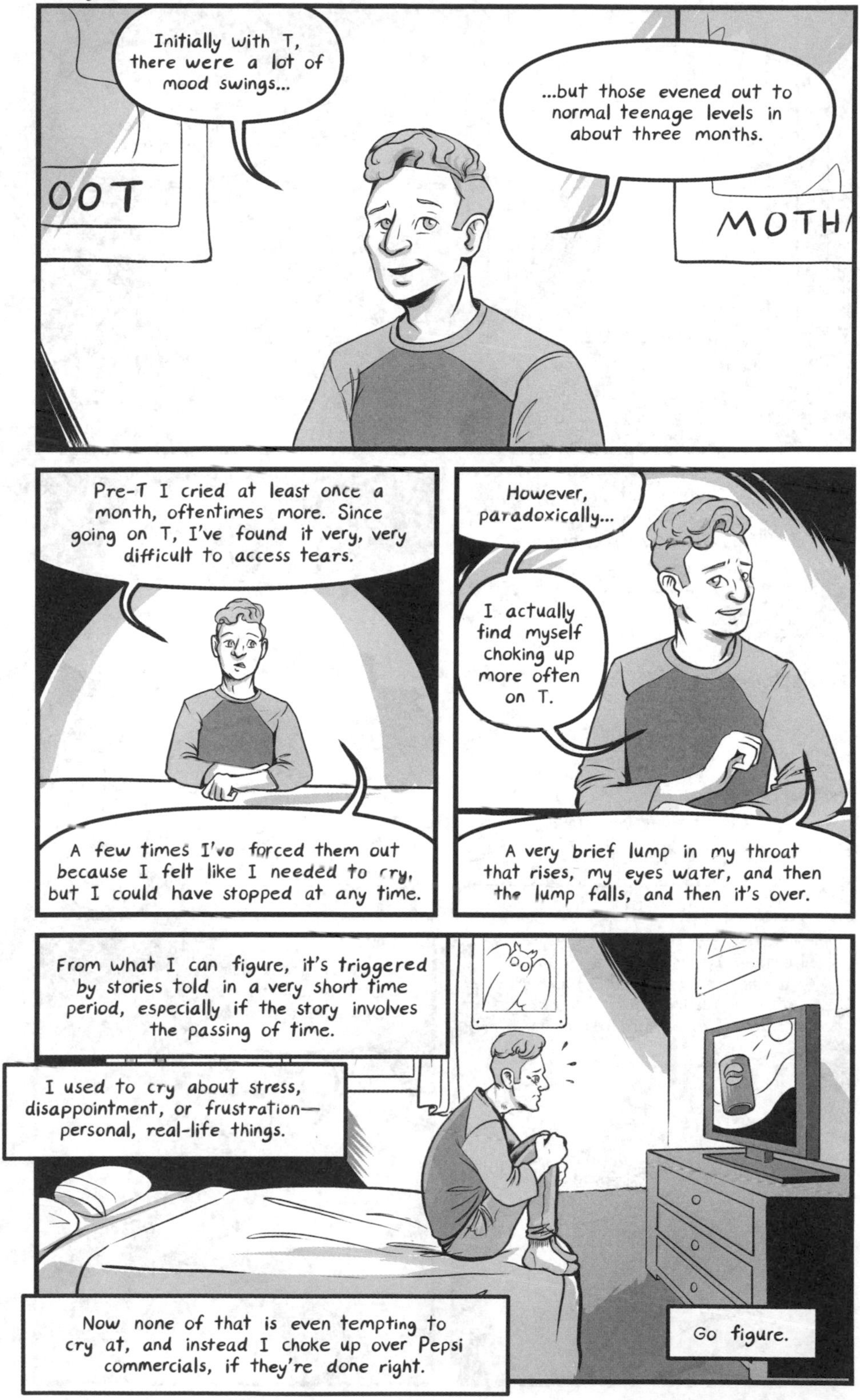
Initially with T, there were a lot of mood swings...
...but those evened out to normal teenage levels in about three months.
OOT
MOTH
Pre-T I cried at least once a month, oftentimes more. Since going on T, I've found it very, very difficult to access tears.
A few times I've forced them out because I felt like I needed to cry, but I could have stopped at any time.
However, paradoxically...
I actually find myself choking up more often on T.
A very brief lump in my throat that rises, my eyes water, and then the lump falls, and then it's over.
From what I can figure, it's triggered by stories told in a very short time period, especially if the story involves the passing of time.
I used to cry about stress, disappointment, or frustration— personal, real-life things.
Now none of that is even tempting to cry at, and instead I choke up over Pepsi commercials, if they're done right.
Go figure.

Mo, 2013

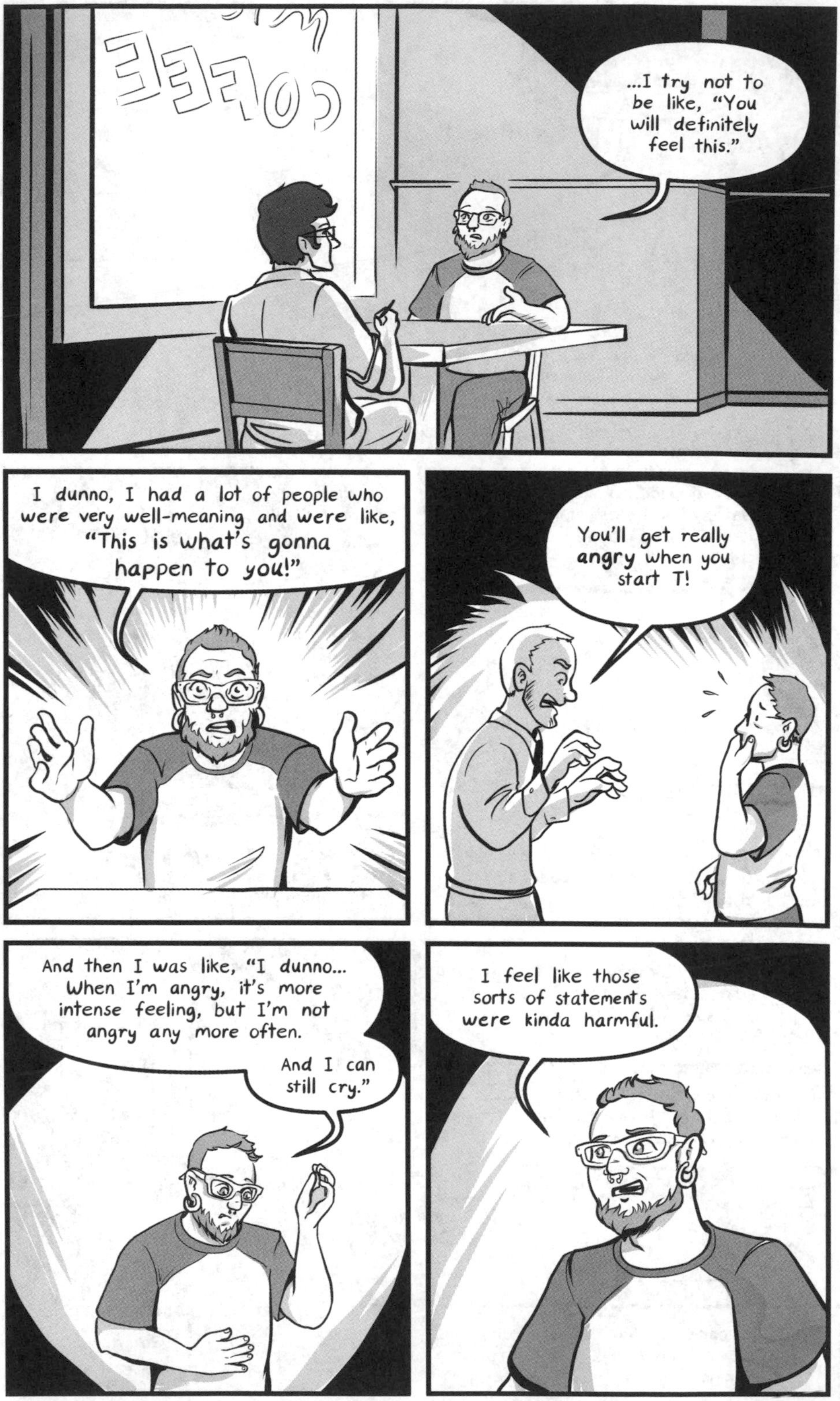
COFFEE
...I try not to be like, "You will definitely feel this."
I dunno, I had a lot of people who were very well-meaning and were like, "This is what's gonna happen to you!"
You'll get really angry when you start T!
And then I was like, "I dunno... When I'm angry, it's more intense feeling, but I'm not angry any more often.
And I can still cry."
I feel like those sorts of statements were kinda harmful.

Rhea, 2012

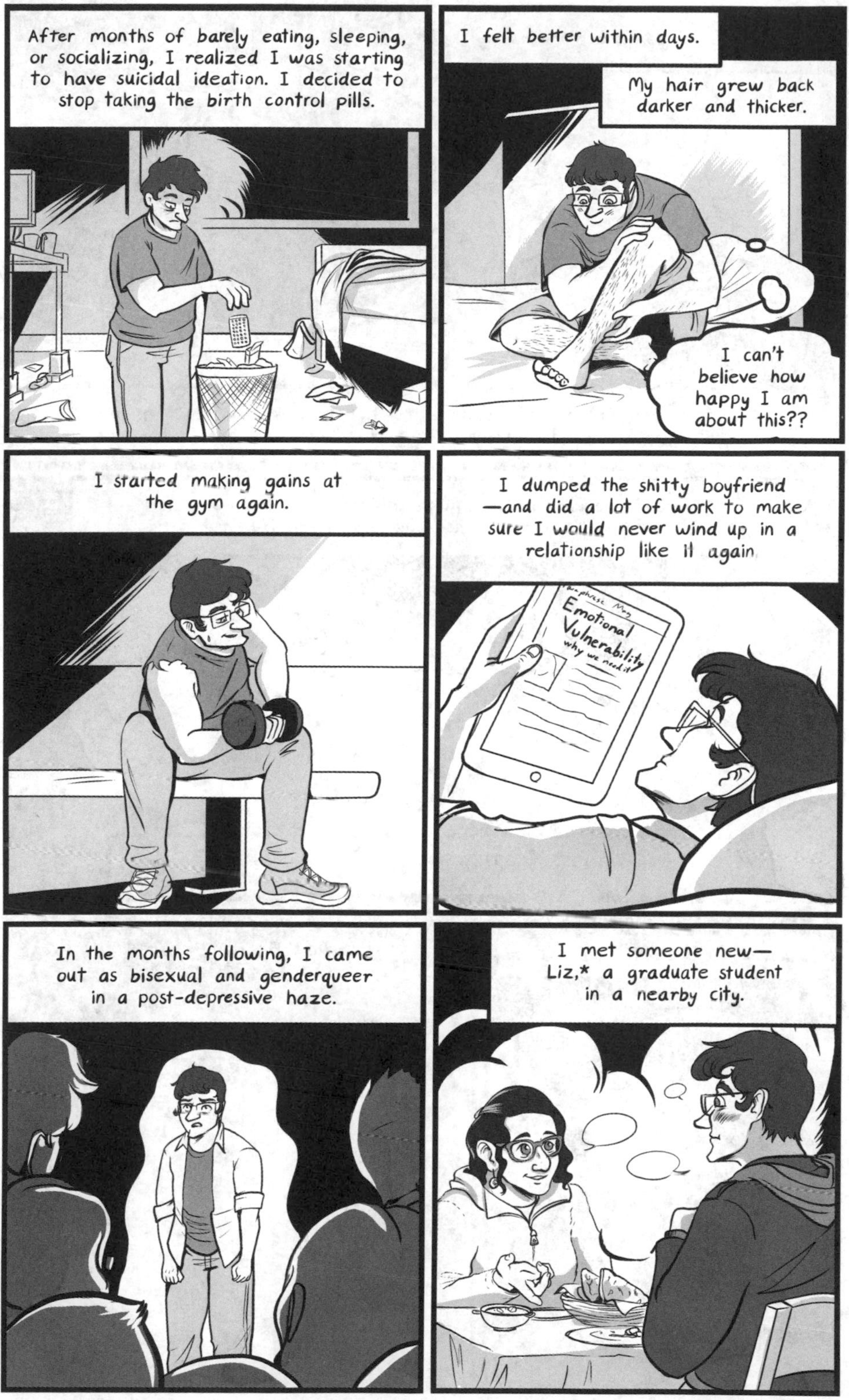
After months of barely eating, sleeping, or socializing, I realized I was starting to have suicidal ideation. I decided to stop taking the birth control pills.
I felt better within days.
My hair grew back darker and thicker.
I can't believe how happy I am about this??
I started making gains at the gym again.
I dumped the shitty boyfriend —and did a lot of work to make sure I would never wind up in a relationship like it again.
Emotional Vulnerability
why we need it
In the months following, I came out as bisexual and genderqueer in a post-depressive haze.
I met someone new— Liz,* a graduate student in a nearby city.

*Ze no longer goes by this name, but did at the time we met, and approved its use in this book.

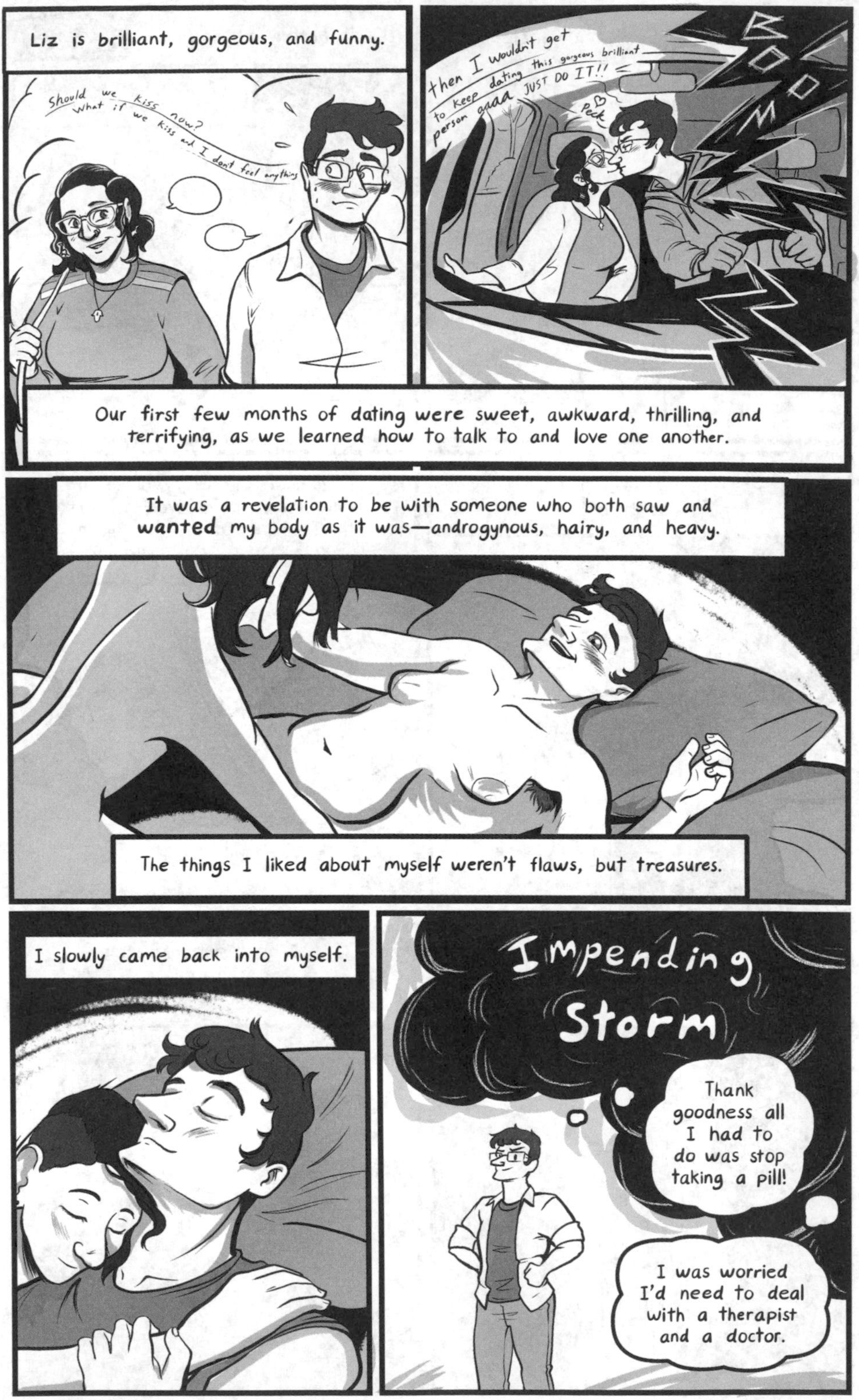
Liz is brilliant, gorgeous, and funny.
Should we kiss now? What if we kiss and I don't feel anything
then I wouldn't get to keep dating this gorgeous brilliant person aaaa JUST DO IT!!
Peck
BOOM
Our first few months of dating were sweet, awkward, thrilling, and terrifying, as we learned how to talk to and love one another.
It was a revelation to be with someone who both saw and **wanted** my body as it was—androgynous, hairy, and heavy.
The things I liked about myself weren't flaws, but treasures.
I slowly came back into myself.
Impending Storm
Thank goodness all I had to do was stop taking a pill!
I was worried I'd need to deal with a therapist and a doctor.

Rhea, 2013

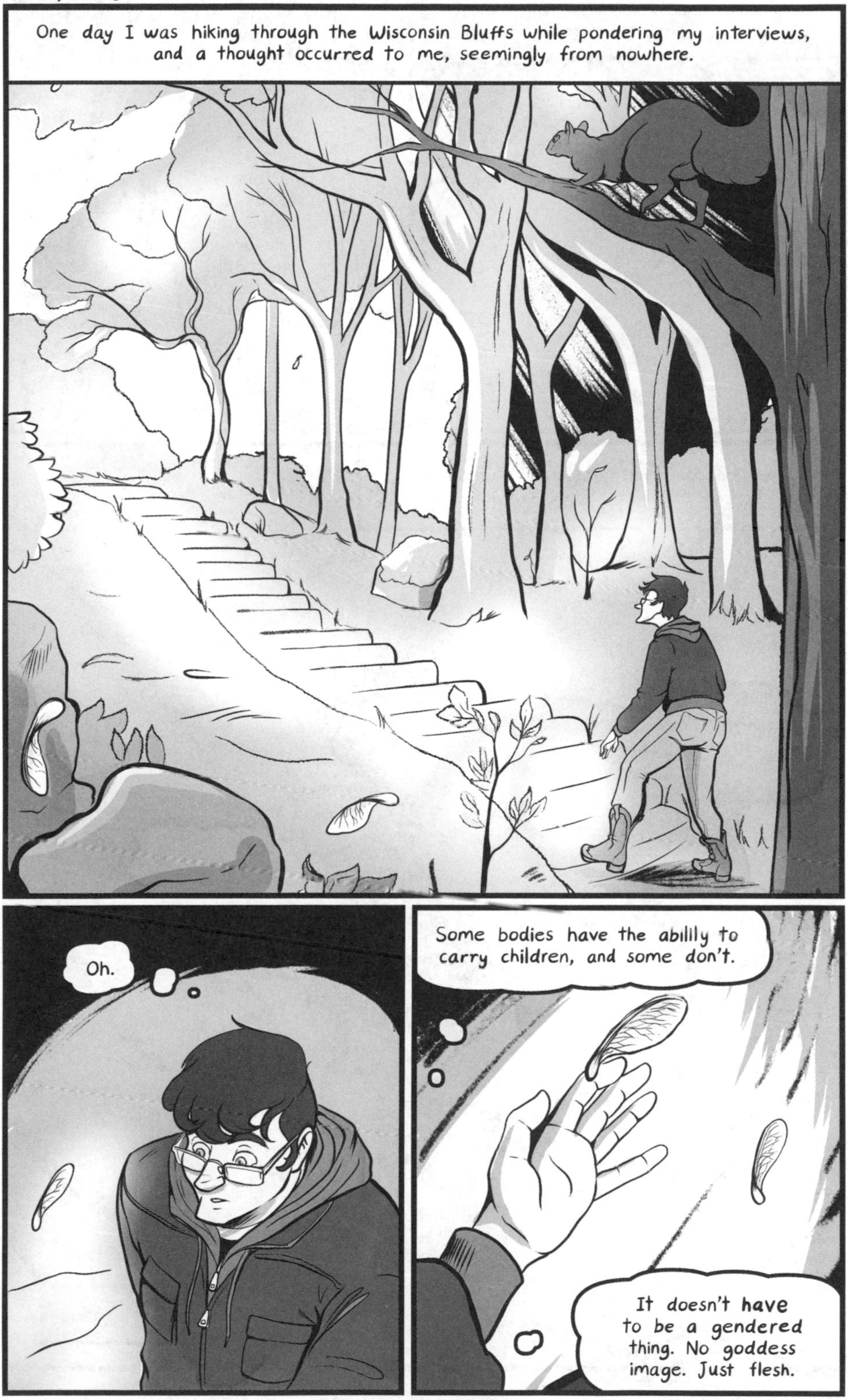

One day I was hiking through the Wisconsin Bluffs while pondering my interviews, and a thought occurred to me, seemingly from nowhere.
Oh.
Some bodies have the abilily to carry children, and some don't.
It doesn't **have** to be a gendered thing. No goddess image. Just flesh.

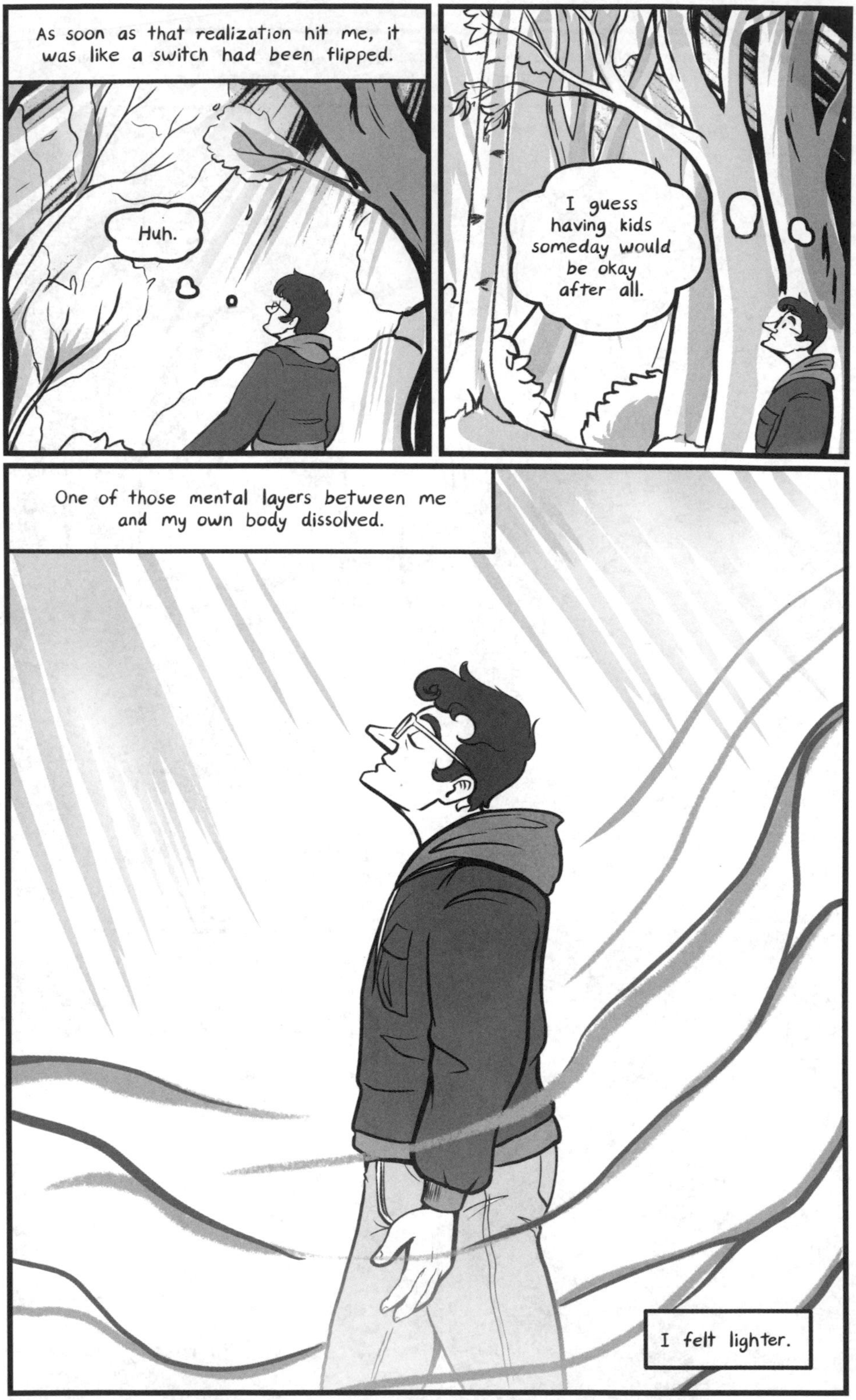
As soon as that realization hit me, it was like a switch had been flipped.
Huh.
I guess having kids someday would be okay after all.
One of those mental layers between me and my own body dissolved.
I felt lighter.

What is the difference between gender and sex?

Gerbil, 2012

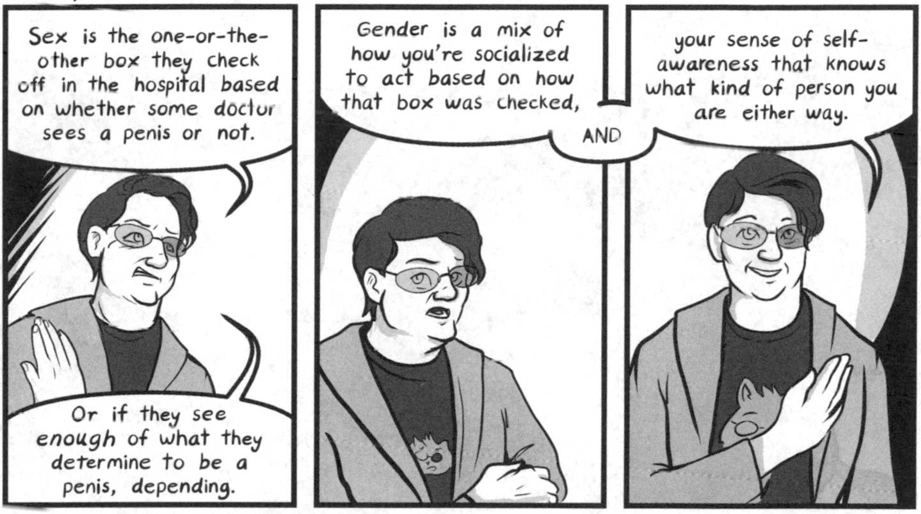
Sex is the one-or-the-other box they check off in the hospital based on whether some doctor sees a penis or not.
Or if they see *enough* of what they determine to be a penis, depending.
Gender is a mix of how you're socialized to act based on how that box was checked,
AND
your sense of self-awareness that knows what kind of person you are either way.

Mo, 2013

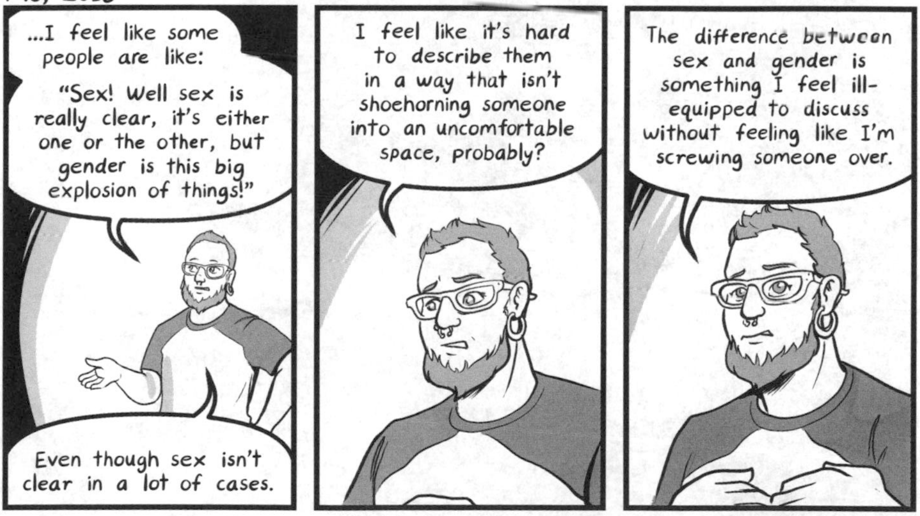
...I feel like some people are like:
"Sex! Well sex is really clear, it's either one or the other, but gender is this big explosion of things!"
Even though sex isn't clear in a lot of cases.
I feel like it's hard to describe them in a way that isn't shoehorning someone into an uncomfortable space, probably?
The difference betwoen sex and gender is something I feel ill-equipped to discuss without feeling like I'm screwing someone over.

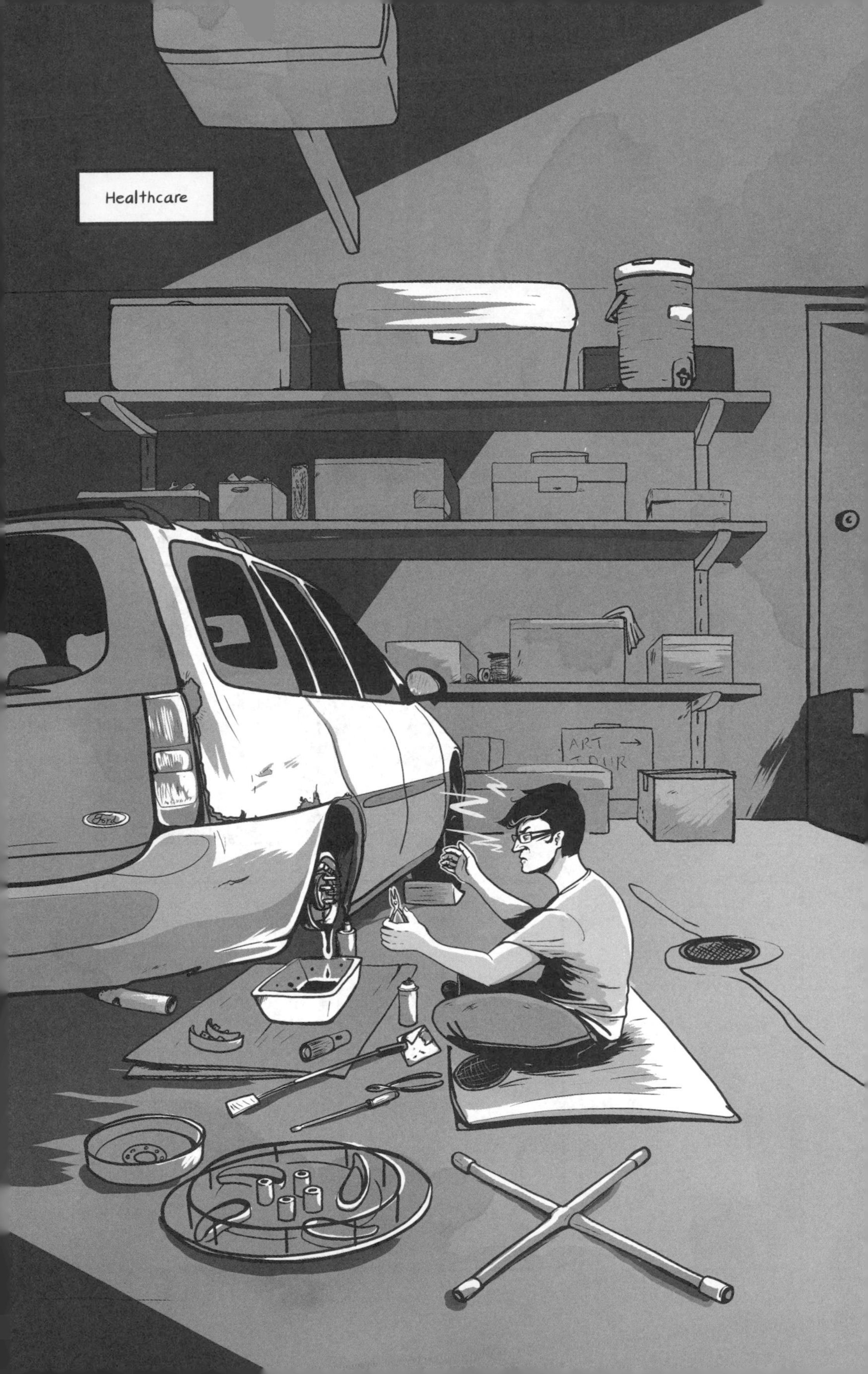
Healthcare
ART →
TOUR

Rhea, 2017

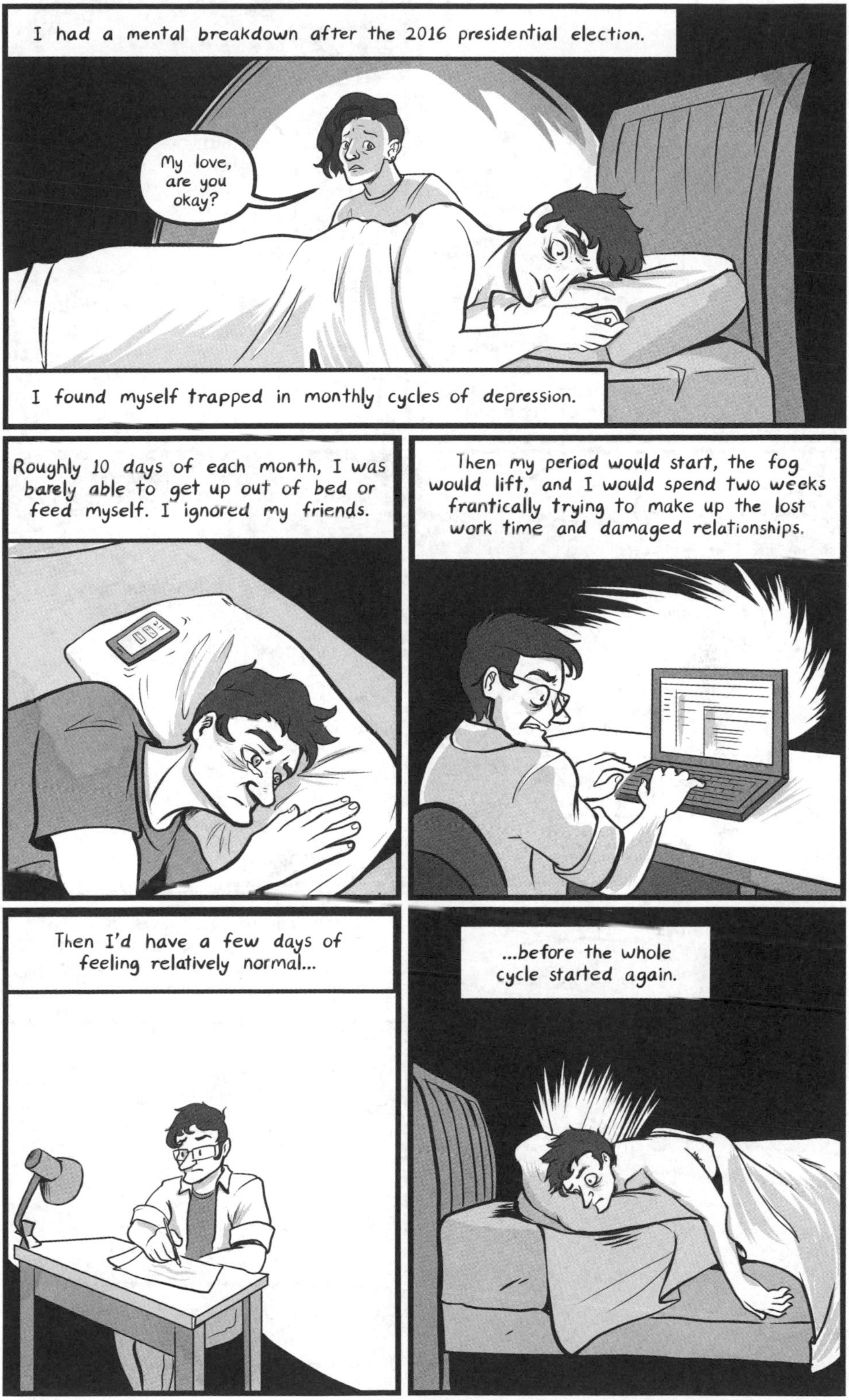
I had a mental breakdown after the 2016 presidential election.
My love, are you okay?
I found myself trapped in monthly cycles of depression.
Roughly 10 days of each month, I was barely able to get up out of bed or feed myself. I ignored my friends.
Then my period would start, the fog would lift, and I would spend two weeks frantically trying to make up the lost work time and damaged relationships.
Then I'd have a few days of feeling relatively normal...
...before the whole cycle started again.

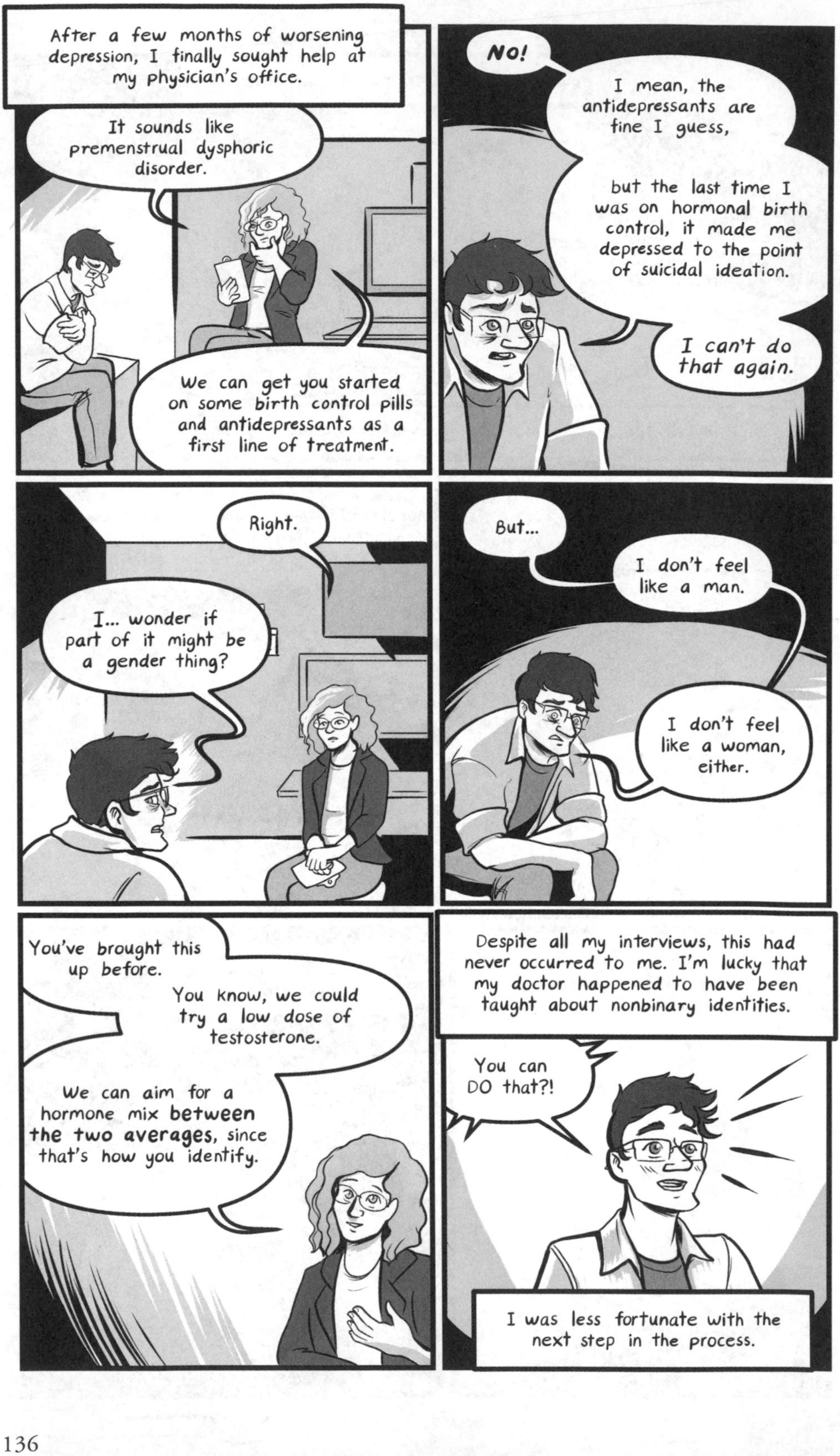
After a few months of worsening depression, I finally sought help at my physician's office.
It sounds like premenstrual dysphoric disorder.
We can get you started on some birth control pills and antidepressants as a first line of treatment.
NO!
I mean, the antidepressants are fine I guess,
but the last time I was on hormonal birth control, it made me depressed to the point of suicidal ideation.
I can't do that again.
Right.
I... wonder if part of it might be a gender thing?
But...
I don't feel like a man.
I don't feel like a woman, either.
You've brought this up before.
You know, we could try a low dose of testosterone.
We can aim for a hormone mix between the two averages, since that's how you identify.
Despite all my interviews, this had never occurred to me. I'm lucky that my doctor happened to have been taught about nonbinary identities.
You can DO that?!
I was less fortunate with the next step in the process.

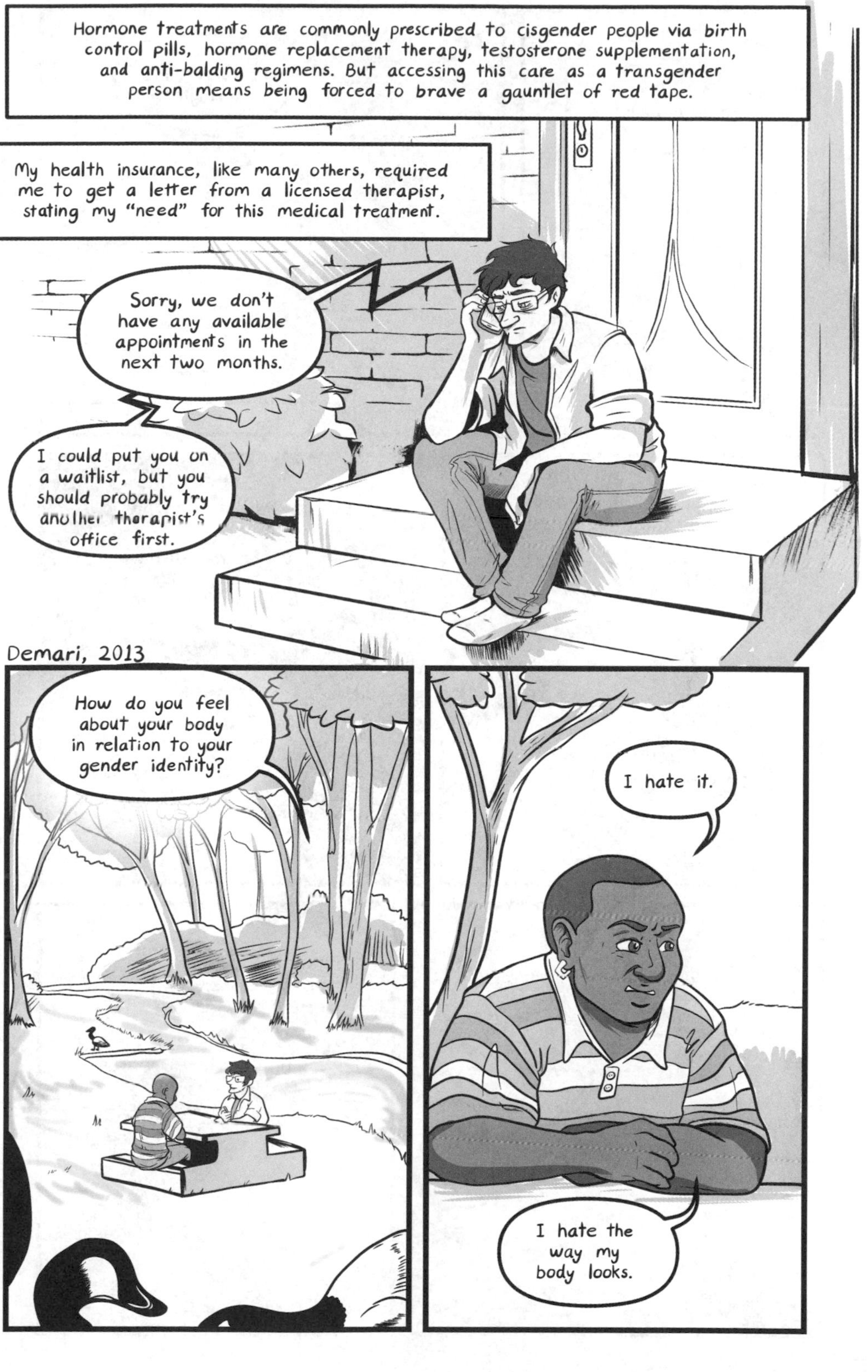

Hormone treatments are commonly prescribed to cisgender people via birth control pills, hormone replacement therapy, testosterone supplementation, and anti-balding regimens. But accessing this care as a transgender person means being forced to brave a gauntlet of red tape.
My health insurance, like many others, required me to get a letter from a licensed therapist, stating my "need" for this medical treatment.
Sorry, we don't have any available appointments in the next two months.
I could put you on a waitlist, but you should probably try another therapist's office first.
Demari, 2013
How do you feel about your body in relation to your gender identity?
I hate it.
I hate the way my body looks.

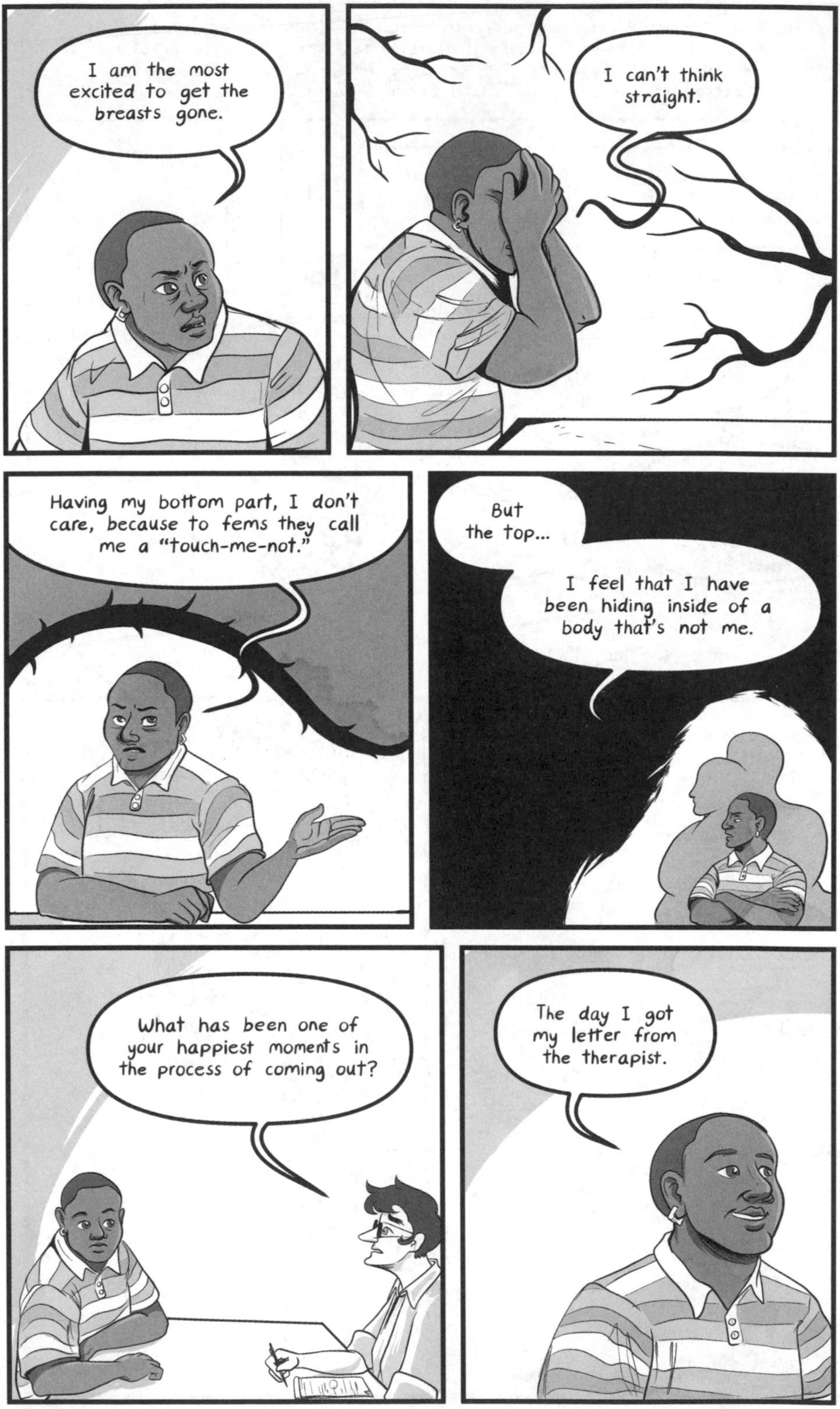
I am the most excited to get the breasts gone.
I can't think straight.
Having my bottom part, I don't care, because to fems they call me a "touch-me-not."
But the top...
I feel that I have been hiding inside of a body that's not me.
What has been one of your happiest moments in the process of coming out?
The day I got my letter from the therapist.

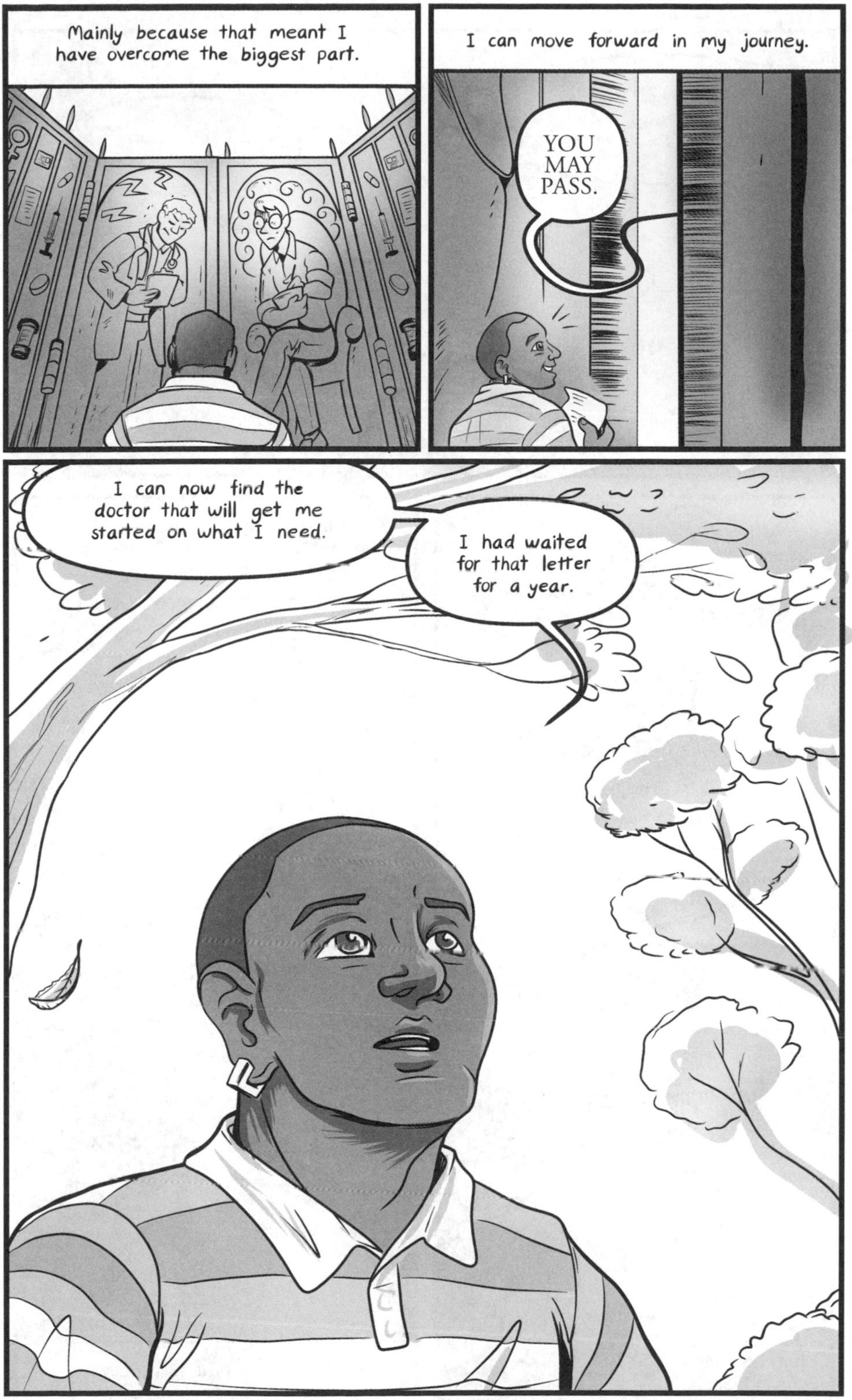
Mainly because that meant I have overcome the biggest part.
I can move forward in my journey.
YOU MAY PASS.
I can now find the doctor that will get me started on what I need.
I had waited for that letter for a year.

Anonymous, 2012

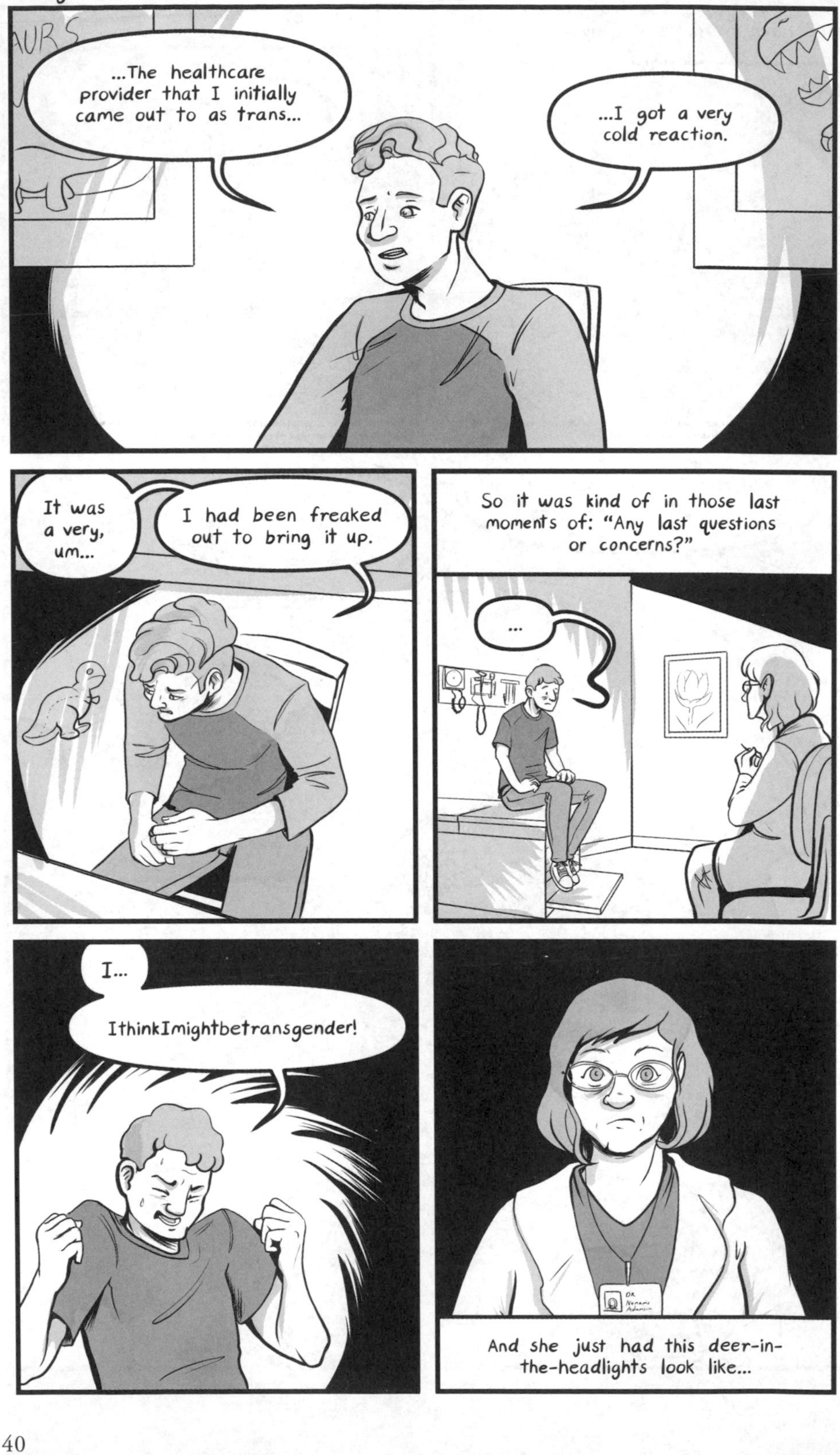
...The healthcare provider that I initially came out to as trans...
...I got a very cold reaction.
It was a very, um...
I had been freaked out to bring it up.
So it was kind of in those last moments of: "Any last questions or concerns?"
...
I...
IthinkImightbetransgender!
And she just had this deer-in-the-headlights look like...

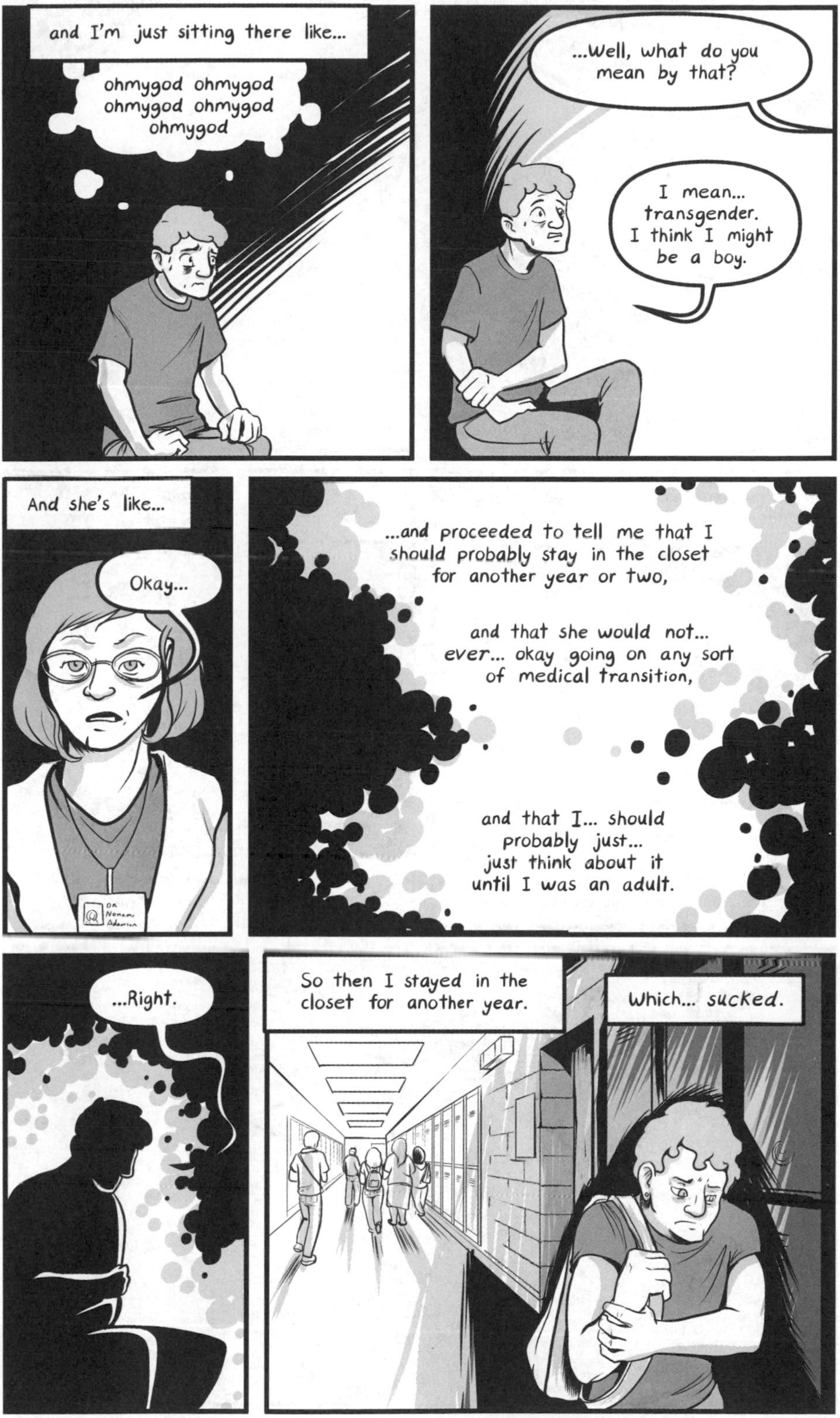
and I'm just sitting there like...
ohmygod ohmygod ohmygod ohmygod ohmygod
...Well, what do you mean by that?
I mean... transgender. I think I might be a boy.
And she's like...
Okay...
DR. Noname Adamson
...and proceeded to tell me that I should probably stay in the closet for another year or two,
and that she would not... ever... okay going on any sort of medical transition,
and that I... should probably just... just think about it until I was an adult.
...Right.
So then I stayed in the closet for another year.
Which... sucked.

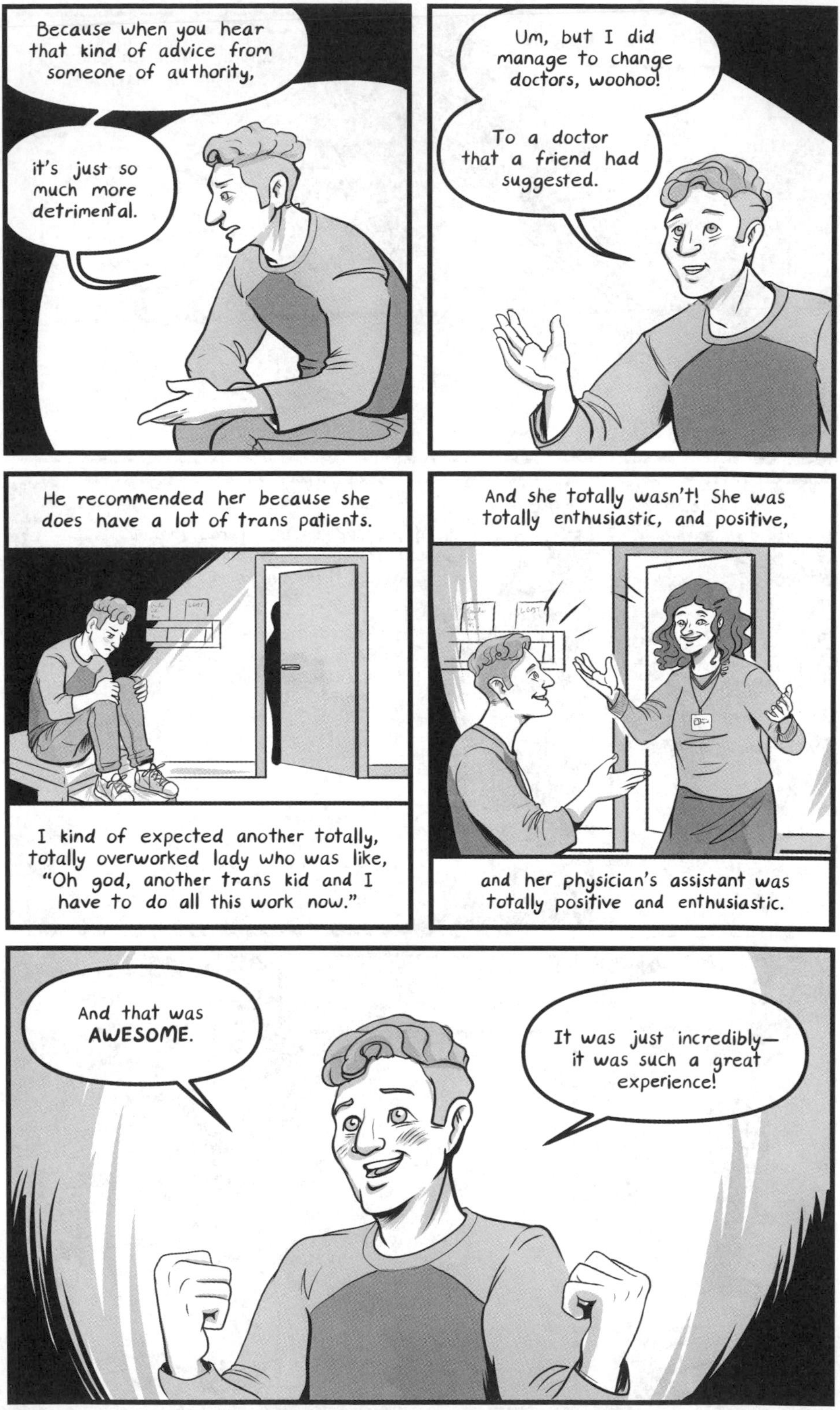
Because when you hear that kind of advice from someone of authority,
it's just so much more detrimental.
Um, but I did manage to change doctors, woohoo!
To a doctor that a friend had suggested.
He recommended her because she does have a lot of trans patients.
I kind of expected another totally, totally overworked lady who was like, "Oh god, another trans kid and I have to do all this work now."
And she totally wasn't! She was totally enthusiastic, and positive,
and her physician's assistant was totally positive and enthusiastic.
And that was **AWESOME**.
It was just incredibly— it was such a great experience!

Corrine, 2011

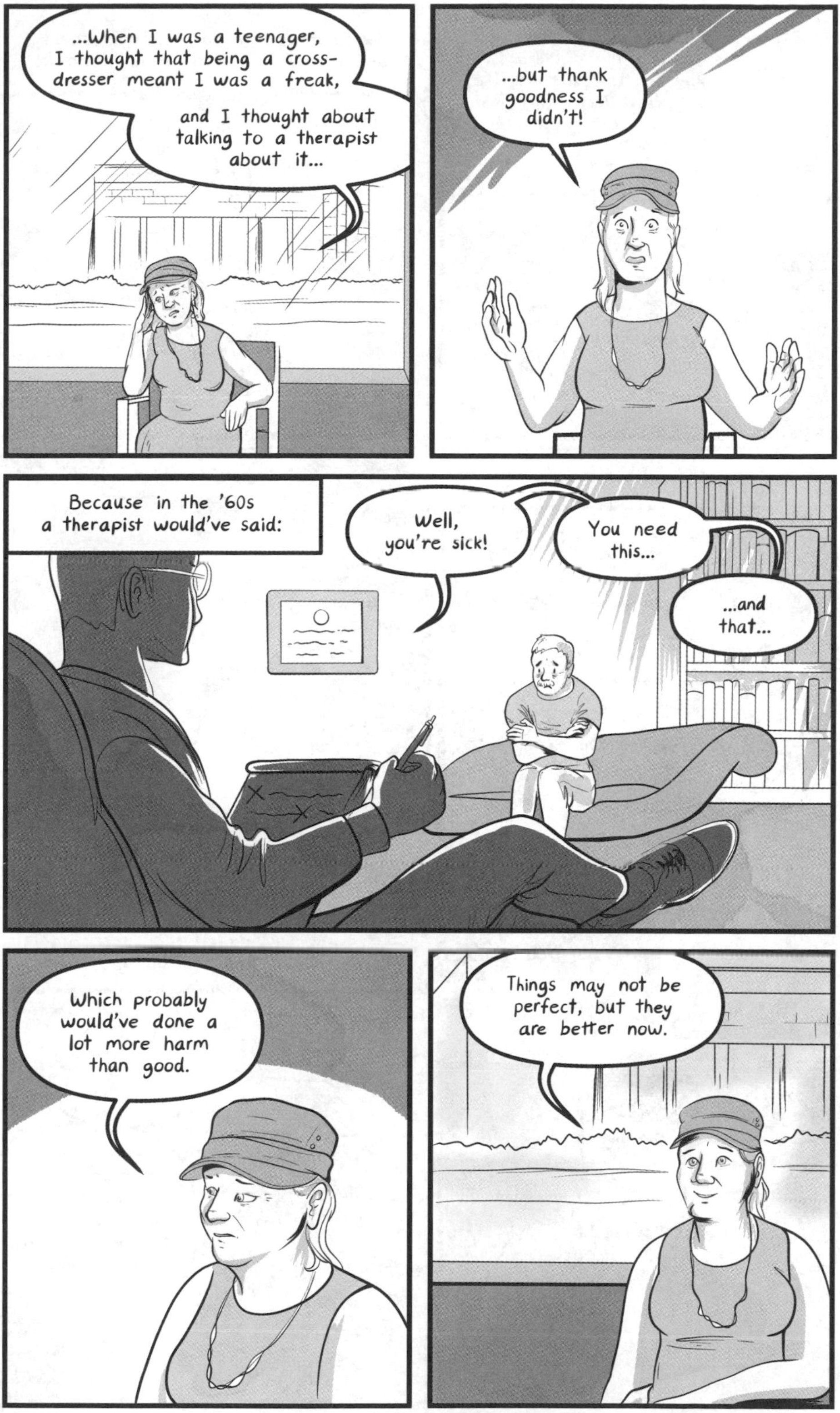

...When I was a teenager, I thought that being a cross-dresser meant I was a freak,
and I thought about talking to a therapist about it...
...but thank goodness I didn't!
Because in the '60s a therapist would've said:
Well, you're sick!
You need this...
...and that...
Which probably would've done a lot more harm than good.
Things may not be perfect, but they are better now.

Rhea, 2017

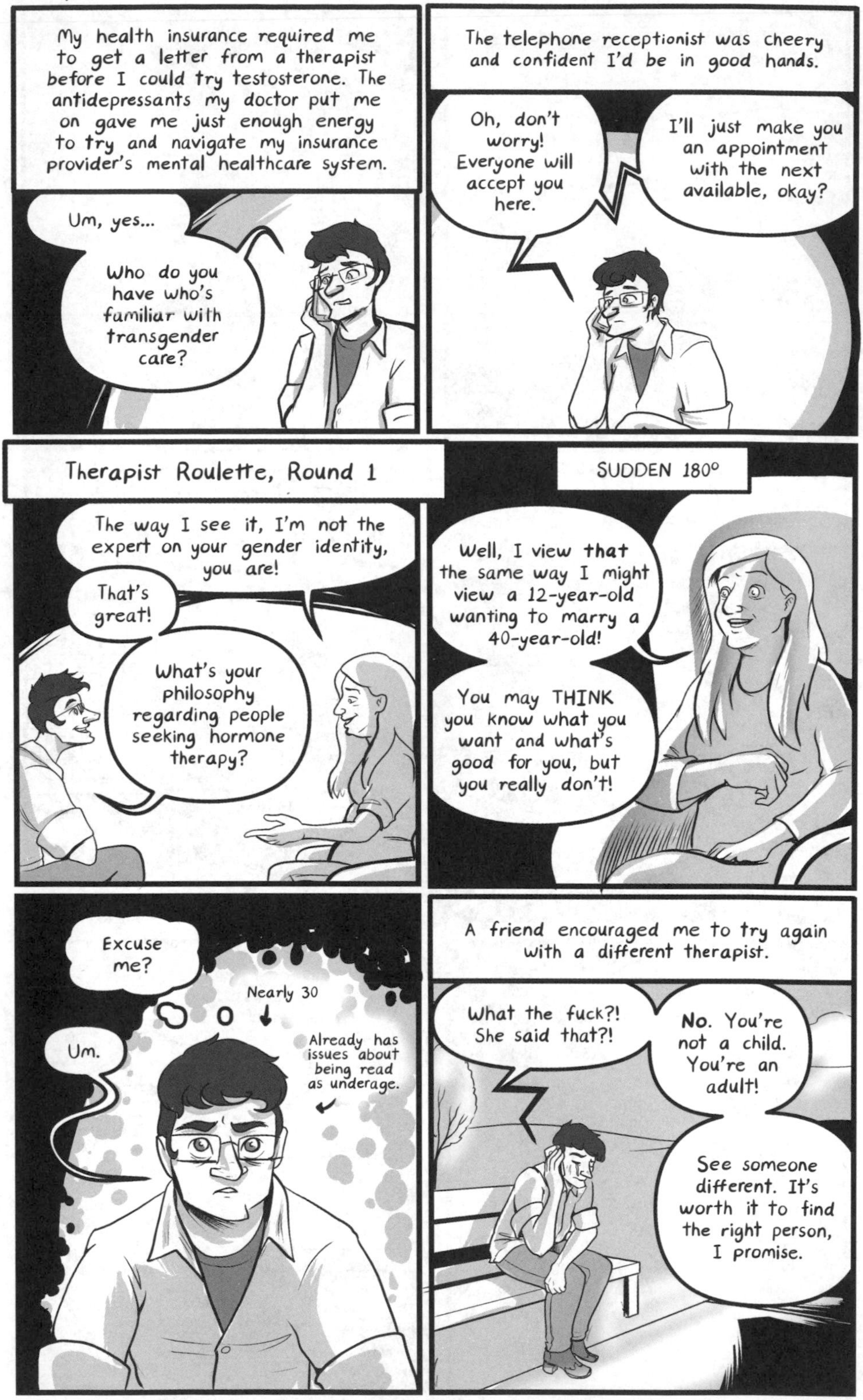
My health insurance required me to get a letter from a therapist before I could try testosterone. The antidepressants my doctor put me on gave me just enough energy to try and navigate my insurance provider's mental healthcare system.
Um, yes...
Who do you have who's familiar with transgender care?
The telephone receptionist was cheery and confident I'd be in good hands.
Oh, don't worry! Everyone will accept you here.
I'll just make you an appointment with the next available, okay?
Therapist Roulette, Round 1
The way I see it, I'm not the expert on your gender identity, you are!
That's great!
What's your philosophy regarding people seeking hormone therapy?
SUDDEN 180°
Well, I view that the same way I might view a 12-year-old wanting to marry a 40-year-old!
You may THINK you know what you want and what's good for you, but you really don't!
Excuse me?
Um.
Nearly 30
Already has issues about being read as underage.
A friend encouraged me to try again with a different therapist.
What the fuck?! She said that?!
No. You're not a child. You're an adult!
See someone different. It's worth it to find the right person, I promise.

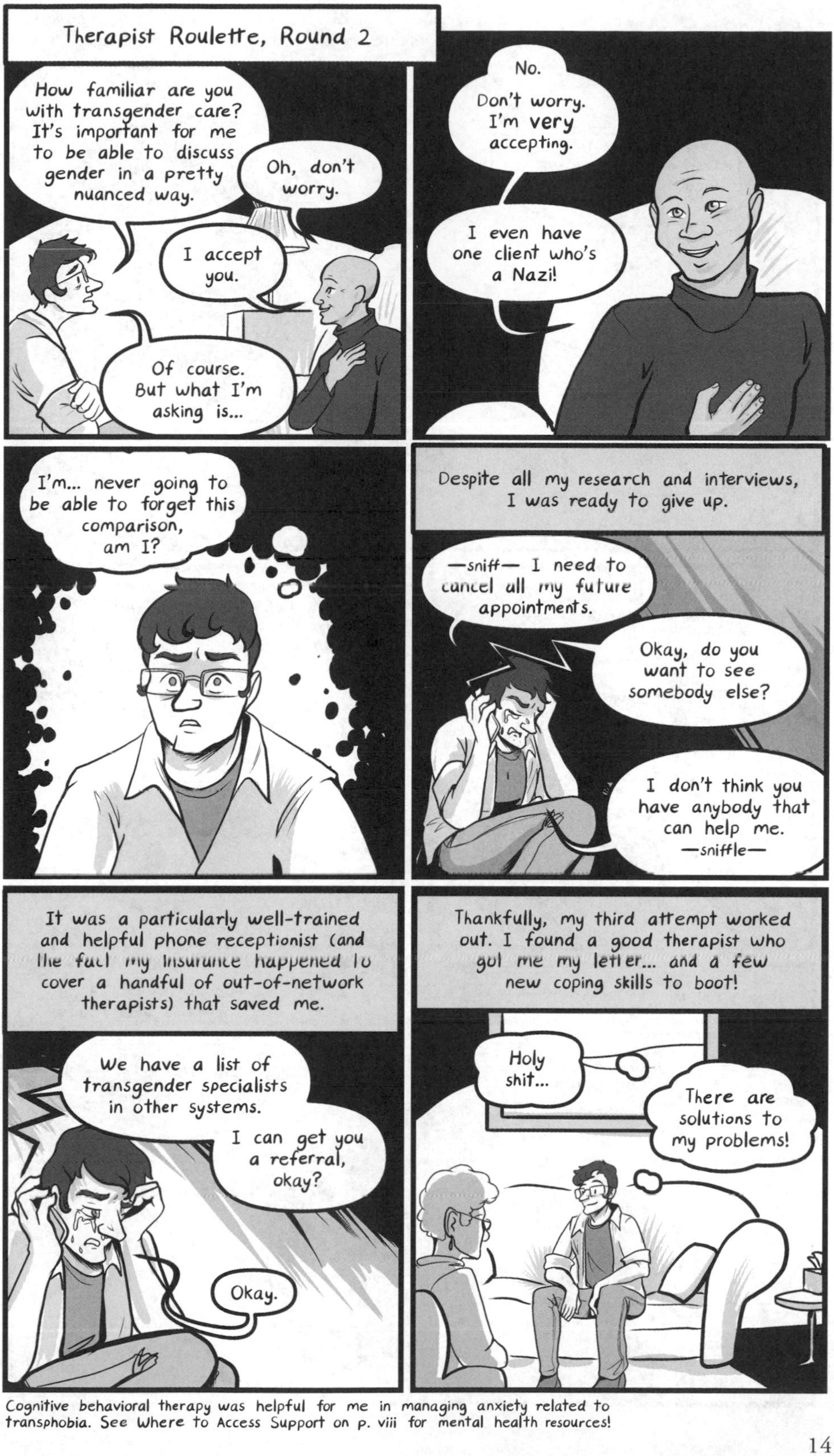
Therapist Roulette, Round 2
How familiar are you with transgender care? It's important for me to be able to discuss gender in a pretty nuanced way.
Oh, don't worry.
I accept you.
Of course. But what I'm asking is...
No.
Don't worry. I'm very accepting.
I even have one client who's a Nazi!
I'm... never going to be able to forget this comparison, am I?
Despite all my research and interviews, I was ready to give up.
—sniff— I need to cancel all my future appointments.
Okay, do you want to see somebody else?
I don't think you have anybody that can help me. —sniffle—
It was a particularly well-trained and helpful phone receptionist (and the fact my insurance happened to cover a handful of out-of-network therapists) that saved me.
We have a list of transgender specialists in other systems.
I can get you a referral, okay?
Okay.
Thankfully, my third attempt worked out. I found a good therapist who got me my letter... and a few new coping skills to boot!
Holy shit...
There are solutions to my problems!

Cognitive behavioral therapy was helpful for me in managing anxiety related to transphobia. See Where to Access Support on p. viii for mental health resources!

Superheroine, 2015

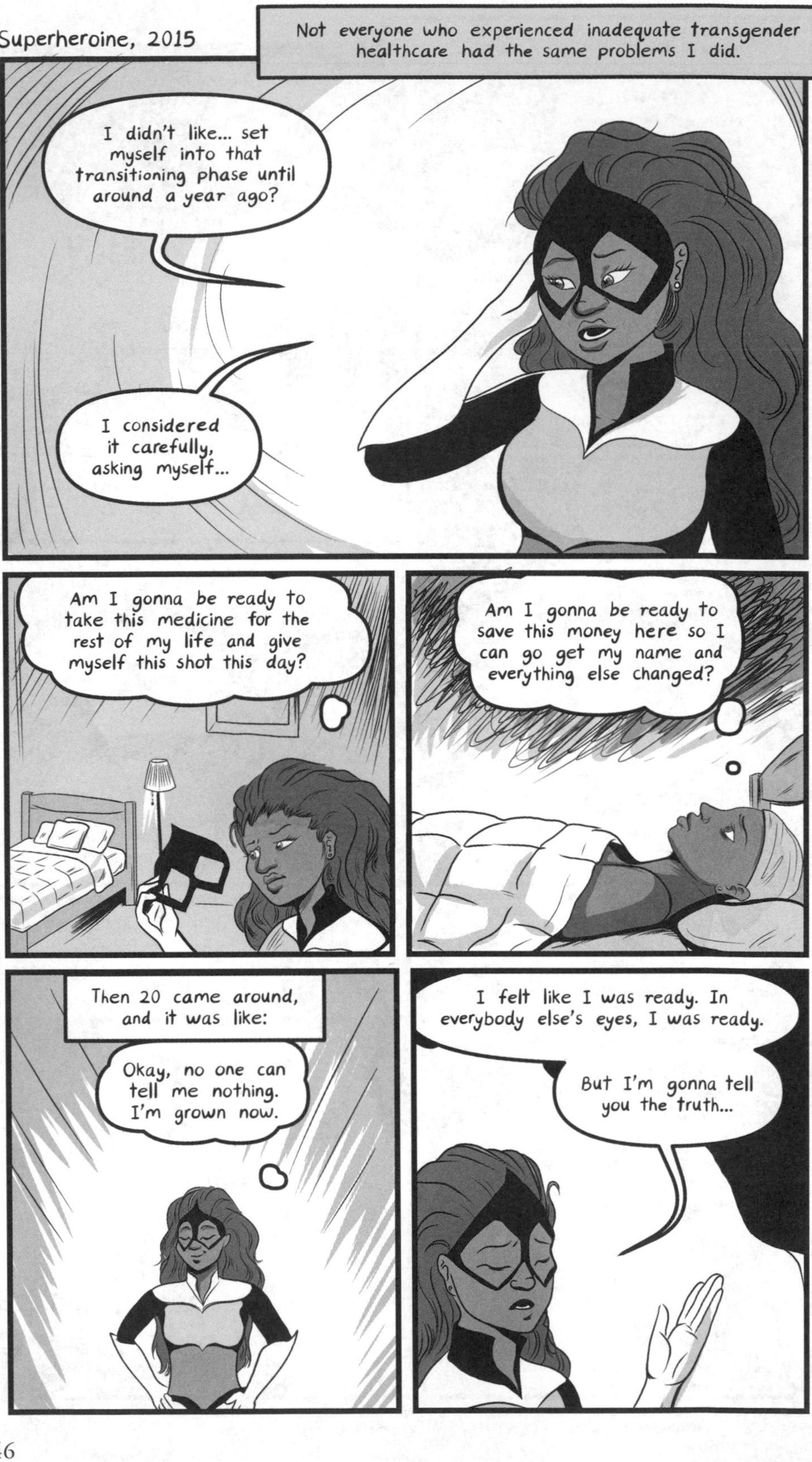
Not everyone who experienced inadequate transgender healthcare had the same problems I did.
I didn't like... set myself into that transitioning phase until around a year ago?
I considered it carefully, asking myself...
Am I gonna be ready to take this medicine for the rest of my life and give myself this shot this day?
Am I gonna be ready to save this money here so I can go get my name and everything else changed?
Then 20 came around, and it was like:
Okay, no one can tell me nothing. I'm grown now.
I felt like I was ready. In everybody else's eyes, I was ready.
But I'm gonna tell you the truth...

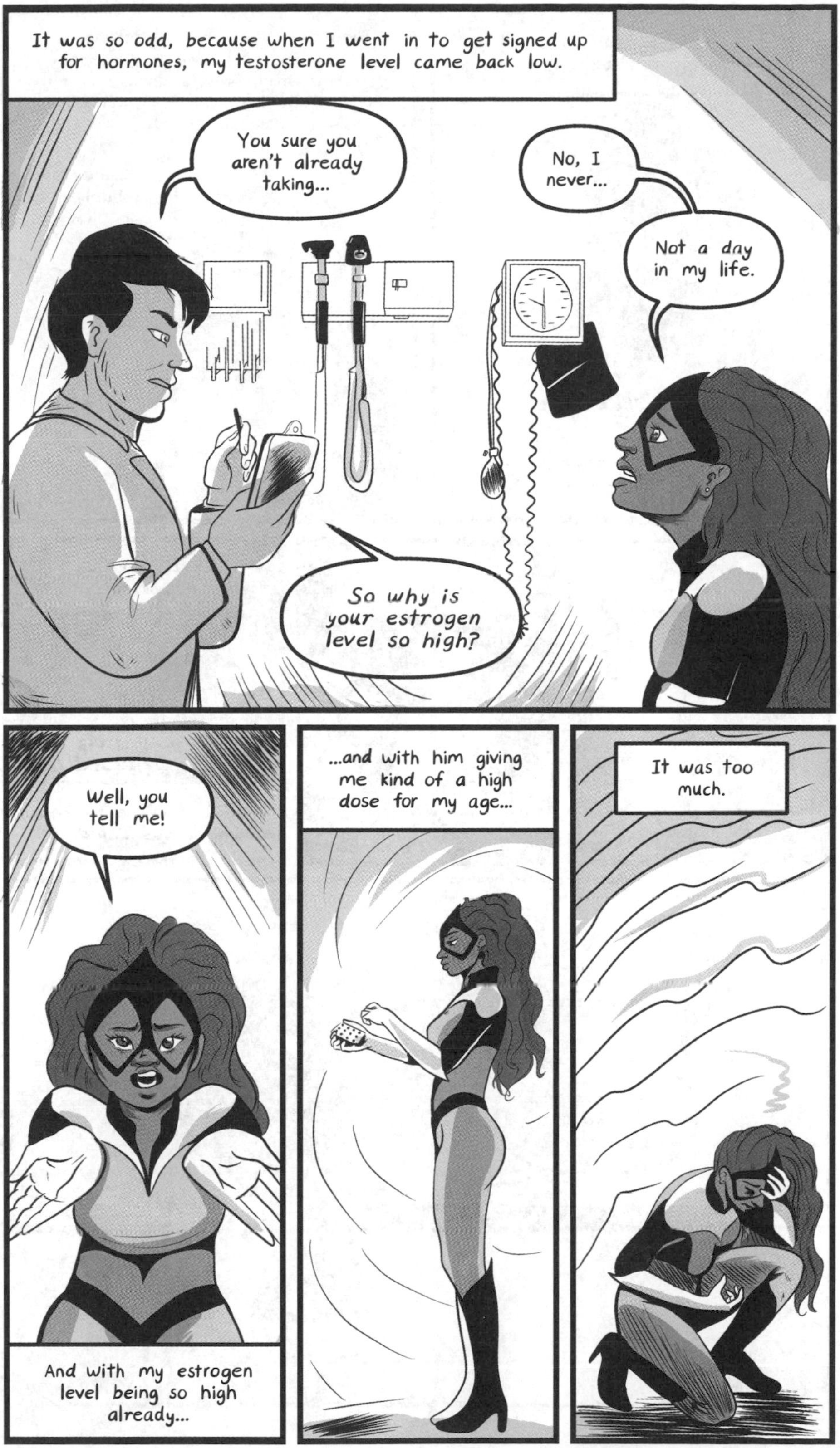
It was so odd, because when I went in to get signed up for hormones, my testosterone level came back low.
You sure you aren't already taking...
No, I never...
Not a day in my life.
So why is your estrogen level so high?
Well, you tell me!
And with my estrogen level being so high already...
...and with him giving me kind of a high dose for my age...
It was too much.

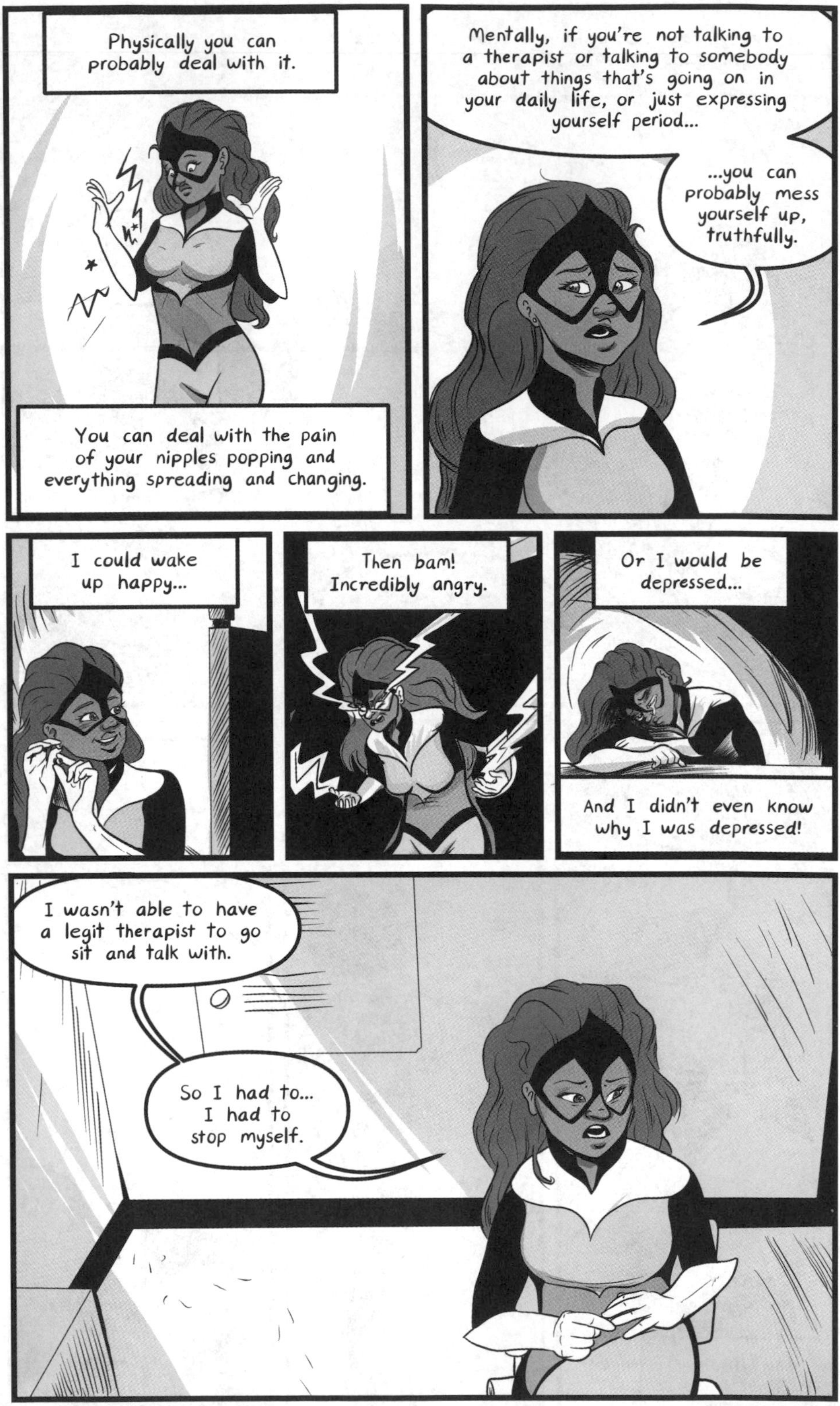

Physically you can probably deal with it.
You can deal with the pain of your nipples popping and everything spreading and changing.
Mentally, if you're not talking to a therapist or talking to somebody about things that's going on in your daily life, or just expressing yourself period...
...you can probably mess yourself up, truthfully.
I could wake up happy...
Then bam! Incredibly angry.
Or I would be depressed...
And I didn't even know why I was depressed!
I wasn't able to have a legit therapist to go sit and talk with.
So I had to... I had to stop myself.

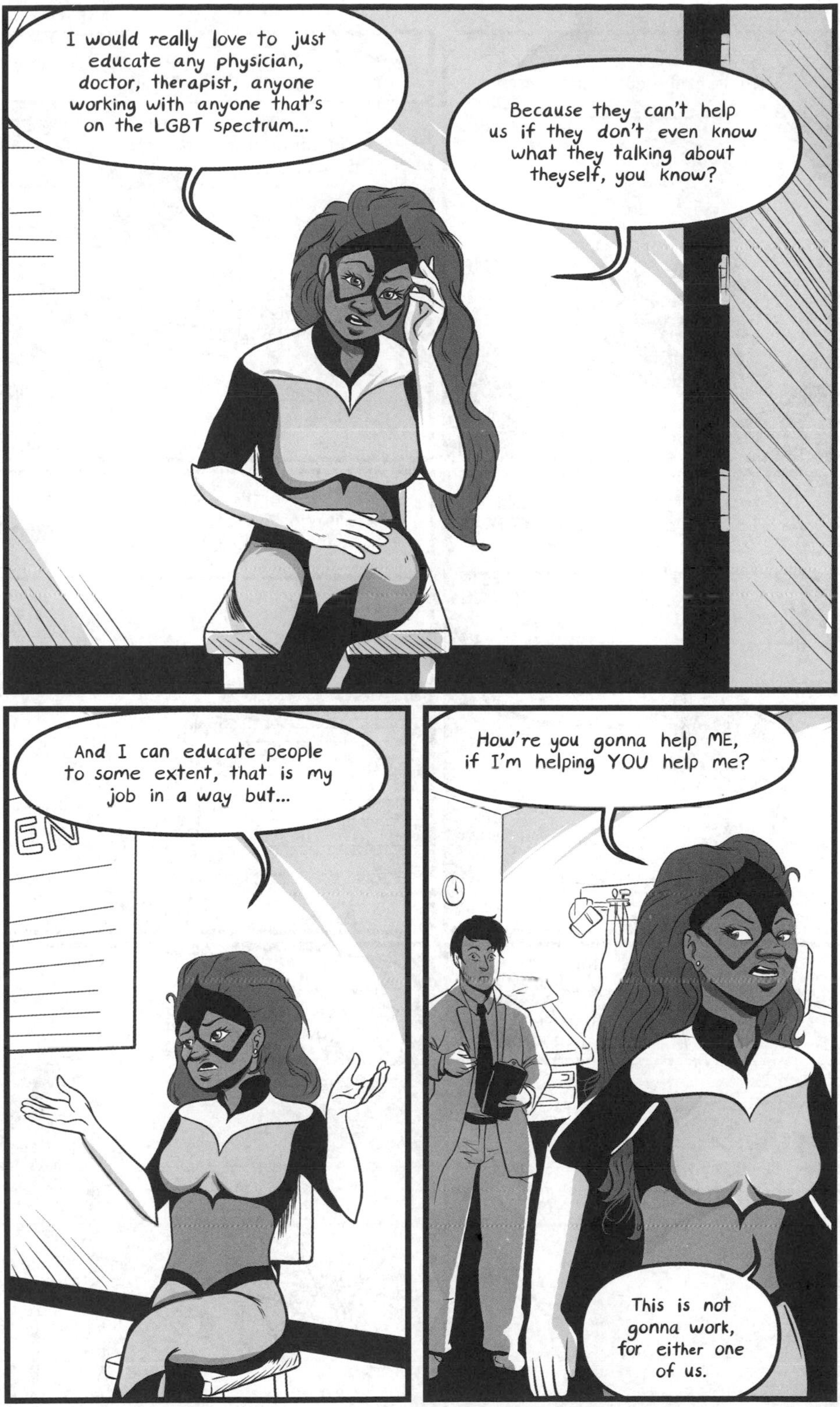
I would really love to just educate any physician, doctor, therapist, anyone working with anyone that's on the LGBT spectrum...
Because they can't help us if they don't even know what they talking about theyself, you know?
And I can educate people to some extent, that is my job in a way but...
How're you gonna help ME, if I'm helping YOU help me?
This is not gonna work, for either one of us.

Cassie, 2013

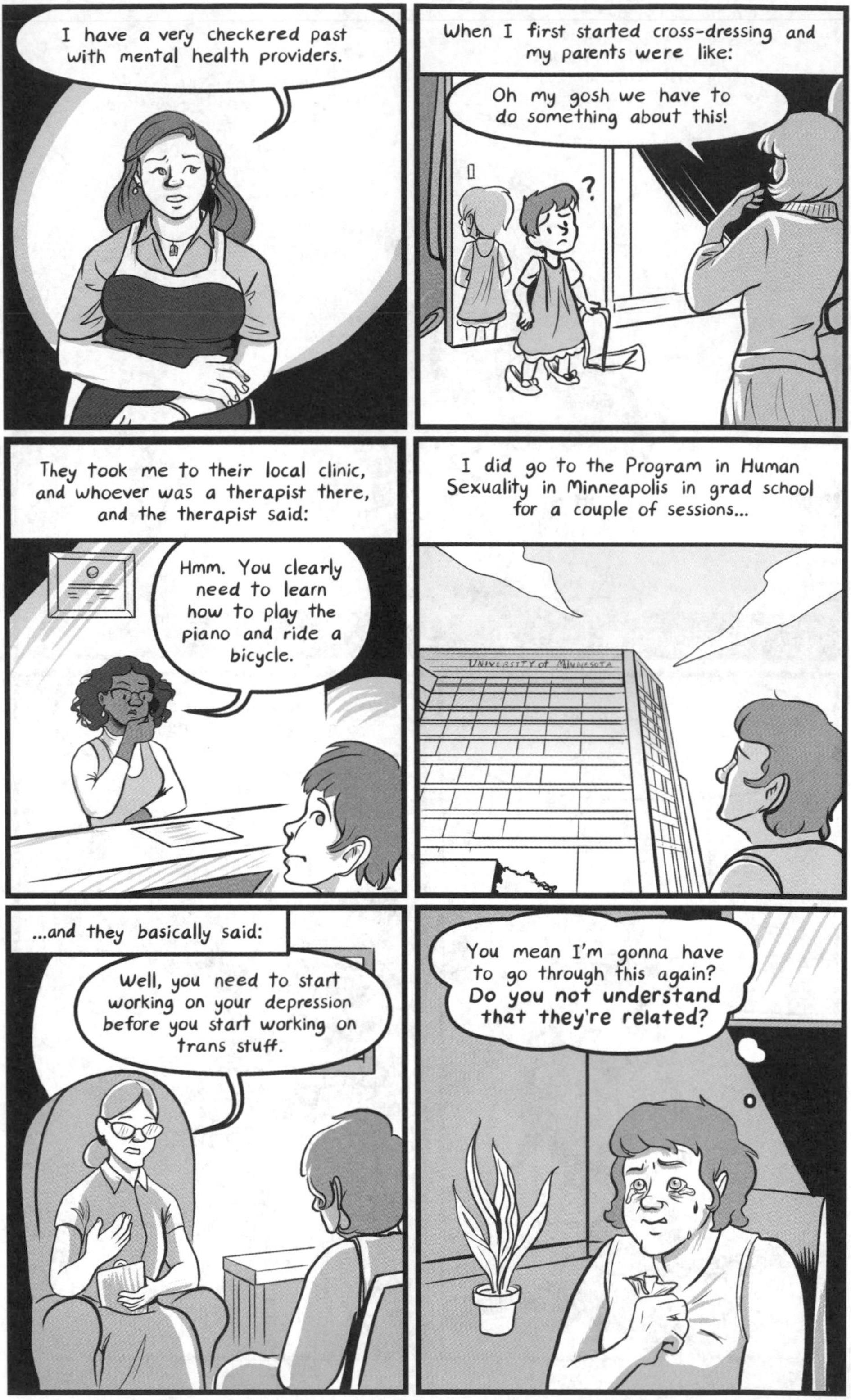
I have a very checkered past with mental health providers.
When I first started cross-dressing and my parents were like:
Oh my gosh we have to do something about this!
?
They took me to their local clinic, and whoever was a therapist there, and the therapist said:
Hmm. You clearly need to learn how to play the piano and ride a bicycle.
I did go to the Program in Human Sexuality in Minneapolis in grad school for a couple of sessions...
UNIVERSITY of MINNESOTA
...and they basically said:
Well, you need to start working on your depression before you start working on trans stuff.
You mean I'm gonna have to go through this again? **Do you not understand that they're related?**

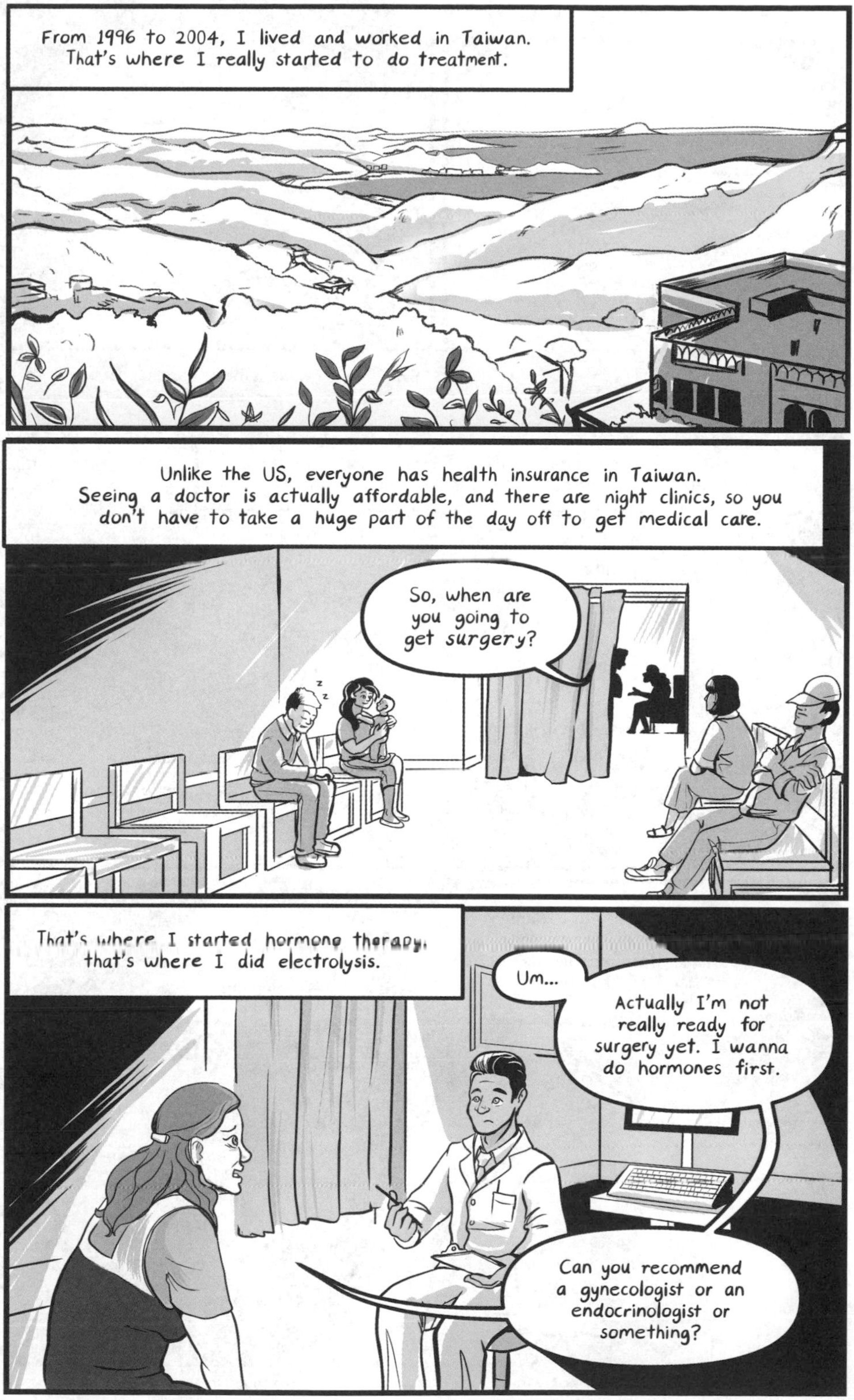
From 1996 to 2004, I lived and worked in Taiwan. That's where I really started to do treatment.
Unlike the US, everyone has health insurance in Taiwan. Seeing a doctor is actually affordable, and there are night clinics, so you don't have to take a huge part of the day off to get medical care.
So, when are you going to get *surgery*?
That's where I started hormone therapy, that's where I did electrolysis.
Um...
Actually I'm not really ready for surgery yet. I wanna do hormones first.
Can you recommend a gynecologist or an endocrinologist or something?

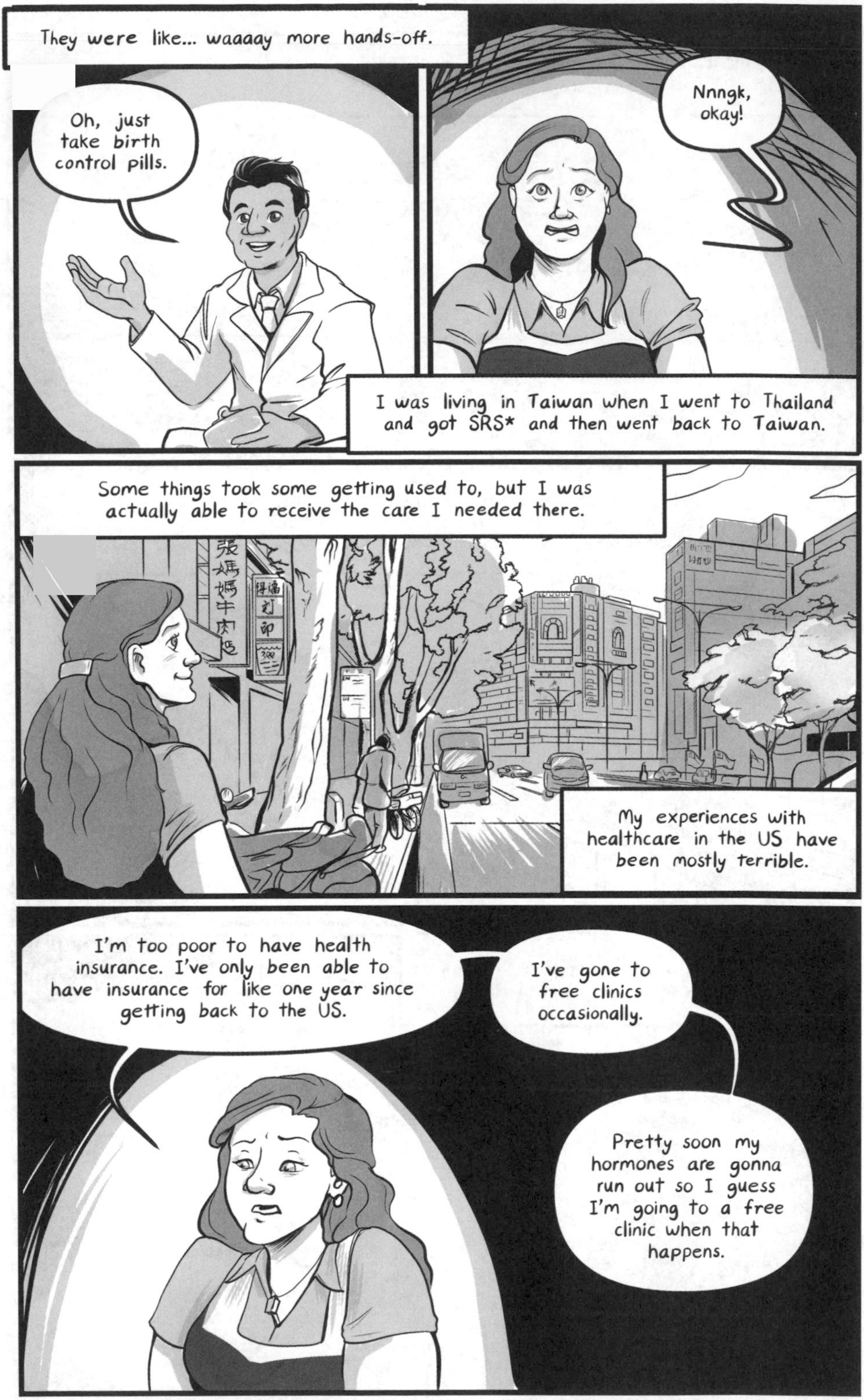
They were like... waaaay more hands-off.
Oh, just take birth control pills.
Nnngk, okay!
I was living in Taiwan when I went to Thailand and got SRS* and then went back to Taiwan.
Some things took some getting used to, but I was actually able to receive the care I needed there.
My experiences with healthcare in the US have been mostly terrible.
I'm too poor to have health insurance. I've only been able to have insurance for like one year since getting back to the US.
I've gone to free clinics occasionally.
Pretty soon my hormones are gonna run out so I guess I'm going to a free clinic when that happens.

*SRS here refers to sex reassignment surgery, also known as gender confirmation surgery.

Was it worth the pain and effort for me to access transgender care?

Rhea, 2017

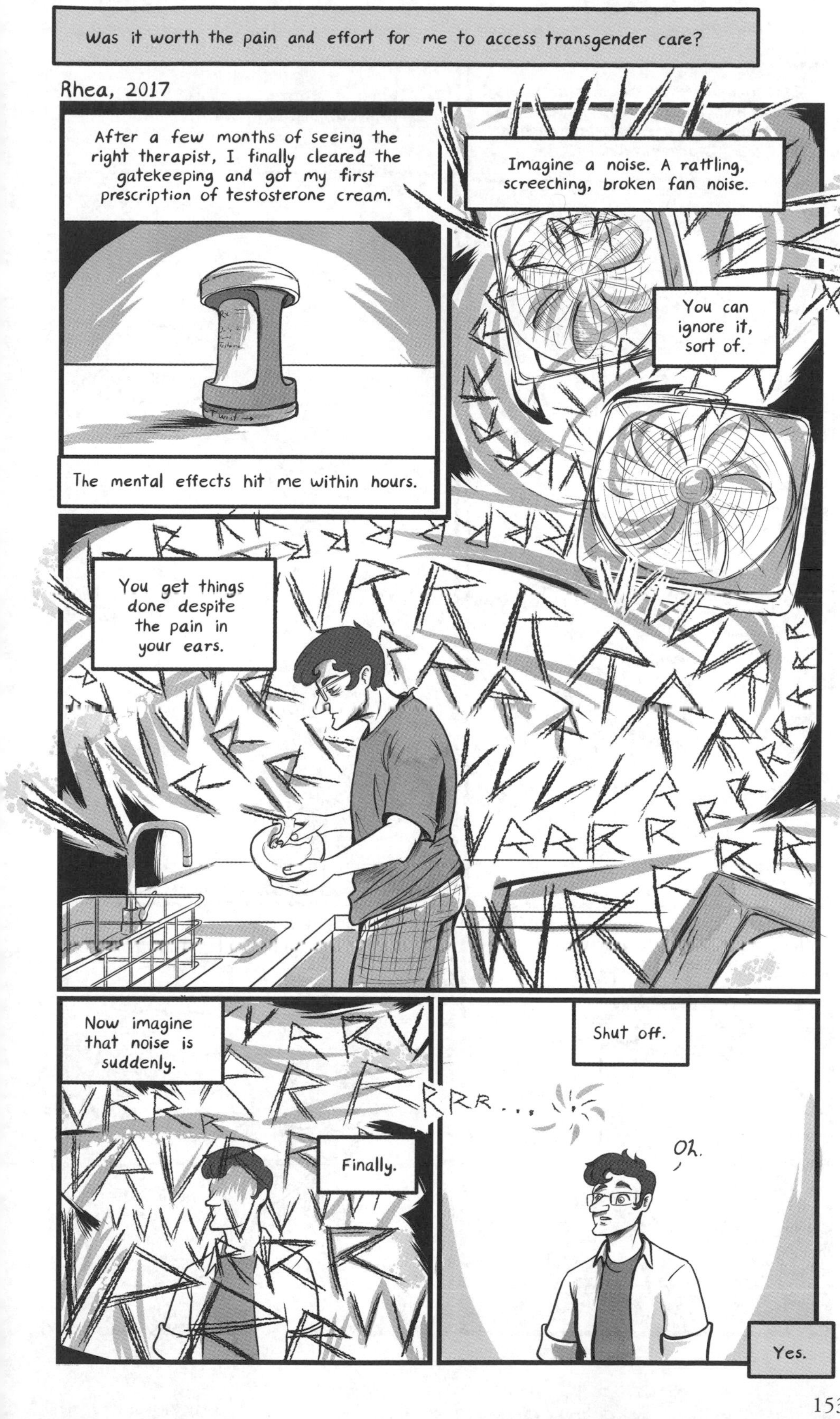
After a few months of seeing the right therapist, I finally cleared the gatekeeping and got my first prescription of testosterone cream.
Twist →
The mental effects hit me within hours.
Imagine a noise. A rattling, screeching, broken fan noise.
You can ignore it, sort of.
You get things done despite the pain in your ears.
Now imagine that noise is suddenly.
Finally.
RRR...
Shut off.
Oh.
Yes.

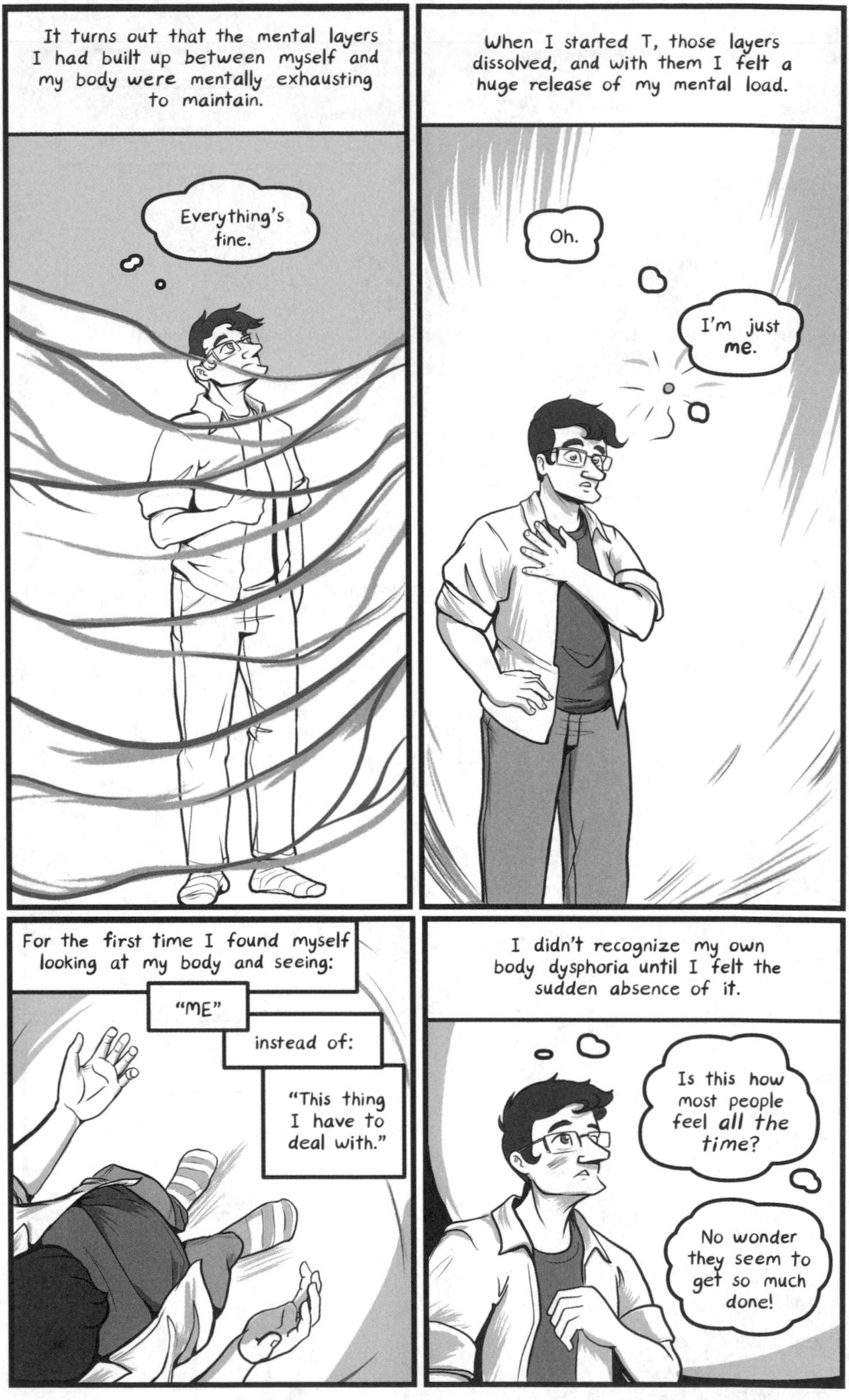
It turns out that the mental layers I had built up between myself and my body were mentally exhausting to maintain.
Everything's fine.
When I started T, those layers dissolved, and with them I felt a huge release of my mental load.
Oh.
I'm just me.
For the first time I found myself looking at my body and seeing:
"ME"
instead of:
"This thing I have to deal with."
I didn't recognize my own body dysphoria until I felt the sudden absence of it.
Is this how most people feel all the time?
No wonder they seem to get so much done!

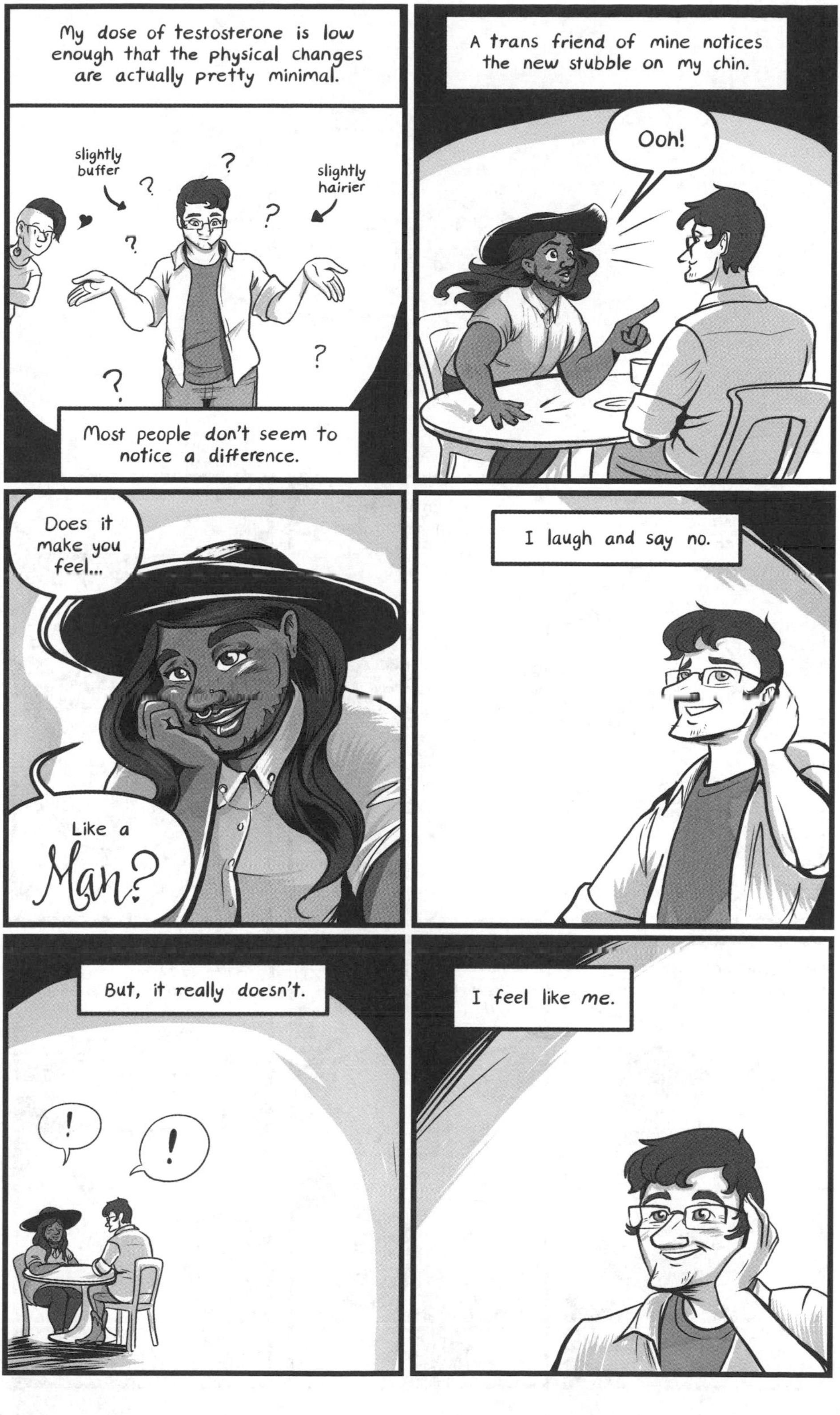
My dose of testosterone is low enough that the physical changes are actually pretty minimal.
slightly buffer
slightly hairier
Most people don't seem to notice a difference.
A trans friend of mine notices the new stubble on my chin.
Ooh!
Does it make you feel...
Like a Man?
I laugh and say no.
But, it really doesn't.
!
!
I feel like me.

What is the difference between gender and sex?

Daiquiri, 2012

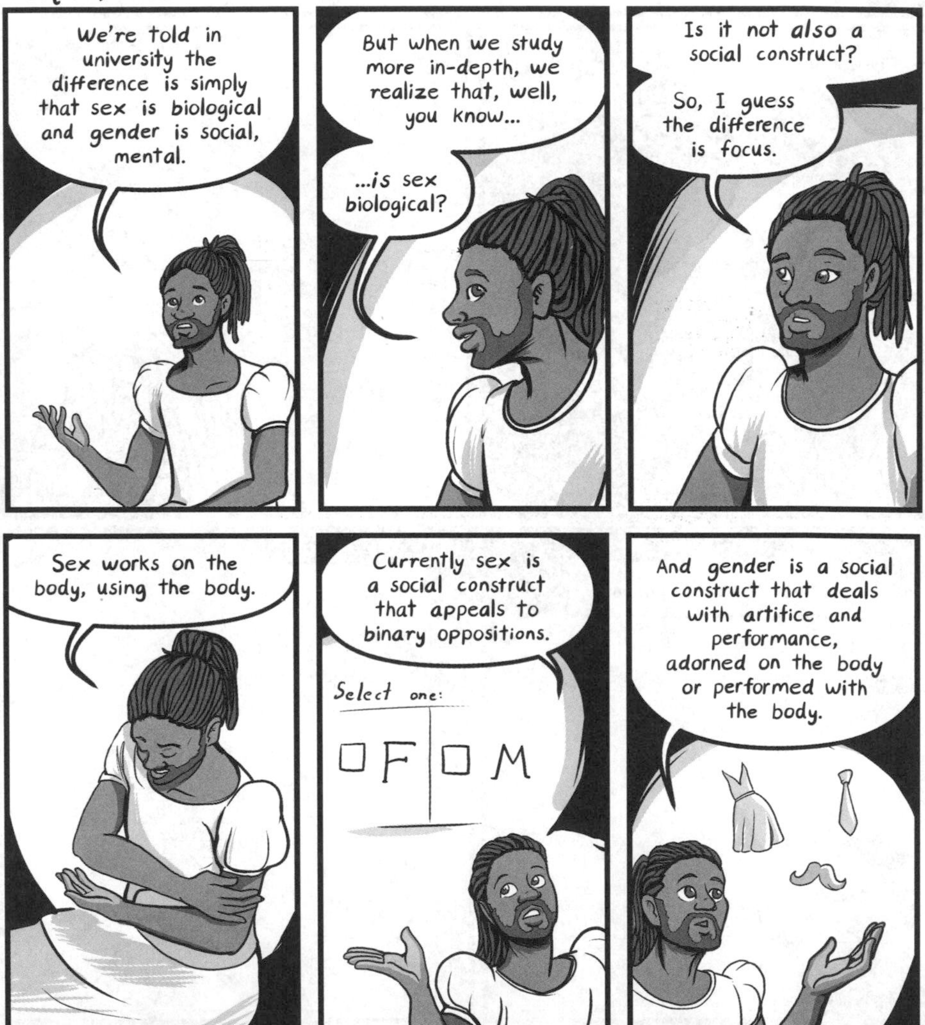
We're told in university the difference is simply that sex is biological and gender is social, mental.
But when we study more in-depth, we realize that, well, you know...
...is sex biological?
Is it not also a social construct?
So, I guess the difference is focus.
Sex works on the body, using the body.
Currently sex is a social construct that appeals to binary oppositions.
Select one:
F
M
And gender is a social construct that deals with artifice and performance, adorned on the body or performed with the body.

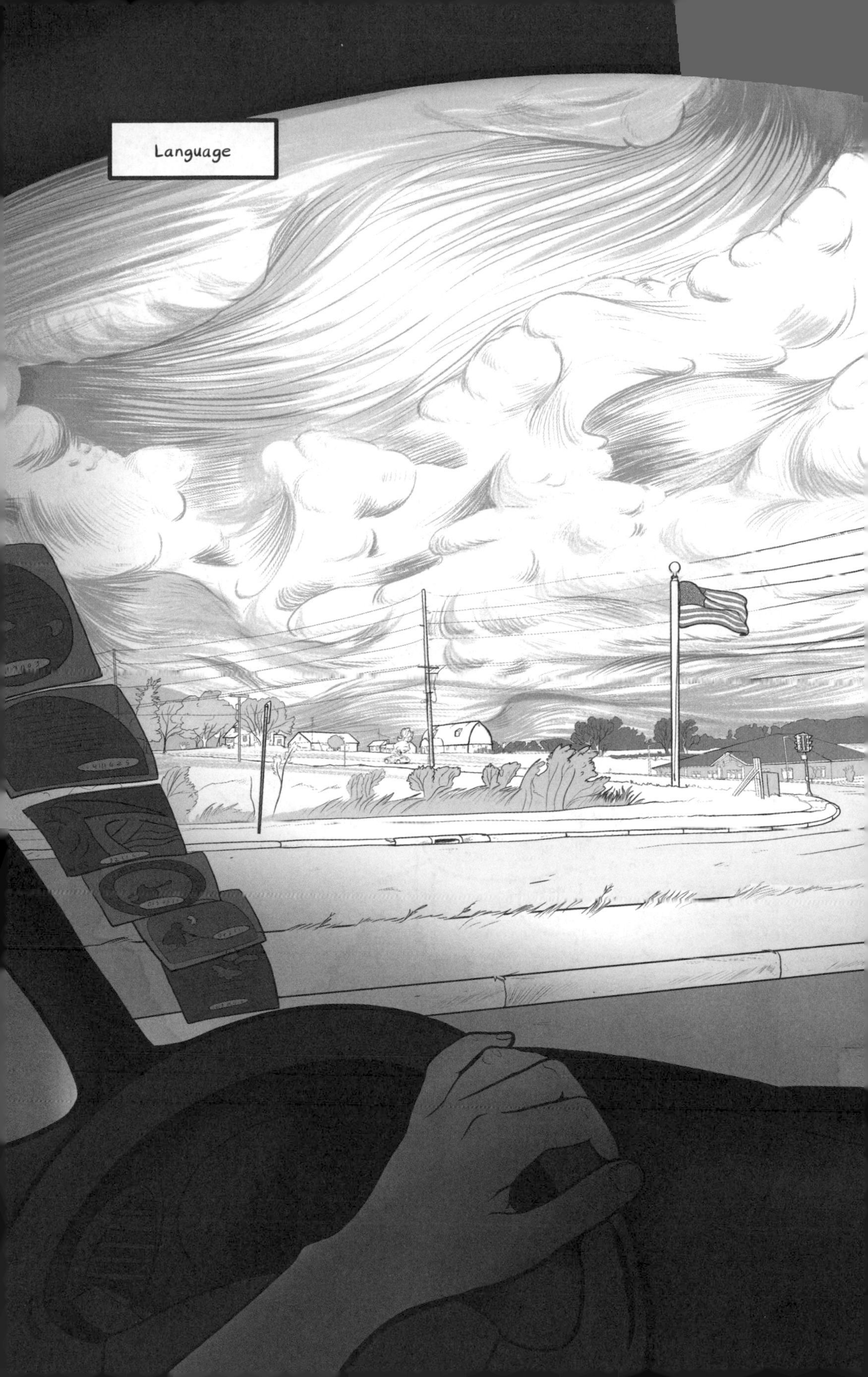

Language

Rhea, 2011

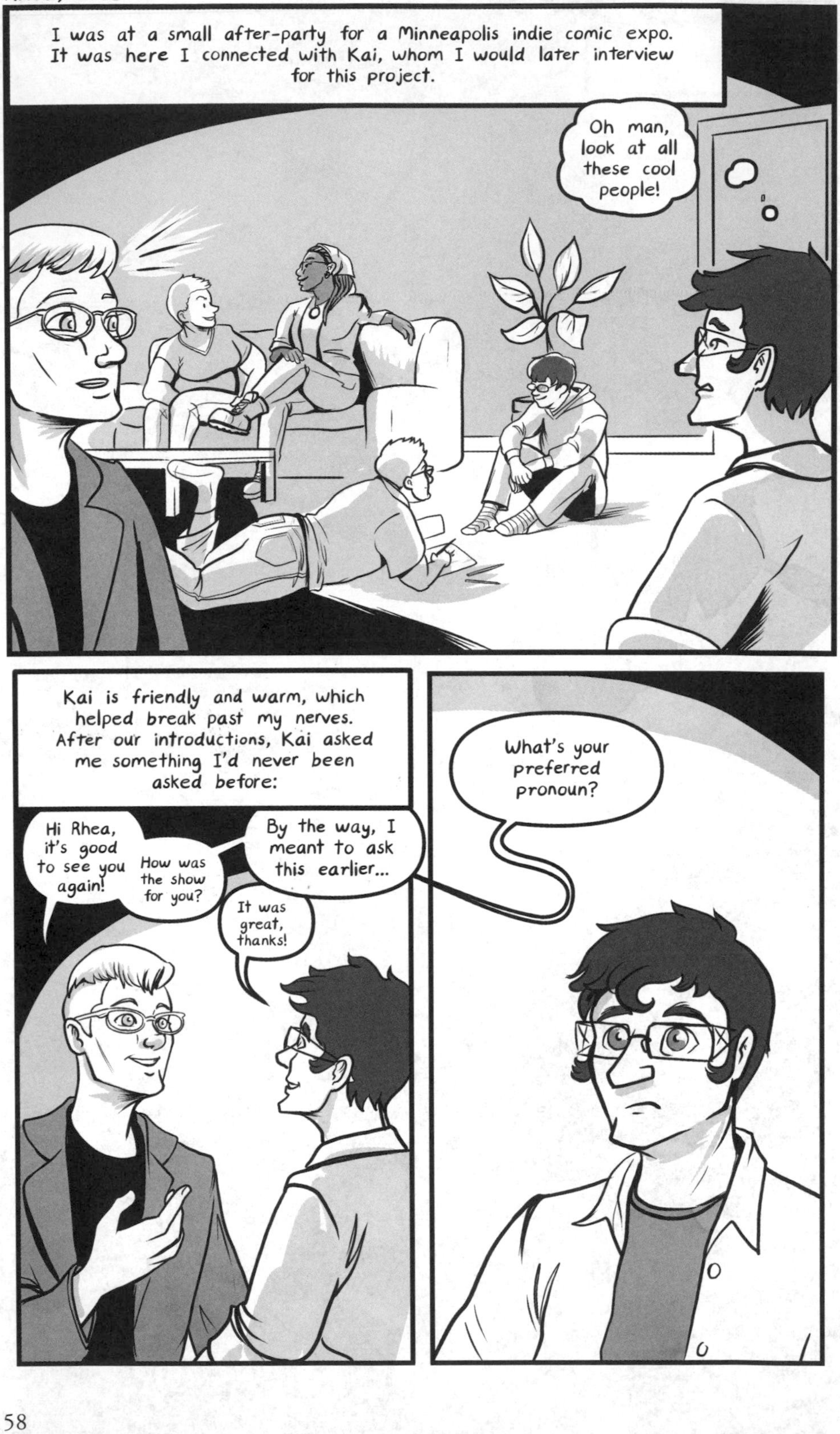
I was at a small after-party for a Minneapolis indie comic expo. It was here I connected with Kai, whom I would later interview for this project.
Oh man, look at all these cool people!
Kai is friendly and warm, which helped break past my nerves. After our introductions, Kai asked me something I'd never been asked before:
Hi Rhea, it's good to see you again!
How was the show for you?
It was great, thanks!
By the way, I meant to ask this earlier...
What's your preferred pronoun?

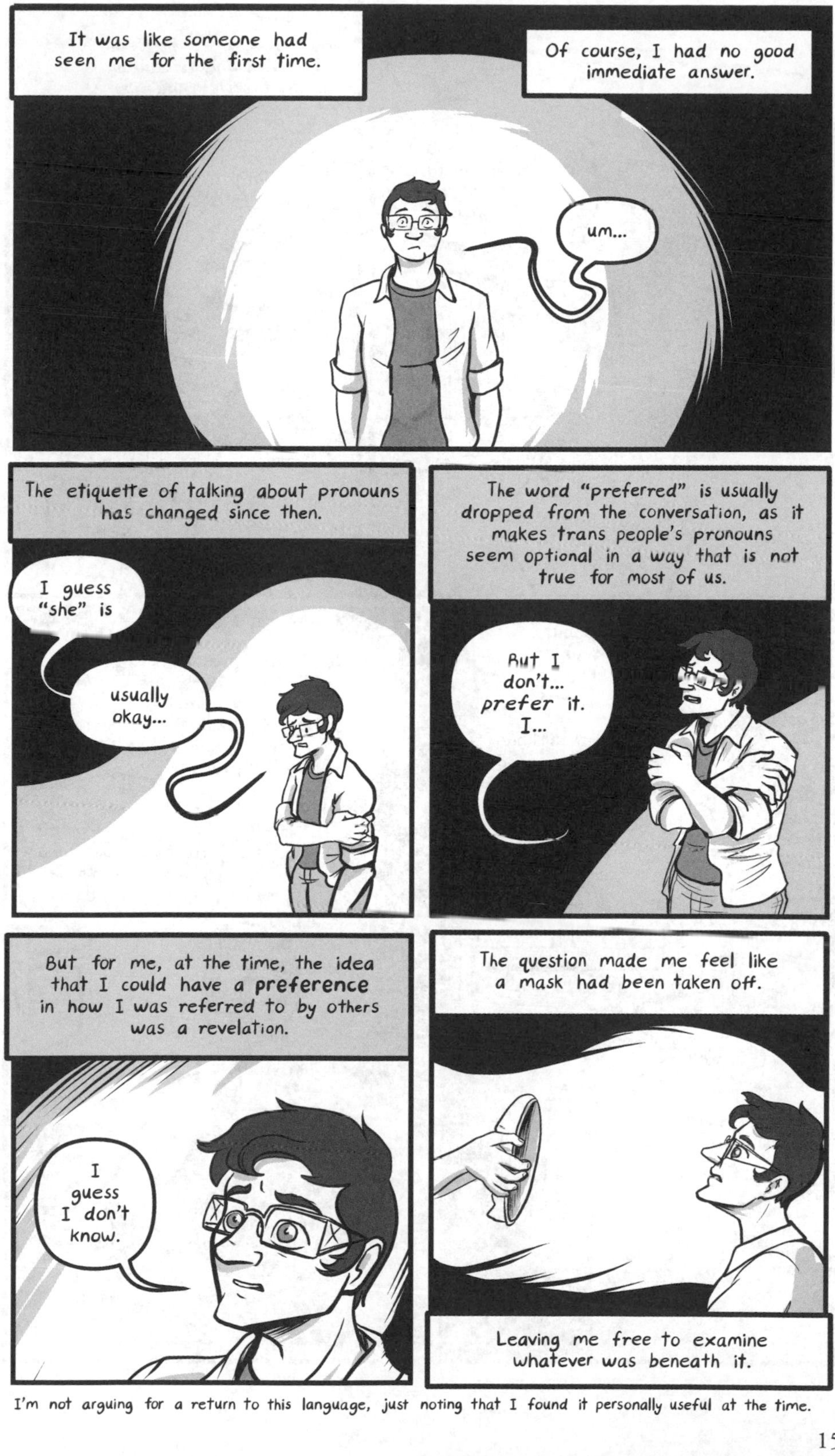
It was like someone had seen me for the first time.
Of course, I had no good immediate answer.
um...
The etiquette of talking about pronouns has changed since then.
I guess "she" is
usually okay...
The word "preferred" is usually dropped from the conversation, as it makes trans people's pronouns seem optional in a way that is not true for most of us.
But I don't... *prefer* it. I...
But for me, at the time, the idea that I could have a **preference** in how I was referred to by others was a revelation.
I guess I don't know.
The question made me feel like a mask had been taken off.
Leaving me free to examine whatever was beneath it.

I'm not arguing for a return to this language, just noting that I found it personally useful at the time.

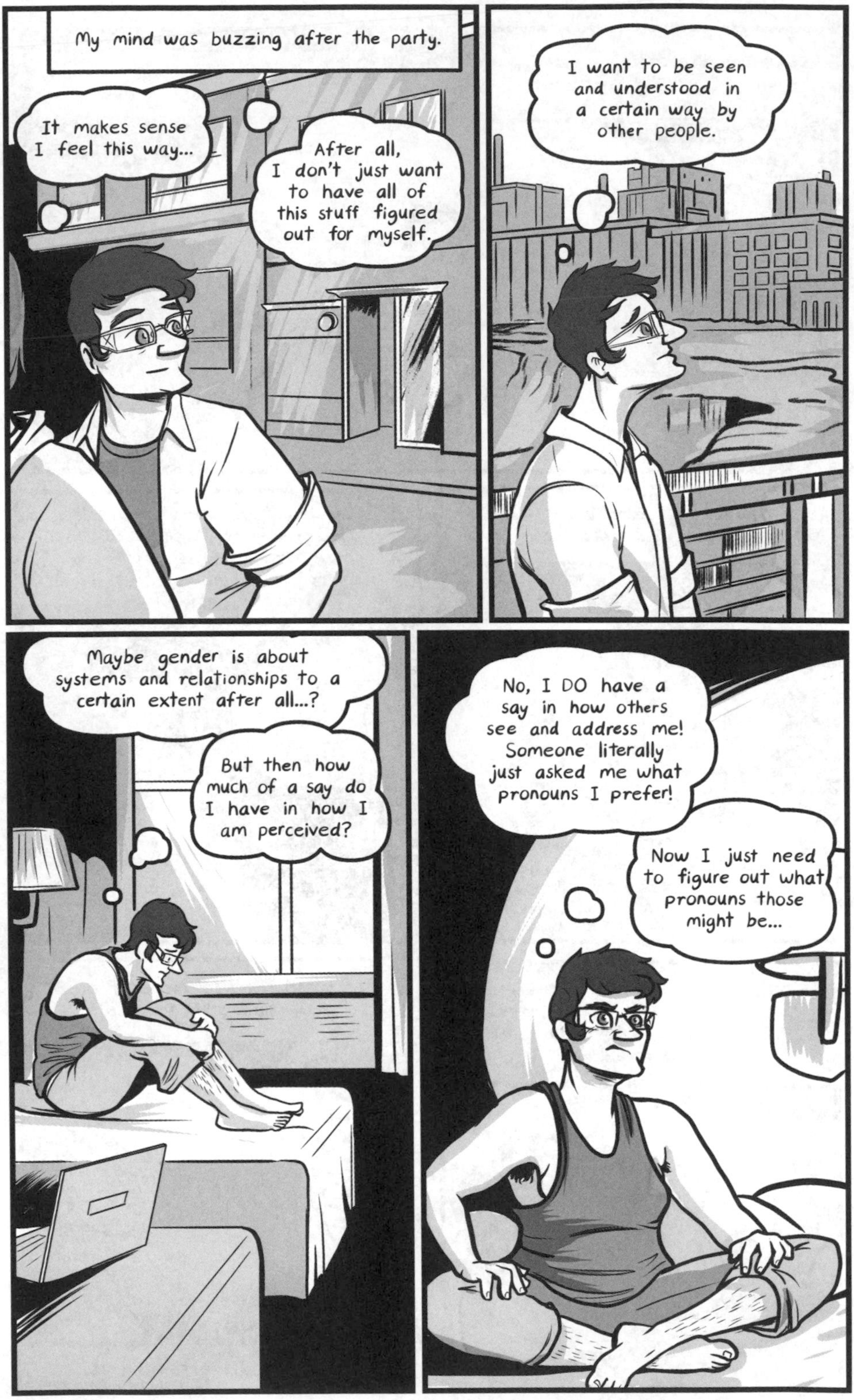
My mind was buzzing after the party.
It makes sense I feel this way...
After all, I don't just want to have all of this stuff figured out for myself.
I want to be seen and understood in a certain way by other people.
Maybe gender is about systems and relationships to a certain extent after all...?
But then how much of a say do I have in how I am perceived?
No, I DO have a say in how others see and address me! Someone literally just asked me what pronouns I prefer!
Now I just need to figure out what pronouns those might be...

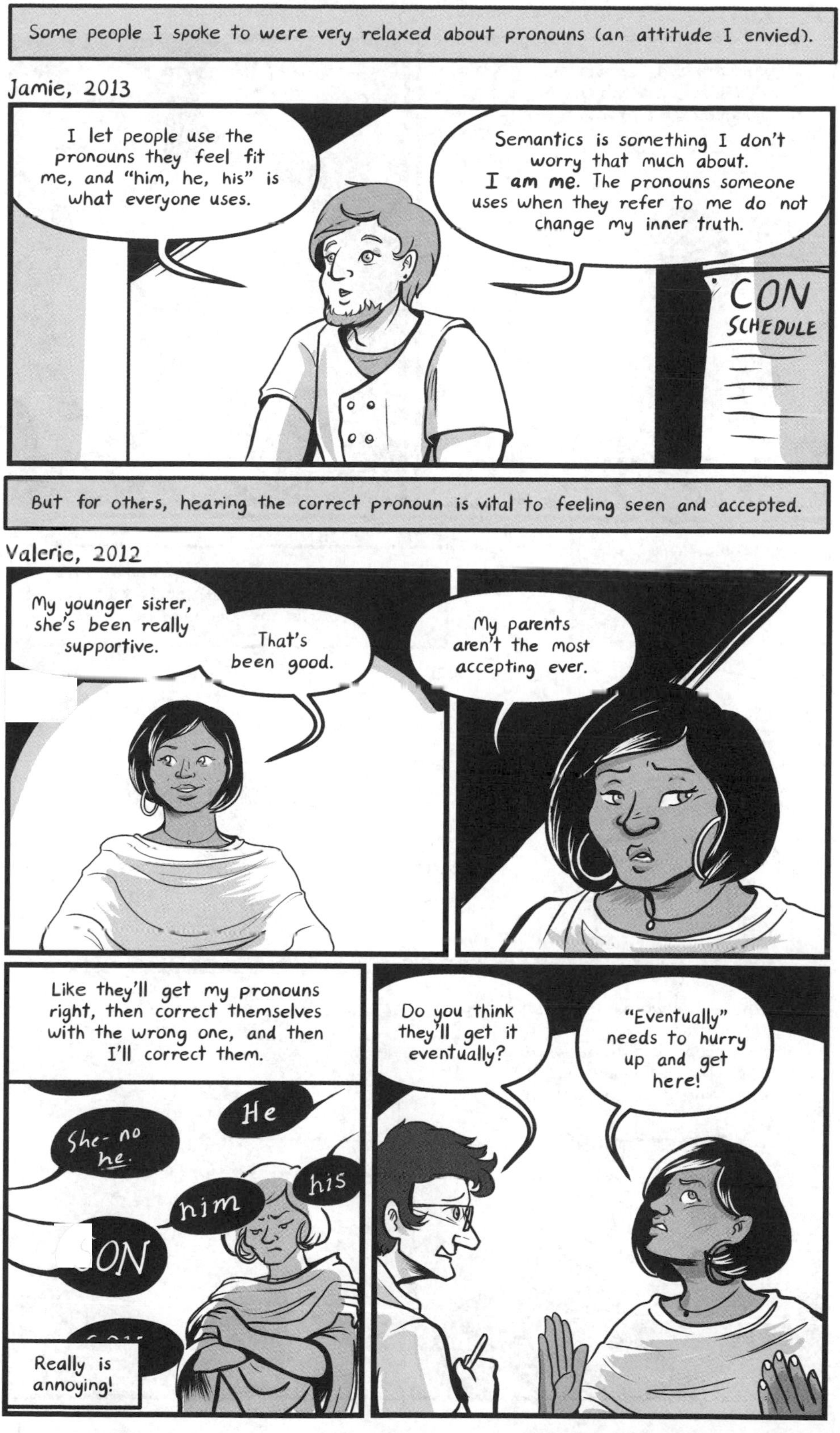
Some people I spoke to were very relaxed about pronouns (an attitude I envied).
Jamie, 2013
I let people use the pronouns they feel fit me, and "him, he, his" is what everyone uses.
Semantics is something I don't worry that much about. **I am me**. The pronouns someone uses when they refer to me do not change my inner truth.
CON SCHEDULE
But for others, hearing the correct pronoun is vital to feeling seen and accepted.
Valerie, 2012
My younger sister, she's been really supportive.
That's been good.
My parents aren't the most accepting ever.
Like they'll get my pronouns right, then correct themselves with the wrong one, and then I'll correct them.
He
She- no he.
his
him
Really is annoying!
Do you think they'll get it eventually?
"Eventually" needs to hurry up and get here!

JAC, 2013

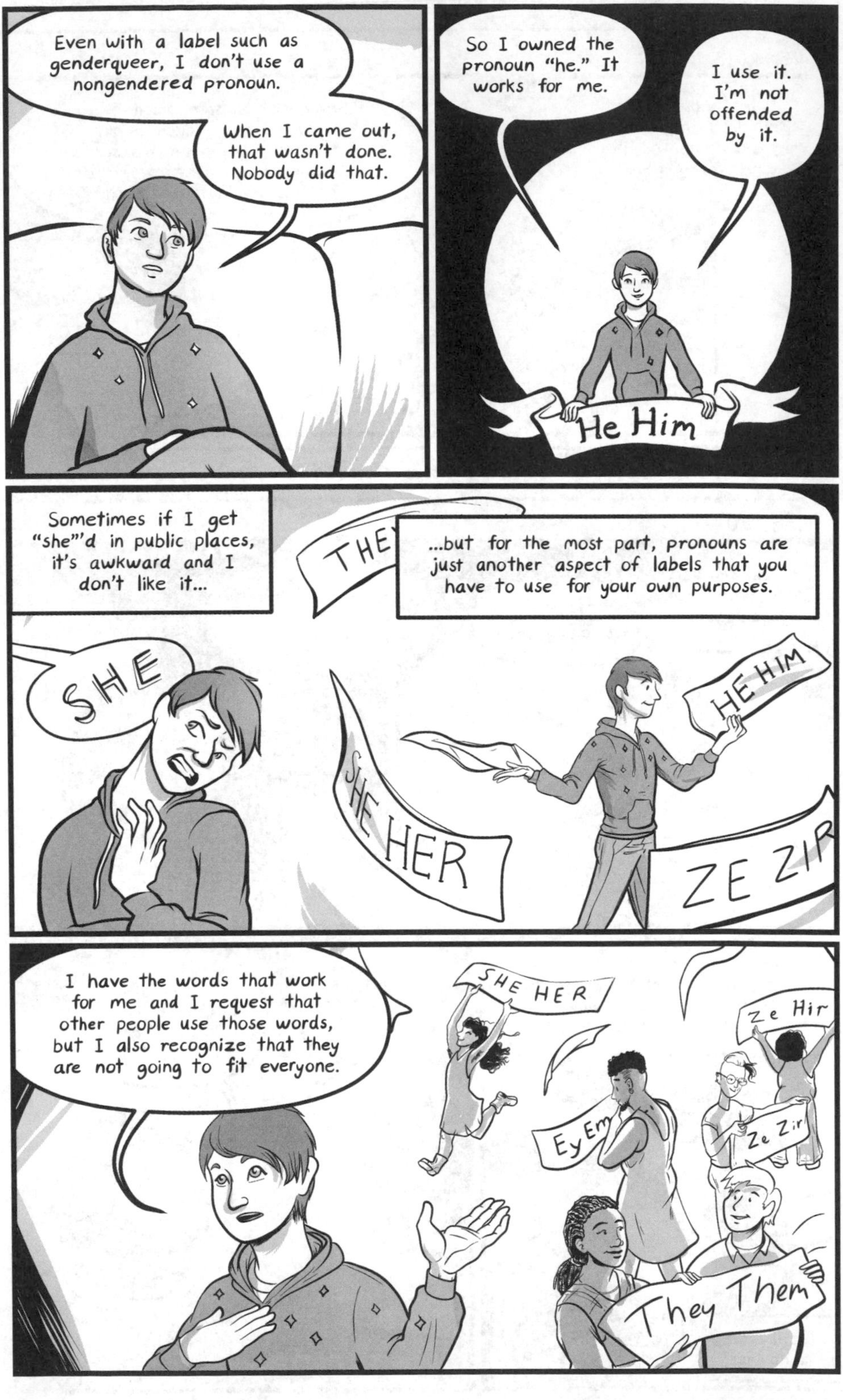
Even with a label such as genderqueer, I don't use a nongendered pronoun.
When I came out, that wasn't done. Nobody did that.
So I owned the pronoun "he." It works for me.
I use it. I'm not offended by it.
He Him
Sometimes if I get "she"'d in public places, it's awkward and I don't like it...
THEY
...but for the most part, pronouns are just another aspect of labels that you have to use for your own purposes.
SHE
SHE HER
HE HIM
ZE ZIR
I have the words that work for me and I request that other people use those words, but I also recognize that they are not going to fit everyone.
SHE HER
Ze Hir
Ey Em
Ze Zir
They Them

Ignacio, 2013

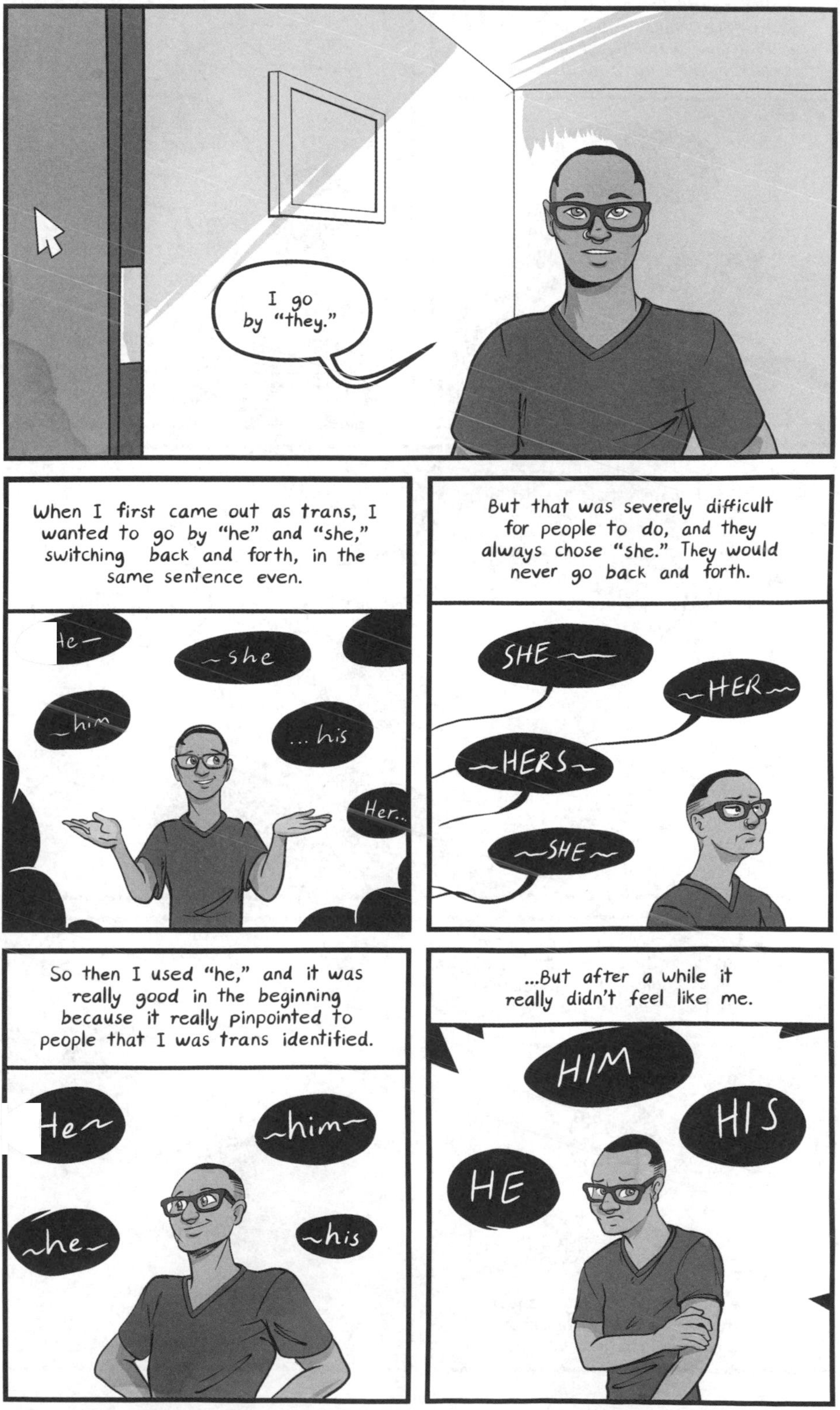
I go by "they."
When I first came out as trans, I wanted to go by "he" and "she," switching back and forth, in the same sentence even.
—she
—him
...his
Her...
But that was severely difficult for people to do, and they always chose "she." They would never go back and forth.
SHE—
—HER—
—HERS—
—SHE—
So then I used "he," and it was really good in the beginning because it really pinpointed to people that I was trans identified.
—him—
—he—
—his
...But after a while it really didn't feel like me.
HIM
HIS
HE

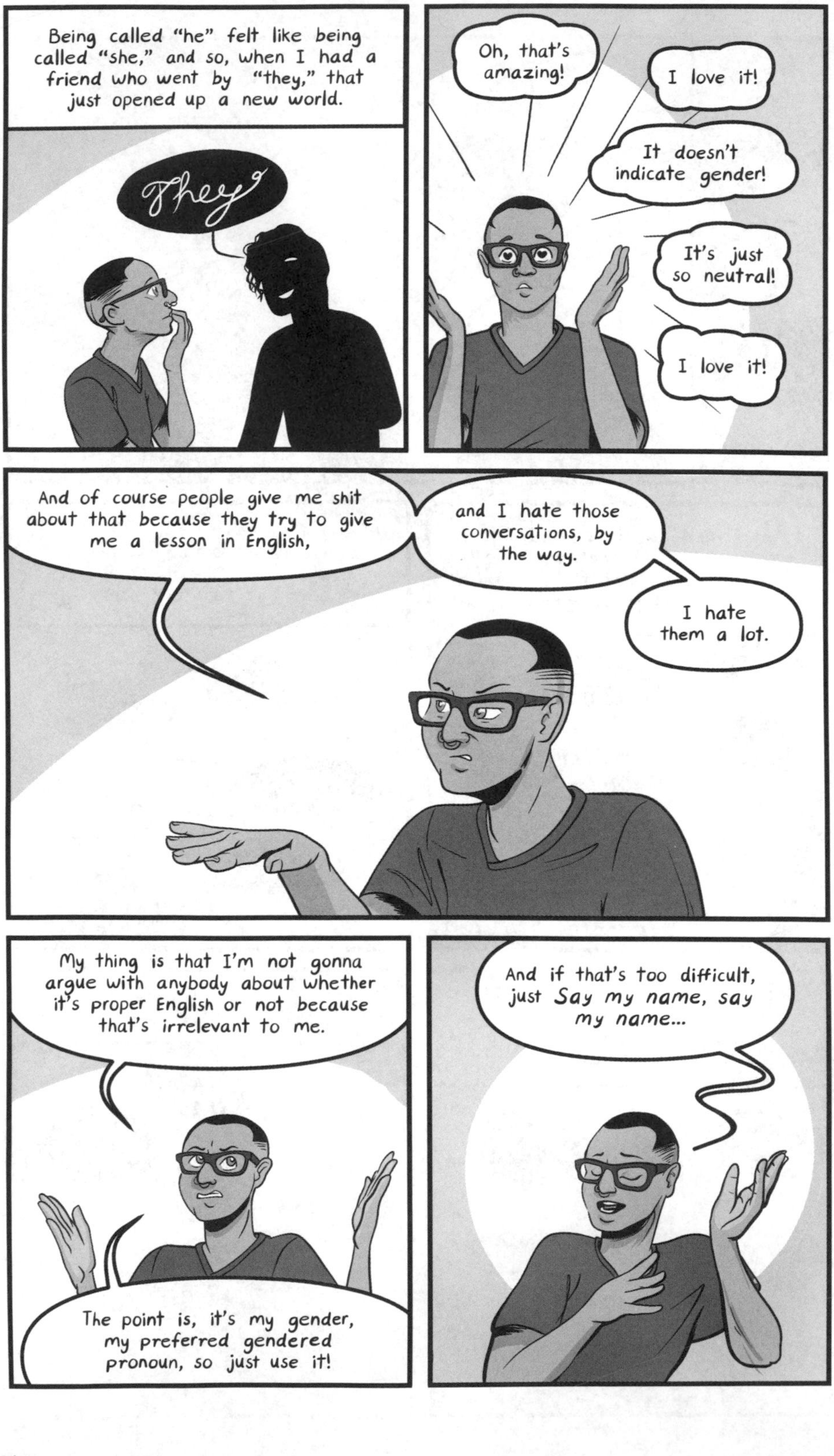
Being called "he" felt like being called "she," and so, when I had a friend who went by "they," that just opened up a new world.
They
Oh, that's amazing!
I love it!
It doesn't indicate gender!
It's just so neutral!
I love it!
And of course people give me shit about that because they try to give me a lesson in English,
and I hate those conversations, by the way.
I hate them a lot.
My thing is that I'm not gonna argue with anybody about whether it's proper English or not because that's irrelevant to me.
The point is, it's my gender, my preferred gendered pronoun, so just use it!
And if that's too difficult, just *Say my name, say my name...*

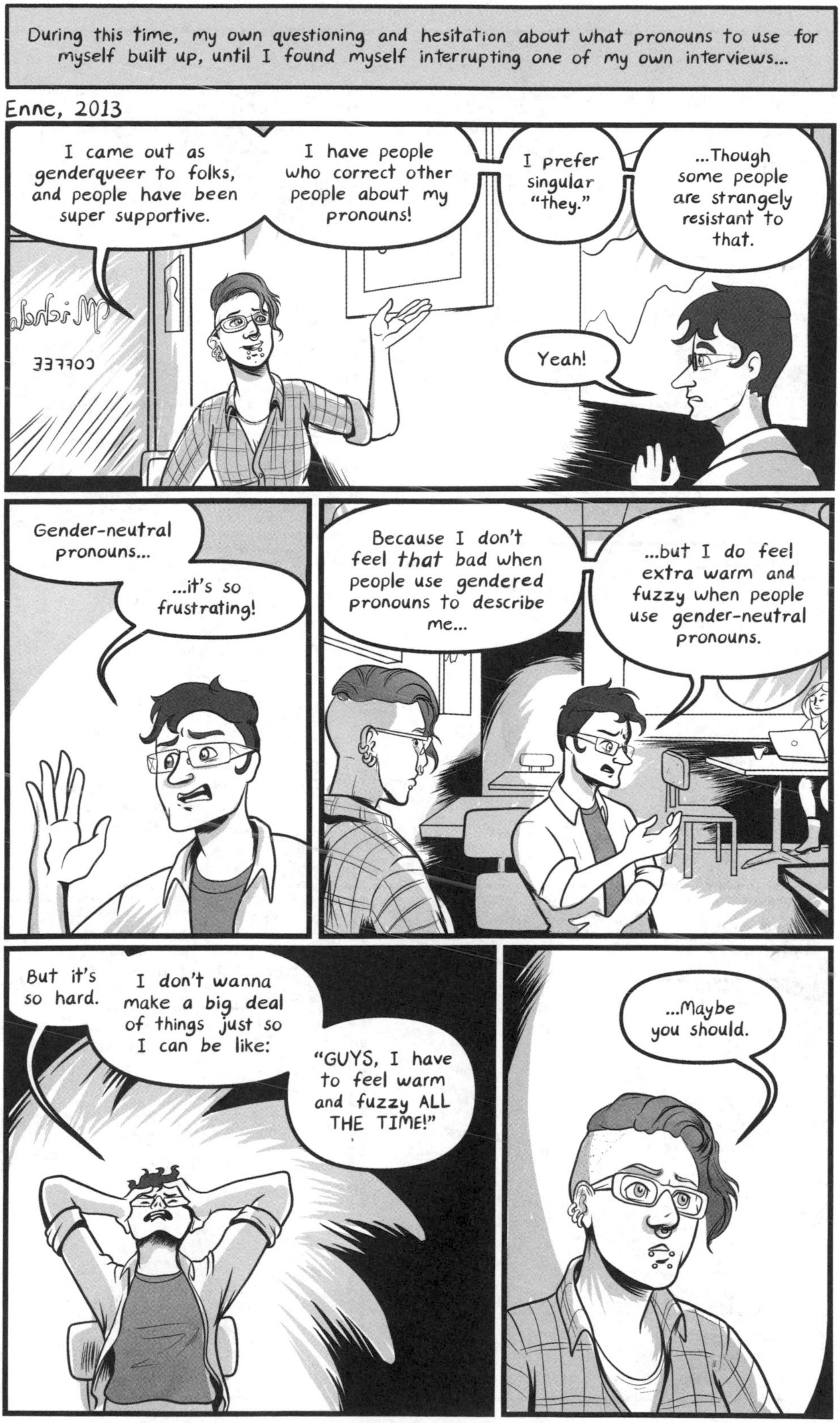
During this time, my own questioning and hesitation about what pronouns to use for myself built up, until I found myself interrupting one of my own interviews...
Enne, 2013
I came out as genderqueer to folks, and people have been super supportive.
I have people who correct other people about my pronouns!
I prefer singular "they."
...Though some people are strangely resistant to that.
Yeah!
Gender-neutral pronouns...
...it's so frustrating!
Because I don't feel *that* bad when people use gendered pronouns to describe me...
...but I do feel extra warm and fuzzy when people use gender-neutral pronouns.
But it's so hard.
I don't wanna make a big deal of things just so I can be like:
"GUYS, I have to feel warm and fuzzy ALL THE TIME!"
...Maybe you should.

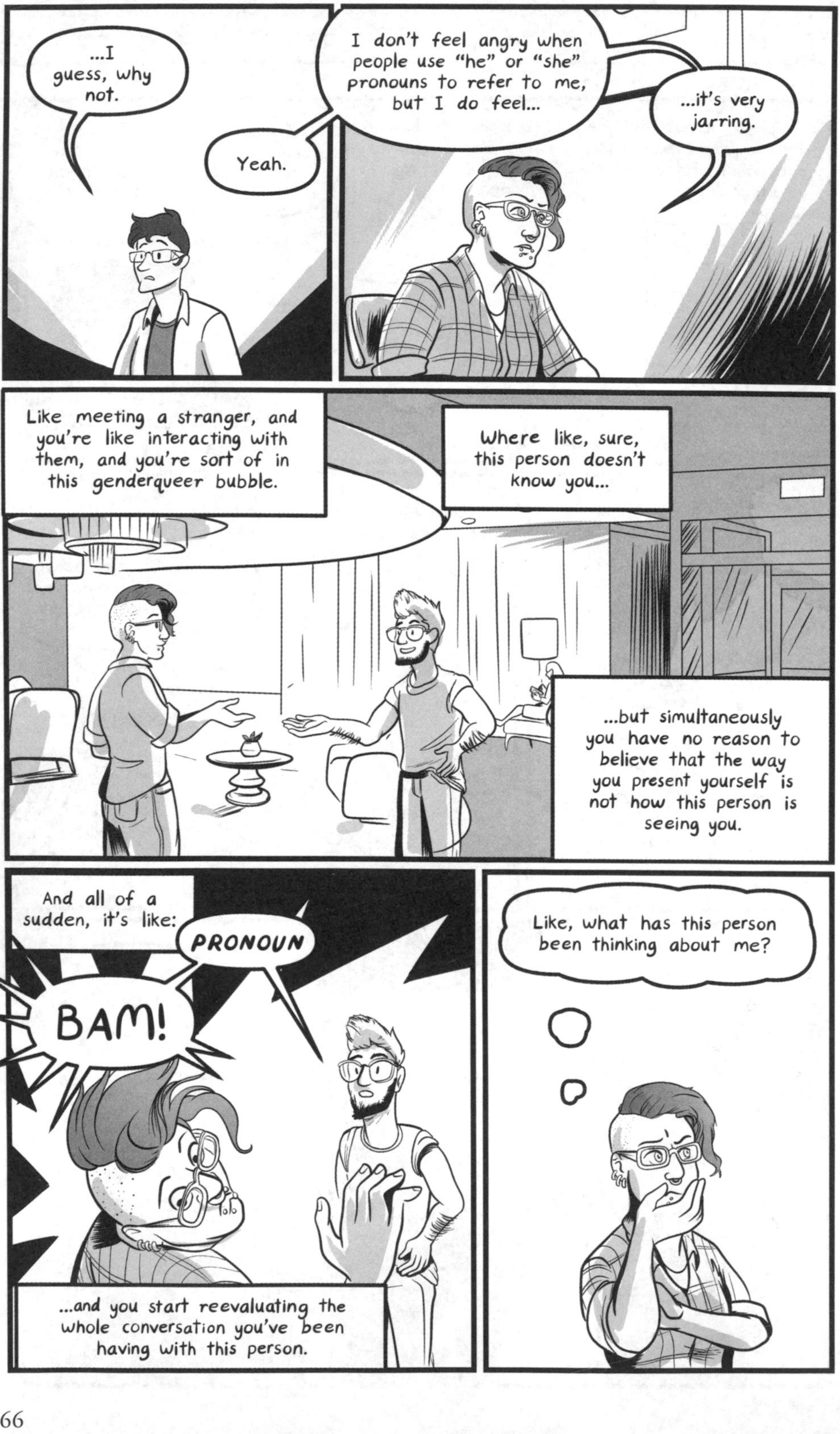
...I guess, why not.
Yeah.
I don't feel angry when people use "he" or "she" pronouns to refer to me, but I do feel...
...it's very jarring.
Like meeting a stranger, and you're like interacting with them, and you're sort of in this genderqueer bubble.
Where like, sure, this person doesn't know you...
...but simultaneously you have no reason to believe that the way you present yourself is not how this person is seeing you.
And all of a sudden, it's like:
PRONOUN
BAM!
...and you start reevaluating the whole conversation you've been having with this person.
Like, what has this person been thinking about me?

Rhea, 2013

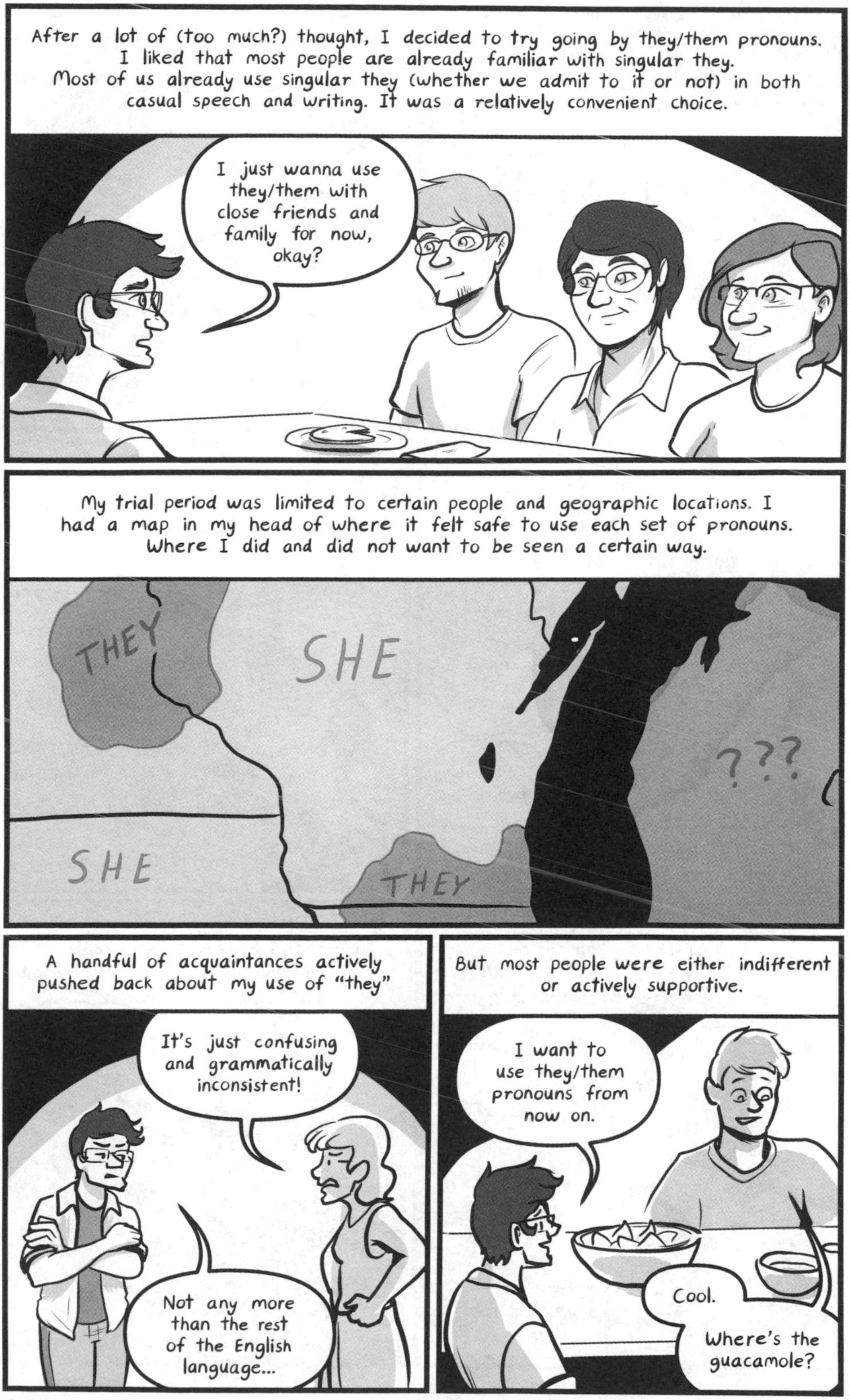
After a lot of (too much?) thought, I decided to try going by they/them pronouns. I liked that most people are already familiar with singular they. Most of us already use singular they (whether we admit to it or not) in both casual speech and writing. It was a relatively convenient choice.
I just wanna use they/them with close friends and family for now, okay?
My trial period was limited to certain people and geographic locations. I had a map in my head of where it felt safe to use each set of pronouns. Where I did and did not want to be seen a certain way.
THEY
SHE
???
SHE
THEY
A handful of acquaintances actively pushed back about my use of "they"
It's just confusing and grammatically inconsistent!
Not any more than the rest of the English language...
But most people were either indifferent or actively supportive.
I want to use they/them pronouns from now on.
Cool.
Where's the guacamole?

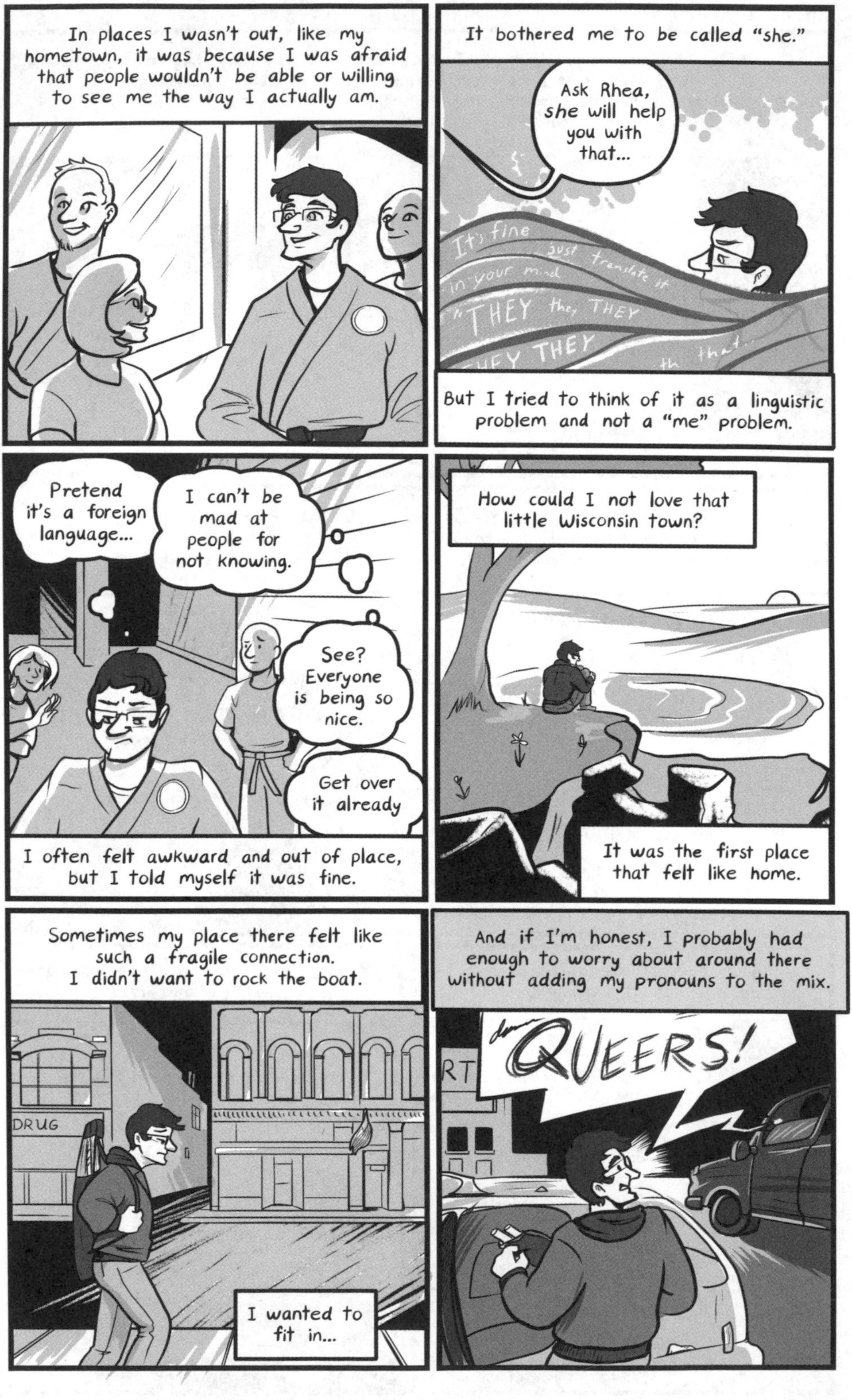

In places I wasn't out, like my hometown, it was because I was afraid that people wouldn't be able or willing to see me the way I actually am.
It bothered me to be called "she."
Ask Rhea, she will help you with that...
It's fine
just translate it
in your mind
"THEY they, THEY
THEY THEY
But I tried to think of it as a linguistic problem and not a "me" problem.
Pretend it's a foreign language...
I can't be mad at people for not knowing.
See? Everyone is being so nice.
Get over it already
I often felt awkward and out of place, but I told myself it was fine.
How could I not love that little Wisconsin town?
It was the first place that felt like home.
Sometimes my place there felt like such a fragile connection. I didn't want to rock the boat.
DRUG
I wanted to fit in...
And if I'm honest, I probably had enough to worry about around there without adding my pronouns to the mix.
QUEERS!

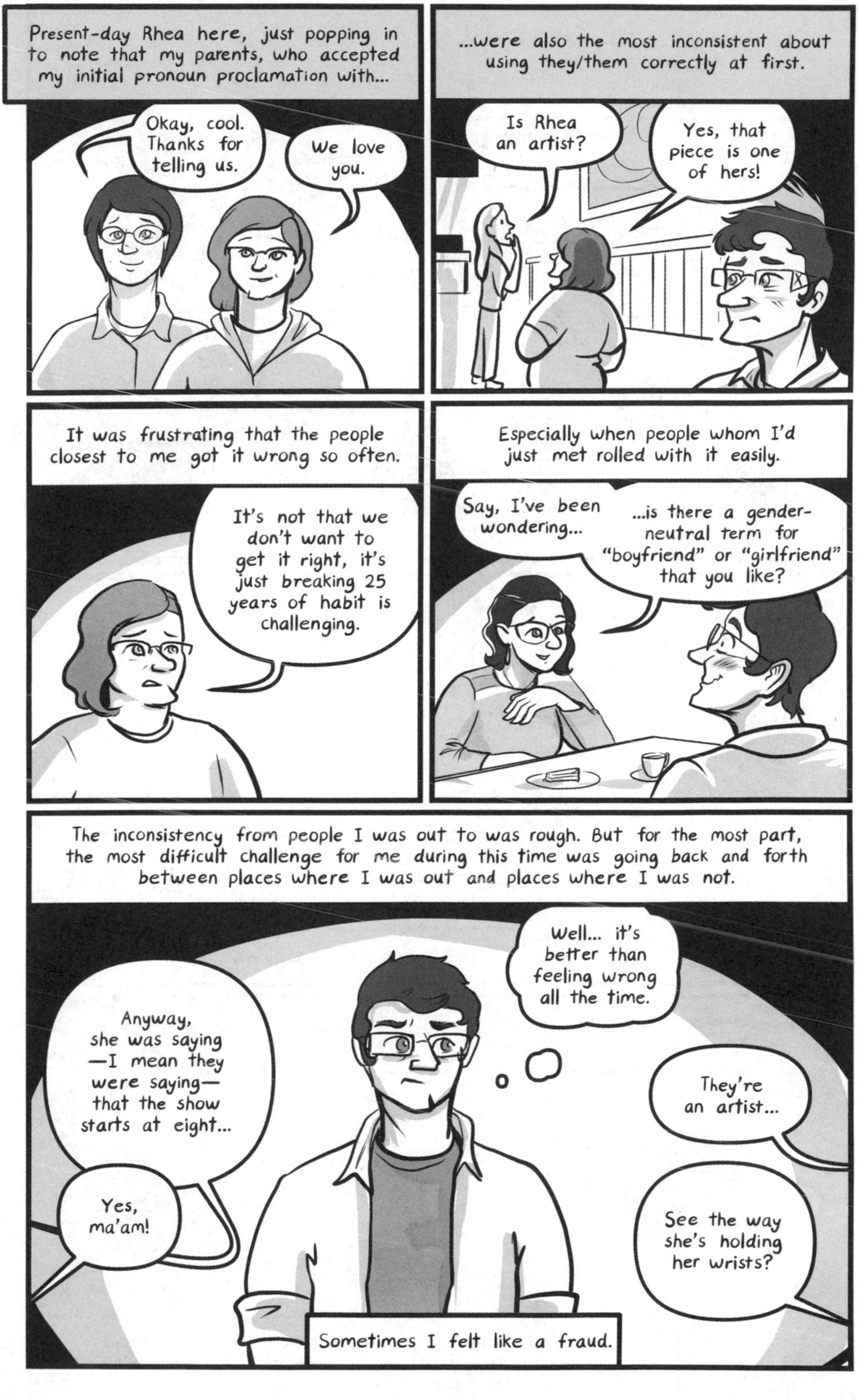
Present-day Rhea here, just popping in to note that my parents, who accepted my initial pronoun proclamation with...
Okay, cool. Thanks for telling us.
We love you.
...were also the most inconsistent about using they/them correctly at first.
Is Rhea an artist?
Yes, that piece is one of hers!
It was frustrating that the people closest to me got it wrong so often.
It's not that we don't want to get it right, it's just breaking 25 years of habit is challenging.
Especially when people whom I'd just met rolled with it easily.
Say, I've been wondering...
...is there a gender-neutral term for "boyfriend" or "girlfriend" that you like?
The inconsistency from people I was out to was rough. But for the most part, the most difficult challenge for me during this time was going back and forth between places where I was out and places where I was not.
Well... it's better than feeling wrong all the time.
Anyway, she was saying —I mean they were saying— that the show starts at eight...
Yes, ma'am!
They're an artist...
See the way she's holding her wrists?
Sometimes I felt like a fraud.

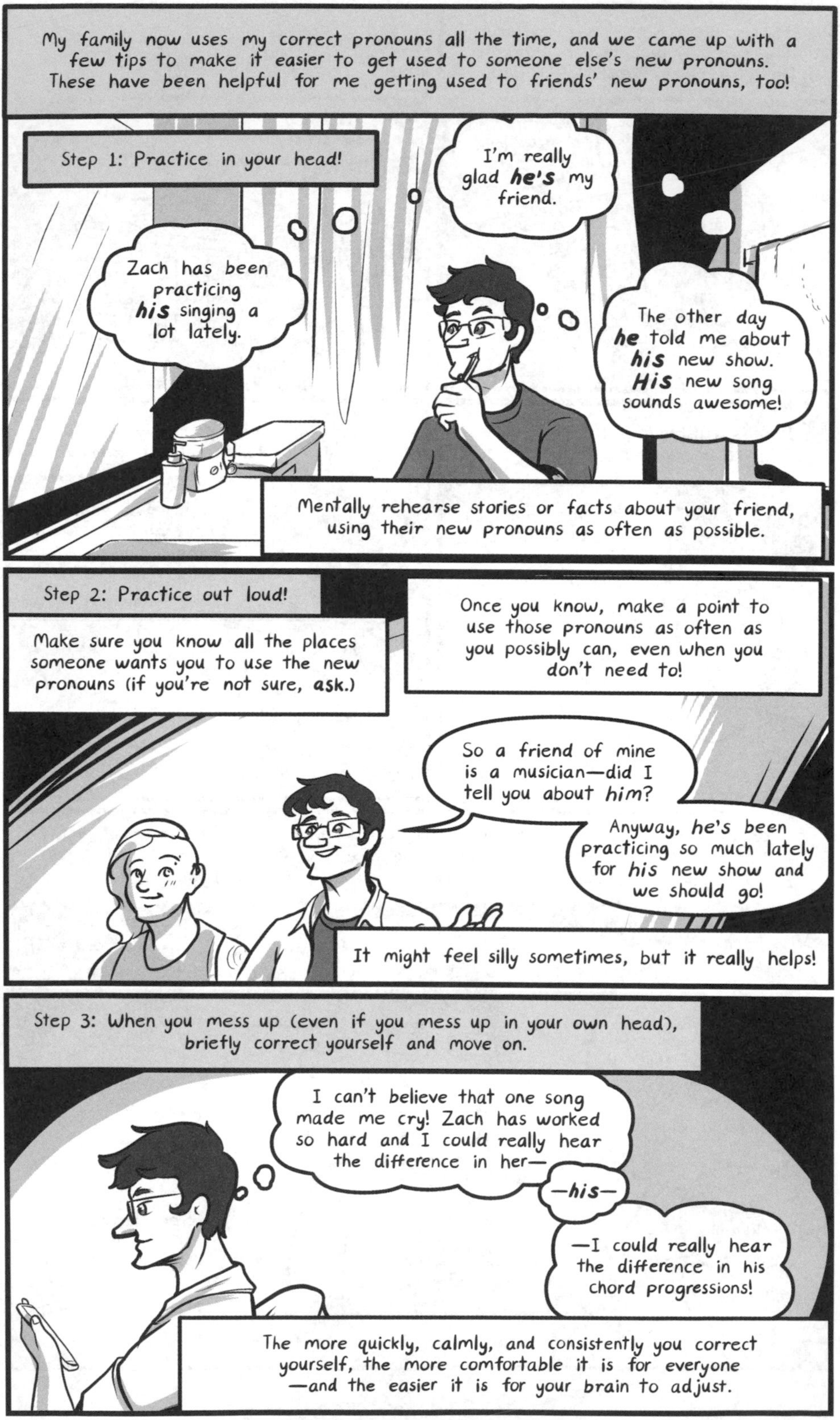
My family now uses my correct pronouns all the time, and we came up with a few tips to make it easier to get used to someone else's new pronouns. These have been helpful for me getting used to friends' new pronouns, too!
Step 1: Practice in your head!
Zach has been practicing **his** singing a lot lately.
I'm really glad **he's** my friend.
The other day **he** told me about **his** new show. **His** new song sounds awesome!
Mentally rehearse stories or facts about your friend, using their new pronouns as often as possible.
Step 2: Practice out loud!
Make sure you know all the places someone wants you to use the new pronouns (if you're not sure, **ask**.)
Once you know, make a point to use those pronouns as often as you possibly can, even when you don't need to!
So a friend of mine is a musician—did I tell you about *him*?
Anyway, *he's* been practicing so much lately for *his* new show and we should go!
It might feel silly sometimes, but it really helps!
Step 3: When you mess up (even if you mess up in your own head), briefly correct yourself and move on.
I can't believe that one song made me cry! Zach has worked so hard and I could really hear the difference in her—
—his—
—I could really hear the difference in his chord progressions!
The more quickly, calmly, and consistently you correct yourself, the more comfortable it is for everyone —and the easier it is for your brain to adjust.

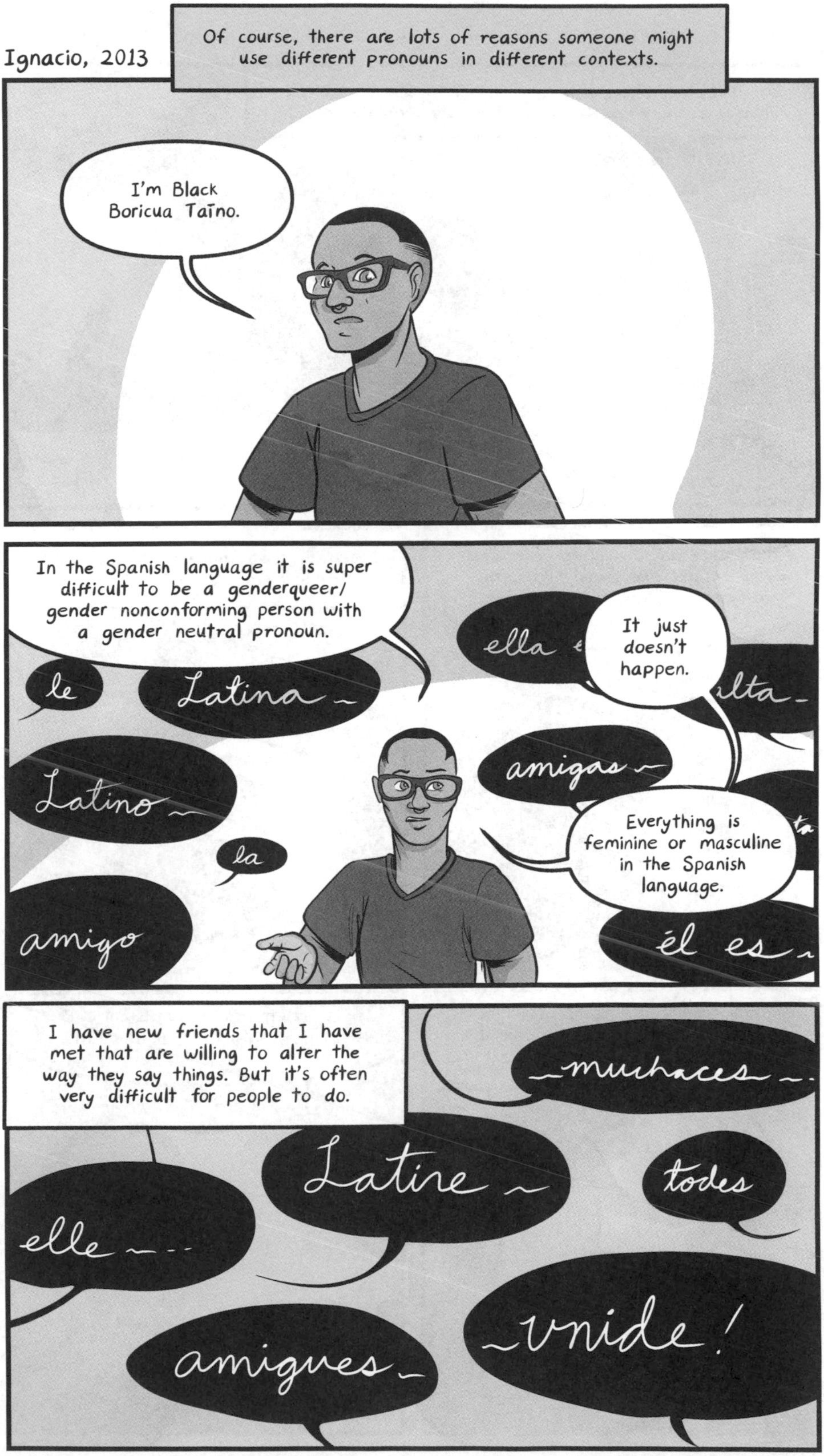

Ignacio, 2013
Of course, there are lots of reasons someone might use different pronouns in different contexts.
I'm Black Boricua Taíno.
In the Spanish language it is super difficult to be a genderqueer/ gender nonconforming person with a gender neutral pronoun.
It just doesn't happen.
ella
le
Latina
amigas
Latino
la
Everything is feminine or masculine in the Spanish language.
amigo
él es
I have new friends that I have met that are willing to alter the way they say things. But it's often very difficult for people to do.
muchaces
Latine
todes
elle
unide!
amigues

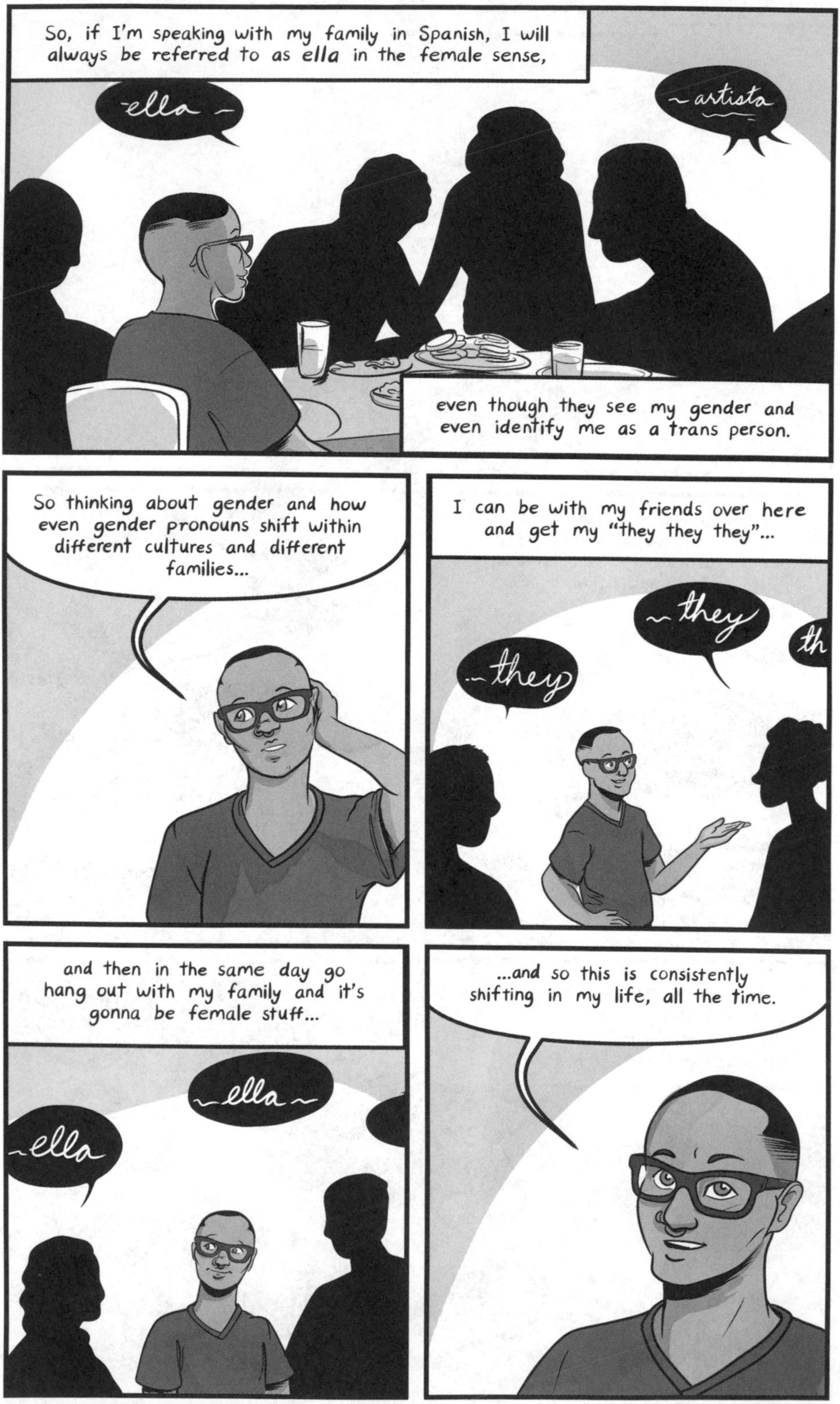
So, if I'm speaking with my family in Spanish, I will always be referred to as *ella* in the female sense,
ella
artista
even though they see my gender and even identify me as a trans person.
So thinking about gender and how even gender pronouns shift within different cultures and different families...
I can be with my friends over here and get my "they they they"...
they
they
and then in the same day go hang out with my family and it's gonna be female stuff...
ella
ella
...and so this is consistently shifting in my life, all the time.

Rhea, 2018

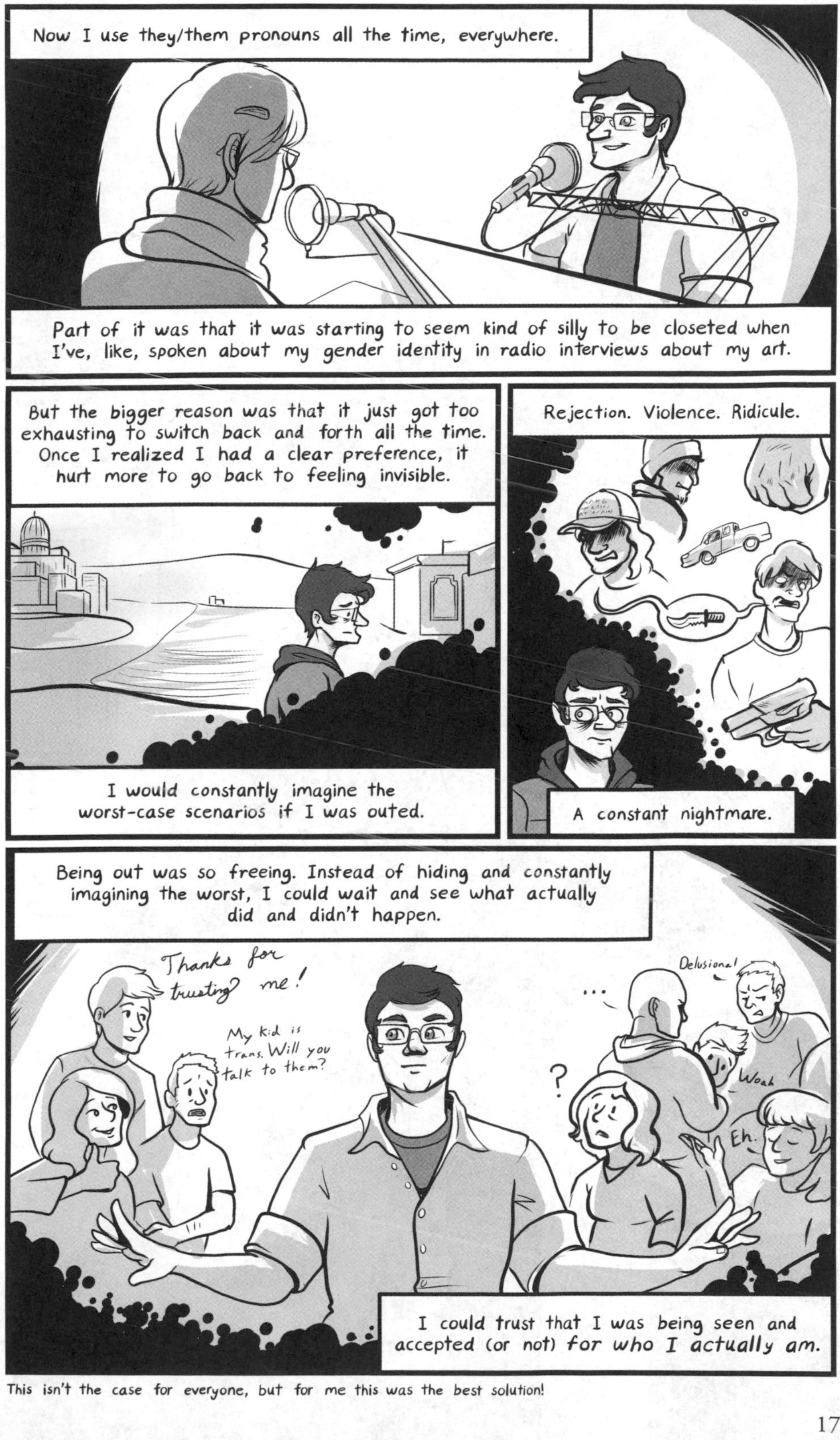
Now I use they/them pronouns all the time, everywhere.
Part of it was that it was starting to seem kind of silly to be closeted when I've, like, spoken about my gender identity in radio interviews about my art.
But the bigger reason was that it just got too exhausting to switch back and forth all the time. Once I realized I had a clear preference, it hurt more to go back to feeling invisible.
I would constantly imagine the worst-case scenarios if I was outed.
Rejection. Violence. Ridicule.
A constant nightmare.
Being out was so freeing. Instead of hiding and constantly imagining the worst, I could wait and see what actually did and didn't happen.
Thanks for trusting me!
My kid is trans. Will you talk to them?
?
...
Delusional
Woah
Eh.
I could trust that I was being seen and accepted (or not) for who I actually am.

This isn't the case for everyone, but for me this was the best solution!

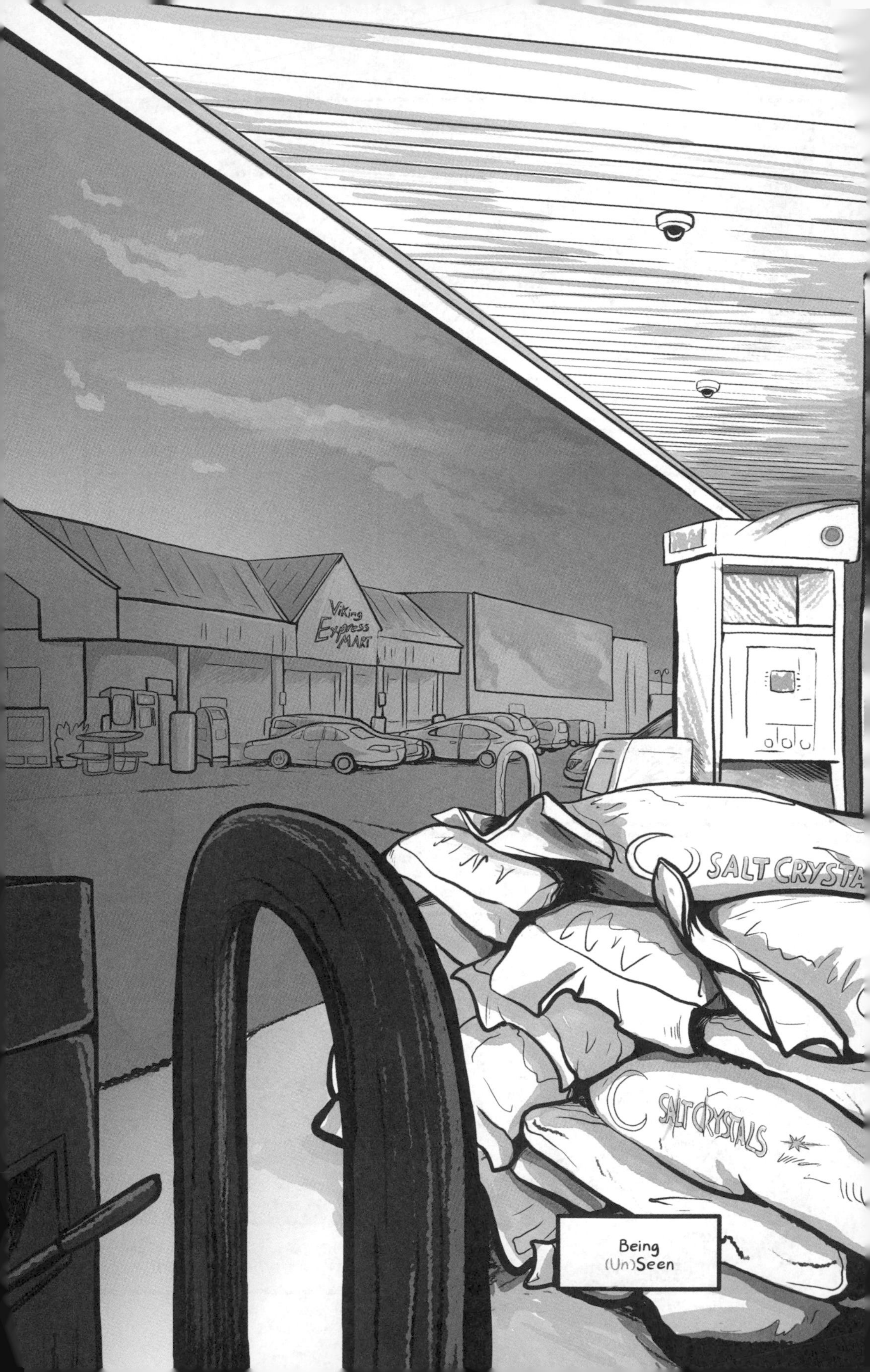
Viking Express MART
SALT CRYSTALS
SALT CRYSTALS
Being
(Un)Seen

Rashida, 2013

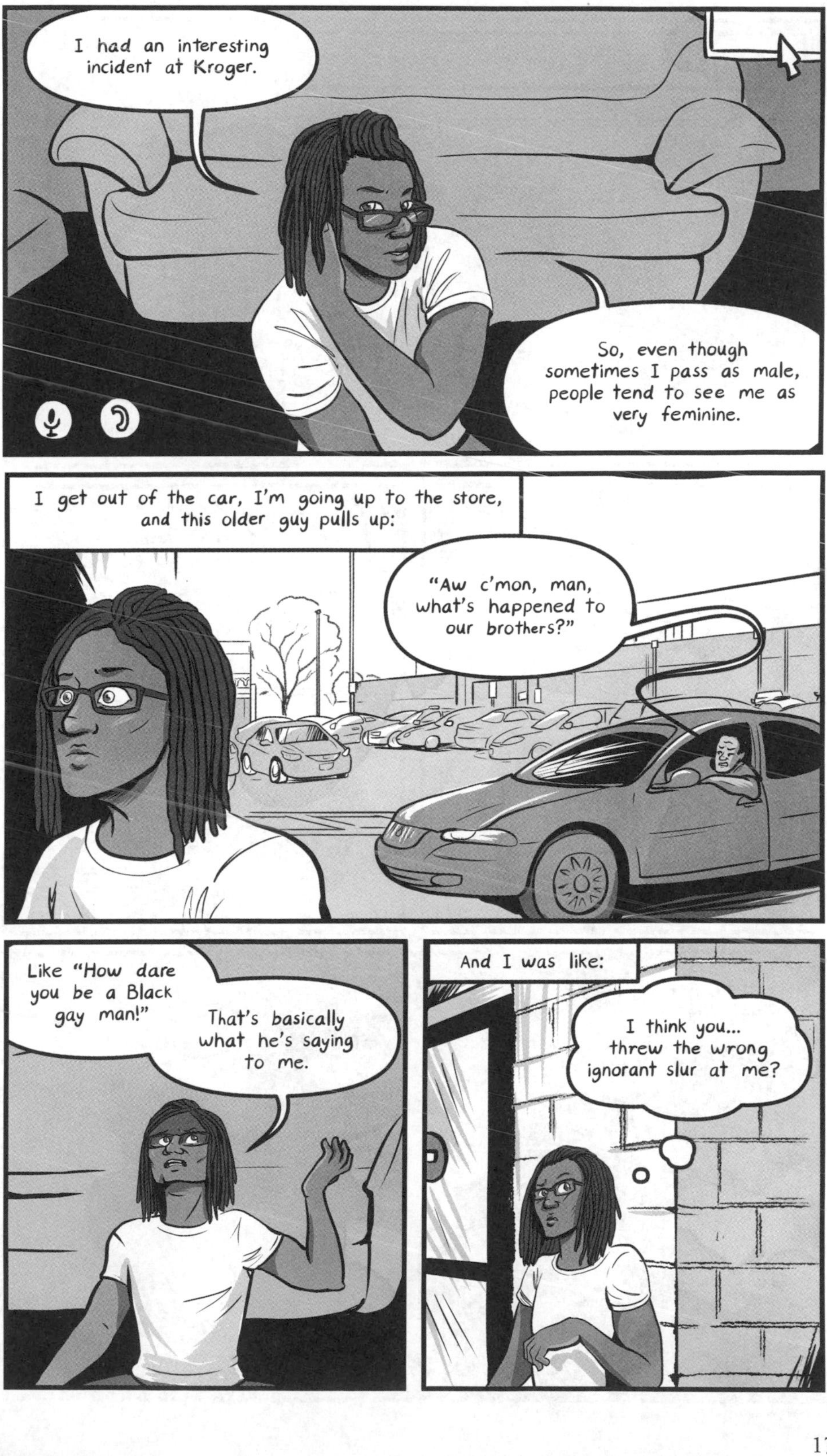

I had an interesting incident at Kroger.
So, even though sometimes I pass as male, people tend to see me as very feminine.
I get out of the car, I'm going up to the store, and this older guy pulls up:
"Aw c'mon, man, what's happened to our brothers?"
Like "How dare you be a Black gay man!"
That's basically what he's saying to me.
And I was like:
I think you... threw the wrong ignorant slur at me?

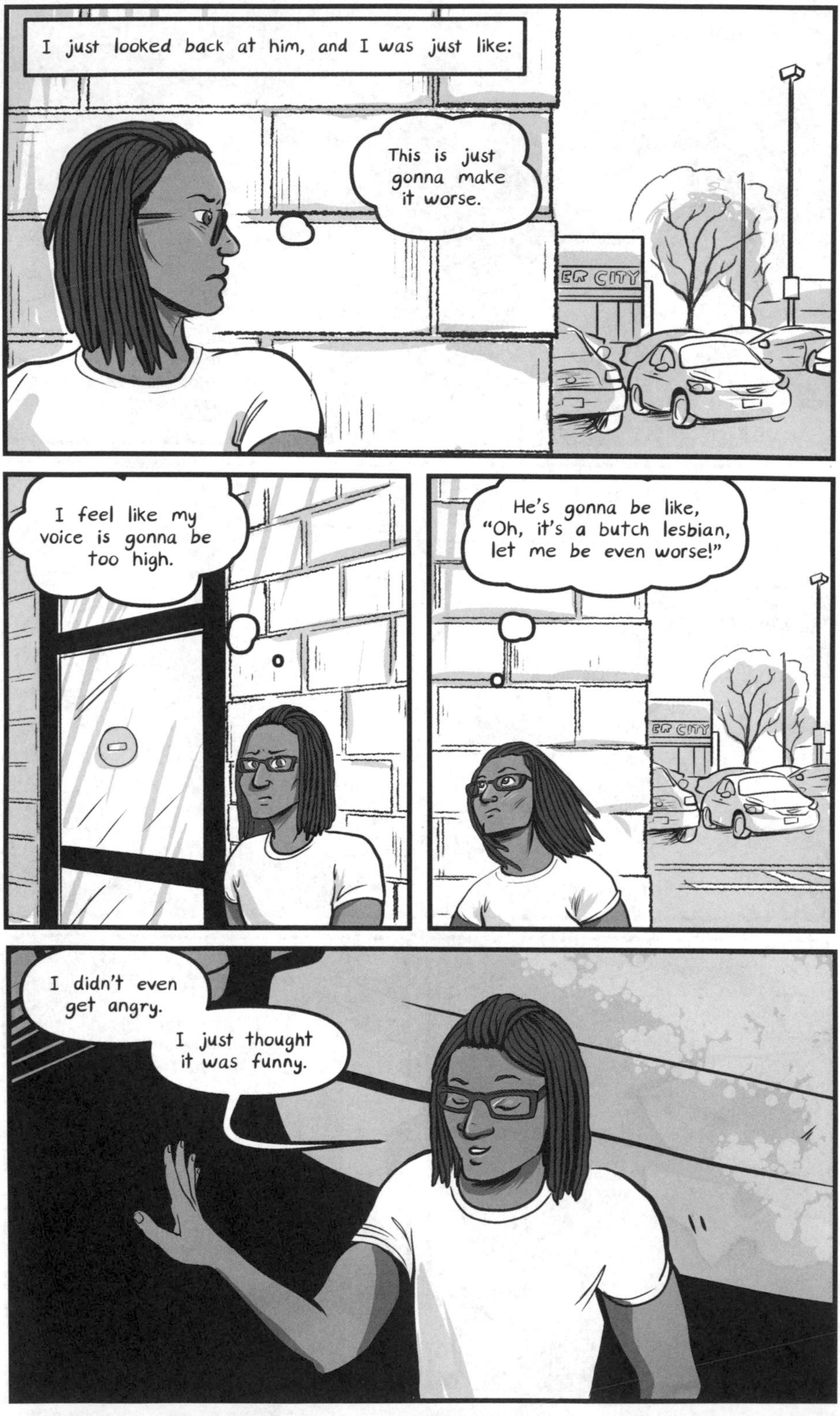
I just looked back at him, and I was just like:
This is just gonna make it worse.
ER CITY
I feel like my voice is gonna be too high.
He's gonna be like, "Oh, it's a butch lesbian, let me be even worse!"
ER CITY
I didn't even get angry.
I just thought it was funny.

Ignacio, 2013

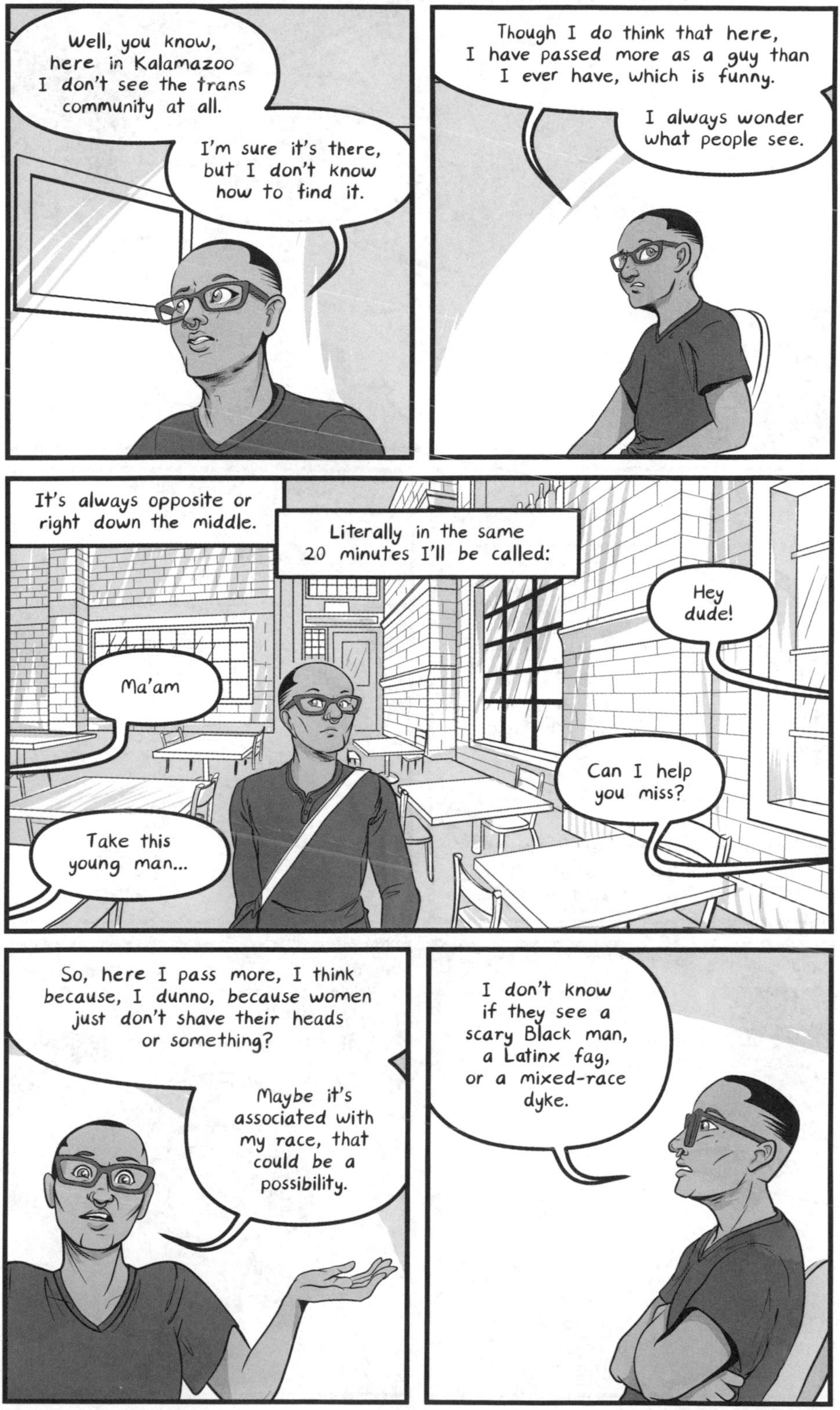
Well, you know, here in Kalamazoo I don't see the trans community at all.
I'm sure it's there, but I don't know how to find it.
Though I do think that here, I have passed more as a guy than I ever have, which is funny.
I always wonder what people see.
It's always opposite or right down the middle.
Literally in the same 20 minutes I'll be called:
Hey dude!
Ma'am
Can I help you miss?
Take this young man...
So, here I pass more, I think because, I dunno, because women just don't shave their heads or something?
Maybe it's associated with my race, that could be a possibility.
I don't know if they see a scary Black man, a Latinx fag, or a mixed-race dyke.

Anonymous, 2012

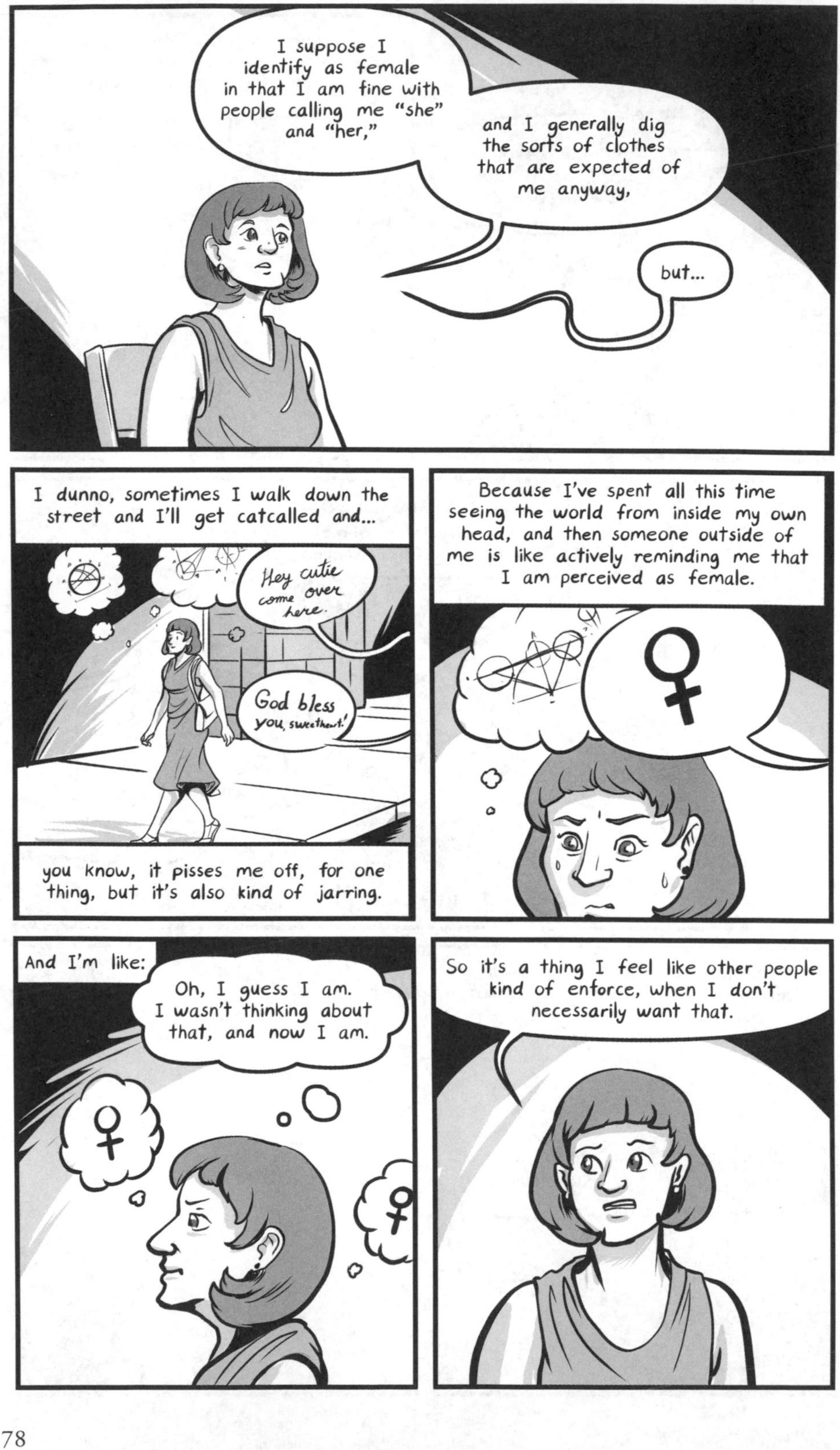
I suppose I identify as female in that I am fine with people calling me "she" and "her,"
and I generally dig the sorts of clothes that are expected of me anyway,
but...
I dunno, sometimes I walk down the street and I'll get catcalled and...
Hey cutie come over here.
God bless you, sweetheart!
you know, it pisses me off, for one thing, but it's also kind of jarring.
Because I've spent all this time seeing the world from inside my own head, and then someone outside of me is like actively reminding me that I am perceived as female.
♀
And I'm like:
Oh, I guess I am. I wasn't thinking about that, and now I am.
♀
♀
So it's a thing I feel like other people kind of enforce, when I don't necessarily want that.

Gerbil, 2012

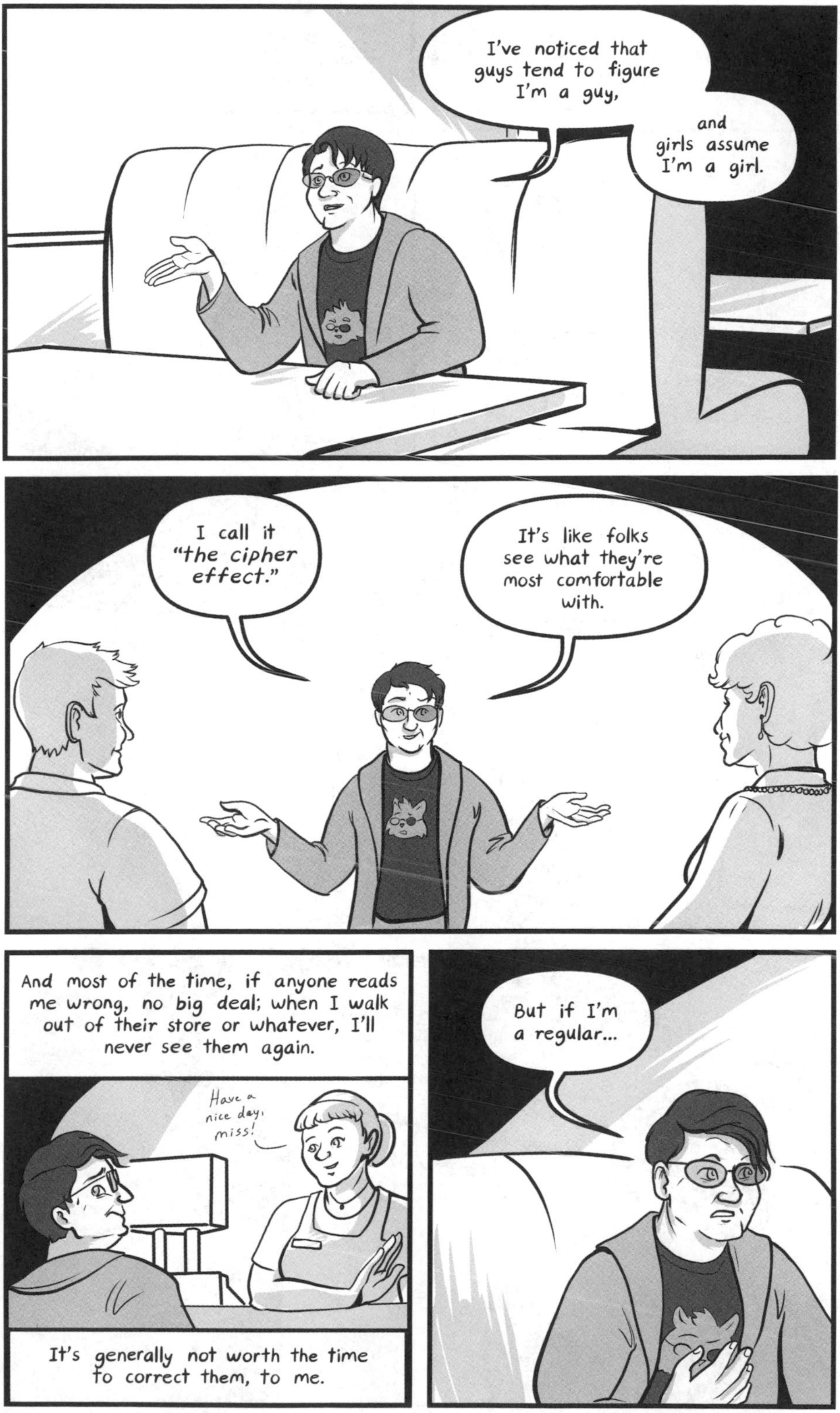
I've noticed that guys tend to figure I'm a guy,
and girls assume I'm a girl.
I call it *"the cipher effect."*
It's like folks see what they're most comfortable with.
And most of the time, if anyone reads me wrong, no big deal; when I walk out of their store or whatever, I'll never see them again.
Have a nice day, miss!
It's generally not worth the time to correct them, to me.
But if I'm a regular...

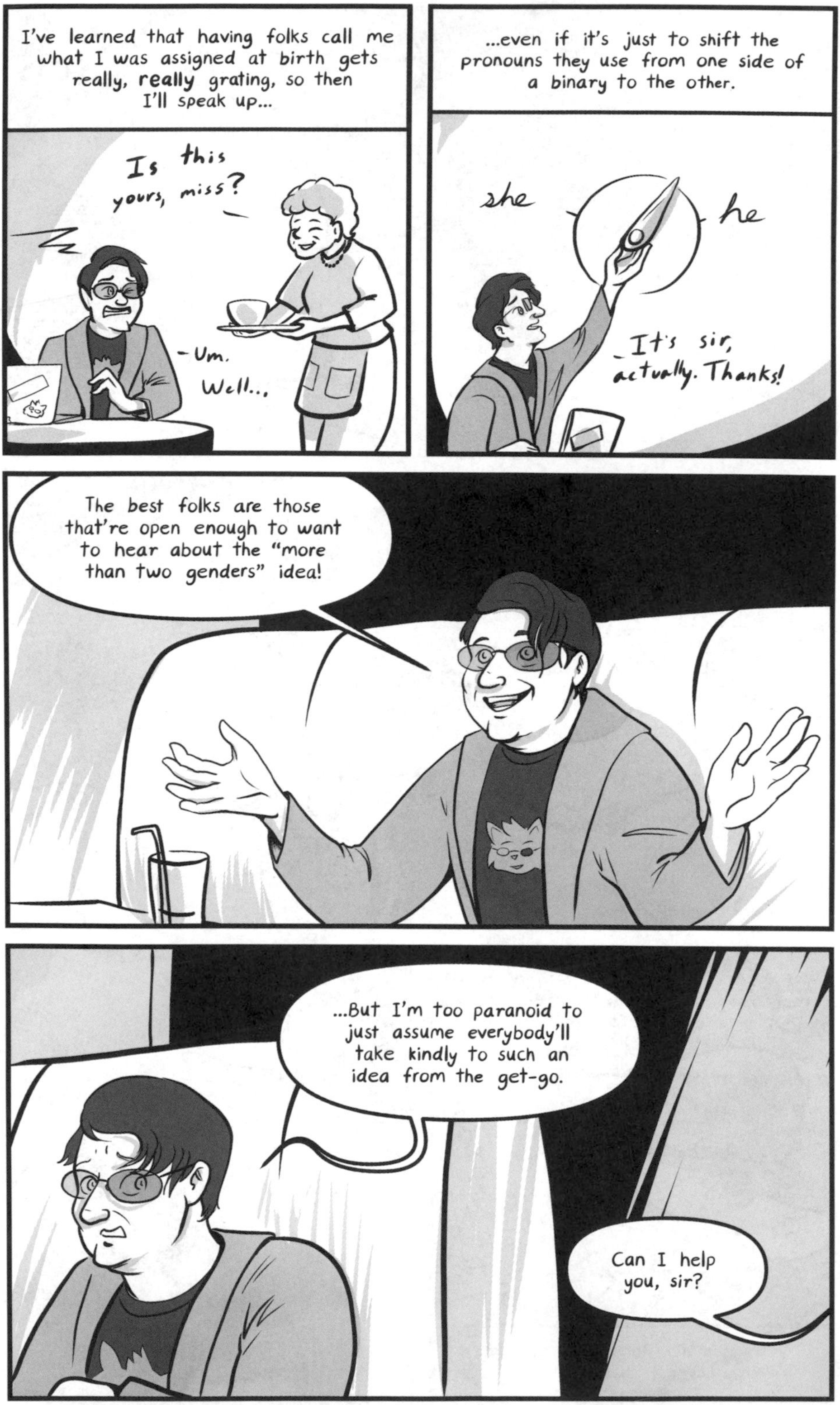
I've learned that having folks call me what I was assigned at birth gets really, **really** grating, so then I'll speak up...
...even if it's just to shift the pronouns they use from one side of a binary to the other.
Is this yours, miss?
-Um. Well...
she
he
It's sir, actually. Thanks!
The best folks are those that're open enough to want to hear about the "more than two genders" idea!
...But I'm too paranoid to just assume everybody'll take kindly to such an idea from the get-go.
Can I help you, sir?

Haley, 2012

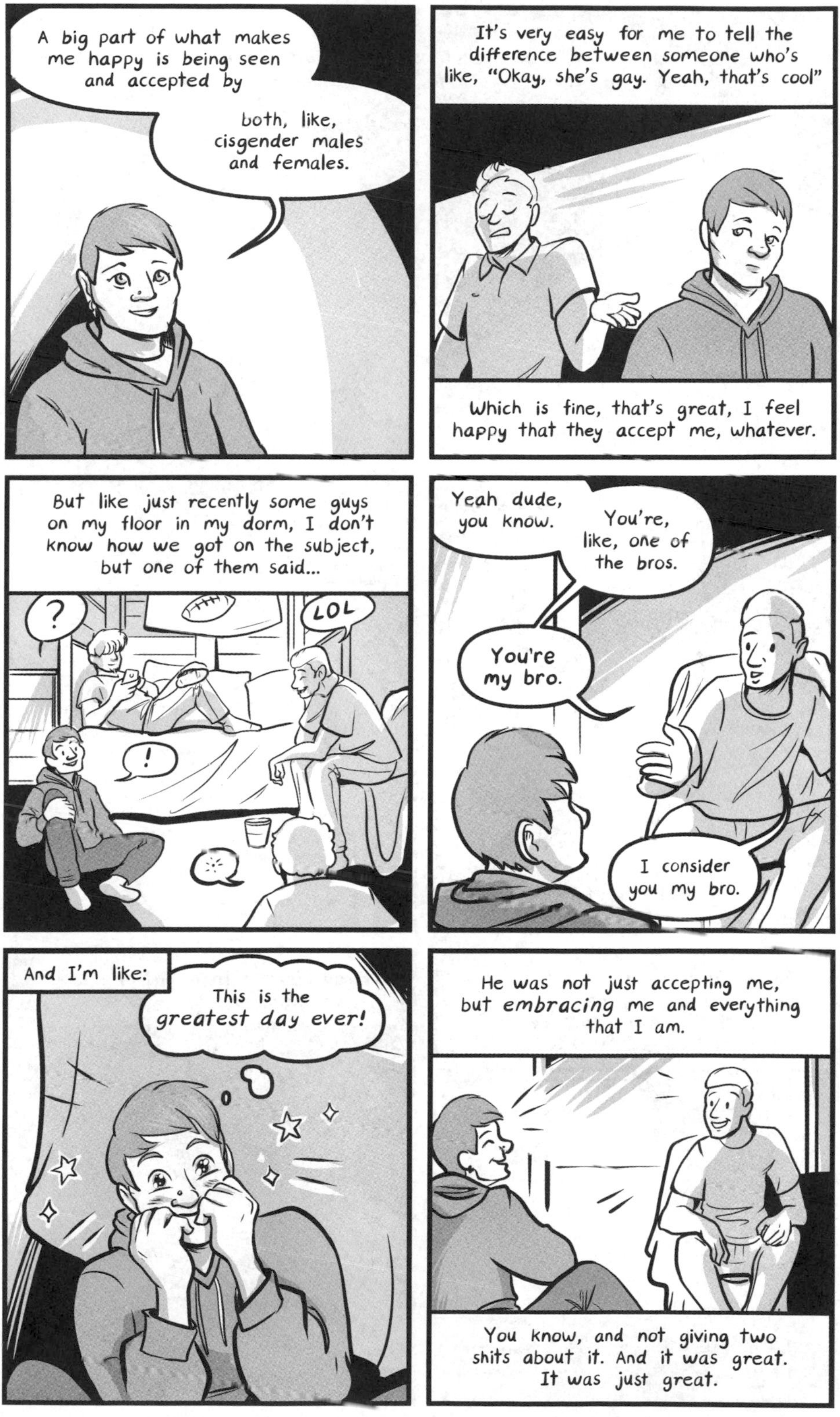
A big part of what makes me happy is being seen and accepted by
both, like, cisgender males and females.
It's very easy for me to tell the difference between someone who's like, "Okay, she's gay. Yeah, that's cool"
Which is fine, that's great, I feel happy that they accept me, whatever.
But like just recently some guys on my floor in my dorm, I don't know how we got on the subject, but one of them said...
?
LOL
!
Yeah dude, you know.
You're, like, one of the bros.
You're my bro.
I consider you my bro.
And I'm like:
This is the *greatest day ever!*
He was not just accepting me, but *embracing* me and everything that I am.
You know, and not giving two shits about it. And it was great. It was just great.

Very Anonymous, 2013

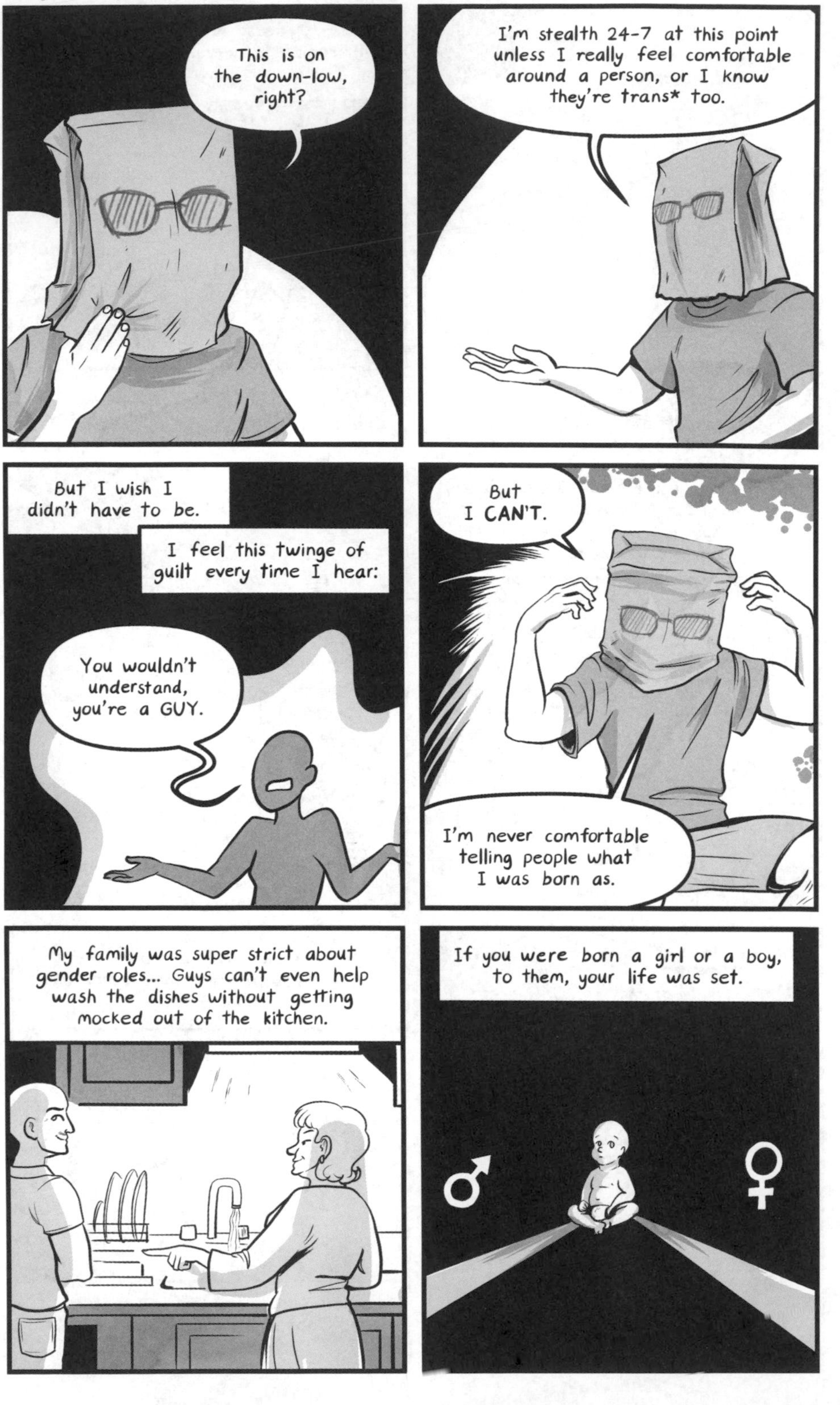

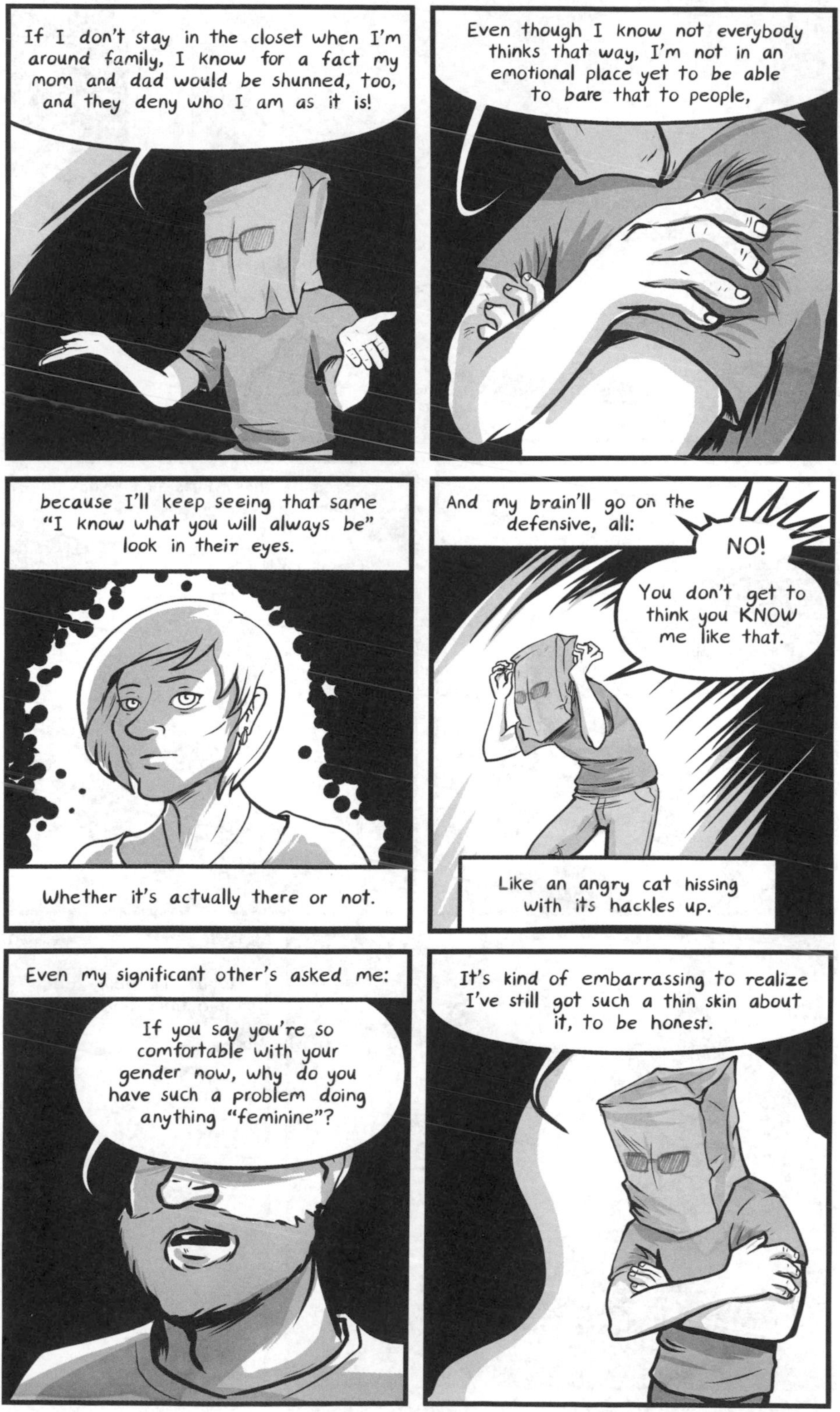

If I don't stay in the closet when I'm around family, I know for a fact my mom and dad would be shunned, too, and they deny who I am as it is!
Even though I know not everybody thinks that way, I'm not in an emotional place yet to be able to bare that to people,
because I'll keep seeing that same "I know what you will always be" look in their eyes.
Whether it's actually there or not.
And my brain'll go on the defensive, all:
NO!
You don't get to think you KNOW me like that.
Like an angry cat hissing with its hackles up.
Even my significant other's asked me:
If you say you're so comfortable with your gender now, why do you have such a problem doing anything "feminine"?
It's kind of embarrassing to realize I've still got such a thin skin about it, to be honest.

Anonymous, 2014

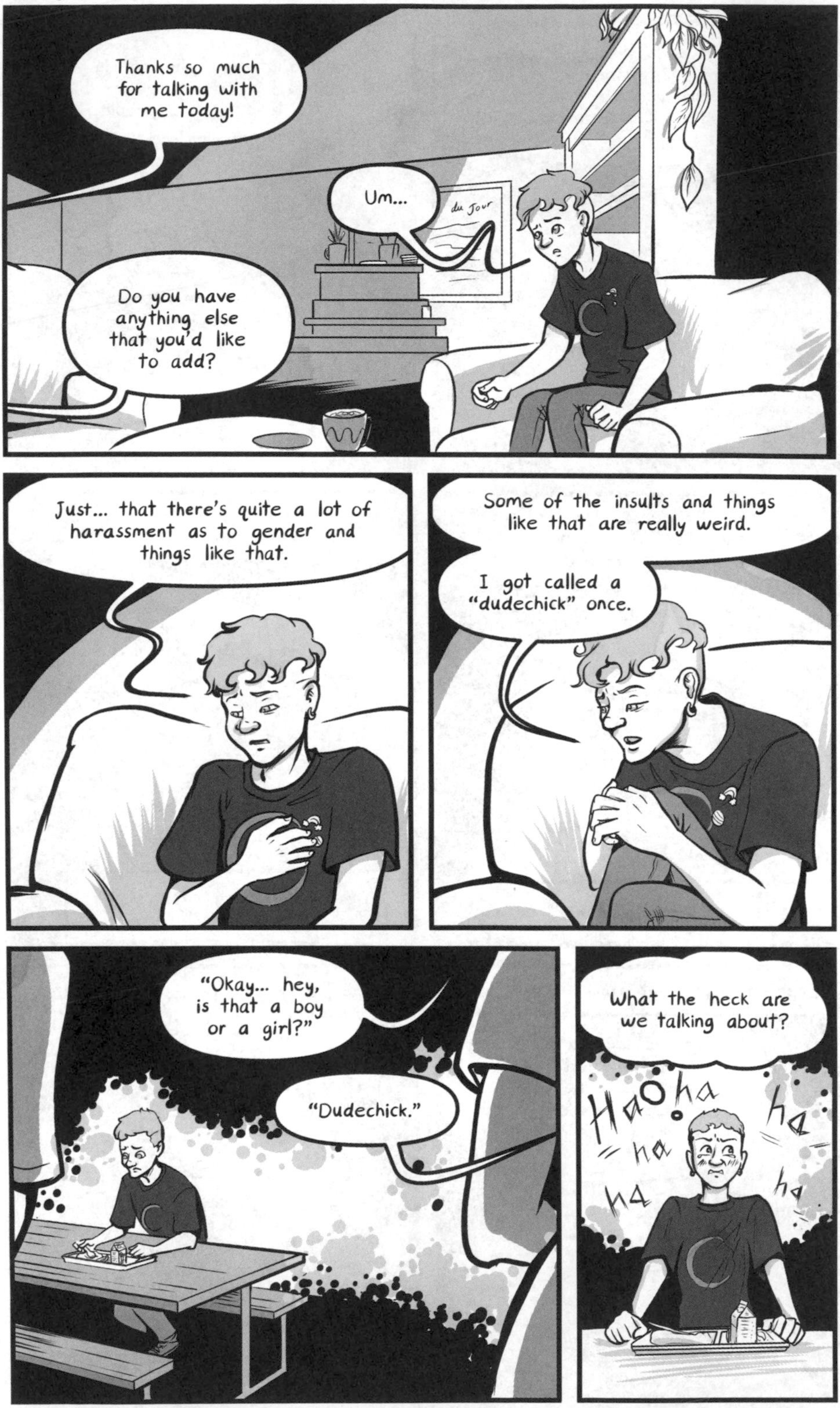
Thanks so much for talking with me today!
Um...
du Jour
Do you have anything else that you'd like to add?
Just... that there's quite a lot of harassment as to gender and things like that.
Some of the insults and things like that are really weird.
I got called a "dudechick" once.
"Okay... hey, is that a boy or a girl?"
"Dudechick."
What the heck are we talking about?
HAHAha ha ha ha ha

Heads Up! The next 2 pages discuss suicide. Do me a favor and skip it if you're not in a space where that's safe for you. See Where to Access Support on page viii for mental health resources.

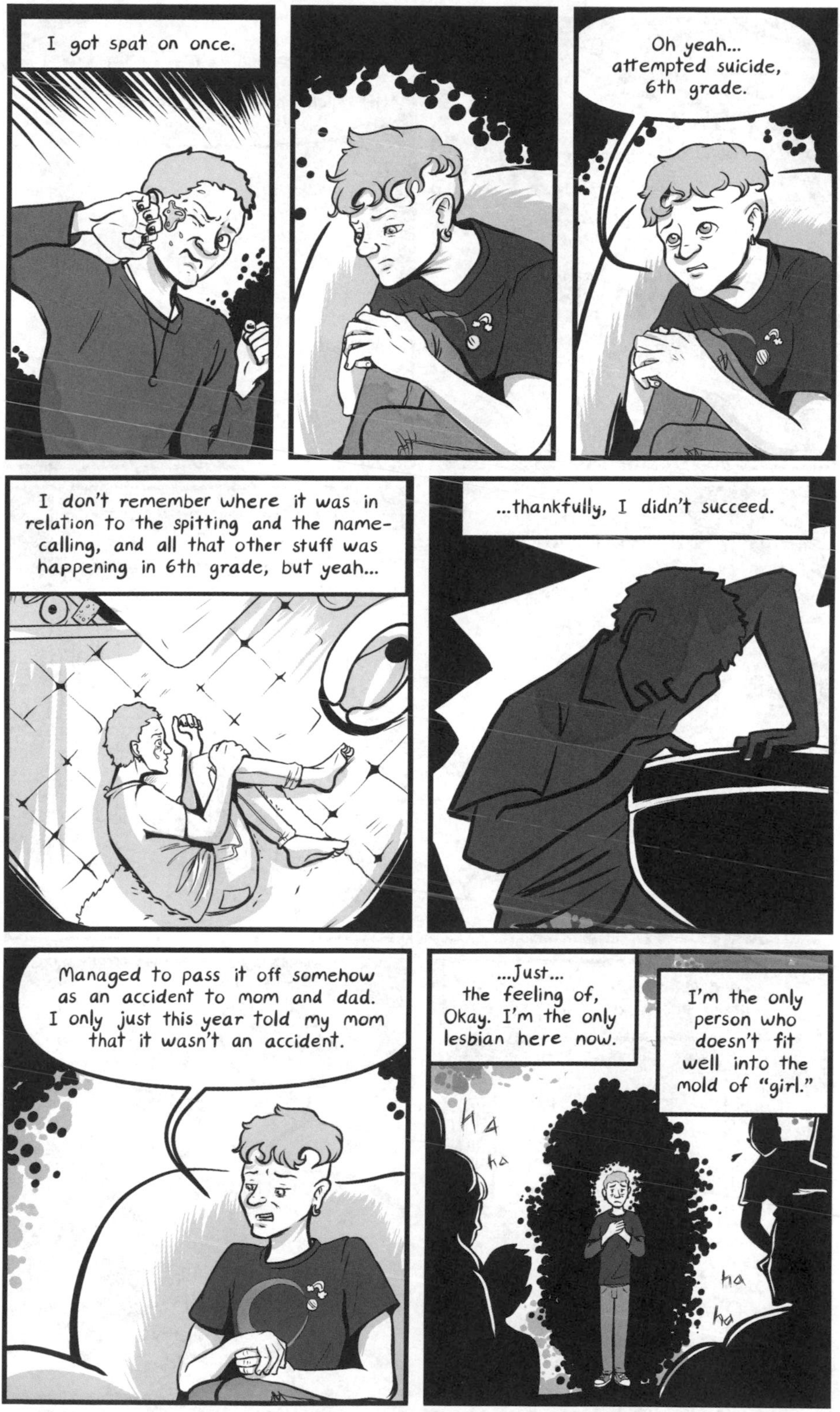
I got spat on once.
Oh yeah... attempted suicide, 6th grade.
I don't remember where it was in relation to the spitting and the name-calling, and all that other stuff was happening in 6th grade, but yeah...
...thankfully, I didn't succeed.
Managed to pass it off somehow as an accident to mom and dad. I only just this year told my mom that it wasn't an accident.
...Just... the feeling of, Okay. I'm the only lesbian here now.
I'm the only person who doesn't fit well into the mold of "girl."
ha
ha
ha
ha

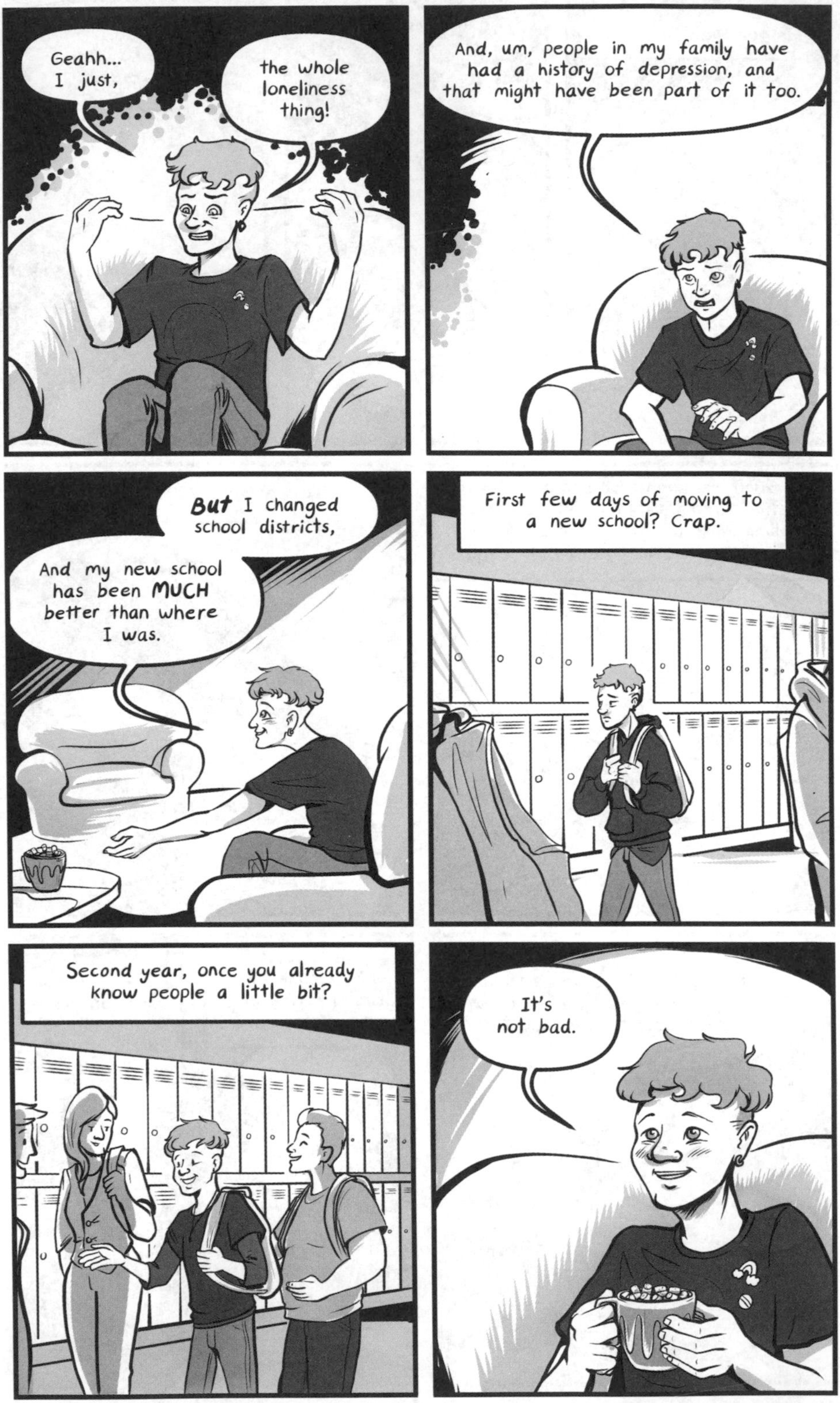
Geahh...
I just,
the whole loneliness thing!
And, um, people in my family have had a history of depression, and that might have been part of it too.
But I changed school districts,
And my new school has been MUCH better than where I was.
First few days of moving to a new school? Crap.
Second year, once you already know people a little bit?
It's not bad.

Rhea, 2015

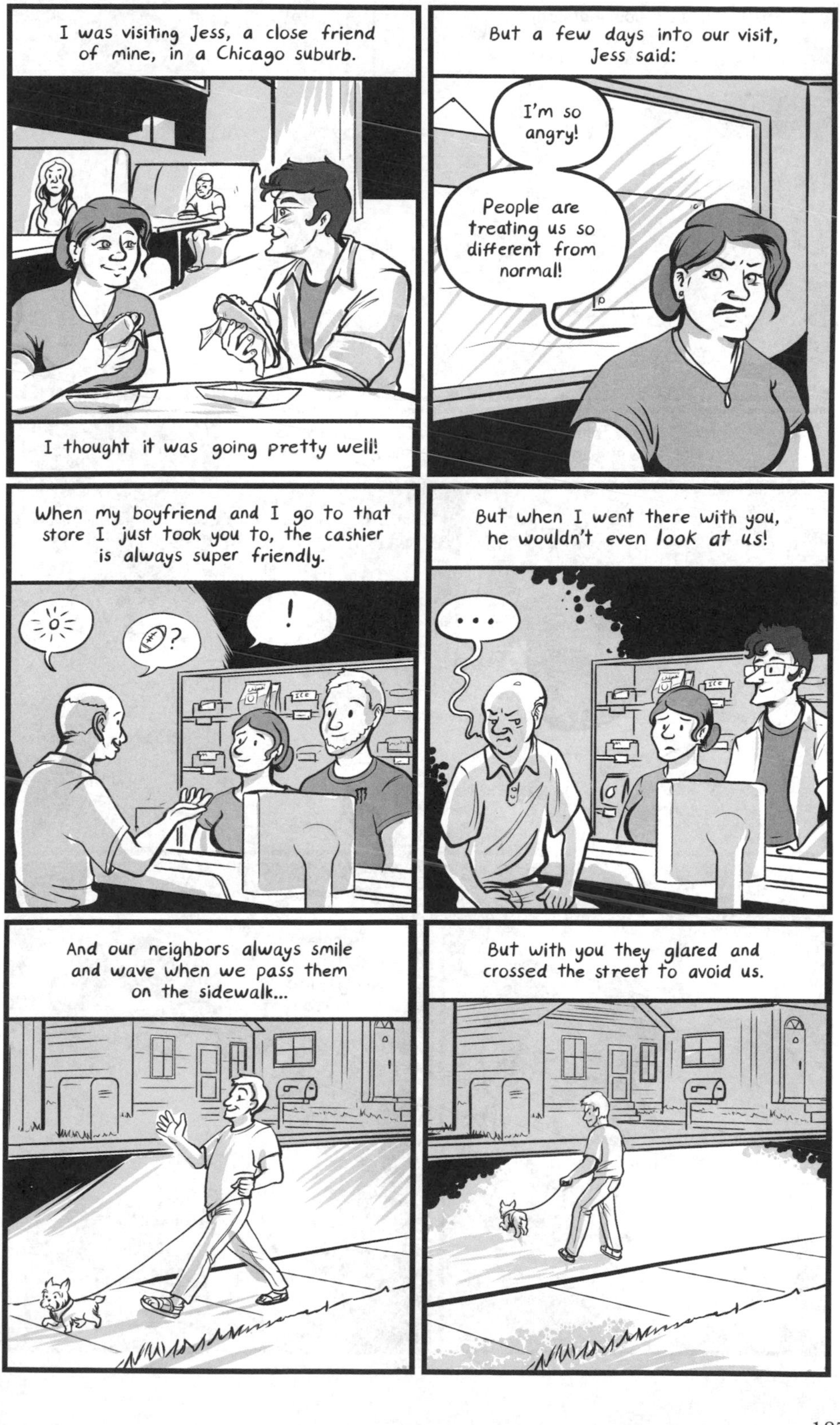
I was visiting Jess, a close friend of mine, in a Chicago suburb.
I thought it was going pretty well!
But a few days into our visit, Jess said:
I'm so angry!
People are treating us so different from normal!
When my boyfriend and I go to that store I just took you to, the cashier is always super friendly.
?
!
But when I went there with you, he wouldn't even look at us!
...
And our neighbors always smile and wave when we pass them on the sidewalk...
But with you they glared and crossed the street to avoid us.

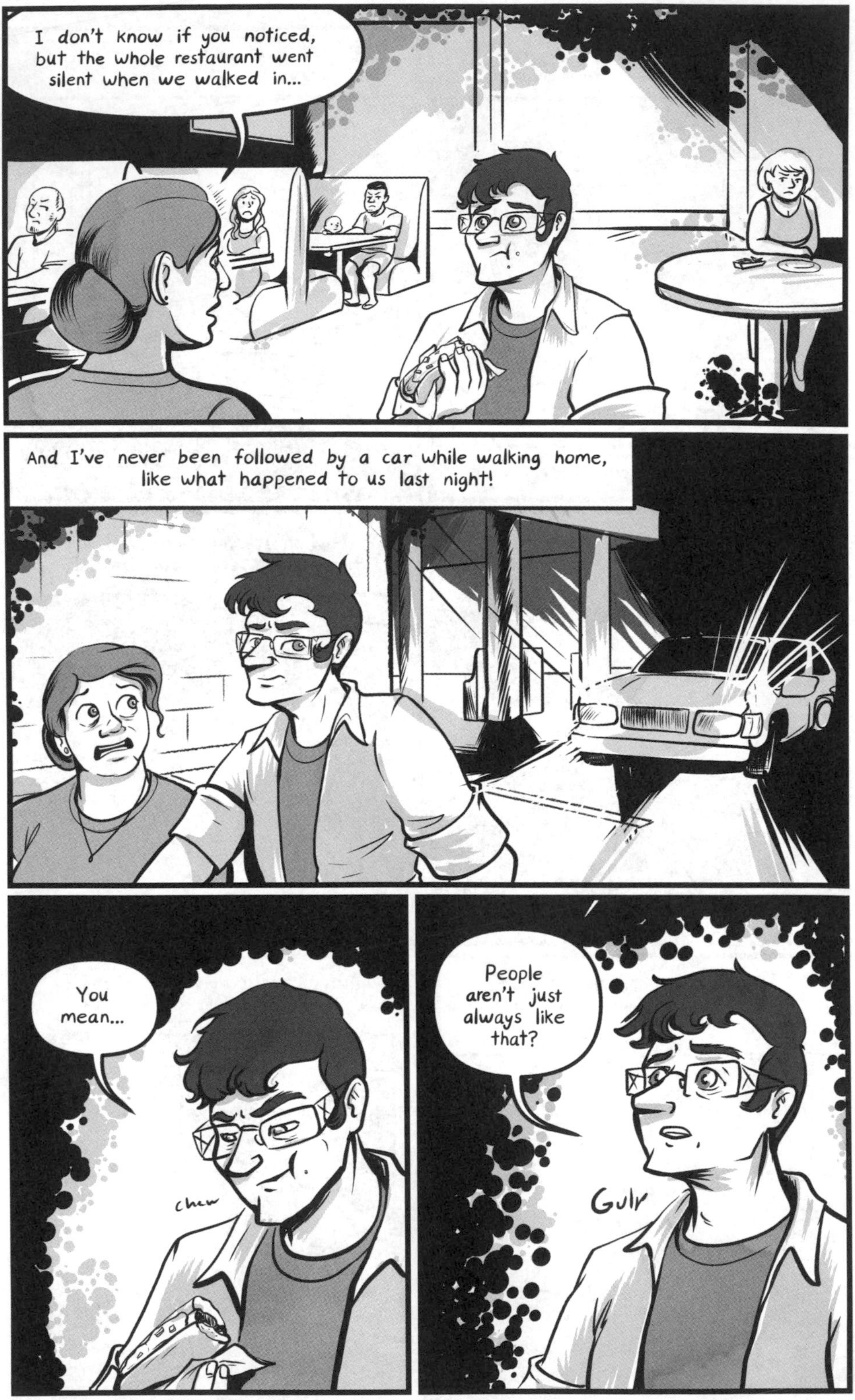

I don't know if you noticed, but the whole restaurant went silent when we walked in...
And I've never been followed by a car while walking home, like what happened to us last night!
You mean...
chew
People aren't just always like that?
Gulp

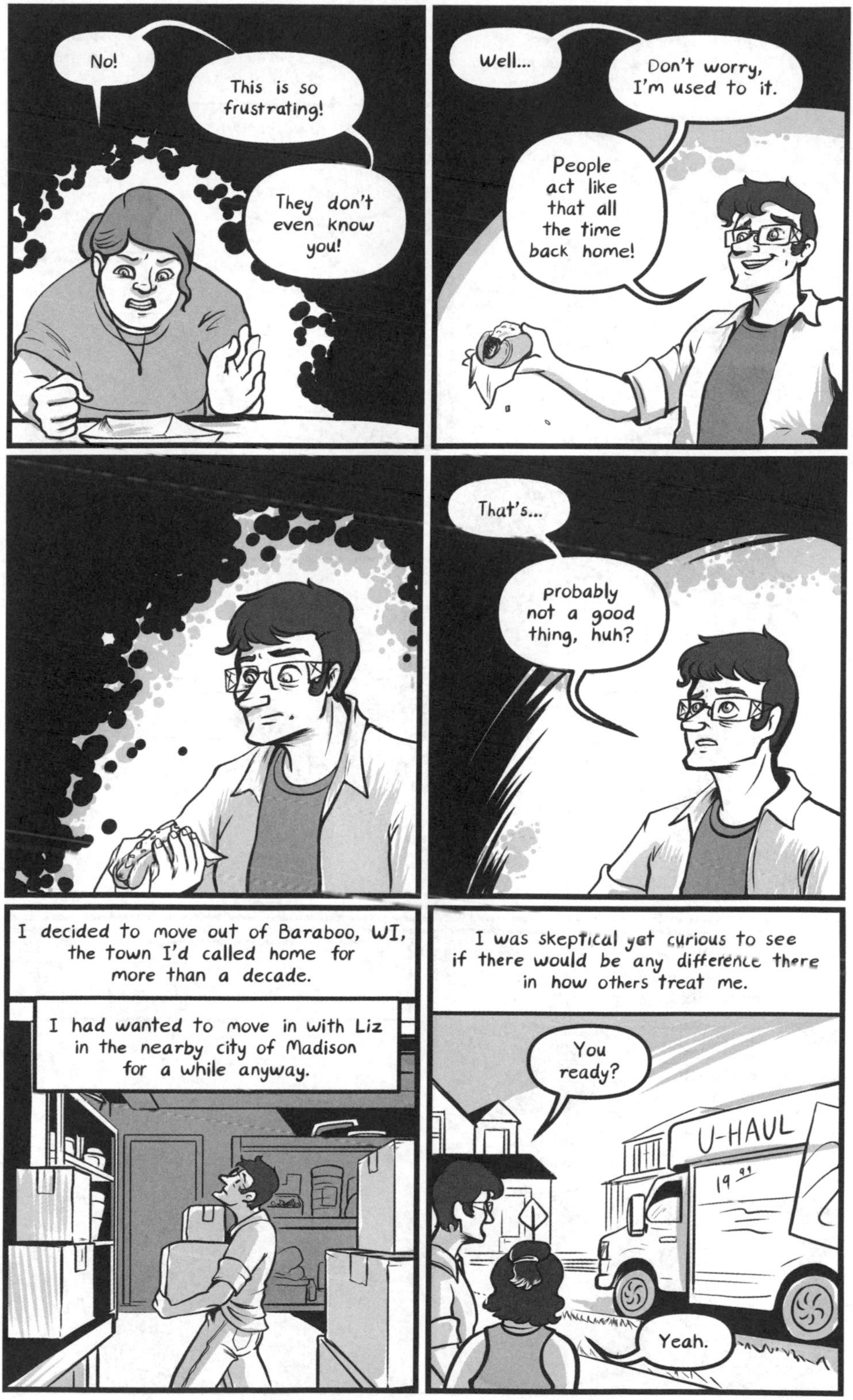

No!
This is so frustrating!
They don't even know you!
Well...
Don't worry, I'm used to it.
People act like that all the time back home!
That's...
probably not a good thing, huh?
I decided to move out of Baraboo, WI, the town I'd called home for more than a decade.
I had wanted to move in with Liz in the nearby city of Madison for a while anyway.
I was skeptical yet curious to see if there would be any difference there in how others treat me.
You ready?
U-HAUL
19.99
Yeah.

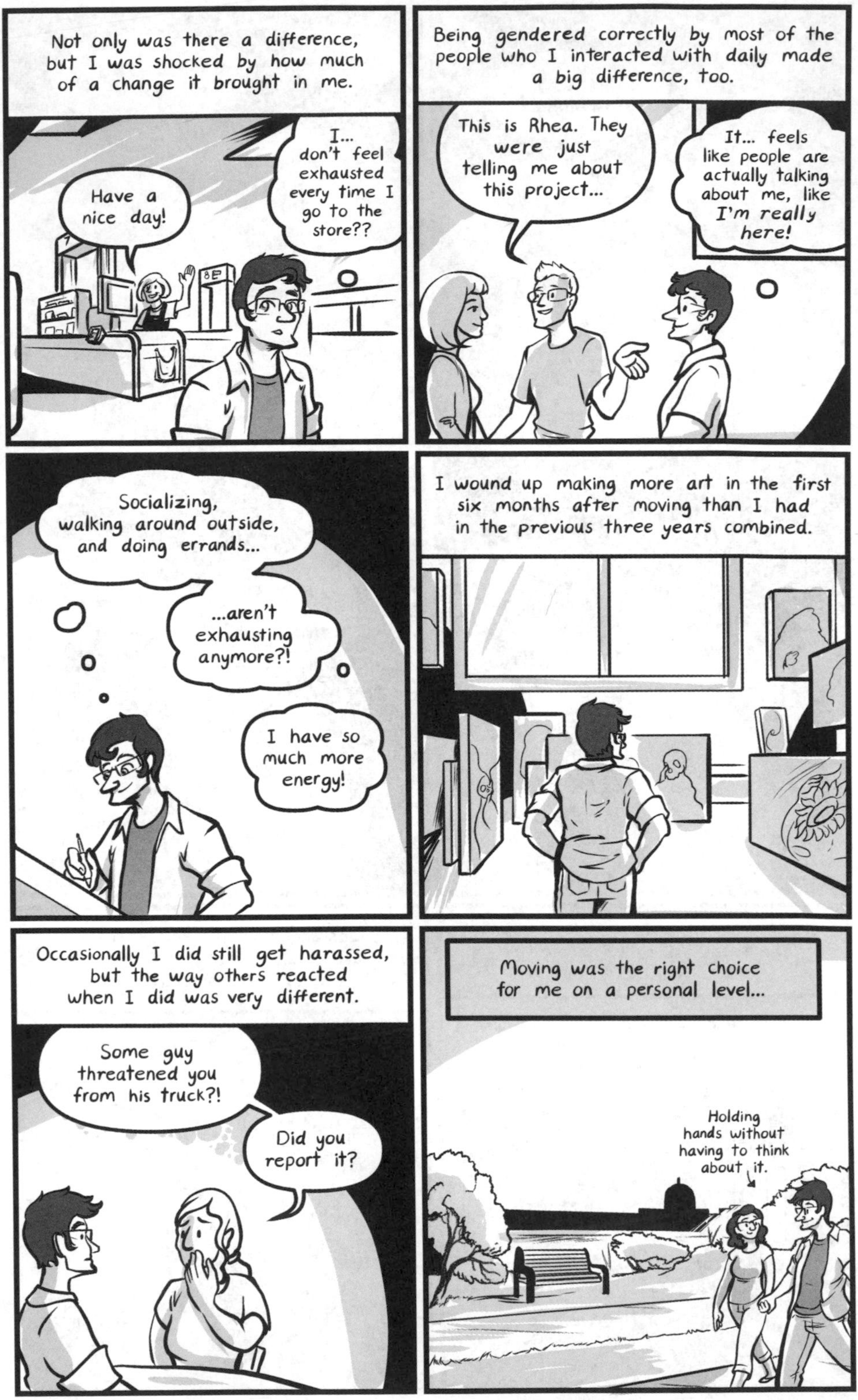
Not only was there a difference, but I was shocked by how much of a change it brought in me.
Have a nice day!
I... don't feel exhausted every time I go to the store??
Being gendered correctly by most of the people who I interacted with daily made a big difference, too.
This is Rhea. They were just telling me about this project...
It... feels like people are actually talking about me, like *I'm really here!*
Socializing, walking around outside, and doing errands...
...aren't exhausting anymore?!
I have so much more energy!
I wound up making more art in the first six months after moving than I had in the previous three years combined.
Occasionally I did still get harassed, but the way others reacted when I did was very different.
Some guy threatened you from his truck?!
Did you report it?
Moving was the right choice for me on a personal level...
Holding hands without having to think about it.

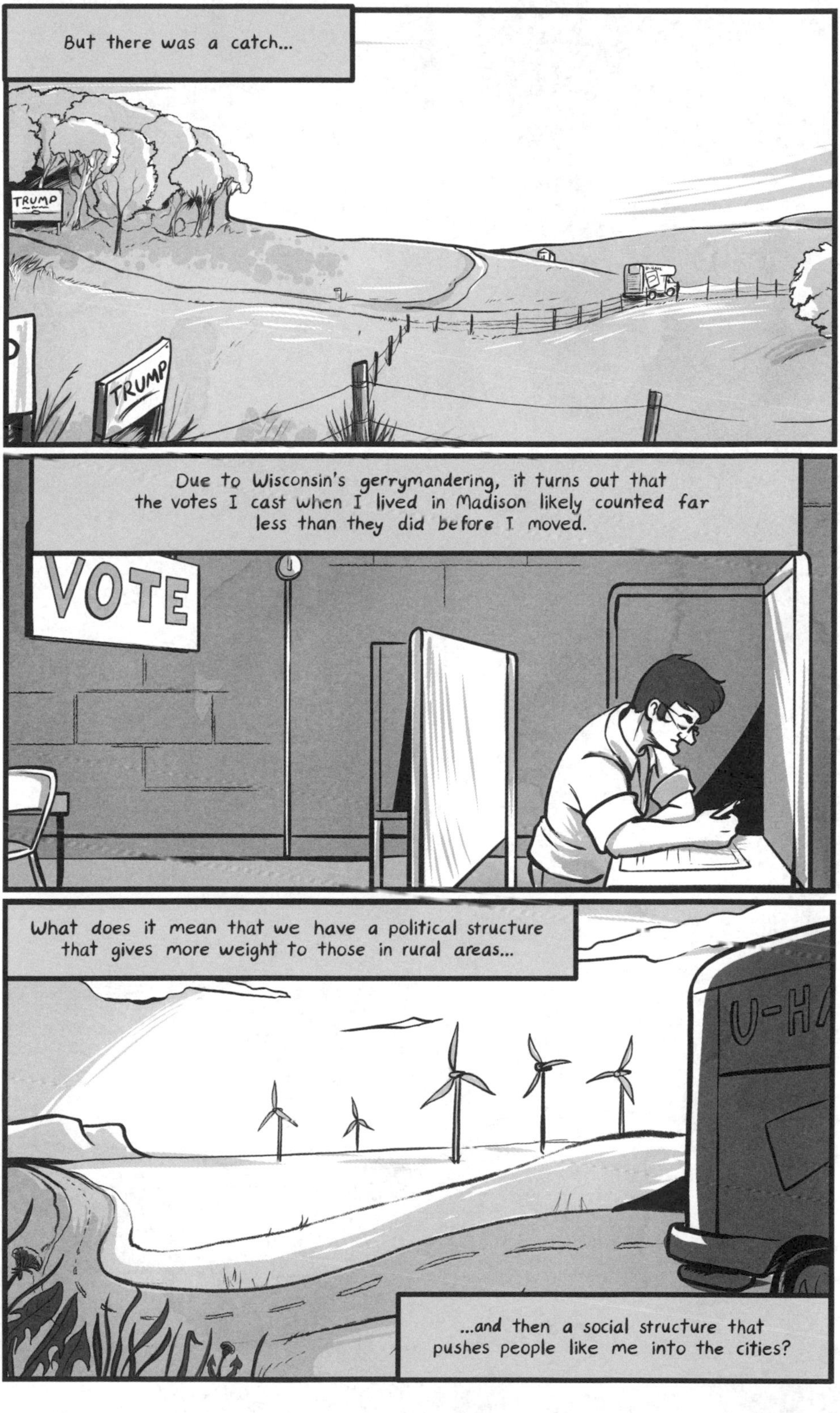
But there was a catch...
TRUMP
TRUMP
Due to Wisconsin's gerrymandering, it turns out that the votes I cast when I lived in Madison likely counted far less than they did before I moved.
VOTE
What does it mean that we have a political structure that gives more weight to those in rural areas...
...and then a social structure that pushes people like me into the cities?

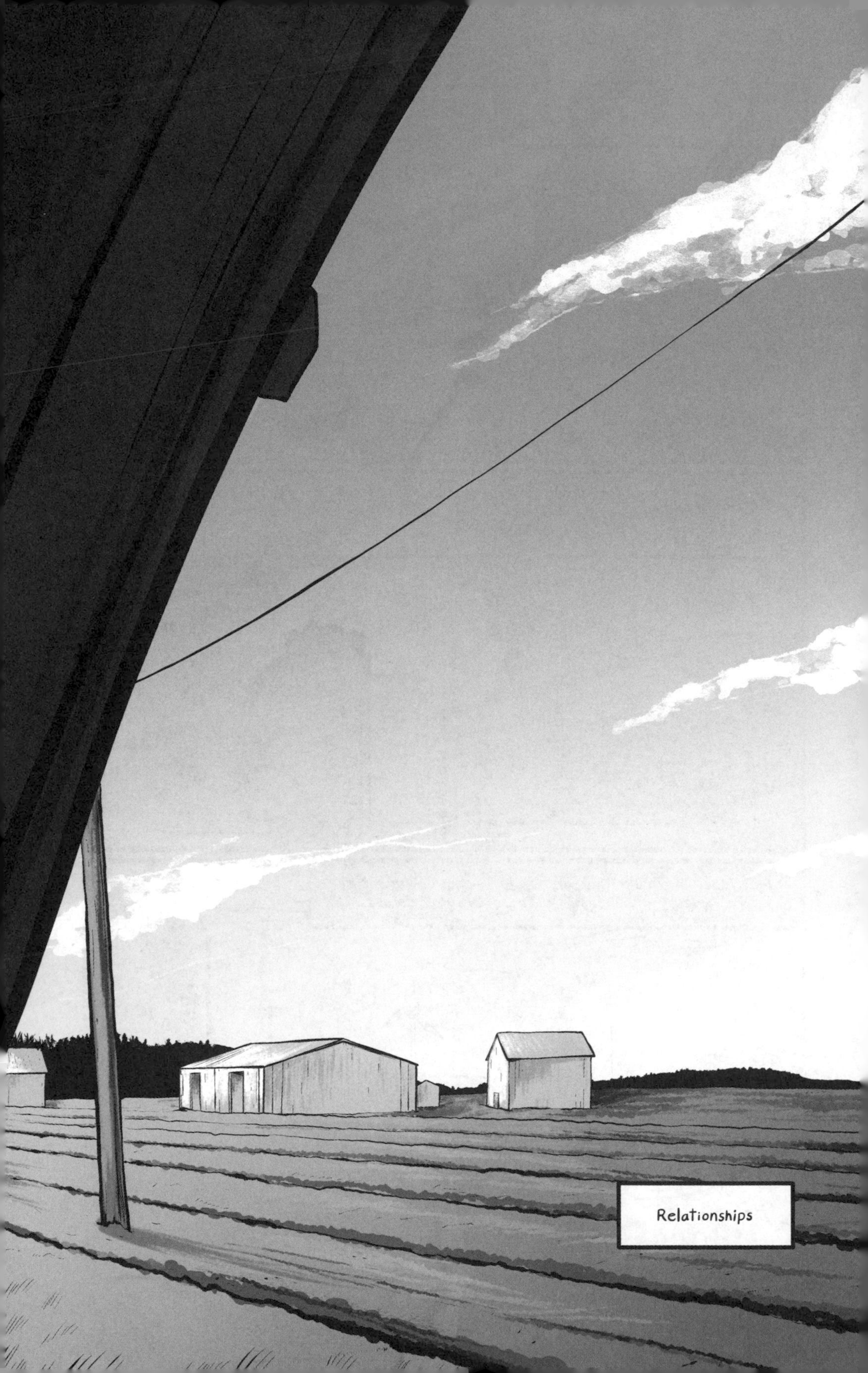
Relationships

Rhea, 2013

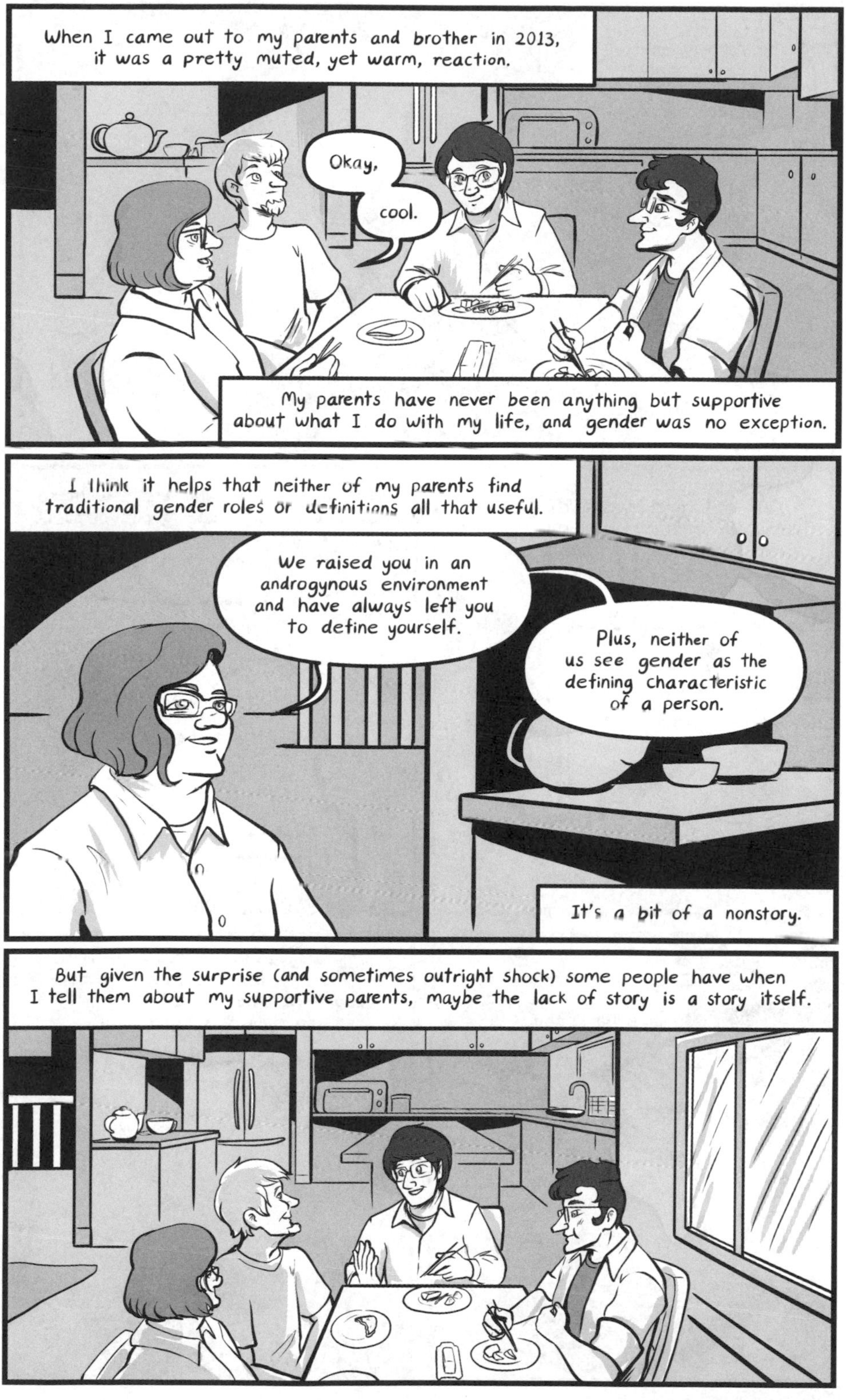
When I came out to my parents and brother in 2013, it was a pretty muted, yet warm, reaction.
Okay,
cool.
My parents have never been anything but supportive about what I do with my life, and gender was no exception.
I think it helps that neither of my parents find traditional gender roles or definitions all that useful.
We raised you in an androgynous environment and have always left you to define yourself.
Plus, neither of us see gender as the defining characteristic of a person.
It's a bit of a nonstory.
But given the surprise (and sometimes outright shock) some people have when I tell them about my supportive parents, maybe the lack of story is a story itself.

Gerbil, 2012

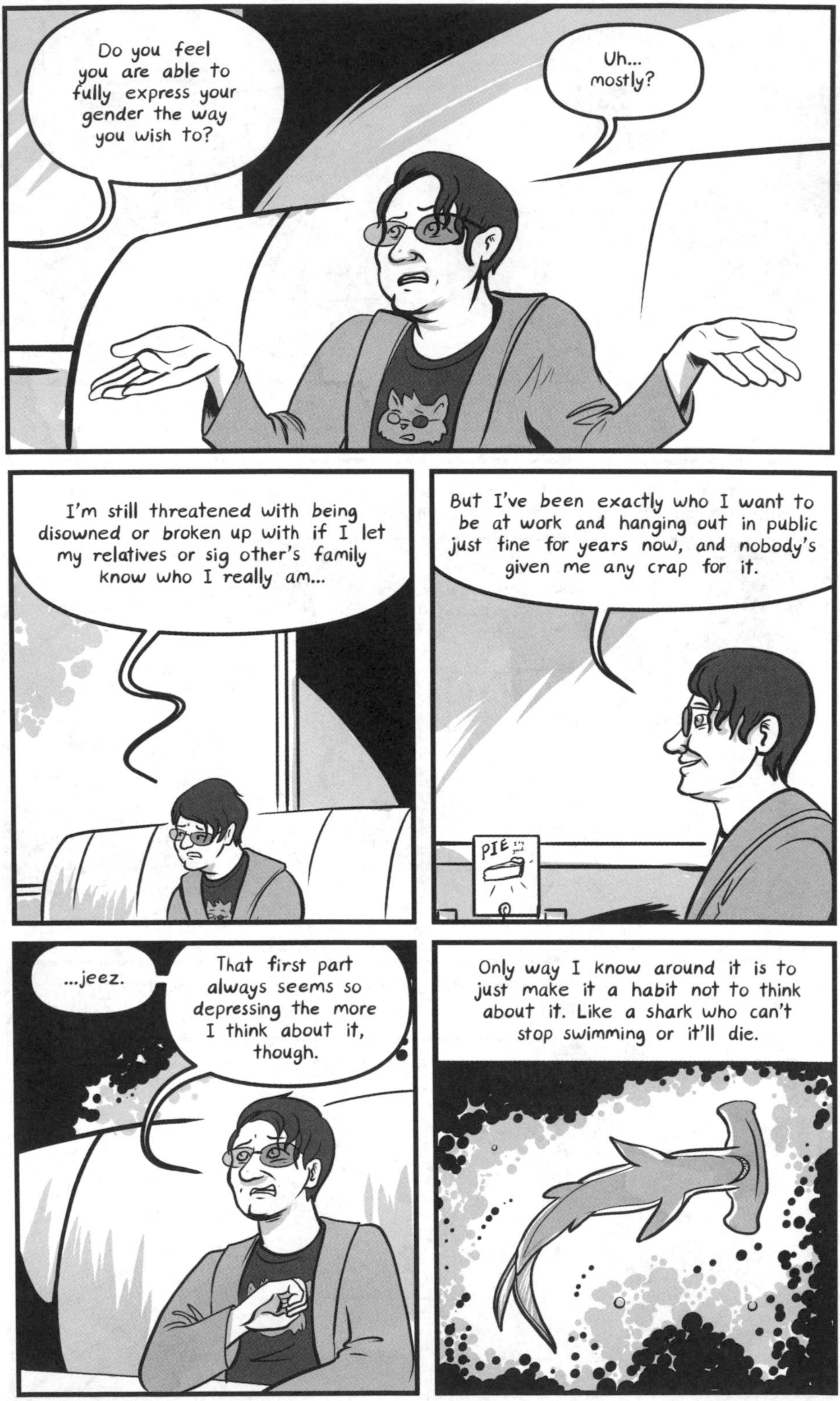
Do you feel you are able to fully express your gender the way you wish to?
Uh... mostly?
I'm still threatened with being disowned or broken up with if I let my relatives or sig other's family know who I really am...
But I've been exactly who I want to be at work and hanging out in public just fine for years now, and nobody's given me any crap for it.
PIE
...jeez.
That first part always seems so depressing the more I think about it, though.
Only way I know around it is to just make it a habit not to think about it. Like a shark who can't stop swimming or it'll die.

Enne, 2013

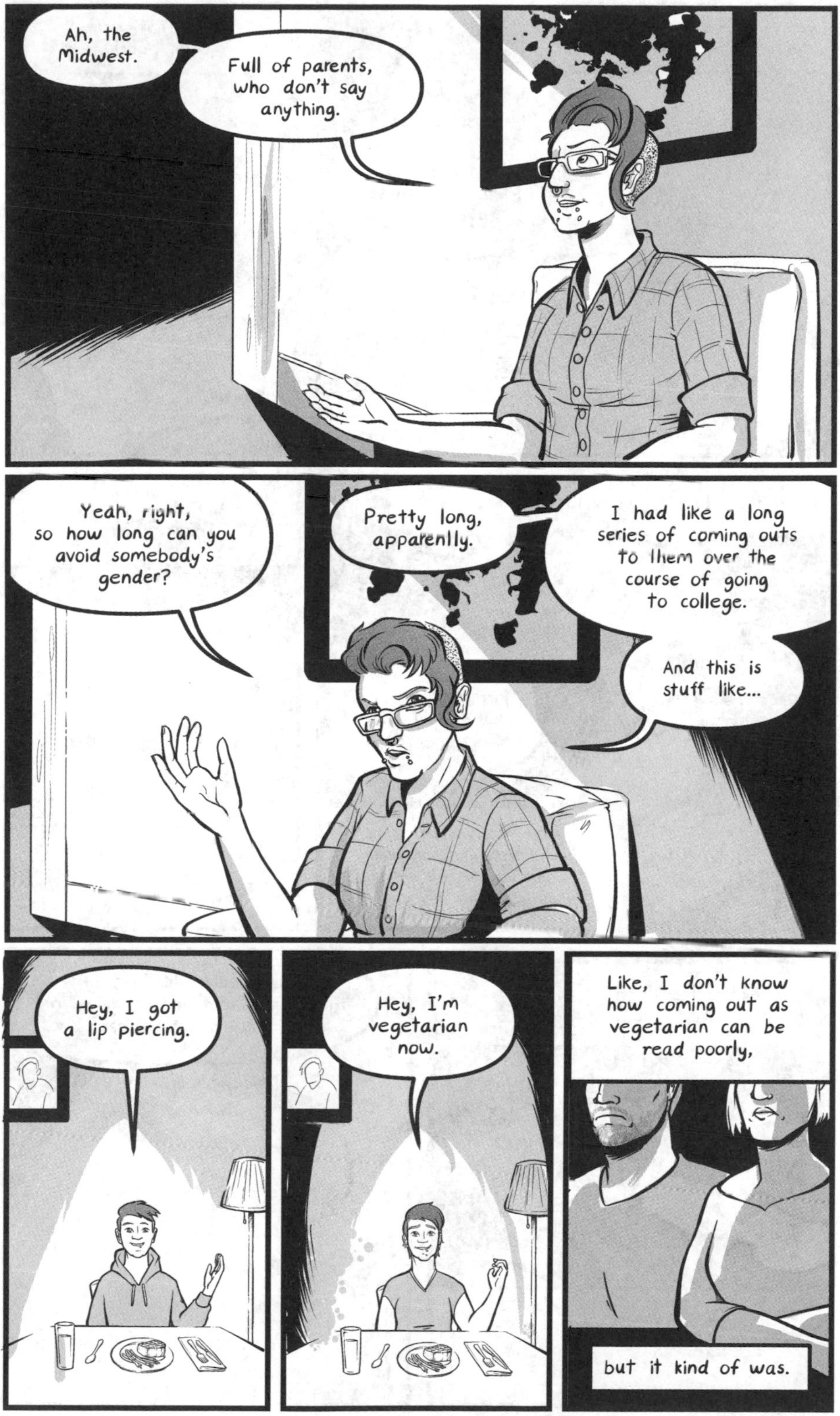

Ah, the Midwest.
Full of parents, who don't say anything.
Yeah, right, so how long can you avoid somebody's gender?
Pretty long, apparently.
I had like a long series of coming outs to them over the course of going to college.
And this is stuff like...
Hey, I got a lip piercing.
Hey, I'm vegetarian now.
Like, I don't know how coming out as vegetarian can be read poorly,
but it kind of was.

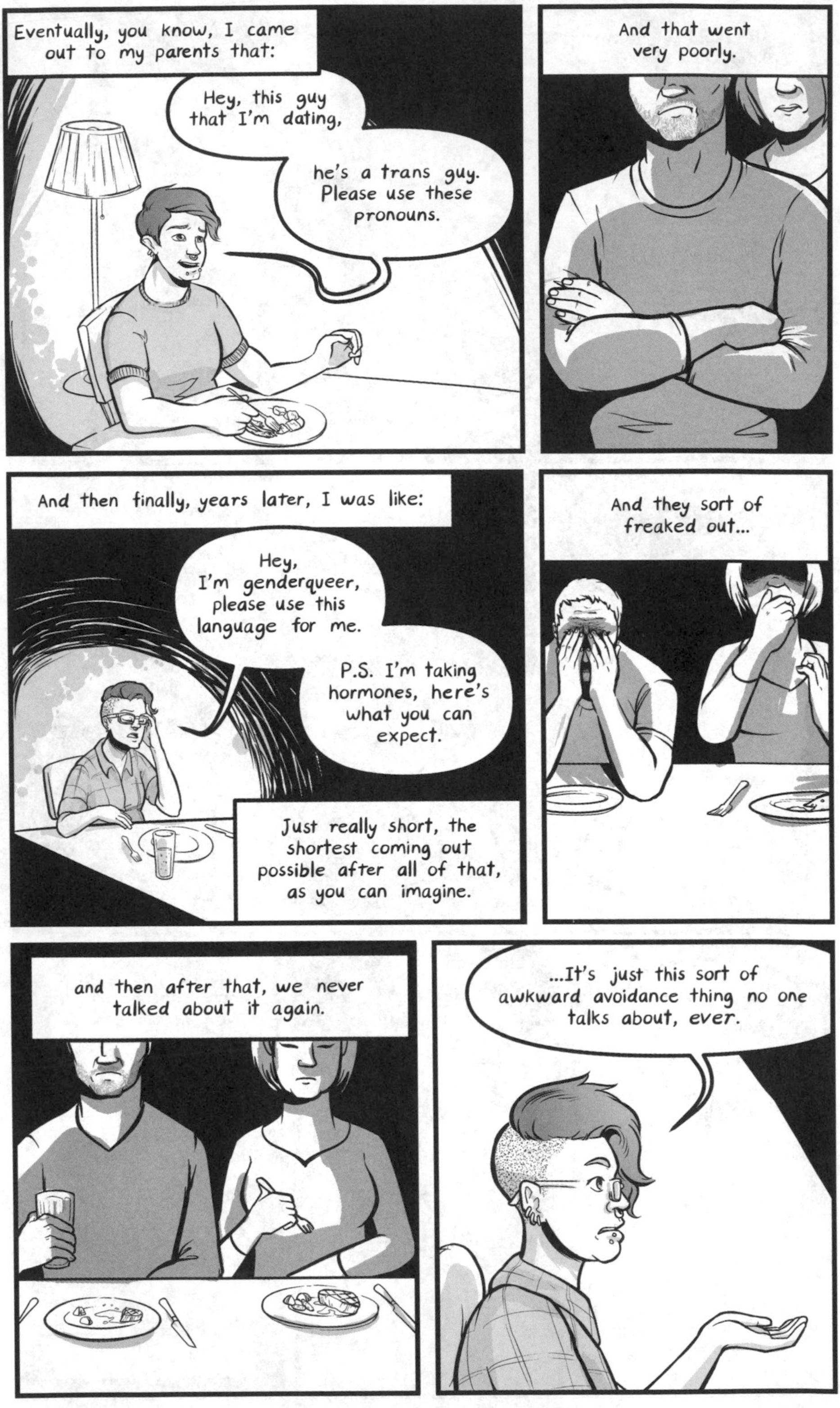
Eventually, you know, I came out to my parents that:
Hey, this guy that I'm dating,
he's a trans guy. Please use these pronouns.
And that went very poorly.
And then finally, years later, I was like:
Hey, I'm genderqueer, please use this language for me.
P.S. I'm taking hormones, here's what you can expect.
Just really short, the shortest coming out possible after all of that, as you can imagine.
And they sort of freaked out...
and then after that, we never talked about it again.
...It's just this sort of awkward avoidance thing no one talks about, *ever*.

Monei, 2015

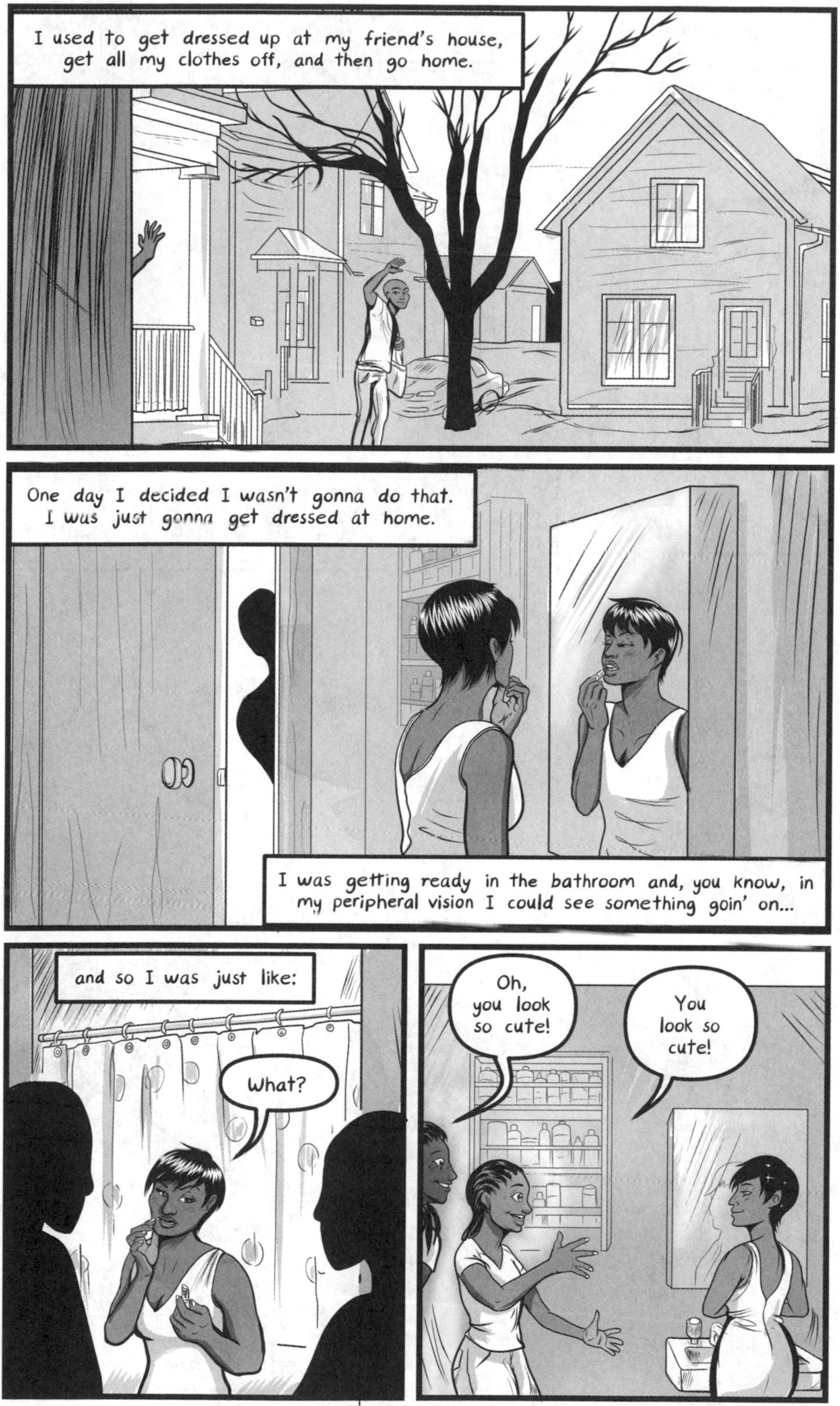

I used to get dressed up at my friend's house, get all my clothes off, and then go home.
One day I decided I wasn't gonna do that. I was just gonna get dressed at home.
I was getting ready in the bathroom and, you know, in my peripheral vision I could see something goin' on...
and so I was just like:
What?
Oh, you look so cute!
You look so cute!

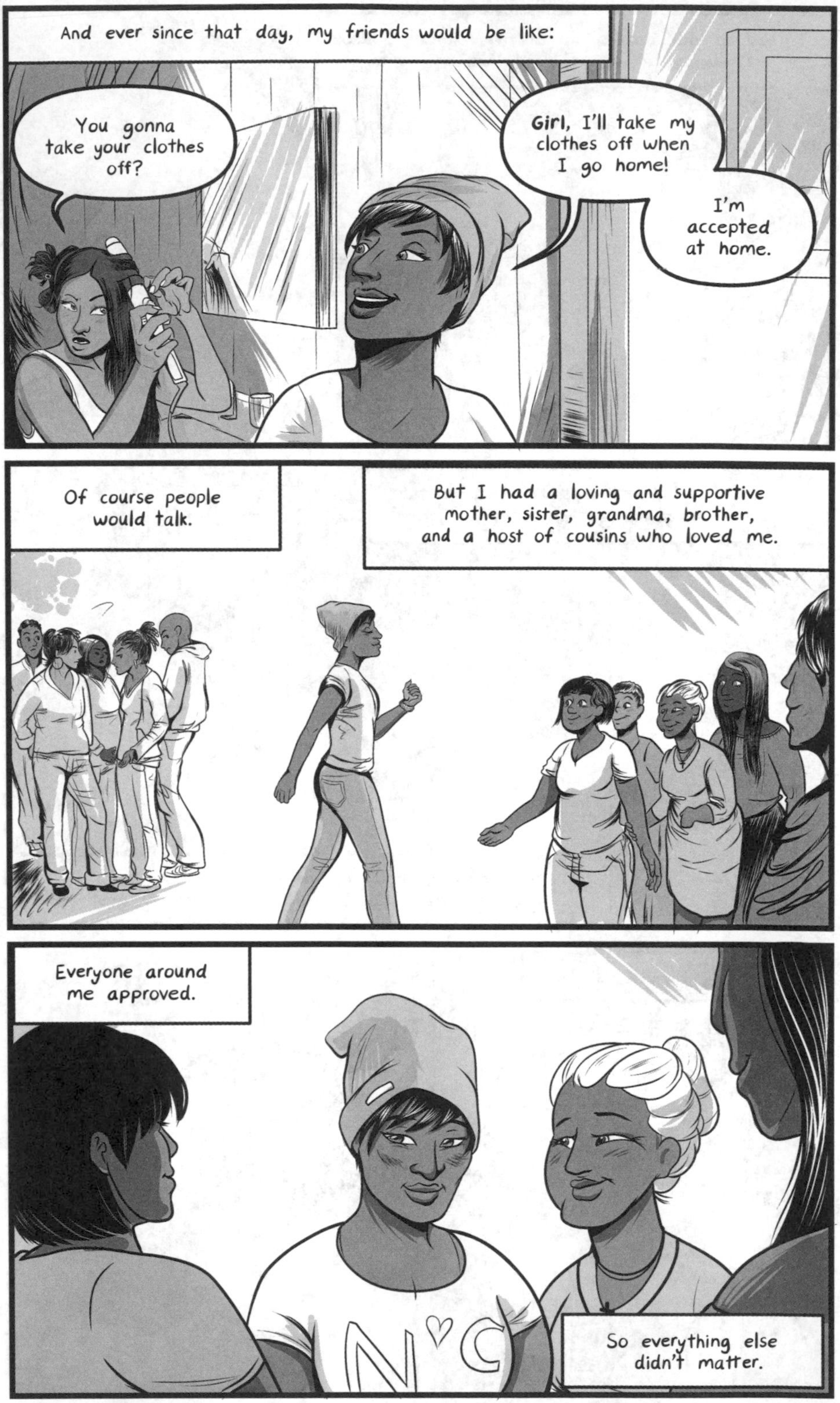
And ever since that day, my friends would be like:
You gonna take your clothes off?
Girl, I'll take my clothes off when I go home!
I'm accepted at home.
Of course people would talk.
But I had a loving and supportive mother, sister, grandma, brother, and a host of cousins who loved me.
Everyone around me approved.
N♡C
So everything else didn't matter.

Paris, 2015

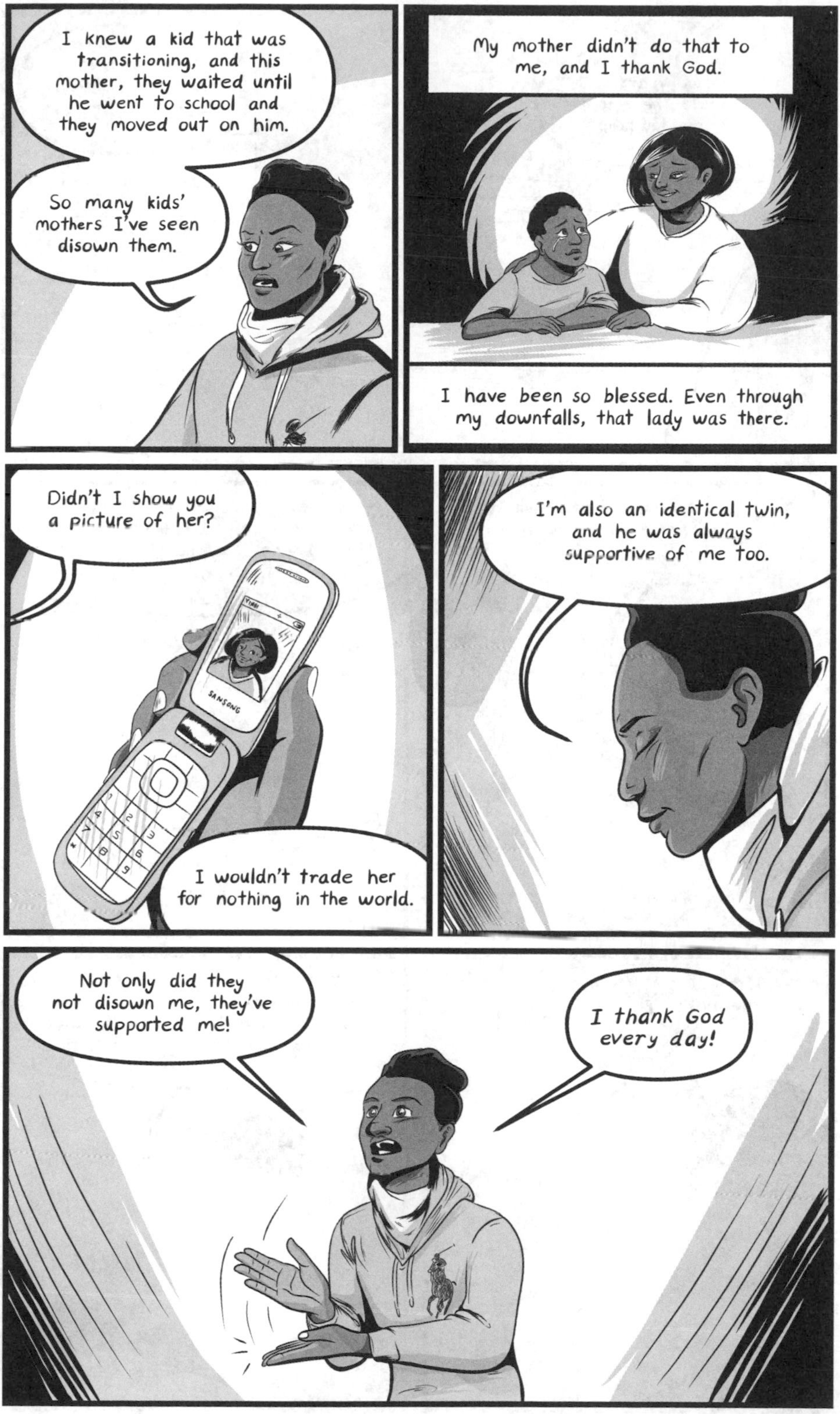
I knew a kid that was transitioning, and this mother, they waited until he went to school and they moved out on him.
So many kids' mothers I've seen disown them.
My mother didn't do that to me, and I thank God.
I have been so blessed. Even through my downfalls, that lady was there.
Didn't I show you a picture of her?
SANSONG
I wouldn't trade her for nothing in the world.
I'm also an identical twin, and he was always supportive of me too.
Not only did they not disown me, they've supported me!
I thank God every day!

Demari, 2013

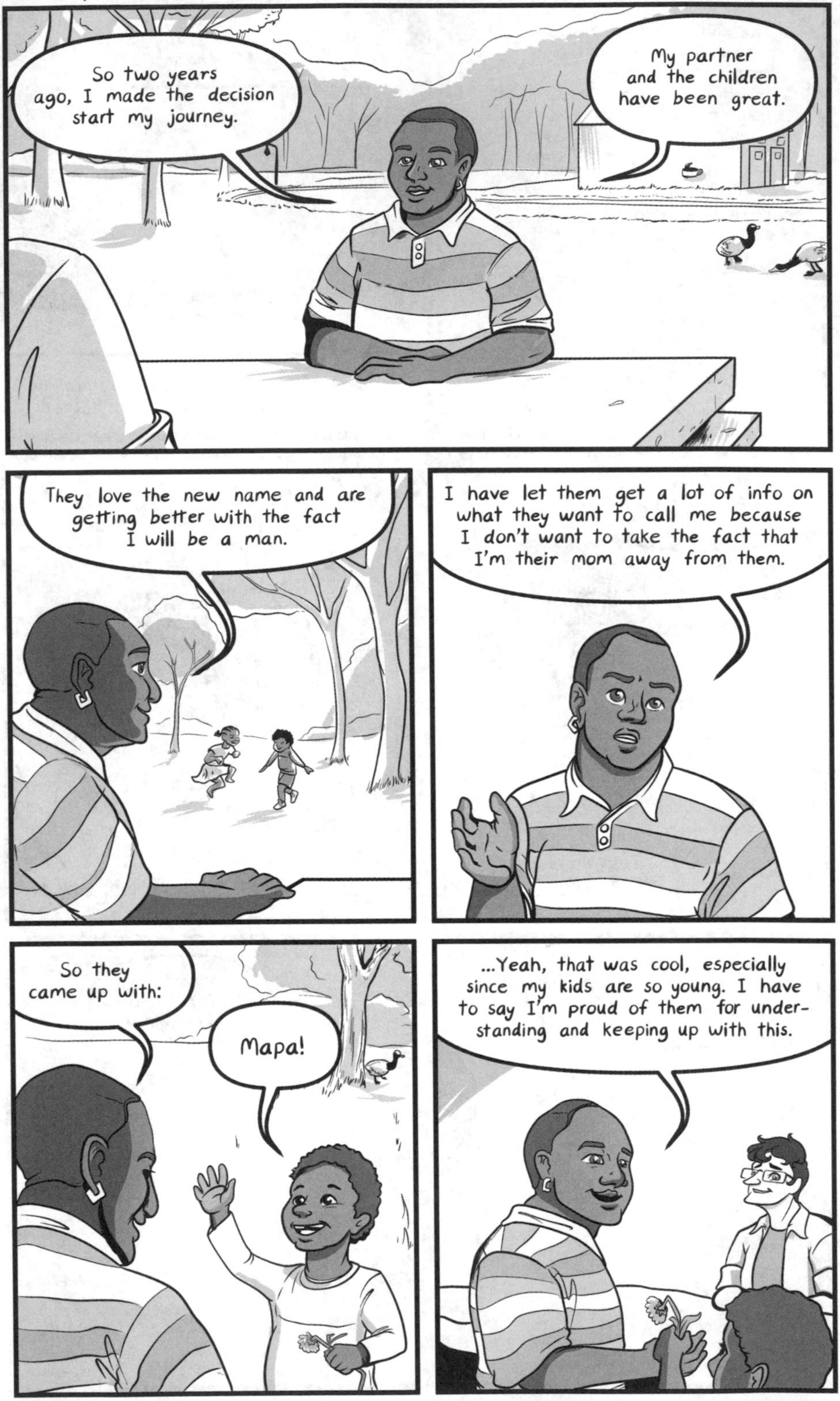
So two years ago, I made the decision start my journey.
My partner and the children have been great.
They love the new name and are getting better with the fact I will be a man.
I have let them get a lot of info on what they want to call me because I don't want to take the fact that I'm their mom away from them.
So they came up with:
Mapa!
...Yeah, that was cool, especially since my kids are so young. I have to say I'm proud of them for understanding and keeping up with this.

Demari, 2014

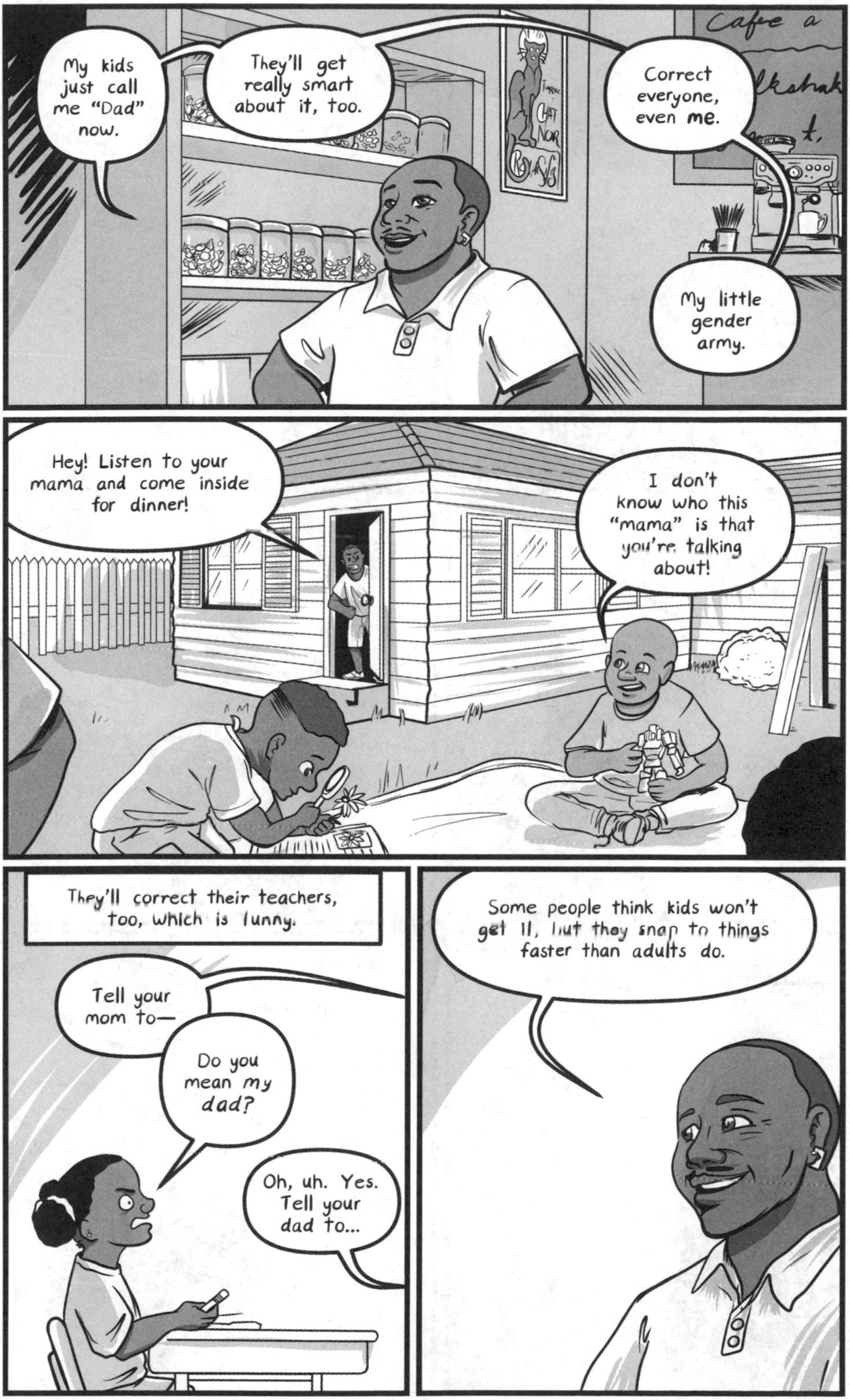

My kids just call me "Dad" now.
They'll get really smart about it, too.
Correct everyone, even **me**.
My little gender army.
Hey! Listen to your mama and come inside for dinner!
I don't know who this "mama" is that you're talking about!
They'll correct their teachers, too, which is funny.
Tell your mom to—
Do you mean my *dad*?
Oh, uh. Yes. Tell your dad to...
Some people think kids won't get it, but they snap to things faster than adults do.

Ignacio, 2013

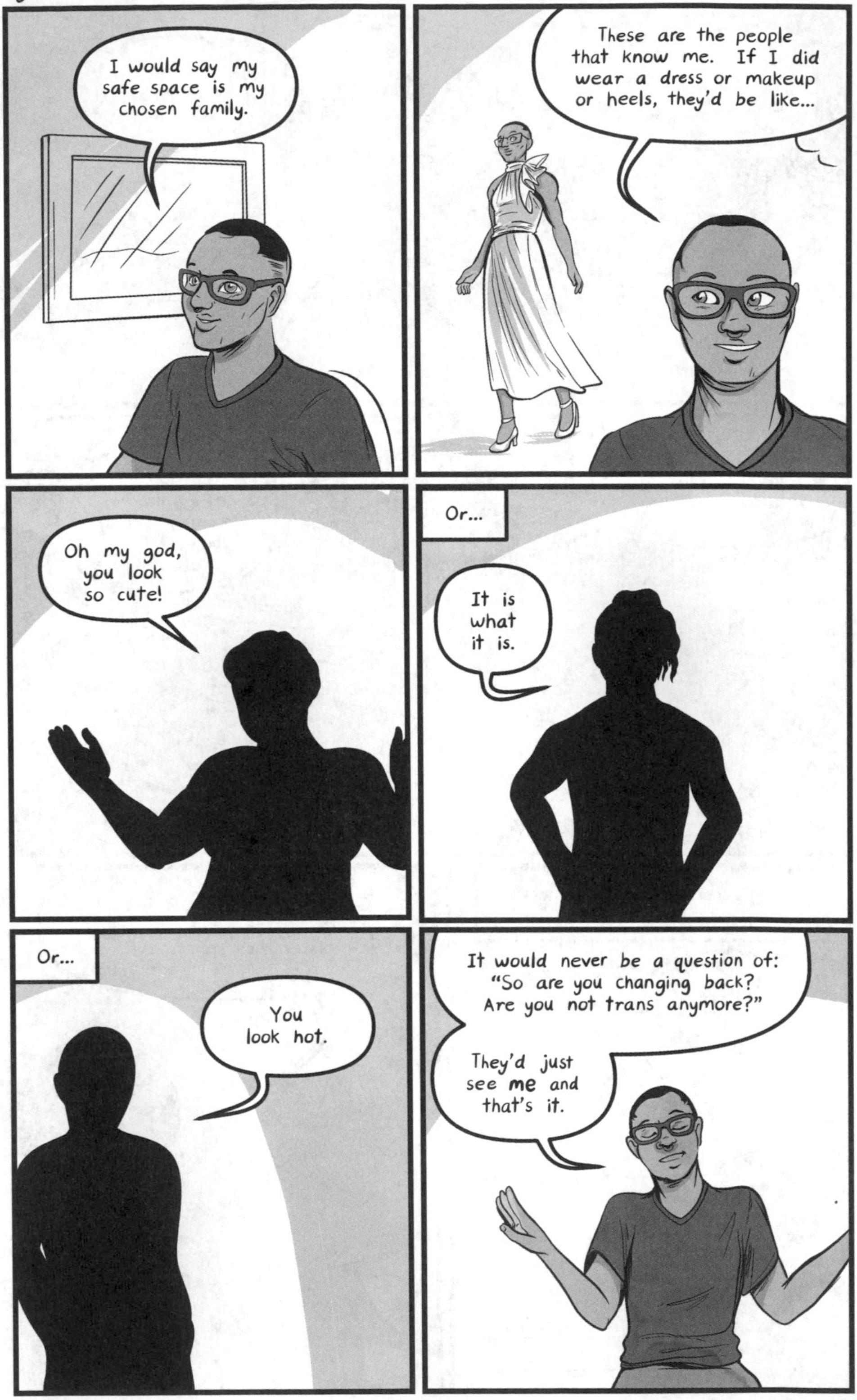
I would say my safe space is my chosen family.
These are the people that know me. If I did wear a dress or makeup or heels, they'd be like...
Oh my god, you look so cute!
Or...
It is what it is.
Or...
You look hot.
It would never be a question of: "So are you changing back? Are you not trans anymore?"
They'd just see **me** and that's it.

Anonymous, 2011

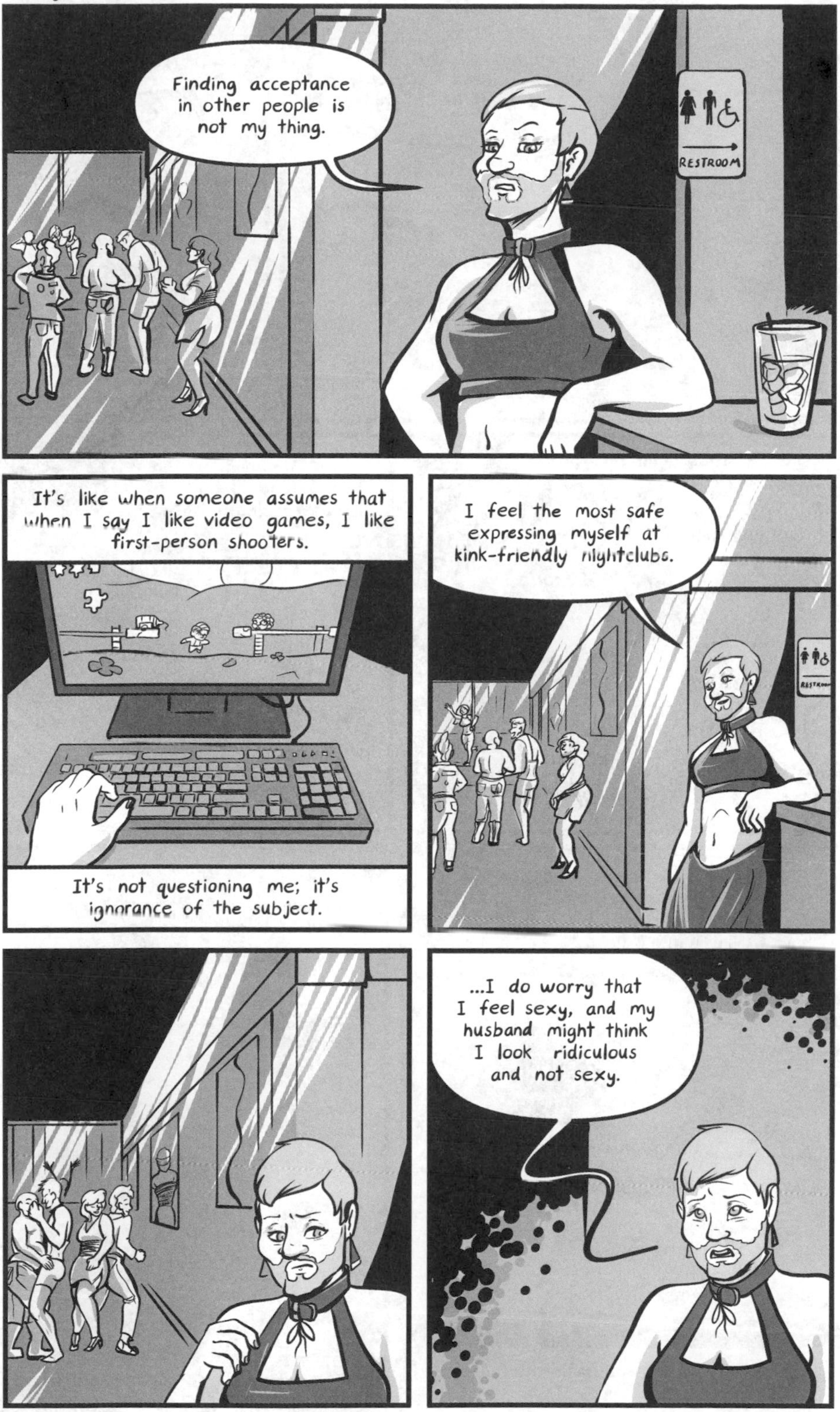
Finding acceptance in other people is not my thing.
RESTROOM
It's like when someone assumes that when I say I like video games, I like first-person shooters.
It's not questioning me; it's ignorance of the subject.
I feel the most safe expressing myself at kink-friendly nightclubs.
RESTROOM
...I do worry that I feel sexy, and my husband might think I look ridiculous and not sexy.

Dutchess, 2015

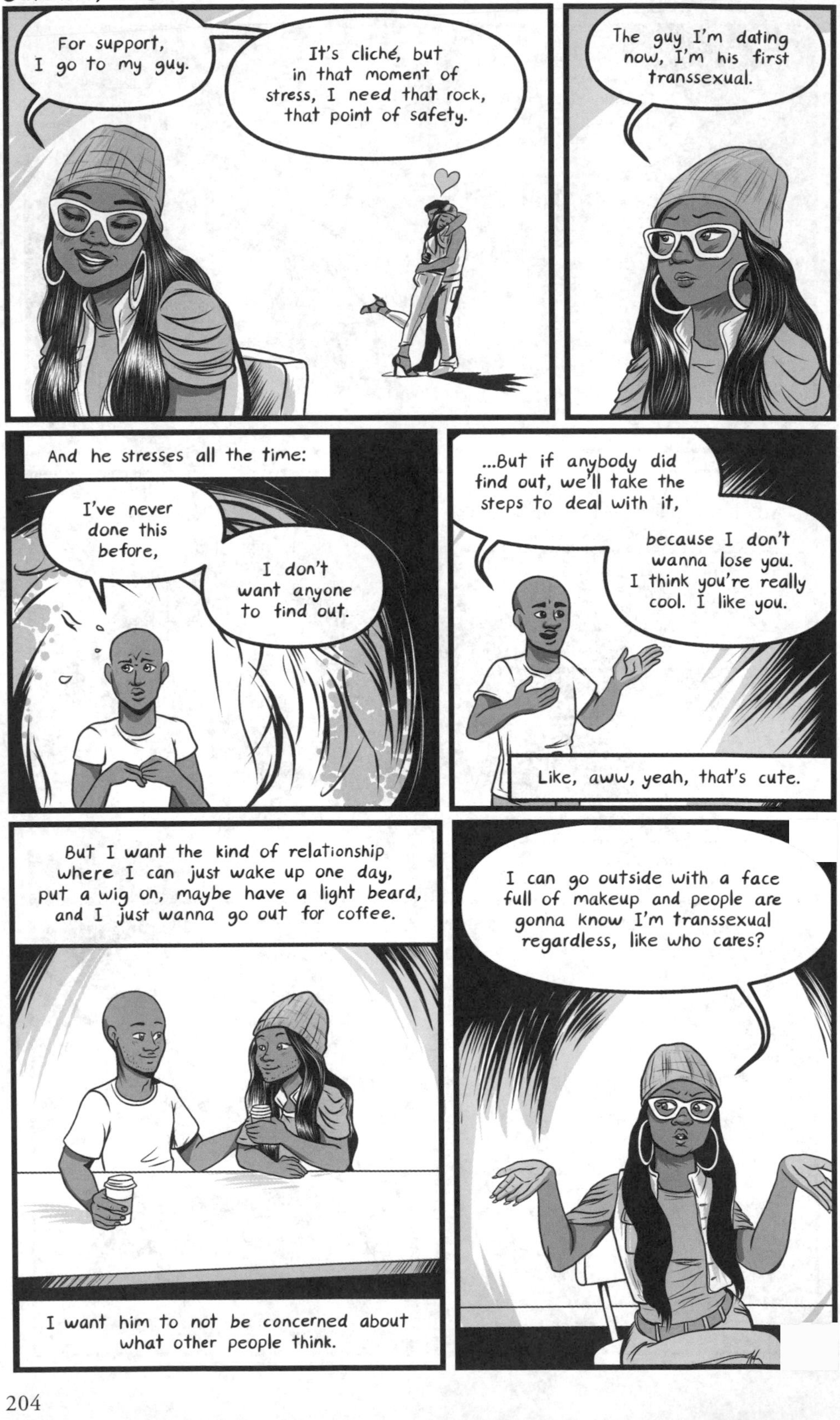
For support, I go to my guy.
It's cliché, but in that moment of stress, I need that rock, that point of safety.
The guy I'm dating now, I'm his first transsexual.
And he stresses all the time:
I've never done this before,
I don't want anyone to find out.
...But if anybody did find out, we'll take the steps to deal with it,
because I don't wanna lose you. I think you're really cool. I like you.
Like, aww, yeah, that's cute.
But I want the kind of relationship where I can just wake up one day, put a wig on, maybe have a light beard, and I just wanna go out for coffee.
I want him to not be concerned about what other people think.
I can go outside with a face full of makeup and people are gonna know I'm transsexual regardless, like who cares?

The Best Couple, 2013

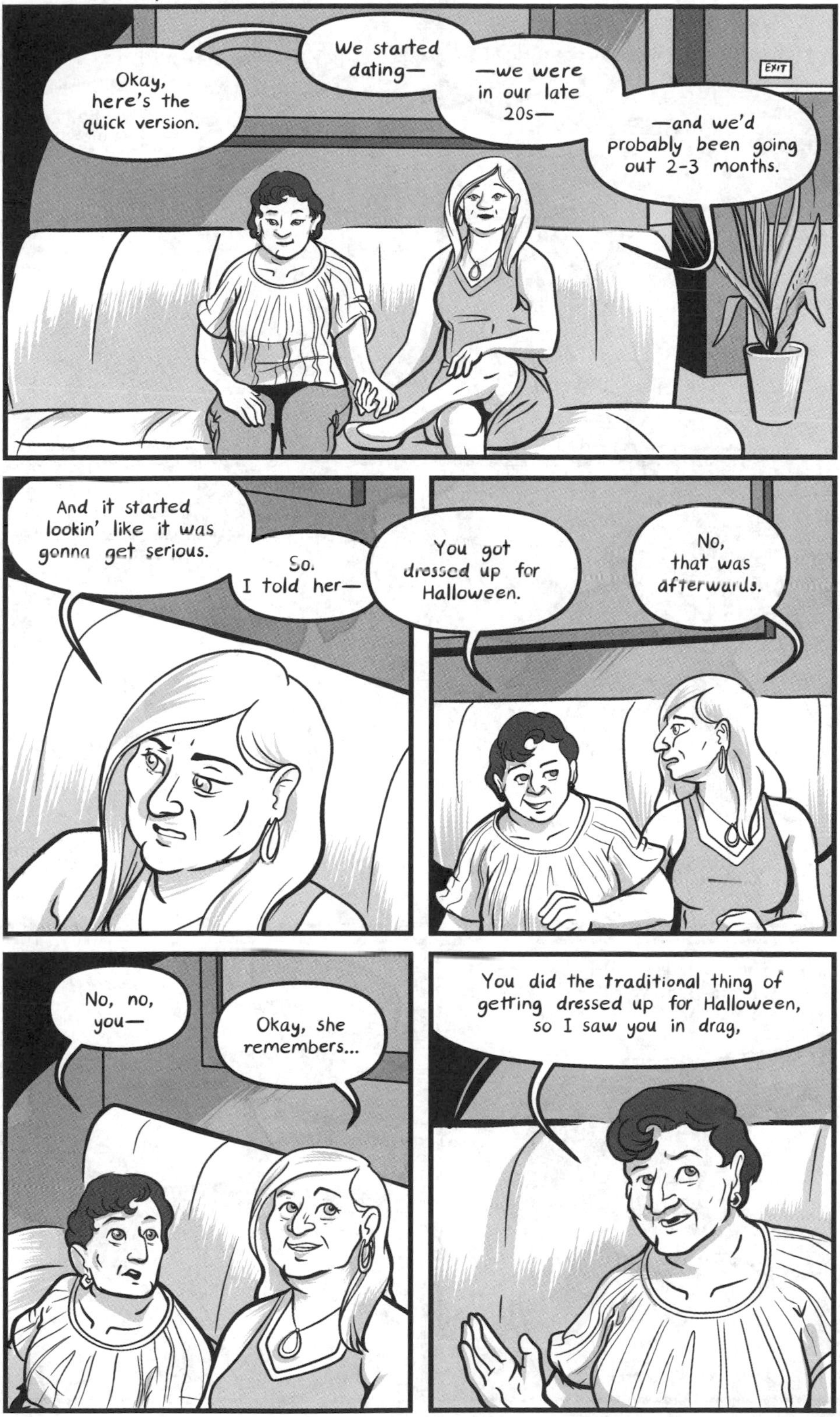
Okay, here's the quick version.
We started dating—
—we were in our late 20s—
—and we'd probably been going out 2-3 months.
EXIT
And it started lookin' like it was gonna get serious.
So. I told her—
You got dressed up for Halloween.
No, that was afterwards.
No, no, you—
Okay, she remembers...
You did the traditional thing of getting dressed up for Halloween, so I saw you in drag,

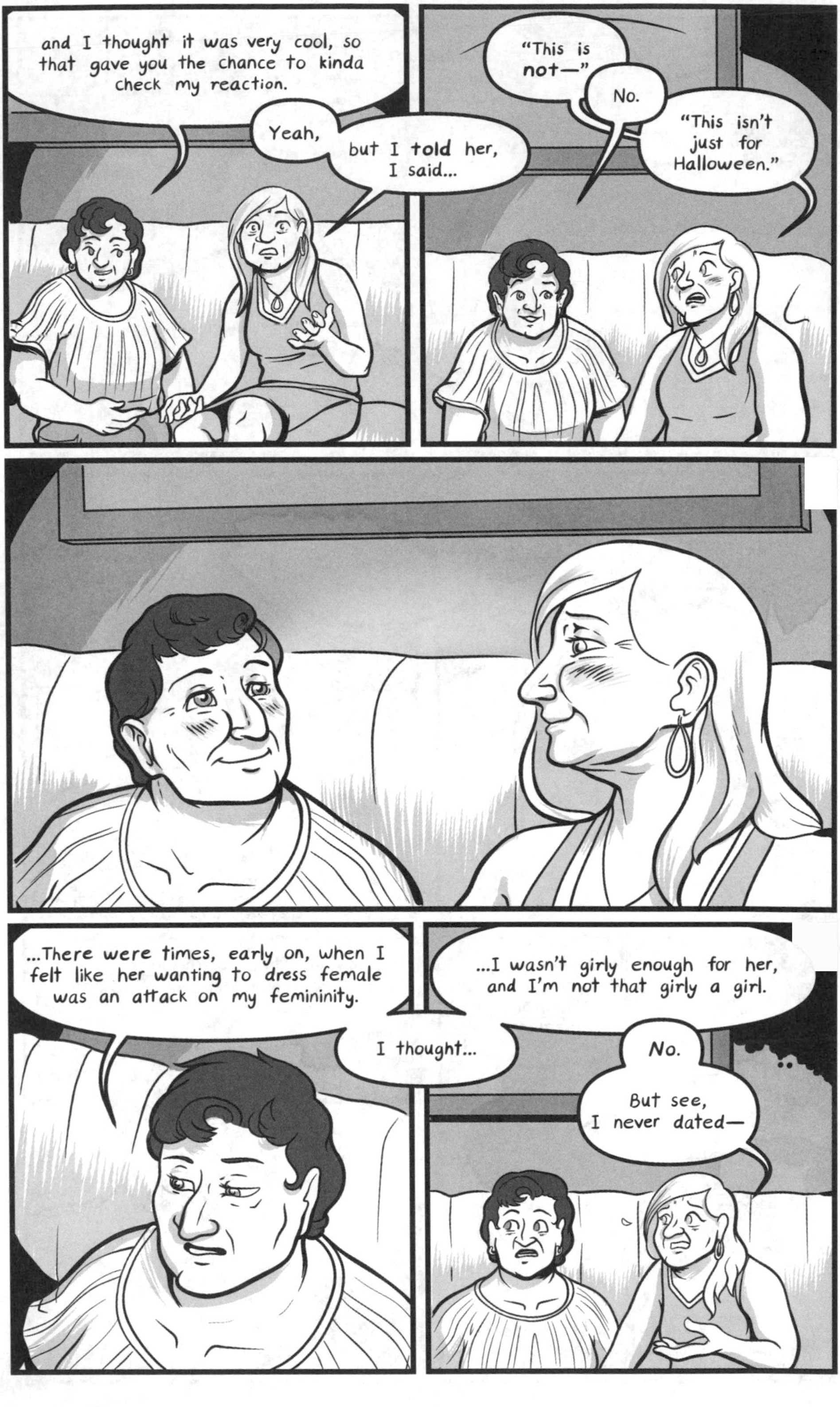

and I thought it was very cool, so that gave you the chance to kinda check my reaction.
Yeah,
but I **told** her, I said...
"This is **not**—"
No.
"This isn't just for Halloween."
...There were times, early on, when I felt like her wanting to dress female was an attack on my femininity.
I thought...
...I wasn't girly enough for her, and I'm not that girly a girl.
No.
But see, I never dated—

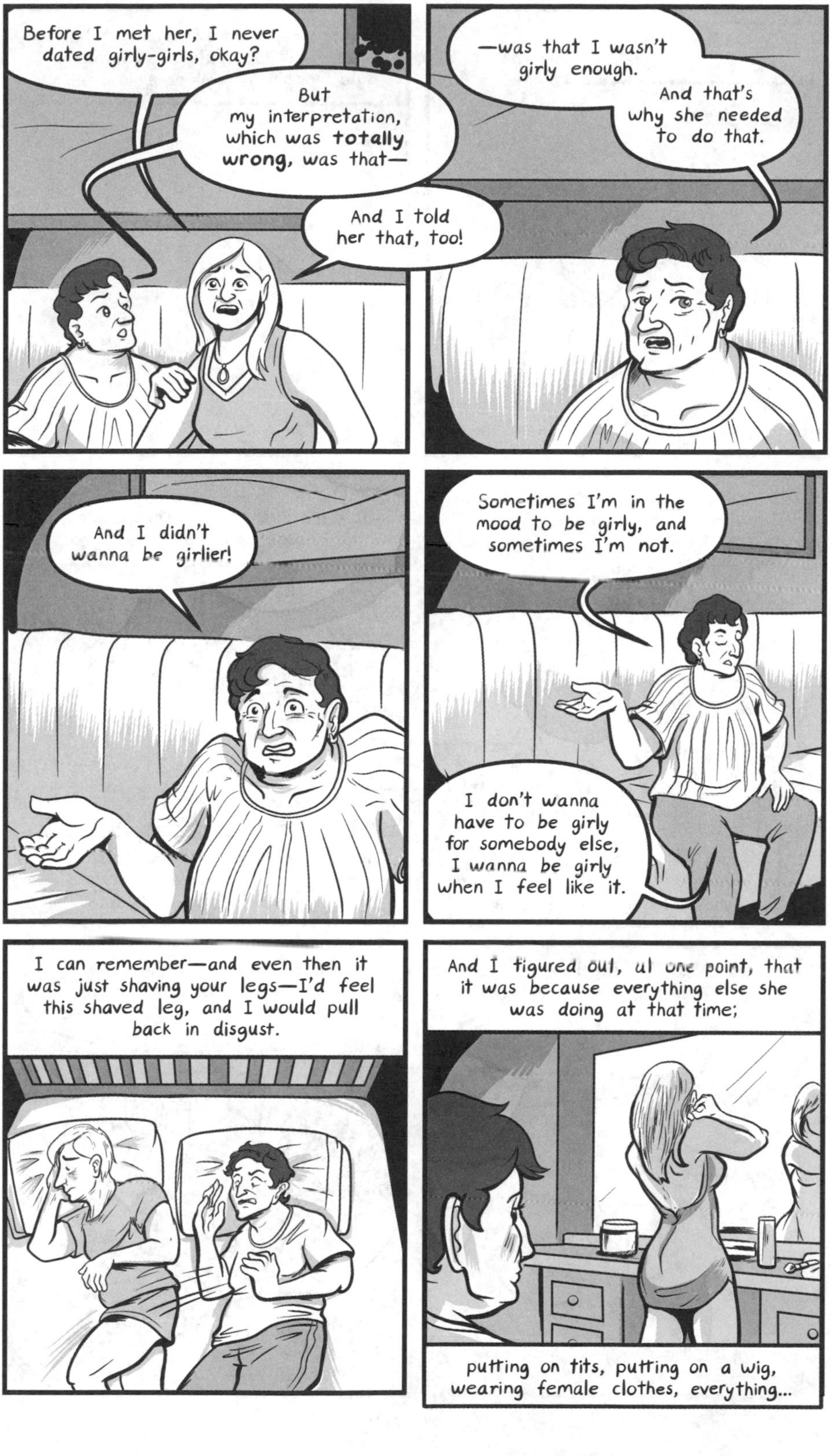
Before I met her, I never dated girly-girls, okay?
But my interpretation, which was **totally wrong**, was that—
And I told her that, too!
—was that I wasn't girly enough.
And that's why she needed to do that.
And I didn't wanna be girlier!
Sometimes I'm in the mood to be girly, and sometimes I'm not.
I don't wanna have to be girly for somebody else, I wanna be girly when I feel like it.
I can remember—and even then it was just shaving your legs—I'd feel this shaved leg, and I would pull back in disgust.
And I figured out, at one point, that it was because everything else she was doing at that time;
putting on tits, putting on a wig, wearing female clothes, everything...

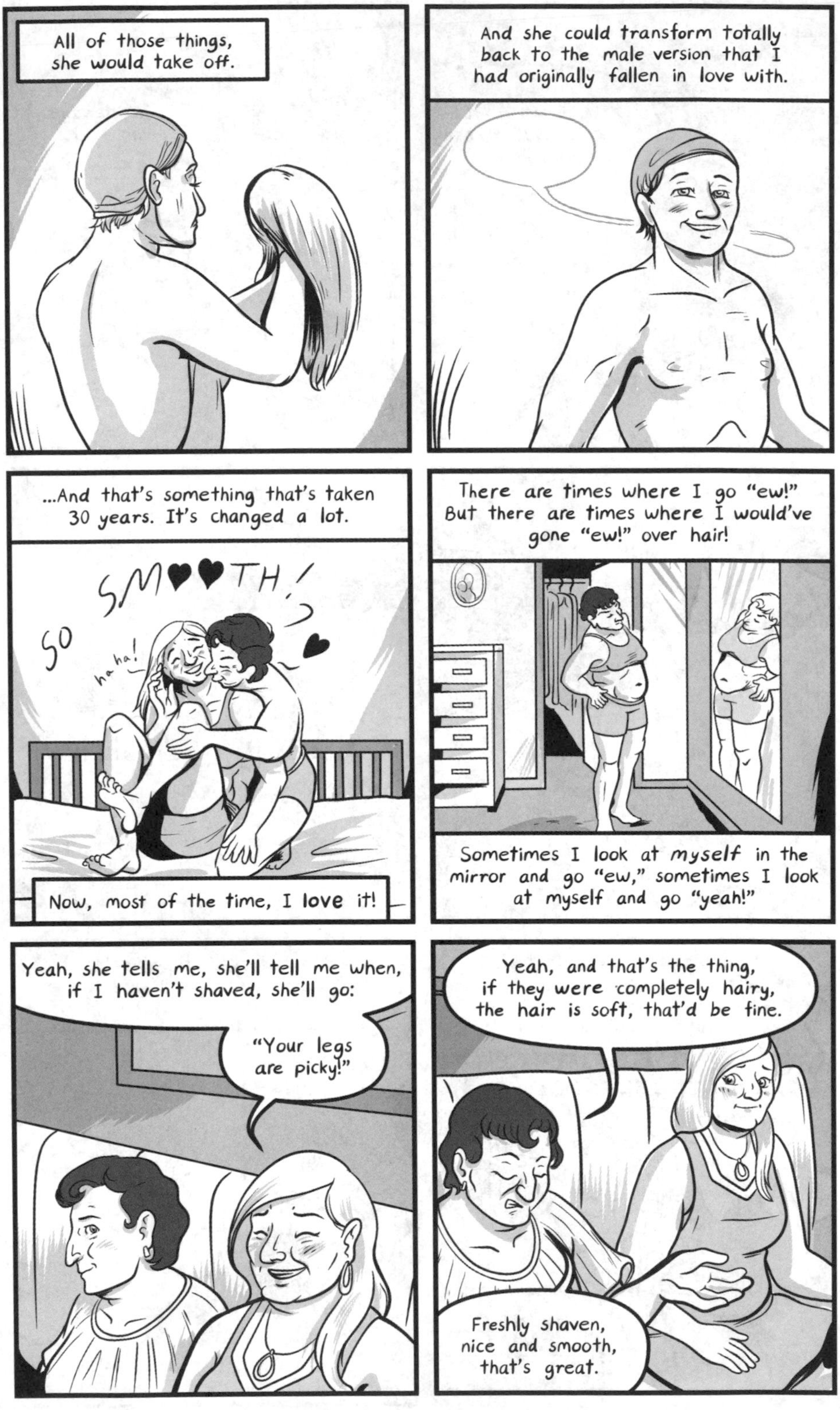
All of those things, she would take off.
And she could transform totally back to the male version that I had originally fallen in love with.
...And that's something that's taken 30 years. It's changed a lot.
SO SM♥♥TH!
ha ha!
Now, most of the time, I **love** it!
There are times where I go "ew!" But there are times where I would've gone "ew!" over hair!
Sometimes I look at *myself* in the mirror and go "ew," sometimes I look at myself and go "yeah!"
Yeah, she tells me, she'll tell me when, if I haven't shaved, she'll go:
"Your legs are picky!"
Yeah, and that's the thing, if they were completely hairy, the hair is soft, that'd be fine.
Freshly shaven, nice and smooth, that's great.

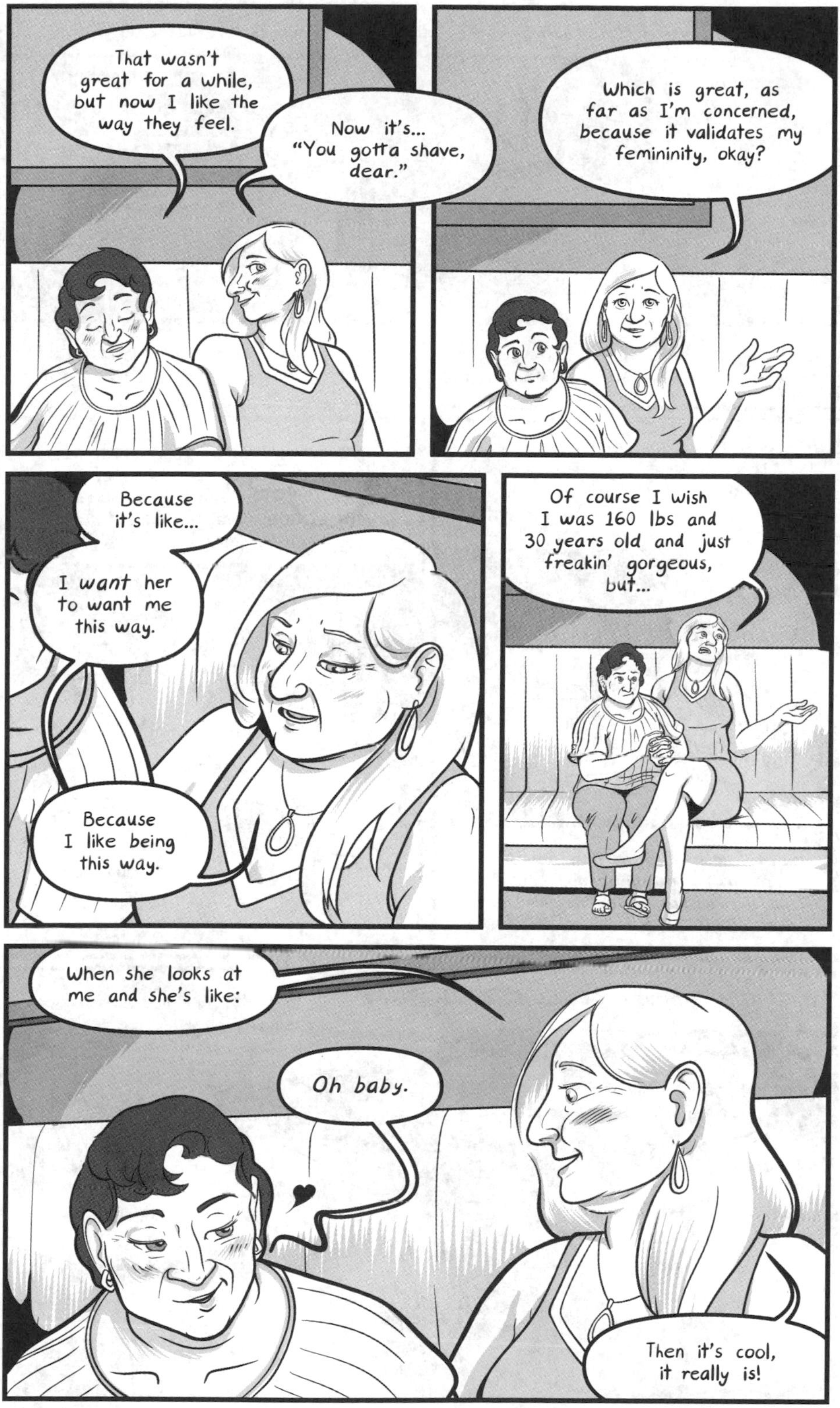

That wasn't great for a while, but now I like the way they feel.
Now it's... "You gotta shave, dear."
Which is great, as far as I'm concerned, because it validates my femininity, okay?
Because it's like...
I *want* her to want me this way.
Because I like being this way.
Of course I wish I was 160 lbs and 30 years old and just freakin' gorgeous, but...
When she looks at me and she's like:
Oh baby.
Then it's cool, it really is!

Rhea, 2015

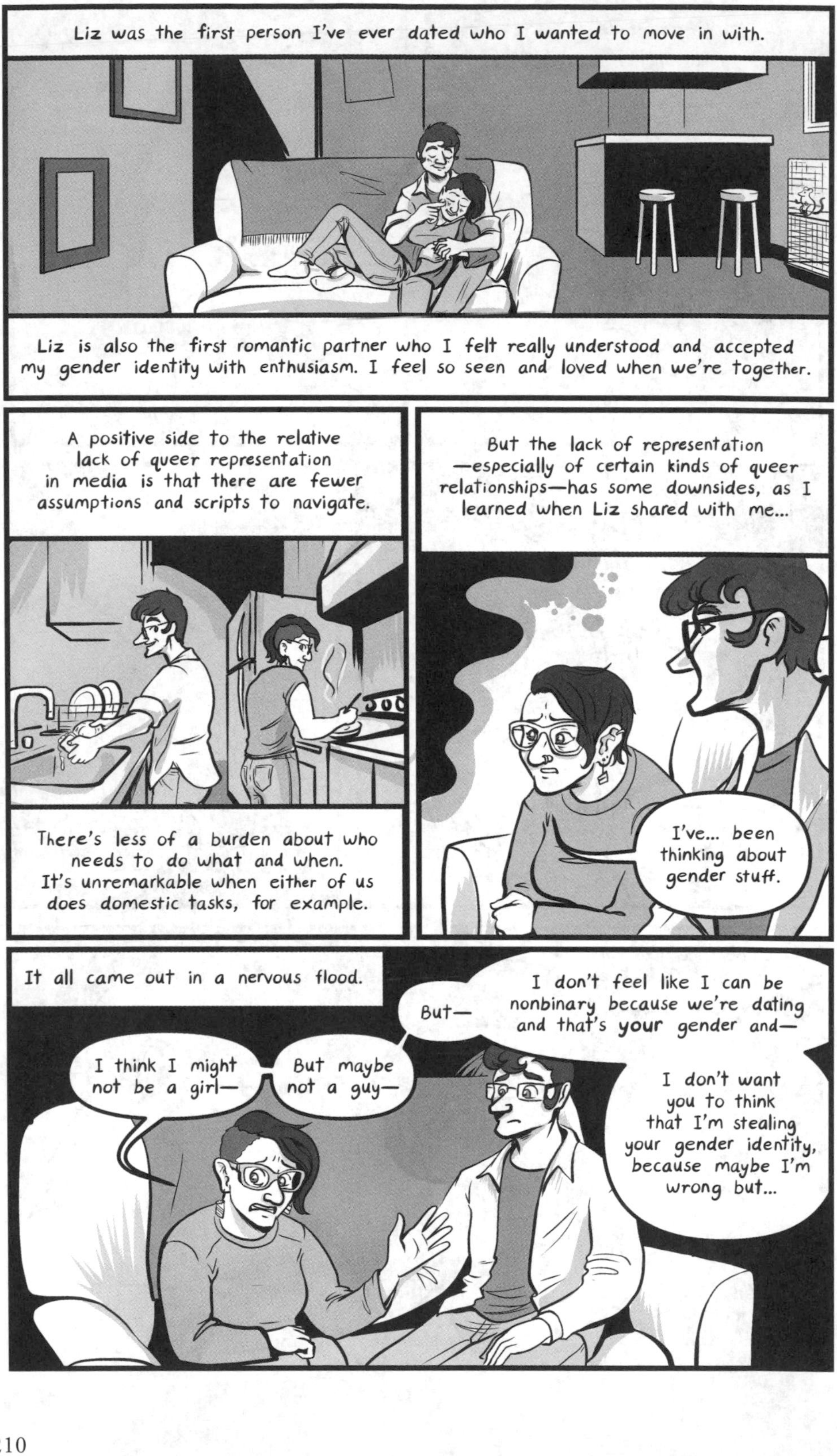
Liz was the first person I've ever dated who I wanted to move in with.
Liz is also the first romantic partner who I felt really understood and accepted my gender identity with enthusiasm. I feel so seen and loved when we're together.
A positive side to the relative lack of queer representation in media is that there are fewer assumptions and scripts to navigate.
There's less of a burden about who needs to do what and when. It's unremarkable when either of us does domestic tasks, for example.
But the lack of representation—especially of certain kinds of queer relationships—has some downsides, as I learned when Liz shared with me...
I've... been thinking about gender stuff.
It all came out in a nervous flood.
I think I might not be a girl—
But maybe not a guy—
But—
I don't feel like I can be nonbinary because we're dating and that's **your** gender and—
I don't want you to think that I'm stealing your gender identity, because maybe I'm wrong but...

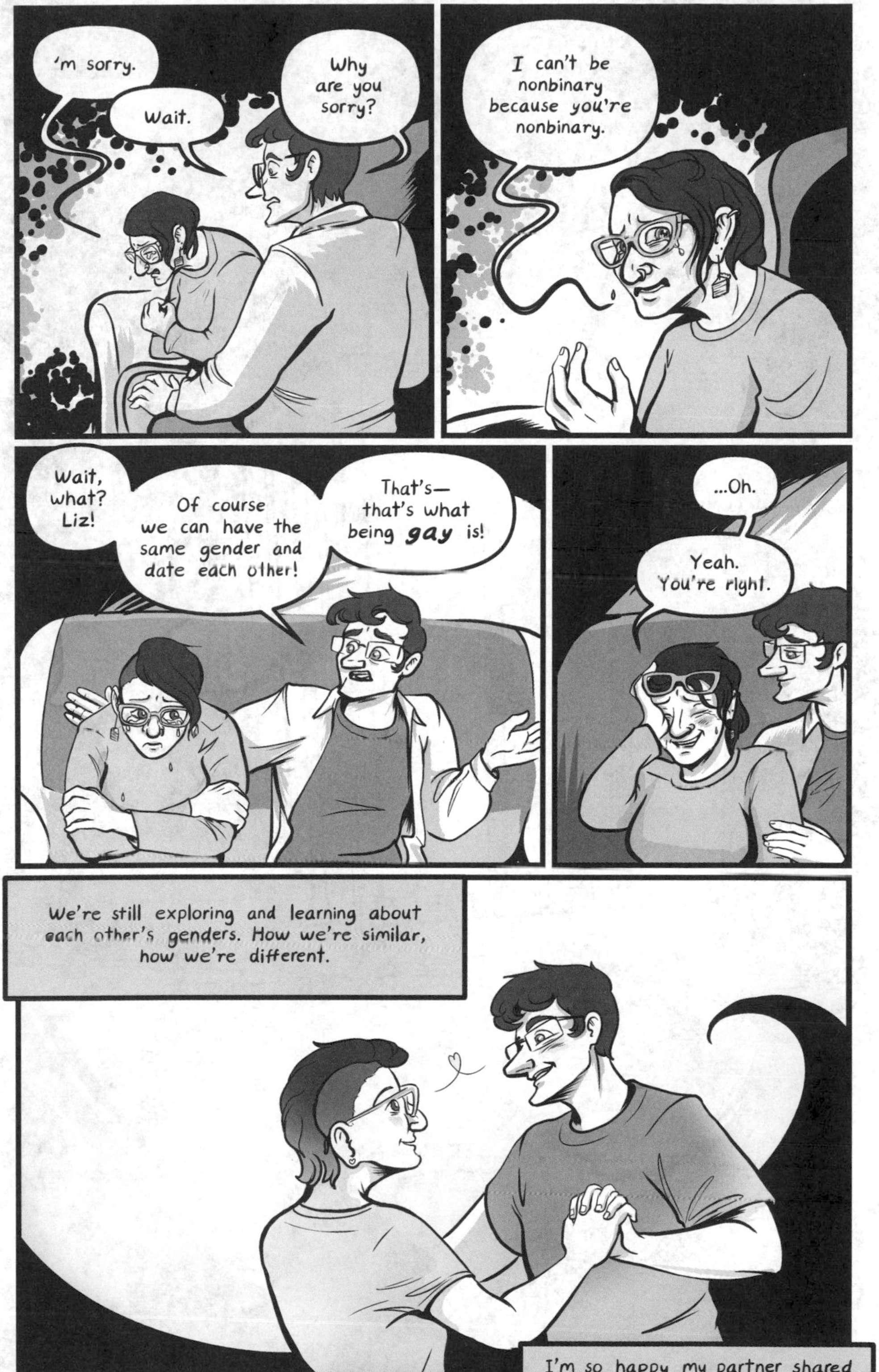
'm sorry.
Wait.
Why are you sorry?
I can't be nonbinary because you're nonbinary.
Wait, what? Liz!
Of course we can have the same gender and date each other!
That's— that's what being **gay** is!
...Oh.
Yeah. You're right.
We're still exploring and learning about each other's genders. How we're similar, how we're different.
I'm so happy my partner shared this truth with me.

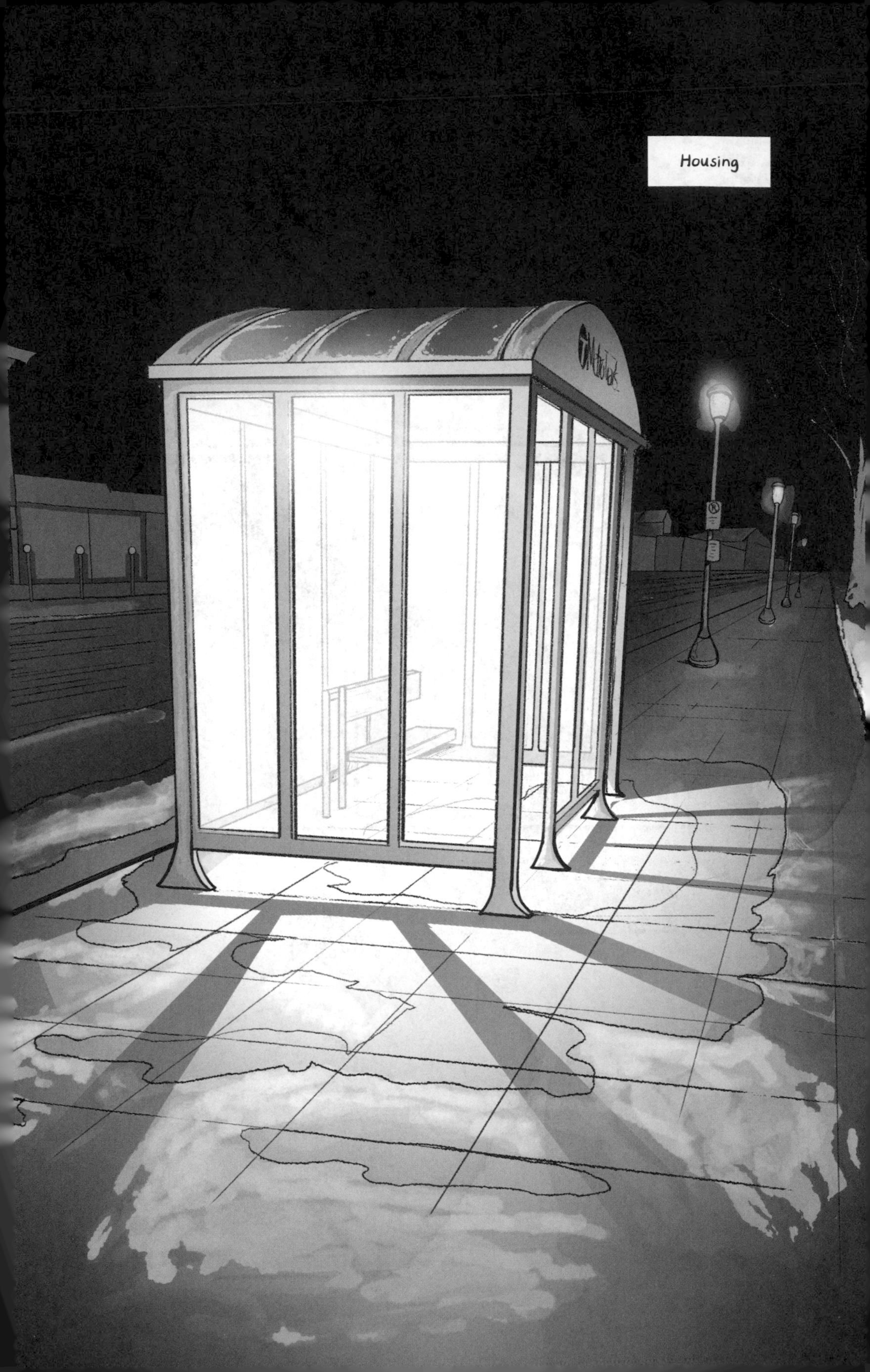
Housing

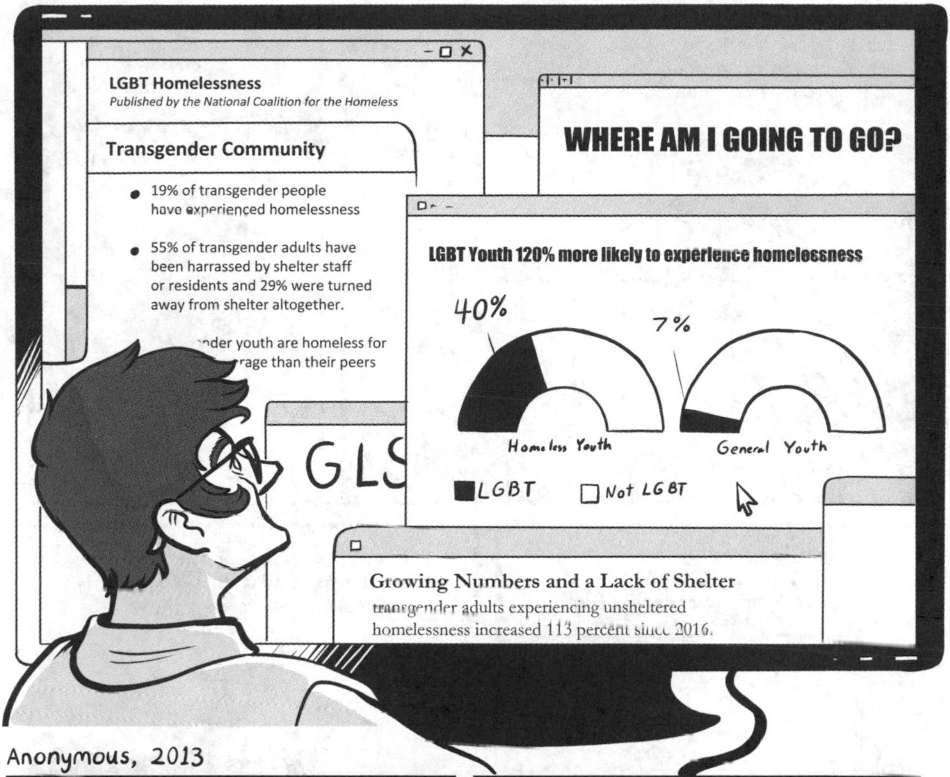
LGBT Homelessness
Published by the National Coalition for the Homeless
Transgender Community
19% of transgender people have experienced homelessness
55% of transgender adults have been harrassed by shelter staff or residents and 29% were turned away from shelter altogether.
WHERE AM I GOING TO GO?
LGBT Youth 120% more likely to experience homelessness
40%
7%
Homeless Youth
General Youth
LGBT
Not LGBT
GLS
Growing Numbers and a Lack of Shelter
transgender adults experiencing unsheltered homelessness increased 113 percent since 2016.

Anonymous, 2013

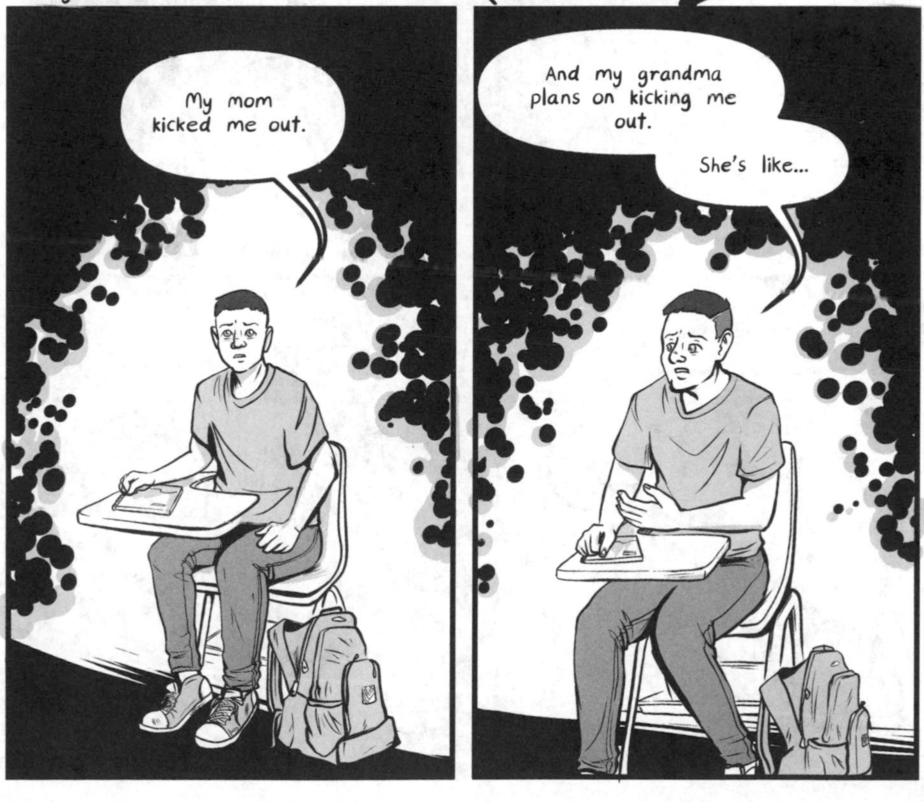
My mom kicked me out.
And my grandma plans on kicking me out.
She's like...

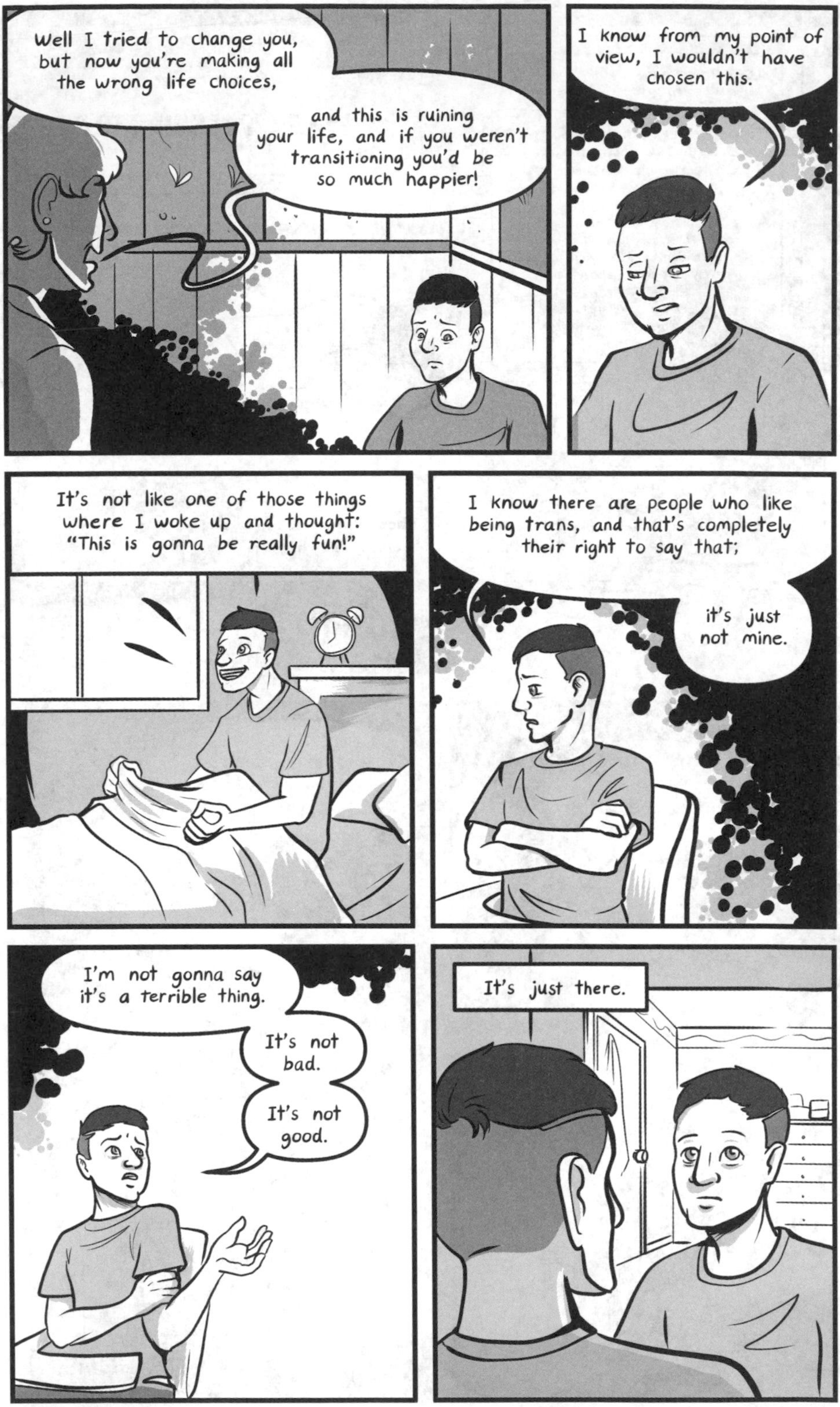
Well I tried to change you, but now you're making all the wrong life choices,
and this is ruining your life, and if you weren't transitioning you'd be so much happier!
I know from my point of view, I wouldn't have chosen this.
It's not like one of those things where I woke up and thought: "This is gonna be really fun!"
I know there are people who like being trans, and that's completely their right to say that;
it's just not mine.
I'm not gonna say it's a terrible thing.
It's not bad.
It's not good.
It's just there.

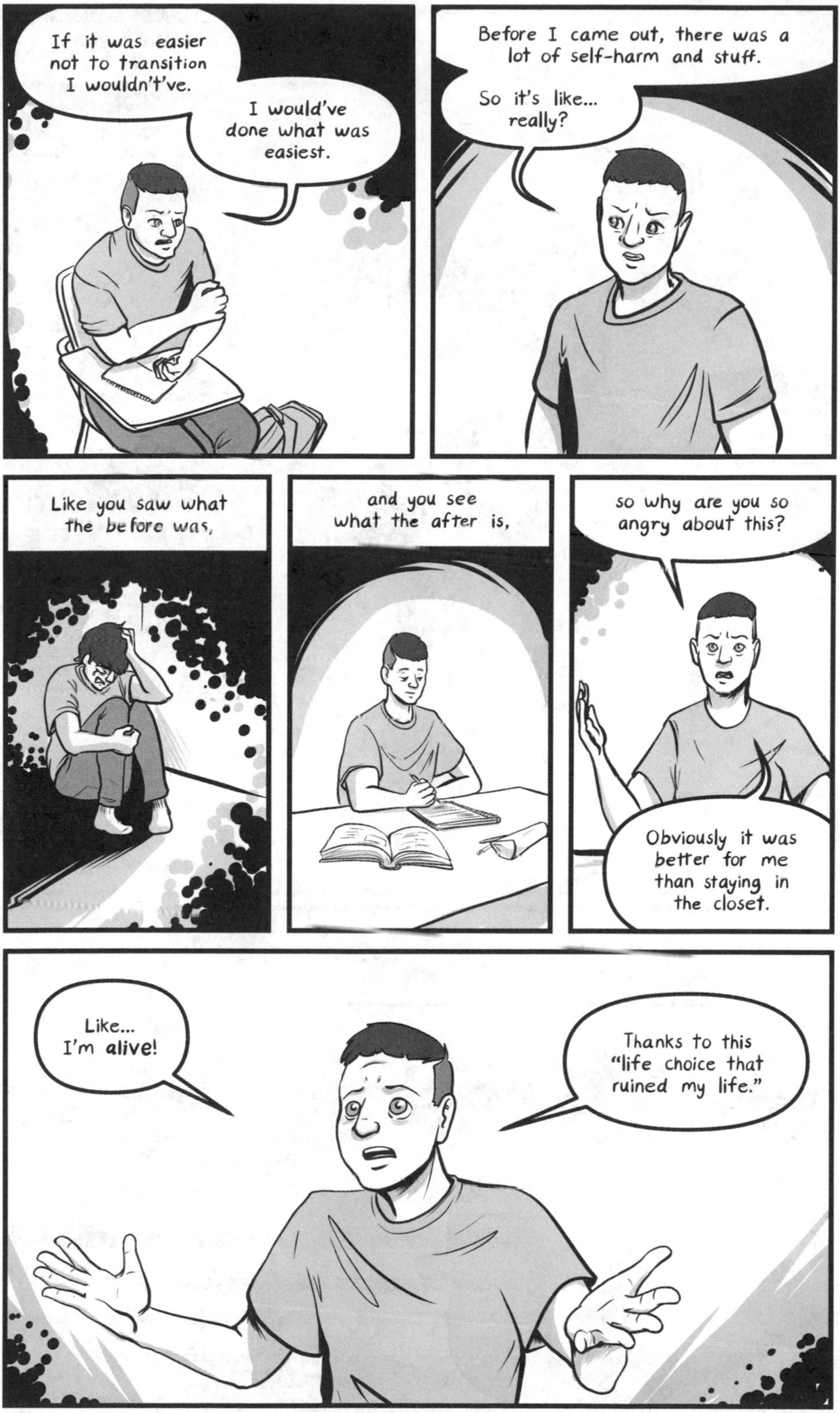
If it was easier not to transition I wouldn't've.
I would've done what was easiest.
Before I came out, there was a lot of self-harm and stuff.
So it's like... really?
Like you saw what the before was,
and you see what the after is,
so why are you so angry about this?
Obviously it was better for me than staying in the closet.
Like... I'm **alive**!
Thanks to this "life choice that ruined my life."

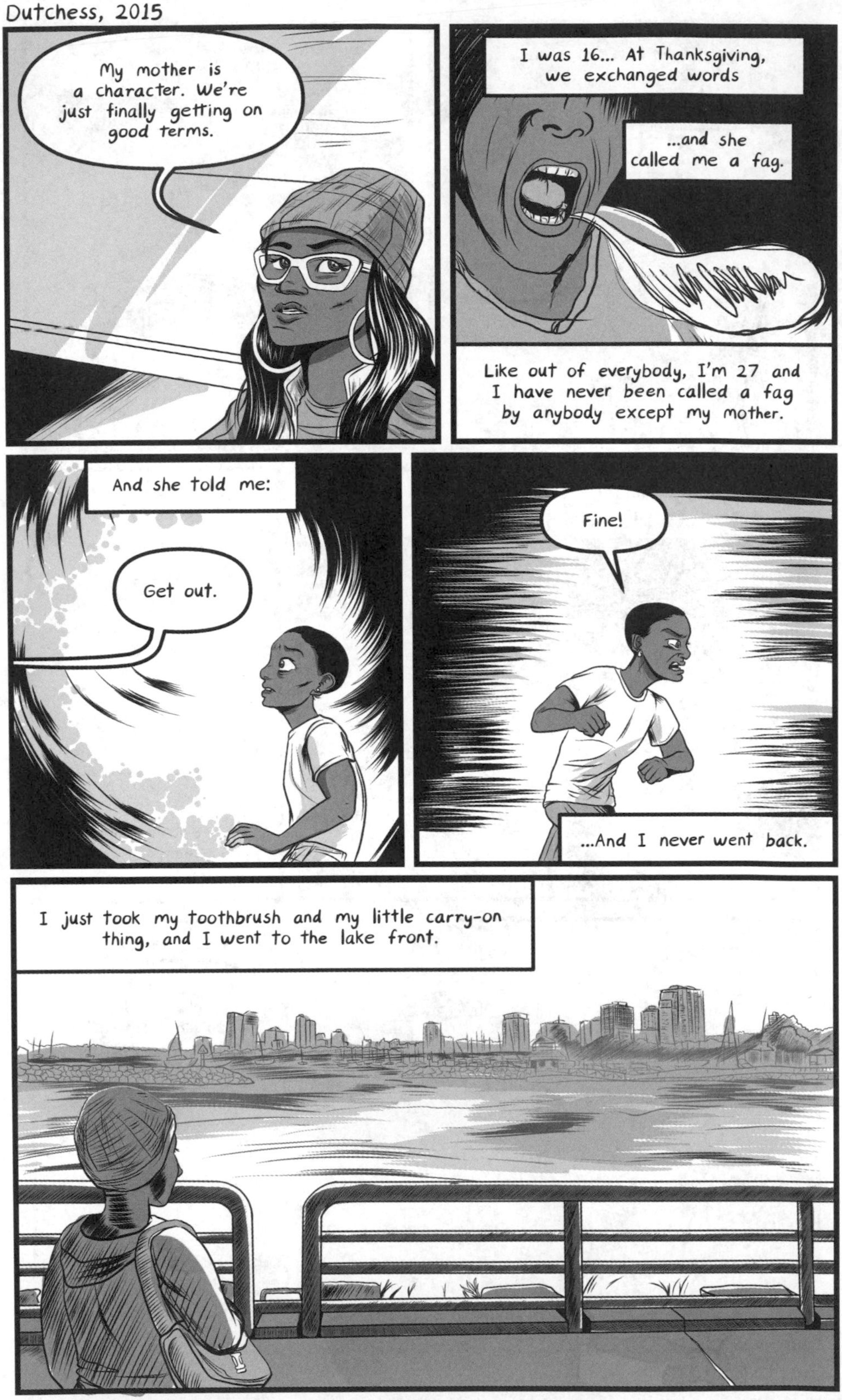
Dutchess, 2015
My mother is a character. We're just finally getting on good terms.
I was 16... At Thanksgiving, we exchanged words
...and she called me a fag.
Like out of everybody, I'm 27 and I have never been called a fag by anybody except my mother.
And she told me:
Get out.
Fine!
...And I never went back.
I just took my toothbrush and my little carry-on thing, and I went to the lake front.

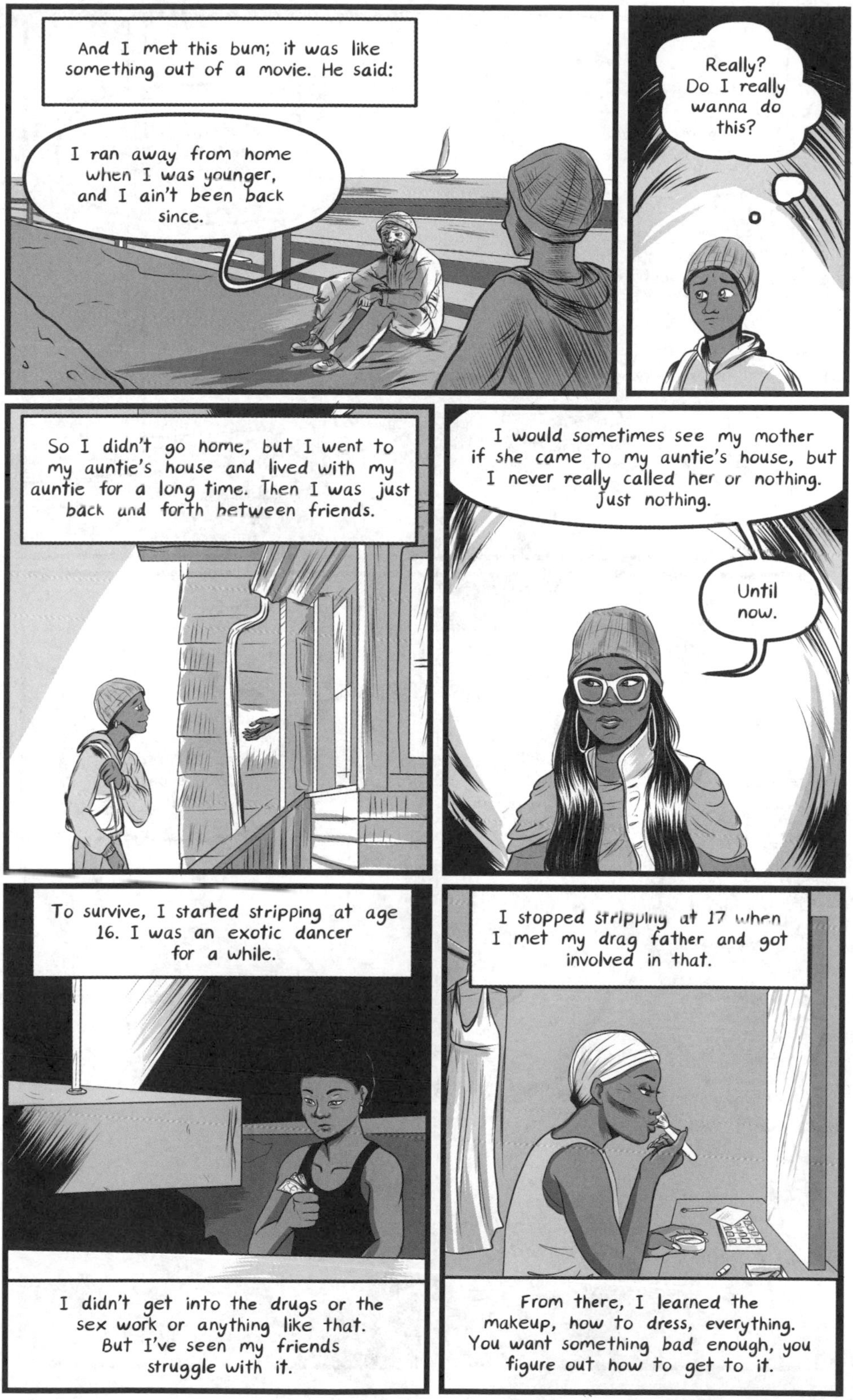

And I met this bum; it was like something out of a movie. He said:
I ran away from home when I was younger, and I ain't been back since.
Really? Do I really wanna do this?
So I didn't go home, but I went to my auntie's house and lived with my auntie for a long time. Then I was just back and forth between friends.
I would sometimes see my mother if she came to my auntie's house, but I never really called her or nothing. Just nothing.
Until now.
To survive, I started stripping at age 16. I was an exotic dancer for a while.
I didn't get into the drugs or the sex work or anything like that. But I've seen my friends struggle with it.
I stopped stripping at 17 when I met my drag father and got involved in that.
From there, I learned the makeup, how to dress, everything. You want something bad enough, you figure out how to get to it.

Monei, 2015

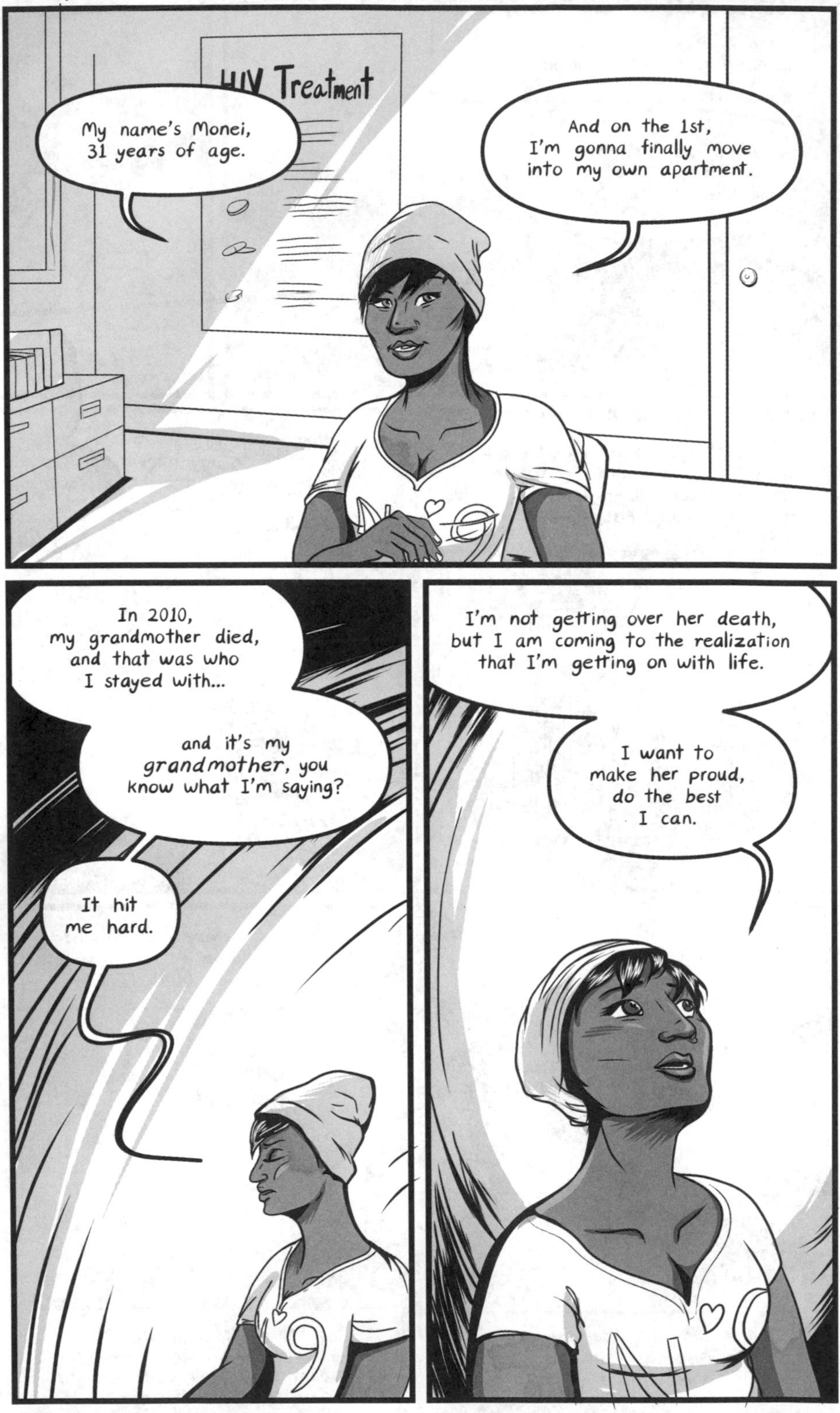
HIV Treatment
My name's Monei, 31 years of age.
And on the 1st, I'm gonna finally move into my own apartment.
In 2010, my grandmother died, and that was who I stayed with...
and it's my *grandmother*, you know what I'm saying?
It hit me hard.
I'm not getting over her death, but I am coming to the realization that I'm getting on with life.
I want to make her proud, do the best I can.

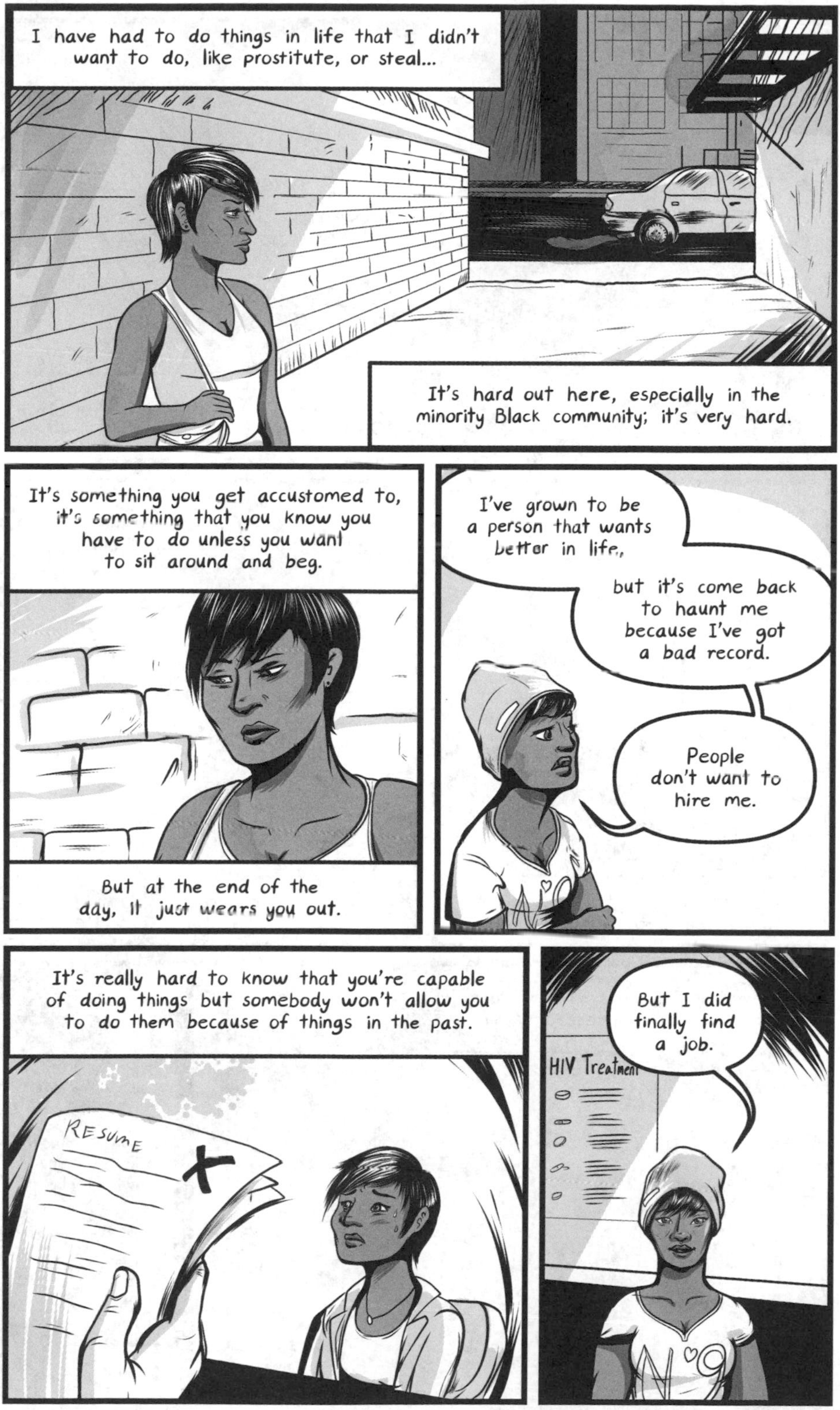
I have had to do things in life that I didn't want to do, like prostitute, or steal...
It's hard out here, especially in the minority Black community; it's very hard.
It's something you get accustomed to, it's something that you know you have to do unless you want to sit around and beg.
But at the end of the day, it just wears you out.
I've grown to be a person that wants better in life,
but it's come back to haunt me because I've got a bad record.
People don't want to hire me.
It's really hard to know that you're capable of doing things but somebody won't allow you to do them because of things in the past.
RESUME
But I did finally find a job.
HIV Treatment

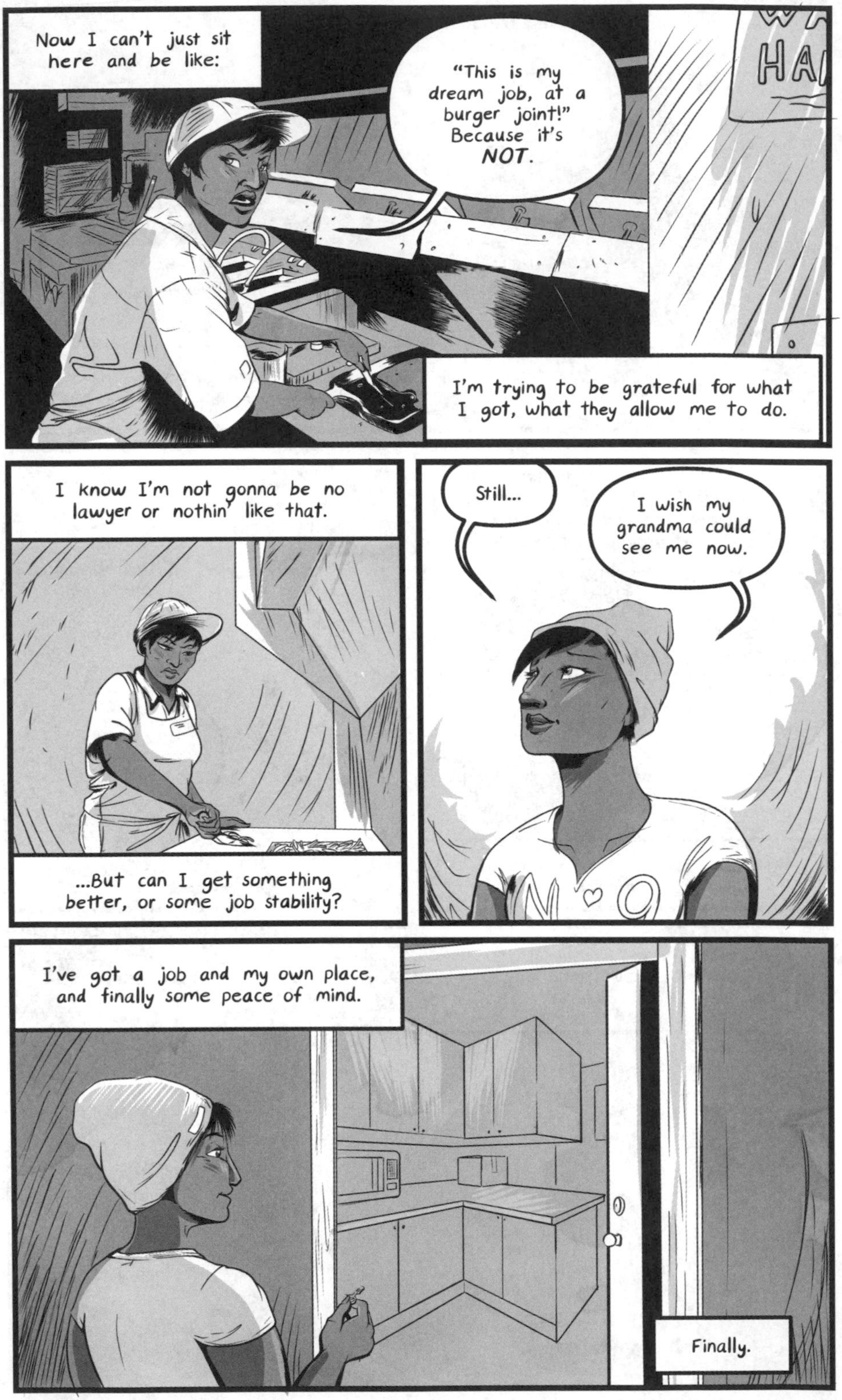

Now I can't just sit here and be like:
"This is my dream job, at a burger joint!" Because it's NOT.
HA
I'm trying to be grateful for what I got, what they allow me to do.
I know I'm not gonna be no lawyer or nothin' like that.
...But can I get something better, or some job stability?
Still...
I wish my grandma could see me now.
I've got a job and my own place, and finally some peace of mind.
Finally.

Ginger, 2012

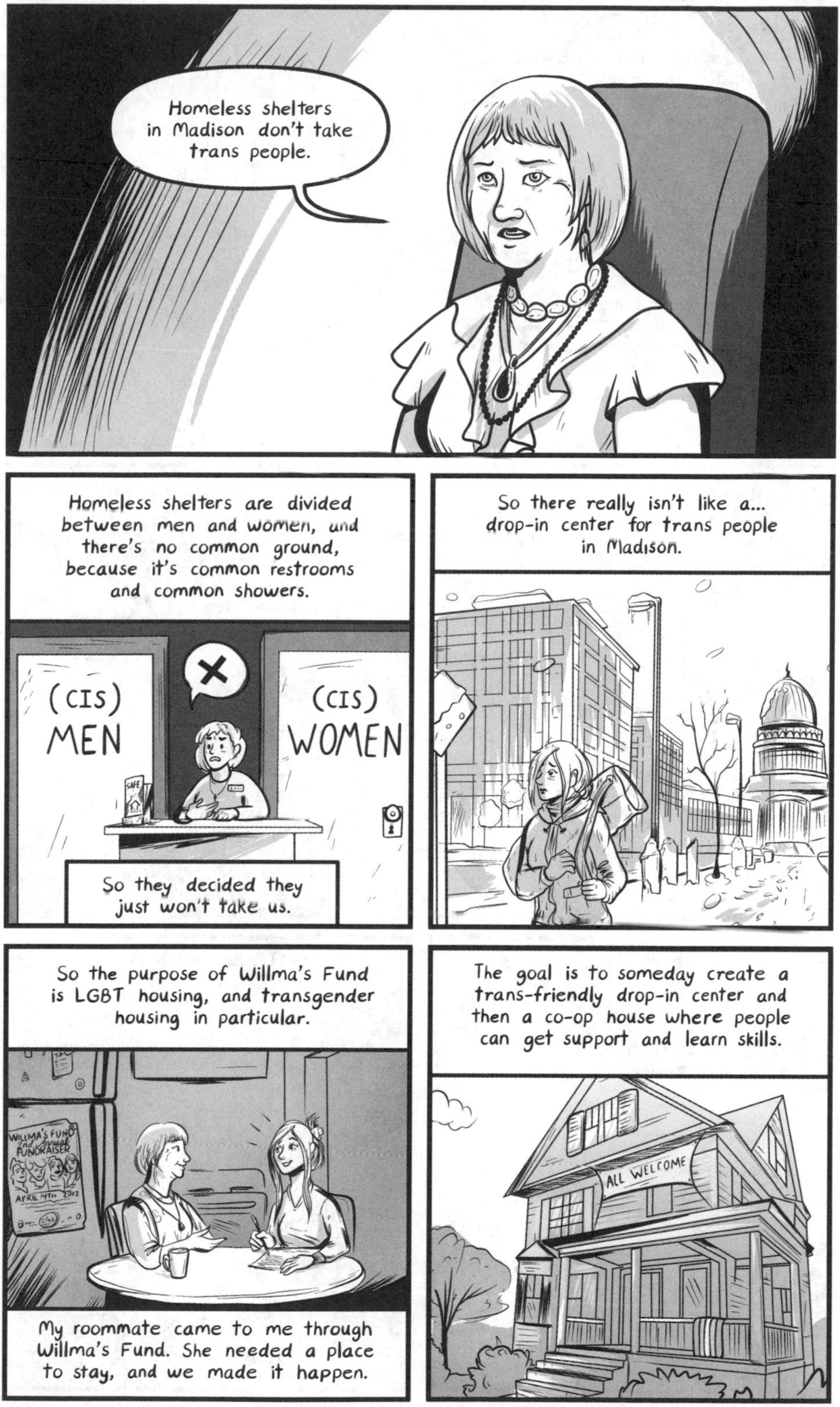
Homeless shelters in Madison don't take trans people.
Homeless shelters are divided between men and women, and there's no common ground, because it's common restrooms and common showers.
(CIS) MEN
(CIS) WOMEN
SAFE
So they decided they just won't take us.
So there really isn't like a... drop-in center for trans people in Madison.
So the purpose of Willma's Fund is LGBT housing, and transgender housing in particular.
WILLMA'S FUND 2nd Annual FUNDRAISER
APRIL 14TH 2012
My roommate came to me through Willma's Fund. She needed a place to stay, and we made it happen.
The goal is to someday create a trans-friendly drop-in center and then a co-op house where people can get support and learn skills.
ALL WELCOME

Lex, 2013

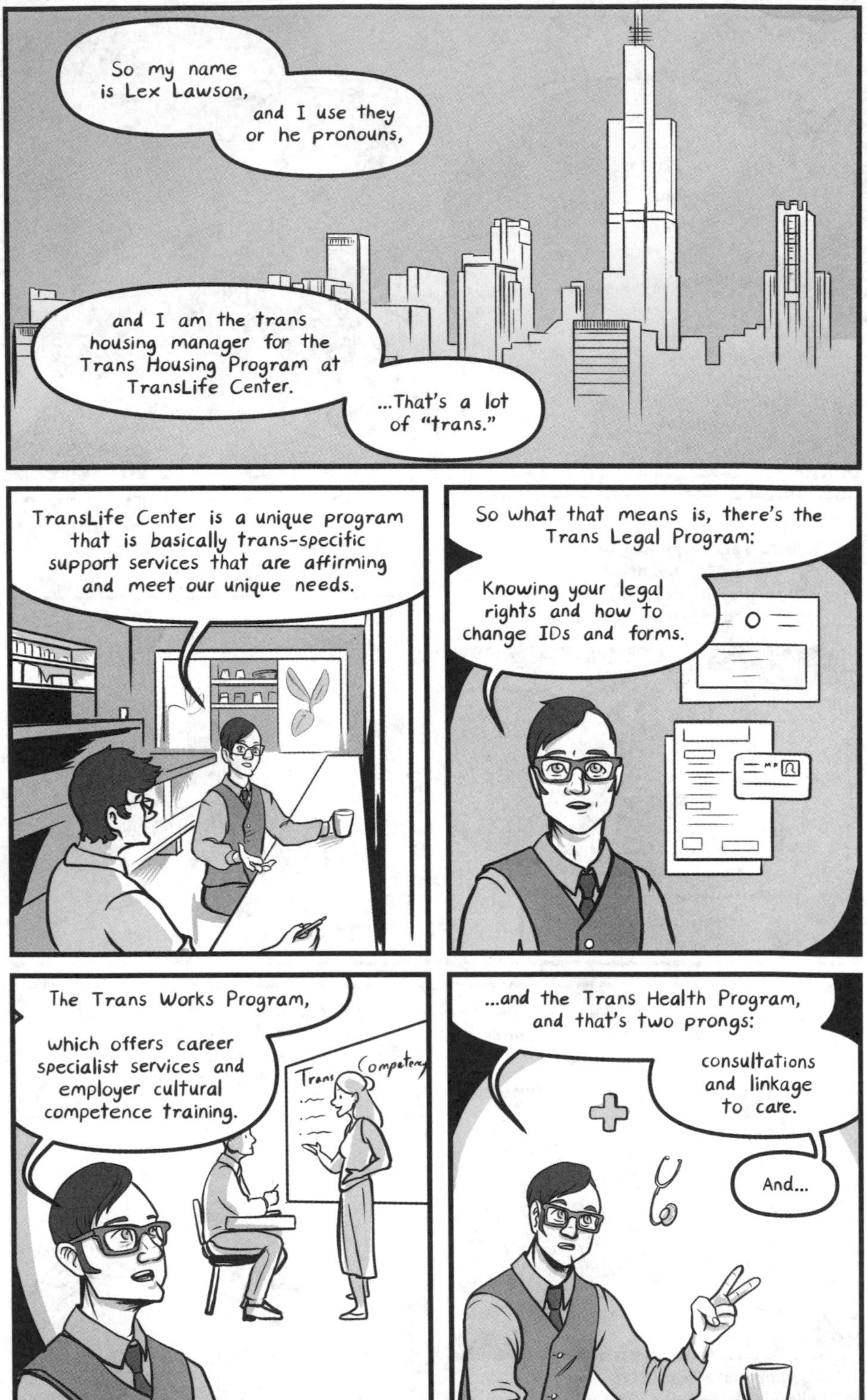

So my name is Lex Lawson,
and I use they or he pronouns,
and I am the trans housing manager for the Trans Housing Program at TransLife Center.
...That's a lot of "trans."
TransLife Center is a unique program that is basically trans-specific support services that are affirming and meet our unique needs.
So what that means is, there's the Trans Legal Program:
Knowing your legal rights and how to change IDs and forms.
The Trans Works Program,
which offers career specialist services and employer cultural competence training.
...and the Trans Health Program, and that's two prongs:
consultations and linkage to care.
And...

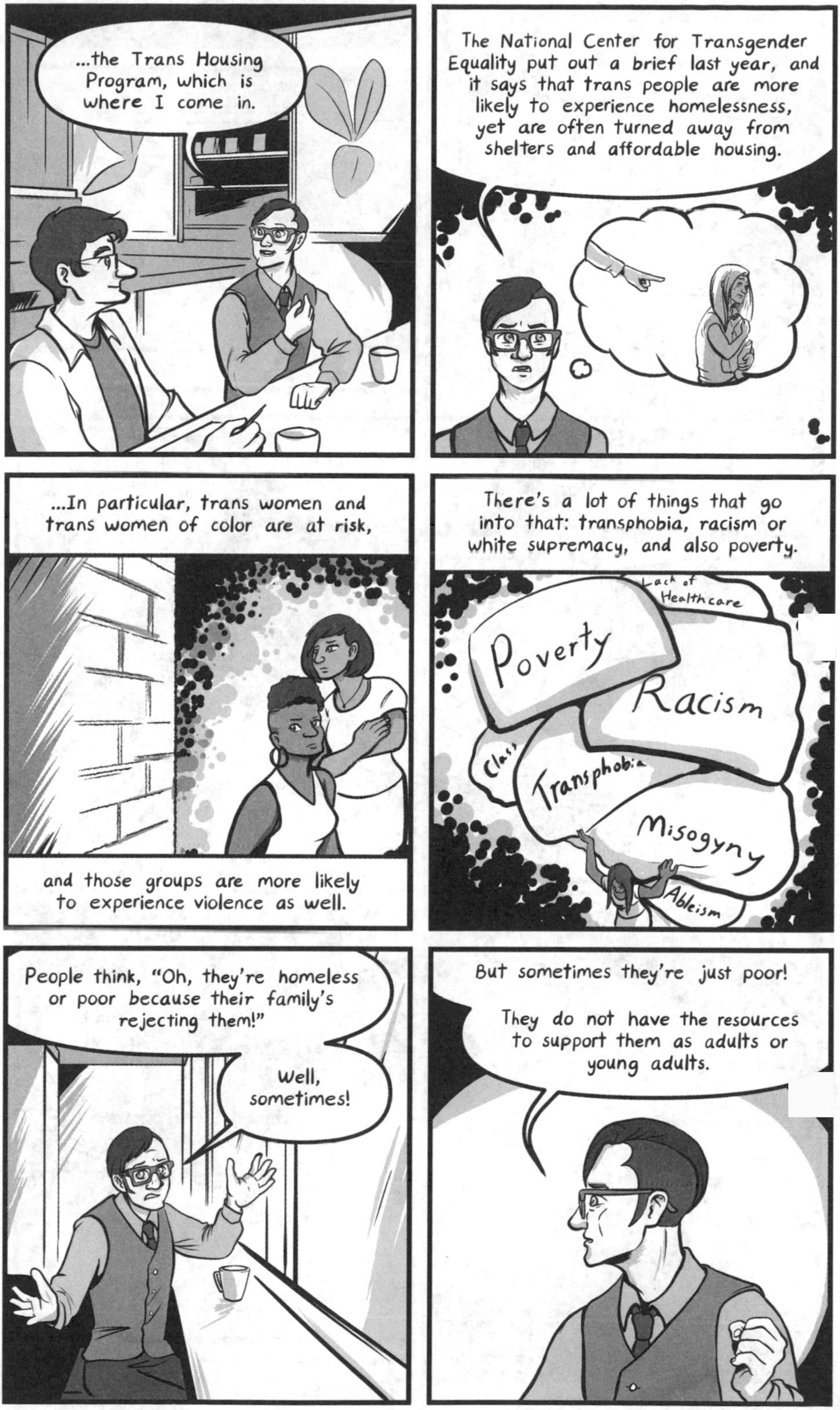
...the Trans Housing Program, which is where I come in.
The National Center for Transgender Equality put out a brief last year, and it says that trans people are more likely to experience homelessness, yet are often turned away from shelters and affordable housing.
...In particular, trans women and trans women of color are at risk,
and those groups are more likely to experience violence as well.
There's a lot of things that go into that: transphobia, racism or white supremacy, and also poverty.
Lack of Healthcare
Poverty
Racism
Class
Transphobia
Misogyny
Ableism
People think, "Oh, they're homeless or poor because their family's rejecting them!"
Well, sometimes!
But sometimes they're just poor!
They do not have the resources to support them as adults or young adults.

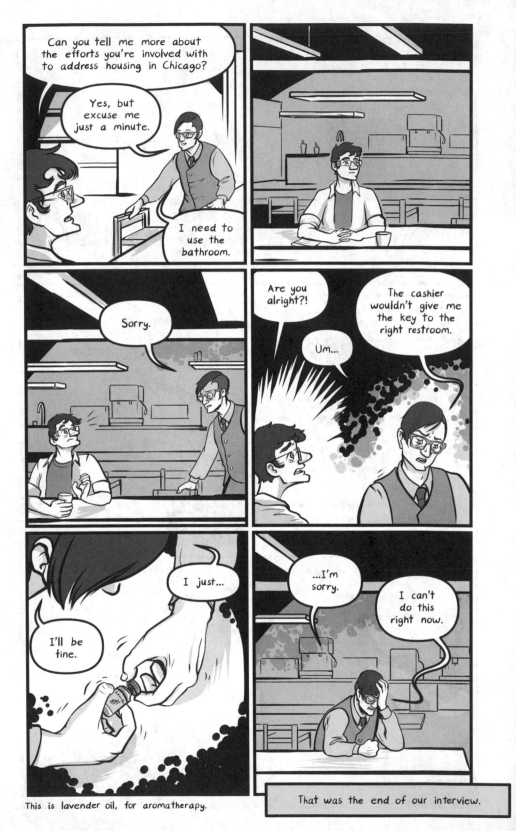

Can you tell me more about the efforts you're involved with to address housing in Chicago?
Yes, but excuse me just a minute.
I need to use the bathroom.
Sorry.
Are you alright?!
Um...
The cashier wouldn't give me the key to the right restroom.
I just...
I'll be fine.
This is lavender oil, for aromatherapy.
...I'm sorry.
I can't do this right now.
That was the end of our interview.

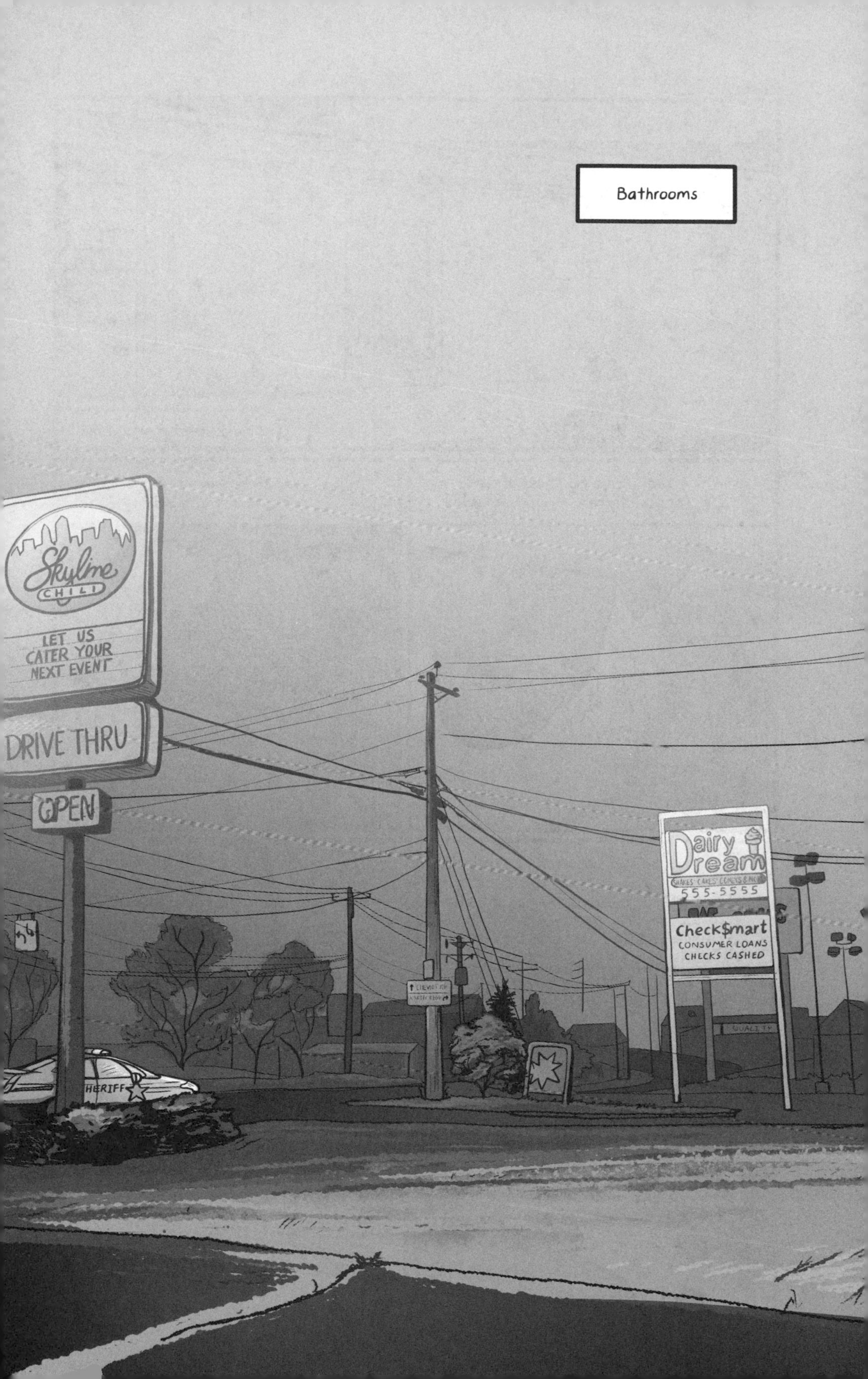
Bathrooms
Skyline
CHILI
LET US CATER YOUR NEXT EVENT
DRIVE THRU
OPEN
HERIFF
Dairy Dream
555-5555
Check$mart
CONSUMER LOANS
CHECKS CASHED

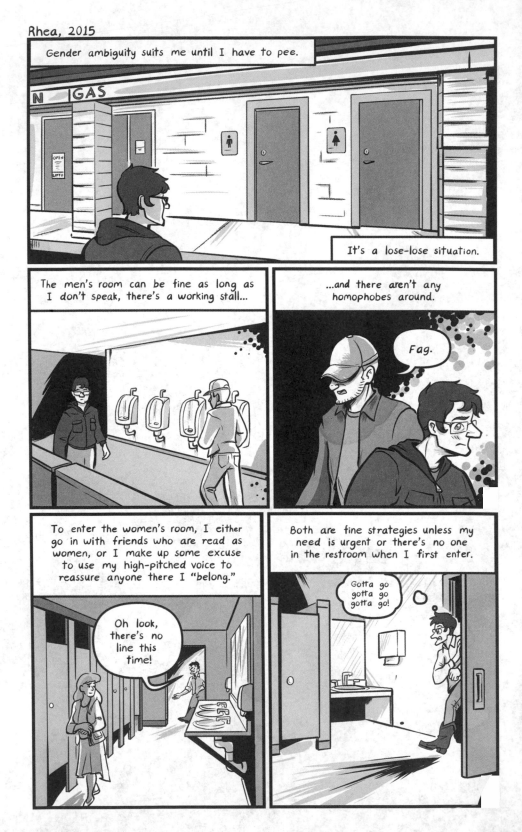

Gender ambiguity suits me until I have to pee.

It's a lose-lose situation.

The men's room can be fine as long as I don't speak, there's a working stall...

...and there aren't any homophobes around.

Fag.

To enter the women's room, I either go in with friends who are read as women, or I make up some excuse to use my high-pitched voice to reassure anyone there I "belong."

Oh look, there's no line this time!

Both are fine strategies unless my need is urgent or there's no one in the restroom when I first enter.

Gotta go gotta go gotta go!

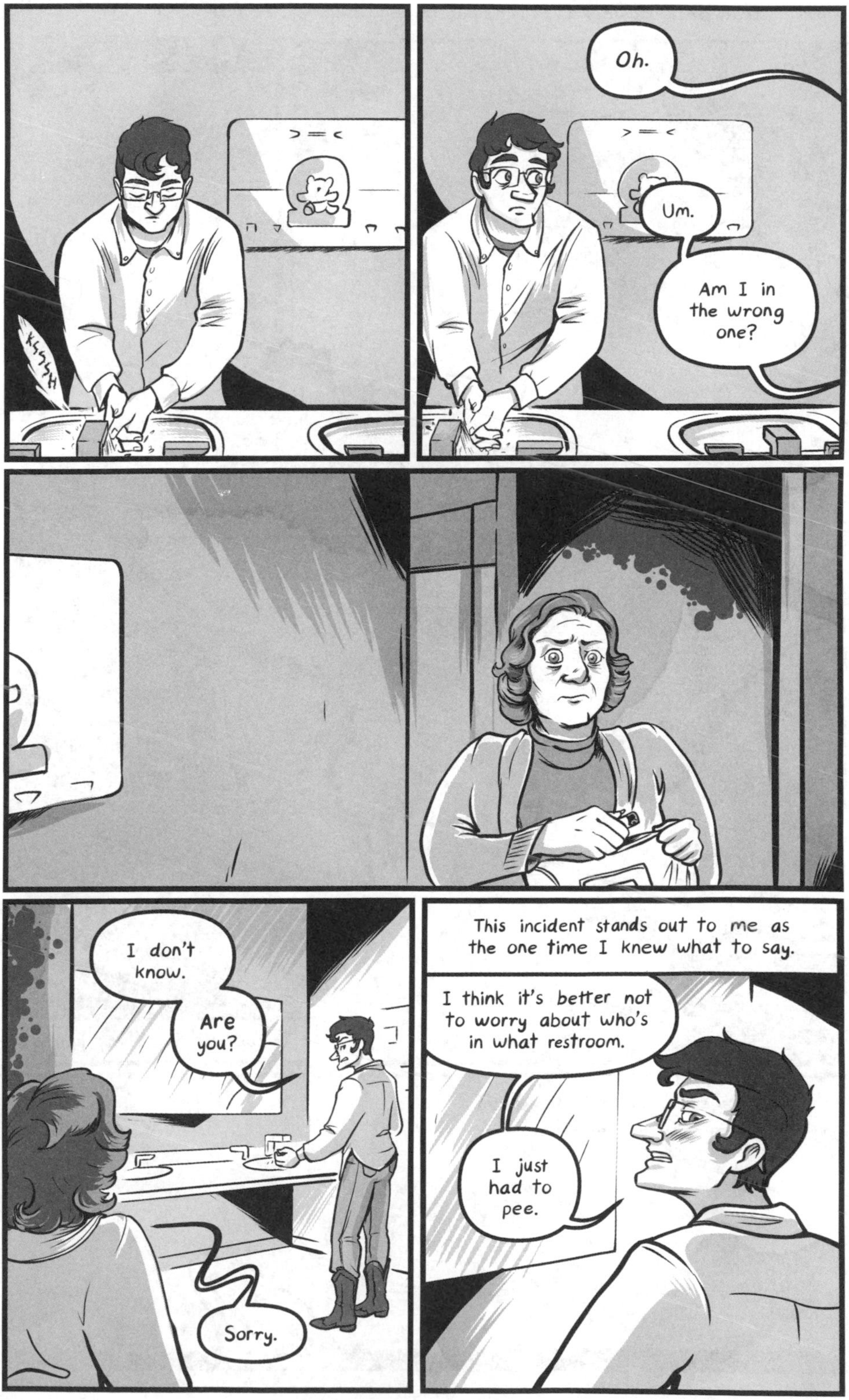
KSSSH
Oh.
Um.
Am I in the wrong one?
I don't know.
Are you?
Sorry.
This incident stands out to me as the one time I knew what to say.
I think it's better not to worry about who's in what restroom.
I just had to pee.

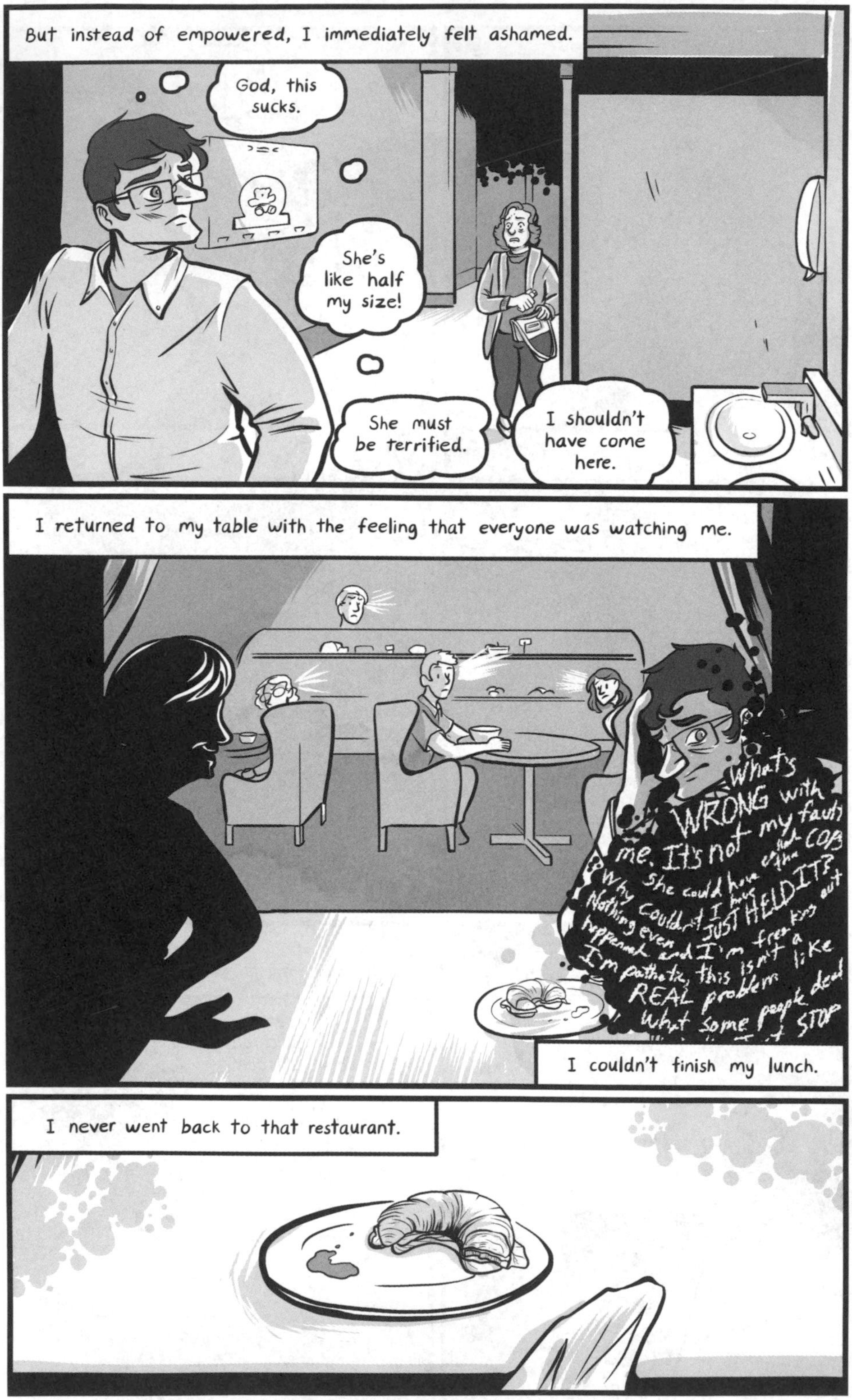
But instead of empowered, I immediately felt ashamed.
God, this sucks.
She's like half my size!
She must be terrified.
I shouldn't have come here.
I returned to my table with the feeling that everyone was watching me.
What's WRONG with me.
It's not my
Why couldn't I JUST HELD IT?
Nothing even happened
I'm pathetic, this isn't a REAL problem like what some people deal
STOP
I couldn't finish my lunch.
I never went back to that restaurant.

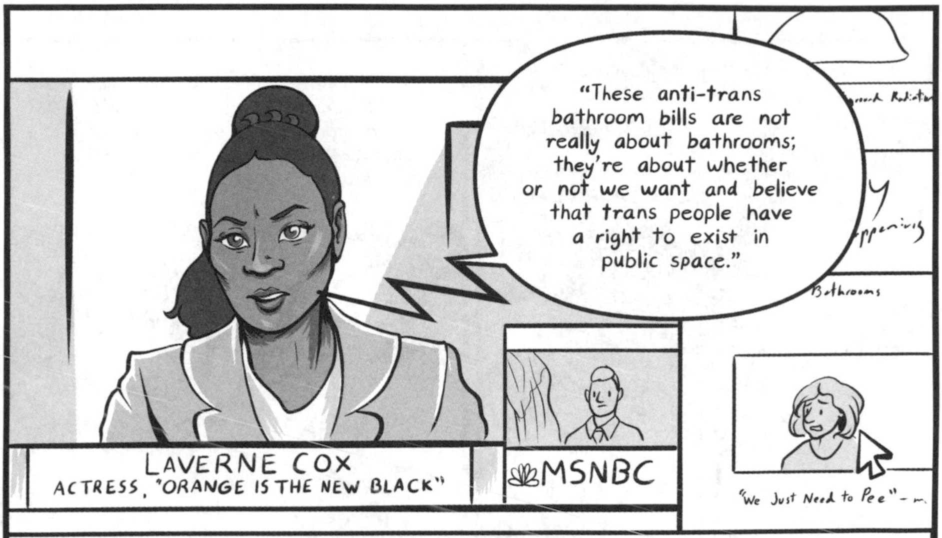
"These anti-trans bathroom bills are not really about bathrooms; they're about whether or not we want and believe that trans people have a right to exist in public space."
LAVERNE COX
ACTRESS, "ORANGE IS THE NEW BLACK"
MSNBC
Bathrooms

Laverne Cox quoting ACLU lawyer Chase Strangio on MSNBC's *Hardball*

Anonymous, 2015

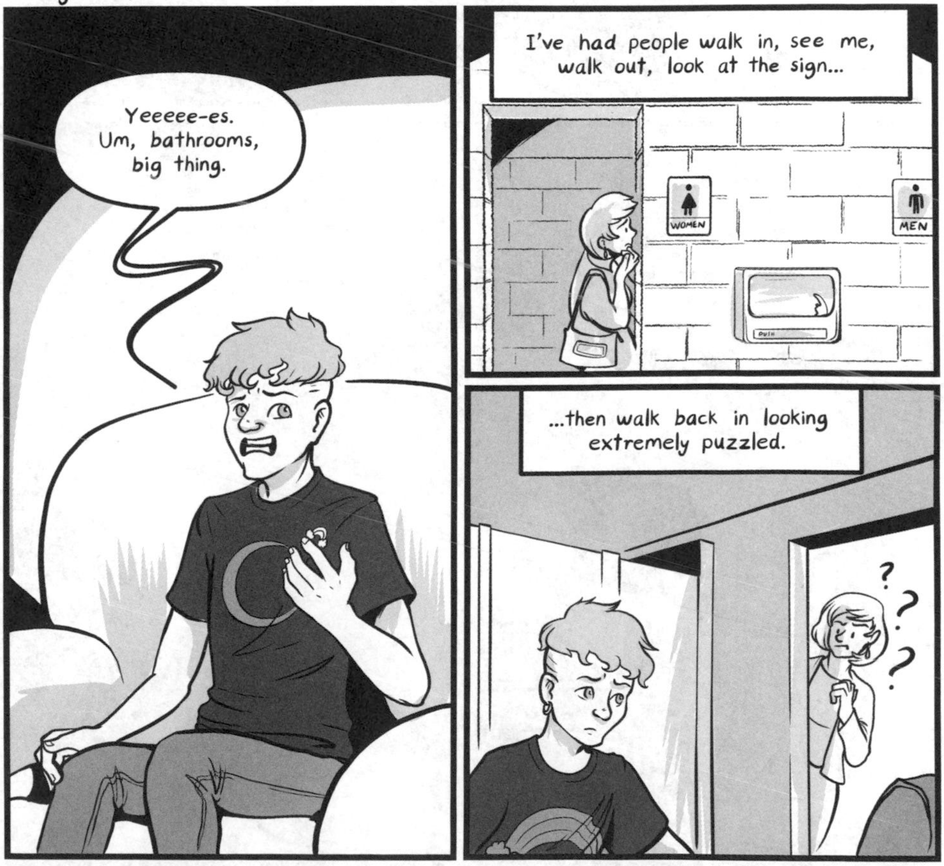
Yeeeee-es. Um, bathrooms, big thing.
I've had people walk in, see me, walk out, look at the sign...
WOMEN
MEN
...then walk back in looking extremely puzzled.
? ? ?

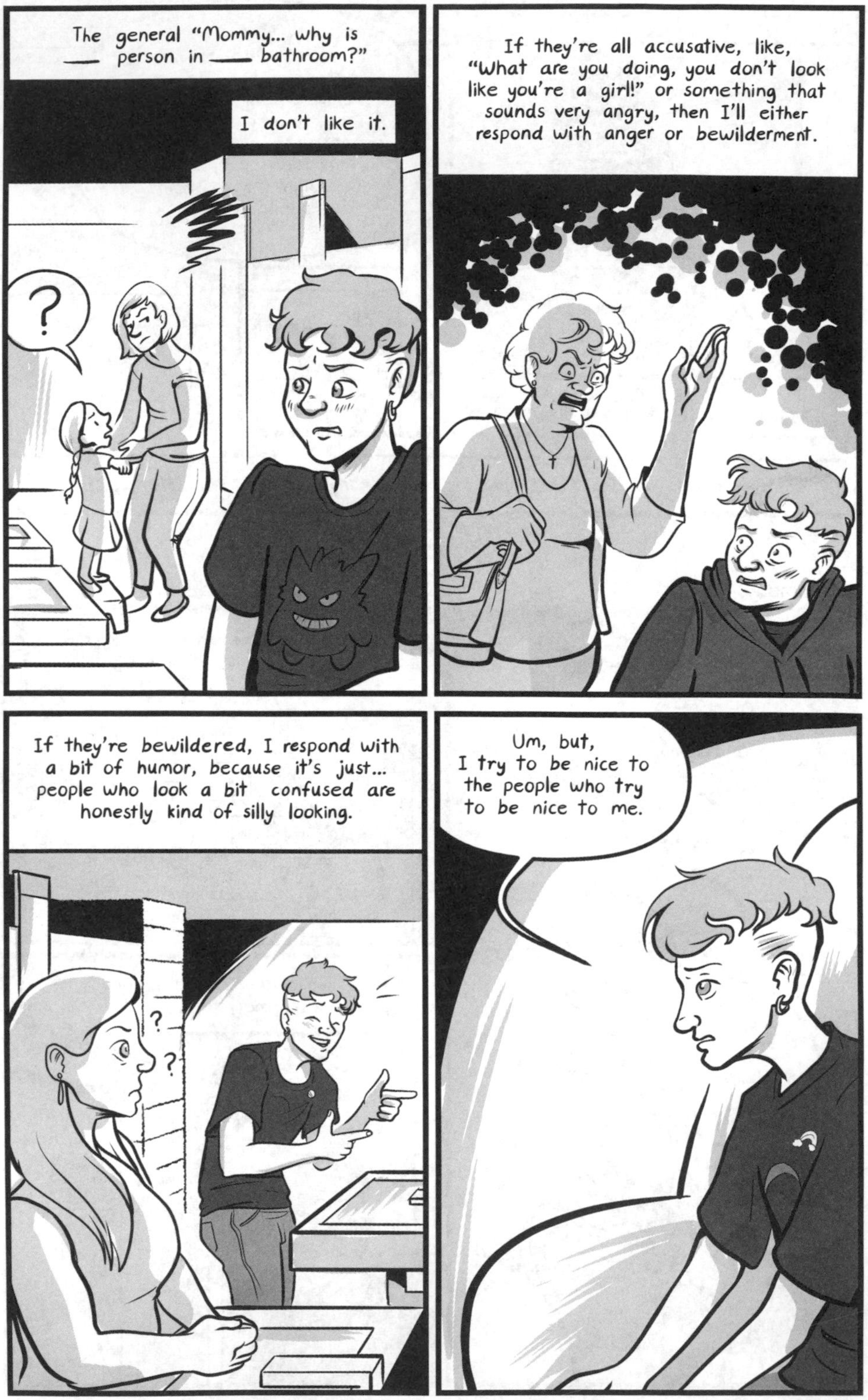
The general "Mommy... why is ___ person in ___ bathroom?"
I don't like it.
?
If they're all accusative, like, "What are you doing, you don't look like you're a girl!" or something that sounds very angry, then I'll either respond with anger or bewilderment.
If they're bewildered, I respond with a bit of humor, because it's just... people who look a bit confused are honestly kind of silly looking.
?
?
Um, but, I try to be nice to the people who try to be nice to me.

Gerbil, 2012

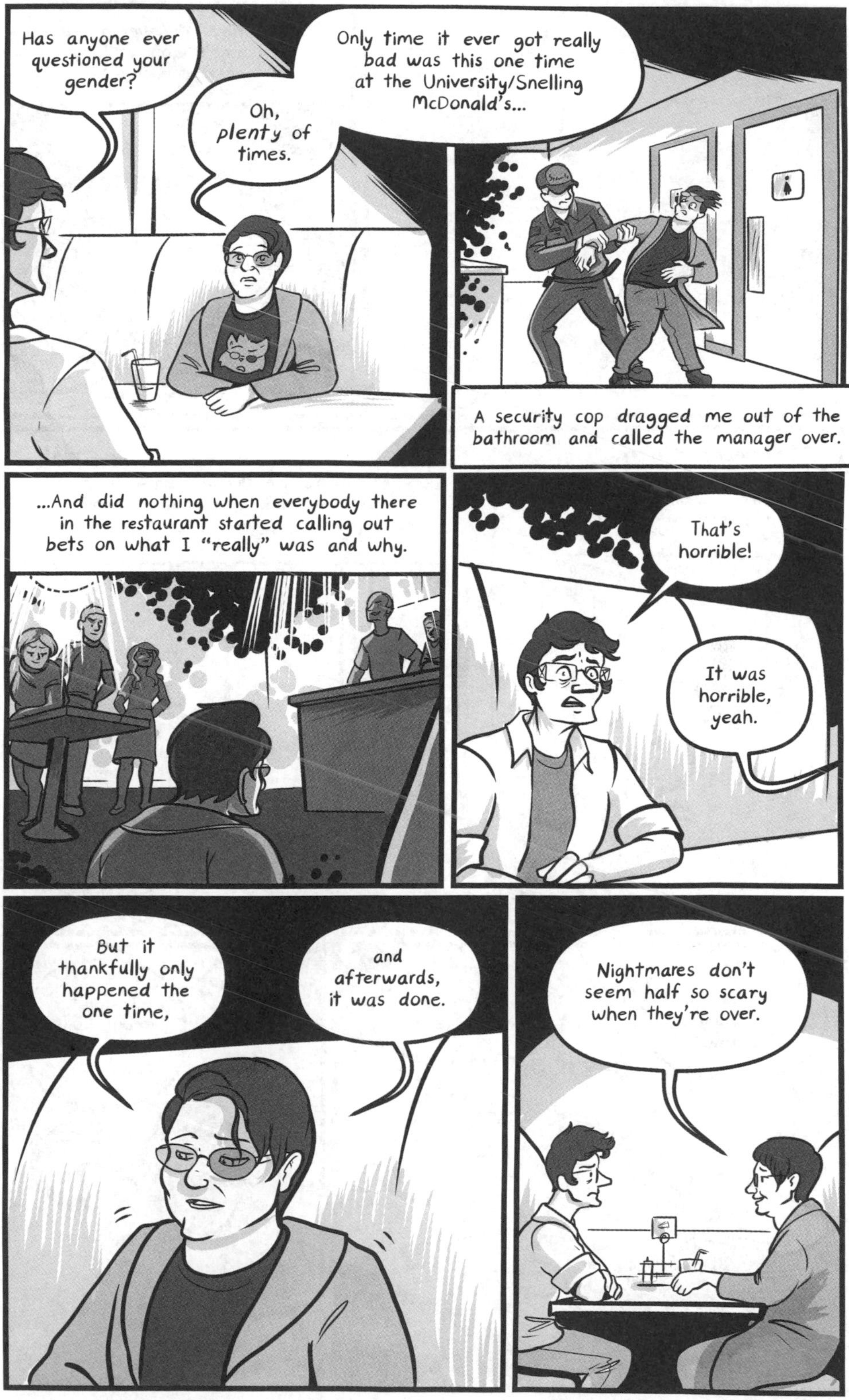
Has anyone ever questioned your gender?
Oh, plenty of times.
Only time it ever got really bad was this one time at the University/Snelling McDonald's...
A security cop dragged me out of the bathroom and called the manager over.
...And did nothing when everybody there in the restaurant started calling out bets on what I "really" was and why.
That's horrible!
It was horrible, yeah.
But it thankfully only happened the one time,
and afterwards, it was done.
Nightmares don't seem half so scary when they're over.

Enne, 2013

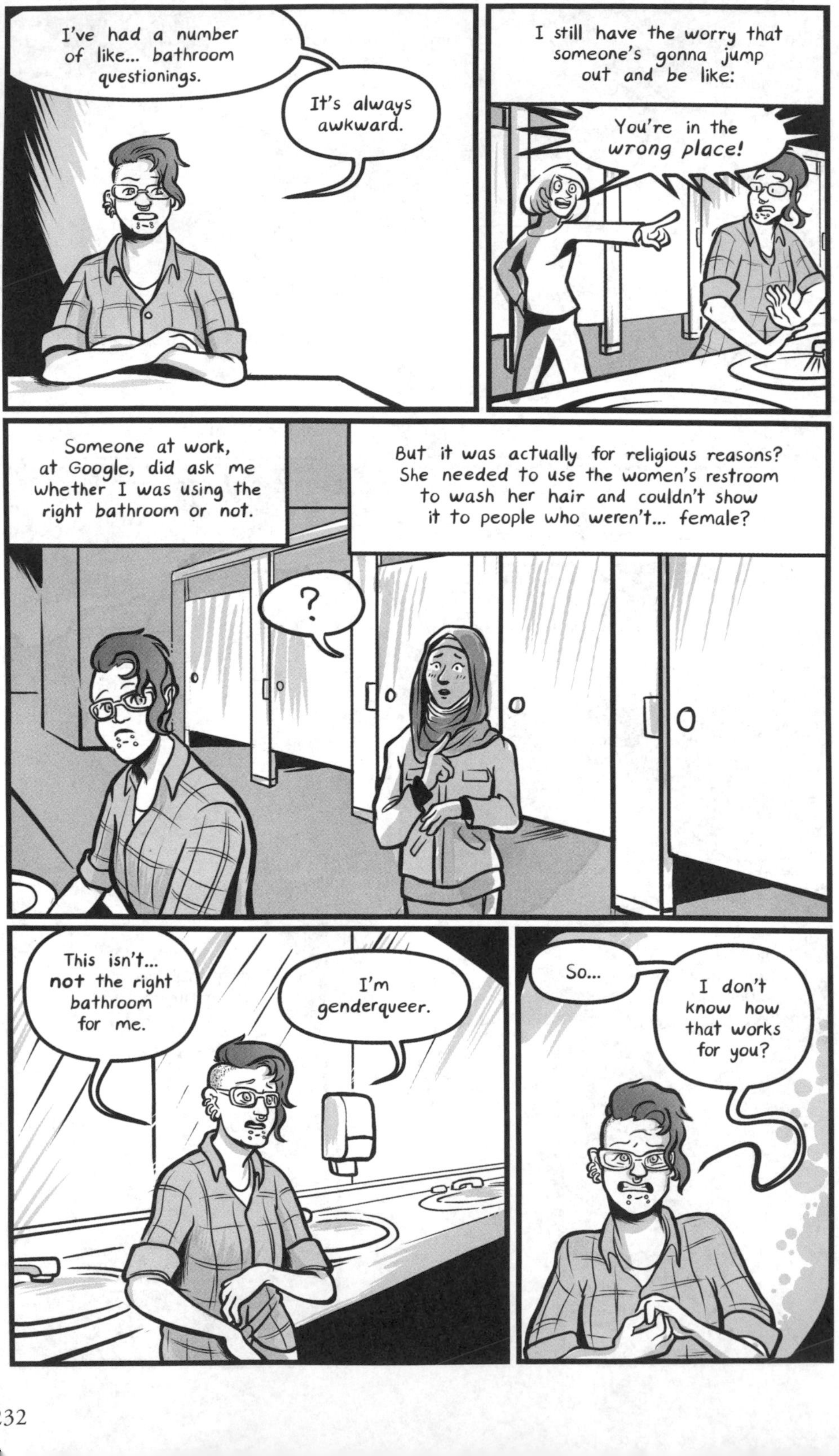
I've had a number of like... bathroom questionings.
It's always awkward.
I still have the worry that someone's gonna jump out and be like:
You're in the *wrong place!*
Someone at work, at Google, did ask me whether I was using the right bathroom or not.
But it was actually for religious reasons? She needed to use the women's restroom to wash her hair and couldn't show it to people who weren't... female?
?
This isn't... **not** the right bathroom for me.
I'm genderqueer.
So...
I don't know how that works for you?

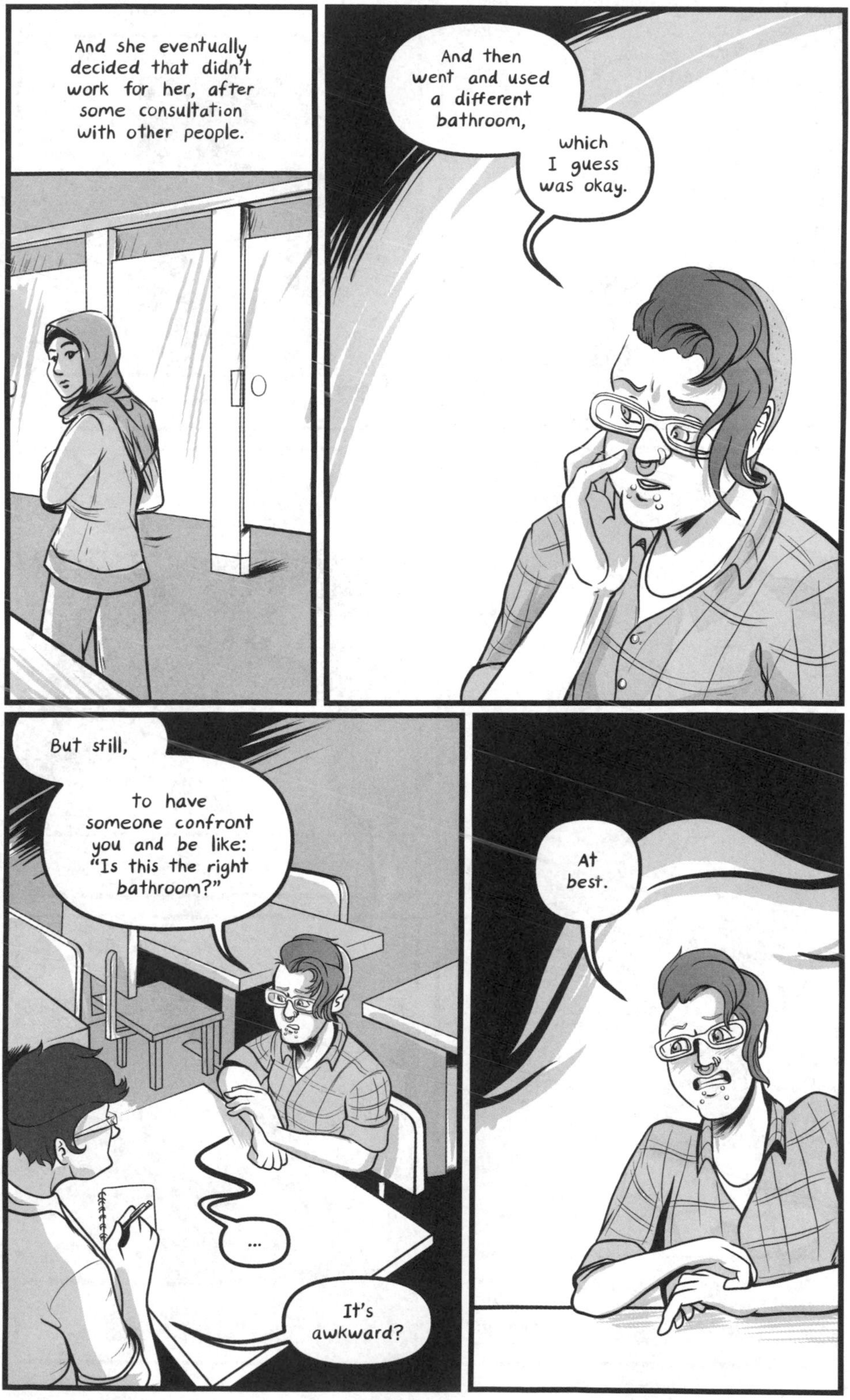
And she eventually decided that didn't work for her, after some consultation with other people.
And then went and used a different bathroom,
which I guess was okay.
But still,
to have someone confront you and be like: "Is this the right bathroom?"
...
It's awkward?
At best.

Rashida, 2013

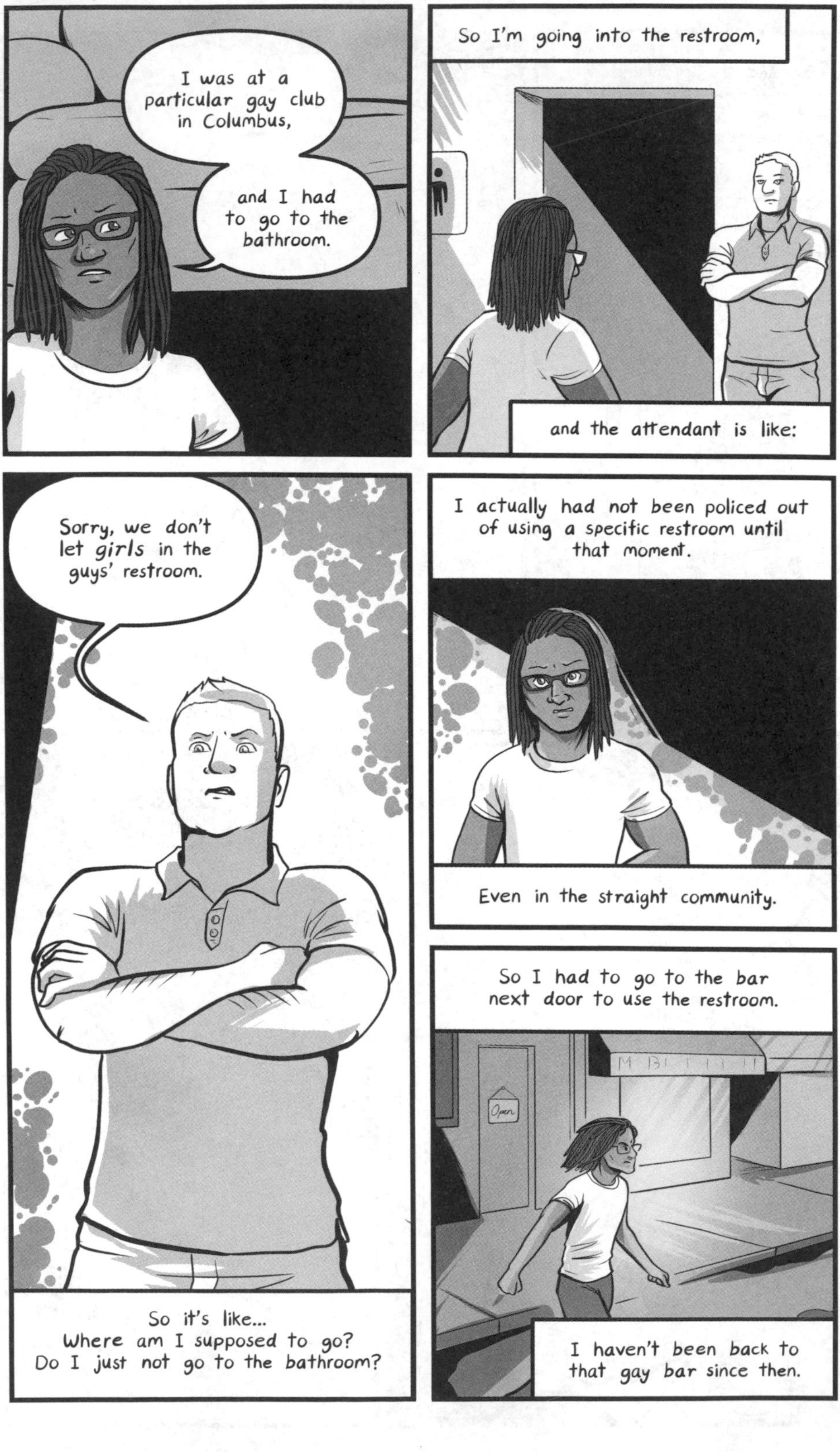

I was at a particular gay club in Columbus,
and I had to go to the bathroom.
So I'm going into the restroom,
and the attendant is like:
Sorry, we don't let *girls* in the guys' restroom.
So it's like... Where am I supposed to go? Do I just not go to the bathroom?
I actually had not been policed out of using a specific restroom until that moment.
Even in the straight community.
So I had to go to the bar next door to use the restroom.
Open
I haven't been back to that gay bar since then.

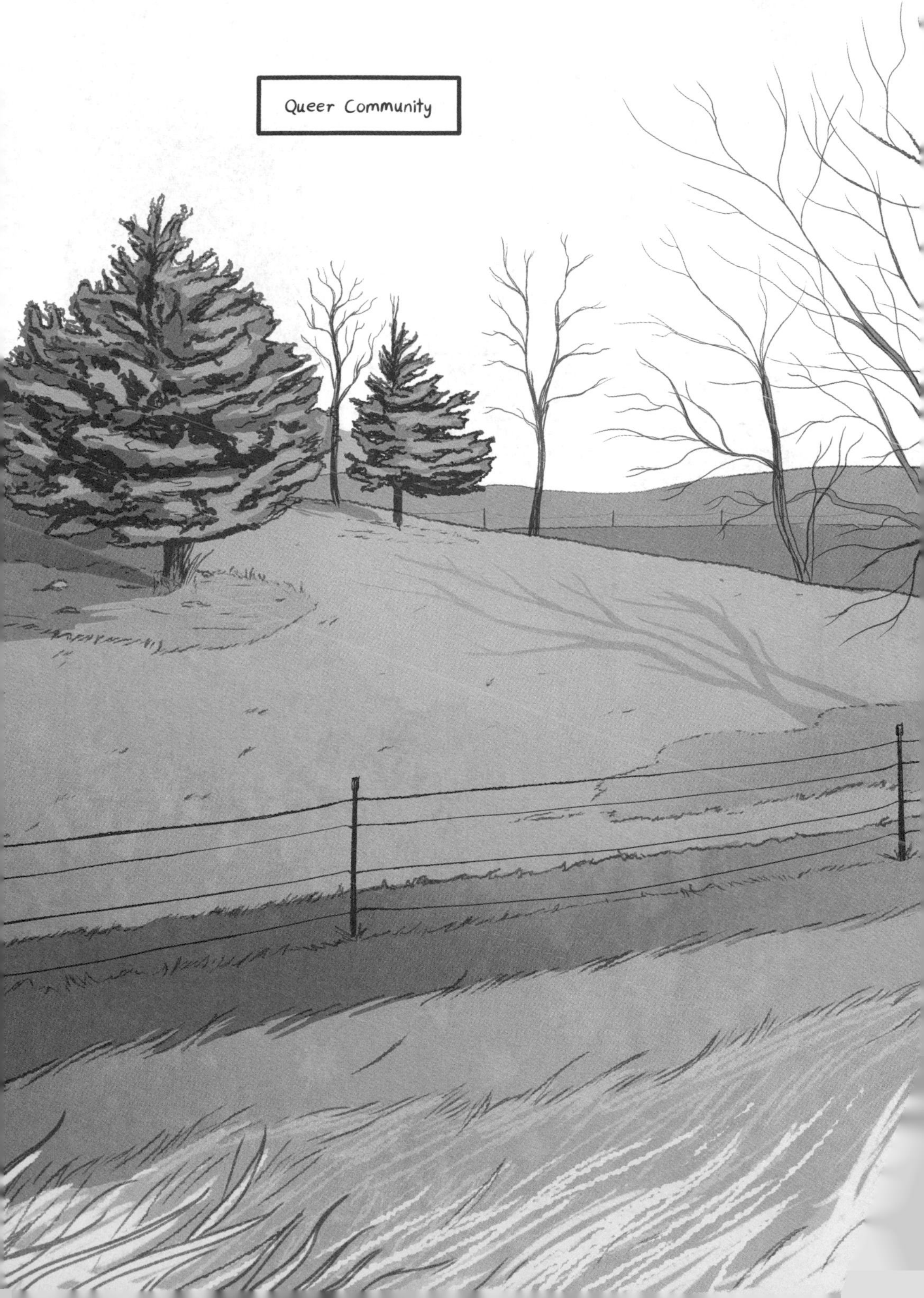
Queer Community

Ginger, 2012

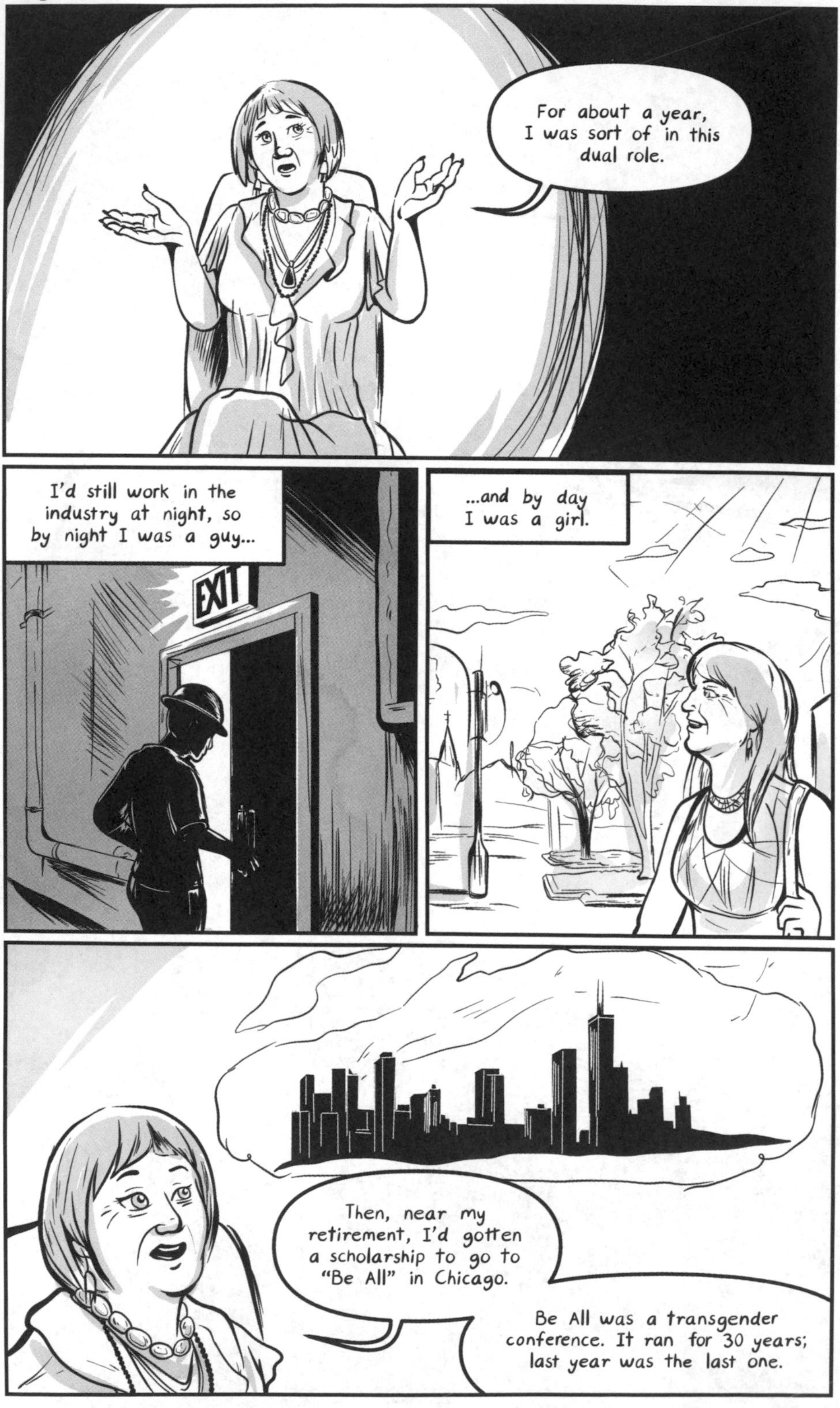
For about a year, I was sort of in this dual role.
I'd still work in the industry at night, so by night I was a guy...
EXIT
...and by day I was a girl.
Then, near my retirement, I'd gotten a scholarship to go to "Be All" in Chicago.
Be All was a transgender conference. It ran for 30 years; last year was the last one.

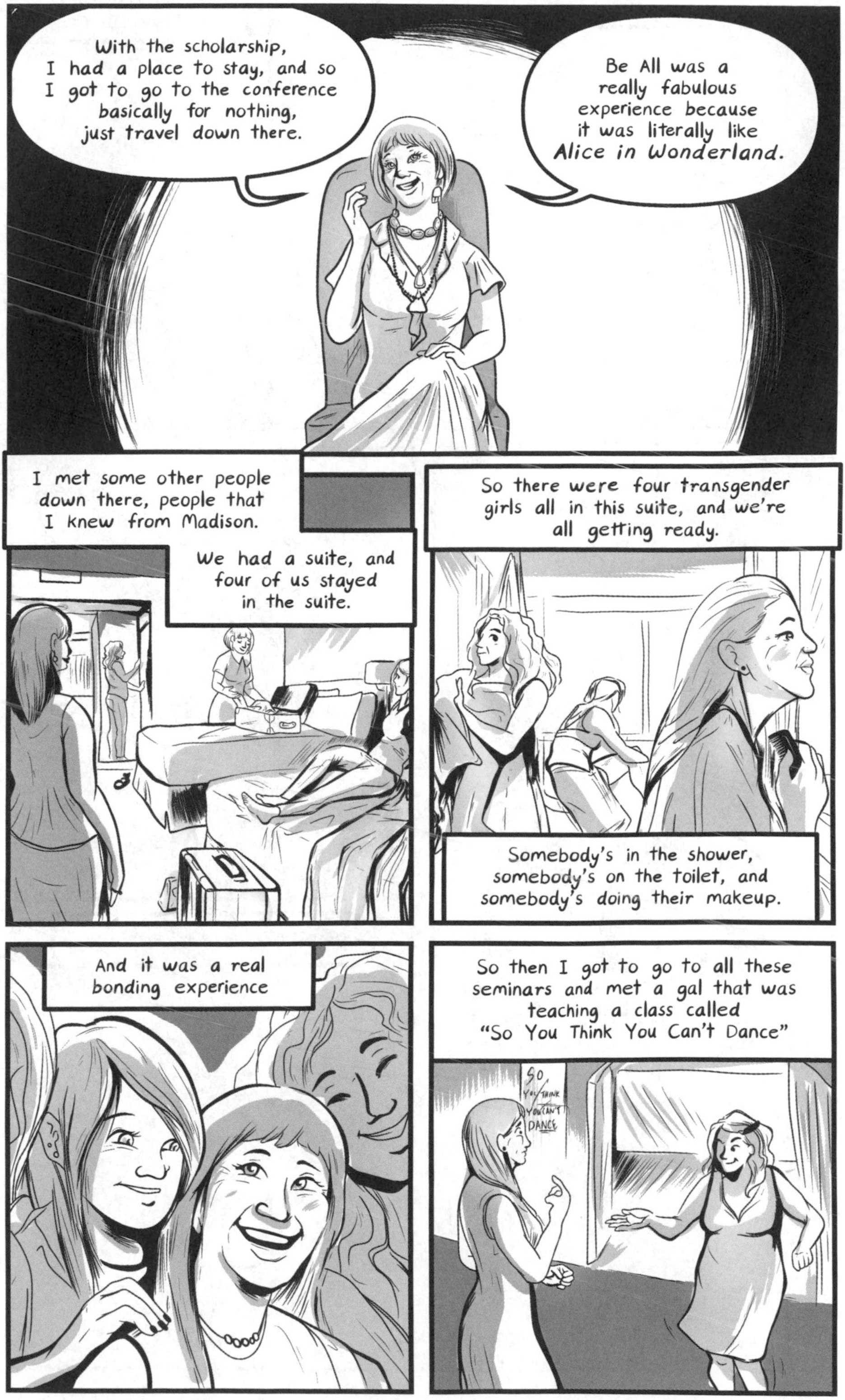
With the scholarship, I had a place to stay, and so I got to go to the conference basically for nothing, just travel down there.
Be All was a really fabulous experience because it was literally like Alice in Wonderland.
I met some other people down there, people that I knew from Madison.
We had a suite, and four of us stayed in the suite.
So there were four transgender girls all in this suite, and we're all getting ready.
Somebody's in the shower, somebody's on the toilet, and somebody's doing their makeup.
And it was a real bonding experience
So then I got to go to all these seminars and met a gal that was teaching a class called "So You Think You Can't Dance"
SO YOU THINK YOU CAN'T DANCE

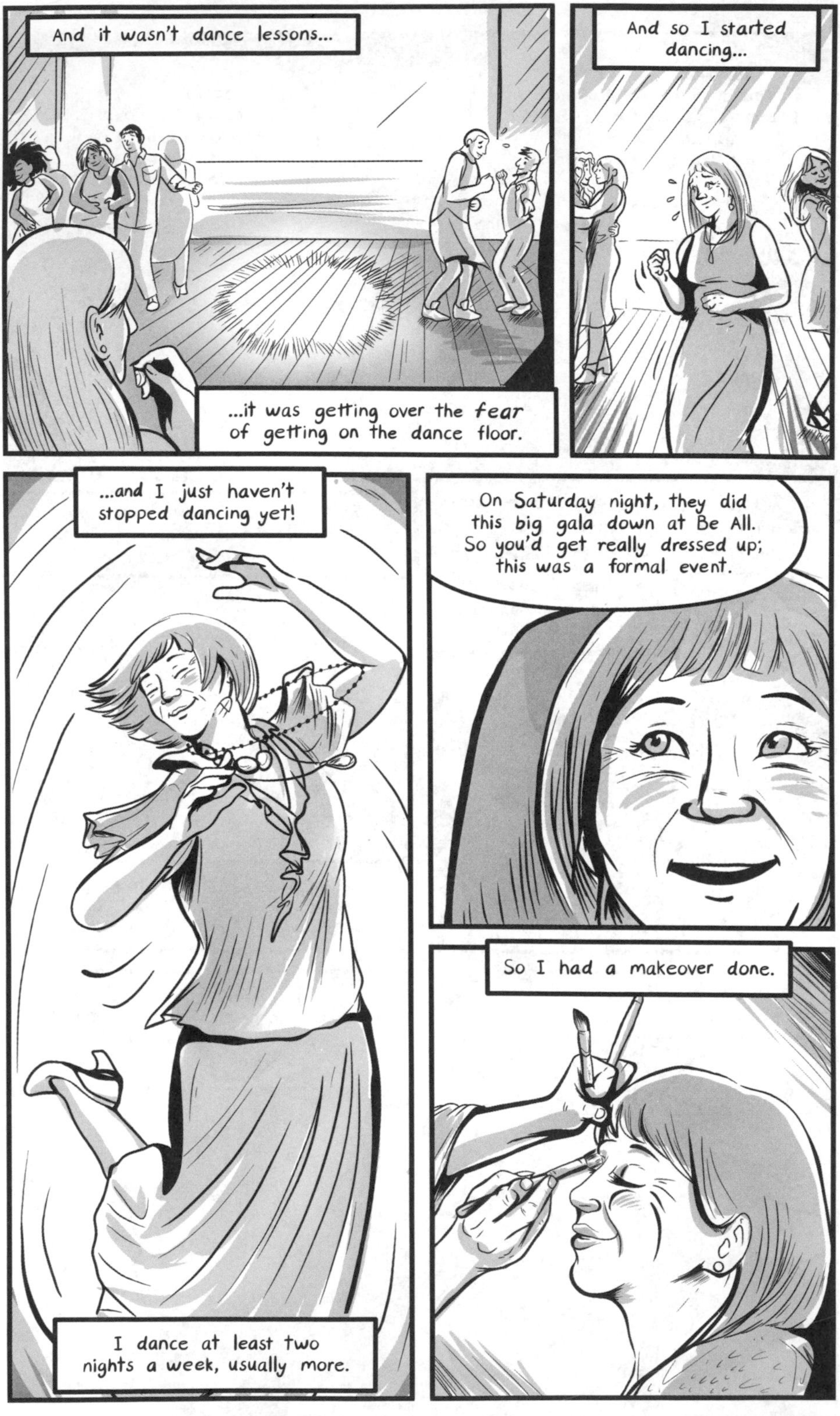
And it wasn't dance lessons...
...it was getting over the *fear* of getting on the dance floor.
And so I started dancing...
...and I just haven't stopped dancing yet!
I dance at least two nights a week, usually more.
On Saturday night, they did this big gala down at Be All. So you'd get really dressed up; this was a formal event.
So I had a makeover done.

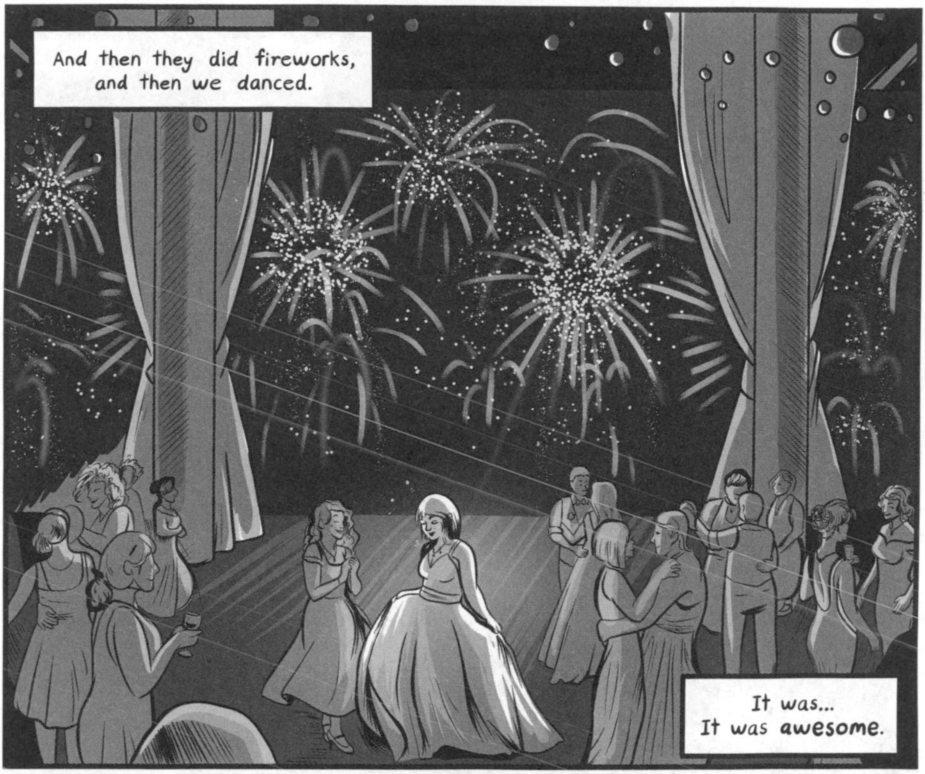
And then they did fireworks, and then we danced.
It was...
It was **awesome**.

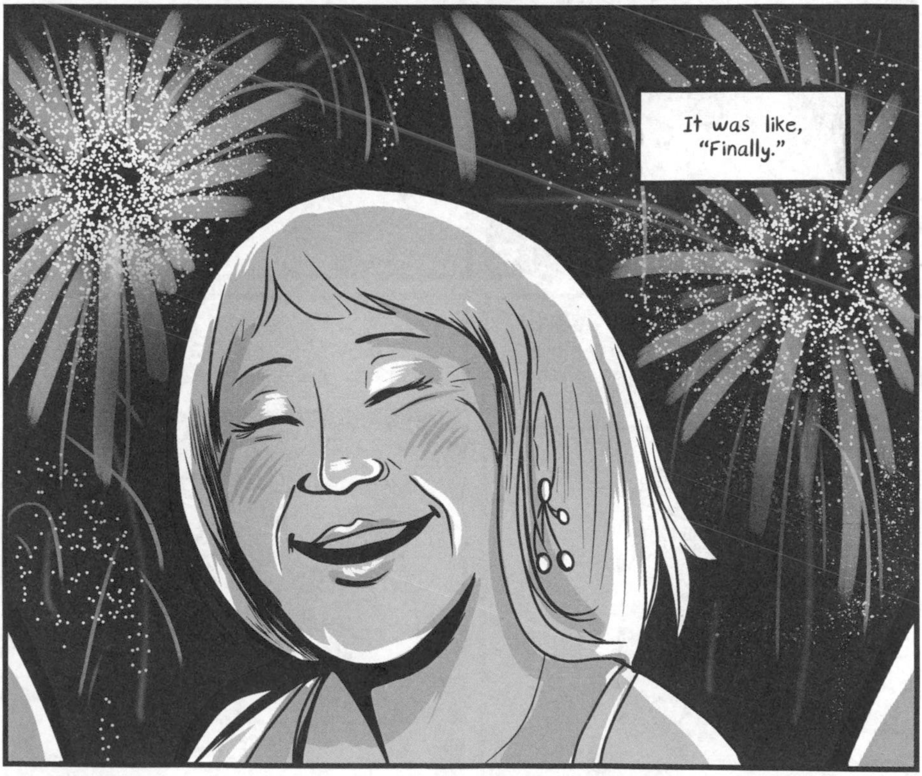
It was like, "Finally."

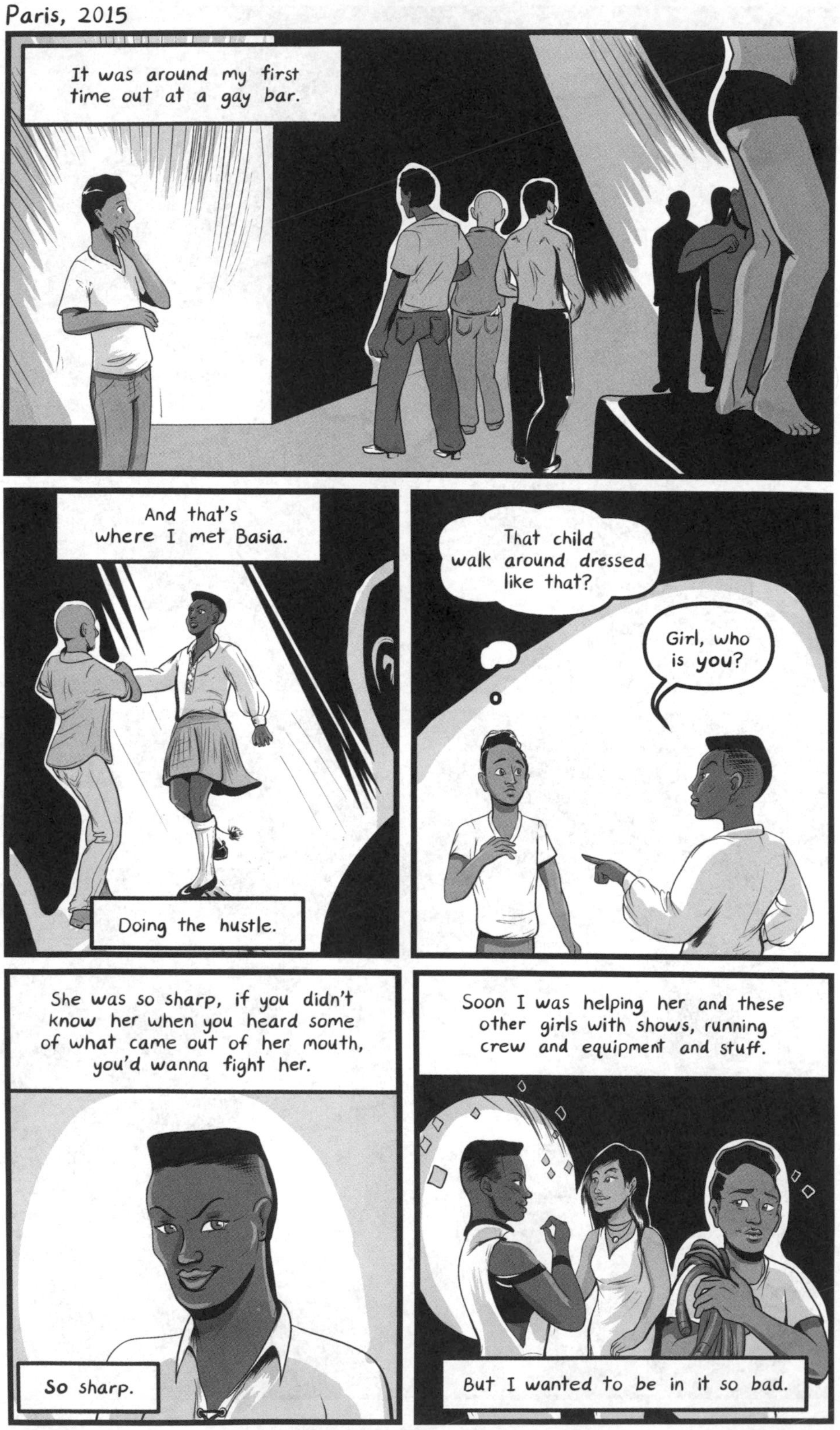
Paris, 2015
It was around my first time out at a gay bar.
And that's where I met Basia.
Doing the hustle.
That child walk around dressed like that?
Girl, who is you?
She was so sharp, if you didn't know her when you heard some of what came out of her mouth, you'd wanna fight her.
So sharp.
Soon I was helping her and these other girls with shows, running crew and equipment and stuff.
But I wanted to be in it so bad.

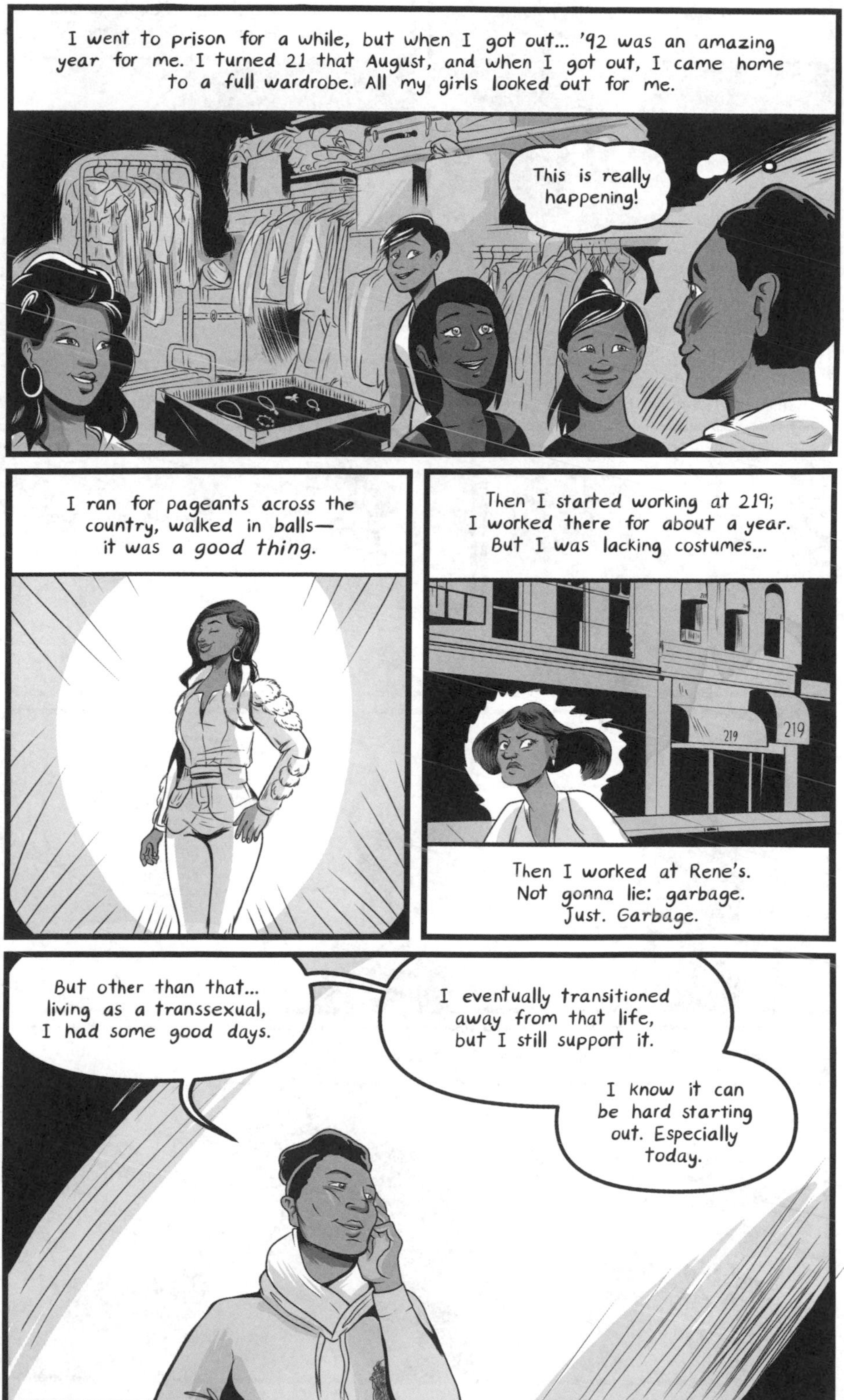
I went to prison for a while, but when I got out... '92 was an amazing year for me. I turned 21 that August, and when I got out, I came home to a full wardrobe. All my girls looked out for me.
This is really happening!
I ran for pageants across the country, walked in balls— it was a *good thing.*
Then I started working at 219; I worked there for about a year. But I was lacking costumes...
219
219
Then I worked at Rene's. Not gonna lie: garbage. Just. Garbage.
But other than that... living as a transsexual, I had some good days.
I eventually transitioned away from that life, but I still support it.
I know it can be hard starting out. Especially today.

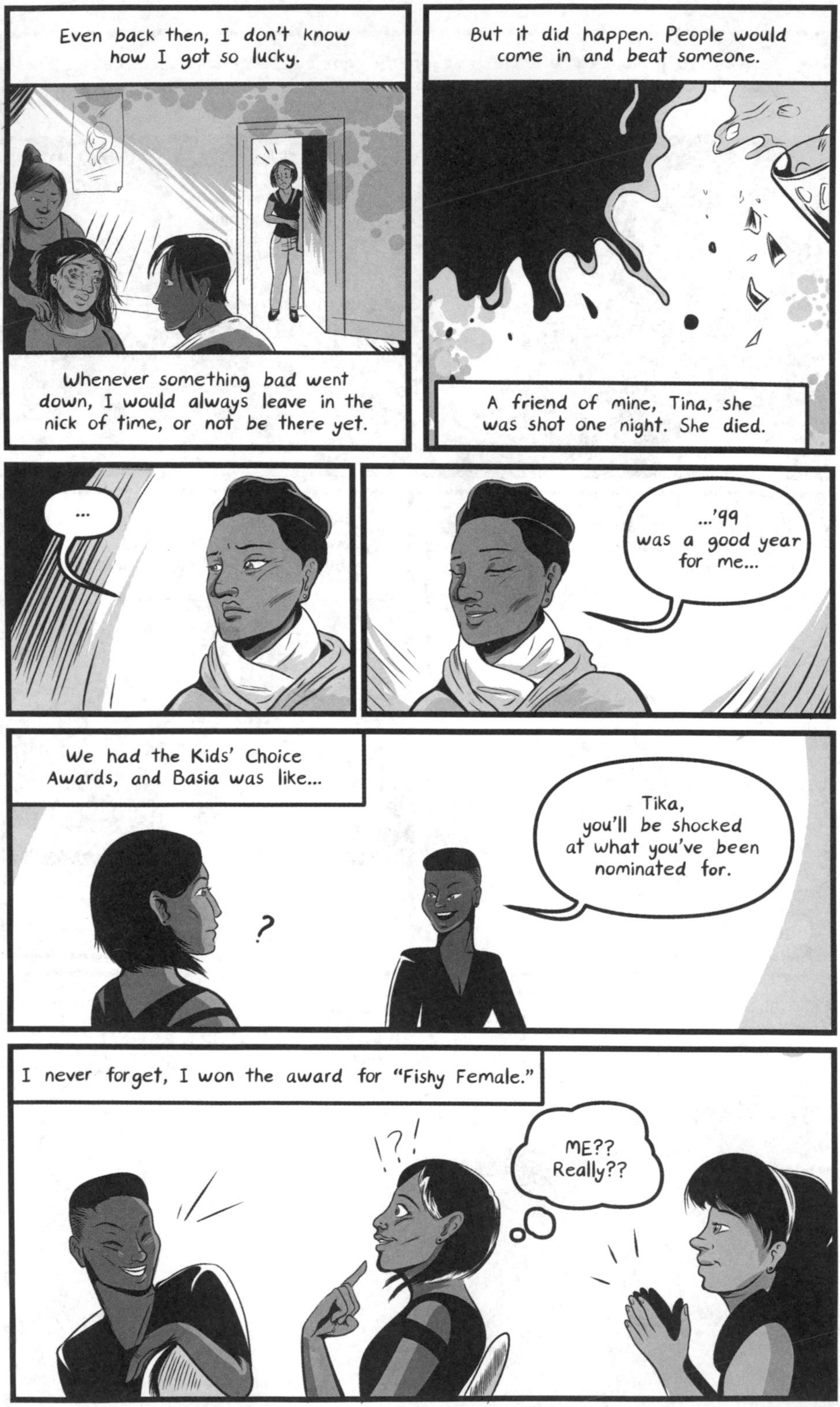
Even back then, I don't know how I got so lucky.
Whenever something bad went down, I would always leave in the nick of time, or not be there yet.
But it did happen. People would come in and beat someone.
A friend of mine, Tina, she was shot one night. She died.
...
...'99 was a good year for me...
We had the Kids' Choice Awards, and Basia was like...
Tika, you'll be shocked at what you've been nominated for.
?
I never forget, I won the award for "Fishy Female."
!?!
ME?? Really??

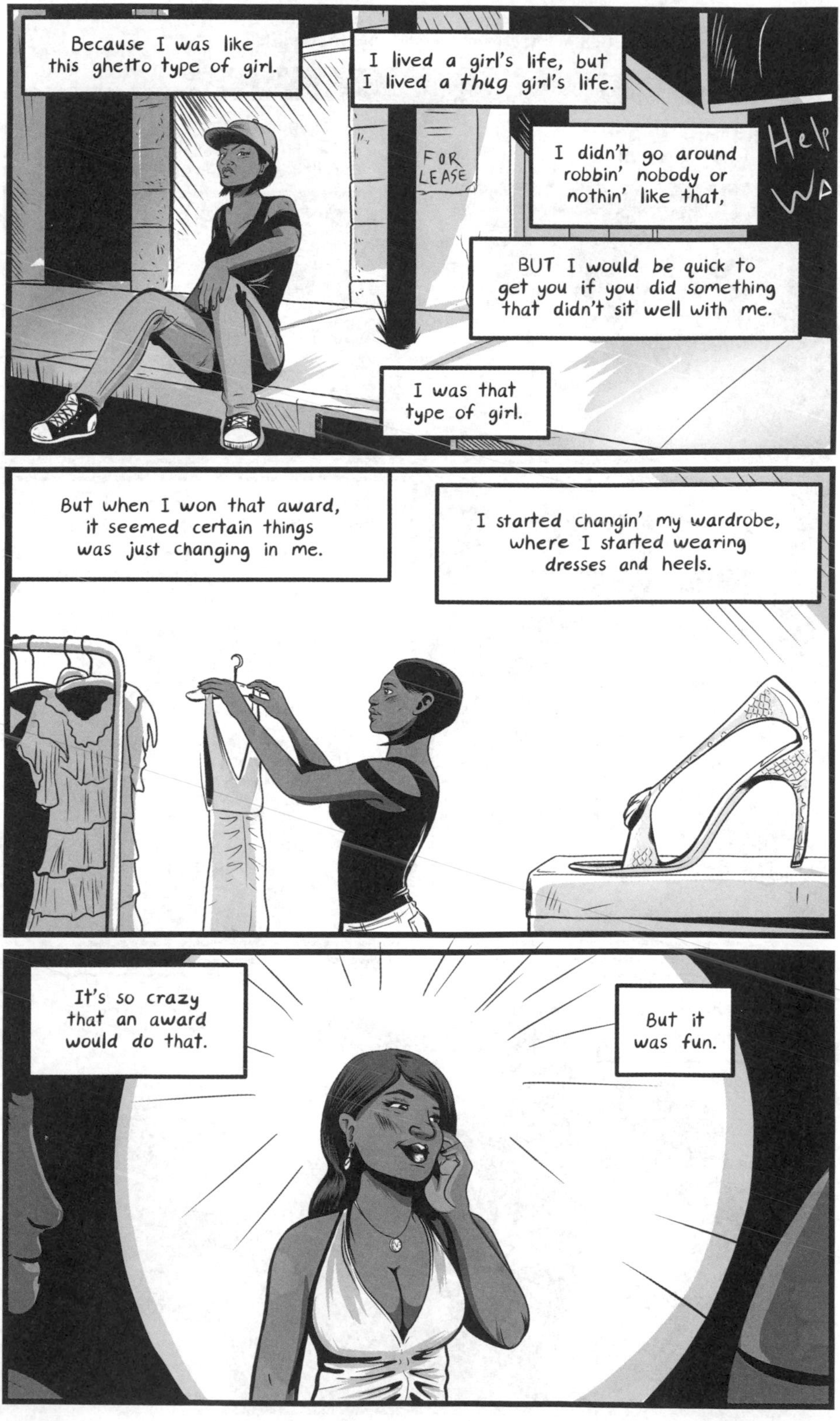

Because I was like this ghetto type of girl.
I lived a girl's life, but I lived a *thug* girl's life.
FOR LEASE
I didn't go around robbin' nobody or nothin' like that,
BUT I would be quick to get you if you did something that didn't sit well with me.
I was that type of girl.
But when I won that award, it seemed certain things was just changing in me.
I started changin' my wardrobe, where I started wearing dresses and heels.
It's so crazy that an award would do that.
But it was fun.

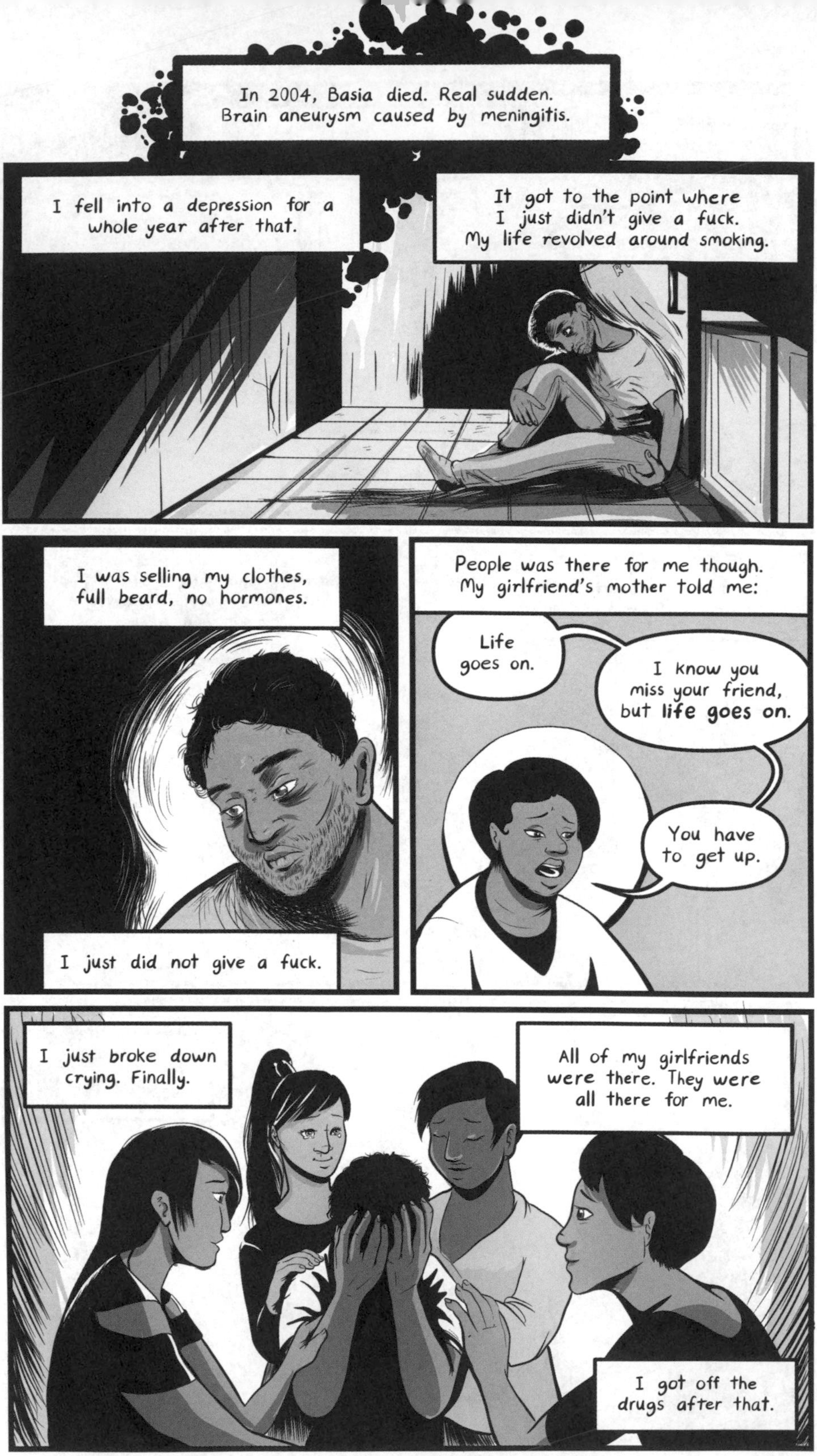
In 2004, Basia died. Real sudden. Brain aneurysm caused by meningitis.
I fell into a depression for a whole year after that.
It got to the point where I just didn't give a fuck. My life revolved around smoking.
I was selling my clothes, full beard, no hormones.
I just did not give a fuck.
People was there for me though. My girlfriend's mother told me:
Life goes on.
I know you miss your friend, but **life goes on.**
You have to get up.
I just broke down crying. Finally.
All of my girlfriends were there. They were all there for me.
I got off the drugs after that.

Marie, 2015

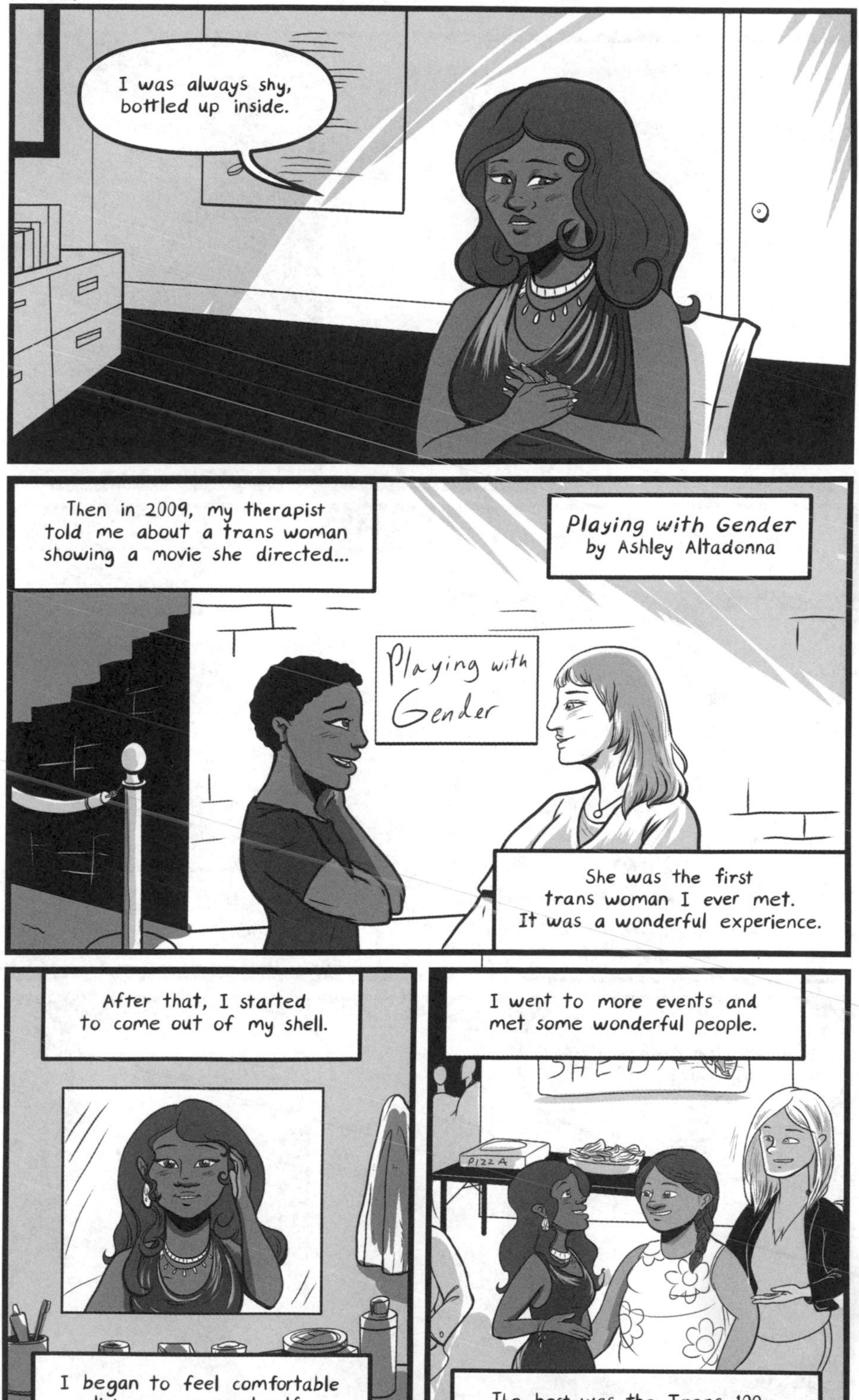
I was always shy, bottled up inside.
Then in 2009, my therapist told me about a trans woman showing a movie she directed...
Playing with Gender by Ashley Altadonna
Playing with Gender
She was the first trans woman I ever met. It was a wonderful experience.
After that, I started to come out of my shell.
I began to feel comfortable living as my real self.
I went to more events and met some wonderful people.
PIZZA
The best was the Trans 100...

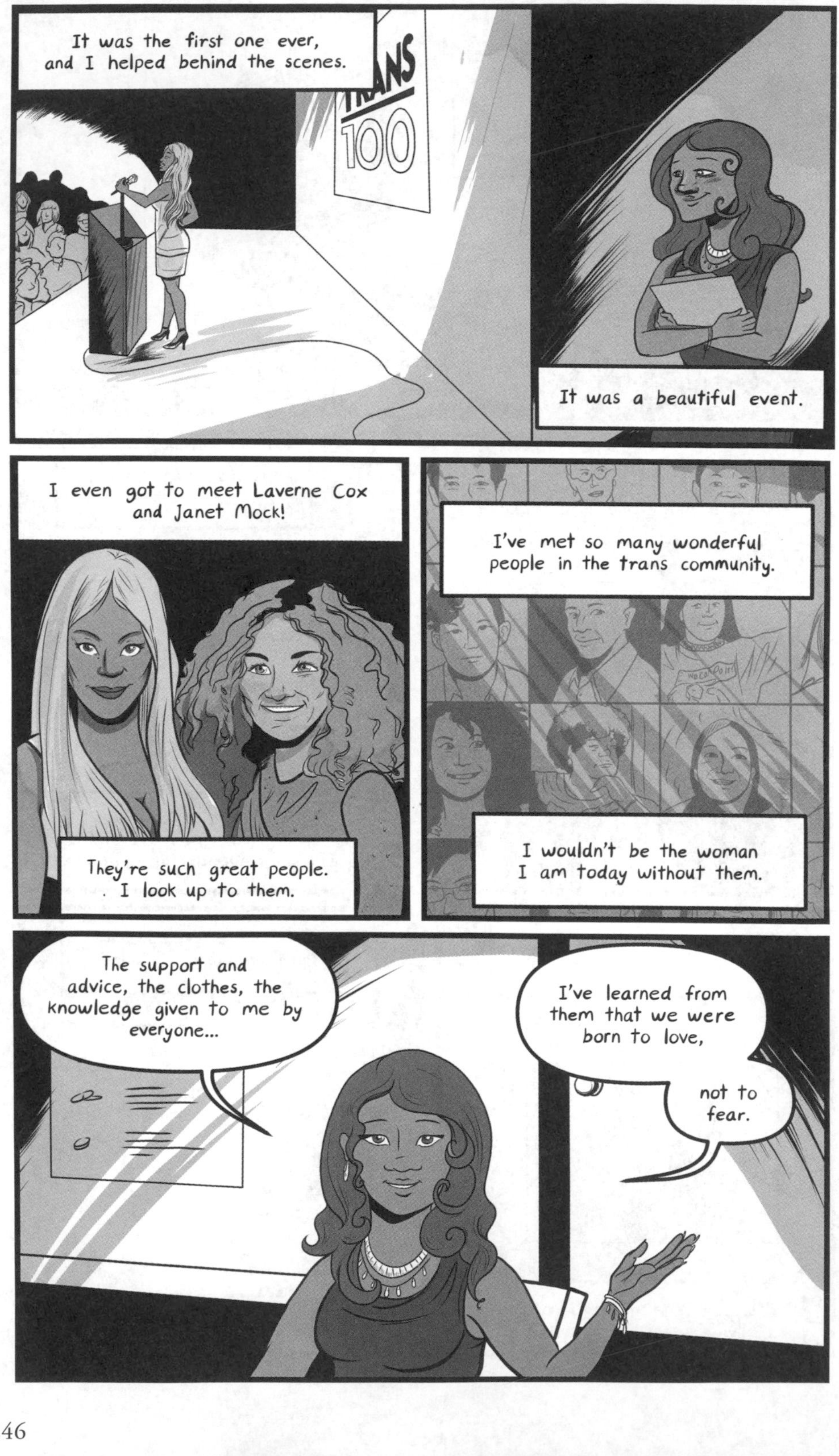

It was the first one ever, and I helped behind the scenes.
TRANS 100
It was a beautiful event.
I even got to meet Laverne Cox and Janet Mock!
They're such great people. I look up to them.
I've met so many wonderful people in the trans community.
I wouldn't be the woman I am today without them.
The support and advice, the clothes, the knowledge given to me by everyone...
I've learned from them that we were born to love,
not to fear.

Dutchess, 2015

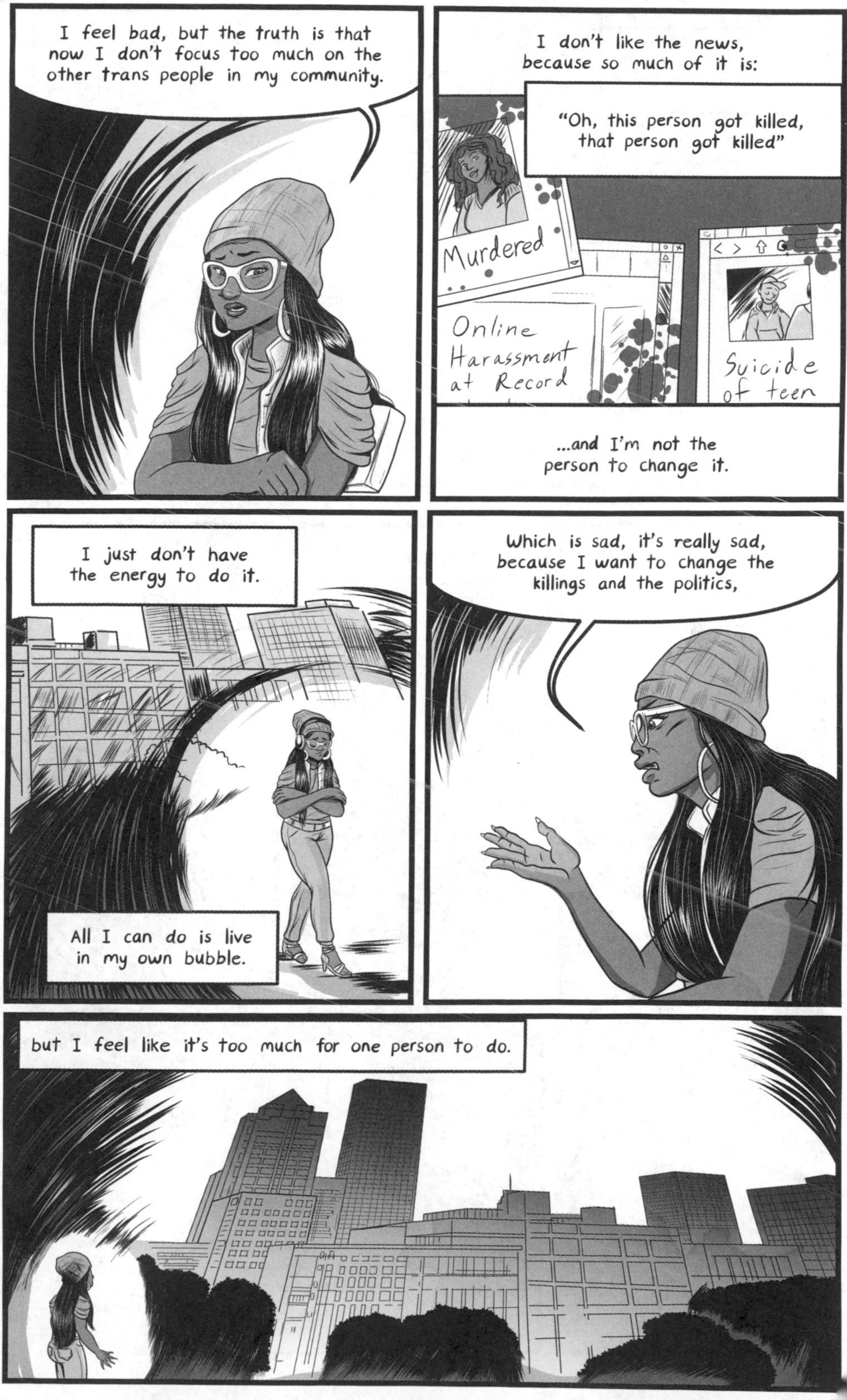

I feel bad, but the truth is that now I don't focus too much on the other trans people in my community.
I don't like the news, because so much of it is:
"Oh, this person got killed, that person got killed"
Murdered
Online Harassment at Record
Suicide of teen
...and I'm not the person to change it.
I just don't have the energy to do it.
All I can do is live in my own bubble.
Which is sad, it's really sad, because I want to change the killings and the politics,
but I feel like it's too much for one person to do.

Superheroine, 2015

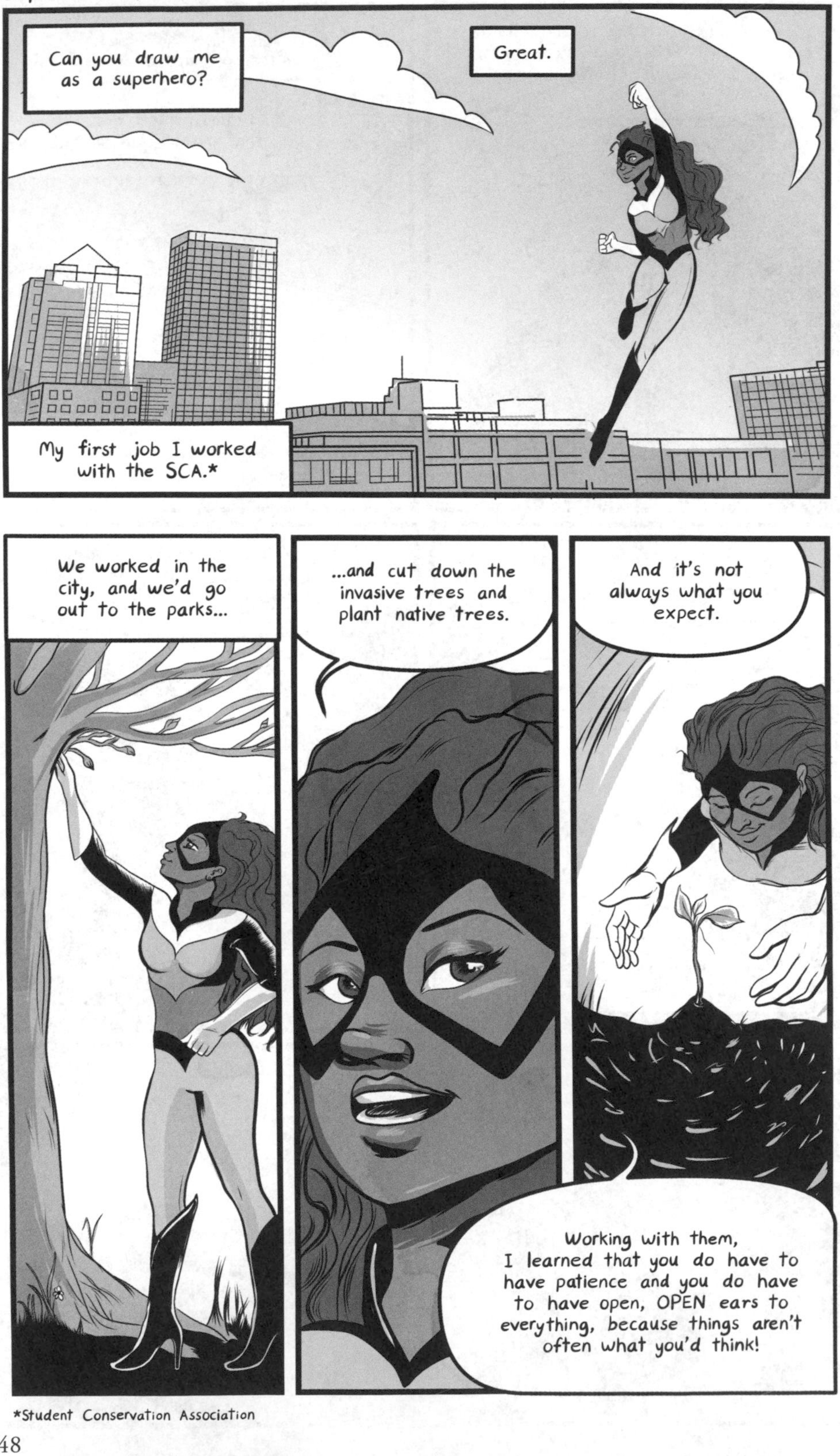
Can you draw me as a superhero?
Great.
My first job I worked with the SCA.*
We worked in the city, and we'd go out to the parks...
...and cut down the invasive trees and plant native trees.
And it's not always what you expect.
Working with them, I learned that you do have to have patience and you do have to have open, OPEN ears to everything, because things aren't often what you'd think!

*Student Conservation Association

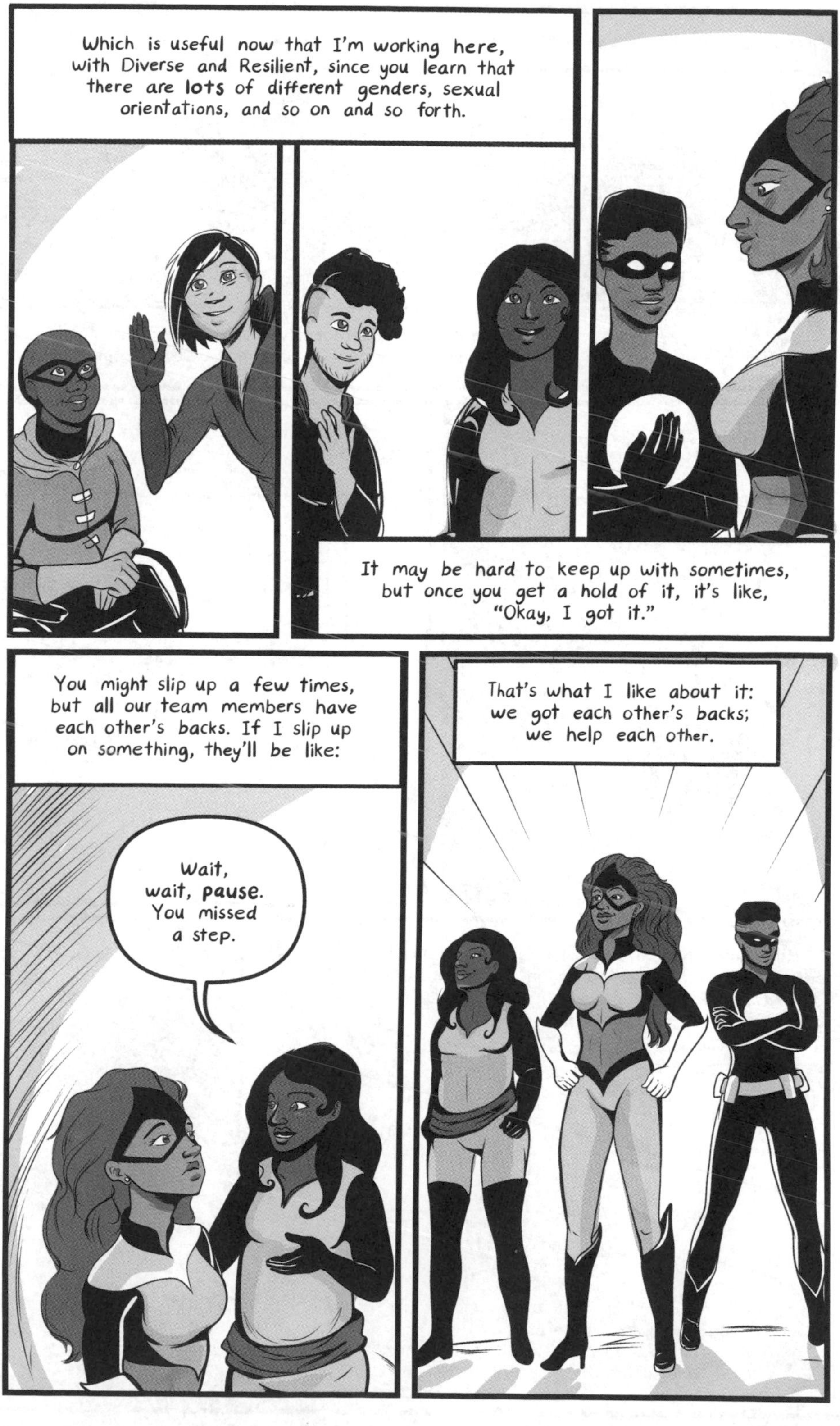
Which is useful now that I'm working here, with Diverse and Resilient, since you learn that there are lots of different genders, sexual orientations, and so on and so forth.
It may be hard to keep up with sometimes, but once you get a hold of it, it's like, "Okay, I got it."
You might slip up a few times, but all our team members have each other's backs. If I slip up on something, they'll be like:
Wait, wait, pause. You missed a step.
That's what I like about it: we got each other's backs; we help each other.

Ronnie, 2015

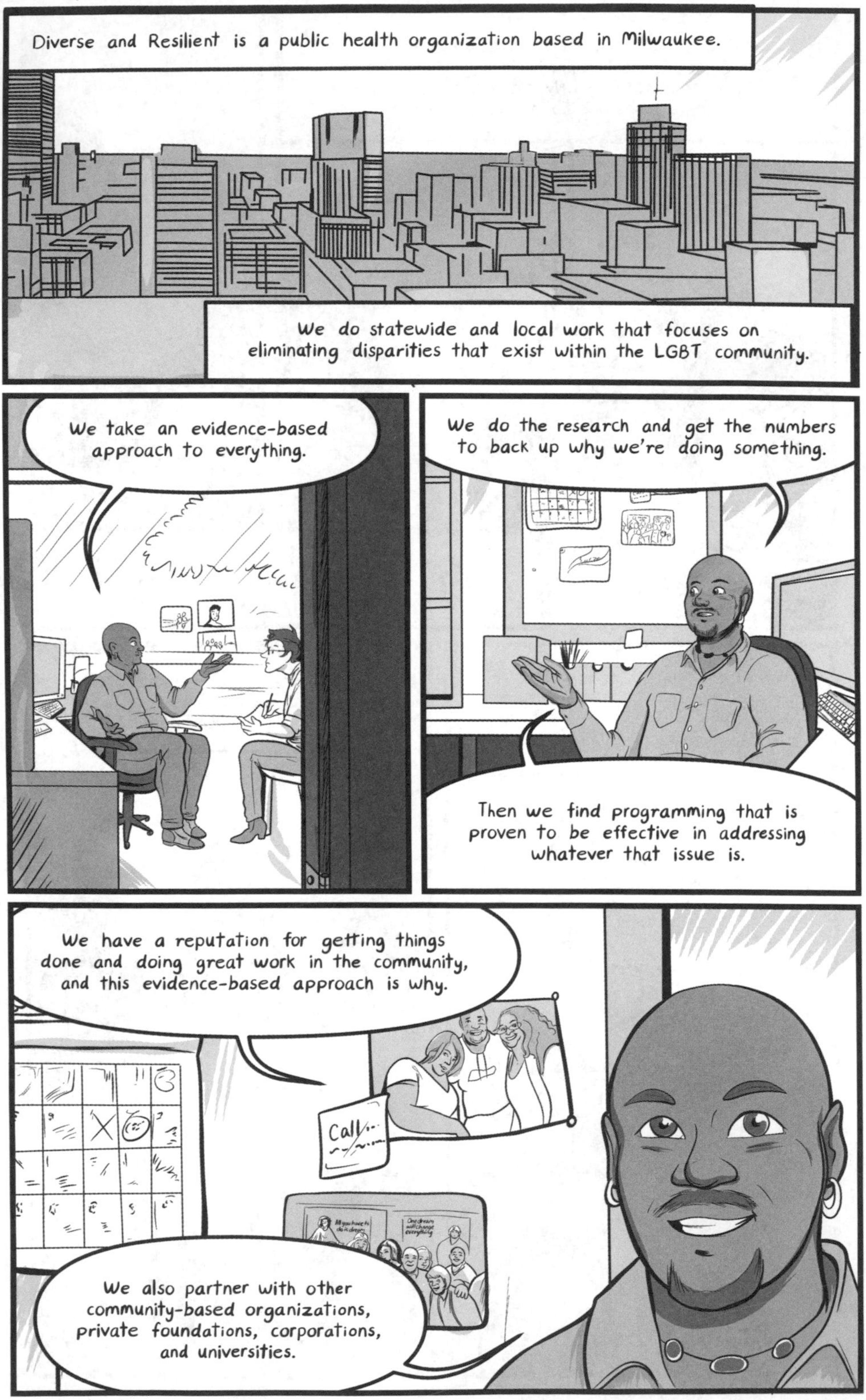
Diverse and Resilient is a public health organization based in Milwaukee.
We do statewide and local work that focuses on eliminating disparities that exist within the LGBT community.
We take an evidence-based approach to everything.
We do the research and get the numbers to back up why we're doing something.
Then we find programming that is proven to be effective in addressing whatever that issue is.
We have a reputation for getting things done and doing great work in the community, and this evidence-based approach is why.
Call
We also partner with other community-based organizations, private foundations, corporations, and universities.

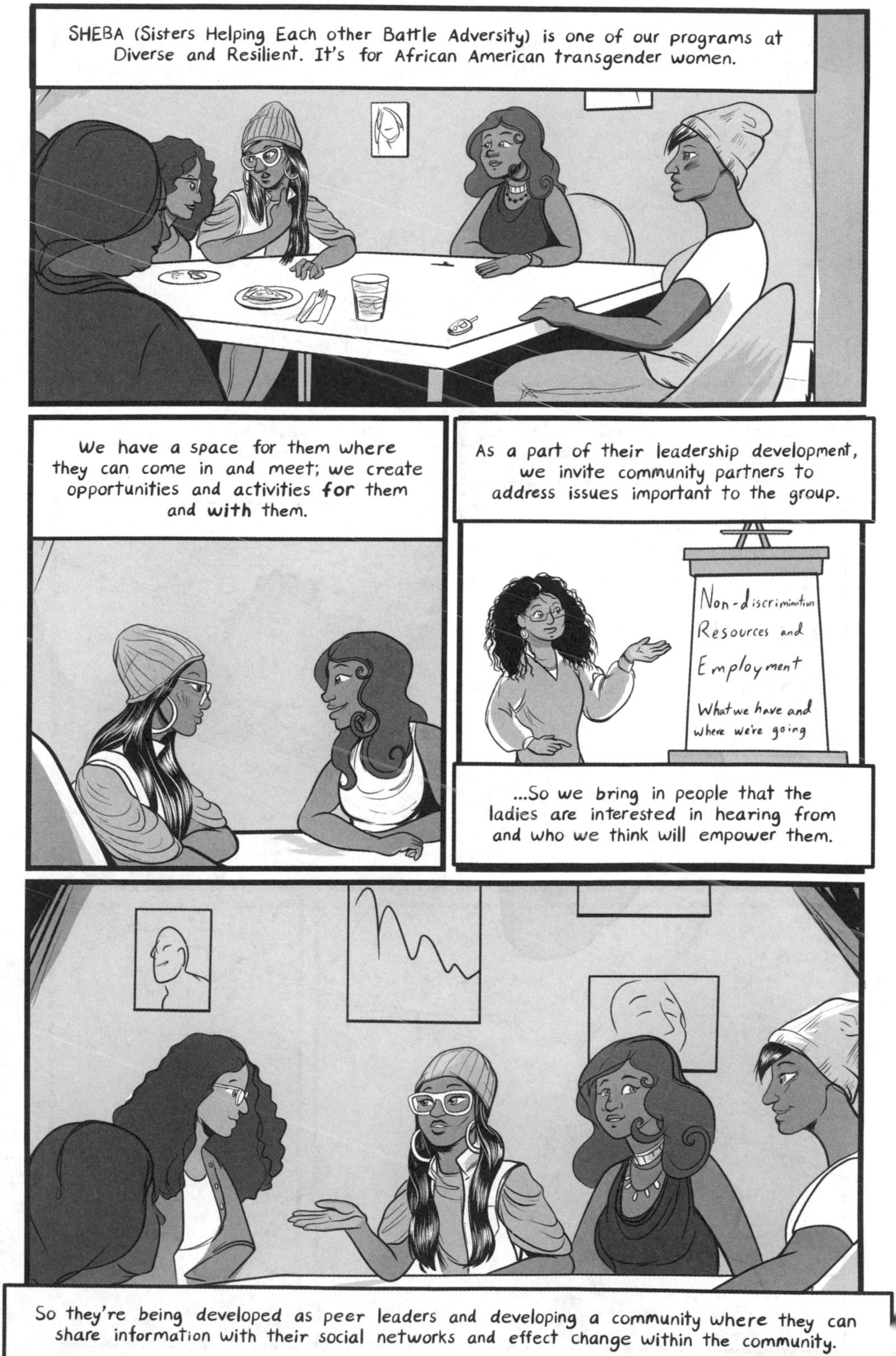
SHEBA (Sisters Helping Each other Battle Adversity) is one of our programs at Diverse and Resilient. It's for African American transgender women.
We have a space for them where they can come in and meet; we create opportunities and activities **for** them and **with** them.
As a part of their leadership development, we invite community partners to address issues important to the group.
Non-discrimination
Resources and
Employment
What we have and where we're going
...So we bring in people that the ladies are interested in hearing from and who we think will empower them.
So they're being developed as peer leaders and developing a community where they can share information with their social networks and effect change within the community.

Jonah, 2013

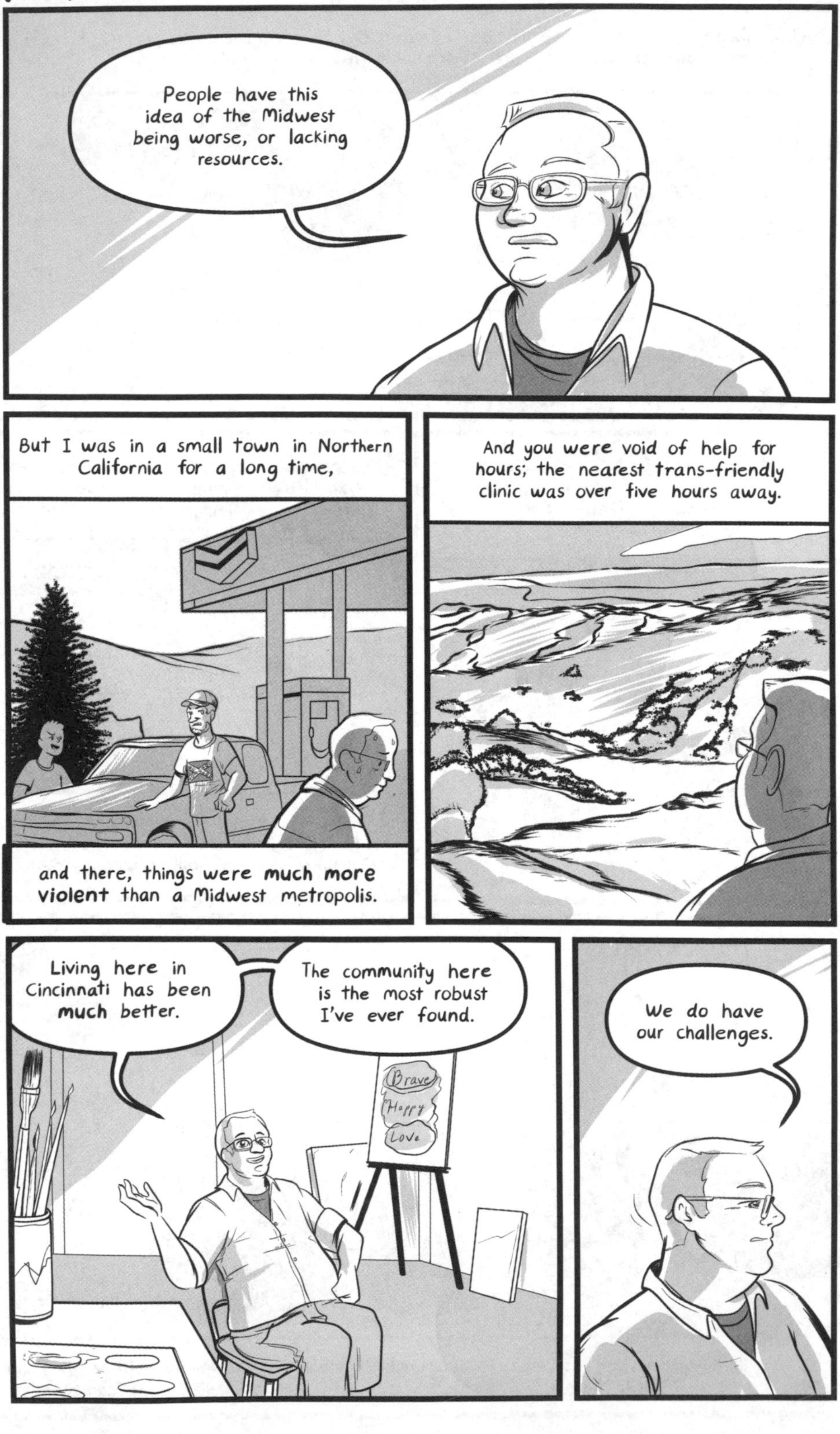

People have this idea of the Midwest being worse, or lacking resources.
But I was in a small town in Northern California for a long time,
and there, things were **much more violent** than a Midwest metropolis.
And you **were** void of help for hours; the nearest trans-friendly clinic was over five hours away.
Living here in Cincinnati has been **much** better.
The community here is the most robust I've ever found.
Brave
Happy
Love
We do have our challenges.

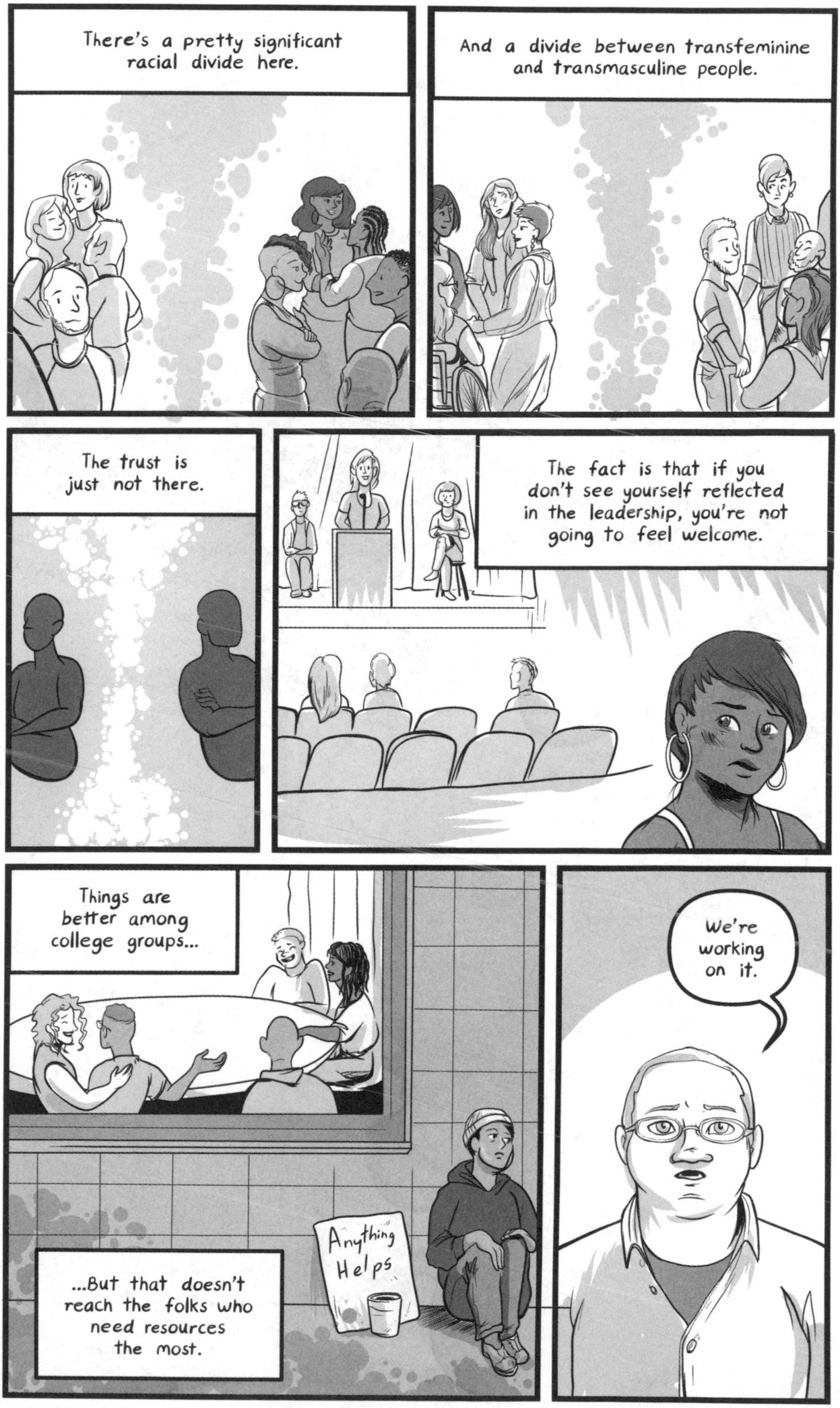
There's a pretty significant racial divide here.
And a divide between transfeminine and transmasculine people.
The trust is just not there.
The fact is that if you don't see yourself reflected in the leadership, you're not going to feel welcome.
Things are better among college groups...
Anything Helps
...But that doesn't reach the folks who need resources the most.
We're working on it.

JAC, 2013

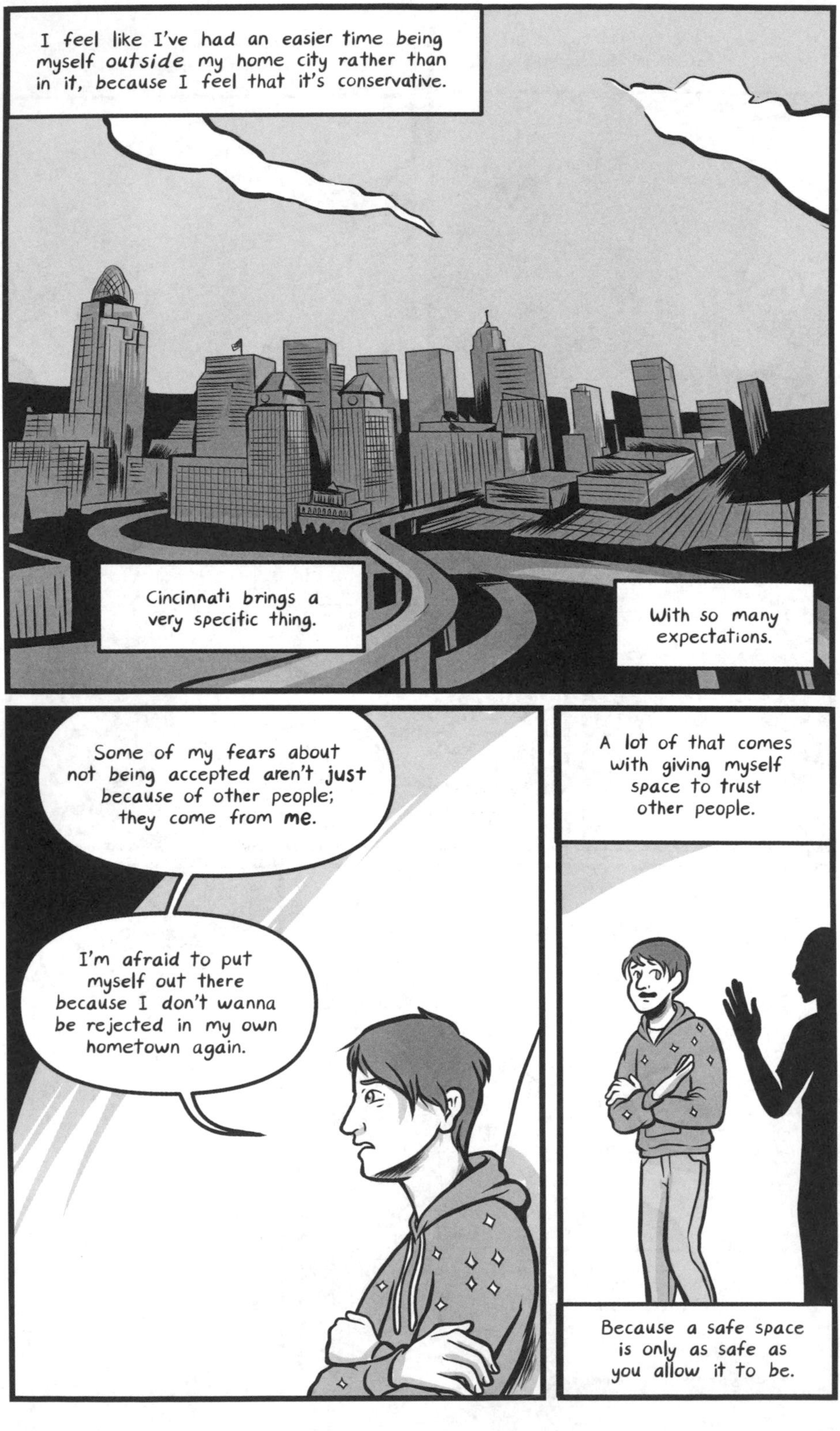
I feel like I've had an easier time being myself *outside* my home city rather than in it, because I feel that it's conservative.
Cincinnati brings a very specific thing.
With so many expectations.
Some of my fears about not being accepted aren't **just** because of other people; they come from **me**.
I'm afraid to put myself out there because I don't wanna be rejected in my own hometown again.
A lot of that comes with giving myself space to trust other people.
Because a safe space is only as safe as you allow it to be.

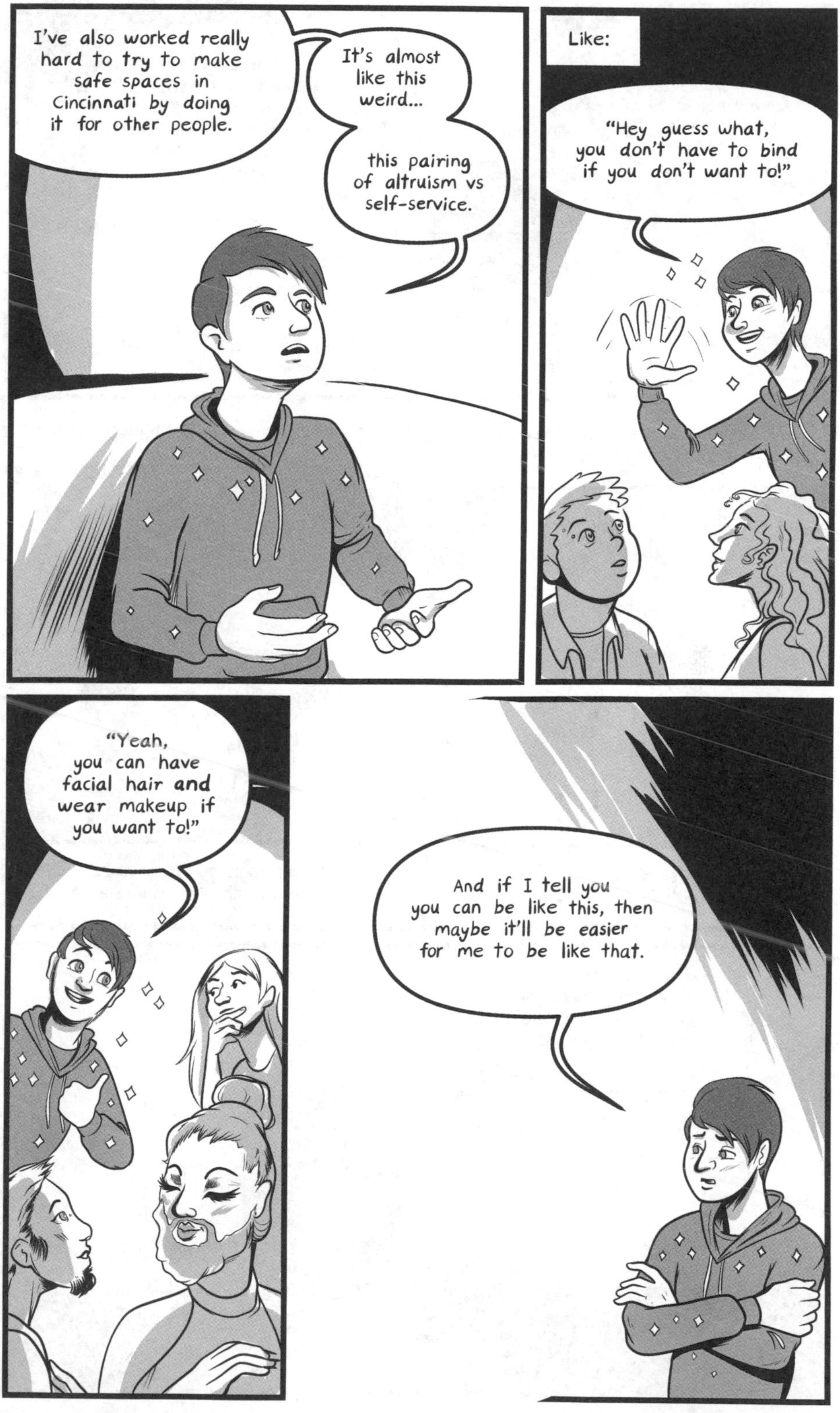
I've also worked really hard to try to make safe spaces in Cincinnati by doing it for other people.
It's almost like this weird...
this pairing of altruism vs self-service.
Like:
"Hey guess what, you don't have to bind if you don't want to!"
"Yeah, you can have facial hair and wear makeup if you want to!"
And if I tell you you can be like this, then maybe it'll be easier for me to be like that.

Rashida, 2013

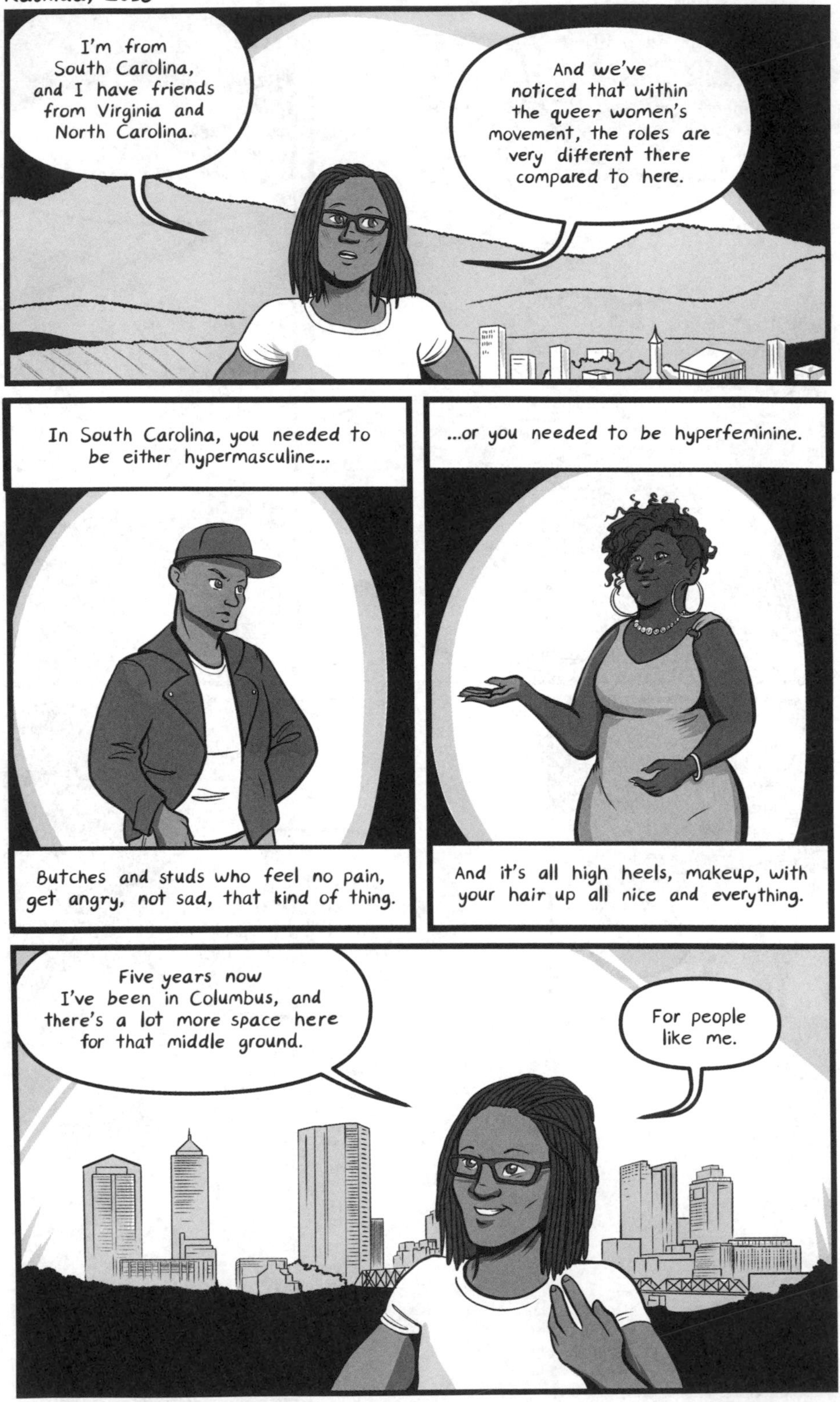
I'm from South Carolina, and I have friends from Virginia and North Carolina.
And we've noticed that within the queer women's movement, the roles are very different there compared to here.
In South Carolina, you needed to be either hypermasculine...
...or you needed to be hyperfeminine.
Butches and studs who feel no pain, get angry, not sad, that kind of thing.
And it's all high heels, makeup, with your hair up all nice and everything.
Five years now I've been in Columbus, and there's a lot more space here for that middle ground.
For people like me.

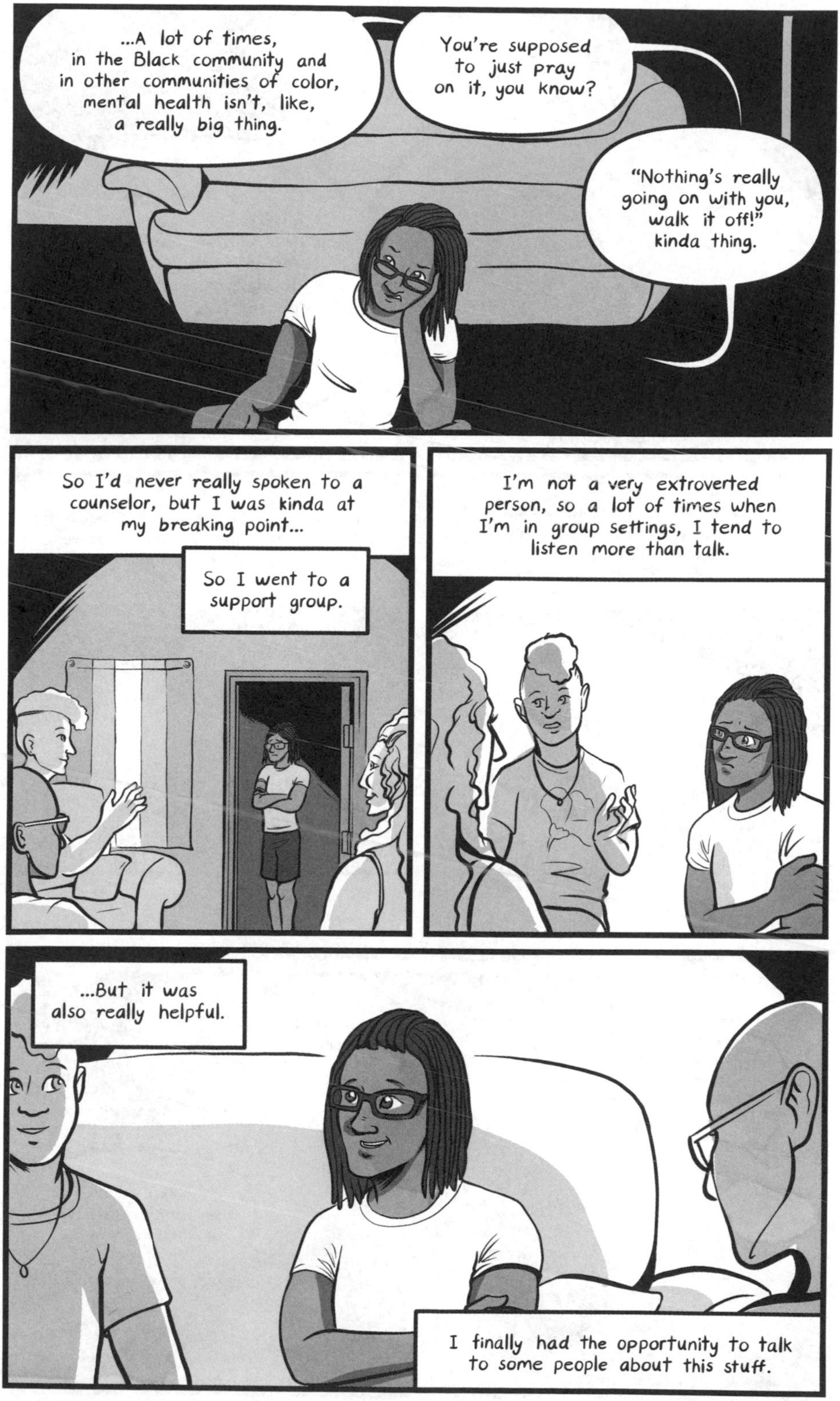
...A lot of times, in the Black community and in other communities of color, mental health isn't, like, a really big thing.
You're supposed to just pray on it, you know?
"Nothing's really going on with you, walk it off!" kinda thing.
So I'd never really spoken to a counselor, but I was kinda at my breaking point...
So I went to a support group.
I'm not a very extroverted person, so a lot of times when I'm in group settings, I tend to listen more than talk.
...But it was also really helpful.
I finally had the opportunity to talk to some people about this stuff.

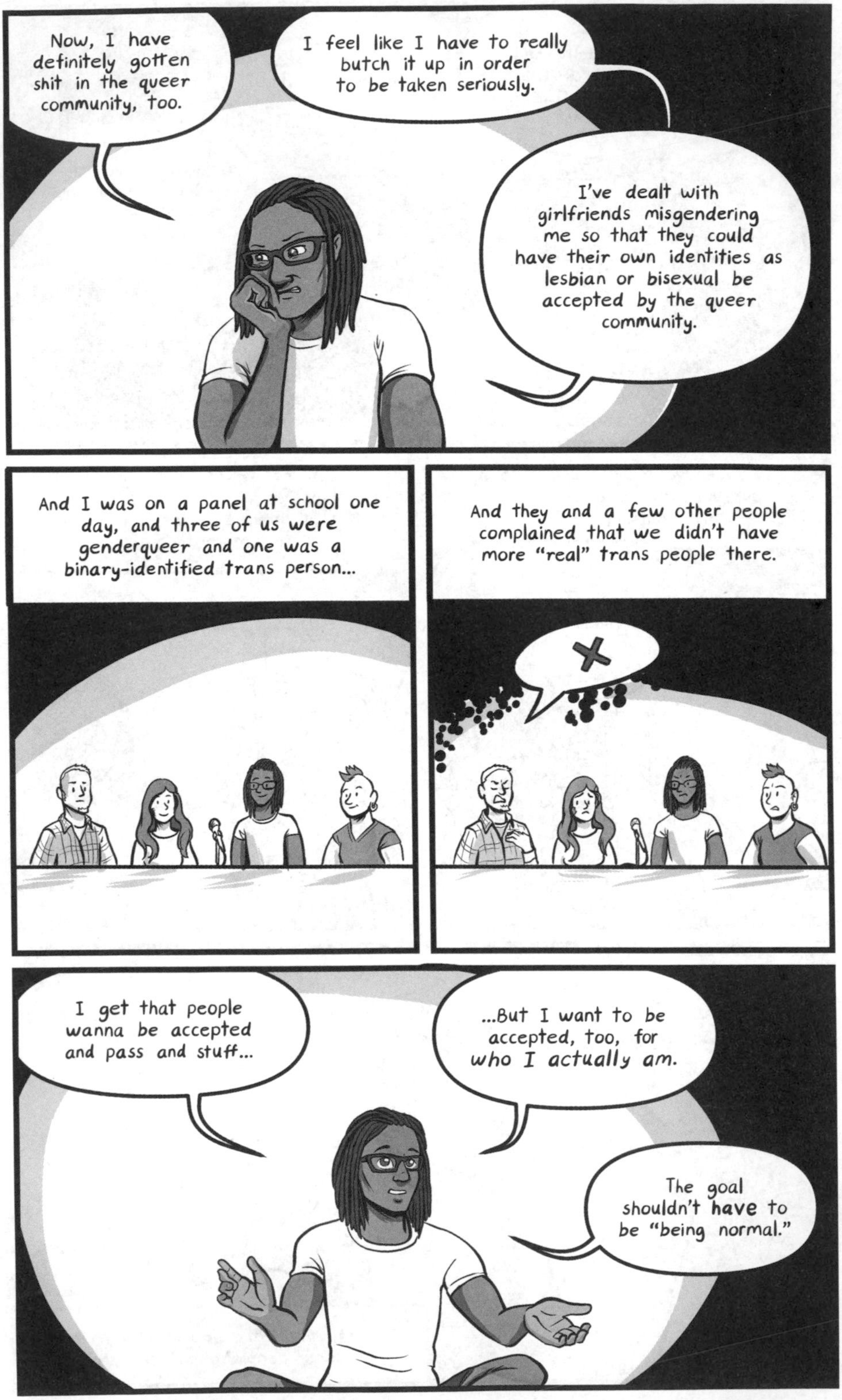
Now, I have definitely gotten shit in the queer community, too.
I feel like I have to really butch it up in order to be taken seriously.
I've dealt with girlfriends misgendering me so that they could have their own identities as lesbian or bisexual be accepted by the queer community.
And I was on a panel at school one day, and three of us were genderqueer and one was a binary-identified trans person...
And they and a few other people complained that we didn't have more "real" trans people there.
I get that people wanna be accepted and pass and stuff...
...But I want to be accepted, too, for *who I actually am.*
The goal shouldn't **have** to be "being normal."

Willow, 2013

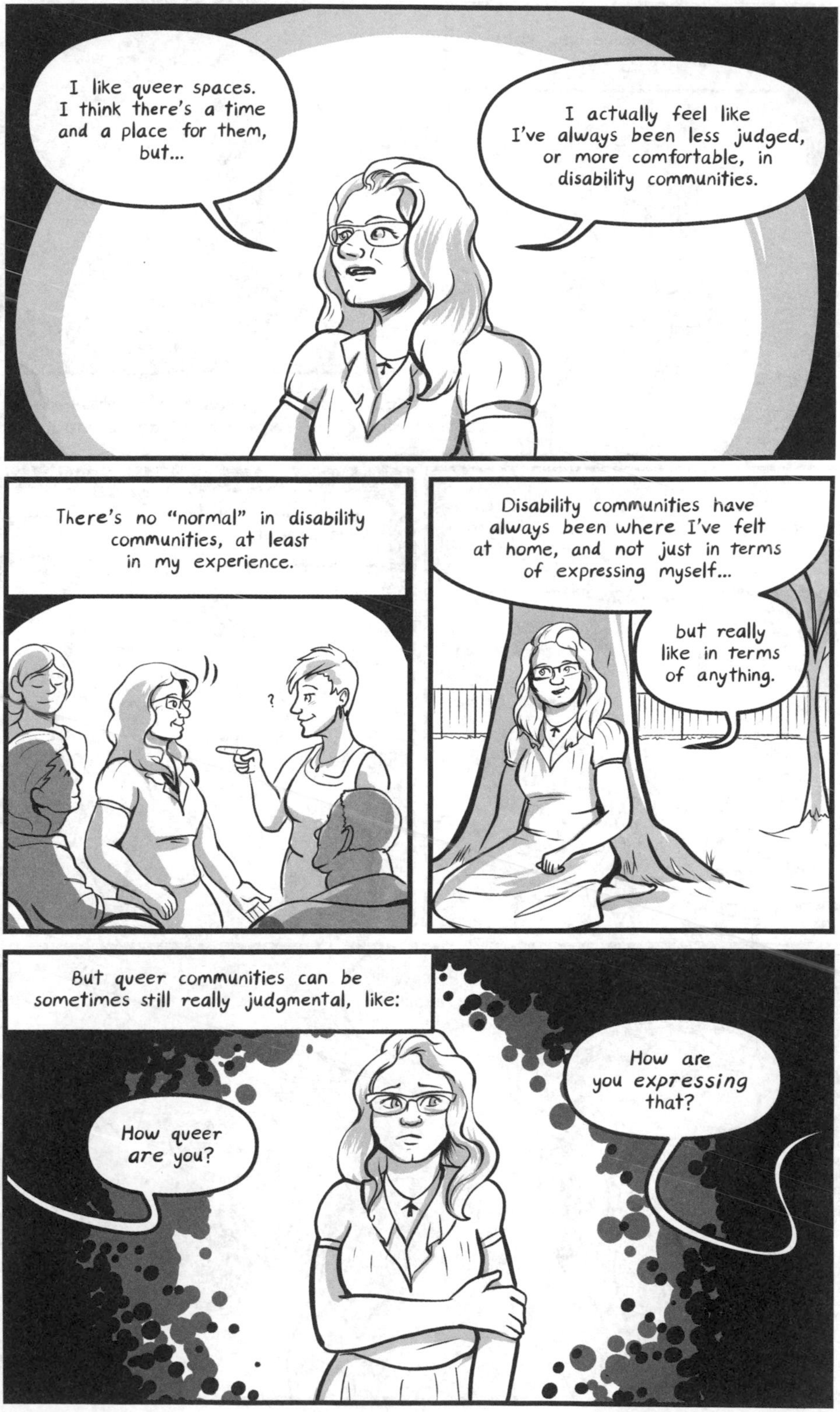
I like queer spaces. I think there's a time and a place for them, but...
I actually feel like I've always been less judged, or more comfortable, in disability communities.
There's no "normal" in disability communities, at least in my experience.
?
Disability communities have always been where I've felt at home, and not just in terms of expressing myself...
but really like in terms of anything.
But queer communities can be sometimes still really judgmental, like:
How queer are you?
How are you *expressing* that?

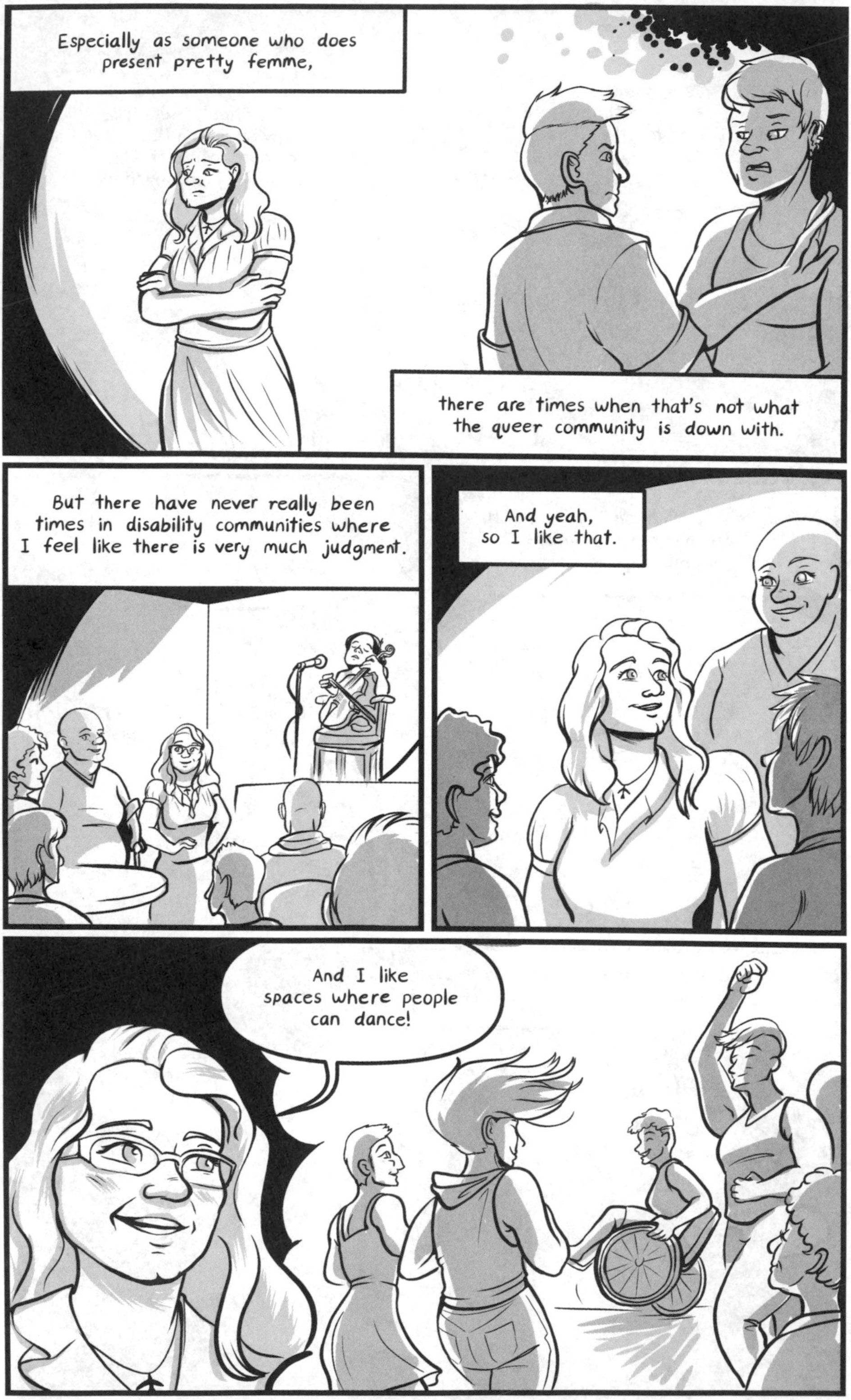
Especially as someone who does present pretty femme,
there are times when that's not what the queer community is down with.
But there have never really been times in disability communities where I feel like there is very much judgment.
And yeah, so I like that.
And I like spaces where people can dance!

Tobias, 2014

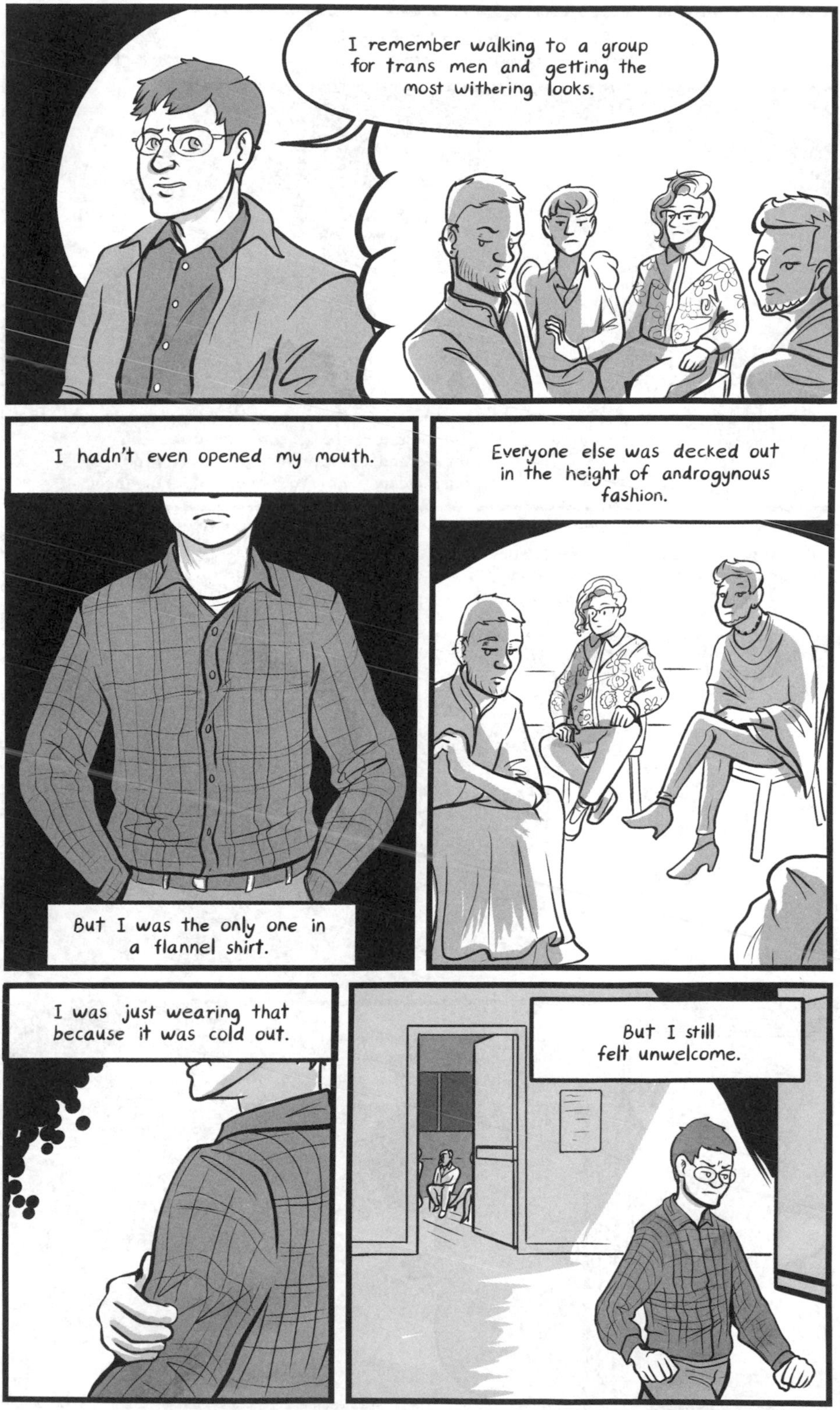
I remember walking to a group for trans men and getting the most withering looks.
I hadn't even opened my mouth.
But I was the only one in a flannel shirt.
Everyone else was decked out in the height of androgynous fashion.
I was just wearing that because it was cold out.
But I still felt unwelcome.

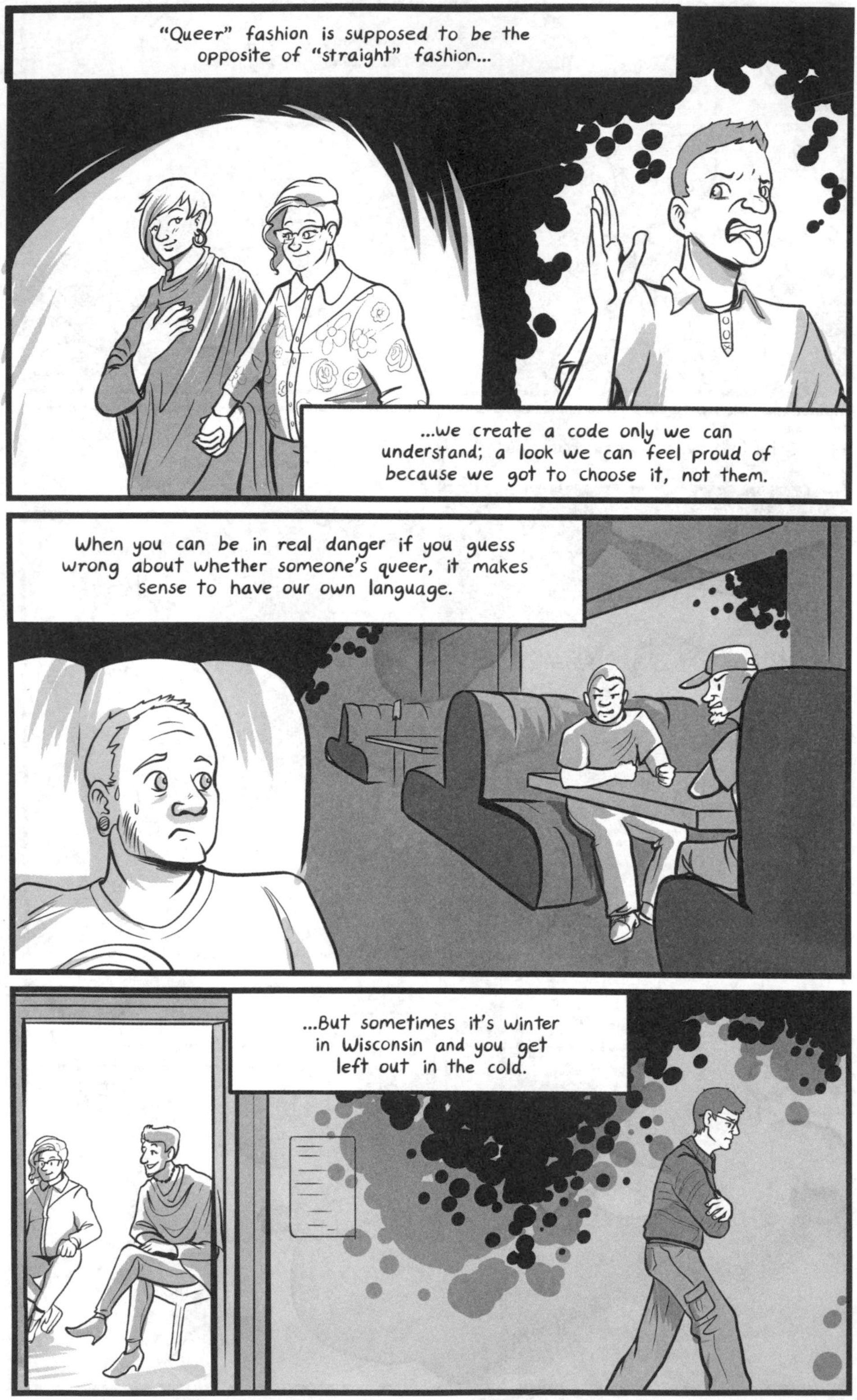
"Queer" fashion is supposed to be the opposite of "straight" fashion...
...we create a code only we can understand; a look we can feel proud of because we got to choose it, not them.
When you can be in real danger if you guess wrong about whether someone's queer, it makes sense to have our own language.
...But sometimes it's winter in Wisconsin and you get left out in the cold.

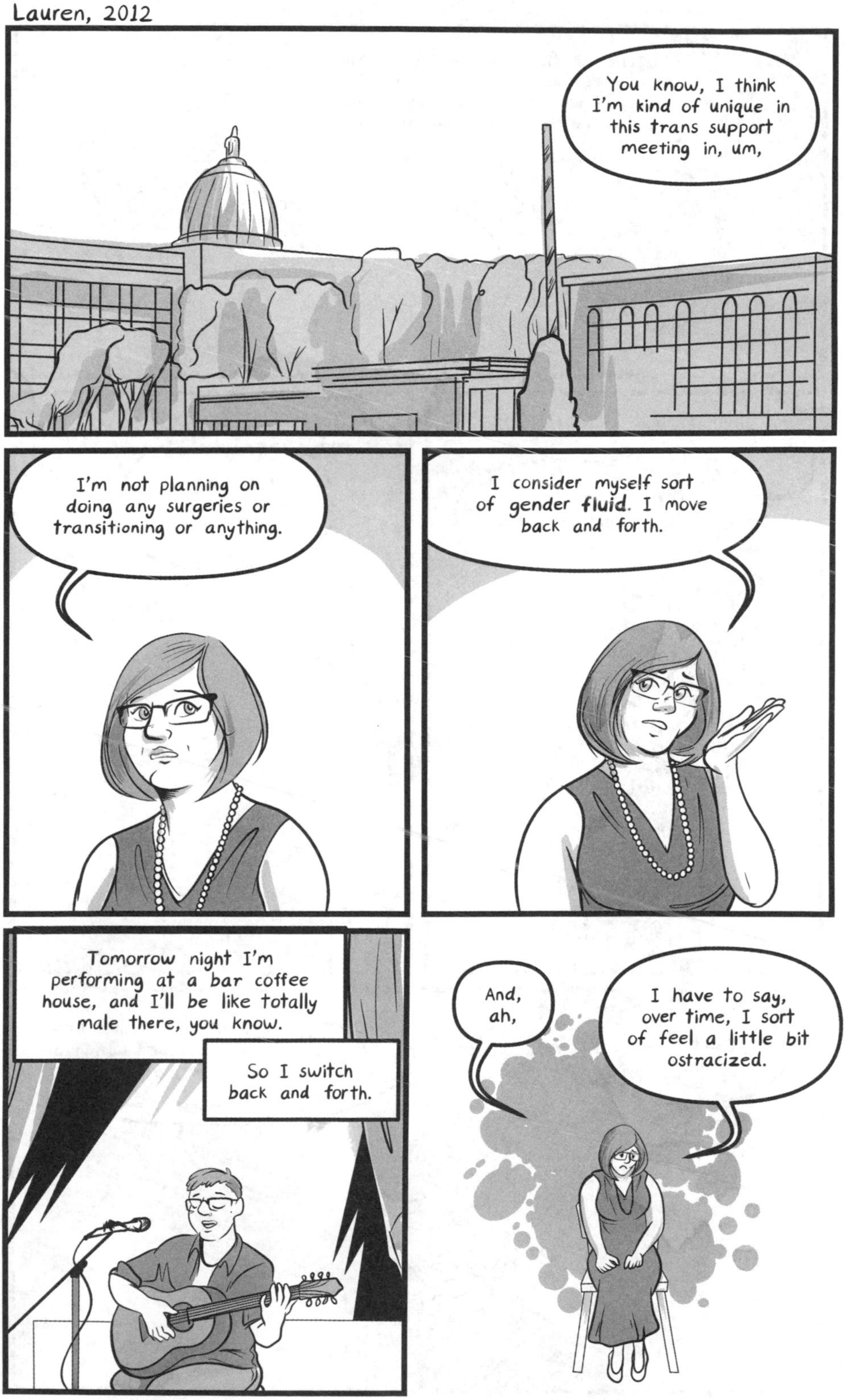
Lauren, 2012
You know, I think I'm kind of unique in this trans support meeting in, um,
I'm not planning on doing any surgeries or transitioning or anything.
I consider myself sort of gender **fluid**. I move back and forth.
Tomorrow night I'm performing at a bar coffee house, and I'll be like totally male there, you know.
So I switch back and forth.
And, ah,
I have to say, over time, I sort of feel a little bit ostracized.

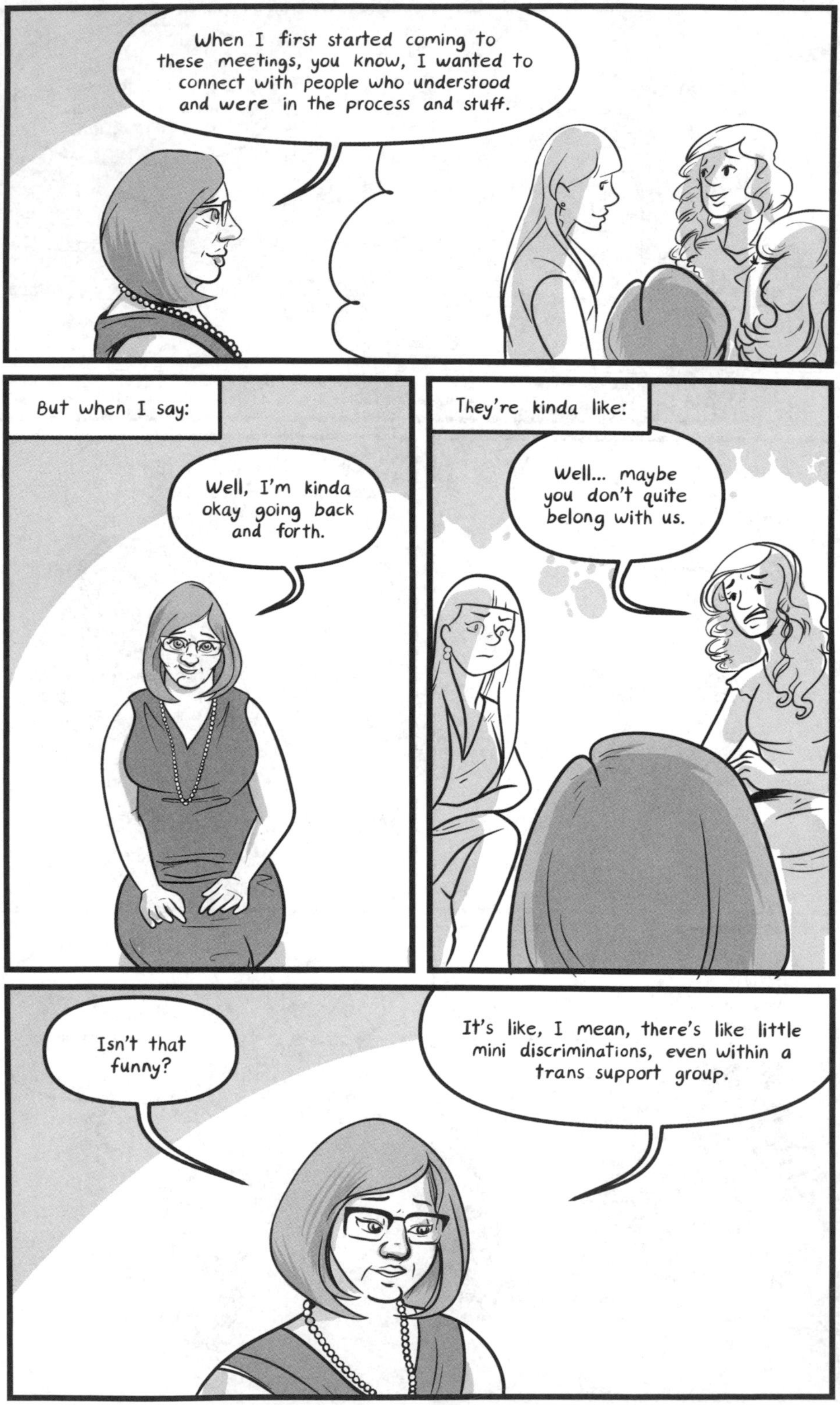
When I first started coming to these meetings, you know, I wanted to connect with people who understood and were in the process and stuff.
But when I say:
Well, I'm kinda okay going back and forth.
They're kinda like:
Well... maybe you don't quite belong with us.
Isn't that funny?
It's like, I mean, there's like little mini discriminations, even within a trans support group.

Lauren, 2017

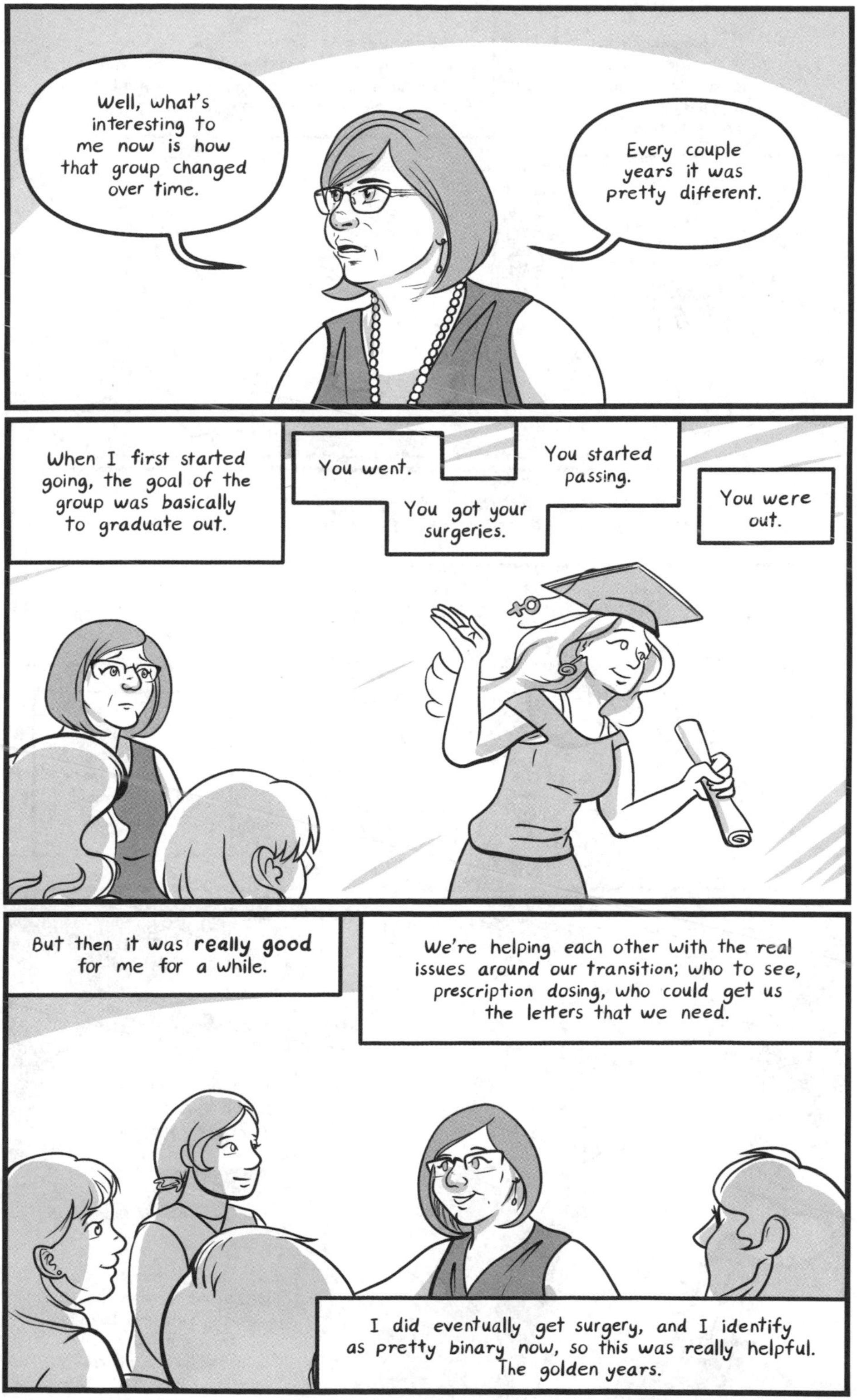

Well, what's interesting to me now is how that group changed over time.
Every couple years it was pretty different.
When I first started going, the goal of the group was basically to graduate out.
You went.
You got your surgeries.
You started passing.
You were out.
But then it was **really good** for me for a while.
We're helping each other with the real issues around our transition; who to see, prescription dosing, who could get us the letters that we need.
I did eventually get surgery, and I identify as pretty binary now, so this was really helpful. The golden years.

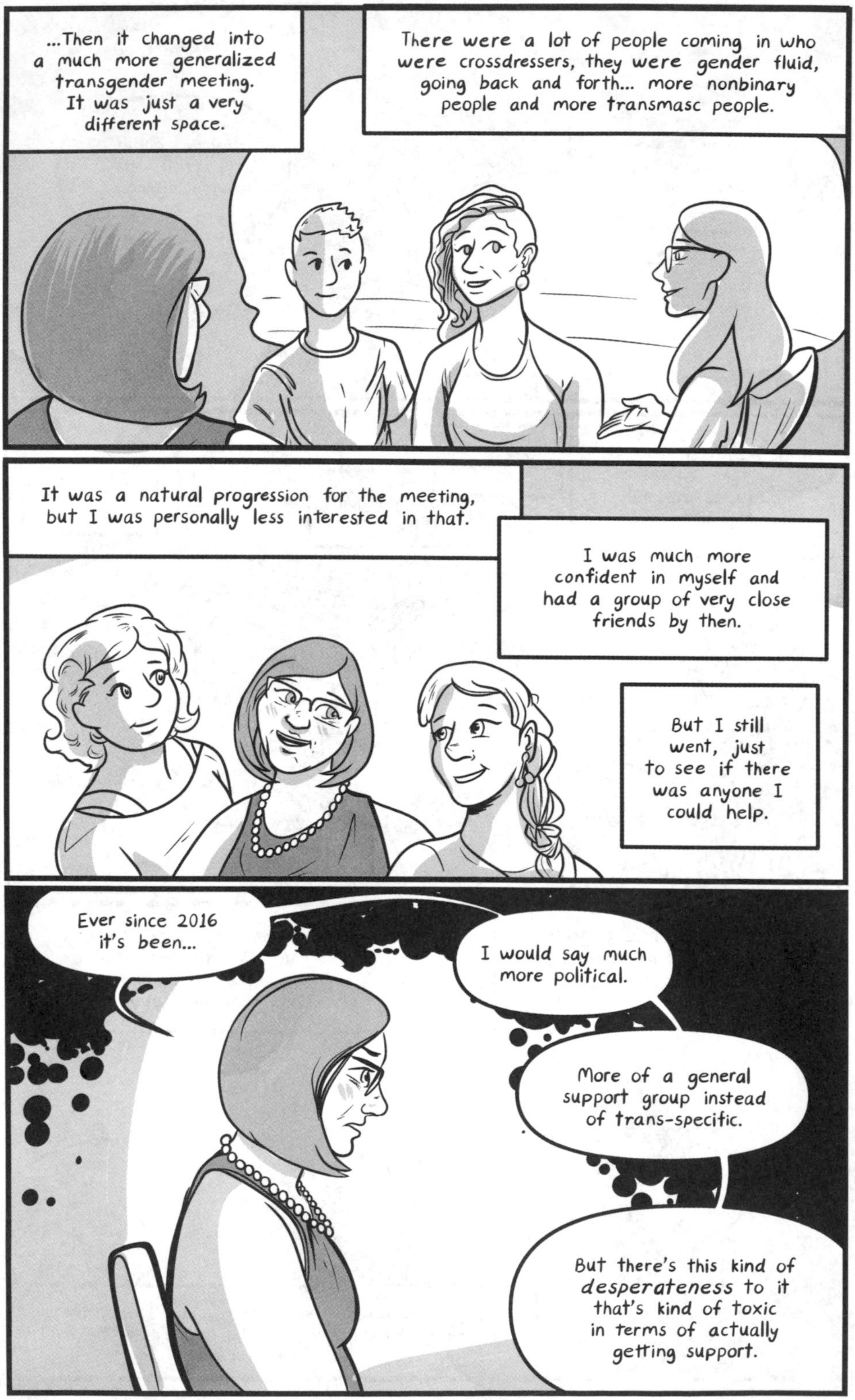
...Then it changed into a much more generalized transgender meeting. It was just a very different space.
There were a lot of people coming in who were crossdressers, they were gender fluid, going back and forth... more nonbinary people and more transmasc people.
It was a natural progression for the meeting, but I was personally less interested in that.
I was much more confident in myself and had a group of very close friends by then.
But I still went, just to see if there was anyone I could help.
Ever since 2016 it's been...
I would say much more political.
More of a general support group instead of trans-specific.
But there's this kind of *desperateness* to it that's kind of toxic in terms of actually getting support.

Bran, 2013

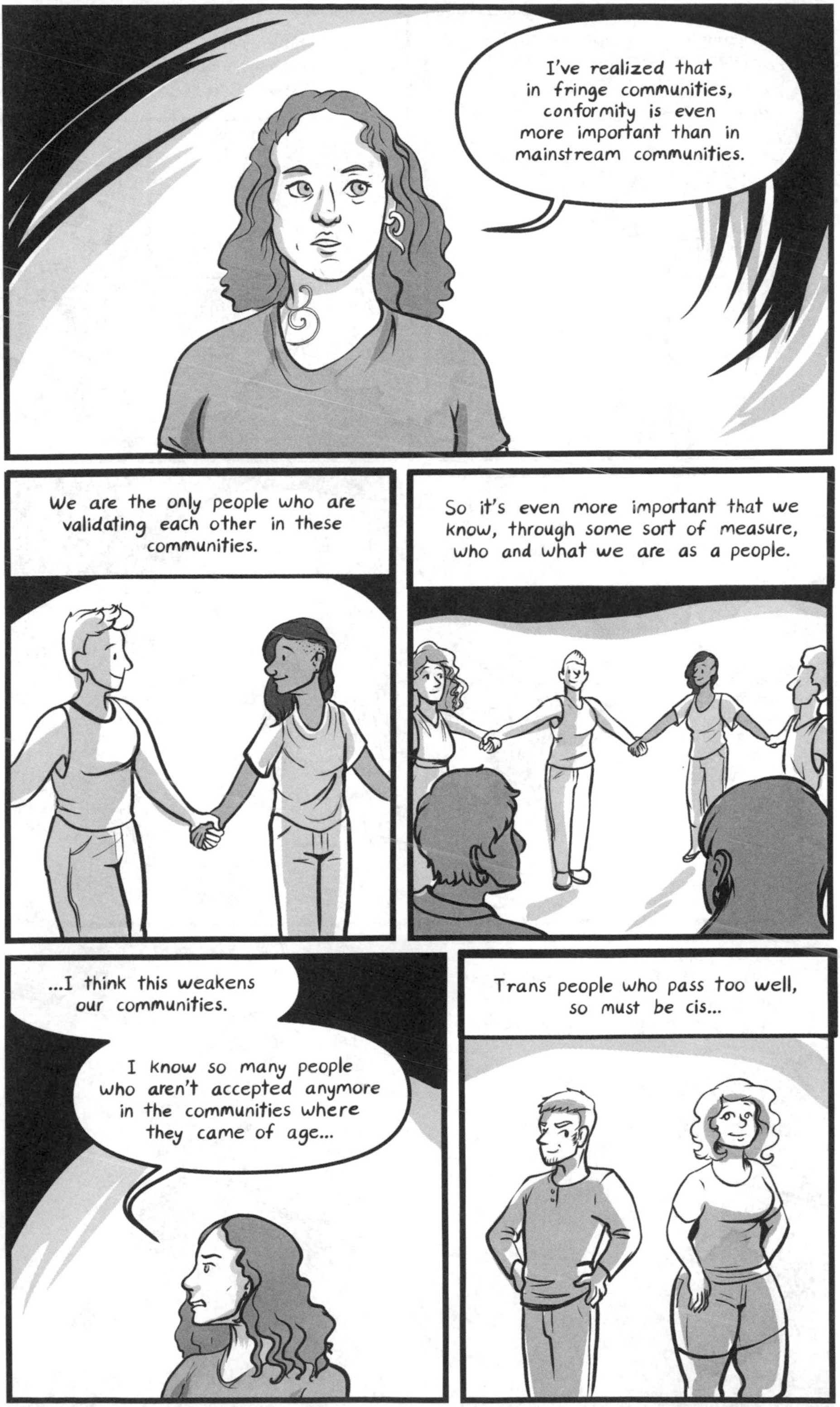
I've realized that in fringe communities, conformity is even more important than in mainstream communities.
We are the only people who are validating each other in these communities.
So it's even more important that we know, through some sort of measure, who and what we are as a people.
...I think this weakens our communities.
I know so many people who aren't accepted anymore in the communities where they came of age...
Trans people who pass too well, so must be cis...

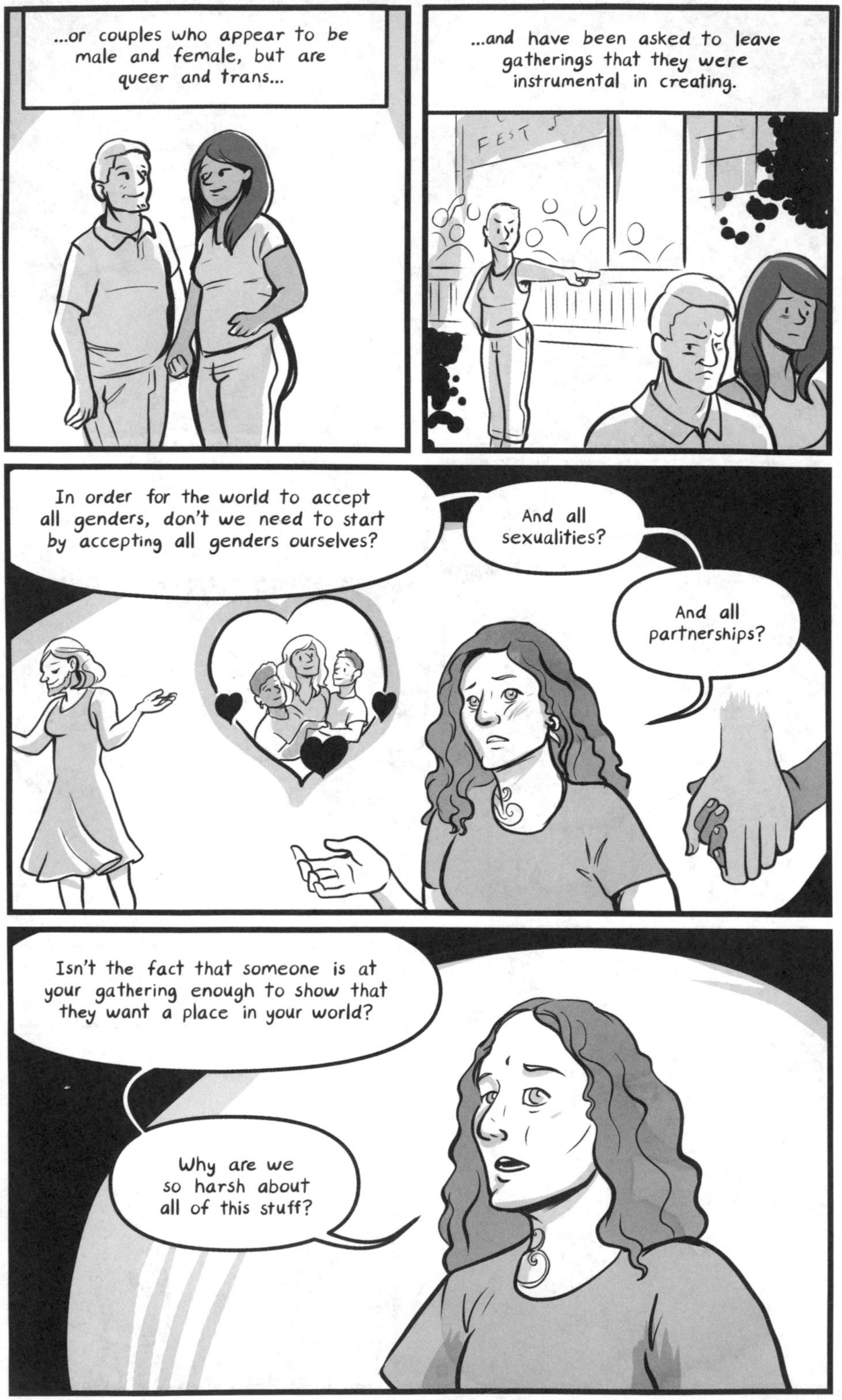
...or couples who appear to be male and female, but are queer and trans...
...and have been asked to leave gatherings that they were instrumental in creating.
FEST
In order for the world to accept all genders, don't we need to start by accepting all genders ourselves?
And all sexualities?
And all partnerships?
Isn't the fact that someone is at your gathering enough to show that they want a place in your world?
Why are we so harsh about all of this stuff?

Lex, 2013

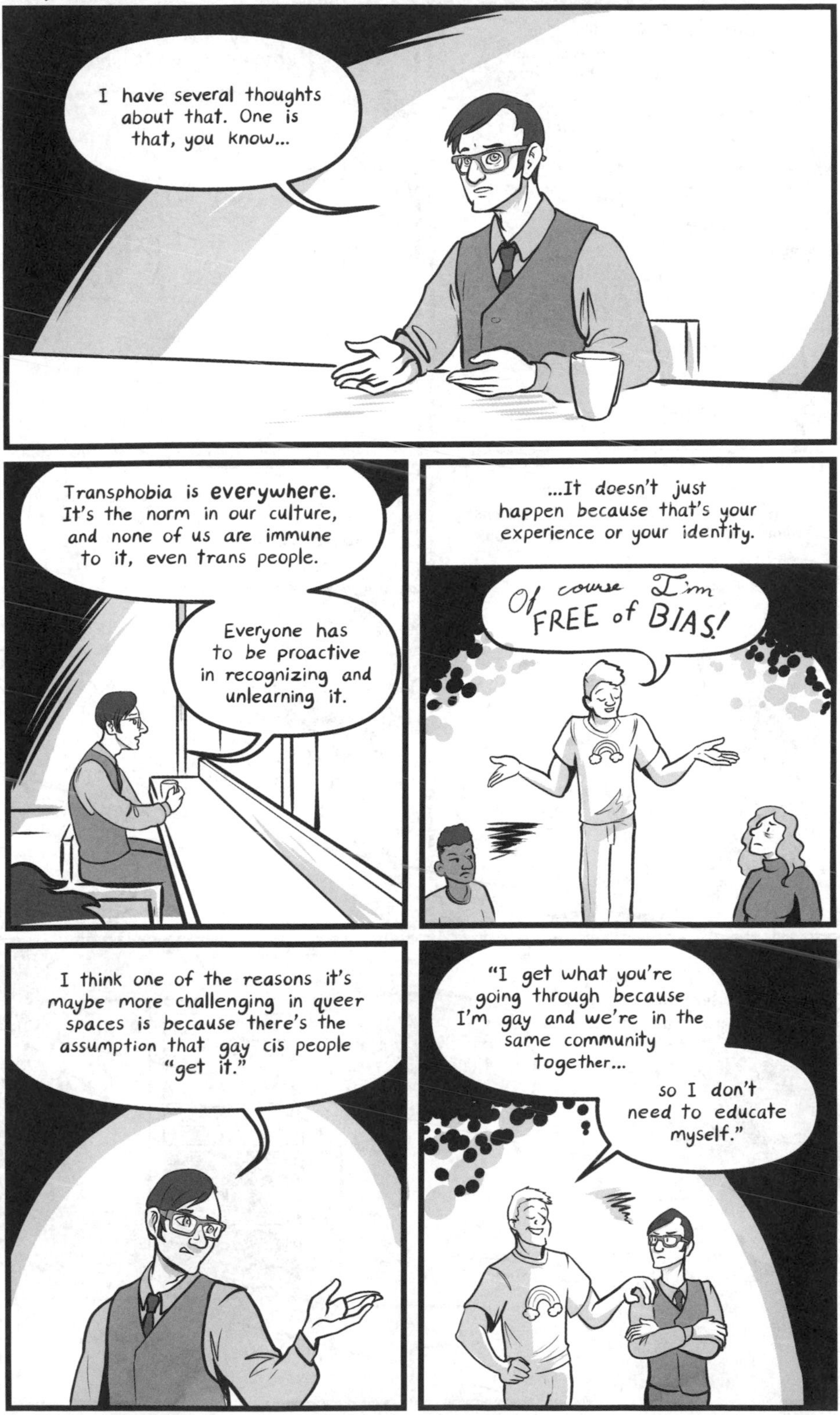
I have several thoughts about that. One is that, you know...
Transphobia is everywhere. It's the norm in our culture, and none of us are immune to it, even trans people.
Everyone has to be proactive in recognizing and unlearning it.
...It doesn't just happen because that's your experience or your identity.
Of course I'm FREE of BIAS!
I think one of the reasons it's maybe more challenging in queer spaces is because there's the assumption that gay cis people "get it."
"I get what you're going through because I'm gay and we're in the same community together...
so I don't need to educate myself."

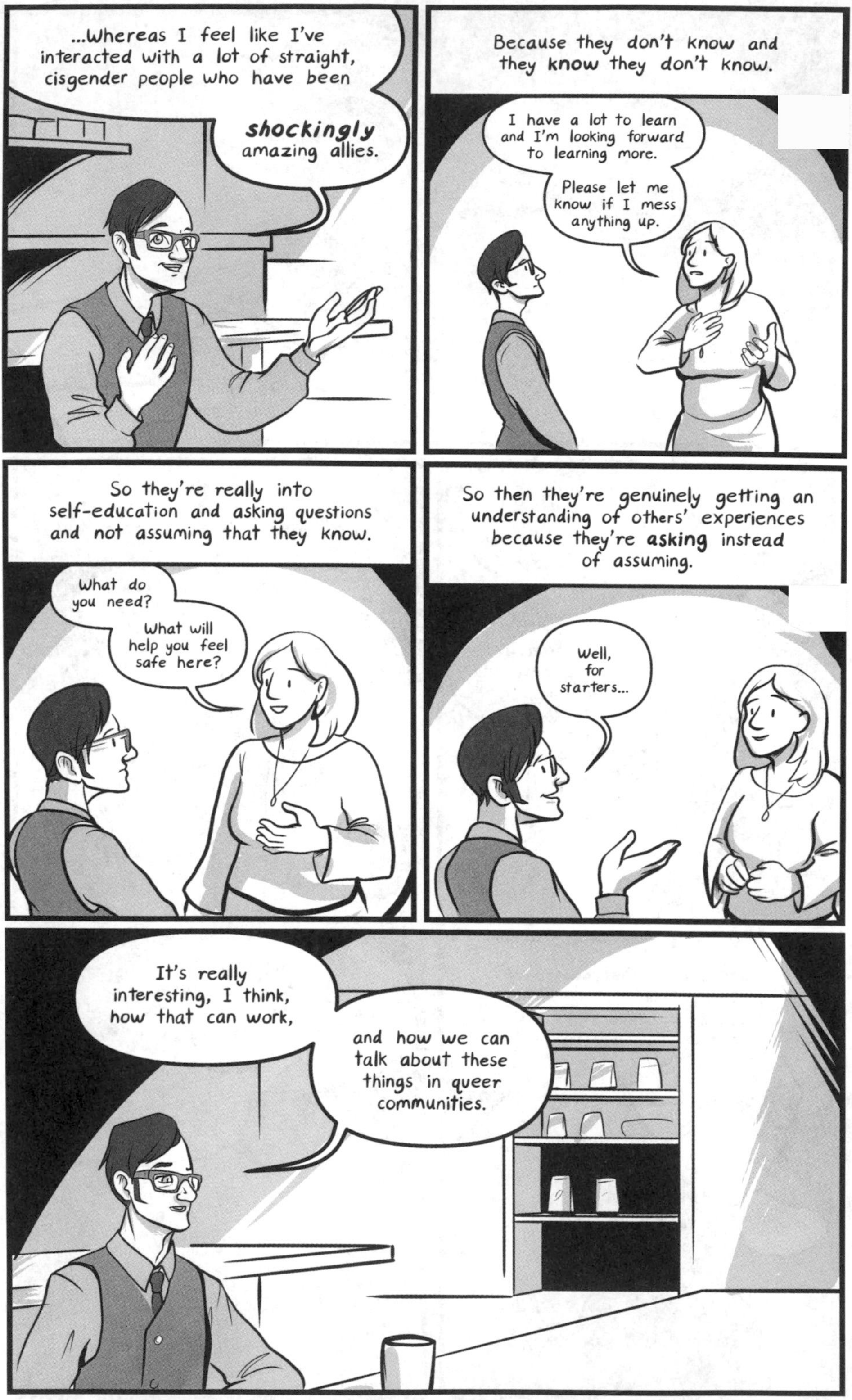
...Whereas I feel like I've interacted with a lot of straight, cisgender people who have been
shockingly amazing allies.
Because they don't know and they **know** they don't know.
I have a lot to learn and I'm looking forward to learning more.
Please let me know if I mess anything up.
So they're really into self-education and asking questions and not assuming that they know.
What do you need?
What will help you feel safe here?
So then they're genuinely getting an understanding of others' experiences because they're **asking** instead of assuming.
Well, for starters...
It's really interesting, I think, how that can work,
and how we can talk about these things in queer communities.

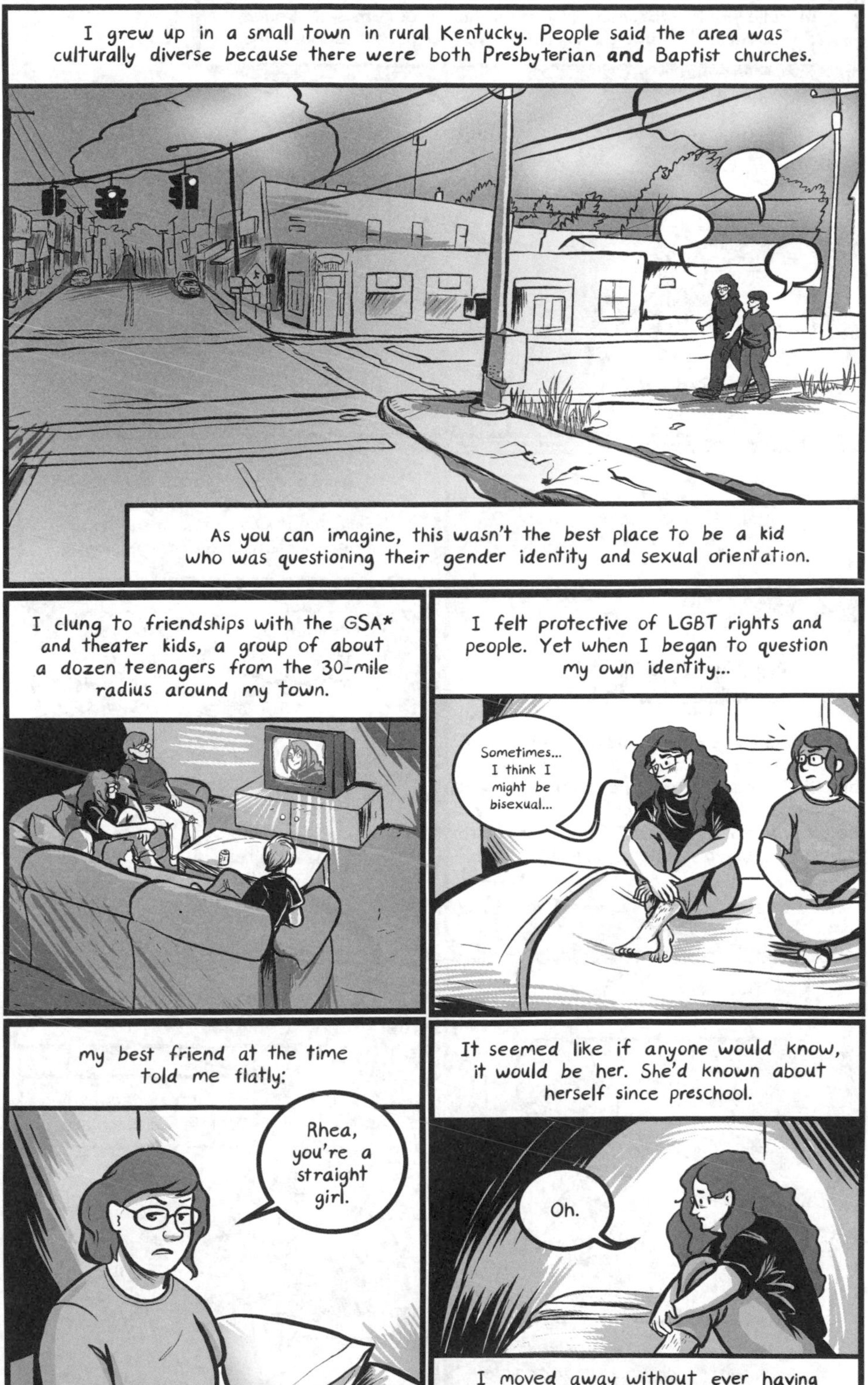
I grew up in a small town in rural Kentucky. People said the area was culturally diverse because there were both Presbyterian **and** Baptist churches.
As you can imagine, this wasn't the best place to be a kid who was questioning their gender identity and sexual orientation.
I clung to friendships with the GSA* and theater kids, a group of about a dozen teenagers from the 30-mile radius around my town.
I felt protective of LGBT rights and people. Yet when I began to question my own identity...
Sometimes... I think I might be bisexual...
my best friend at the time told me flatly:
Rhea, you're a straight girl.
It seemed like if anyone would know, it would be her. She'd known about herself since preschool.
Oh.
I moved away without ever having another conversation about my identity.

*Gay-Straight Alliance

2008

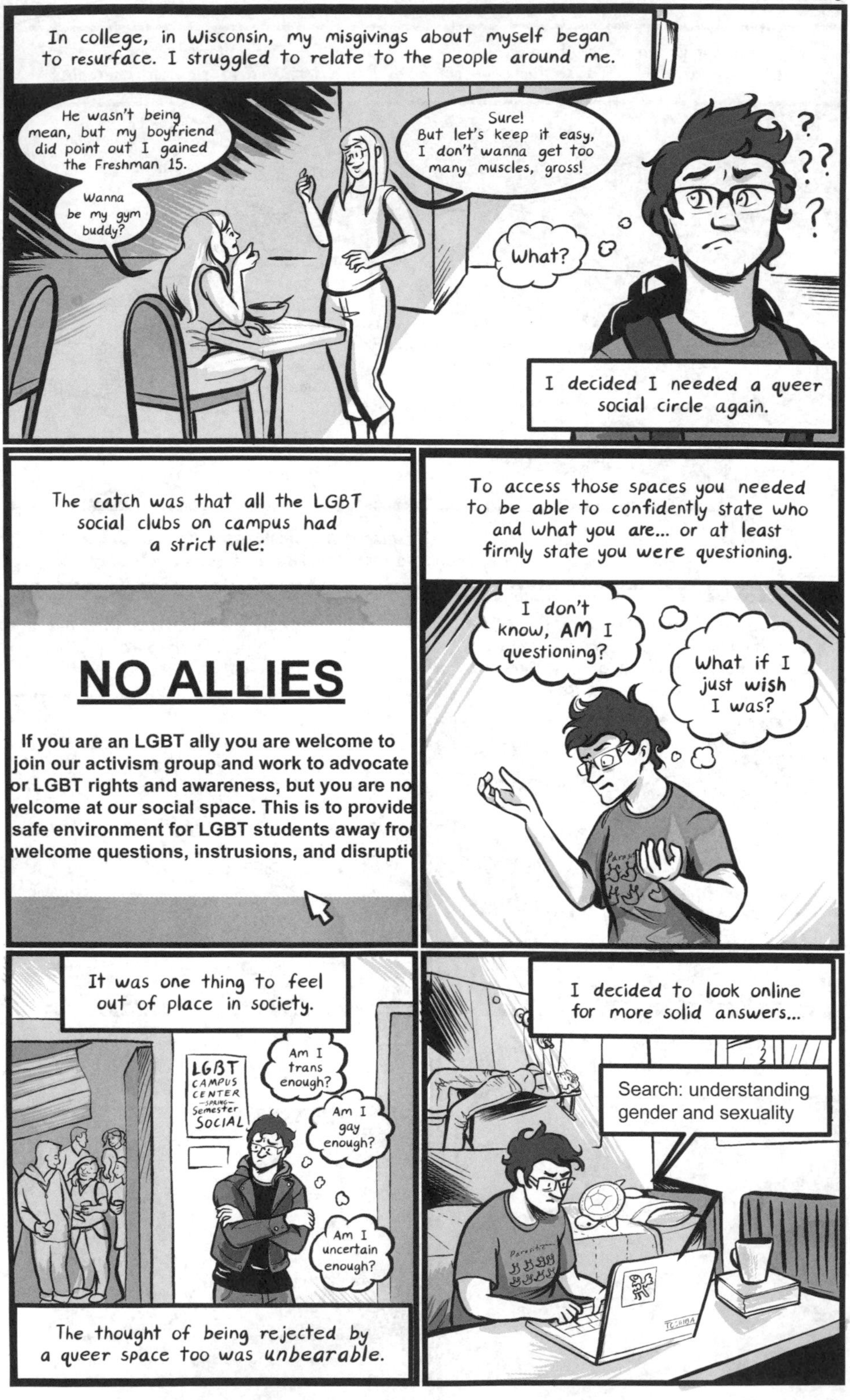

In college, in Wisconsin, my misgivings about myself began to resurface. I struggled to relate to the people around me.
He wasn't being mean, but my boyfriend did point out I gained the Freshman 15.
Wanna be my gym buddy?
Sure! But let's keep it easy, I don't wanna get too many muscles, gross!
What?
? ?? ?
I decided I needed a queer social circle again.
The catch was that all the LGBT social clubs on campus had a strict rule:
NO ALLIES
If you are an LGBT ally you are welcome to
join our activism group and work to advocate
or LGBT rights and awareness, but you are no
velcome at our social space. This is to provide
safe environment for LGBT students away fro
welcome questions, instrusions, and disrupti
To access those spaces you needed to be able to confidently state who and what you are... or at least firmly state you were questioning.
I don't know, AM I questioning?
What if I just wish I was?
It was one thing to feel out of place in society.
LGBT
CAMPUS
CENTER
—SPRING—
Semester
SOCIAL
Am I trans enough?
Am I gay enough?
Am I uncertain enough?
The thought of being rejected by a queer space too was unbearable.
I decided to look online for more solid answers...
Search: understanding gender and sexuality

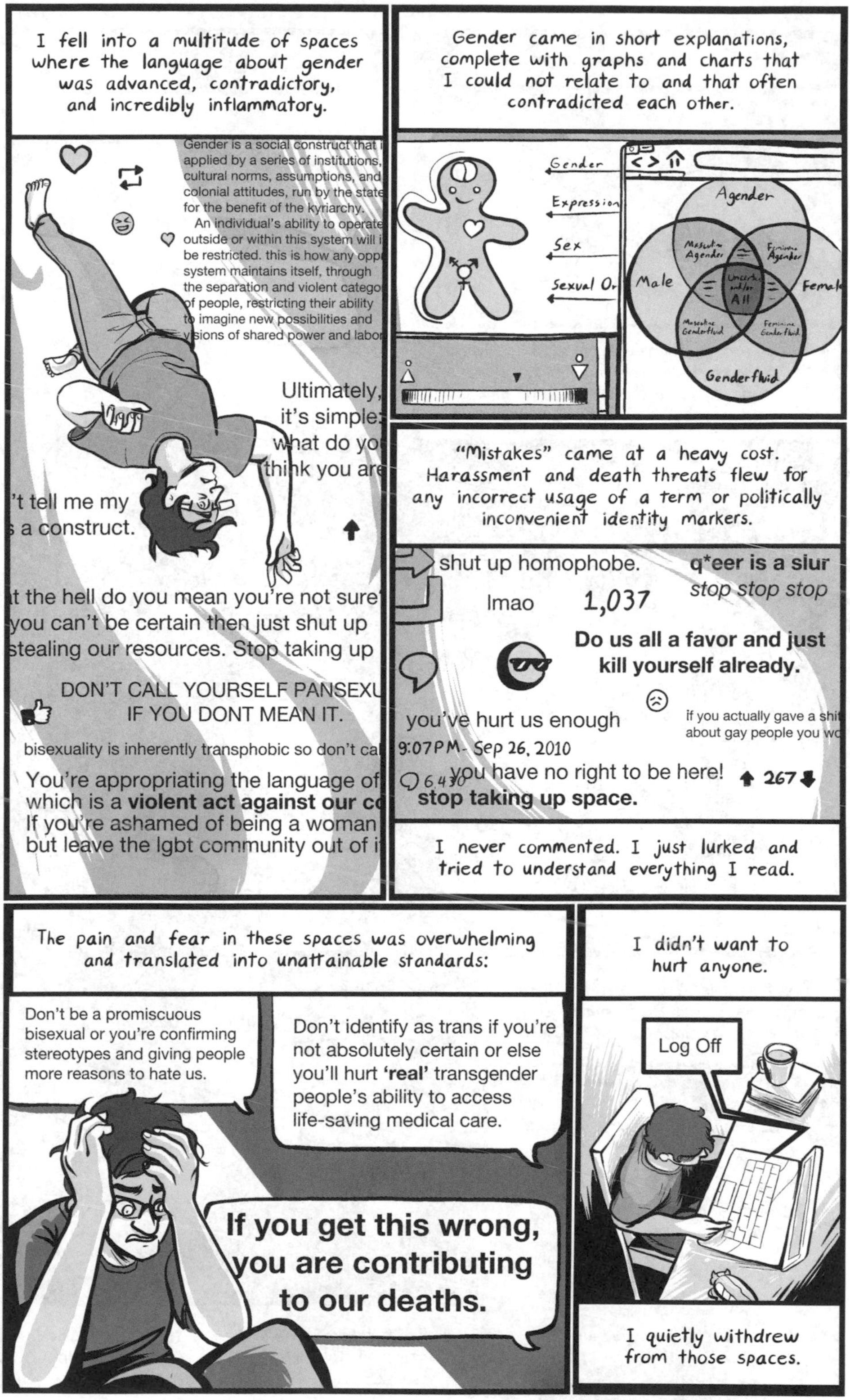

I fell into a multitude of spaces where the language about gender was advanced, contradictory, and incredibly inflammatory.
Gender is a social construct that i
applied by a series of institutions,
cultural norms, assumptions, and
colonial attitudes, run by the state
for the benefit of the kyriarchy.
An individual's ability to operate
outside or within this system will i
be restricted. this is how any opp
system maintains itself, through
the separation and violent catego
of people, restricting their ability
to imagine new possibilities and
visions of shared power and labor
Ultimately,
it's simple:
what do yo
think you are
't tell me my
s a construct.
t the hell do you mean you're not sure
you can't be certain then just shut up
stealing our resources. Stop taking up
DON'T CALL YOURSELF PANSEXU
IF YOU DONT MEAN IT.
bisexuality is inherently transphobic so don't ca
You're appropriating the language of
which is a **violent act against our c**
If you're ashamed of being a woman
but leave the lgbt community out of i
Gender came in short explanations, complete with graphs and charts that I could not relate to and that often contradicted each other.
Gender
Expression
Sex
Sexual O.
Agender
Male
Female
Genderfluid
All
"Mistakes" came at a heavy cost. Harassment and death threats flew for any incorrect usage of a term or politically inconvenient identity markers.
shut up homophobe.
q*eer is a slur
stop stop stop
lmao
1,037
Do us all a favor and just kill yourself already.
you've hurt us enough
if you actually gave a shi
about gay people you w
9:07PM - Sep 26, 2010
6,430
you have no right to be here!
267
stop taking up space.
I never commented. I just lurked and tried to understand everything I read.
The pain and fear in these spaces was overwhelming and translated into unattainable standards:
Don't be a promiscuous bisexual or you're confirming stereotypes and giving people more reasons to hate us.
Don't identify as trans if you're not absolutely certain or else you'll hurt **'real'** transgender people's ability to access life-saving medical care.
If you get this wrong, you are contributing to our deaths.
I didn't want to hurt anyone.
Log Off
I quietly withdrew from those spaces.

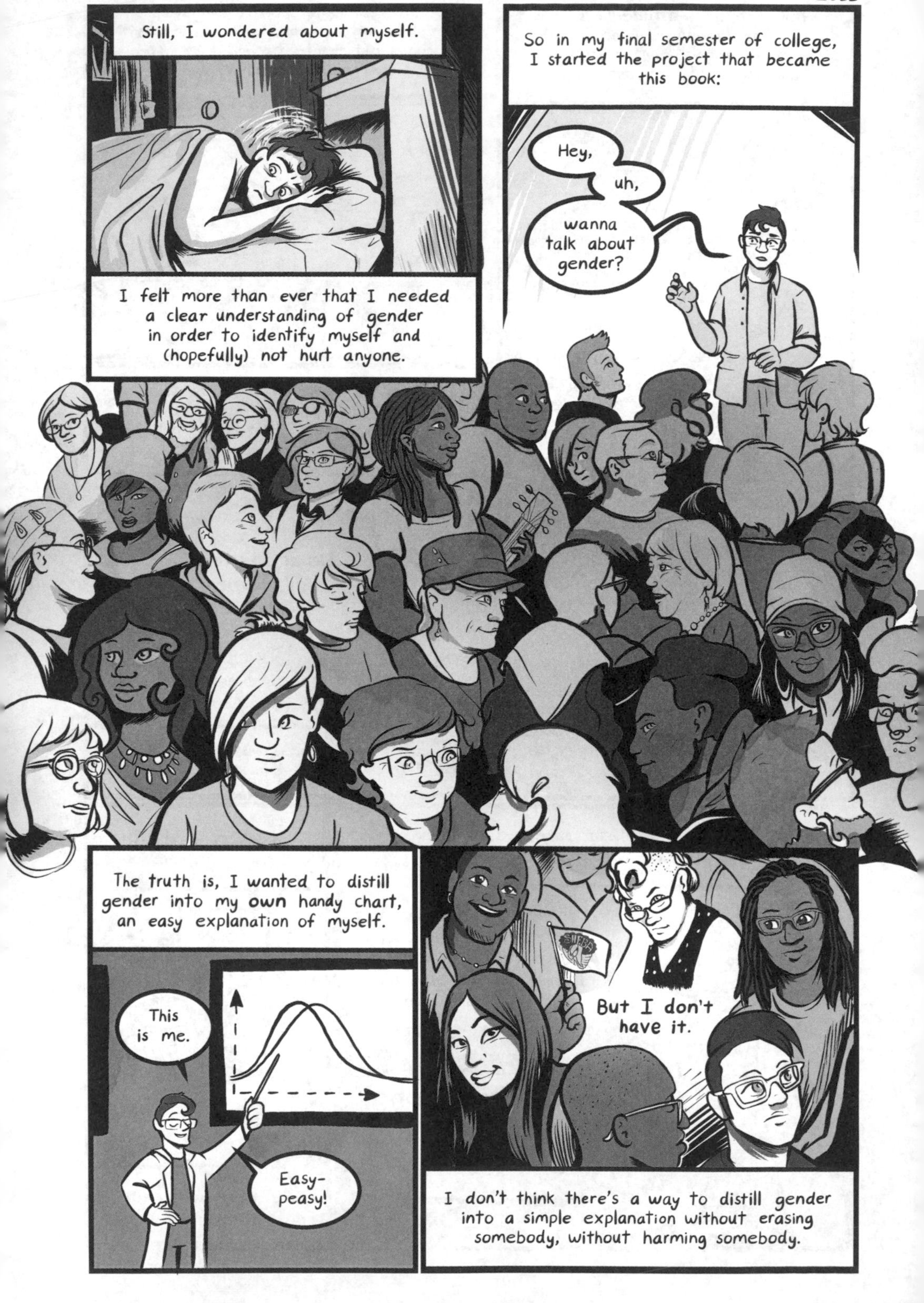
Still, I wondered about myself.
I felt more than ever that I needed a clear understanding of gender in order to identify myself and (hopefully) not hurt anyone.
So in my final semester of college, I started the project that became this book:
Hey,
uh,
wanna talk about gender?
The truth is, I wanted to distill gender into my **own** handy chart, an easy explanation of myself.
This is me.
Easy-peasy!
But I don't have it.
I don't think there's a way to distill gender into a simple explanation without erasing somebody, without harming somebody.

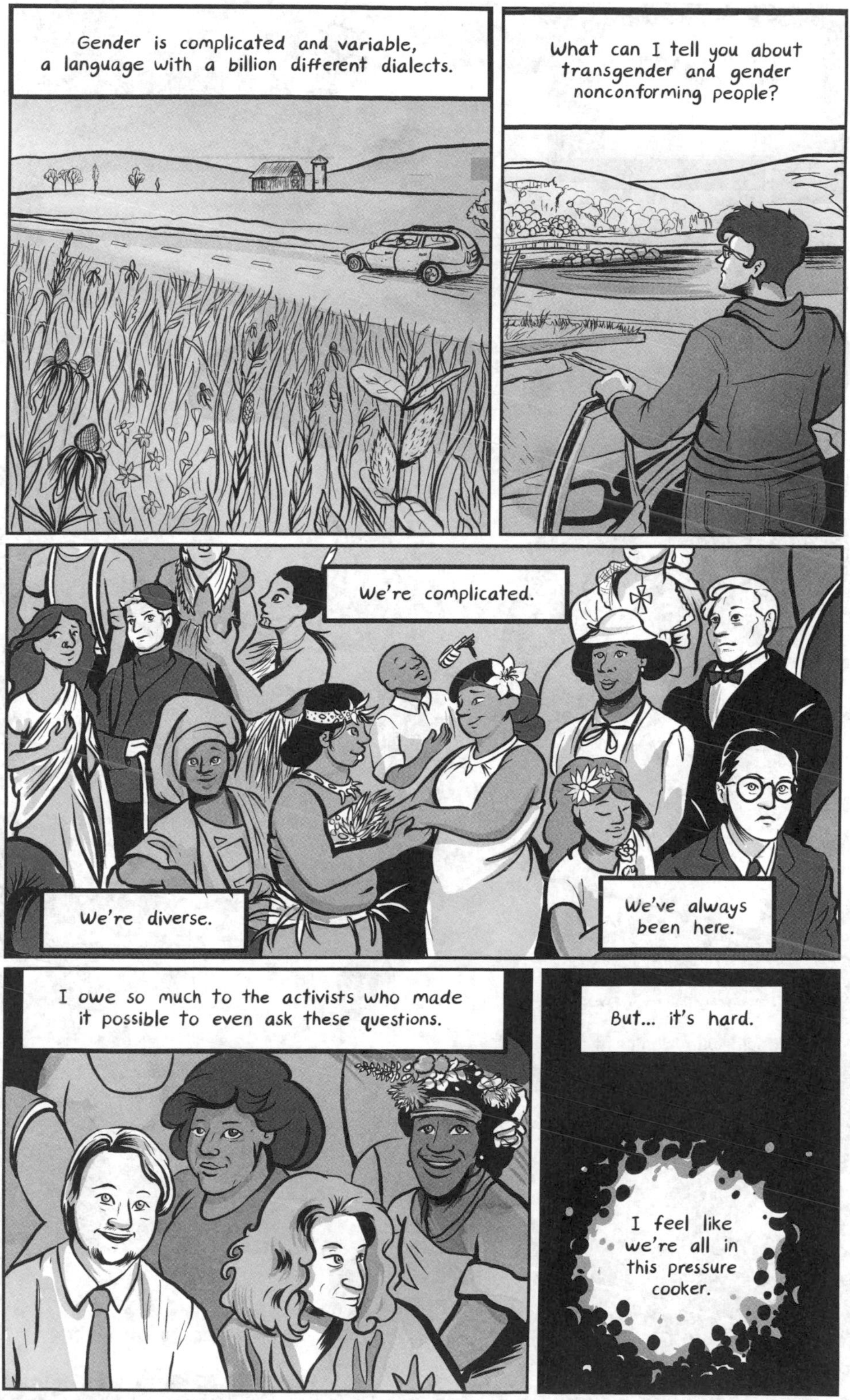
Gender is complicated and variable, a language with a billion different dialects.
What can I tell you about transgender and gender nonconforming people?
We're complicated.
We're diverse.
We've always been here.
I owe so much to the activists who made it possible to even ask these questions.
But... it's hard.
I feel like we're all in this pressure cooker.

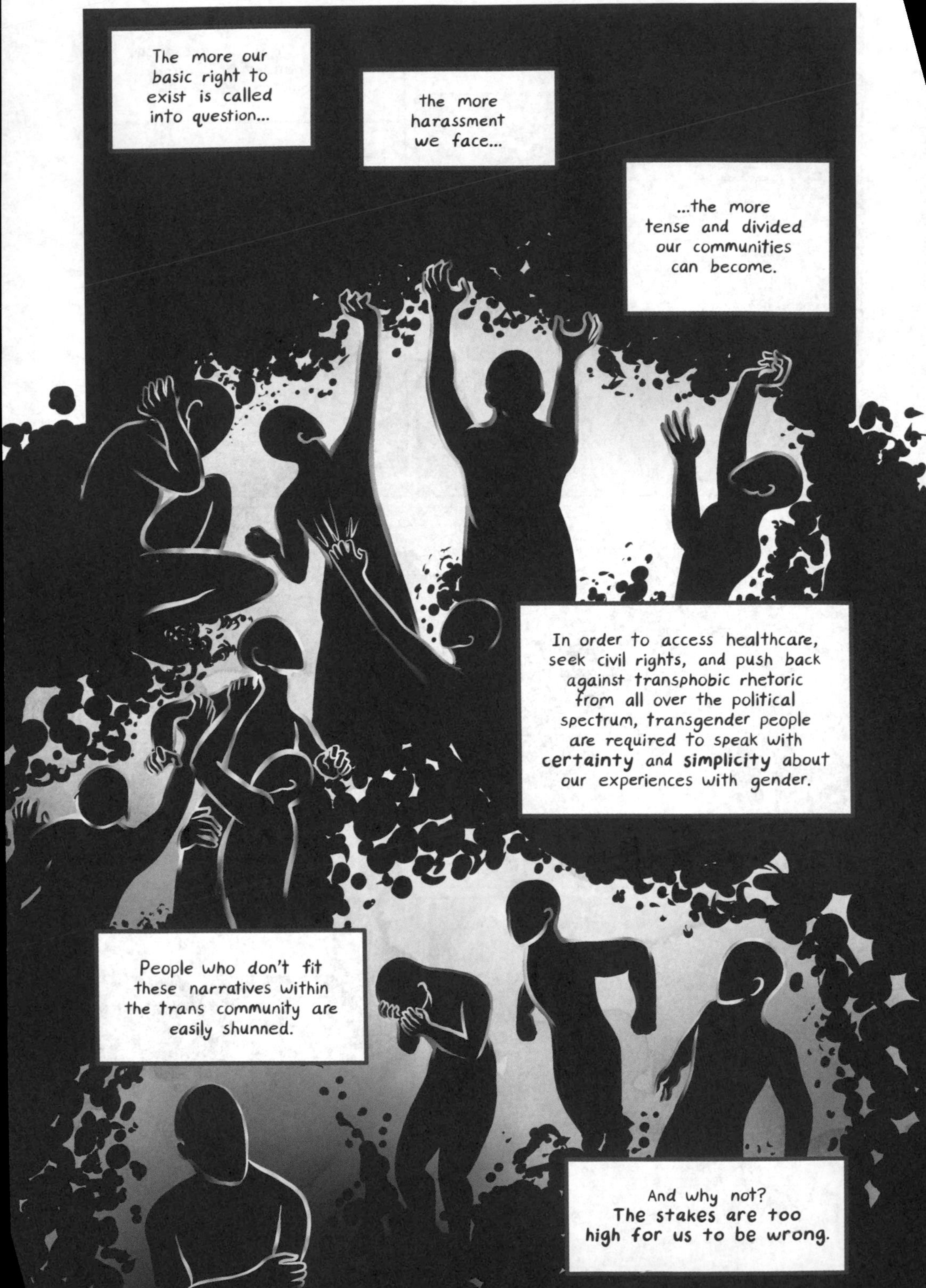
The more our basic right to exist is called into question...
the more harassment we face...
...the more tense and divided our communities can become.
In order to access healthcare, seek civil rights, and push back against transphobic rhetoric from all over the political spectrum, transgender people are required to speak with **certainty** and **simplicity** about our experiences with gender.
People who don't fit these narratives within the trans community are easily shunned.
And why not?
The stakes are too high for us to be wrong.

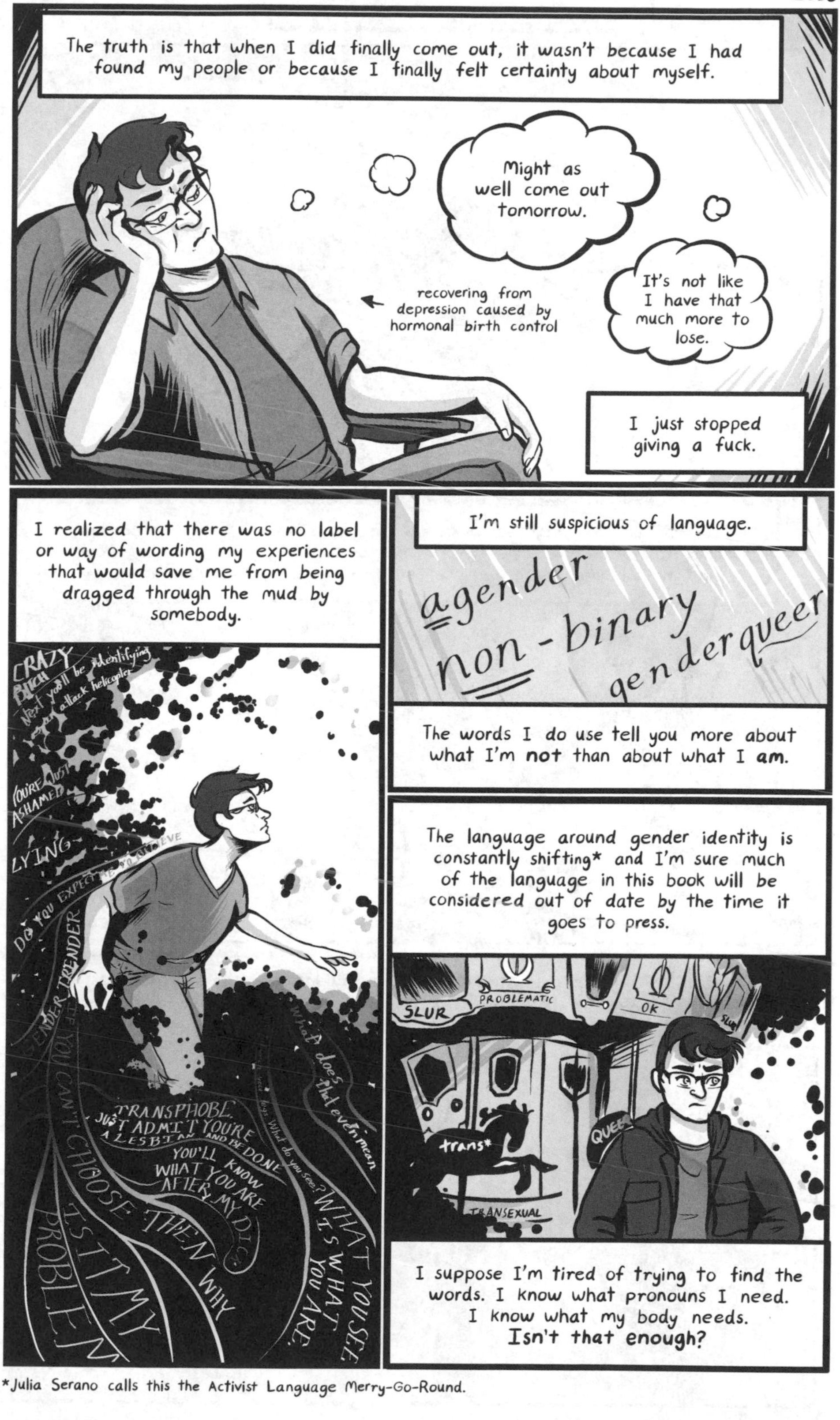
The truth is that when I did finally come out, it wasn't because I had found my people or because I finally felt certainty about myself.
Might as well come out tomorrow.
It's not like I have that much more to lose.
recovering from depression caused by hormonal birth control
I just stopped giving a fuck.
I realized that there was no label or way of wording my experiences that would save me from being dragged through the mud by somebody.
CRAZY BITCH
Next you'll be identifying as an attack helicopter
YOU'RE JUST ASHAMED
LYING
DO YOU EXPECT ME TO JUST BELIEVE
GENDER TRENDER
TRANSPHOBE
JUST ADMIT YOU'RE A LESBIAN AND BE DONE
YOU'LL KNOW WHAT YOU ARE AFTER MY DICK
IF YOU CAN'T CHOOSE THEN WHY IS IT MY PROBLEM
WHAT does that even mean
What do you see?
WHAT YOU SEE IS WHAT YOU ARE.
I'm still suspicious of language.
agender
non-binary
genderqueer
The words I do use tell you more about what I'm **not** than about what I **am**.
The language around gender identity is constantly shifting* and I'm sure much of the language in this book will be considered out of date by the time it goes to press.
SLUR
PROBLEMATIC
OK
trans*
QUEER
TRANSEXUAL
I suppose I'm tired of trying to find the words. I know what pronouns I need. I know what my body needs.
Isn't that enough?

*Julia Serano calls this the Activist Language Merry-Go-Round.

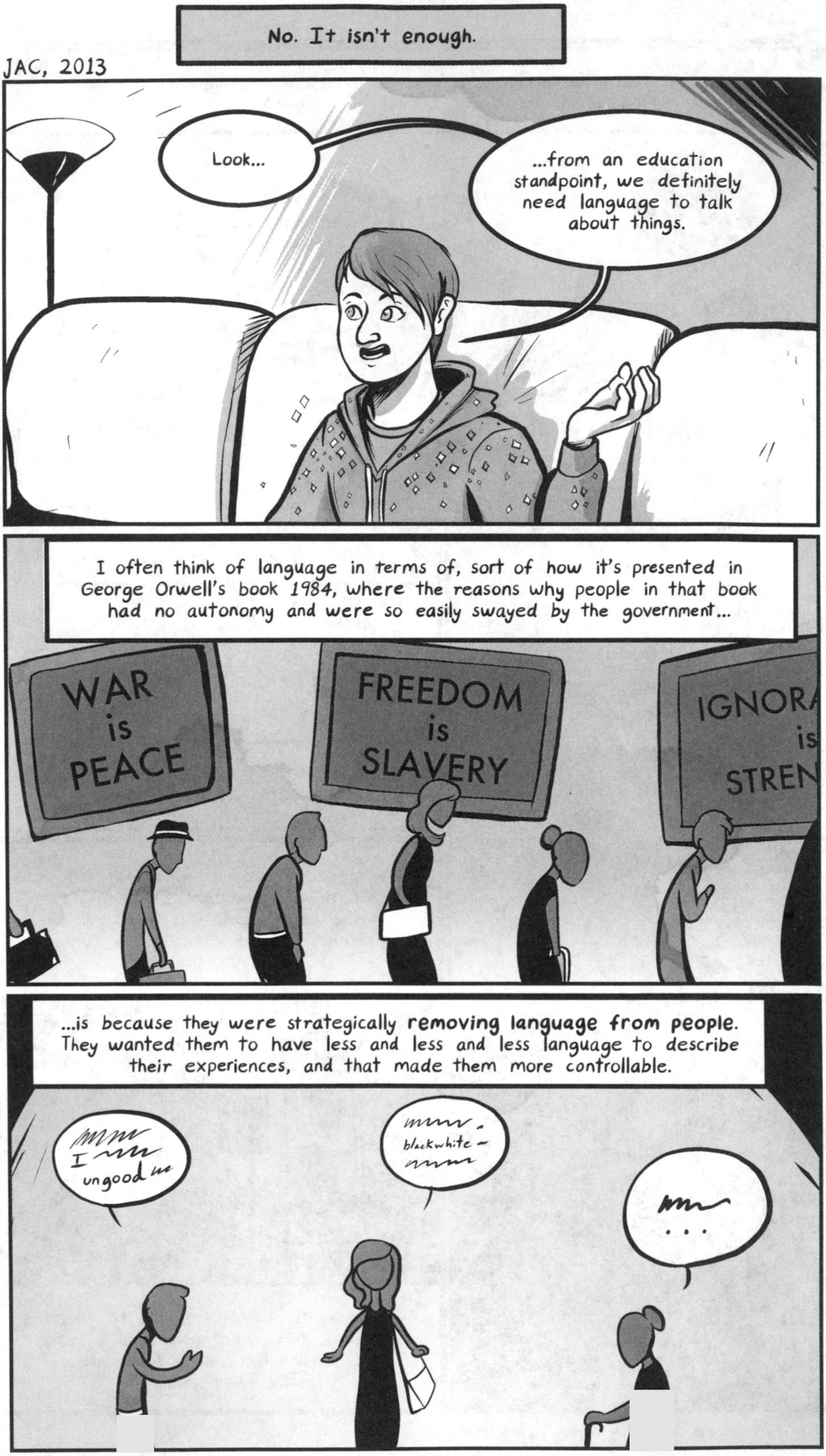
No. It isn't enough.
JAC, 2013
Look...
...from an education standpoint, we definitely need language to talk about things.
I often think of language in terms of, sort of how it's presented in George Orwell's book 1984, where the reasons why people in that book had no autonomy and were so easily swayed by the government...
WAR is PEACE
FREEDOM is SLAVERY
...is because they were strategically **removing language from people**. They wanted them to have less and less and less language to describe their experiences, and that made them more controllable.
I ungood
blackwhite
...

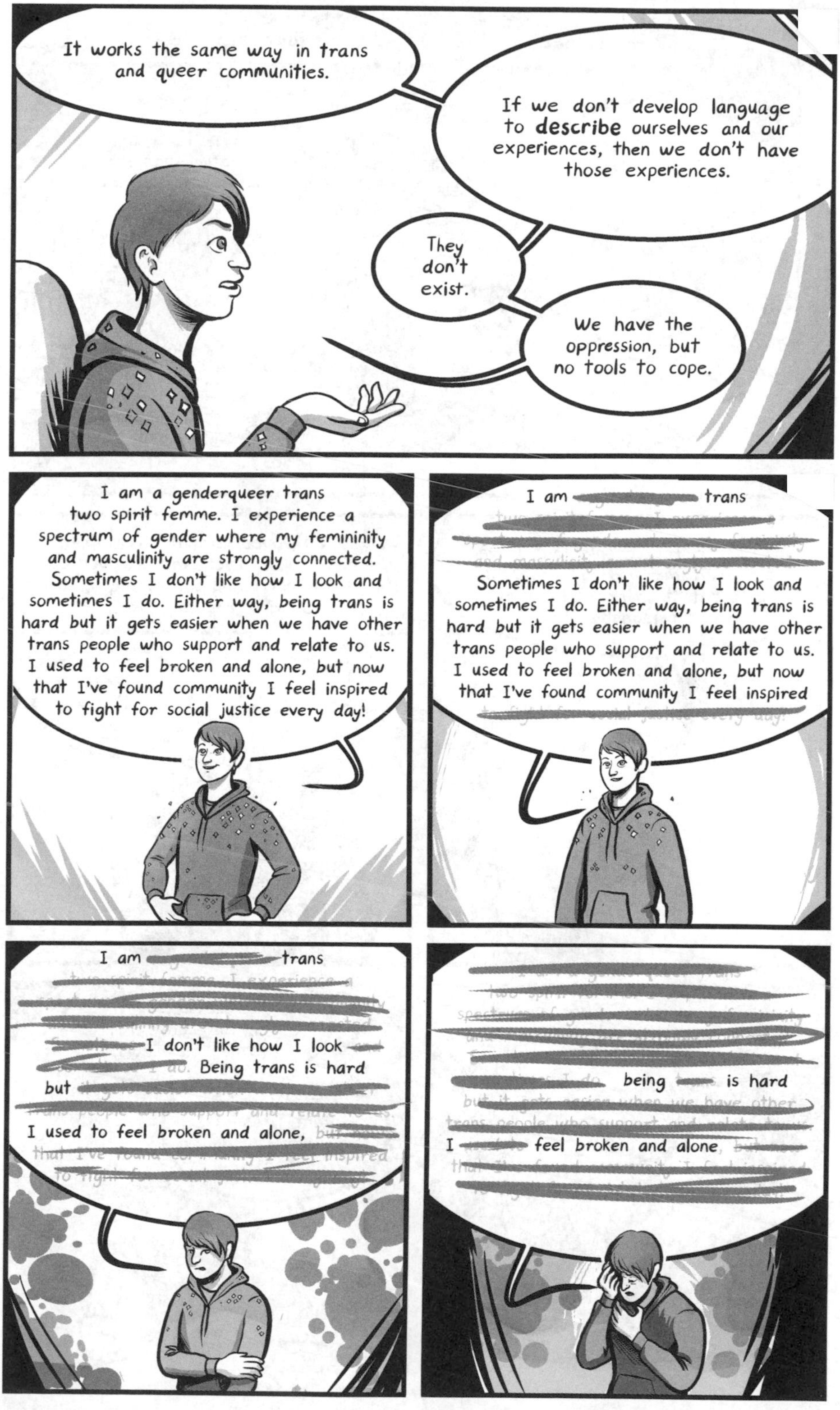
It works the same way in trans and queer communities.
If we don't develop language to **describe** ourselves and our experiences, then we don't have those experiences.
They don't exist.
We have the oppression, but no tools to cope.
I am a genderqueer trans two spirit femme. I experience a spectrum of gender where my femininity and masculinity are strongly connected. Sometimes I don't like how I look and sometimes I do. Either way, being trans is hard but it gets easier when we have other trans people who support and relate to us. I used to feel broken and alone, but now that I've found community I feel inspired to fight for social justice every day!
I am trans
Sometimes I don't like how I look and sometimes I do. Either way, being trans is hard but it gets easier when we have other trans people who support and relate to us. I used to feel broken and alone, but now that I've found community I feel inspired
I am trans
I don't like how I look
Being trans is hard
but
I used to feel broken and alone,
being is hard
I feel broken and alone

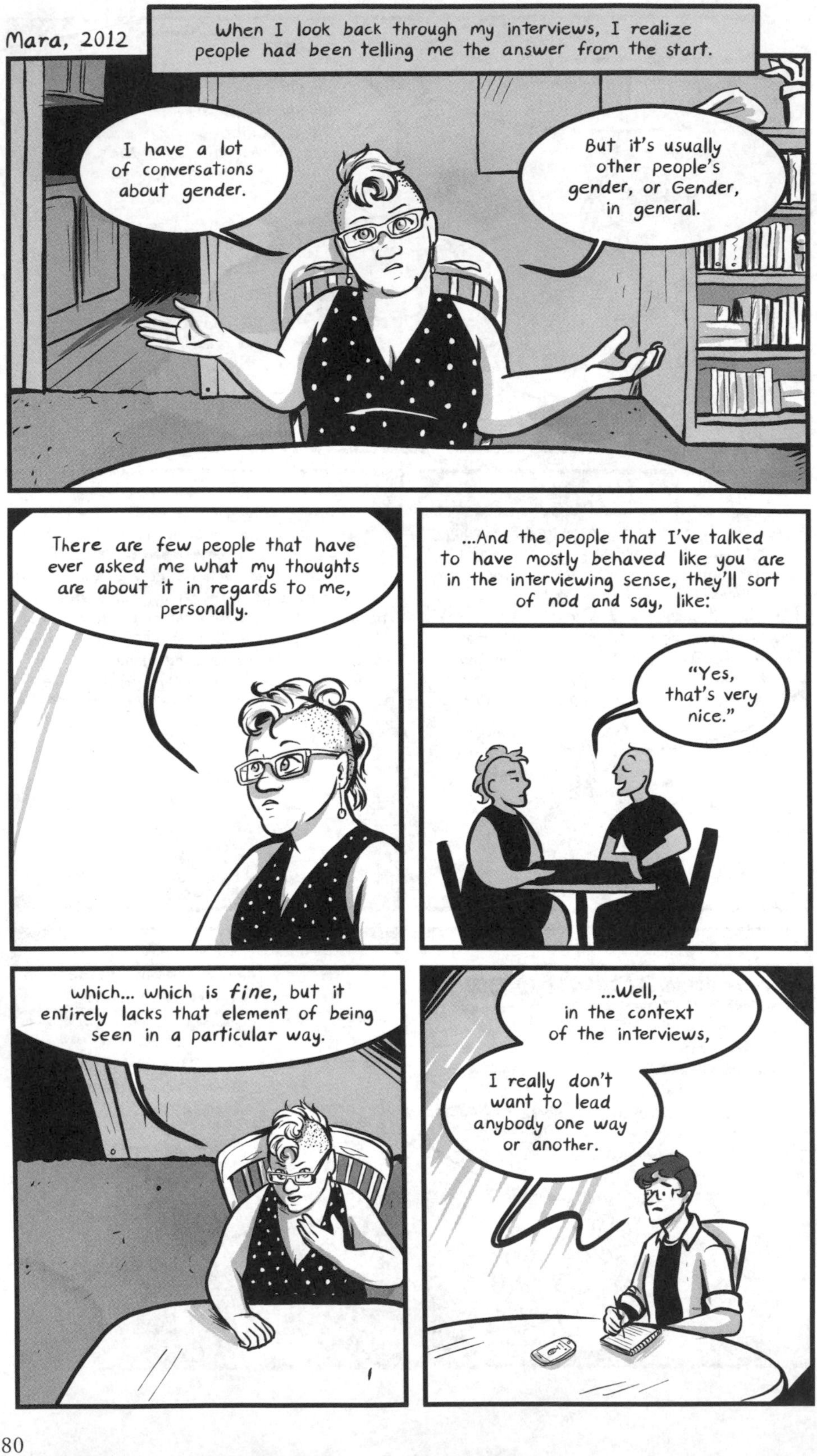
Mara, 2012
When I look back through my interviews, I realize people had been telling me the answer from the start.
I have a lot of conversations about gender.
But it's usually other people's gender, or Gender, in general.
There are few people that have ever asked me what my thoughts are about it in regards to me, personally.
...And the people that I've talked to have mostly behaved like you are in the interviewing sense, they'll sort of nod and say, like:
"Yes, that's very nice."
which... which is *fine*, but it entirely lacks that element of being seen in a particular way.
...Well, in the context of the interviews,
I really don't want to lead anybody one way or another.

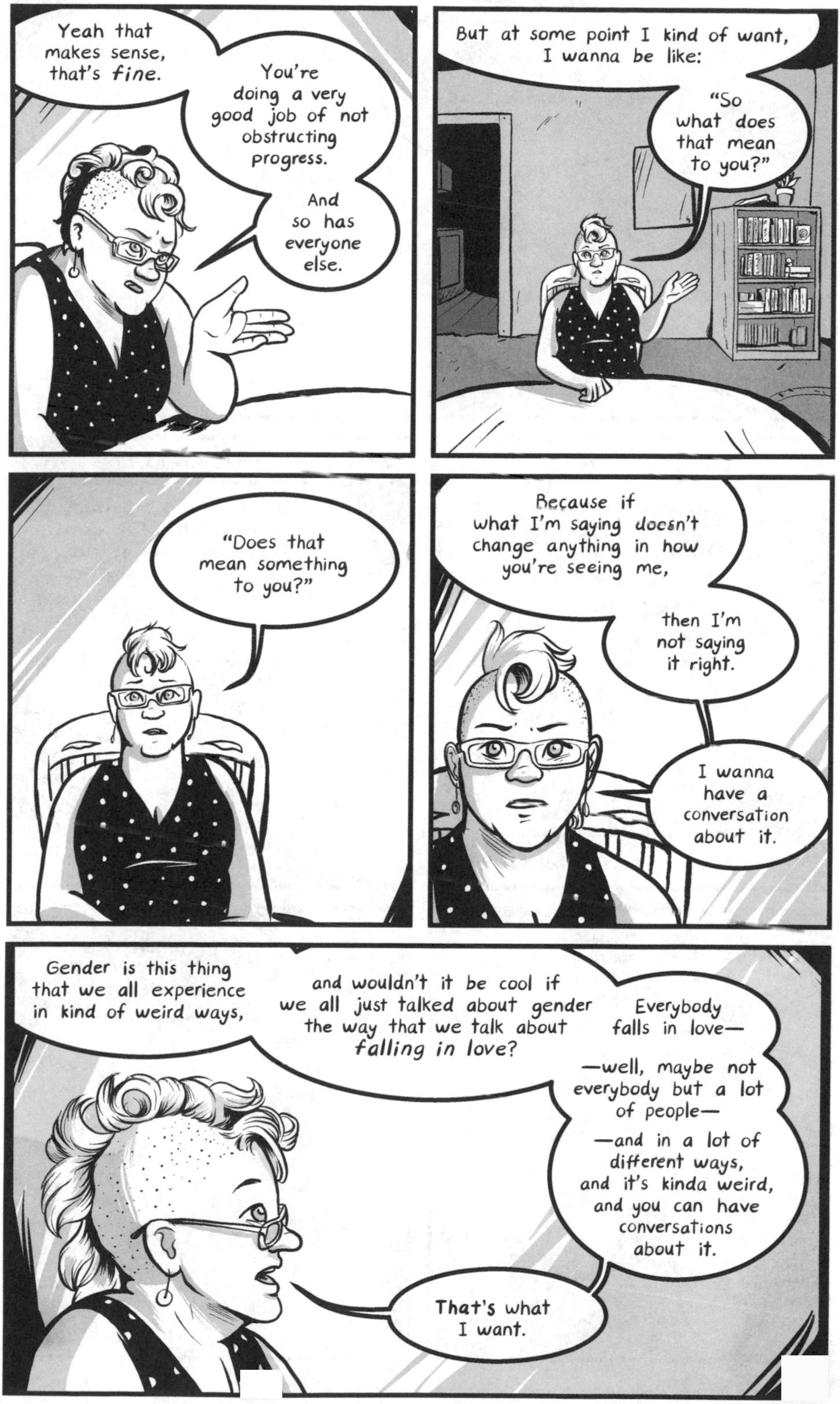
Yeah that makes sense, that's *fine.*
You're doing a very good job of not obstructing progress.
And so has everyone else.
But at some point I kind of want, I wanna be like:
"So what does that mean to you?"
"Does that mean something to you?"
Because if what I'm saying doesn't change anything in how you're seeing me,
then I'm not saying it right.
I wanna have a conversation about it.
Gender is this thing that we all experience in kind of weird ways,
and wouldn't it be cool if we all just talked about gender the way that we talk about *falling in love?*
Everybody falls in love—
—well, maybe not everybody but a lot of people—
—and in a lot of different ways, and it's kinda weird, and you can have conversations about it.
That's what I want.

Mo, 2013

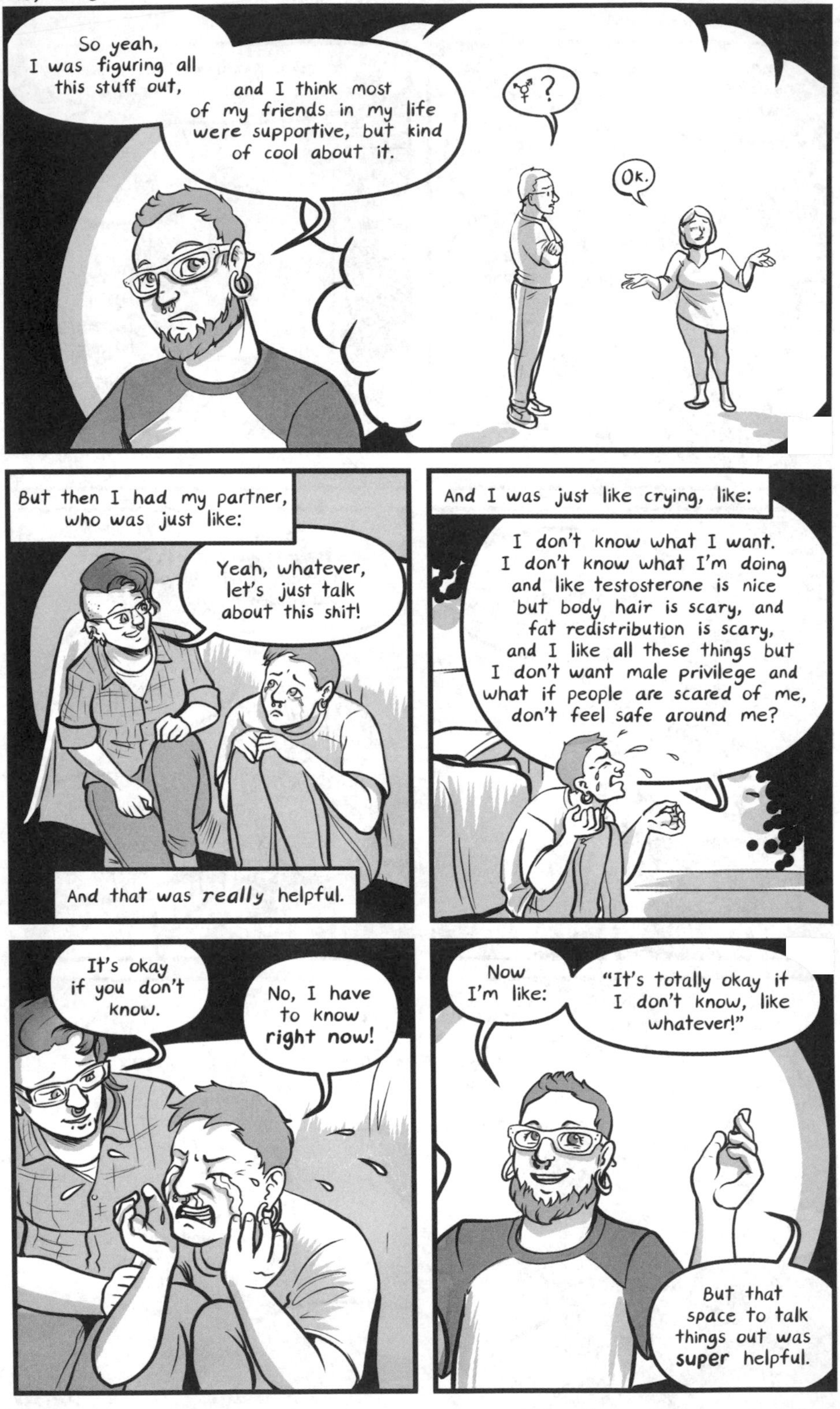
So yeah, I was figuring all this stuff out,
and I think most of my friends in my life were supportive, but kind of cool about it.
⚧ ?
Ok.
But then I had my partner, who was just like:
Yeah, whatever, let's just talk about this shit!
And that was *really* helpful.
And I was just like crying, like:
I don't know what I want. I don't know what I'm doing and like testosterone is nice but body hair is scary, and fat redistribution is scary, and I like all these things but I don't want male privilege and what if people are scared of me, don't feel safe around me?
It's okay if you don't know.
No, I have to know **right now**!
Now I'm like:
"It's totally okay if I don't know, like whatever!"
But that space to talk things out was **super** helpful.

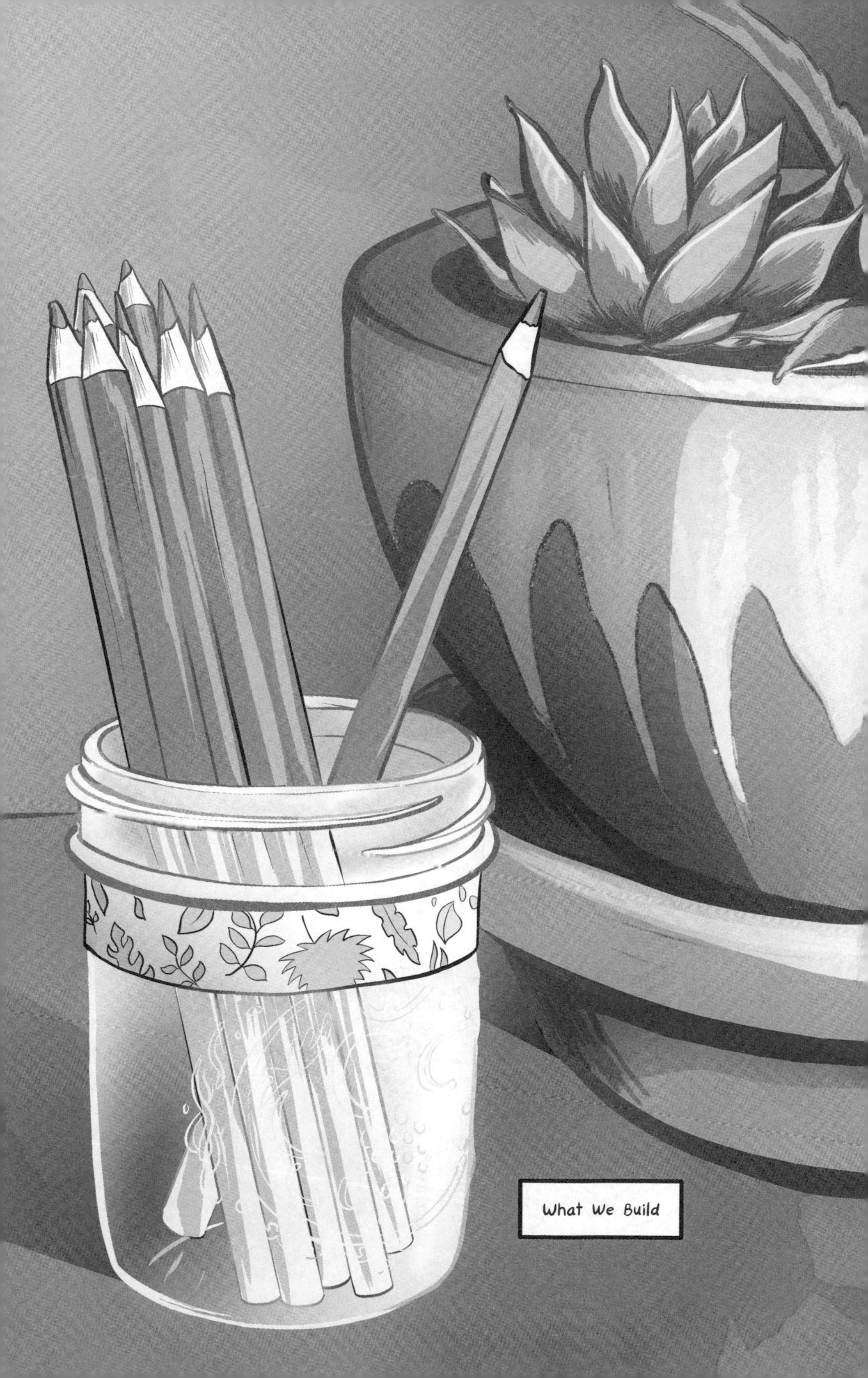
What We Build

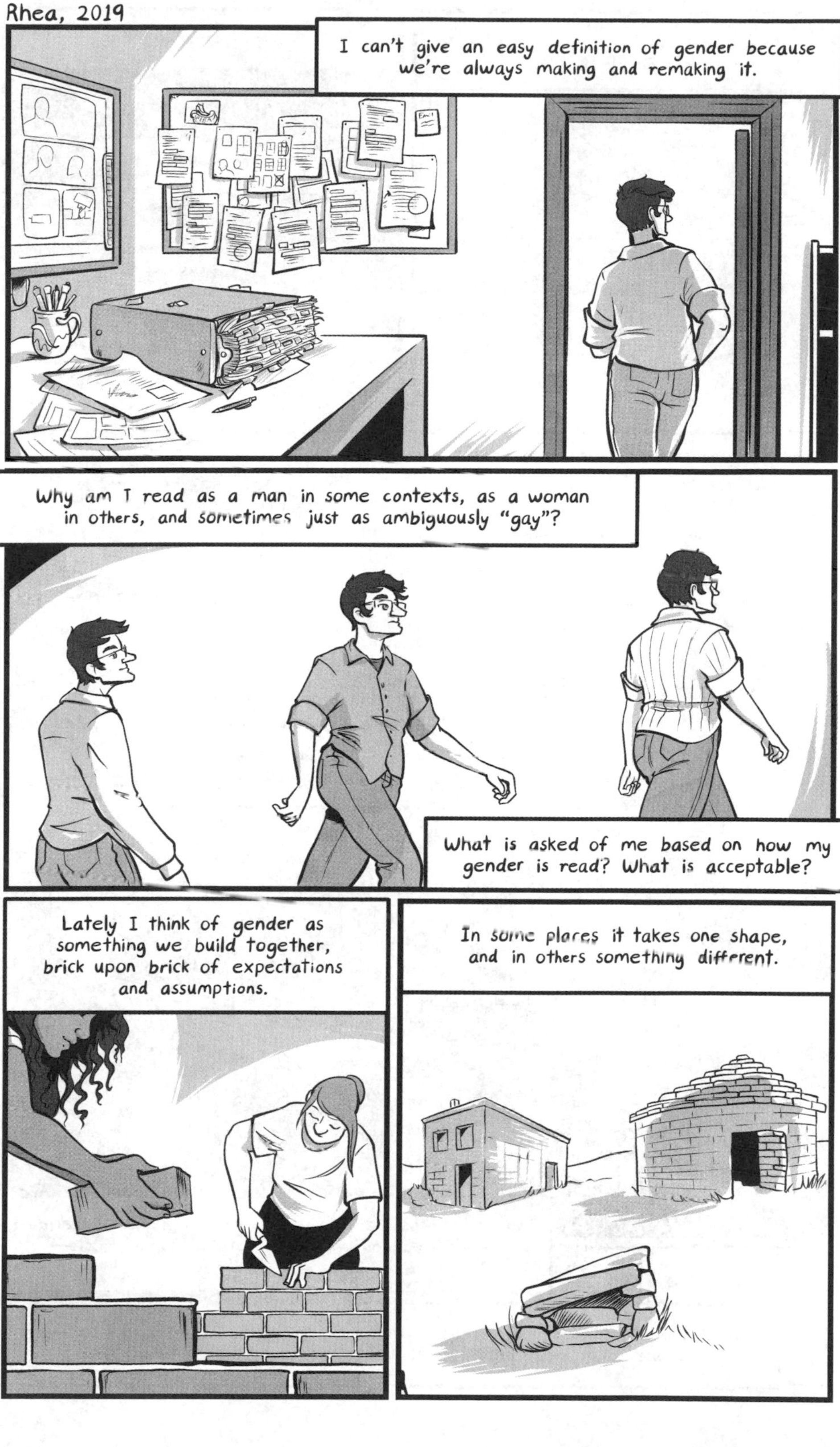
Rhea, 2019
I can't give an easy definition of gender because we're always making and remaking it.
Why am I read as a man in some contexts, as a woman in others, and sometimes just as ambiguously "gay"?
What is asked of me based on how my gender is read? What is acceptable?
Lately I think of gender as something we build together, brick upon brick of expectations and assumptions.
In some places it takes one shape, and in others something different.

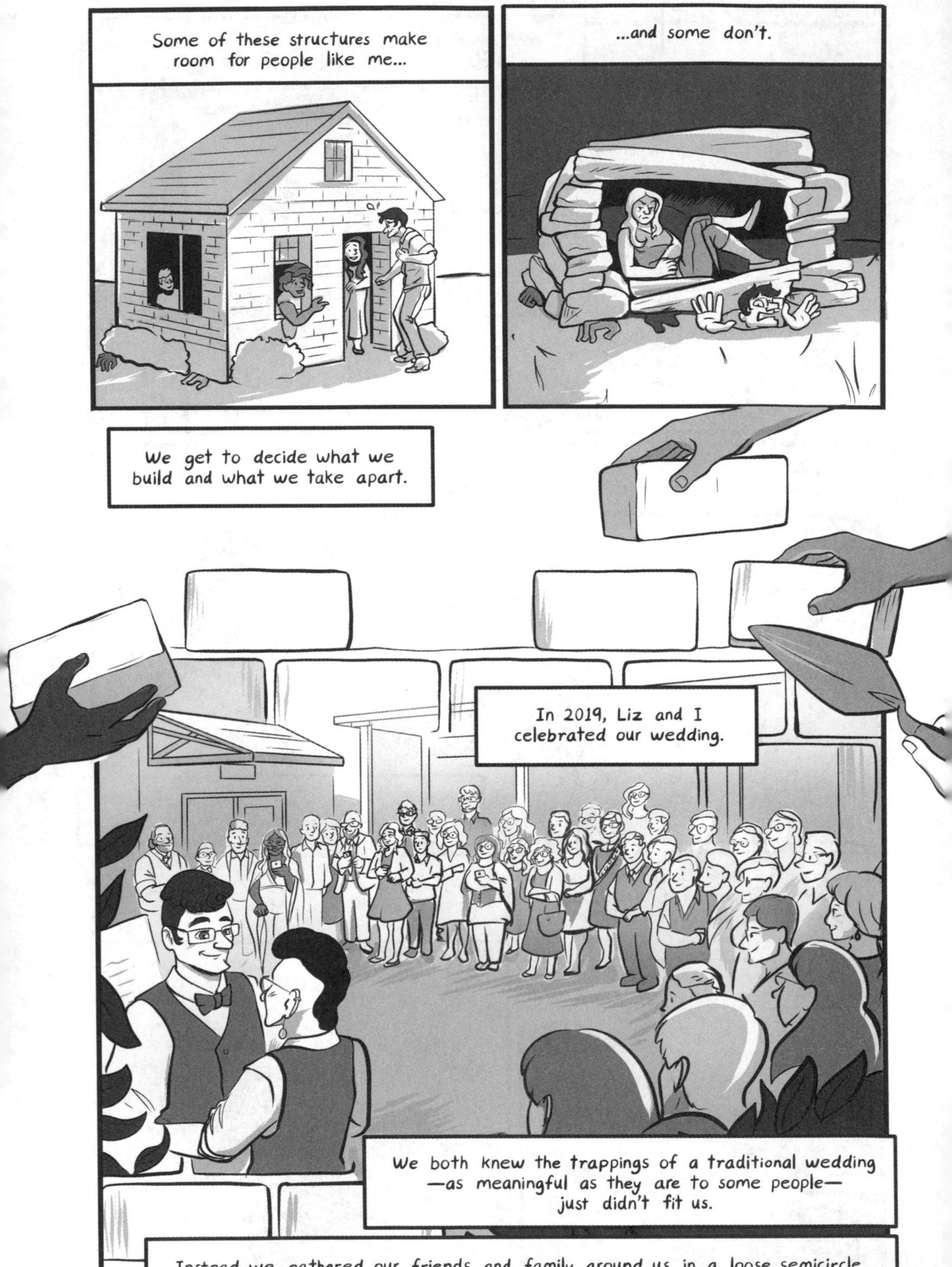
Some of these structures make room for people like me...
...and some don't.
We get to decide what we build and what we take apart.
In 2019, Liz and I celebrated our wedding.
We both knew the trappings of a traditional wedding —as meaningful as they are to some people— just didn't fit us.
Instead we gathered our friends and family around us in a loose semicircle. Everyone could wear whatever they liked. Come as their whole selves.

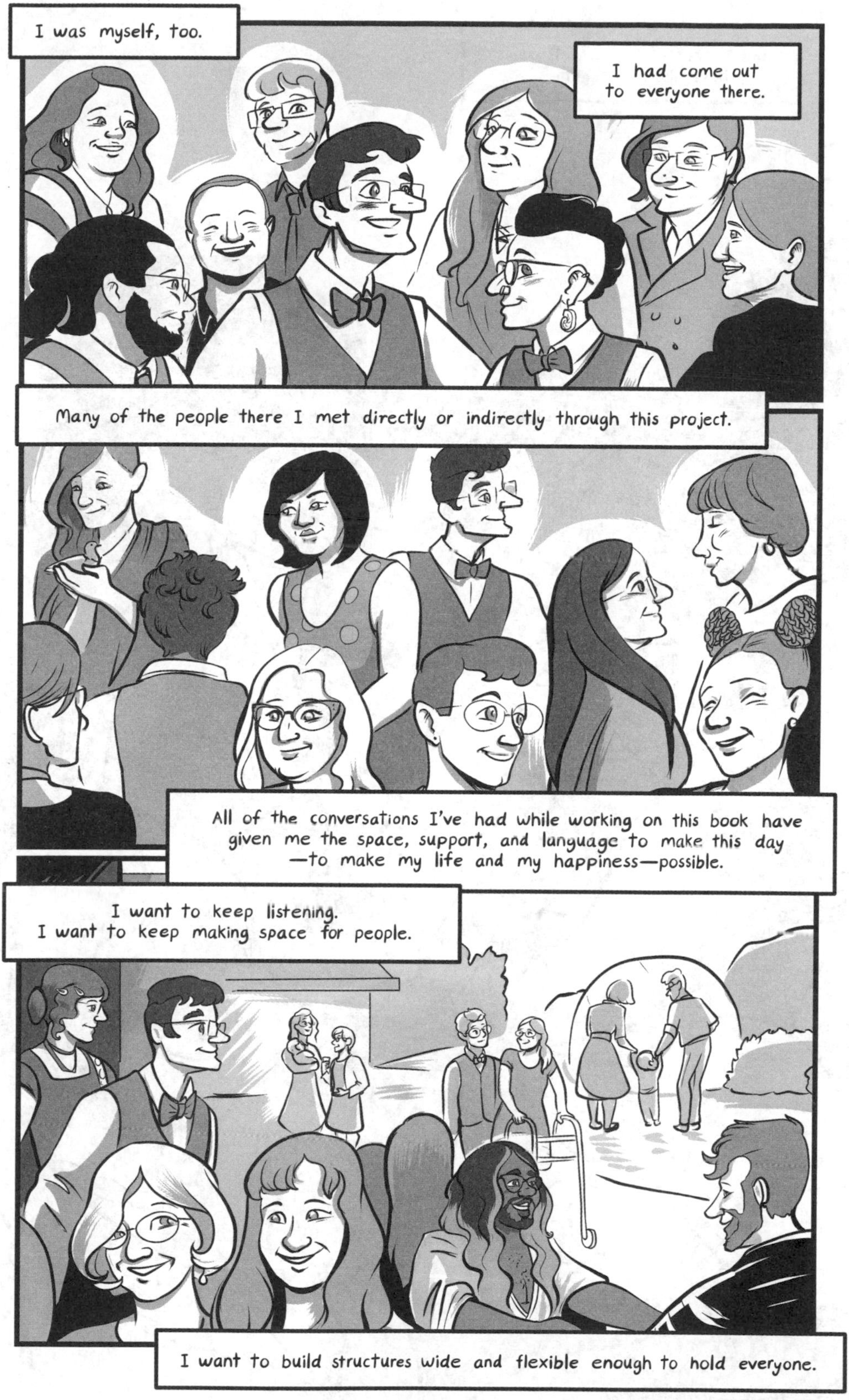

I was myself, too.
I had come out to everyone there.
Many of the people there I met directly or indirectly through this project.
All of the conversations I've had while working on this book have given me the space, support, and language to make this day —to make my life and my happiness—possible.
I want to keep listening.
I want to keep making space for people.
I want to build structures wide and flexible enough to hold everyone.

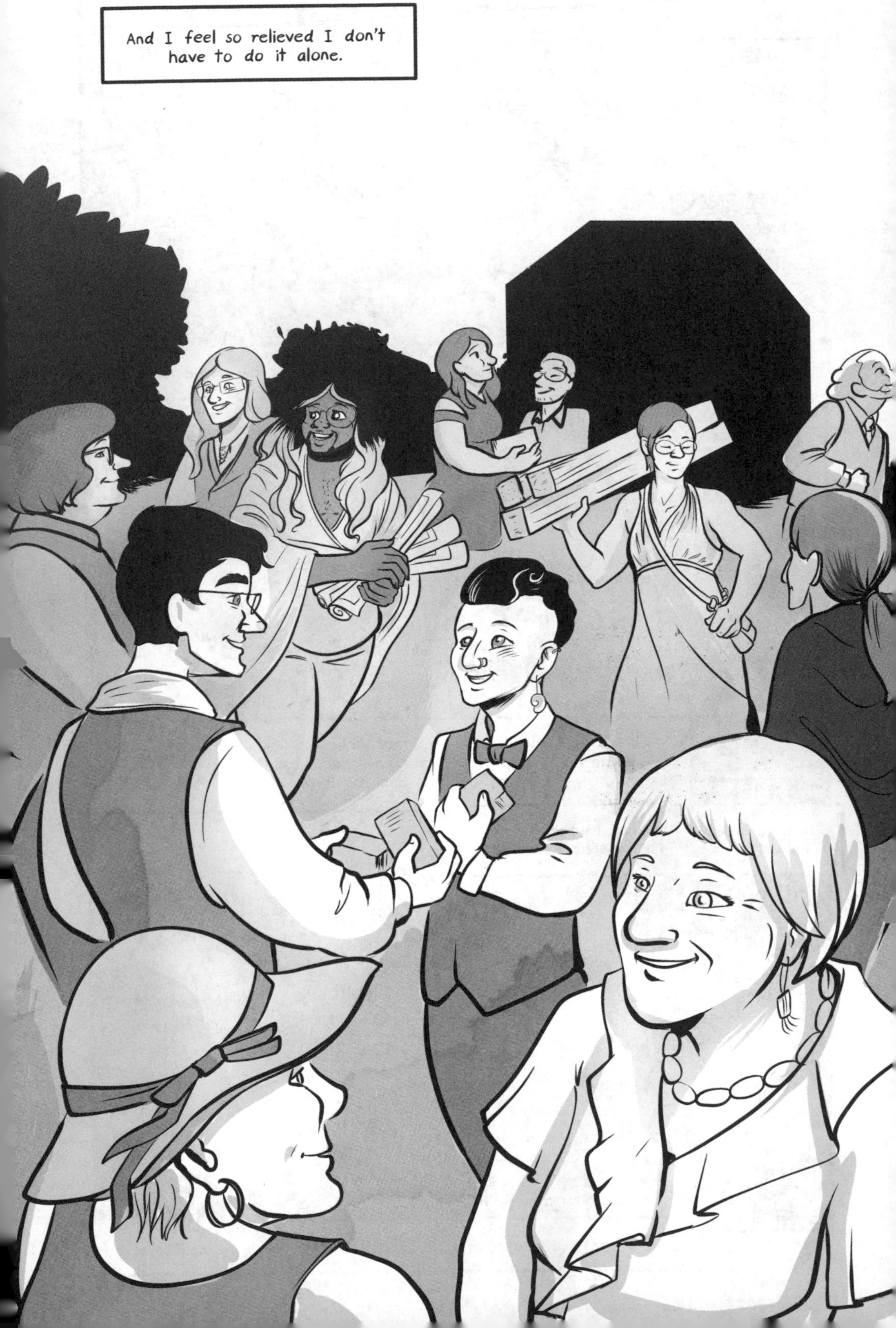
And I feel so relieved I don't have to do it alone.

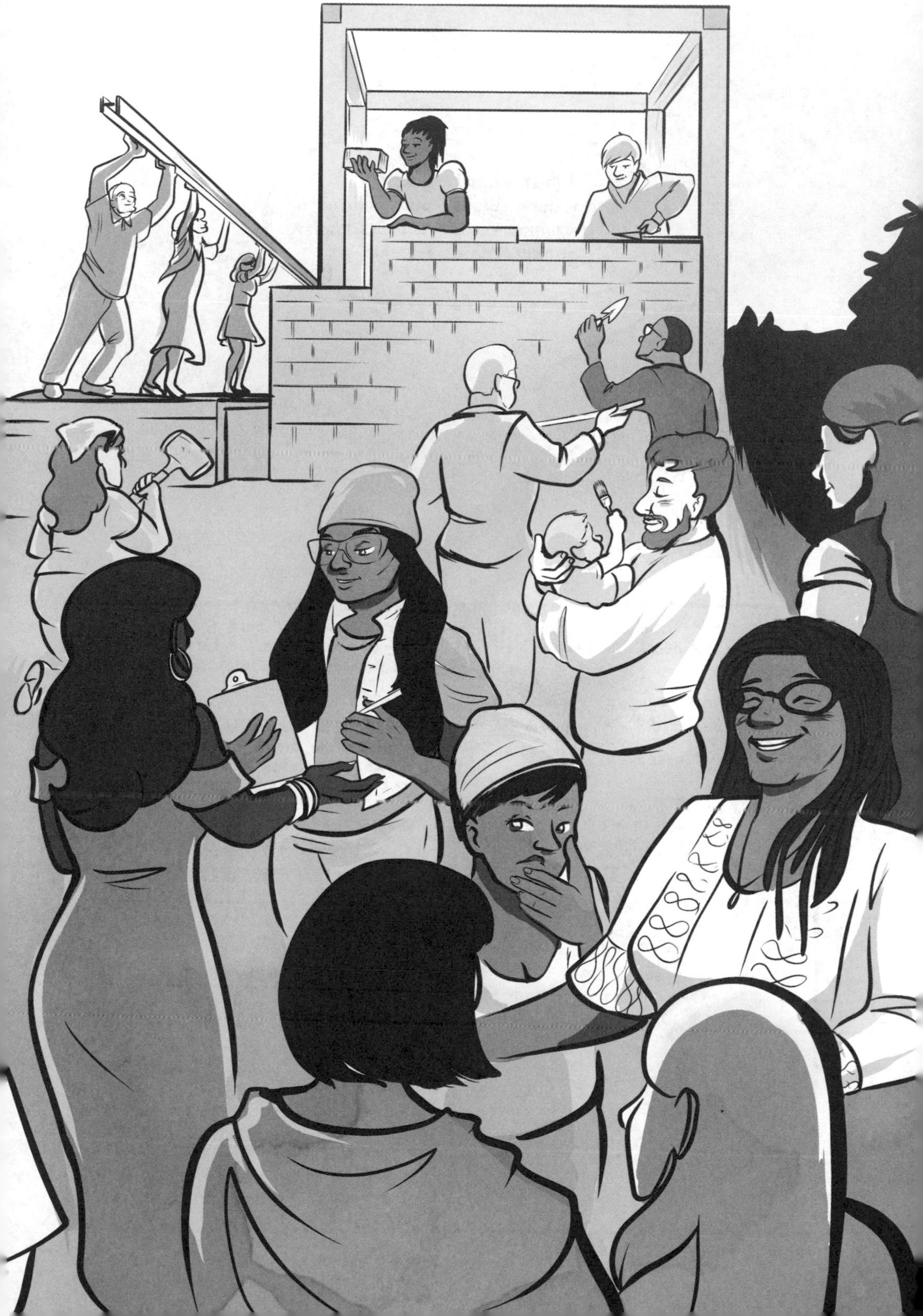

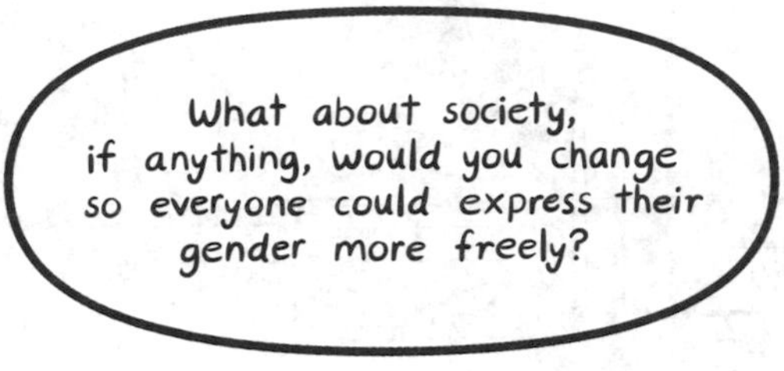
What about society, if anything, would you change so everyone could express their gender more freely?

Kim, 2011

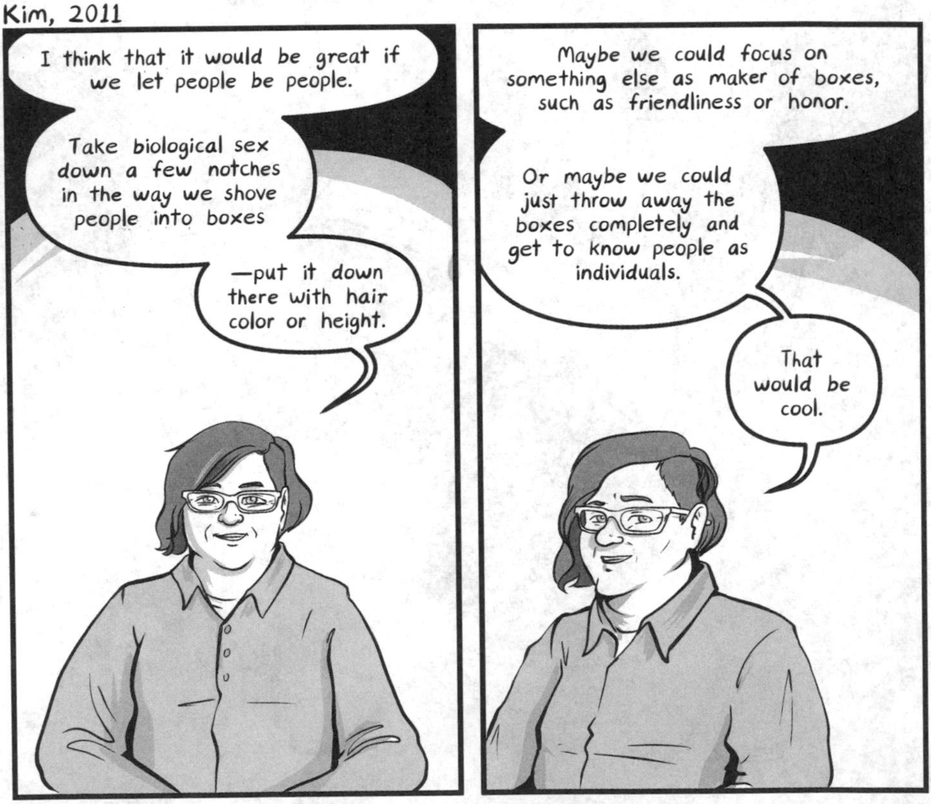
I think that it would be great if we let people be people.
Take biological sex down a few notches in the way we shove people into boxes
—put it down there with hair color or height.
Maybe we could focus on something else as maker of boxes, such as friendliness or honor.
Or maybe we could just throw away the boxes completely and get to know people as individuals.
That would be cool.

Wayne, 2012

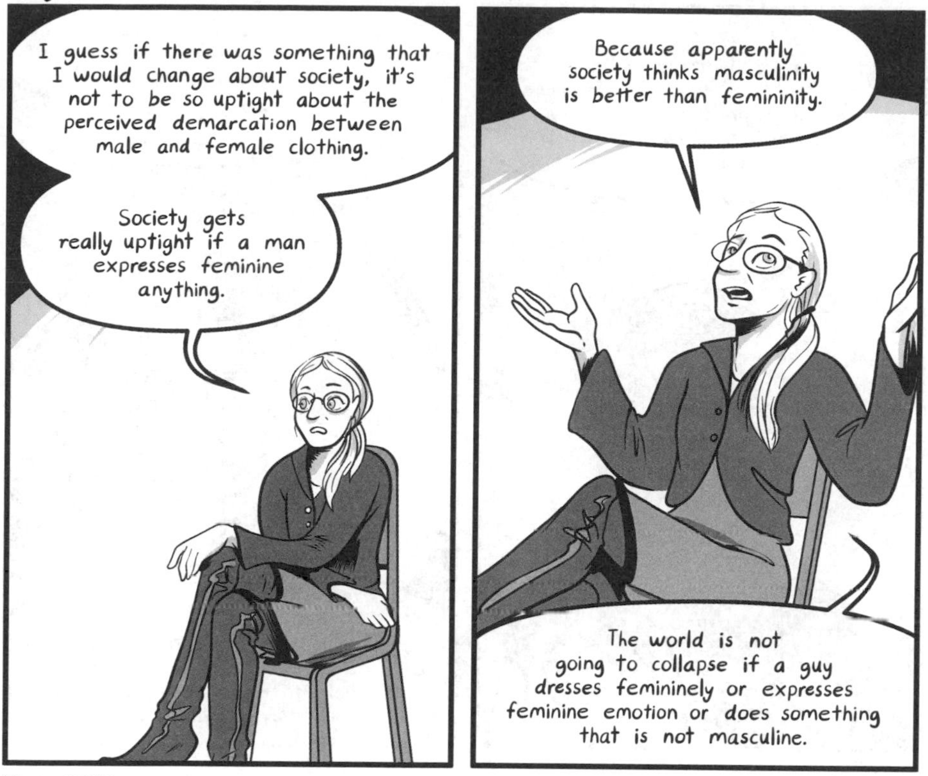
I guess if there was something that I would change about society, it's not to be so uptight about the perceived demarcation between male and female clothing.
Society gets really uptight if a man expresses feminine anything.
Because apparently society thinks masculinity is better than femininity.
The world is not going to collapse if a guy dresses femininely or expresses feminine emotion or does something that is not masculine.

Kai, 2012

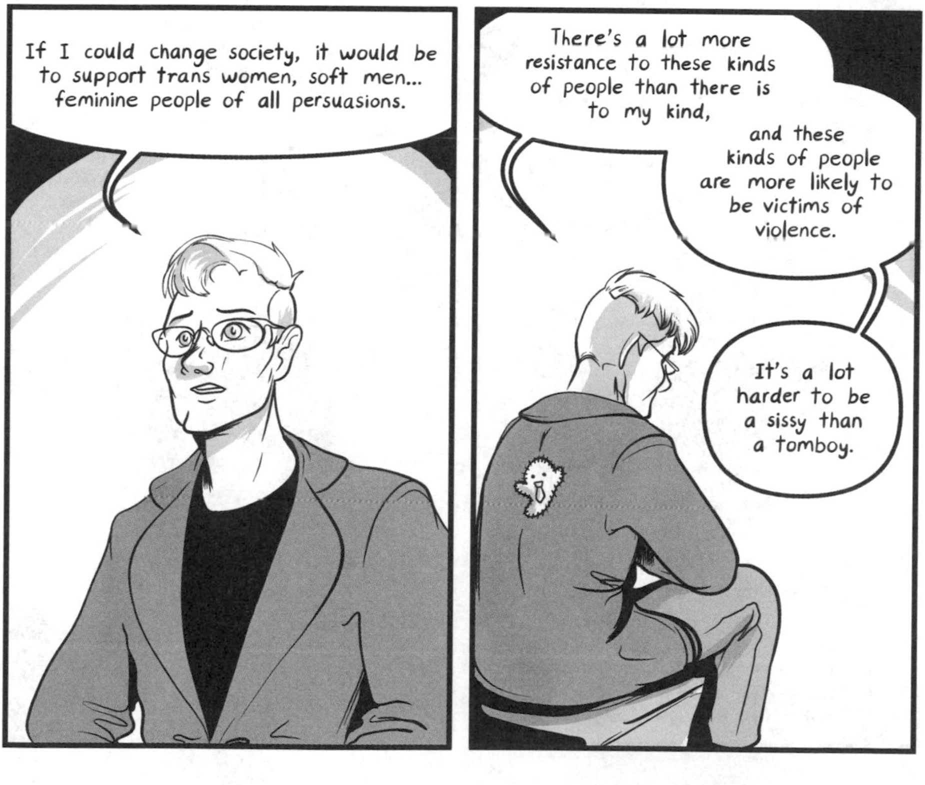
If I could change society, it would be to support trans women, soft men... feminine people of all persuasions.
There's a lot more resistance to these kinds of people than there is to my kind,
and these kinds of people are more likely to be victims of violence.
It's a lot harder to be a sissy than a tomboy.

Mo, 2013

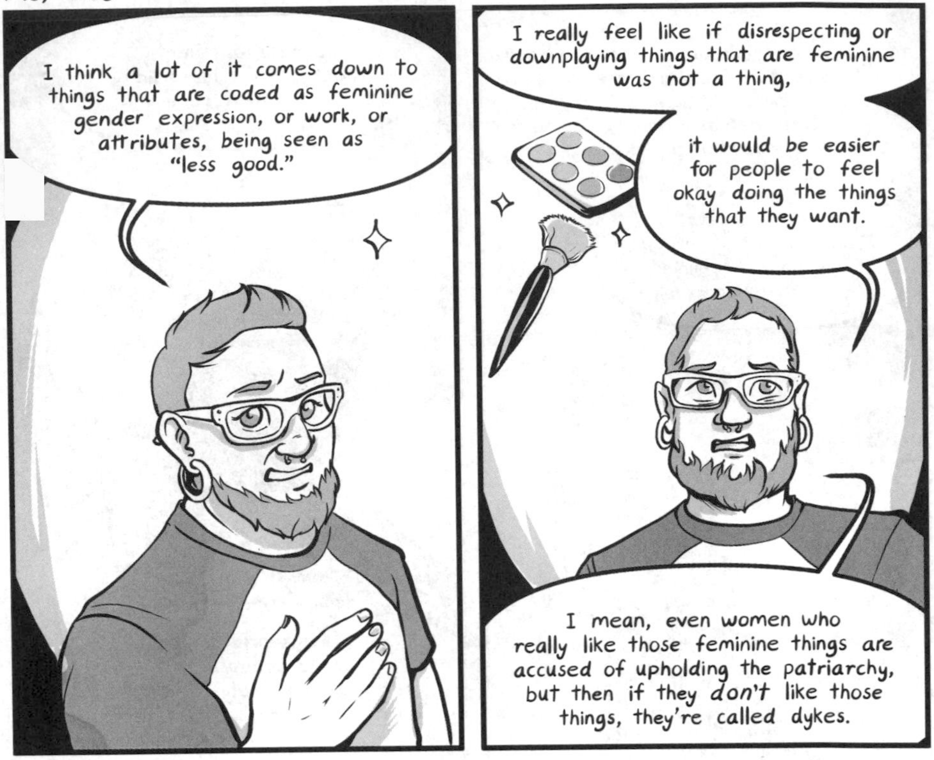
I think a lot of it comes down to things that are coded as feminine gender expression, or work, or attributes, being seen as "less good."
I really feel like if disrespecting or downplaying things that are feminine was not a thing,
it would be easier for people to feel okay doing the things that they want.
I mean, even women who really like those feminine things are accused of upholding the patriarchy, but then if they *don't* like those things, they're called dykes.

LaShawn, 2013

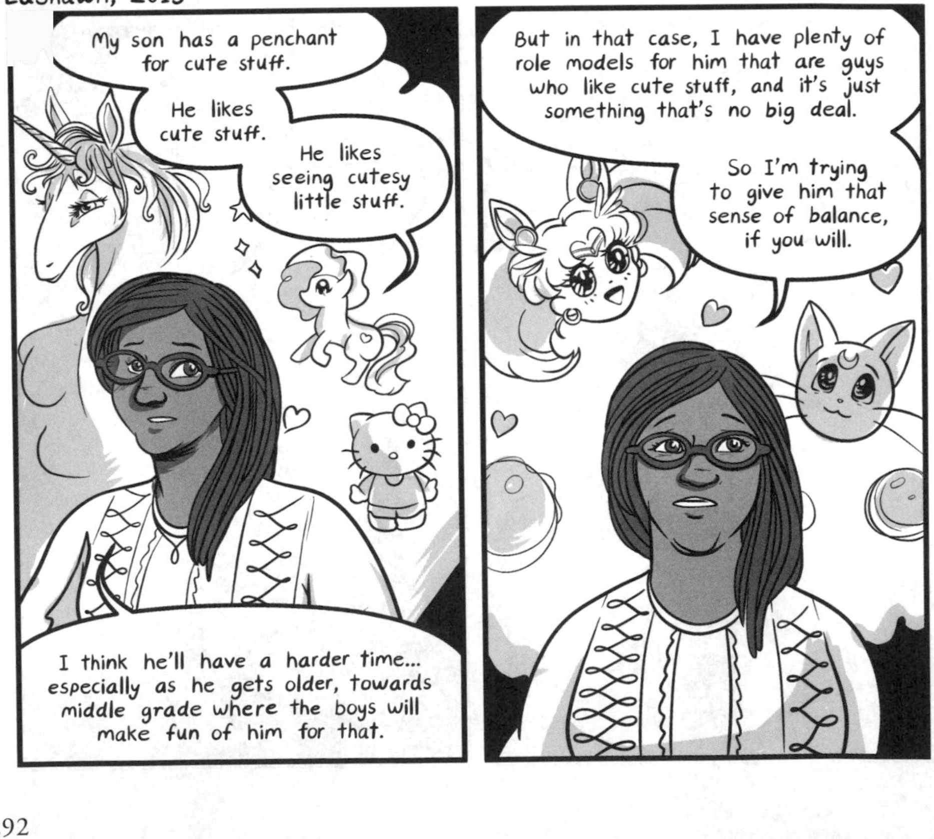
My son has a penchant for cute stuff.
He likes cute stuff.
He likes seeing cutesy little stuff.
I think he'll have a harder time... especially as he gets older, towards middle grade where the boys will make fun of him for that.
But in that case, I have plenty of role models for him that are guys who like cute stuff, and it's just something that's no big deal.
So I'm trying to give him that sense of balance, if you will.

Daiquiri, 2012

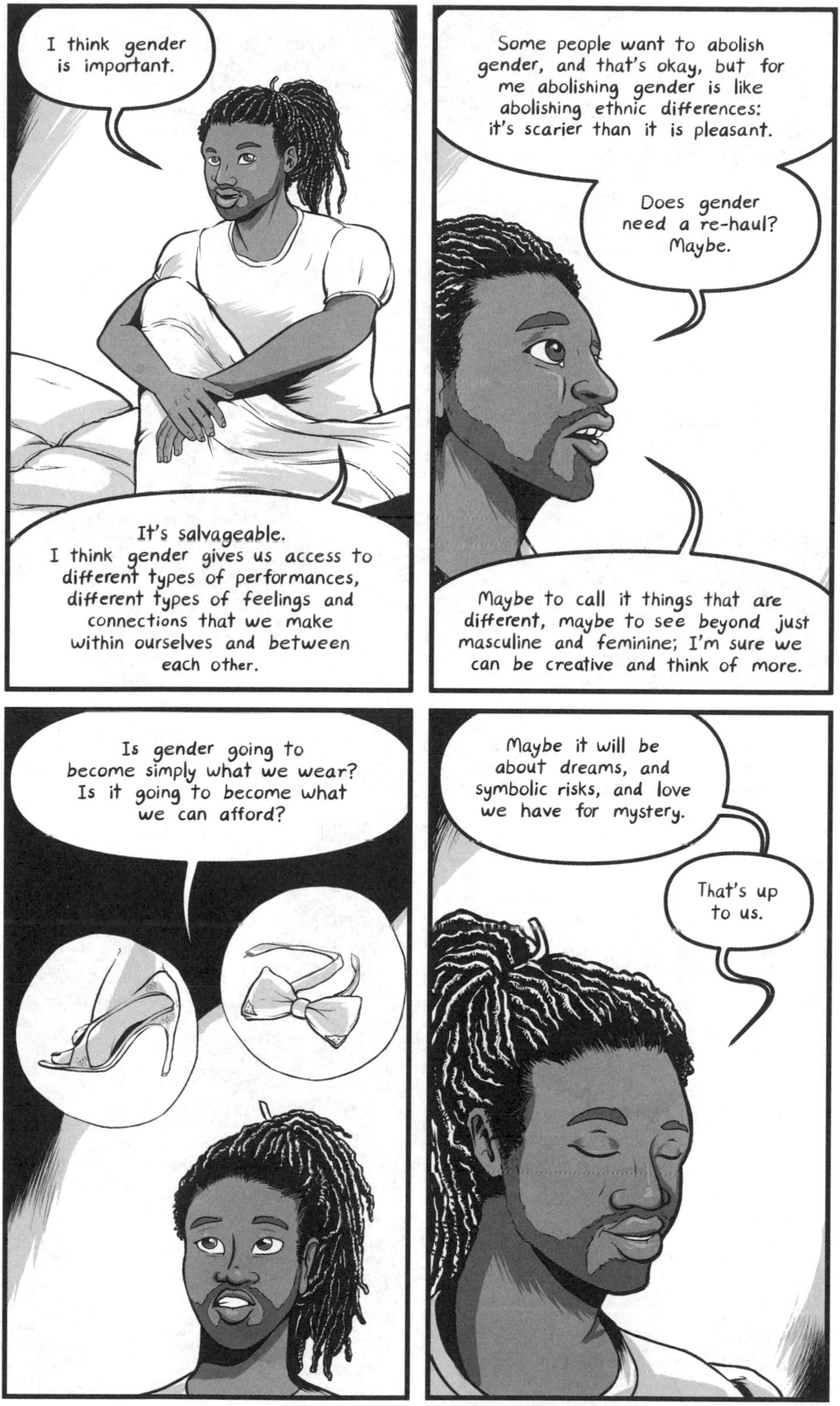
I think gender is important.
Some people want to abolish gender, and that's okay, but for me abolishing gender is like abolishing ethnic differences: it's scarier than it is pleasant.
It's salvageable. I think gender gives us access to different types of performances, different types of feelings and connections that we make within ourselves and between each other.
Does gender need a re-haul? Maybe.
Maybe to call it things that are different, maybe to see beyond just masculine and feminine; I'm sure we can be creative and think of more.
Is gender going to become simply what we wear? Is it going to become what we can afford?
Maybe it will be about dreams, and symbolic risks, and love we have for mystery.
That's up to us.

Ignacio, 2013

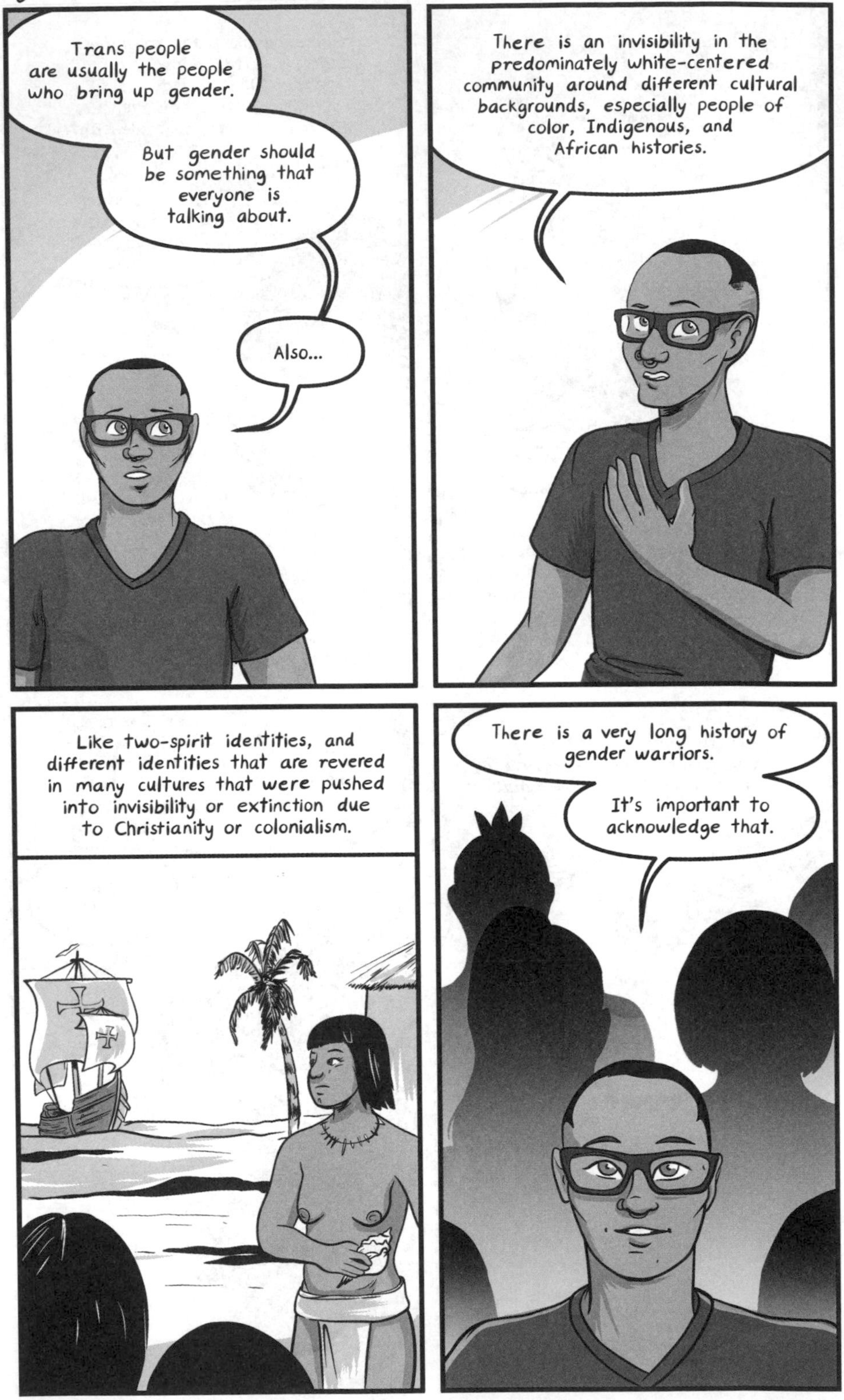
Trans people are usually the people who bring up gender.
But gender should be something that everyone is talking about.
Also...
There is an invisibility in the predominately white-centered community around different cultural backgrounds, especially people of color, Indigenous, and African histories.
Like two-spirit identities, and different identities that are revered in many cultures that were pushed into invisibility or extinction due to Christianity or colonialism.
There is a very long history of gender warriors.
It's important to acknowledge that.

Demari, 2012

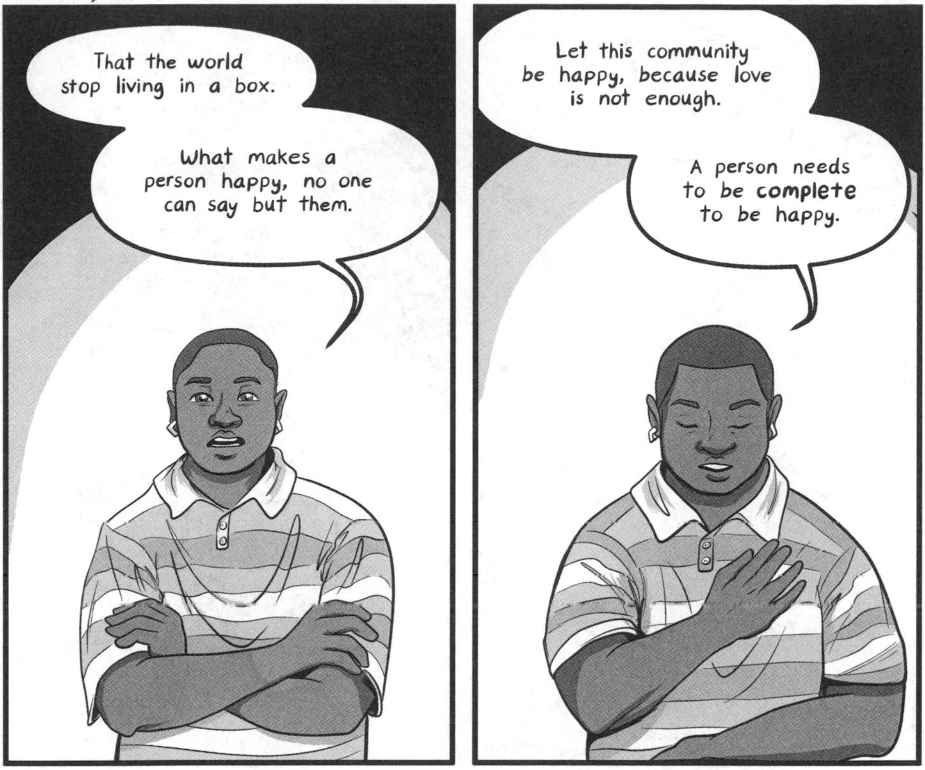
That the world stop living in a box.
What makes a person happy, no one can say but them.
Let this community be happy, because love is not enough.
A person needs to be **complete** to be happy.

Marie, 2012

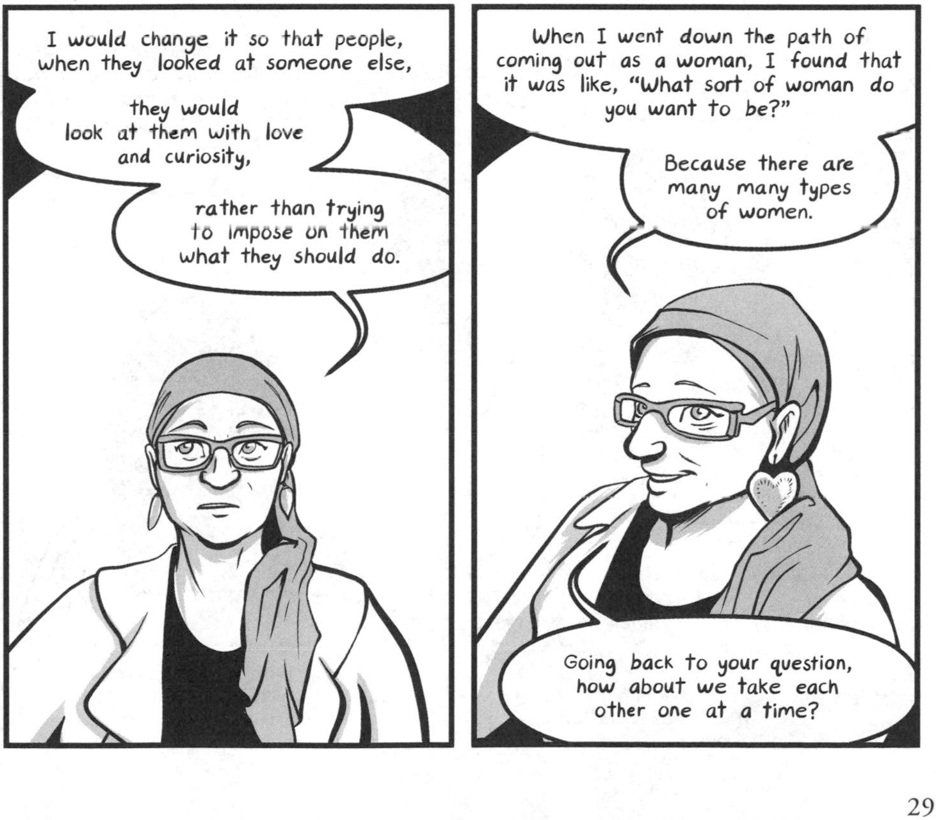
I would change it so that people, when they looked at someone else,
they would look at them with love and curiosity,
rather than trying to impose on them what they should do.
When I went down the path of coming out as a woman, I found that it was like, "What sort of woman do you want to be?"
Because there are many many types of women.
Going back to your question, how about we take each other one at a time?

"A Person," 2011

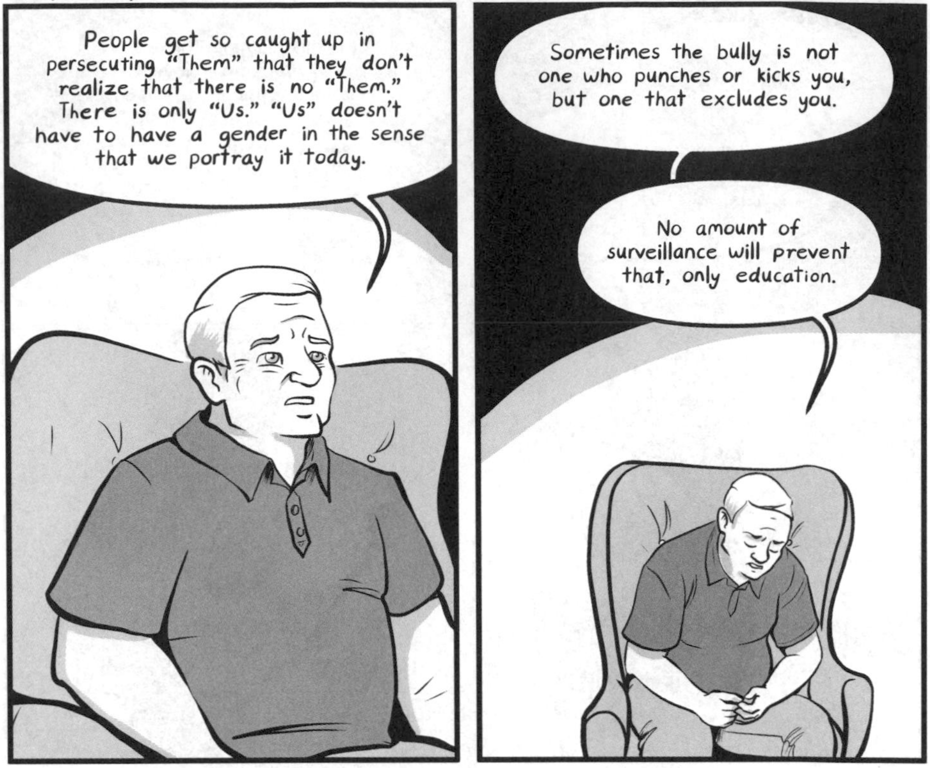
People get so caught up in persecuting "Them" that they don't realize that there is no "Them." There is only "Us." "Us" doesn't have to have a gender in the sense that we portray it today.
Sometimes the bully is not one who punches or kicks you, but one that excludes you.
No amount of surveillance will prevent that, only education.

LaShawn, 2013

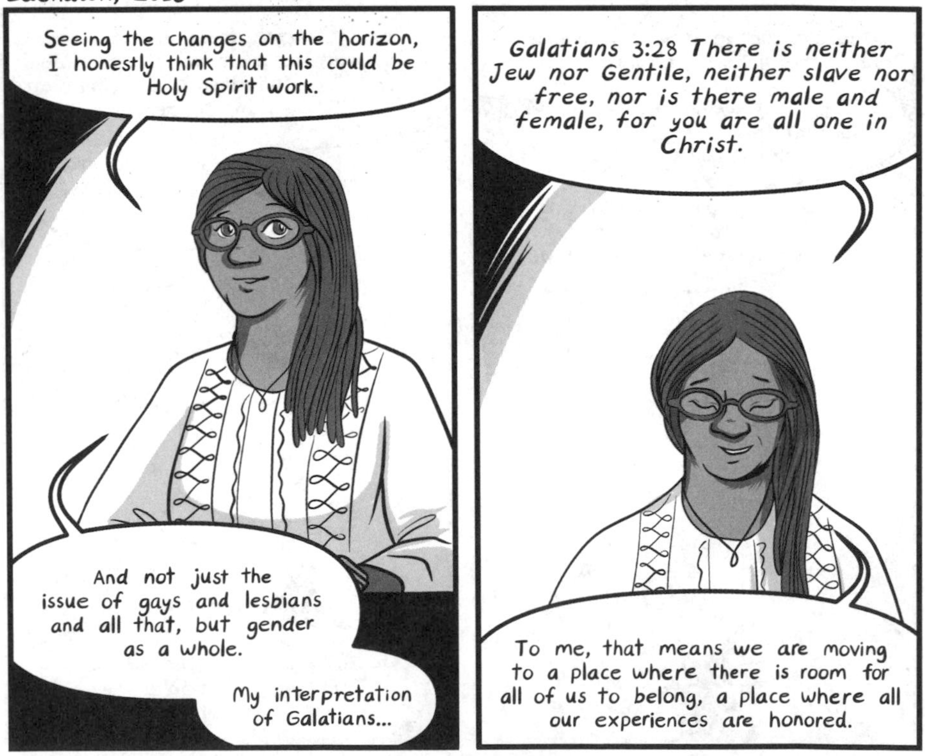
Seeing the changes on the horizon, I honestly think that this could be Holy Spirit work.
And not just the issue of gays and lesbians and all that, but gender as a whole.
My interpretation of Galatians...
Galatians 3:28 There is neither Jew nor Gentile, neither slave nor free, nor is there male and female, for you are all one in Christ.
To me, that means we are moving to a place where there is room for all of us to belong, a place where all our experiences are honored.

Anonymous, 2012

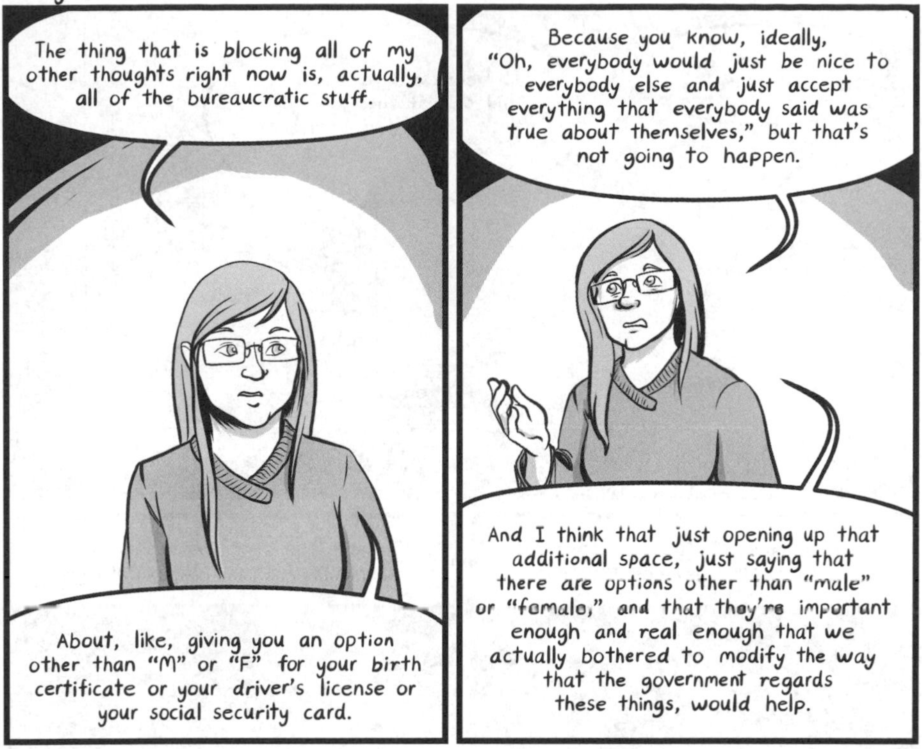
The thing that is blocking all of my other thoughts right now is, actually, all of the bureaucratic stuff.
About, like, giving you an option other than "M" or "F" for your birth certificate or your driver's license or your social security card.
Because you know, ideally, "Oh, everybody would just be nice to everybody else and just accept everything that everybody said was true about themselves," but that's not going to happen.
And I think that just opening up that additional space, just saying that there are options other than "male" or "female," and that they're important enough and real enough that we actually bothered to modify the way that the government regards these things, would help.

The Best Couple, 2014

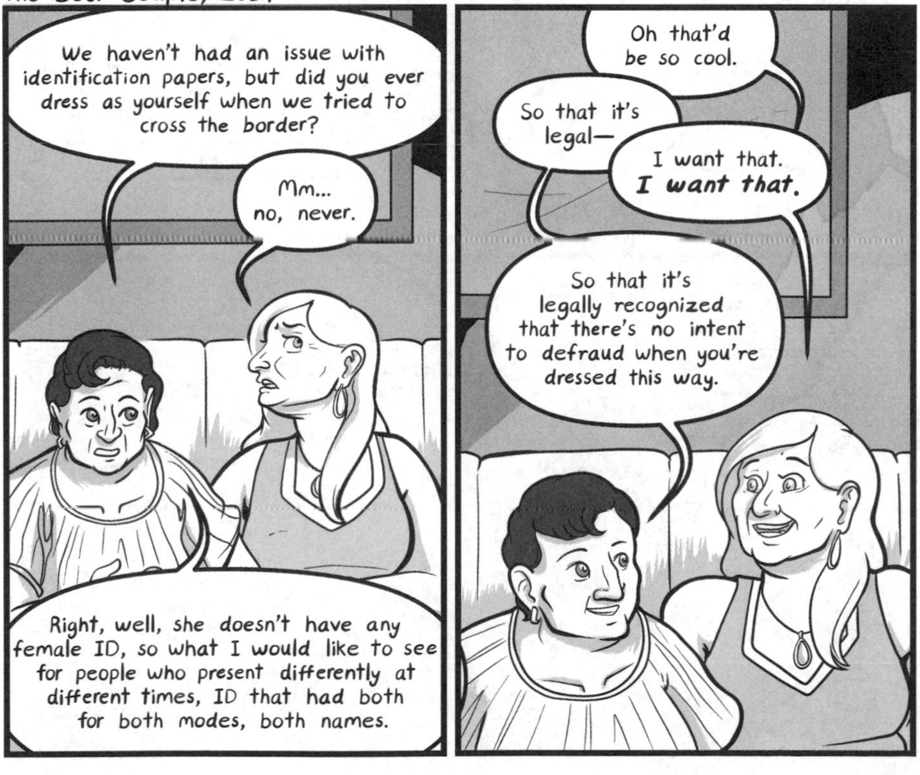
We haven't had an issue with identification papers, but did you ever dress as yourself when we tried to cross the border?
Mm... no, never.
Right, well, she doesn't have any female ID, so what I would like to see for people who present differently at different times, ID that had both for both modes, both names.
Oh that'd be so cool.
So that it's legal—
I want that. ***I want that.***
So that it's legally recognized that there's no intent to defraud when you're dressed this way.

Monei, 2016

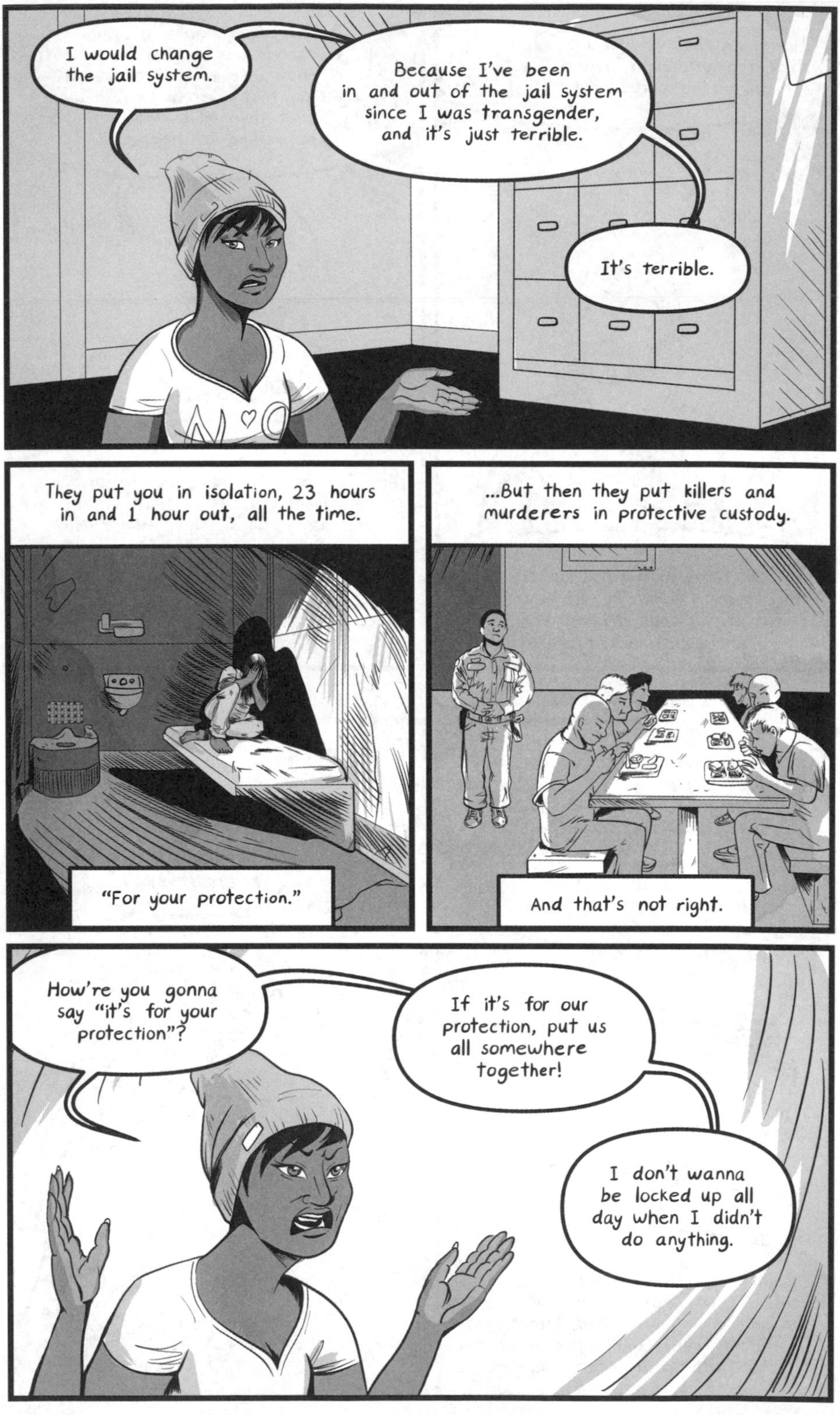
I would change the jail system.
Because I've been in and out of the jail system since I was transgender, and it's just terrible.
It's terrible.
They put you in isolation, 23 hours in and 1 hour out, all the time.
"For your protection."
...But then they put killers and murderers in protective custody.
And that's not right.
How're you gonna say "it's for your protection"?
If it's for our protection, put us all somewhere together!
I don't wanna be locked up all day when I didn't do anything.

Superheroine, 2016

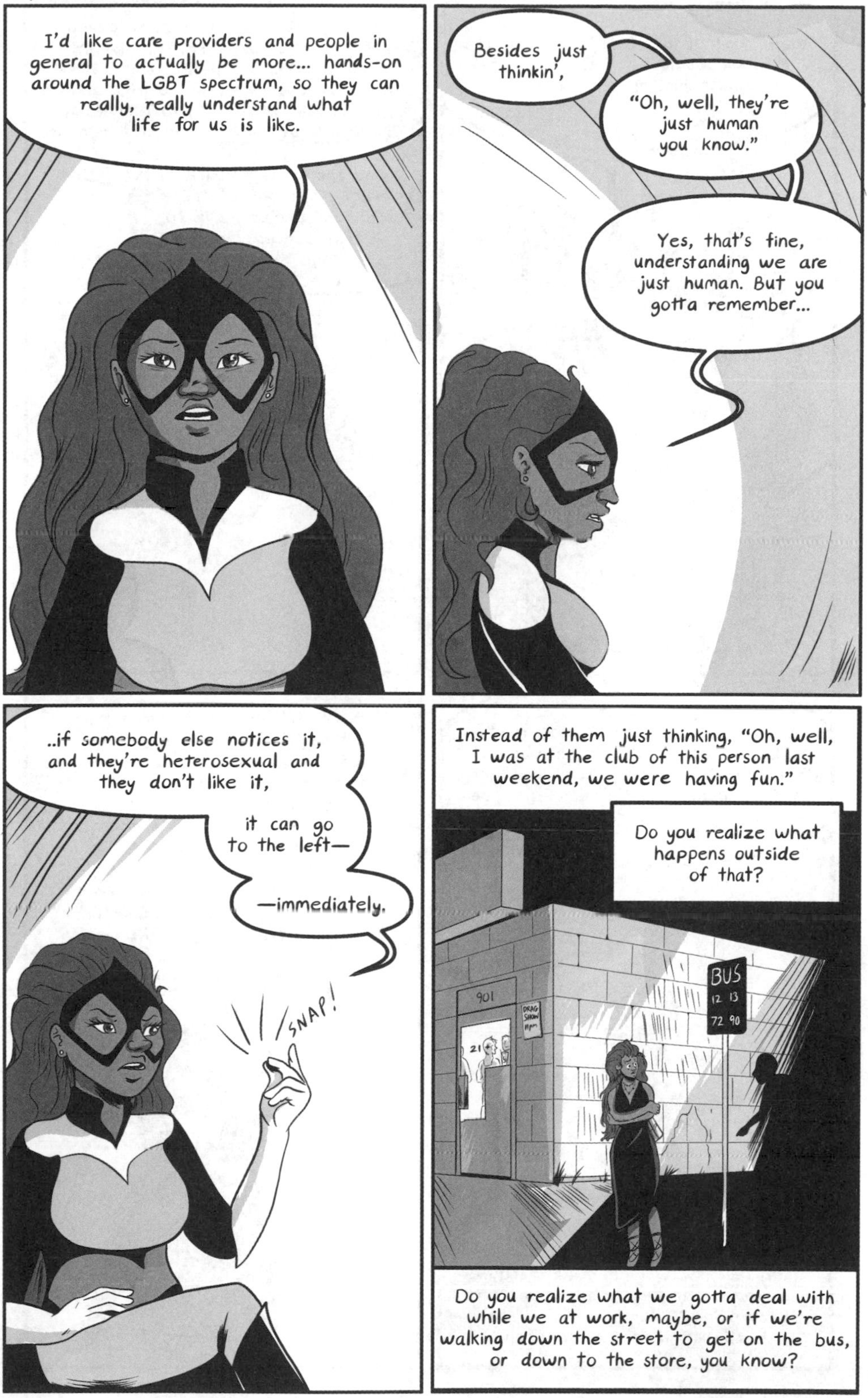

I'd like care providers and people in general to actually be more... hands-on around the LGBT spectrum, so they can really, really understand what life for us is like.
Besides just thinkin',
"Oh, well, they're just human you know."
Yes, that's fine, understanding we are just human. But you gotta remember...
..if somebody else notices it, and they're heterosexual and they don't like it,
it can go to the left—
—immediately.
SNAP!
Instead of them just thinking, "Oh, well, I was at the club of this person last weekend, we were having fun."
Do you realize what happens outside of that?
BUS
12 13
72 90
901
DRAG SHOW
21
Do you realize what we gotta deal with while we at work, maybe, or if we're walking down the street to get on the bus, or down to the store, you know?

Anne, 2012

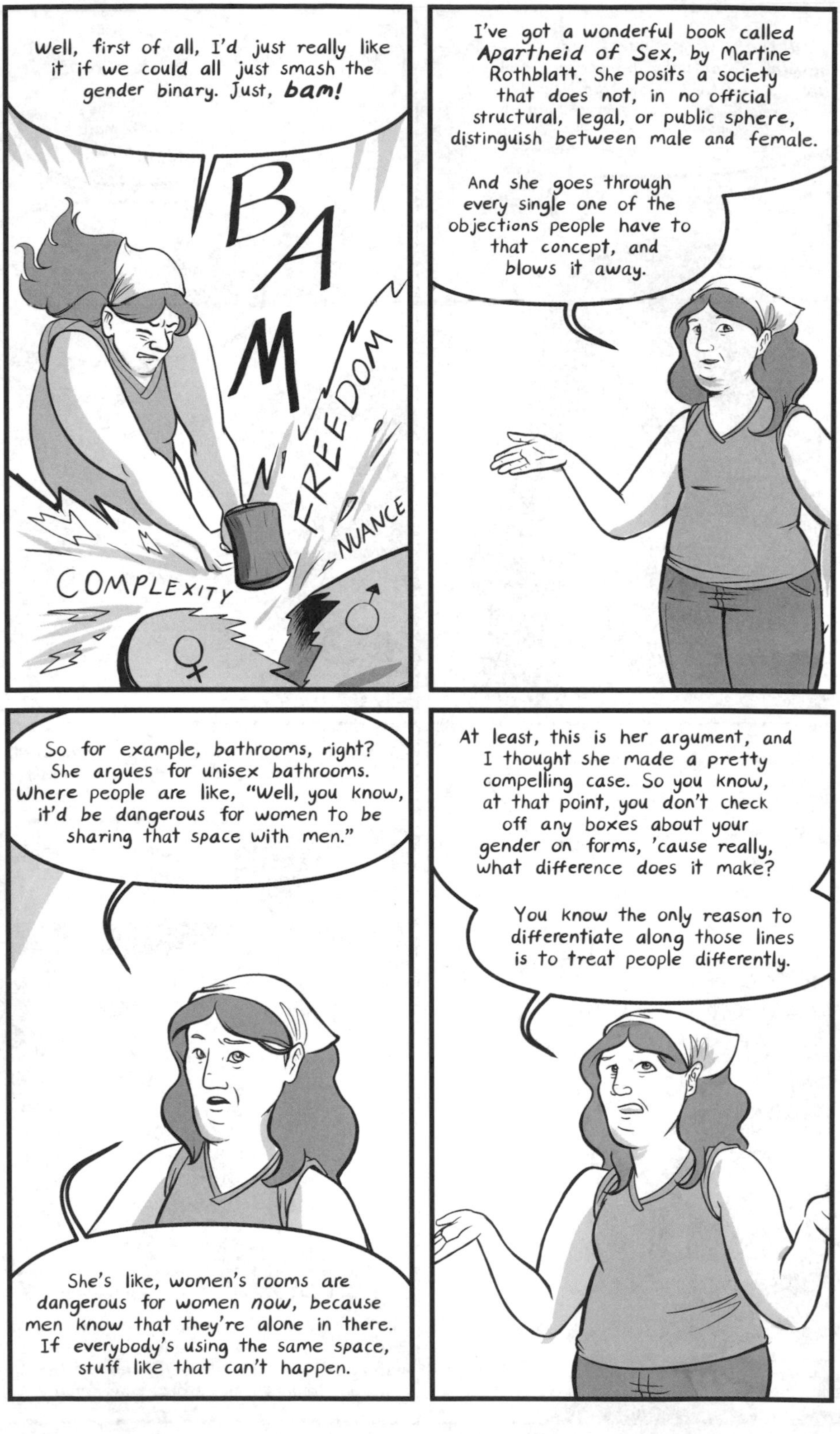
Well, first of all, I'd just really like it if we could all just smash the gender binary. Just, *bam!*
BAM
FREEDOM
NUANCE
COMPLEXITY
I've got a wonderful book called *Apartheid of Sex*, by Martine Rothblatt. She posits a society that does not, in no official structural, legal, or public sphere, distinguish between male and female.
And she goes through every single one of the objections people have to that concept, and blows it away.
So for example, bathrooms, right? She argues for unisex bathrooms. Where people are like, "Well, you know, it'd be dangerous for women to be sharing that space with men."
She's like, women's rooms are dangerous for women *now*, because men know that they're alone in there. If everybody's using the same space, stuff like that can't happen.
At least, this is her argument, and I thought she made a pretty compelling case. So you know, at that point, you don't check off any boxes about your gender on forms, 'cause really, what difference does it make?
You know the only reason to differentiate along those lines is to treat people differently.

Enne, 2013

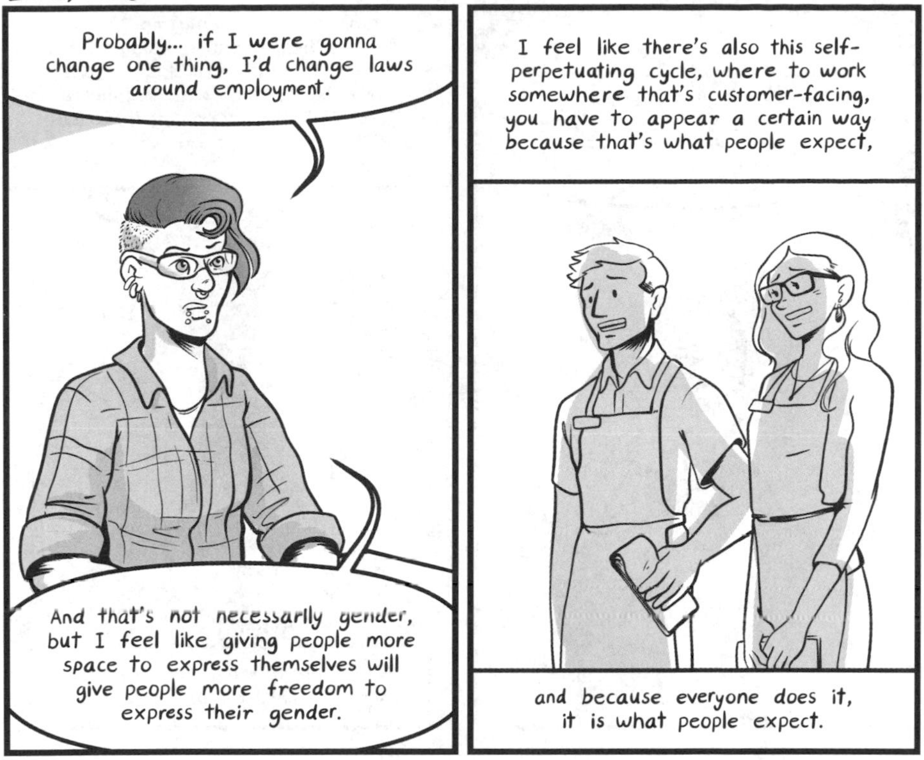
Probably... if I were gonna change one thing, I'd change laws around employment.
And that's not necessarily gender, but I feel like giving people more space to express themselves will give people more freedom to express their gender.
I feel like there's also this self-perpetuating cycle, where to work somewhere that's customer-facing, you have to appear a certain way because that's what people expect,
and because everyone does it, it is what people expect.

Mo, 2013

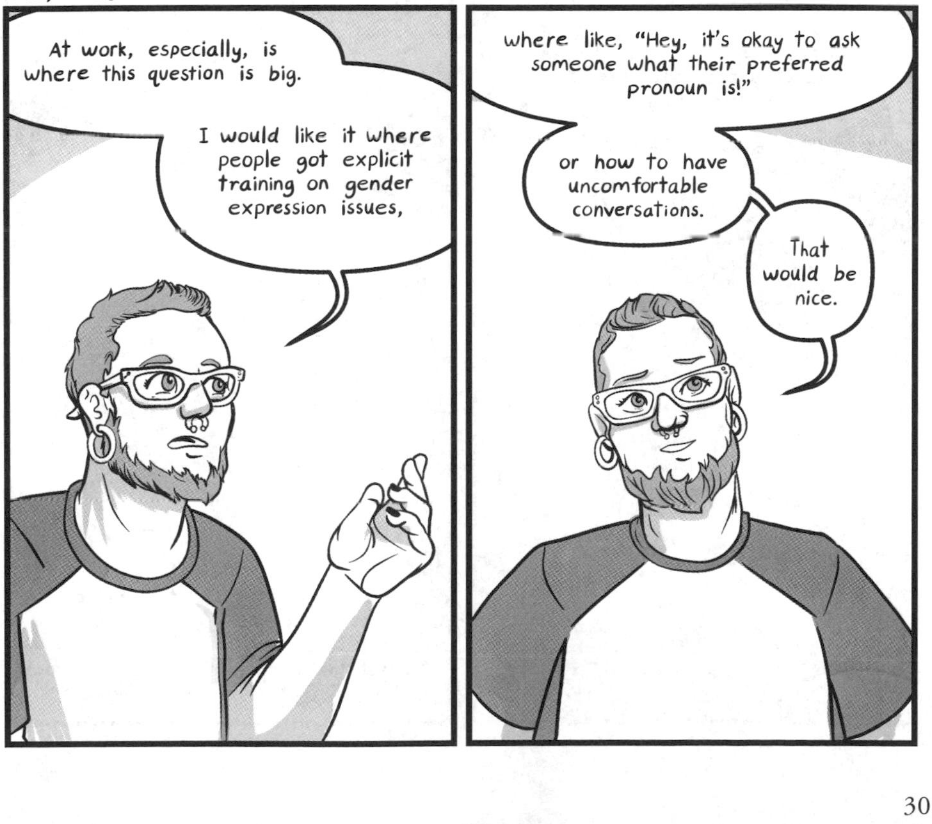
At work, especially, is where this question is big.
I would like it where people got explicit training on gender expression issues,
where like, "Hey, it's okay to ask someone what their preferred pronoun is!"
or how to have uncomfortable conversations.
That would be nice.

Gerbil, 2012

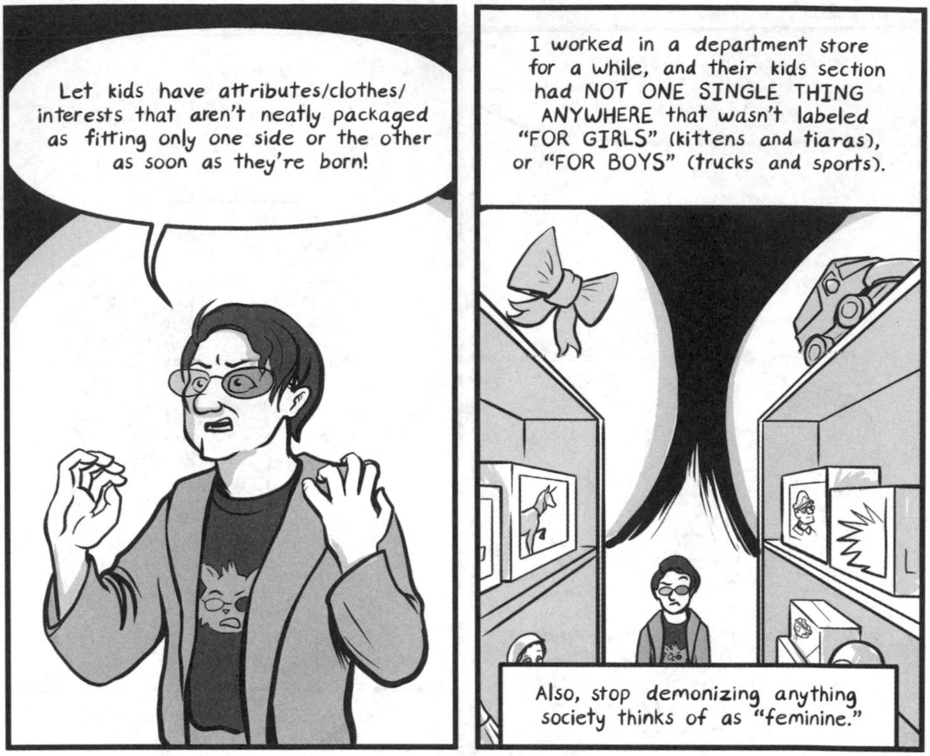
Let kids have attributes/clothes/ interests that aren't neatly packaged as fitting only one side or the other as soon as they're born!
I worked in a department store for a while, and their kids section had NOT ONE SINGLE THING ANYWHERE that wasn't labeled "FOR GIRLS" (kittens and tiaras), or "FOR BOYS" (trucks and sports).
Also, stop demonizing anything society thinks of as "feminine."

Corrine, 2012

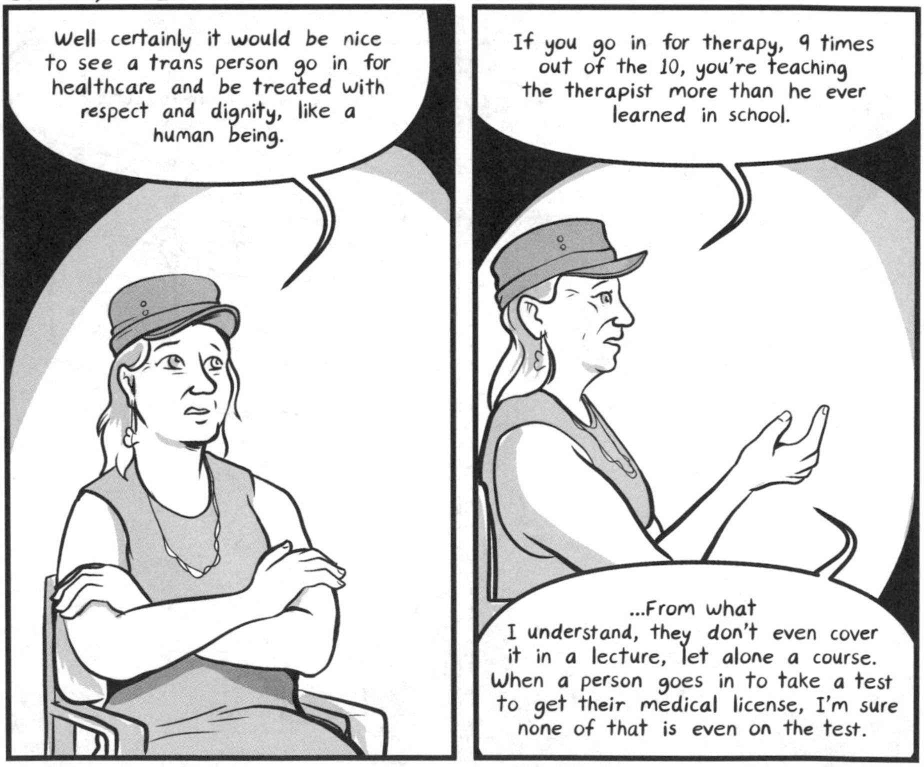
Well certainly it would be nice to see a trans person go in for healthcare and be treated with respect and dignity, like a human being.
If you go in for therapy, 9 times out of the 10, you're teaching the therapist more than he ever learned in school.
...From what I understand, they don't even cover it in a lecture, let alone a course. When a person goes in to take a test to get their medical license, I'm sure none of that is even on the test.

Lex, 2013

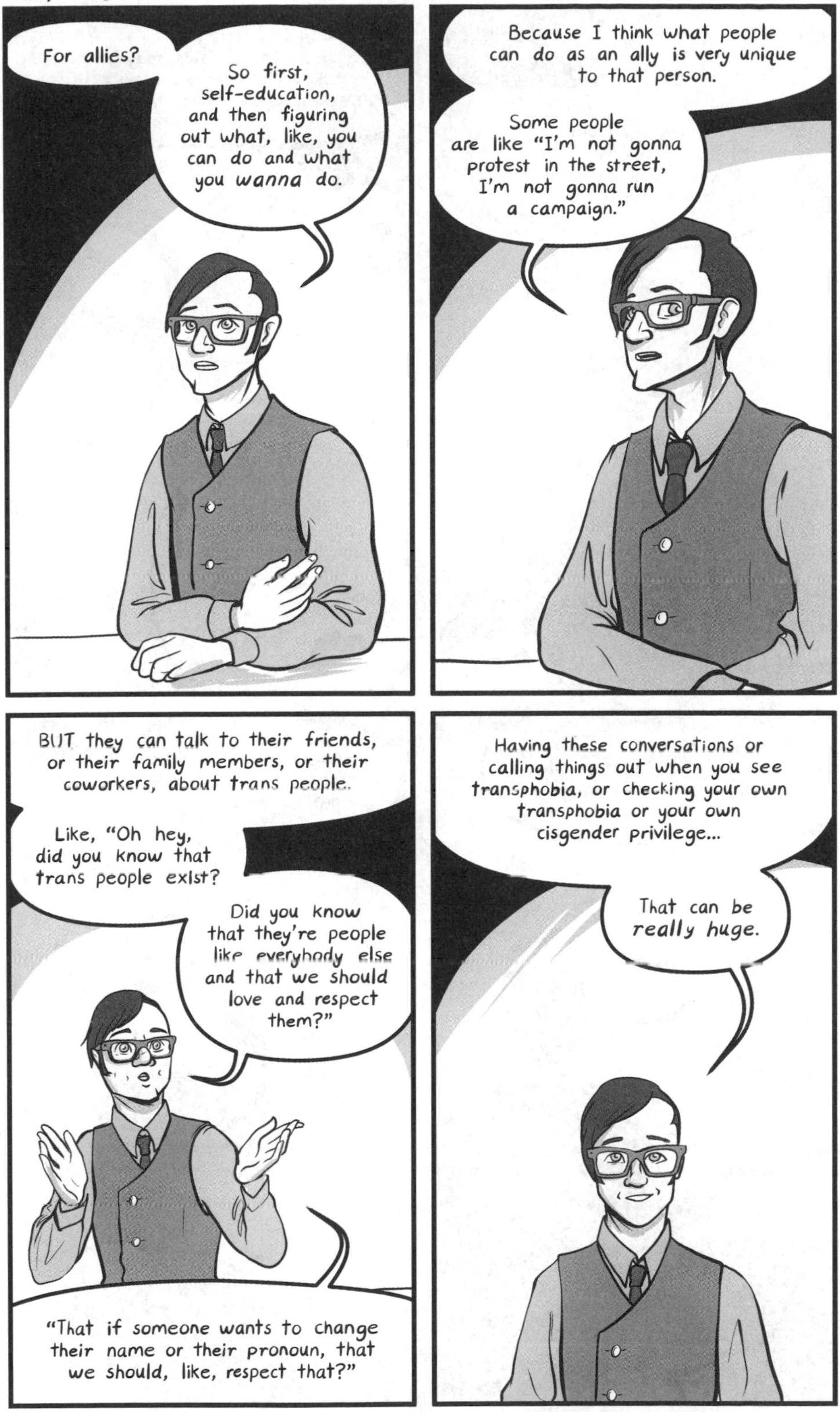
For allies?
So first, self-education, and then figuring out what, like, you can do and what you *wanna* do.
Because I think what people can do as an ally is very unique to that person.
Some people are like "I'm not gonna protest in the street, I'm not gonna run a campaign."
BUT they can talk to their friends, or their family members, or their coworkers, about trans people.
Like, "Oh hey, did you know that trans people exist?
Did you know that they're people like everybody else and that we should love and respect them?"
"That if someone wants to change their name or their pronoun, that we should, like, respect that?"
Having these conversations or calling things out when you see transphobia, or checking your own transphobia or your own cisgender privilege...
That can be *really huge*.

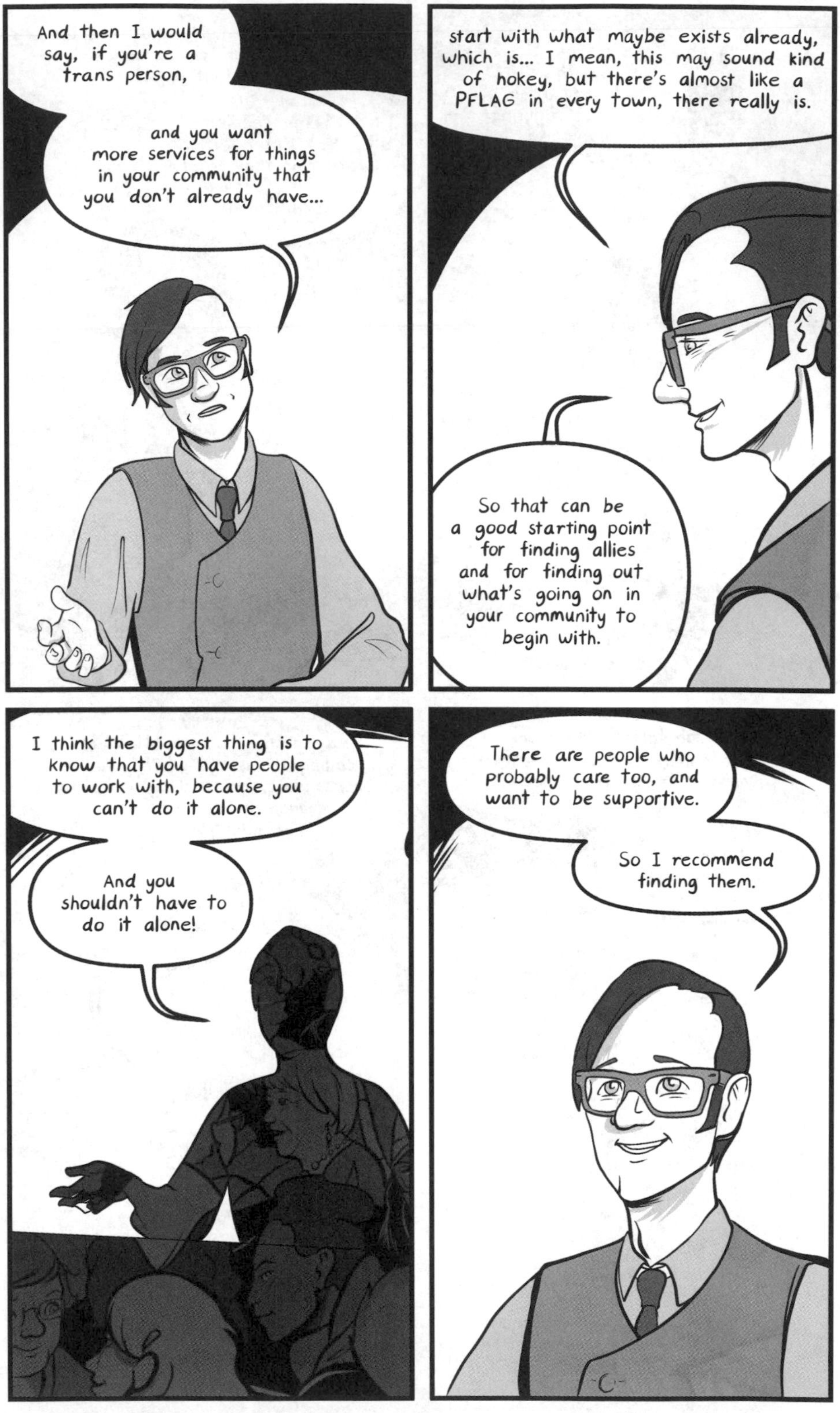
And then I would say, if you're a trans person,
and you want more services for things in your community that you don't already have...
start with what maybe exists already, which is... I mean, this may sound kind of hokey, but there's almost like a PFLAG in every town, there really is.
So that can be a good starting point for finding allies and for finding out what's going on in your community to begin with.
I think the biggest thing is to know that you have people to work with, because you can't do it alone.
And you shouldn't have to do it alone!
There are people who probably care too, and want to be supportive.
So I recommend finding them.

JAC, 2013

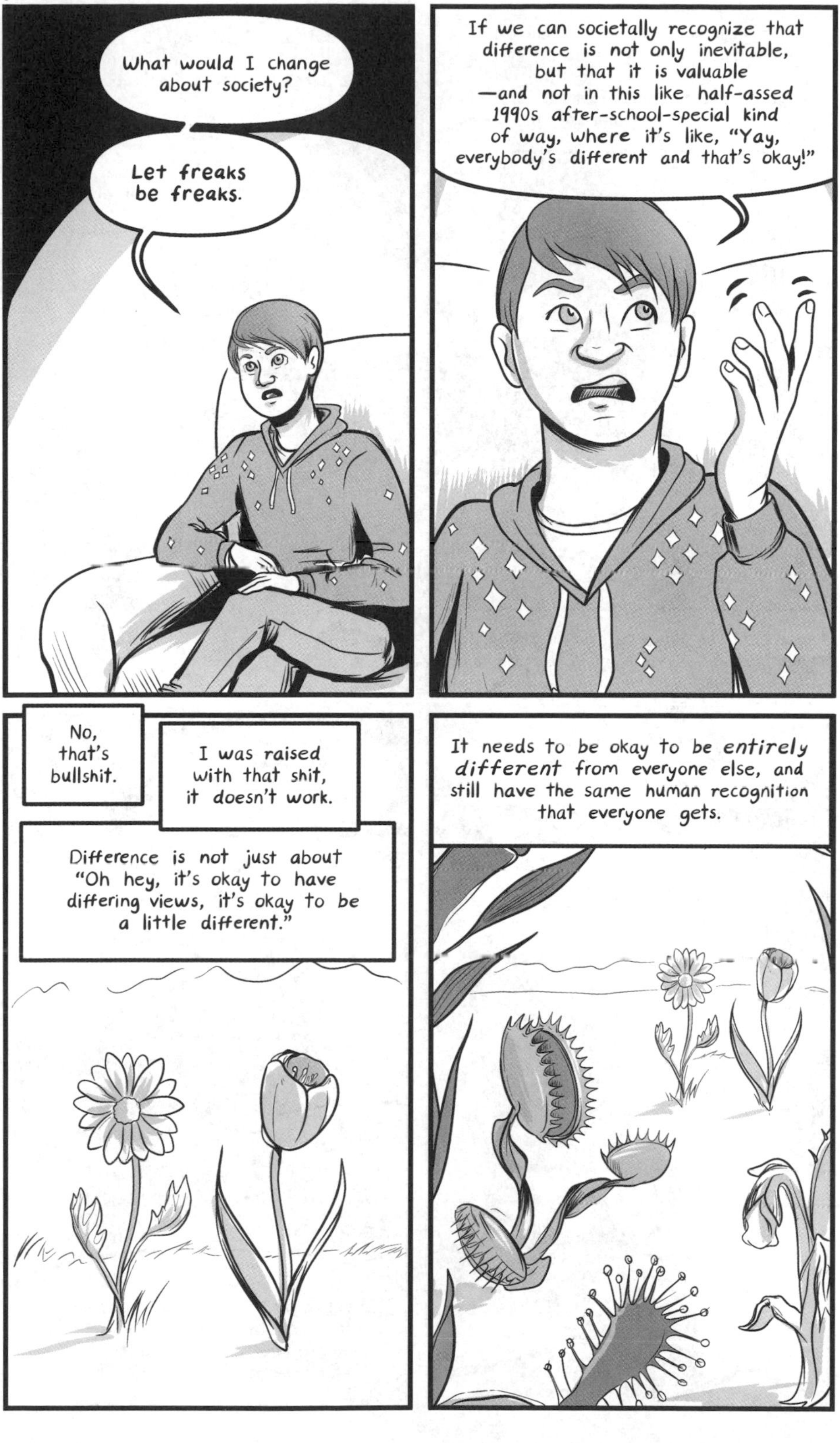
What would I change about society?
Let freaks be freaks.
If we can societally recognize that difference is not only inevitable, but that it is valuable —and not in this like half-assed 1990s after-school-special kind of way, where it's like, "Yay, everybody's different and that's okay!"
No, that's bullshit.
I was raised with that shit, it doesn't work.
Difference is not just about "Oh hey, it's okay to have differing views, it's okay to be a little different."
It needs to be okay to be *entirely different* from everyone else, and still have the same human recognition that everyone gets.

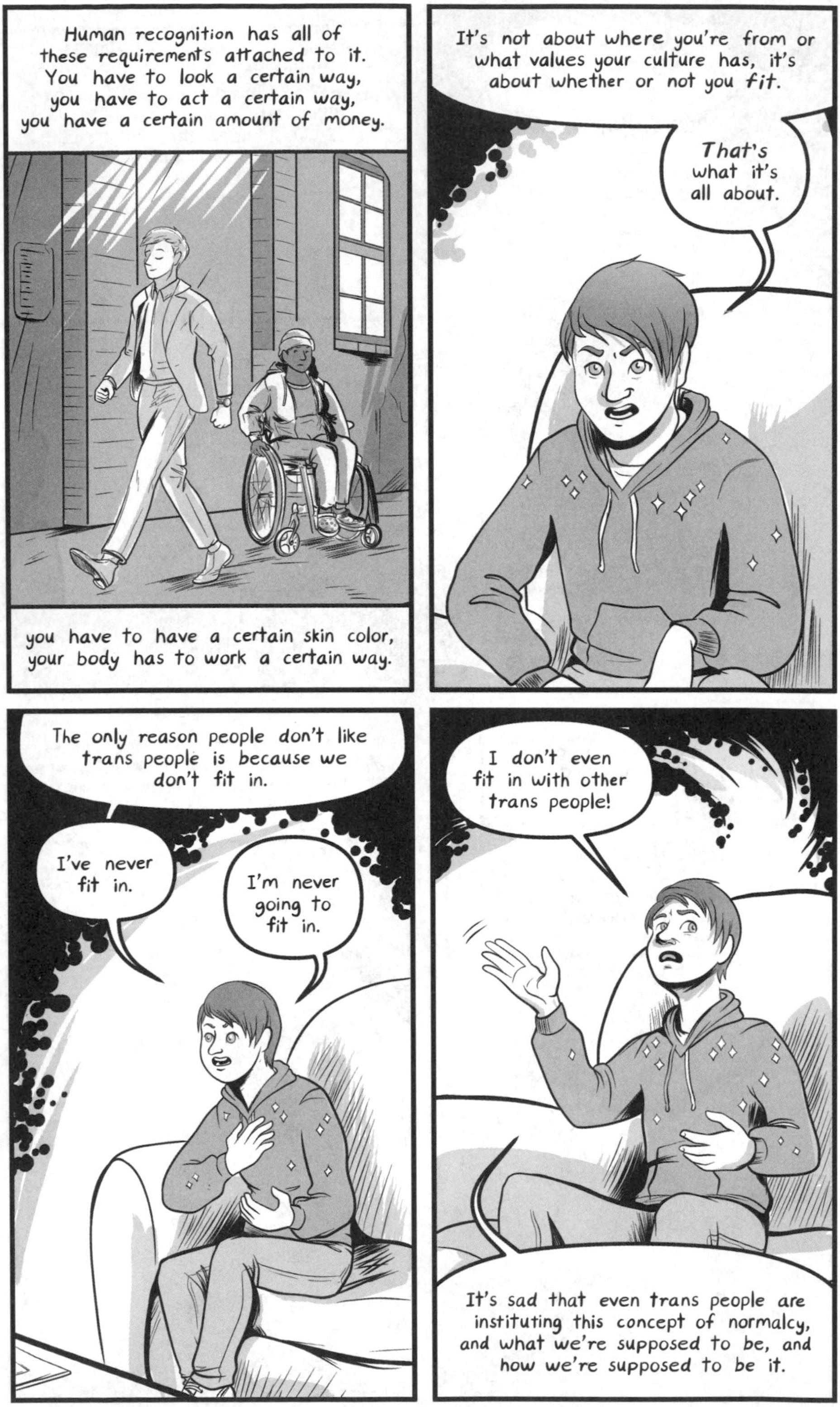
Human recognition has all of these requirements attached to it. You have to look a certain way, you have to act a certain way, you have a certain amount of money.
you have to have a certain skin color, your body has to work a certain way.
It's not about where you're from or what values your culture has, it's about whether or not you *fit*.
That's what it's all about.
The only reason people don't like trans people is because we don't fit in.
I've never fit in.
I'm never going to fit in.
I don't even fit in with other trans people!
It's sad that even trans people are instituting this concept of normalcy, and what we're supposed to be, and how we're supposed to be it.

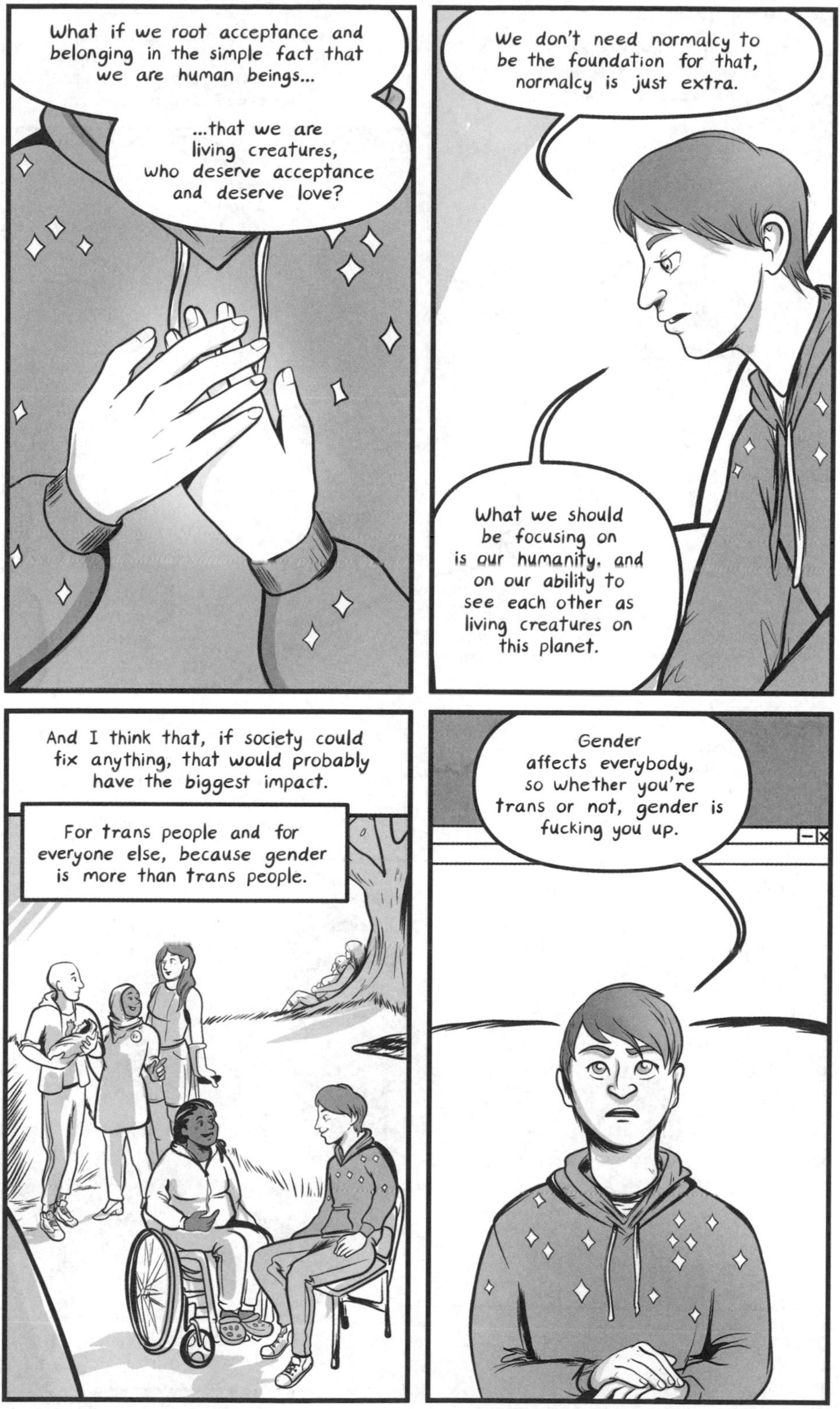
What if we root acceptance and belonging in the simple fact that we are human beings...
...that we are living creatures, who deserve acceptance and deserve love?
We don't need normalcy to be the foundation for that, normalcy is just extra.
What we should be focusing on is our humanity, and on our ability to see each other as living creatures on this planet.
And I think that, if society could fix anything, that would probably have the biggest impact.
For trans people and for everyone else, because gender is more than trans people.
Gender affects everybody, so whether you're trans or not, gender is fucking you up.

Rhea, 2019

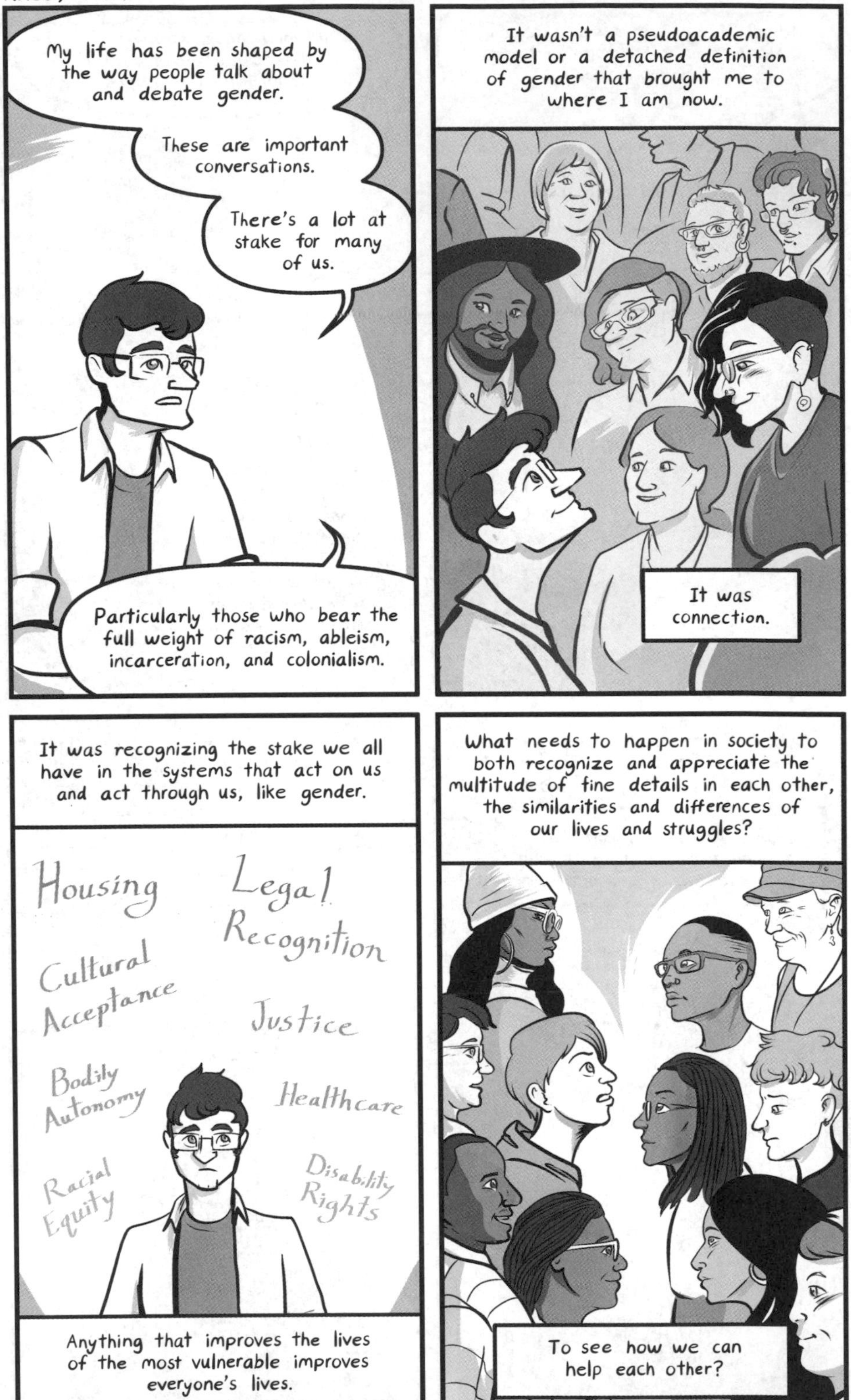
My life has been shaped by the way people talk about and debate gender.
These are important conversations.
There's a lot at stake for many of us.
Particularly those who bear the full weight of racism, ableism, incarceration, and colonialism.
It wasn't a pseudoacademic model or a detached definition of gender that brought me to where I am now.
It was connection.
It was recognizing the stake we all have in the systems that act on us and act through us, like gender.
Housing
Legal Recognition
Cultural Acceptance
Justice
Bodily Autonomy
Healthcare
Racial Equity
Disability Rights
Anything that improves the lives of the most vulnerable improves everyone's lives.
What needs to happen in society to both recognize and appreciate the multitude of fine details in each other, the similarities and differences of our lives and struggles?
To see how we can help each other?

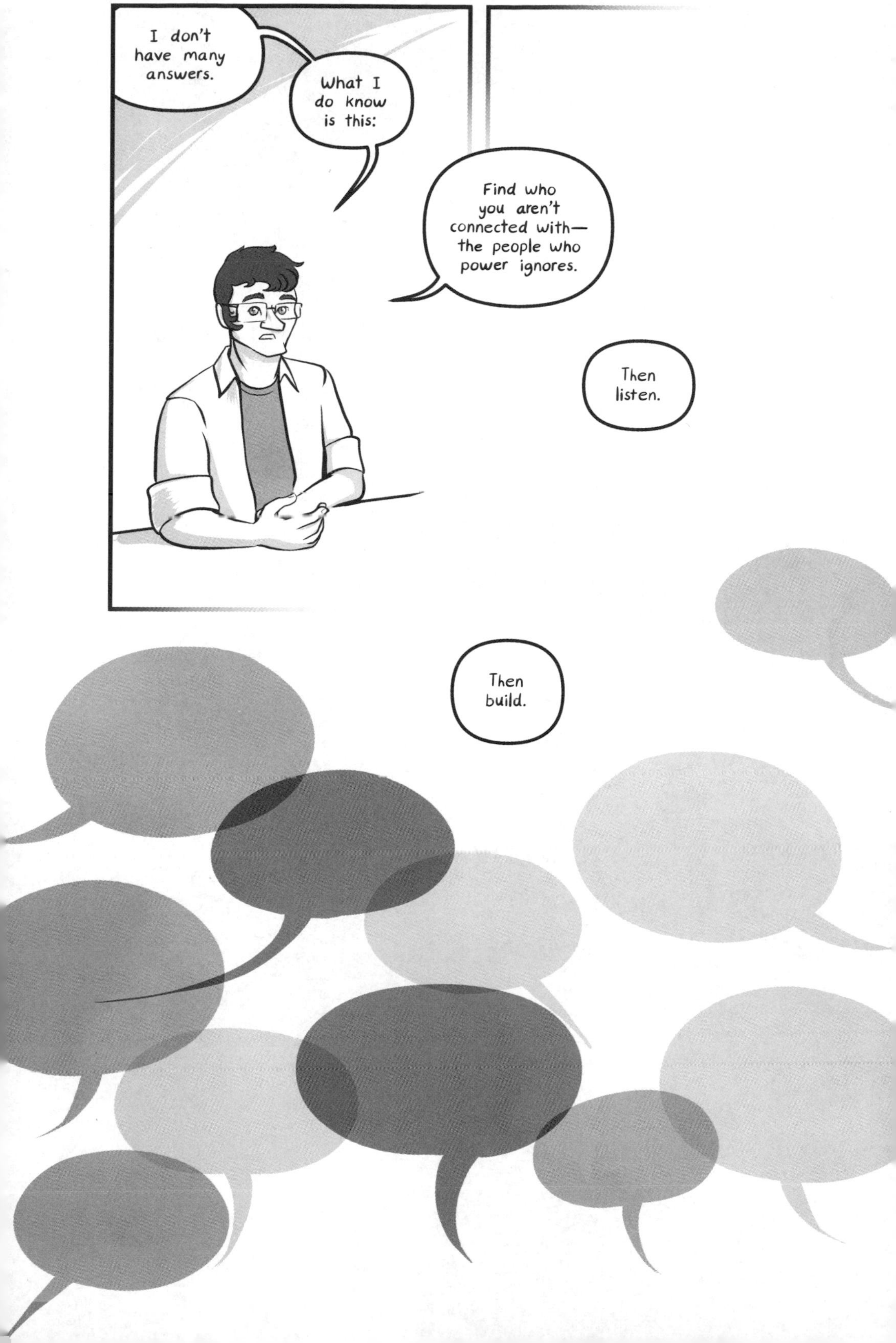
I don't have many answers.
What I do know is this:
Find who you aren't connected with— the people who power ignores.
Then listen.
Then build.

ACKNOWLEDGMENTS

I owe my deepest thanks . . .

To all the fantastic, generous, and brilliant people who sat and interviewed with me. I'm honored to have been trusted with your truths. You have all changed my life for the better.

To my inkers and art assistants, 19 and Sally Scott, whose encouragement and skill made this book possible and pushed me to keep working on it, even when I felt hopeless.

To my agent, Anjali, who pushed me to make the book the best it can be and found it a home.

To the incredible publishing team I was privileged to work with for this book. Marie for believing in and championing the project, and Gina for gently coaxing me into vulnerability and clarity, and to Anna, Amy, Ashley, Cordelia, Nick, and Yang for making the book shine.

To my parents, who let me live with them and supported me when I needed it. You're both incredible humans, and I'm glad you're in my life. This book would not have been possible without you.

To my friends, especially Mark and Kelly and Jess, who know me best of all. Thank you for your support, insight, and laughter over the years. Thanks for always encouraging me on this book, even when it took years longer than I first thought.

To Ezra, my incredible spouse and love of my life. Thank you for inviting me to be my best and most authentic self. Thank you for being vulnerable in my book, even when it's a little embarrassing. Thank you for telling me what you need to be safe in this together. I can't wait to tell the next story.

NOTES

HOW DO YOU KNOW WHAT TO CALL YOURSELF

1   These three landscapes are from areas where I grew up, in Kentucky and Wisconsin. I think our sense of place can deeply inform our identities and experiences, so I wanted to start with these three images.

7   And now we meet some of our characters. I developed each person's appearance in the book a little differently. Early on, I lacked the foresight to ask to sketch or photograph people at the time of our interview, which led to some awkwardness. My favorite portraits are the ones I was able to develop from snapshots I took of people during their interviews. Surprisingly, it was the folks who wanted to be very anonymous who were the most challenging to draw. Each anonymous person needed a character that roughly represented key aspects of who they are—their age, race, ability, build, fashion, etc.—but would still be different enough as to be unrecognizable.

FEMININITY

23   I juxtaposed these two answers to show how both can be true at once. Kai and Kim have a lot in common but are from different geographic areas and are different ages. Expectations around gender shift wildly between places, cultures, and times.

MASCULINITY

35   Erin Horáková describes the shift from the original portrayal of Captain Kirk versus what we remember of Kirk today in the essay "Freshly Remember'd: Kirk Drift" (*Strange Horizons*, no. 10, April 2017). Horáková's essay is a valuable insight into the way specific images of James T. Kirk have been taken out of their original context to be used

to uphold particular visions of toxic masculinity, while ignoring original aspects of his character that challenge toxic masculinity. Regardless of their accuracy to the original *Star Trek* series, J's life has been shaped by these images and rememberings of masculinity, so I decided to include them in this book, but I would encourage readers to consider what our culture likes to remember about media from the past and what gets ignored.

RACE

51   I just want to acknowledge the extra work Ignacio did here to educate me and help me find appropriate images for these pages.

52   Transgender Day of Remembrance is an annual vigil for transgender people who have been murdered due to transphobia. Overwhelmingly these victims are women of color. The women depicted in panel 4 were killed in 2012. Their names are Brandy Martell (37, Oakland, CA), Deja Jones (33, Miami, FL), Tiffany Gooden (19, Chicago, IL), and Tyrell Jackson (23, Riviera Beach, FL). May they rest in power.

BODY FEELINGS

81   I spent most of my childhood in Kentucky absolutely covered in mosquito bites, if you're wondering what those marks on my legs in panel 2 are about. As for panel 5, I know someone is going to wonder, so I'll just say it here: While I was sometimes more aware of interest from adults than I would have preferred, I was never sexually assaulted as a child. It's weird to have to say that, but since there are people who believe (wrongly) that being transgender is caused by childhood trauma, it seems important to clarify.

    As an aside, it's interesting to me how many assumptions about the "causes" of being transgender echo the homophobic arguments about the "causes" of homosexuality that I remember while I was growing up in the '90s and early '00s.

84   The Goddess image here is inspired largely by the sculpture *The Millennial Gaia* by artist Oberon Zell, created in 1998.

HORMONES

130 Fun fact: We didn't kiss until our third or fourth date because I was so terrified that I would turn out to be straight after all, and then I wouldn't get to keep going out with this amazing and extremely attractive person! Very silly, but hindsight is 20/20.

HOUSING

224 Some folks (including me) find aromatherapy helpful for managing stress . . . but lavender oil is a poor substitute for harassment-free access to public facilities.

QUEER COMMUNITY

260 The person on stage in panel 2 is one of my favorite musicians, Gaelynn Lea.

268 The communities depicted here are entirely fictional. Unfortunately, the stories they are based on are not.

275 The people depicted in panel 3 represent people who exist outside the gender binary in various cultures, such as the *hijra* in India, *burrnesha* in Albania, *fa'afafine* of Samoa, and two-spirit people of various Indigenous North American tribes.

There are also drawings of specific transgender historical figures, including Willmer Broadnax, Lucy Hicks Anderson, the Chevalier d'Éon, Dr. James Barry, and Alan L. Hart.

Panel 4 depicts Lou Sullivan, Miss Major Griffin-Gracy, Sylvia Rivera, and Marsha P. Johnson.

WHAT WE BUILD

286 My own wedding is a nice way to wrap up my story in this project, but it is important to note that marriage is not the only, or even most important, relationship or life marker a person could have. Many queer and trans people do not choose this path, and I think marriage as a cultural and legal institution is limited in its ability to acknowledge the broad

network of familial and found-family relationships queer, trans, and even straight cis people form. Events of joy and community connection heal the world, but they don't have to be weddings.

Not everyone whom I interviewed became a close friend, due in no small part to my own awkwardness and social anxiety. The fact that I was able to gather such a supportive and wonderful network around me despite my tendency to isolate myself is a testament to the way trans and queer people seek each other out and find ways to support one another.

289 This page is all anachronistic symbolism. I wanted to capture the way that all of these connections have strengthened and improved my life, and how my interviewees are all continuing to create new constructions of gender.

296 LaShawn asked to clarify that this verse has been used to erase and harm people, and that she disagrees with such interpretations of the verse. She writes: "I am fully aware that the Bible verse I quoted from Galatians has been used to erase experiences and history of those of Jewish descent, as well as gender. I hope that my interpretation is able to clarify that those experiences are deeply valued."

BIBLIOGRAPHY

Romero, Adam P., Shoshana K. Goldberg, and Luis A. Vasquez. *LGBT People and Housing Affordability, Discrimination, and Homelessness.* Los Angeles: The Williams Institute, 2020. https://williamsinstitute.law.ucla.edu/publications/lgbt-housing-instability/.

Morton, Matthew H., Amy Dworsky, and Gina M. Samuels. *Missed Opportunities: Youth Homelessness in America, National Estimates.* Chicago: Chapin Hall at the University of Chicago, 2017. https://voicesofyouthcount.org/brief/national-estimates-of-youth-homelessness/.

National Coalition for the Homeless. *LGBTQ Homelessness.* Washington, DC: National Coalition for the Homeless, 2017. https://nationalhomeless.org/wp-content/uploads/2017/06/LGBTQ-Homelessness.pdf.

National Alliance to End Homelessness. *Transgender Homeless Adults & Unsheltered Homelessness: What the Data Tell Us.* Washington, DC: National Alliance to End Homelessness, 2020. https://endhomelessness.org/resource/transgender-homeless-adults-unsheltered-homelessness-what-the-data-tell-us/.

Quintana, Nico Sifra, Josh Rosenthal, and Jeff Krehely. *On the Streets: The Federal Response to Gay and Transgender Homeless Youth.* Washington, DC: Center for American Progress, 2010. https://cdn.americanprogress.org/wp-content/uploads/issues/2010/06/pdf/lgbtyouthhomelessness.pdf?_ga=2.9804210.669032182.1624547272-47732862.1624547272.

Abramovich, Alex, and Jama Shelton, eds. *Where Am I Going to Go? Intersectional Approaches to Ending LGBTQ2S Youth Homelessness in Canada & the U.S.* Toronto: Canadian Observatory on Homelessness Press, 2017. Digital book. https://www.homelesshub.ca/WhereAmIGoingToGo.

Choi, Soon Kyu, Bianca D. M. Wilson, Jama Shelton, and Gary Gates. *Serving Our Youth 2015: The Needs and Experiences of Lesbian, Gay, Bisexual, Transgender, and Questioning Youth Experiencing Homelessness.* Los Angeles: The Williams Institute with True Colors Fund, 2015. https://williamsinstitute.law.ucla.edu/publications/serving-our-youth -lgbtq/.

Kerlin, Scott P. "The Presence of Gender Dysphoria, Transsexualism, and Disorders of Sex Differentiation in Males Prenatally Exposed to Diethylstilbestrol: Initial Evidence from a 5-Year Study." Paper presented at the 6th Annual E-Hormone Conference, New Orleans, LA, October 27–30, 2004. https://diethylstilbestrol.co.uk/the -presence-of-gender-dysphoria-transsexualism-and-disorders-of-sex -differentiation-in-males-prenatally-exposed-to-des/.

FURTHER READING

Looking for more graphic novels and quick reads about gender? I recommend:

A Quick & Easy Guide to Queer & Trans Identities by Mady G.

A Quick & Easy Guide to They/Them Pronouns by Archie Bongiovanni and Tristan Jimerson

Beyond the Gender Binary by Alok Vaid-Menon

My New Gender Workbook: A Step-by-Step Guide to Achieving World Peace through Gender Anarchy and Sex Positivity by Kate Bornstein

Gender: A Graphic Guide by Meg-John Barker and Jules Scheele

For a more complete list of recommended reading and resources, go to **finecomic.com.**